The Context of Business
Understanding the Canadian Business Environment

Len Karakowsky
York University

Natalie Guriel
York University

Toronto

Vice-President, Editorial Director: Gary Bennett
Managing Editor: Claudine O'Donnell
Acquisitions Editor: Deana Sigut
Senior Marketing Manager: Leigh-Anne Graham
Program Manager: Karen Townsend
Project Manager: Rachel Thompson
Developmental Editor: Suzanne Simpson Millar
Production Services: Aptara®, Inc.
Permissions Project Manager: Joanne Tang
Photo Permissions Research: Christina Simpson
Text Permissions Research: Khalid Shakhshir
Art Director: Zeneth Denchik
Cover Designer: Bruce Kenselaar
Interior Designer: Anthony Leung
Cover Image: © Aslan Alphan/Gettyimages

Credits and acknowledgments for material borrowed from other sources and reproduced, with permission, in this textbook appear on the appropriate page within the text.

If you purchased this book outside the United States or Canada, you should be aware that it has been imported without the approval of the publisher or the author.

10 9 8 7 6 5 4 3 2 1 [CKV]

Library and Archives Canada Cataloguing in Publication

Karakowsky, Len, author
The context of business: understanding the Canadian business environment/Len Karakowsky, York University, Natalie Guriel, York University.

Includes bibliographical references and index.
ISBN 978-0-13-291300-3 (pbk.)

1. Canada–Economic conditions–21st century–Textbooks.
2. Canada–Economic policy–Textbooks. 3. Business enterprises–
Canada–Textbooks. 4. International business enterprises–
Textbooks. I. Guriel, Natalie, author II. Title.

HC115.K342 2013 338.971 C2013-907169-5

ISBN 978-0-13-291300-3

Brief Contents

Contents

Part 3 The External Challenges   193

6 Economic Forces

7 Competitive and Technological Forces

12 Confronting Change

How Do Businesses Address the Challenge of Change? 448

Preface

There is much to be proud of with regard to the Canadian business sector. According to many observers, Canada is poised to earn a distinguished reputation on the world scene. In fact, Canada has been consistently cited in the media as "one of the best countries to do business in." Recently *Forbes* ranked Canada fifth overall in the world for business, based on such factors as low corporate tax rates and one of the most stable banking systems.

Beyond its economic stability, Canada is also reputed for its world-class university system, which is much more affordable than most privately funded colleges in the United States. In turn, Canada is known for its ability to attract and retain a highly educated workforce. Our strong business reputation is also based on having among the highest investment rates in education as a percentage of its GDP. Its enviable status is also based on comparatively low poverty and crime rates.

The positive climate for business has also made this country a popular location for entrepreneurs. Based on a study conducted by management consulting firm Ernst & Young, Canada was ranked among the top five places in the world to start a business, given its strong entrepreneurial culture. The Ernst & Young report considered such factors as small business tax burden, access to financing, and intangibles such as the value placed on research and innovation as well as attitudes toward entrepreneurs in the business community.

There is no doubt that Canada is fast becoming a major player on the global scene. However, at the same time significant challenges exist. The past two decades have witnessed tremendous change and turmoil across our organizational landscape—from numerous bankruptcies of once-great Canadian companies to massive reductions in the workforce of many others to the growth in foreign ownership across corporate Canada. Is all this cause for concern or just the natural evolution of business? Are we headed for the best of times or the worst of times?

Indeed, what lies ahead for Canadian business? To address that question, we need to systematically examine the context of business and the factors that shape our business environment. To do so we must look both "inside" and "outside" of the corporate walls. That is, we need to consider key challenges and opportunities that exist within the boundaries of the organization, as well in the organization's external environment.

The aim of this book is to help facilitate the following learning goals for students:

1. To examine the context within which all businesses operate. Specifically, we consider the internal context and the external context of business and the range of unique challenges and opportunities each possesses.
2. To obtain a deeper understanding of the nature of the Canadian business environment. What differentiates Canada from other business environments? What are the major strengths and weaknesses of Canada as a place to do business? What does the future hold for Canadian business?
3. To encourage critical thinking regarding the nature of business and its environment. This text presents a range of ideas, perspectives, and conceptual frameworks for identifying and analyzing key issues in the business environment.

4. To gain exposure to major voices and leading thinkers in the field of business and organizational studies. This book draws upon many ideas from a wide range of business scholars, experts, and practitioners.

The study of business is really about the study of society. It is an obvious fact that we are a society of organizations—from our hospitals to our schools to our multinational organizations, it is hard to imagine life without organizations. And, for better or worse, those very institutions and organizations that we have grown up with are continuing to undergo dramatic change. We need to understand where change is coming from and how organization's can best respond to the changing business context.

The Context of Business takes the reader on a journey that explores the environment within which business operates—both within the Canadian context and within the global context. The reader will be introduced to a variety of perspectives, theories, and concepts that shed light on real business issues. While this text does introduce the reader to many fundamentally important business terms and concepts, our emphasis is on helping students develop analytical thinking skills. Our aim is to present ideas, frameworks for discussion, and concepts that students can use as tools to help analyze "what is going on out there" in the "real" business world.

We hope that *The Context of Business* takes you on an enriching journey into the environment of business. There is much to learn about Canadian business and, as you will see, there is also much to be proud of. As a current or prospective member of the Canadian workforce, you have every reason to be interested in what the future holds for Canadian business. We hope this book helps you think more critically and thoughtfully about what lies ahead.

Enjoy the journey!

Len Karakowsky

Natalie Guriel

STRENGTHS AND FEATURES OF THIS TEXT

This text differs in a number of significant ways from the typical introductory business textbook. There are at least three key areas of emphasis that distinguish this text, as outlined below.

1. Emphasis on Critical Thinking Skills

The Context of Business will be the foundation for an introductory course in business that first introduces students to the business environment—both internal and external. The aim of this text is to provide a critical examination of the nature of business organizations and the fundamental challenges that they face within the Canadian context. The central objective is to provide insight into the business environment in Canada while encouraging students to think critically about how organizations are managed and how business leaders confront current challenges. This emphasis on critical thinking skills may be what largely differentiates this book from many other introductory business textbooks.

Consequently, while we clearly set out descriptions necessary to understand the "mechanics" of business issues, ranging from the economic context to the political context, our aim is to engage students in a way that will stimulate them to think critically about these contexts. Students will be inspired to ask questions about how business operates and how the environment impacts business. We ask questions central to understanding what is "going on out there" in the Canadian business world, including: What kind of competition exists in Canada in different industries? How has the number of telecommunications companies impacted the consumer? Do government subsidies to business impact competitiveness in Canada? What did the tragedy at Lac-Mégantic teach us about corporate social responsibility? These kinds of questions demand more than simply memorizing business jargon.

We believe that our approach in this text will help students better understand and appreciate the purpose behind their further studies in specific functional areas of business while also nurturing the skills they need to succeed in later courses.

2. Emphasis on Concept Application

Each chapter sets out clearly the **learning objectives** for that chapter. We believe that we have set challenging but achievable learning objectives for each chapter, and we have ensured our chapters provide all the information students require to engage in a thoughtful and informed analysis of each of the topics. Our fundamental aim is to get students to take business ideas, concepts, and frameworks and use them to make sense of business events and challenges.

In writing this book, we endeavoured to make fundamental business concepts "come alive" through the application of these concepts to important, real-world situations. This text includes a wealth of current business cases drawn from the popular press to help clarify ideas presented within each chapter. Specifically, each chapter begins with **The Business World** case, which reports on important, current, real-life business issues and themes that are explored within the chapter. The chapters are also filled with real-life business illustrations summarized within the **Talking Business** boxes. Interspersed throughout the text, these features often present current business news or situations that further explore the concepts discussed in the chapter in a real, applied way. These are ideal for class discussion and also offer media accounts that may differ from the authors' perspectives of business happenings. Instructors may wish to use some of these as mini-cases for class discussion on a daily basis when a lengthier, end-of-chapter case is not assigned.

Each chapter also contains an **end-of-chapter Case Application with questions**. These cases are also drawn from the Canadian popular press and are intended to give students an opportunity to apply chapter concepts to real business contexts. We have used these kinds of cases in our own classes with much success. The cases are of relatively short length. While the cases are intended to focus on the material in the accompanying chapter, many of the cases in this book carry ramifications that spill over into several areas. However, we have found that the ability to integrate different concepts from different chapters takes time. Consequently, our focus was on building this skill by keeping the cases relatively focused, though certainly many of these cases could be revisited from different chapter perspectives. The *Instructor's Resource Manual* provides suggestions and possible discussions relating to each of these cases.

3. Emphasis on "Real" Canadian Business Context

In addition to offering frameworks and principles central to an understanding of the context of business in general, we have endeavoured to provide an interesting and up-to-date presentation of relevant business events and business cases. We have made every effort to infuse this text with "real-life" illustrations. References are made to major business stories from across the globe. However, we are particularly interested in the Canadian context. Consequently, we focus on Canadian stories and give ample attention to current Canadian business policies and practices for the topics covered throughout this book. The end-of-chapter cases are drawn from both Canadian and global contexts. And this text was authored by Canadian scholars—it is not a Canadian adaptation of a US text.

While this text relates ideas and theories drawn from the work of management scholars and management research, we are also concerned with relating ideas and issues voiced by practitioners and communicated through such popular press sources as *Canadian Business*, *Globe and Mail*, *Fortune*, *Report on Business*, and the *Huffington Post*.

End-of-Chapter Pedagogical Features

We have included discussion questions at the end of every chapter, ranging from short answer to essay-type responses. These questions provide various levels of challenge and will ensure students have understood the issues presented in the chapter. In addition, we have included multiple-choice questions. The *Instructor's Resource Manual* provides suggestions and discussions for taking up all of these end-of-chapter questions.

Supplements   The following supplements are available for instructors:

Instructor's Resource Manual. The Instructor's Resource Manual includes chapter learning objectives, chapter outlines and summaries, discussion questions and answers for in-text features, as well as answers for the discussion and review questions.

Pearson MyTest. MyTest helps instructors easily create and print quizzes and exams with hundreds of questions, including multiple-choice, true/false, short answer, and essay questions. For each question we have provided the correct answer, a reference to the relevant section of the text, a difficulty rating, and a classification (recall/applied). MyTest software enables instructors to view and edit the existing questions, add questions, generate tests, and distribute tests in a variety of formats. Powerful search and sort functions make it easy to locate questions and arrange them in any order desired. Questions and tests can be authored online, allowing instructors ultimate flexibility and the ability to efficiently manage assessments anytime, anywhere, visit www.pearsonmytest.com.

PowerPoint Lecture Slides. Prepared by the authors, the PowerPoint presentations are colourful and varied, designed to hold students' interest and reinforce each chapter's main points.

peerScholar. Firmly grounded in published research, peerScholar is a powerful online pedagogical tool that helps develop students' critical and creative thinking skills. peerScholar facilitates this through the process of creation, evaluation, and reflection. Working in stages, students begin by submitting written assignments. peerScholar then circulates their work for others to review, a process that can be anonymous or not, depending on your preference. Students receive peer feedback and evaluations immediately, reinforcing their learning and driving the development of higher-order thinking skills. Students can then resubmit revised work, again depending on your preference. Contact your Pearson Canada representative to learn more about peerScholar and the research behind it.

Innovative Solutions Team. Pearson's Innovative Solutions Team works with faculty and campus course designers to ensure that Pearson products, assessment tools, and online course materials are tailored to meet your specific needs. This highly qualified team is dedicated to helping schools take full advantage of a wide range of educational technology by assisting in the integration of a variety of instructional materials and media formats.

Pearson Custom Library. For enrollments of 25 students or more, you can create your own textbook by choosing the chapters that best suit your own course needs. To begin building your custom text, visit www.pearsoncustomlibrary.com.

CourseSmart for Instructors. CourseSmart goes beyond traditional expectations—providing instant, online access to textbooks and course materials at a lower cost for students. And even as students save money, you can save time and hassle with a digital eTextbook that allows you to search for the most relevant content at the very moment you need it. Whether it's evaluating textbooks or creating lecture notes to help students with difficult concepts, CourseSmart can make life a little easier. Find out how when you visit www.coursesmart.com/instructors.

The following supplements are available for students:

CourseSmart for Students. CourseSmart goes beyond traditional expectations—providing instant, online access to the textbooks and course materials you need at an average savings of 60%. With instant access from any computer and the ability to search your text, you'll find the content you need quickly, no matter where you are. And with online tools like highlighting and note-taking, you can save time and study efficiently. See all the benefits at www.coursesmart.com/students.

Acknowledgements

There are many people to acknowledge for their contributions to and support of this book. First, we would like to express gratitude to those individuals at Pearson Canada who were responsible for making this book a reality. Our gratitude goes to the expertise provided by Deana Sigut, Acquisitions Editor; Suzanne Simpson Millar, Developmental Editor; Leanne Rancourt, Copyeditor; Rachel Thompson, Project Manager; and Rashmi Tickyani, Production Editor. Suzanne merits our deep gratitude for her dedicated attention to and rigorous work on this text.

Thanks also go to those who reviewed our proposals and earlier drafts of this text:

Julius Bankole	University of Northern British Columbia
Edith Callaghan	Acadia University
Cuiping Chen	University of Ontario Institute of Technology
Shawna DePlonty	Sault College
Susan Graham	University of Prince Edward Island
Brent Groen	Trinity Western University
Eytan Lasry	York University
Anthony Mallette	Southern Alberta Institute of Technology
Angelo Papadatos	Dawson College
Raymond Paquin	Concordia University
Jennifer Percival	University of Ontario Institute of Technology
Robert Soroka	Dawson College
Trent Tucker	University of Guelph
Michael Wade	Seneca College
Kent Walker	University of Windsor
Bill Waterman	Mount Allison University

We would also like to express gratitude to our colleagues, Professors David Doorey, You-Ta Chuang, and Eytan Lasry for authoring Chapters 2, 5, and 7, respectively. We are grateful as well to our students, who have provided comments on a regular basis.

We wish to thank our colleagues for their insights and suggestions, including Paulette Burgher, Keith Lehrer, Peter Modir, Peter Tsasis, Indira Somwaru, and Vita Lobo. Our thanks also go to textbook contributors Joseph Adubofuor, Amy Bitton, Anya Cyznielewski, Ziv Deutsch, Melanie Gammon, Jason Guriel, Gillian Gurney, Shu-Hui Huang, Imran Kanga, Ezra Karakowsky, Miri Katz, Chris Kirkpatrick, Orlando Lopez, Karen Rabideau, Akiva Stern, Paul Thomson, and Janu Yasotharan. Your input and assistance were much appreciated!

Finally, we wish to express appreciation to our family members for their patience, understanding, and support. We dedicate this book to you.

Len Karakowsky

Natalie Guriel

About the Authors

Len Karakowsky is a professor of management at York University. He earned his Ph.D. from the Joseph L. Rotman School of Management at the University of Toronto, his MBA from the Schulich School of Business at York University, and his Bachelor of Commerce from the University of Toronto. He has served on the faculty of York University since 1997.

Professor Karakowsky is an award-winning instructor who has been teaching business management courses for almost 20 years. In 2004, he helped launch Canada's first executive master's degree program in the School of Human Resource Management at York University. Several years later he assisted in the establishment of the doctoral program in human resource management at York University.

Professor Karakowsky's research and consulting interests include the areas of leadership development, organizational change, demographic diversity, and corporate social responsibility. His research has been published extensively in such journals as *Leadership Quarterly, Journal of Applied Psychology, Administration and Society, Journal of Management Studies, Group and Organization Management, Journal of Management Development, Small Group Research, Journal of Management Systems, International Business Review,* and many others. He has authored award-winning papers and co-authored the text *Business and Society: Ethics and Stakeholder Management* (Canadian Edition) for Thomson Nelson publishers.

Natalie Guriel is a faculty member in the School of Administrative Studies at York University. She holds a master's degree in management and professional accounting from the Joseph L. Rotman School of Management, University of Toronto, and an honours bachelor of arts degree in political science from the University of Toronto. Her professional designations were earned from the Canadian Institute of Management and include Chartered Manager, Certified in Management, and Professional Manager.

Professor Guriel has enjoyed teaching business management courses at York University for over 10 years. She has also taught undergraduate and graduate business courses at several other universities across Canada. Her teaching interests are varied and range from business management to financial accounting, management accounting, and taxation. She has received recognition for her teaching excellence and for her contributions to curriculum development.

Professor Guriel began her career as a taxation and accounting specialist for Deloitte. She later worked in a variety of management-related roles in the software, retail, and service industries. She is a member of the Canadian Institute of Management as well as the Academy of Management in the United States.

Chapter 1
Exploring Canadian Business: A Critical Approach
What Are the Major Challenges Facing Business?

© Age Fotostock

Is Canadian business headed for a dismal future, or one that is bright? How does one make sense of the current state of Canadian business? Assessing the prospects of organizations requires a careful examination of the contexts within which they operate. This chapter introduces the framework for this book—a critical examination of the internal and external forces that can significantly impact the functioning and fate of business.

Learning Objectives

After studying this chapter, you should be able to

1. Identify the key internal forces that shape any business.

2. Identify the forces that compose the specific and general environments of organizations.

3. Discuss the nature of the external forces confronting organizations.

4. Explain the importance of each of the external forces within the Canadian business context.

1

THE BUSINESS WORLD

Can Canadian Tire Flourish in a Rapidly Changing Business Context?

Canadian Tire has certainly become part of the fabric of Canadian society. It's been around since 1922 and has established itself as a solid Canadian retailer. Like the proverbial "underdog" Canadian hockey team, this Canadian retailer has managed quite well against a growing list of formidable US opponents. Over its 90-plus years, it has established approximately 500 stores across Canada, and with revenues close to $13 billion in 2012, this is no retail slouch.

However, as the expression goes, the times they are a changin'. And the question is, "Can Canadian Tire continue to flourish in these changing times amidst the onslaught of US retailers to Canada?"

US retailers have been invading our retail sector for many years now. It's an invasion welcomed by most Canadian consumers, but certainly not by Canadian retailers. Home Depot, Walmart, and Target are just a few of Canadian Tire's adversaries. And the competition continues to heat up.[1]

So what's a good ol' Canadian business to do? This is the question Canadian Tire is attempting to address. While the company clearly must have done something right to survive this long, some observers are puzzled by its success. In a recent *Maclean's* article, writer Chris Sorensen had this to say:

> Newer stores, located in towns and cities across the country, are brighter and more airy, but largely house the same eclectic inventory—none of it particularly cheap and none of it terribly aspirational either. Customer service, meanwhile, varies wildly from store to store, the result of the company's independent—and bureaucratic—dealer ownership model. It all seems like a recipe for retail disaster, particularly as an army of well-oiled U.S. big box chains—Wal-Mart, Home Depot and soon Target—continue their relentless march north of the border. Yet somehow, Canadian Tire remains standing, earning profits of $453 million on $10.3 billion in retail sales last year, which was up three percent from a year earlier (Canadian Tire Corporation Ltd. also makes money through a banking operation, Canadian Tire Financial Services).[2]

How has Canadian Tire managed to retain its place among the top 20 Canadian brands over the past several years?

Experts believe that a big part of Canadian Tire's appeal is a combination of familiarity and convenience. But that doesn't tell the whole story. Obviously, Canadian Tire has succeeded by understanding its environment and responding to changing business contexts. The entrance of Target to the Canadian retail landscape has certainly made companies like Canadian Tire more vigilant and aware of the need to constantly evolve to best meet market demands. After feeling increased pressure from competitors, Canadian Tire has recently been revisiting its strategy. While not a direct competitor, Canadian

---

[1] Hulsman, N. (2013, March 7). Canadian Tire going small in fight against Target, Yahoo Finance. Retrieved from http://ca.finance.yahoo.com/blogs/insight/canadian-tire-going-small-fight-against-target-180021300.html.

[2] Sorenson, C. (2011, October 11). Canadian Tire's baffling strategy to sell you everything. *Maclean's*. Retrieved from http://www2.macleans.ca/2011/10/11/so-wrong-that-its-right. Reprinted with permission of MacLean's Magazine.

Tire competes with Target on a number of product lines, including small appliances, and Canadian Tire's subsidiary Mark's Work Wearhouse competes for clothing sales.

In an effort to streamline its decision making, Canadian Tire cut several senior management positions in 2012. It has taken a systematic approach to analyzing the industry and adopting strategies to keep ahead of the game. For example, among recent changes was Canadian Tire's decision to spend less of its advertising budget on small, grassroots events and more on mainstream media. The aim is to build more brand awareness of Canadian Tire. The nature of advertising will also change, with a greater emphasis on the Canadian Tire image rather than on specific products. While some have suggested that Canadian Tire should play up its Canadian roots to appeal to loyal Canadians, others feel that a strategy based on national sentiment is a waste of time; they believe that other more tangible actions should be taken. As Susan Krashinsky of the *Globe and Mail* observed:

> Canadian Tire has survived past incursions by U.S. retailers such as Home Depot Inc. and Wal-Mart Stores Inc. The entry of Wal-Mart particularly caused the company to rethink the layout of its stores, change pricing policies and in more recent years, appeal to female shoppers more directly. It's efforts such as this, not Canadian roots, that proved most effective.[3]

In 2013, Canadian Tire announced plans to significantly improve its digital technology practices, including a partnership with Communitech, a technology company based in Kitchener, Ontario.[4] The aim is to develop apps, content, and other digital innovations to improve the shopping experience of Canadian Tire customers, both online and in the store. Canadian Tire also recently relaunched its online store after executives aborted a previous attempt in 2009. Among the items sold online are tires and wheels, which have to be picked up at Canadian Tire stores where many will also be installed. This effort was in response to a growing trend of Canadians buying their tires online through US-based websites and having them shipped directly to local mechanics.

Among other changes has been a renewed focus on its automotive roots. In 2013, Canadian Tire opened a number of automotive concept stores that feature drive-in reception areas, express oil and lube services, and auto detailing. Canadian Tire also owns 87 specialty automotive PartSource stores. This is part of its strategic emphasis on auto parts, tools, home supplies, and sporting goods to combat increased competition.

Another area of change is in the customer services offered by Canadian Tire. For example, it recently began offering home installation services for Canadian Tire garage door openers, followed by central vacuum installations and heating and cooling systems.

Canadian Tire has also ventured more deeply into the world of sports.[5] In 2013, it announced a host of deals with amateur sports organizations to strengthen its ties to a major market: up-and-coming athletes. Among the sponsorships is an eight-year agreement

[3] Krashinsky, S. (2012, September 13). Pumping up the "Canada" in Canadian Tire. *Globe and Mail*. Retrieved from www.theglobeandmail.com/report-on-business/industry-news/marketing/pumping-up-the-canada-in-canadian-tire/article4543680.

[4] Boodoosingh, C. (2013, March 22). Canadian Tire steps up digital strategy, *Digital Home*. Retrieved from www.digitalhome.ca/2013/03/canadian-tire-steps-up-digital-strategy.

[5] McDiarmid, J. (2013, January 23). Canadian Tire digs deeper into amateur sport, *Toronto Star*. Retrieved from www.thestar.com/business/2013/01/23/canadian_tire_digs_deeper_into_amateur_sport.html.

with the Canadian Olympic Committee and new or expanded deals with other amateur organizations. These arrangements reflect Canadian Tire's shift to a greater presence in amateur sport following its 2011 acquisition of sports retailer Forzani Group Ltd. for $771 million. This move entrenched Canadian Tire's status in the sporting goods market as well as provided it with access to a younger demographic of Canadian consumers (who like to shop at malls). Forzani continues to serve as an independent unit, operating Sport Chek, Sport Mart, and Athletes World stores.

Some observers believe that a continuing challenge for Canadian Tire is to make it clear in consumers' minds that it offers more than automotive parts, tools, or sporting goods. On the other hand, marketing experts believe that Canadian Tire must also be cautious to not deviate far from its core business—that is, offering Canadians "everyday" household items rather than upscale home décor. As the old adage goes, you can't be all things to all people.

Sorensen sums it up nicely:

> Canadian Tire will need to stay on its toes as its territory is further invaded by big U.S. retailers. But despite its sometimes ungainly appearance, there's no reason to think the inverted orange triangle and green maple leaf will disappear from the Canadian landscape anytime soon. It may never be a chic proposition. But neither is weatherproofing windows or fixing a clogged toilet.[6]

In fact, in 2013 Canadian Tire announced that it would launch smaller stores in city centres, admitting that it needed to adopt a new approach to dealing with existing competitors like Walmart as well as combating new entrants like Target. Canadian Tire attempted the small-store concept in previous years. However, when Walmart began opening Supercentres across Canada (each about seven times the size of the new Canadian Tire format), it reconsidered that approach. Given that Walmart has recently begun toying with the "small box" concept (opening smaller, express versions of its big box stores) and with the entrance of Target, Canadian Tire has been open to revisiting just about anything, including a focus on smaller stores in core city shopping areas and malls. The plan is for these new "express" stores to be about 10,000 square feet.

Big or small, Canadian Tire has a lot to be proud of. It has been an iconic figure in the Canadian marketplace for many years. It has understood well the environmental forces that it must confront and address to survive. And for those patriotic Canadian consumers, let's hope this good ol' Canadian retailer sticks around for many more years. Way to go Canadian Tire—may the force(s) be with you, eh!

THE INTERNAL CONTEXT OF BUSINESS

Objective 1 Identify the key internal forces that shape any business.

leadership How people are managed within an organization.

strategy The decisions made by business managers about how the company will address political, economic, global, societal, competitive, and technological forces.

What goes on within the walls of an organization? That is, what comprises the internal context of organizations? In Part 2 of this book, we will consider more closely the internal context of organizations, focusing on four fundamental concepts: the employment relationship, **leadership**, organizational structure, and **strategy**. Looking inside organizations involves a consideration of how people within organizations are managed.

---

[6] Sorensen, 2011.

Chapter 2 explores the employment relationship; we will identify and examine the nature of responsibilities that employers have toward their workforce. Chapter 3 considers the notion of leadership and discusses perspectives on managing people, which is particularly important considering that organizations' fates are intrinsically bound to the quality of decisions that are generated inside the organization. Chapter 4 looks at how organizations are designed and why they sometimes decide to undergo dramatic **change**. Chapter 5 introduces the notion of business strategy and its relevance to organizational success or failure.

Exhibit 1.1 illustrates the framework we adopt in this book and also identifies the internal environment of business, which we discuss next.

Exhibit 1.1 Inside and Outside Organizations: The Framework for This Book

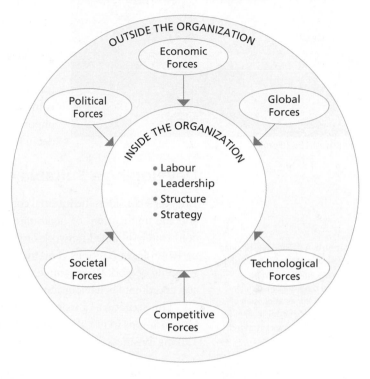

The Employment Relationship: Responsibilities Toward Labour

The ability to attract qualified workers and to extract maximum effort from them can be crucial to business success. However, navigating the **labour** relationship can be difficult and is fraught with risks. The context in which the labour relationship operates is a highly complex one. Workers are usually interested in maximizing the income they receive from the sale of their labour, whereas businesses usually desire to maximize profit. These two objectives can clash, creating conflicts that can have negative effects on productivity and profits, as well as the economy and society more generally. Chapter 2 considers the complexities associated with the legal context of managing labour. Societies and economies are influenced dramatically by how work is organized. We will discuss how debates about the best way to organize work are long-standing and influenced by perspectives on markets, power, and the role of the state in capitalist societies. The result is a complex web of rules and forces that businesses must learn and adapt to if they are to operate successfully. The next chapter considers some of these rules more closely, including rules and processes relating to unemployment and the loss of work, and rules that attempt to address Canada's diverse labour force.

change A shift in how an organization operates.

labour One of the five factors of production. Includes all workers in an organization who contribute their talents and strengths to create goods and services.

Leadership and Effectively Managing People

Chapter 3 considers the nature of the members who comprise an organization and how they manage and are managed. It does not matter whether we are talking about a nonprofit organization,

Philip Date/Shutterstock

© ohmega1982/Fotolia

a small business, or a giant multinational corporation; any type of organization must be managed. Organizations are made up of people and, consequently, this factor is clearly one that we must carefully examine. How do we manage people within the organization? Regardless of your role in organizations, no doubt at some point in your career you will be required to apply some sort of management or leadership skills in the conduct of your job. Simply working in organizations is a reason to be familiar with how organizational life operates and to understand what exactly is involved in the art and science of management. Given the importance of this issue, we will take a closer look at it in more detail in Chapter 3.

Developing a Suitable Organizational Structure

Chapter 4 considers the internal context of the organization with regard to how it is designed and the implications of organizational design and redesign. Organizational structure is a deliberately planned network or pattern of relationships that exists among individuals in various roles or positions. This includes the formal hierarchy of authority, the distribution or grouping of work (for example, into departments) and the rules or procedures that control and coordinate behaviour in the organization.

structure A deliberately planned network or pattern of relationships that exists among individuals within an organization. It determines such things as division of labour, span of control, level of formalization, and how centralized decision making is.

The **structure** of many organizations has been radically redesigned in recent years. Organizations in just about every industrialized nation have been undergoing change. (See Talking Business 1.1.) While some companies have reduced their levels of hierarchy or

---

TALKING BUSINESS 1.1

Changing GM's Organizational Structure

GM Global Design . . . announced a revised organizational structure and executive appointments that align it more closely with the company's brands across its network of 10 Design Centers around the world.

"This new structure provides a foundation to build and grow the design language for each of our brands moving forward," said Ed Welburn, GM vice-president for Global Design. "It gives our design teams a greater opportunity to create products and brands that have an emotional connection with our customers and that continue to move our company forward."

The benefits of a more brand-focused design organization include:

- Drive stronger—and common—messaging across a brand's portfolio

- Allow designers to better understand—and design for—customers when they live the brand on a day-to-day basis

- Provide for greater parts sharing across brands

- Foster more creativity and provide a clear, single purpose for each design team member.

The revised structure also increases the role of GM's Advanced Design Centers, which are strategically located in the United States, Germany, Korea, China and Australia.

"Strengthening our Advanced Design organization will allow us to help the company develop innovative new technologies and strategies to meet the future transportation needs of the global marketplace," Welburn said. "One thing is clear: Success will require a variety of mobility solutions that are striking both in their execution and their efficiency."

Source: Excerpted from GM press release. (2012, June 18). GM Design announces changes to its global organization and leadership team; moves strengthen brand focus and advanced design capabilities. Available at www.autoblog.com/2012/06/18/general-motors-design-ranks-get-big-overhaul. Reprinted with permission from General Motors Corporation

laid off employees at all levels, others have undergone a concurrent change in their whole business process, while others have simply closed down. To understand what is happening, and more importantly *why* it is happening, we need to understand more about the design or structure of organizations. This is the aim of Chapter 4—to offer insight into the anatomy of organizations and, ultimately, to explain why organizations are being redesigned.

Generating a Winning Business Strategy

Deciding what strategies the organization should pursue is a key task of managers. Managers are continually faced with making decisions, both minor and major, on a daily basis. The aim of Chapter 5 is to describe the nature and purpose of strategic management. The chapter examines issues that are of critical importance to strategic management. What are the key forces in determining an industry's structure, and what are the strategic implications? We will consider the roles of organizational resources and capabilities in firm performance. Our exploration will also include a discussion of corporate strategy and an identification of three generic strategies as well as how organizations go about implementing strategy. This examination reflects a central internal force that all organizations must contend with—the ability to generate a game plan to succeed.

THE EXTERNAL CONTEXT OF BUSINESS

We can refer to the external context of organizations as its *environment*. Management scholars have typically defined the environment of an organization along two dimensions: the organization's **specific or task environment** and the organization's **general environment**. Each factor in an organization's external environment can be considered as existing in two spheres: a specific sphere or environment within which the organization directly operates, and a general sphere or environment that would encompass the external environments of all organizations in a society. The *specific sphere* has been referred to as the environmental domain of the organization. For example, changes in the international environment may be a common factor for all organizations with, say, trade agreements affecting Canadian industry in general. However, some industries may be differentially affected by changes in the international environment via trade agreements. Not all organizations within an industry or within different industries are equally affected by changes in the environment. There are changes that affect all or some industries, and there are changes or factors that influence the direct sphere or environment of specific organizations.

Specific or Task Environment

Any organization is surrounded by **external stakeholders**. These are parties or groups that have direct influence on the organization's ability to obtain resources and generate outputs. Stakeholders have some kind of *stake* or interest in the organization and could include such parties as the organization's customers or suppliers, the labour pool from within which the organization obtains employees, competitors, unions, distributors, creditors, the local public, and the government (see Exhibit 1.2). While not all of these stakeholders may exist or exert influence on every organization, they are the types of factors that potentially constitute the specific environment of an organization.

Objective 2 Identify the forces that compose the specific and general environments of organizations.

specific or task environment The environment within which a particular organization operates, which is ultimately shaped by the general environment and includes stakeholders, customers, competitors, suppliers, and so on.

general environment The environment shared by all organizations in a society, such as the economic and political environments, and technological, societal, competitive and global forces.

external stakeholders Individuals or groups who bear some kind of risk, whether financial, physical, or other, as a result of a corporation's actions. They include such parties as suppliers, the government, and society in general. There are ethical as well as practical reasons to attend to all of their interests, even when they conflict.

Exhibit 1.2 The External Context of Organizations

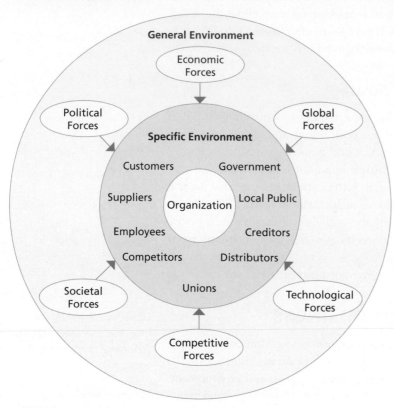

General Environment

Economic Forces

Political Forces

Global Forces

Specific Environment

Customers — Government

Suppliers — Local Public

Organization

Employees — Creditors

Competitors — Distributors

Unions

Societal Forces

Technological Forces

Competitive Forces

General Environment

The sphere surrounding the organization's specific environment is typically referred to as the *general environment*. The forces that make up the general environment ultimately shape the specific environment of the organization. Consequently, the general environment will also influence the organization's ability to obtain resources. General environmental factors typically include economic, competitive, technological, global, political, and societal forces. (See Exhibit 1.2.)

Economic Forces   Whether the Canadian economy is experiencing a recession or strong economic health, **economic forces** act as a strong influence on the present and future prospects of any organization. Moreover, given the strong global ties in Canada, we can also consider the international economic environment as exerting an influence on Canadian organizations. Certainly, we understand the strong influence that the United States and its economy exert on Canadian business.

In considering how it will obtain resources from the environment, any organization must ask the question, "Is the economy healthy or weak?" Organizations are continuously forced to adapt to changing economic conditions. Downsizings are more likely to occur in lean times than in rich. For example, the development of a temporary workforce was partly an outcome of the recession that occurred in the 1990s and the consequent introduction of massive downsizings and layoffs of permanent members of the workforce. Economic changes have also facilitated changes to the nature of the employer–employee relationship. Lifetime employment appears to be a thing of the past. Consider the 1950s or the 1970s—those were times when employment actually meant security. In fact, the dominant model was long-term employment stability. However, a change to these implicit employment promises occurred sometime in the 1980s, when large, secure organizations began to layoff employees and the age of downsizing began. Today, part-time and temporary work arrangements have become much more common than in the past. The economic context of business will be explained in Chapter 6.

Competitive Forces   **Competitive forces** operate at two levels for any organization. As mentioned, an organization will have its own set of competitors, yet the force of competition can be viewed from a more general level as well. For example, globalization (which will be discussed elsewhere in this book) opens the floodgates for competitors in many industries. Clearly, the number of competitors and the nature of competition will dictate changes in organizational strategy. Competition, both domestic and foreign, certainly has demanded an

Objective 3 Discuss the nature of the external forces confronting organizations.

economic forces The economic influences on organizations, such as the state of the economy, unemployment, inflation, interest rates, and gross domestic product. For example, high unemployment numbers may indicate lower overall consumer spending, and business sales could be negatively affected. If sales go down significantly, businesses may need to reduce production, cut costs, or lay off workers.

competitive forces The domestic and foreign competitor influences on organizational decisions. Competitors are organizations operating in the same industry and selling similar products and services. However, competitors may compete in different ways.

acceleration in innovation among firms in many industries. To compete effectively, organizations must continually create new and better methods of serving customers. So while globalization has opened up larger markets for businesses, it has also facilitated much higher levels of competition. Chapter 7 examines the nature of competitive forces and includes a consideration of the different stages of the industry life cycle model. That chapter also identifies the key drivers of industry evolution and how competitive forces change during the life cycle of a business. What are the key success factors for firms at each stage of the life cycle?

Technological Forces   Chapter 7's discussion of innovation acknowledges the importance of **technological forces** that surround organizations. Technology plays a central role in how an organization functions, how it obtains resources, and, ultimately, how effectively it competes. We will consequently examine different types of innovations and explore the relationship between technological evolution and industry evolution. Furthermore, we will discuss the impact of technology on competitive business practices and technology life-cycle models.

The technological environment exerts influence across industries. For example, in the case of Bell Canada, the increase in the number of competitors in the telecommunications industry was partly a consequence of the ability of smaller businesses to enter the industry. Technological advances led to reduced operating costs, which led to more competitors being able to enter the industry; formerly, the costly nature of the sophisticated technology required in this industry created a barrier to entry.

Change in technology is a constant force that permits and demands organizational change. One benefit of technology is increased flexibility in work arrangements. For instance, telework, or telecommuting, essentially means that an employee can work from home thanks to the technology available today. Technology has also facilitated business process redesign or "reengineering," an issue examined further in Chapter 4.

Global Forces   **Global forces**, in many ways, are forces that could be considered part of general economic, political, technological, competitive, or societal forces, but are international in nature. For example, the tragic and devastating events of September 11, 2001, resulted in a chain reaction of international consequences, including changes in economic and political forces acting on organizations. Global events have an increasingly important impact on local organizations, too.

While there is no universally agreed-upon definition of **globalization**, it is useful to consider this concept as a process—that is, a process involving the integration of world economies. The presence of trade blocs reflects the accelerating pace with which nations are integrating their economies. Globalization also includes the globalization of markets—the notion that consumer preferences are converging around the world. Whether it is for products made by McDonald's, Sony, Gap, or Nike, organizations are increasingly marketing their goods and services worldwide. On the other side, production is also increasingly becoming a global affair. Businesses will set up operations wherever it is least costly to do so.

Certainly, international trade agreements are global agreements among governments that are changing the nature and functions of many businesses. A Canadian organization may not simply consider consumers within the domestic borders, but may have a significant consumer market overseas; this demands a knowledge of global societies, global competitors, and other forces that exist on an international level.

The global forces of the general environment underscore the increasingly tangled web of players in the global business context: domestic and foreign competitors, workers,

technological forces The technological environment that exerts influence across industries, playing a central role in how an organization functions, obtains resources, and competes. Changes in technology both permit and demand organizational change.

global forces The global influences on organizations that could be considered as part of the general economic, political, technological, competitive, or societal forces, but are international in nature.

globalization Although there is no universally agreed-upon definition, it may be considered as a process involving the integration of national economies and the worldwide convergence of consumer preferences; the process of generating a single world economic system.

industry, government, national cultures, and economies. How business is conducted in light of trade agreements and global arrangements is a key issue for our entire society, and it is a theme we will explore more fully in Chapter 8.

Political Forces

political forces Governmental influences on an organization's decisions through laws, taxes, trade relationships, and other related political factors.

Political forces can exert influence at both the specific and general levels. The government's push toward deregulating many industries was designed to welcome more competitors into the Canadian business sector and facilitate freer trade between Canada and the United States. The reduction in trade barriers worldwide has also opened the doors for the increasing presence of foreign competition in many industries. Deregulation and privatization, discussed in Chapter 9, are clear examples of the importance of considering the effects of governmental changes on business strategy.

Are government regulations facilitating or restricting certain business strategies? The political environment can dictate changes in how a business competes or what services it offers and how they can be offered. As we will discuss in Chapter 9, the deregulation of protected industries in the 1980s and 1990s created competition for companies where no real competition had previously existed. Industries such as telecommunications, banking, energy, and aerospace were dramatically affected by these governmental/regulatory changes. As the dominant companies in these industries were forced to compete in an open market, some responded by downsizing their workforce.

In a general sense, the traditional relationship of government with business is clearly undergoing change. The trend toward increased government involvement after World War II seems to have reversed by about 1980. In fact, some observers have suggested that the massive disposal of government-owned assets and the reduction of government controls in the business sector indicate a minor revolution of sorts. We will examine this issue in more detail in Chapter 9.

Societal Forces

societal forces A wide range of influences in society in general, including, for example, changes in public opinion on ethical issues like organizational justice (how employees are treated), that affect all organizations and to which businesses must respond.

Societal forces have an important impact on organizations. The nature of a society certainly is an entrenched part of any organization's general environment. For example, we have witnessed an increasing concern for individual welfare in the workplace as societies become more cognizant of human rights and how people should be treated. Consequently, the workplace increasingly emphasizes organizational justice—that is, how employees are treated. This has translated into more laws governing fairness in the workplace. One such area that has been dramatically affected is compensation. Pay equity has been a key issue examined in redressing inconsistencies in pay treatment between men and women. We have also witnessed an increasing emphasis on merit-based pay and pay for performance, which attempt to more closely link actual effort to performance instead of seniority-based pay, which bases pay solely on the number of years an employee has been with the organization.

Businesses must respond to society. Consumer tastes change, for example, and businesses must adapt to such changes. Similarly, the types of organizations that serve societal demands can change. The aging population in Canada suggests that greater emphasis needs to be placed on industries such as the health care sector. In addition, society has a certain set of ethics or values, and these can influence the type of behaviour that organizations will manifest in that society. From a societal standpoint, it is not difficult to understand the importance of adequately addressing ethical behaviour of business organizations and their constituents. All sectors of society, including organizations themselves, are drastically affected by many forms of unethical behaviour. There is a growing belief that organizations are social actors responsible for the ethical and unethical behaviour of their employees.

Critics of business argue that organizational leaders must examine more closely the "moral sense-making" within organizations and responsibilities to external constituents. The tolerance of unethical behaviour in a society would seem to be a precursor to the acceptance of corporate unethical behaviour. This is an issue that we will more fully explore in Chapter 10, which also emphasizes the requirement for organizations to address stakeholders in the global context.

© SerrNovik/Fotolia

From the description of the external environment, it can be observed that there is overlap between the general environment and the specific environment. An organization may have a specific market niche or set of consumers, but demographic changes in the general environment, such as an aging society, will certainly translate into changes in consumer tastes at the specific level. Similarly, as noted above, the government's aim to reduce trade barriers at a national level can translate into regulatory changes or increased competition within an organization's specific environment. This underlines the importance of understanding the impact of both the general external environment and the specific environment of the organization.

Sustainability

What is the most critical issue in the world today that needs to be solved? The answer will likely depend on whom you ask and where you live. For example, there is less fresh water to drink and less viable farmland to grow food on than there was 100 years ago. Sources of oil continue to be extracted worldwide as the number of cars increase. And the climate is getting steadily warmer across the globe. Preserving the environment for future generations to enjoy and for the economy to prosper is clearly an important issue. What currently threatens the planet? Two key concerns are the depletion of natural resources by overconsumption and the ongoing release of greenhouse gas emissions. As a society, how do we continue to grow and prosper while also ensuring that our way of life is sustainable now and in the future?

Traditionally, growing the economy and protecting the environment were viewed as two separate goals, often conflicting with one another. Why should businesses want to be sustainable? What are the motivating factors for businesses to implement sustainable practices? While the primary goal of a business is to make a profit, sustainable practices can contribute to this goal and help create value on a number of levels. Business leaders now recognize that society, the economy, and the environment are interrelated systems that have an important effect on one another; one system cannot survive without the others.

Today, sustainable development can be viewed as a long-term approach to balancing the needs of people while growing the economy and preserving the environment. In a general sense, **sustainability** involves the relationship between the three Ps: people, profits, and the planet (also referred to as the three Es: social equity, the economy, and the environment). This accounting framework is known as the **triple bottom line**. However, since the movement toward sustainability is still relatively new, the development of a common standard of global measures is still underway. What measures currently exist and how can businesses

sustainability In business, the relationship between the three Ps: people, profits, and the planet.

triple bottom line An accounting framework that can be voluntarily used by organizations to report performance on social, economic, and environmental results for a project or reporting period.

implement more sustainable practices? There are a number of indicators of sustainable development that measure changes on a national or global basis that can be examined.

Implementing sustainable business practices is a new challenge many managers face. Time, money, and lack of knowledge are a few obstacles. Yet sustainable businesses that achieve their economic, social, and environmental goals can expect to receive many benefits. Sustainable business practices have proven to help businesses in the long term by reducing costs, reducing risks, and improving consumer relations. Clearly, environmental degradation cannot quickly be fixed, and businesses need to continue to consider their impact on the environment and society now and in the future. All of these issues will be addressed in Chapter 11.

The Challenge of Change

We are a society of organizations—from our hospitals to our schools to our multinational organizations, it is hard to imagine life without organizations. And, for better or worse, those very institutions and organizations that we have grown up with are continuing to undergo dramatic change. In fact, over the years, we witnessed tremendous change and turmoil across our organizational landscape—from bankruptcies of once great Canadian companies like Nortel, to massive reductions in the workforce of many well-known organizations such as GM and Bell Canada, to the rise (and possible fall) of successful Canadian companies like Research In Motion (now known as BlackBerry). What is going on?

While predicting the next big change may be futile, sensible questions that can be addressed include, "What are the sources of change directed at organizations?" "How do these changes affect the nature of organizations and work?" In every chapter in this book, from management through to globalization, we recognize that just about every important area of business is undergoing some kind of change. Chapter 12 considers how organizations respond (or fail to respond) to these shifts in the environment of business. It's all about adaption and change.

Organizations that effectively change or adapt to their environment are ones that have first "learned" —they have learned how to recognize the need for change, and they have learned what actions are necessary to adapt. Some management scholars have suggested that organizational learning represents the collective experience of individuals within the organization and happens when organizational procedures change as a result of what has been learned. **Organizational learning**, in this sense, involves a three-stage evolution in which the highest stage incorporates three aspects of learning: adapting to the environment, learning from employees, and contributing to the learning of the wider community or context. This idea will be explored more fully in Chapter 12.

The ability of organizations to adapt to and change with a changing environment is dependent on the ability of their members to change and adapt. The best business leaders are essentially facilitators of change. Such facilitators are individuals with vision who can encourage others to leap into a new paradigm—a concept we will also examine in Chapter 12.

THE CANADIAN CONTEXT: HOW'S BUSINESS IN CANADA, EH?

How is business doing in Canada? Some economists believe we are doing well; others believe Canada's economy is slowly contracting and losing its competitive edge in the growing global economy. Some factors that are important to a country's success in the global marketplace

organizational learning The detection and correction of error, or the collective experience of individuals within the organization that results in changes in organizational procedure. Three aspects of learning are adapting to the environment, learning from employees, and contributing to the learning of the wider community or context. Two types of learning are single-loop learning and double-loop learning.

Objective 4 Explain the importance of each of the external forces within the Canadian business context.

identified by economists include a country's need for strong trading partners, low corporate taxes, an educated and skilled workforce, a stable financial and banking system, and a sustainable competitive advantage. Let's consider how business is doing in Canada in these terms by revisiting each of the external environmental forces with regard to the Canadian context.

Economic Forces in Canada

What are some of the indicators of the current state of health of the Canadian economic scene? One indicator of the health of the economy is **gross domestic product (GDP)**: the total value of a country's output of goods and services in a given year. The money that is earned from producing goods and services goes to the employees who produce them, to the people who own businesses, and to the governments in the form of taxes. The general trend of governments worldwide is to reduce their share of GDP. Obviously, it is good for GDP to grow: From 1979–1989 Canada's GDP grew about 3.2% annually. The compound annual growth of GDP between 2002 and 2011 was 2.6%. Currently, Canada's economy is expected to see compounded annual growth of 2.5% until 2025. (See Exhibit 1.3 for GDP growth between 2002 and 2011.) Canada experienced solid economic growth between 1993 and 2007. However, it went into a severe recession in 2008–2009, but has since emerged strong after this global financial crisis ended.

The future health of the Canadian economy, as in most economies, is continually the subject of speculation. It appears that economists are not necessarily more accurate in their predictions of economic well-being than are those looking into the proverbial crystal ball. Nonetheless, it is crucial to understand what underlying forces are ultimately shaping the state of our business system in Canada. This amounts to distinguishing between short-term changes in the domestic economy and ongoing trends in the nature of the business enterprise system. It may be more manageable for us to consider what has been going on around us in recent years and assess what conditions will continue to persist in the coming years.

One important economic factor is the unemployment rate. In Canada, the unemployment rate increased sharply in the early part of the 1990s because of the severe 1991–1992 recession and the steepest drop in economic activity since the Great Depression of the 1930s. While much of the 1990s was not bright for employment, we have witnessed vast

gross domestic product (GDP) The total value of a country's output of goods and services in a given year.

Exhibit 1.3 Gross Domestic Product (GDP) and GDP Growth

Between 2002 and 2011, GDP for all industries in the Canadian economy increased from $1,068 billion to $1,266 billion. In each year during this time period, GDP growth was positive with the exception of 2009. The compound annual growth rate of GDP between 2002 and 2011 measured 2.6%.

Source: Statistics Canada. (2013, March 31). Canadian economic accounts, first quarter 2013 and March 2013. *The Daily.* Reproduced and distributed on an "as is" basis with the permission of Statistics Canada. Canadian economic accounts, first quarter 2013 and March 2013.

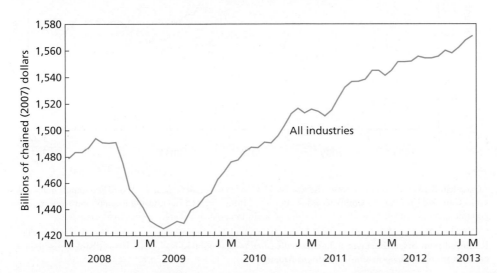

© Francis Vachon/Alamy

improvements in recent years. By 1999, the unemployment rate dropped to 7.6%; in 2005 it dropped to 6.7%, which was the lowest level achieved in three decades. This decrease in unemployment continued to drop in 2007, reaching a low of about 6%. (See Exhibit 1.4.)

The soundness of Canada's banking system is another important economic factor for Canada's economy. In 2010, the World Economic Forum ranked Canada's banking system as the world's soundest for the third year in a row.[7] This type of international recognition is good for Canada because it gives businesses, investors, and consumers the confidence that Canada is a safe and stable place to conduct business.

Why are Canadian banks more secure than banks in other countries? The Canadian Bankers Association attributes this financial stability to three key factors: Canada's banks are well regulated, well capitalized, and well managed.[8]

Canada's Banks Are Well Regulated Under the federal government, two primary regulatory bodies oversee banking activities in Canada: the Office of the Superintendent of Financial Institutions (OSFI) for prudential regulation, and the Financial Consumer Agency of Canada (FCAC) for consumer issues. The Canadian Bank Act is also reviewed and updated every five years to reflect changes in the industry. In comparison, the United States has a much more complex arrangement of regulators, but with less stringent rules. After the US economic collapse in 2009, the US federal government had to bail out many of its banks with billions of dollars to prevent bankruptcies and a potential economic depression. Similar

Exhibit 1.4 The Unemployment Rate in Canada, 2008–2013 (percent of labour force)

In 2009, the unemployment rate was 8.3%. Between 1976 and 2009, the unemployment rate reached its highest levels in 1983 (12.0%) and 1993 (11.4%), following two major recessions. In 2007, Canada recorded its lowest unemployment rate (6.0%) since the mid-1970s. By May 2013, the unemployment rate was 7.1%.

Source: Statistics Canada. (2013, May). Labour Force Survey, May 2013. *The Daily.* Reproduced and distributed on an "as is" basis with the permission of Statistics Canada.

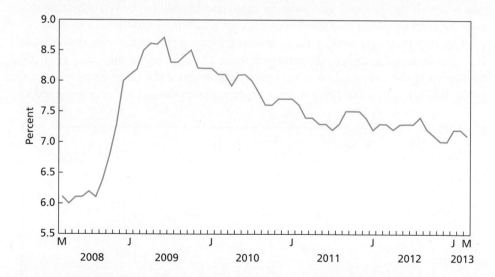

[7] Canadian Bankers Association. (2010, September 9). Good news for all Canadians: World Economic Forum again ranks Canada's banks as the world's soundest. Retrieved from www.cba.ca/en/media-room/65-news-releases/536-good-news-for-all-canadians-world-economic-forum-again-ranks-canadas-banks-as-the-worlds-soundest.

[8] Canadian Bankers Association. (2010, May 14). Canada's strong banking system: Benefiting Canadians. Retrieved from http://cba.stage6.industrialmedia.ca/en/media-room/50-backgrounders-on-banking-issues/469-canadas-strong-banking-system-benefiting-canadians.

bank bailouts occurred across Europe. Canadian banks, however, did not require any government assistance and kept doing business as usual throughout the crisis.

Some economists blamed the US mortgage lending system for the collapse. There were many high-risk mortgage products in the United States, which Canadian regulators did not allow. Canadian bank mortgages also require at least a 20% down payment for a home or the mortgage would need to be insured; this requirement was not mandatory in the United States. Today, the US government is seeking bank regulation reform and is looking to Canadian models to help improve its system.

Canadian Banks Are Well Capitalized

Canada has also been commended for the fact that its banks are well capitalized. This means that banks hold sufficient reserves to cover potential defaults on loans and other losses. According to Erik Heinrich, "the average capital reserves for Canada's Big Six banks—defined as Tier 1 capital (common shares, retained earnings, and non-cumulative preferred shares) to risk-adjusted assets—is 9.8%, several percentage points above the 7% required by Canada's federal bank regulators."[9] Canada even exceeds international norms and surpasses the Bank for International Settlement's requirements.[10]

Canadian Banks Are Well Managed

Although Canadian banks may not have the same level of competition (as US banks) to motivate them to succeed, they have remained well managed. Canada's six largest banks (known collectively as the "**Big Six**") include the Canadian Imperial Bank of Commerce (CIBC), Scotiabank, TD Canada Trust, Bank of Montreal (BMO), Royal Bank of Canada (RBC), and National Bank of Canada. Investment advisers frequently refer to these companies as Canada's blue-chip stocks. Historically, these companies have proven to be safe and conservative investments that usually profit year after year.

Big Six Canada's six largest banks, including CIBC, Scotiabank, TD Canada Trust, BMO, RBC, and National Bank.

Why can the Big Six banks be relied upon to be consistently profitable? Stringent lending requirements constitute one factor that has proven effective in preventing huge losses. According to the Canadian Bankers Association, "in a survey by the Strategic Counsel, 81% of respondents believe that prudent lending is a key reason why Canadian banks have performed better than their international peers."[11] But are Canadian banks as competitive as they can be? Can they compete on a global scale? Here are three challenges industry analysts point to that Canada's banking industry needs to overcome in order to become a successful global competitor.

1. *Canadian banks are less competitive:* Some analysts believe that Canada's banks pay a cost for being safe. They tend to take fewer risks and, therefore, are not high-growth companies. In Canada, the banking industry is more stable, but it does not have the same competition that other countries do. The Canadian financial market is dominated by a few large players—the Big Six. Although consumers have begun to see smaller players enter the market, there have been few so far. President's Choice Financial (PCF), for example, offers many of the same banking services as the Big Six, but it does not have the same number of in-person branches that many of the traditional banks have. PCF provides mainly phone and online services so it can reduce overhead expenses and offer customers greater benefits. With lower

---

[9] Heinrich, E. (2008, November 10). Why Canada's banks don't need help. *Time.* Retrieved from www.time.com/time/business/article/0,8599,1855317,00.html.

[10] Canadian Bankers Association (2010, May 14).

[11] Canadian Bankers Association (2010, May 14).

administrative costs, this bank has typically offered customers higher interest rates on deposits and lower (sometimes zero) banking fees.

2. *Too small to compete globally:* Many banks would like to be more competitive but have faced some limitations. Some Canadian banks would need to double in size to compete as international players. A couple of the Big Six banks have attempted to merge in the past, but government approval was denied. Many opponents argue that merged banks would be too powerful, and consumers would have less choice and potentially face higher fees.

3. *Too much regulation:* In addition, many argue that our banking system is too regulated. For example, stringent bank loan policies can make it difficult for small businesses to gain the funds needed to invest and to expand. This can impact Canada's economic growth, since the majority of new jobs are created by small businesses. For banks, this means more of the same slow and stable growth and less opportunity for high-growth results. Nonetheless, media attention promoting the fiscal well-being of Canadian banks has helped give them international recognition and, perhaps, a competitive advantage.

Competitive Forces in Canada

Imagine a situation where there is only one provider of an important good. If you require this good, then you must be willing to accept whatever price the provider demands. There is also no assurance regarding the quality of the good. There is little incentive for the provider of this good to be efficient in operations—any high costs can simply be passed on to the consumer in the form of higher prices. Similarly, there is little need to innovate or produce higher quality products for the consumer, given that there is no risk of losing this captive market. Consequently, competition is considered to be an important element: This entails firms competing with each other to provide better products at lower prices if they want to increase sales and profits.

Our economic system is based on the assumption that sufficient competition exists. Competition is the "invisible hand" that ensures the market works in this manner. However, if an industry is relatively concentrated then businesses can act as price setters, not price takers. Of course, with extreme concentration, as is the case with a monopoly, then businesses can set whatever price they want or collude with other businesses. Observers suggest that Canada has not taken as strict a stance on this issue as the United States, where legislation has been aimed at preventing industry concentration.

Now, when you think "Canadian business," what picture do you conjure in your mind? Looking back over Canada's past, it has been argued that we established a certain pattern for ourselves in terms of the types of business activities we emphasized here. During most of our existence, we have developed as a largely open economy, trading internationally primarily in resources. It has been suggested that our emphasis on the export of our natural resources, typically in a relatively unprocessed state, has made us more akin to a simple supplier of raw materials, whether it has been logs and lumber, pulp and newsprint, unrefined minerals, agricultural crops, and so on. But is that resource industry Canada's competitive advantage?

First of all, what is a competitive advantage? A **competitive advantage** is achieved when an organization excels in one or more attributes that allow it to outperform its competitors. An **attribute** might be having a highly skilled staff, a patented technology, a unique marketing strategy, a well-known brand, or something else that makes the company a leader in its field.

In the global economic environment, countries compete through trade and strive for a competitive advantage based on the goods and services they sell. Some countries are

competitive advantage
Achieved when an organization excels in one or more attributes that allow it to outperform its competitors.

attribute A business advantage of some kind, which might include having a highly skilled staff, a patented technology, a unique marketing strategy, a well-known brand, or something else that makes the company a leader in its field.

recognized for their superior products. The United States, for example, is known for producing world-class Hollywood movies. Belgium is known for crafting decadent chocolates. And England is recognized for its fine bone china. But what is Canada known for?

When people think of Canada's economy, they often think of its natural resources. These are Canada's forests, farms, fisheries, mines, and oil and gas sectors. Traditionally, Canada's economy was built on extracting and exporting these raw materials. As early as the 1600s, companies began selling Canadian resources abroad. In 1670, for example, the Hudson's Bay Company was formed and began trading fur with European countries.[12]

By the early 1900s, significant industry had developed in Canada. Numerous mining companies began extracting minerals and coal from Alberta's landscape. Similarly, other companies saw great opportunity to extract and manufacture forestry products. In 1909, for example, a pulp and paper mill was established in Grand Falls, Newfoundland. Similarly, the Maritime provinces had flourishing fishing industries with easy access to the Atlantic Ocean and other bodies of water.

Across Canada, individuals moved to places of employment, and towns grew around industry leaders. The resource sector became the foundation of Canada's economy and economic growth for the next century, creating jobs and prosperity for many. Today, the resource sector is still an important part of Canada's economy, but faces a number of challenges:

- *Depleting resources:* Over the past century, many renewable and non-renewable resources have been significantly depleted. Mining companies have had to rely on lower-grade ores; in the forestry industry, depletion of high-quality fibre has led companies to exploit second- and third-growth timber in less accessible areas; and in the fishing sector, the Newfoundland cod fishery had been essentially exhausted by the late 1980s.[13]

- *New technology and equipment:* Costs have increased significantly for improved technology and extraction equipment. New equipment has been required to improve production efficiency, to extract resources requiring advanced extraction systems, to gain greater value from production inputs, and to sustain Canada's competitive position in the global commodities marketplace.[14]

- *Foreign competition:* Foreign competition presents another challenge to Canada's natural resource industries. The US softwood lumber producers, for example, have been a major competitor to Canada, resulting in several legal battles over unfair competition practices. Inexpensive labour costs have also been a competitive advantage for foreign producers. In 2009, AbitibiBowater Inc. (now known as Resolute Forest Products), closed its Grand Falls pulp and paper mill because of reduced demand for paper and increasing labour costs.

- *Pressure from environmental groups:* Similarly, environmental concerns have resulted in new regulations for Canadian companies, to which foreign producers are not subject. The high rate of extraction of natural resources has led environmental groups to lobby governments to protect wilderness areas, reduce yields extracted, and require

---

[12] Canadiana.org. (2001–2002). The Hudson's Bay Company Is Formed. Retrieved from www.canadiana.ca/hbc/hist/hist6_e.html.

[13] Howlett, M., & Brownsey, K. (2008). *Canada's resource economy in transition* (p. 43). Toronto, ON: Edmond Montgomery Publications Limited.

[14] Howlett & Brownsey, 2008, 44.

higher standards for extraction processes. Substitute products that are more sustainable, like bamboo, have also been encouraged. As the fastest growing wood in the world, bamboo has advantages over traditional woods such as cherry, maple, and walnut. Bamboo is highly renewable and, therefore, environmentally friendly.[15]

Clean energy consumption presents another environmental concern. Increased demand for cleaner energy sources means lower demand for dirtier energy like coal. Subsequently, many coal mines across Canada have faced closures. Some have even become tourist attractions that serve as historical sites, such as the Bellevue coal mine in Crowsnest Pass, Alberta.

Animal protection organizations have had a similar impact. Today, many consumers opposing cruelty to animals have stopped purchasing fur products and refrain from shopping at stores that sell them. Hudson's Bay was one of these stores, and after 300 years of selling furs the company finally ended its fur trade business in 1991 because of societal pressures.

Many economists will agree that Canada's resources sector is in transition. But is the sector still important to the Canadian economy? Some business leaders contend that mining and natural resources is still Canada's competitive advantage. Other business leaders argue that Canada needs to diversify into other areas, so that when our non-renewable resources run out we will still have a thriving economy. In fact, it has been argued that Canadian corporations are much more involved in the extraction and processing of natural resources than most other countries at comparable stages of economic development. This pattern has led critics to suggest that we have not developed the entrepreneurial and technological expertise of other nations—nations that have used our "raw materials" and added value through their own technological resources. However, it would be unfair to suggest that this is the whole picture. The fact is we have witnessed major changes in the nature of our economic sector, and we continue to see a major transformation in our economy and in the types of business competitors we have created. As with any capitalist-based system, Canada views competition as an important part of the business enterprise system.

Technological Forces in Canada

Traditionally, Canada's economy has been resource based. This refers to our emphasis on industries like agriculture, mining, forestry, fisheries, minerals, and energy. Natural resources have constituted the bulk of Canada's exports. Given the nature of our primary industries, one important implication for businesses in these industries is that prices for the output are very much influenced by the world market. That is, these natural resource industries are highly affected by any fluctuations in the global supply and demand for these commodities, suggesting that many of our industries are highly sensitive to changes in the global or world market. A general criticism that has been levelled at the Canadian business environment is that we need to catch up in the area of technology and innovation rather than relying on our natural resources (which are exported mostly in an unprocessed form).

However, the Canadian economy has been transforming. While much of Canada's economic strength lies in the diversity of its natural resource industries that supply ore, oil and gas, lumber, and other commodities internationally, our rapidly growing high-tech sectors are earning high marks for leading-edge research and development. This includes such

---

[15] Howlett & Brownsey, 2008, 46.

areas as information and communications technology (ICT), biotechnology, nanotechnology, advanced manufacturing, electronics, aeronautics, pharmaceuticals, and agri-food.

We have already seen significant changes in the sectoral composition of Canada's economy throughout the 20th century. At the beginning of the 20th century, there was a balance between employment in the primary sectors of the economy and the industrial and service sectors. The *primary sector* consists of agriculture, mining, logging, fishing, hunting, and trapping. The *industrial sector* is akin to the manufacturing or goods-producing sectors, while the *service sector* can include things like the hotel or restaurant industry. At the beginning of the 20th century, we had an abundance of employment in the primary sector, with most of this coming from the agricultural sector. However, even early in the century Canada witnessed a steady decline in agricultural employment right up until World War II—after which time this decline was more rapid.

Canada's employment has clearly shifted away from the agricultural sector. Why? A number of reasons have been offered. Perhaps one of the most obvious reasons for the decline in agricultural employment is a reduced need for human capital; that is, technological advances have helped many agricultural practices become increasingly mechanized and, consequently, fewer workers are required to achieve the same level of output. Concurrent with this decline has been the increasing urbanization of the Canadian population. Increasing numbers of Canadians continue to flock to cities from rural areas in search of employment, and it is the cities that attract the largest share of new immigrants.

If there has been a significant shift in employment away from the agriculture sector, the question is, "Where has it shifted to?" What we have seen happening in conjunction with agricultural employment decline in Canada is an increase in the number of Canadians employed in goods-producing and service industries. The manufacturing sector produces tangible goods, such as clothes, oil, food, machines, and automobiles. The service sector includes things like banking, insurance, information, marketing, accounting, hospitality and food services, recreation, and so on.

The shift to the manufacturing and service sectors was particularly striking in the first 15 years following World War II, after which growth in these areas slowed, although it certainly continued throughout the 1960s, 1970s, and 1980s. However, what is particularly striking in the later postwar period is the simultaneous rise in service-sector employment and, at least since the 1950s, the rapid decline in goods-producing industries. We continue to witness this trend, albeit at a reduced rate. Consider this: In 1950, only 42% of Canadians were employed in service-producing industries; by 1993, the figure had risen to over 72%. Whereas at the turn of the 20th century we shifted from an agricultural to an industrial economy, the second shift has been the transition from a goods-producing to a service-oriented economy.

Why are we moving away from the natural resources and the manufacturing sector to the service sector? What is driving this shift? Well, there is not really one accepted reason for this transformation to a service economy. But probably the most oft-cited reason is technology: Just as mechanization of agricultural production decreased the need for human capital, the increasing mechanization of manufacturing facilities has similarly reduced the need for human labour in this sector. We can produce comparable levels of output with far less labour than we did in the past. But productivity still remains a challenge across Canada. (See Talking Business 1.2 and Exhibit 1.5.)

And as far as productivity is concerned, what we have seen is labour productivity growth in manufacturing outpacing productivity growth in services. Why? Consider the

Growth in Provincial Labour Productivity: A Problem from Coast to Coast

Over the next two decades, Canada and its regions will have to contend with the challenges of more and more aging baby boomers leaving the workforce. The result will be slower growth in our economy while simultaneously adding to demand and expenditures for health care. One part of the solution to slower growth would be to lift our productivity—a sure fire way to boost income per capita and help us pay for those public services we want and need.

While we're hopeful for the future, our past performance on the productivity front has not been strong. Numerous past studies have highlighted our poor labour productivity performance relative to the United States but few have looked at the issue from a regional perspective. Productivity is not just a federal issue. Here, we look at productivity among the provinces and find that with just one exception, poor productivity growth is a problem that exists from coast-to-coast. With the baby boomers contributing to slower economic growth and to rising health care expenditures across all regions, it's vital that all provinces develop an agenda to boost their productivity growth.

Over the 1998 to 2011 time period, the U.S. posted average annual compound growth in labour productivity of 2.5 percent while Canada posted average growth of 1.3 percent. But it's no wonder that productivity growth for Canada as a whole has been so low when its three biggest provinces are productivity growth laggards. Quebec and Ontario, for instance, posted gains of 1.1 and 1.2 percent respectively, and in Alberta, the headline number is even worse, with growth of just 0.5 percent. (See chart "Business Sector Labour Productivity Growth.")

Only one province posted stronger business sector labour productivity growth than the United States and that was Newfoundland and Labrador. While Newfoundland and Labrador does have programs to promote productivity, the primary reason behind its productivity miracle was a structural shift in its economy where an oil boom increased the contribution of the highly productive mineral fuels industry from an estimated 1.5 percent of real GDP in 1997 to 19.4 percent in 2011. Therefore, its success cannot be benchmarked by the other provinces. Moreover, looking only at the headline productivity growth rates does not tell the whole story. For example, Alberta has the weakest growth among the provinces, but it also has the highest level of labour productivity in the country.

Nevertheless, the data clearly shows that labour productivity *growth* is a problem across the country. By embracing a productivity strategy, provinces would have the ability to make themselves more competitive, increase the standard of living for their residents and experience faster economic growth. So how can provinces boost their productivity growth?

There are three main factors that drive labour productivity growth: the composition of labour, capital intensity and multifactor productivity (MFP) growth. Labour composition basically refers to the skill set of the working population, and all provinces perform fairly well on this metric. This is not to suggest that there is no room for improving the quality of the labour force, but it is not the driving force behind weak productivity growth.

When it comes to capital intensity (the amount of capital per worker), the provincial performance has been mixed. Half the provinces experienced larger increases in capital intensity over the 1998 to 2010 period than the U.S., led by the resource intensive economies of Saskatchewan

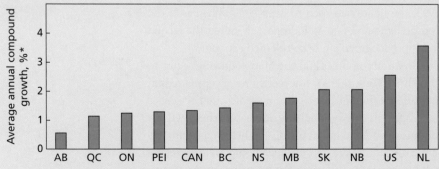

*Canadian data are based on 2002 $; US data are based on 2005 $.
Sources: Statistics Canada; U.S Bureau of Labor Statistics; The Conference Board of Canada.

and Alberta. But that leaves half the provinces still trailing in capital investment. Policies such as adopting a harmonized sales tax (where it is not already in place), investment tax credits and reducing corporate tax rates and regulatory burdens are steps provinces can take to boost investment and, subsequently, productivity.

MFP, the final component, captures increases in labour productivity not attributable to increases in capital or labour composition. MFP is essentially the efficiency with which capital and labour mix to create output. This captures a wide range of factors from the industrial structure of an economy to its innovation performance. With the exception of Newfoundland and Labrador (which as noted above benefited from a structural economic shift), all provinces posted sub-par MFP growth relative to the U.S. That is the main reason why labour productivity growth in the provinces (and for Canada as a whole) is so much weaker than in the U.S. While there is no easy answer to improving MFP growth, research has shown that initiatives such as credits and programs that encourage business spending on research and development; investments in public infrastructure; and a reduction in barriers to interprovincial trade and labour mobility can help provinces boost their MFP growth.

Governments at a variety of levels have understood for years the need to address lagging productivity performance, but the data show that we have not made nearly enough progress. With every province facing an aging population and budget challenges, the time is now to develop and implement productivity strategies with a focus on improving MFP growth.

Source: Excerpted from Macdonald, A. (2013, February 20). Growth in provincial labour productivity: A problem from coast to coast. Reprinted with permission from The Conference Board of Canada. Retrieved from www.conferenceboard.ca/economics/ hot_eco_topics/default/13-02-20/growth_in_provincial_labour_ productivity_a_problem_from_coast_to_coast.aspx.

nature of many service-oriented jobs: Social workers who counsel youths, waiters who serve customers, and medical caregivers who treat patients are not easily replaced by machinery. Productivity growth in this sector is thus much slower than in the manufacturing sector. The result of this difference in productivity growth rates is that more Canadians need to be employed in services to maintain the relative levels of service and manufacturing output.

Whatever the source, there is little question that services are playing a much greater role in our economy than they have in the past. However, one final question that we can ask related to all this has to do with whether this shift is a good thing. Let's consider several implications of this transition.

On an individual level, anyone planning on entering the job market or remaining employable must consider his or her skill set. Obviously, our workforce must be better educated and capable of attaining the relatively higher skill levels required in the well-paying service-sector jobs (in comparison to the manufacturing sector). The notion of the **knowledge worker**, a relatively recent buzzword, underscores the increasing importance of higher education and the value of transferable skills.

But in broader terms, is the service sector better for our economy? Or is manufacturing still a critical element? A number of observers suggest that we should say "good riddance" to the old, outdated manufacturing sector and welcome the growing service sector with open arms. For example, economist Nuala Beck, in her popular book *Shifting Gears: Thriving in the New Economy*, referred to a "new knowledge economy" that is quickly replacing the old mass-manufacturing economy. Beck observed that these "knowledge workers" now make up 30% of North America's workforce, while only 10% are actually involved in production. Further, it is the more knowledge-intensive industries (like the high-tech industries) that are creating most of the jobs and driving the economy.

knowledge workers People employed in knowledge-intensive industries, such as the high-tech industries, where specialized and frequently changing knowledge is required. Knowledge work is thus harder to routinize than, for instance, service work.

Exhibit 1.5 Canadian Employment by Industry (in thousands)

	2008	2009	2010	2011	2012
Total, all industries	17,087.4	16,813.1	17,041.0	17,306.2	17,507.7
Goods-producing sector	4,013.4	3,724.3	3,740.0	3,804.9	3,872.0
Agriculture	323.6	316.1	300.7	305.6	309.2
Forestry, fishing, mining, quarrying, oil and gas	344.6	317.9	329.4	337.2	369.1
Forestry and logging with support activities	54.4	46.2	51.4	46.5	51.8
Fishing, hunting, and trapping	21.6	20.7	20.6	19.4	18.4
Mining, quarrying, and oil and gas	268.6	251.1	257.5	271.3	298.8
Utilities	151.5	147.6	148.3	139.8	140.7
Construction	1,231.0	1,160.8	1,217.2	1,262.2	1,267.5
Manufacturing	1,962.7	1,781.8	1,744.3	1,760.2	1,785.5
Durables	1,168.4	1,037.0	1,019.4	1,042.9	1,083.4
Nondurables	794.3	744.8	724.9	717.3	702.1
Services-producing sector	13,074.0	13,088.8	13,301.0	13,501.3	13,635.7
Trade	2,684.9	2,652.2	2,677.8	2,669.9	2,643.8
Wholesale trade	632.0	631.8	628.9	632.8	611.9
Retail trade	2,052.9	2,020.4	2,048.9	2,037.1	2,031.9
Transportation and warehousing	848.9	816.2	805.7	843.4	849.4
Finance, insurance, real estate, and leasing	1,073.6	1,092.1	1,095.7	1,083.4	1,093.2
Finance and insurance	776.4	769.9	783.5	758.0	783.2
Real estate and leasing	297.2	322.3	312.2	325.4	309.9
Professional, scientific, and technical services	1,189.3	1,191.9	1,266.7	1,309.2	1,299.3
Business, building and other support services	685.0	654.9	672.2	677.0	690.5
Educational services	1,186.3	1,188.8	1,217.8	1,219.4	1,287.7
Health care and social assistance	1,893.0	1,949.2	2,030.7	2,091.5	2,128.0
Information, culture, and recreation	758.4	769.6	766.0	784.2	790.4
Accommodation and food services	1,080.6	1,056.6	1,058.4	1,093.4	1,102.4
Other services	748.3	787.0	753.5	758.7	795.3
Public administration	925.7	930.3	956.4	971.2	955.9

Source: Statistics Canada, CANSIM Table 282-0008. Reproduced and distributed on an "as is" basis with the permission of Statistics Canada.

Global Forces in Canada

Clearly, our proximity to the United States is an element that influences the nature of our business environment. Keep in mind that the United States has a population that is approximately 10 times that of Canada. And though we possess one of the largest countries in terms of land mass, the bulk of our population lives within 200 kilometres of the Canada–US border. In fact, the US presence in the Canadian business sector is a defining characteristic of our environment. Moreover, the trade agreements we have entered into with the United States have critical implications for our business sector (an issue we will deal with later in this book).

It is hard to imagine Canada's economy without the United States. With a market of over 300 million people, the United States has always been a significant player when Canada's economy grows or contracts. After all, 75% of Canadian exports go to the United States,[16] and of those exports 85% of the goods are Canadian.[17] These numbers make sense, though, when you consider the contributing factors. Canada and the United States share an adjacent border, a similar culture, and a common language. The United States also makes an efficient and effective trading partner. The Canada–US trade relationship is supported by accessible railways, trucking, air services, and oceans linking the two nations to shipped goods.

Although trade had existed for many years, in 1988 the partnership became formalized under the Canada–US Free Trade Agreement (FTA). By 1994, the countries expanded their trading relationship to include Mexico. Subsequently, the agreement became known as the North American Free Trade Agreement (NAFTA).

Today, the Canada–US trade relationship remains unique. It represents the largest cross-border trading relationship between any two countries globally.[18] But what does this really mean? According to the Government of Canada, goods and services traded between the two countries totalled $740 billion in 2008—that's about $1.4 million in trade per minute.[19] Canada's exports to the United States make up about $306.6 billion,[20] an important part of our GDP, which was approximately $1.5 trillion in 2009.[21]

But what does Canada trade with the United States, and what are the dominant industries? Over half of Canada's food exports go to the United States, making our southern neighbour Canada's leading agricultural export market. In recent years, Canada's main exports to the United States were automobiles, machinery, mineral fuels, and oils. According to the Government of Canada, "Canadians and Americans share the closest energy relationship in the world. Energy infrastructure—including oil and gas pipeline networks and electricity grids—is tightly integrated. Canada is the United States' largest and most secure supplier of oil, natural gas, electricity, and uranium."[22]

Currently, Canada exports over 40% of its total annual production (GDP), compared to 25% a decade ago. This underscores the fact that Canada is considered to be a major trading nation. A key concern regarding our international business activity is whether we are selling more to other countries (exporting) than we are importing (buying from other countries).

A number of issues regarding our trade status have received much attention in the past decade or so: the FTA and NAFTA and the consequent increase in the degree of openness to international trade. As mentioned earlier, Canada's traditional reliance on trade in unprocessed natural resources has received much criticism, and its reliance on US trade has been scrutinized.

---

[16] Lam, E. (2011, October 3). Canada weaning itself off exports to U.S. *Financial Post*. Retrieved from http://business.financialpost.com/2011/10/03/is-canada-weaning-itself-off-the-u-s.

[17] Mandal-Campbell, A. (2007). *Why Mexicans don't drink Molson*, p. 25. Toronto, ON: Douglas and McIntyre.

[18] Mandal-Campbell, 2007, 19.

[19] Government of Canada. (2011). NAFTA Advantage. Retrieved from http://investincanada.gc.ca/eng/advantage-canada/nafta-advantage.aspx.

[20] Prime Minister of Canada. (2011, February 4). Canada/U.S. trade and investment. Retrieved from http://pm.gc.ca/eng/media.asp?id=3935.

[21] Statistics Canada. (2010). Gross domestic product, expenditure-based. Retrieved from http://www40.statcan.gc.ca/l01/cst01/econ04-eng.htm.

[22] Prime Minister of Canada, 2011.

So how "Canadian" is Canadian business? In other words, what proportion of the corporations doing business in Canada are actually controlled by Canadian sources? While the level of foreign ownership varies among different industries (for example, about 67% of chemical product and textile manufacturers are foreign owned, while only about 9% of communications companies are), the average level of foreign ownership is relatively high by world standards. *Annual foreign investment* in Canadian companies refers to ownership of assets like factories, land, buildings, machinery, equipment, and companies themselves.

So we have a pretty high level of foreign ownership, largely US-based, in Canadian corporations—but what difference does that make to the nature of business in Canada? That is, what are the implications of foreign investment? There is much debate about this topic. In fact, Canadians have traditionally been ambivalent when it comes to the issue of foreign investment. For some, interest in the Canadian economy is a good thing. We want to attract investors to our country to generate more business and more jobs. The source of ownership shouldn't make a difference when the results are the same—more jobs for Canadians and more money invested in the Canadian economy.

What impact does foreign ownership have on the personality of our corporate sector? Keep in mind that these foreign-owned corporations are largely subsidiaries of US-based "parent" companies. One important consideration are the activities the corporation carries out to conduct its business—that is, strategic planning, research and development, marketing, and so on. Many foreign-owned firms, like the car manufacturers or the multinational oil companies, operate Canadian subsidiaries largely to produce or simply market the product. These products are typically designed outside Canada, usually using imported components. These Canadian subsidiaries, then, do not perform the complete range of functions necessary to offer a product in the marketplace. These are the traditional so-called **branch plants**.

branch plants Subsidiaries (of companies in another country) that do not perform the complete range of functions necessary to offer a product in the marketplace. Typically, subsidiaries defer responsibility of higher-level strategic functions to the parent company.

Some observers believe that we will continue to see the rapid spread of branch plants in Canada, with progressively less important activities being allocated to the Canadian subsidiary. This has led many critics to suggest that these subsidiaries are nothing more than "sales offices" for the US parent company. Mel Hurtig made the following critical observation regarding the significance of foreign ownership in Canada:

> In . . . just over 20 years, there were 11,380 companies in Canada taken over by non-resident controlled corporations . . . 569 companies a year on average. Or you can think of it as 3 companies every two days, and an average of 47 a month, EVERY month for the last 20 years![23]

Some critics argue that we have built up a dependence on foreign capital to supply us with the funds for business development. While this financial assistance was welcome, it brought a major cost with it—the establishment of these branch plants and an economy that is approximately 30% foreign owned. It has been suggested that this branch-plant economy has impeded the development of an innovative or entrepreneurial spirit in Canadian business. In other words, there is a sense that, historically, Canadian managers have not been challenged to do the strategic planning, to engage in the research and

---

[23] US Energy Information Administration.

development, and to develop the technological expertise to add value to the present supply of products or services. However, we are witnessing the increasing presence of Canadian-owned and global competitors, and it is expected that Canada will continue to move beyond its history and carve a bigger niche in the global environment.

Political Forces in Canada

The Canadian economic system has been described as a **mixed system**. This refers to the notion that while we possess a capitalist economy, government nonetheless plays an important role. In fact, government has historically played a critical role in the Canadian economy. (See Talking Business 1.3.) In Canada, we have a long history of government involvement in business in the sense of promoting and protecting our industries. Tariffs

mixed system An economic system that involves a capitalist economy with an important government role. Most economies today are considered mixed systems.

TALKING BUSINESS 1.3

Jobs, Productivity, and Innovation: How Health Care Drives the Economy

As one of the biggest recipients of public revenues, health care plays a major role within Canada's economic performance. While most people are generally aware of the sector's high costs (over $200 billion, or about 11.7 percent of gross domestic product in 2011), there is less understanding of its economic benefits. The health care sector delivers economic benefits on three levels: jobs, productivity and innovation.

First, the health care sector is a major employer. The sector directly employs about 1.4 million physicians, nurses, and other health care providers and clerical and administrative staff, which represent about nine percent of total jobs in Canada. Indirectly, the sector also supports thousands of additional jobs through its supply chain: the purchase of medical supplies, clinical equipment, and professional services. About 45,000 Canadians are employed in pharmaceutical, medicine, medical equipment, and medical supplies manufacturing in Canada. Therefore, directly or indirectly, the sector has a major influence on the careers of thousands of Canadians, many of whom are highly qualified professionals who pay taxes and purchase goods and services from all sectors of the economy.

Second, the health care sector contributes to a more productive and engaged workforce. Productivity, how efficiently goods and services are produced, is the single most important determinant of a country's per capita income over the longer term. Countries with high productivity have a superior standard of living. Unfortunately, this is an area where Canada has faced challenges. In 2012, Canada's

level of labour productivity (that is, the dollar value of output per hour worked) was US$42, much lower than that of the United States, at US$52. More worrisome is that despite a broad and growing consensus that Canadian productivity needs to be improved, the gap with the U.S. is widening, not narrowing. Canada's productivity level has fallen to 80 percent of the U.S. level from a high of 90 percent in the mid-1980s. Efforts to improve labour productivity are needed to sustain or improve Canada's standard of living.

How does this relate to Canada's health care systems? According to Statistics Canada, Canadian workers lost an average of 7.7 days from work in 2011 due to illness or disability. Direct and indirect costs of disease and injury in 2000 were estimated at around $188 billion, a figure that is likely to be higher now. Disease outbreaks are very costly too. The Severe Acute Respiratory Syndrome (SARS) drained billions of dollars from Canada's economy in 2003. Because health care services touch the life of every Canadian, the sector plays a key role in decreasing employee absence due to illness, stress, and disability, which bring significant economic burden to Canada. Put simply, healthier workers are more productive workers.

Third, the health care sector is a major pillar of science and technology research. It also is a leader in putting the result of research to work. Advancements in life sciences have resulted in additional economic output of trillions of dollars that exceeds health research and health care costs over the same

(continued)

period by orders of magnitude. For example, at the turn of the 20th century, an individual had a life expectancy of 50 years. In 1961, the average Canadian could expect to live to age 71, and in 2006, the estimated average life expectancy in Canada was 80 years. This represents an impressive gain of 30 years of life over one century. These health gains represent the benefits of improvements in determinants of health (e.g., education, income) but also health advancements which were the product of research and innovation that was properly translated into health care services. In the United States, 1970–2000 life expectancy gains have been estimated to be worth US$95 trillion (US$3.2 trillion per year). Further improvements in the treatment of cancer and cardiovascular diseases are estimated to bring additional value in the magnitude of billions of dollars to the United States. (See below Table 1.)

Table 1: Current Value of a 10 Percent Reduction in Mortality from Major Diseases (2004 US$ billions)

Major Cause of Death	Males	Females	Total
All causes	$10,651	$7,885	$18,536
Cardiovascular diseases	$3,254	$2,471	$5,725
Cancer	$2,415	$2,261	$2,676
Diabetes	$237	$249	$486
Infectious diseases	$500	$148	$648
Accidents and adverse effects	$977	$421	$1,398

A 2008 report from the United Kingdom also highlighted the value of advancements resulting from medical research. It found that public investments in cardiovascular research in the U.K.—conducted from 1975 to 1992—yielded returns of about 39 percent. In other words, for each £1 invested in public cardiovascular research, the U.K. earned £0.39 per year in perpetuity. This demonstrates that when health research and development leads to health innovations that are appropriately and timely integrated into health and health care systems, it results in healthier and longer lives, which creates more value than the investments they require. Combined with the shift over the past century from physical labour to knowledge work, this means that Canadians have the ability to remain in the labour force for longer and hence make a greater contribution to wealth creation as well as consumption. The returns on research, therefore, also contribute to productivity growth.

Despite its escalating costs, the health care sector may be creating more value than it consumes. It is no exaggeration to say that the Canadian health care system lies at the heart of Canada's national economy and innovation system, both as a contributor of inputs and as an attractor or demander of its outputs.

Source: Prada. G. (2013, April 2). Jobs, productivity and innovation: How health care drives the economy. Reprinted with permission from The Conference Board of Canada. Retrieved from www.conferenceboard.ca/commentaries/healthinnovation/default/13-04-02/jobs_productivity_and_innovation_how_health_care_drives_the_economy.aspx.

on imported goods were designed to protect our domestic business by making the cost of foreign goods more expensive relative to those of Canadian goods. It can be argued that a large portion of Canada's industrial development is due to protectionism through tariffs first imposed in 1879 by Sir John A. Macdonald's National Policy.

Eventually, the government also offered direct incentives for industrial and resource development. *Incentive programs* were established to encourage managers to conduct business in a manner desired by the government. Managers may decide to, say, invest in new product development, engage in greater export activities, or locate in an underdeveloped region. Government incentives will be offered to engage in such activities. Receiving government financial support or reward for such activities would influence decisions to engage in these activities.

In Canada, an ongoing concern is the degree to which government can or should help businesses compete—whether in the form of direct subsidies, tax incentives, or some other form of protectionism. For example, one recurring controversy in recent years is the level of government subsidies to businesses operating in the global marketplace and government support for research and development programs. For example, one controversy involved a dispute regarding government subsidies to Canada's aerospace giant Bombardier and its main competitor in the jet market, Embraer SA (Empresa Brasileira de Aeronáutica S.A.) of Brazil.

Taxation The government's ability to levy taxes on corporations is another aspect of political forces acting on businesses. All profits earned by a Canadian resident corporation are subject to Canadian corporate income taxes, which are calculated on the basis of the company's net profits. But how much tax should corporations pay?

Canada is often admired by other countries for its low corporate tax rate. Over the past five years, Canada has gone from having the highest tax rate to the lowest of the G7 countries. In 2012, the federal tax rate was further reduced to 15%, which is closer to Ireland's 12.5%, one of the lowest tax rates in the world. When provincial tax rates are added, the combined corporate tax rate jumps to between 26 and 32%.

What are the benefits of low corporate income taxes? Clearly, businesses benefit by keeping more of their profits, but what are the benefits to the economy and the rest of society?

- *Long-term economic growth:* Many economists and business leaders agree: Reduce the expenses of companies and the economy will grow. According to Jeff Brownlee, vice-president of public affairs and partnerships for Canadian Manufacturers and Exporters, "to increase after-tax cash flow, leave more money in the hands of business to invest."[24] In other words, if you give businesses money by reducing taxes, they will be able to purchase efficient machinery or expand a product line. Either way, it is a step in the right direction toward higher productivity and a better economy.

  In 2008, the Organisation for Economic Co-operation and Development (OECD) researched the relationship between different types of taxes and economic growth. The OECD study concluded that corporate income tax was the most harmful tax out of personal income taxes, sales taxes, and property taxes because of the impact it has on long-term economic growth. One finding, for example, was that corporate income taxes had a negative impact on GDP per capita.[25]

- *Improved competitiveness:* Another benefit of low corporate taxes is improved competitiveness. Lower corporate tax rates generally mean lower costs for businesses. In turn, lower costs turn into lower prices for consumers. Lower costs also help businesses be more competitive not only domestically but globally as well.

- *Increased wages and improved living standards:* Economists today recognize that the corporate tax burden is ultimately passed on to other stakeholders in society. In a February 2011 paper, the Canadian Chamber of Commerce stated, "Business taxes are borne directly or indirectly by people—workers through lower wages, consumers in the form of higher prices for goods and services, and shareholders through lower returns."[26] In one research study, the Oxford University Centre for Business Taxation examined over 55,000 European companies in nine countries and found that for every $1 increase in corporate taxes, a reduction in real wages occurred by 75%.[27]

---

[24] *CBC News*. (2011, April 15). Canada's corporate income tax fight. Retrieved from www.cbc.ca/news/business/story/2011/04/14/f-corporate-tax-cuts-for-against.html.

[25] Hodge, S. (2011, May). Special report: Ten benefits of cutting the U.S. corporate tax rate. Tax Foundation, *192*, 2. www.taxfoundation.org/files/sr192.pdf.

[26] *CBC News*, 2011.

[27] Hodge, 2011.

But who actually pays the tax? Opponents of lower corporate taxes argue that if corporations pay less taxes then individuals will have to pay more. When individuals pay more tax, they have less disposable income to spend on goods and services; businesses will therefore profit less. Clearly, the debate on who should pay the tax is far from over.

Societal Forces in Canada

There is much to be proud of with regard to Canadian society. In an OECD study, Canada ranked second out of 17 peer countries in education and skills (see Exhibit 1.6). What does this mean? Canada has a good public education system that provides the basic skills necessary for adults to enter the workplace. With one of the highest high school and college completion rates in the world, Canada is a leader in education.

Given our strengths in educating our population, Canadian society has the potential to create a productive and innovative business environment. Recent studies suggest that countries with more educated and skilled workers have a higher chance of economy prosperity. According to the OECD Secretary-General, Angel Gurria, "better educational outcomes are a stronger predictor for future economic growth."[28] Why? Generally, earnings will increase with each level of education achieved, giving individuals more income to spend on goods and services. Individuals are also better equipped as employees to contribute more knowledge to their organizations. In comparing education to earnings, Americans with a university degree earned $180 for every $100 earned by Americans with a high school diploma. Similarly, a worker with a college degree earned $114, whereas non–high school graduates earned only $65 for every $100 earned by high school graduates.[29] Indeed, Canada is poised to earn a distinguished reputation on the world scene.

At the same time, it is important to consider how we can maintain and strengthen such a reputation. Perhaps central among the factors to consider is the manner in which we conduct business in this country—that is, the integrity of our business environment. Unfortunately, we have witnessed that Canada, like any other country, is not immune to scandal and corruption. In recent years, both the private and public sectors have been forced to confront a host of misdeeds that speak to the issue of corporate governance, social responsibility, and business ethics. The challenge for Canadian business leaders is to ensure that along with our industrial development comes an equally well-developed sense of corporate ethics and social responsibility.

In a recent article for the *Ottawa Citizen*, journalist Derek Abma[30] observed that Canadian business is at risk of losing its "clean cut" image if scandals continue to accumulate. Abma cites a number of recent scandals, including a Vancouver-based mining company. Bear Creek Mining sought to open a silver mine in Peru, which sparked a violent protest by local citizens who were concerned that the company's activities would pollute

---

[28] OECD. (2010, July 12). Education: Korea and Finland top OECD's latest PISA survey of educational performance. Retrieved from www.oecd.org/newsroom/koreaandfinlandtopoecdslatestpisasurveyofeducationperformance.htm.

[29] The Conference Board of Canada. (2013). Education and skills. *How Canada performs: A report card on Canada.* Retrieved from www.conferenceboard.ca/hcp/details/education.aspx.

[30] Abma, D. (2011, July 2). Scandals pile up in world of Canadian business. *Ottawa Citizen*.

local water sources while providing few economic benefits. Five people died and about a dozen were wounded in clashes in 2011.

Sadly, Canadian companies have increasingly been appearing in the news in a less than flattering light. Calgary-based Niko Resources was found guilty in 2011 of bribing a government official in Bangladesh. The RCMP had been investigating the case against Niko for six years, along with at least 22 other ongoing investigations involving Canadian companies suspected of bribery. Elsewhere, an engineering firm based in Montreal (SNC-Lavalin Group) was recently exposed in the media as playing a role in building prisons for the Lybian regime of Muammar Gaddafi. In 2009, Toronto-based Barrick Gold (among the work's largest gold miners) faced public embarrassment after Norway's government pension fund sold off about $230 million worth of Barrick stock because of what it saw as irresponsible environmental practices of the mining company in Papua New Guinea.

Other socially irresponsible practices have been occurring in a host of industries and for many years in Canada. The Canadian oil sands industry in general has been criticized globally for its production of "dirty oil." In terms of criticism, Canada has also been pointed out by the anti-corruption group Transparency International for being the only G7 country that continually provides "little or no enforcement" of the OECD's Anti-Bribery Convention.[31]

All those scandals may be "exceptions to the rule," in that business in Canada normally operates with integrity and with a social conscience. These scandals do not detract from the fact that we do have a lot to be proud of in terms of our Canadian business practices. However, it would be foolish to ignore these events and to assume that they will never reappear. We need to better recognize that the societal context within which business operates must be fully addressed to ensure continued prosperity and success in our business sector.

CHAPTER SUMMARY

Understanding the environment of business is the only way to get a sense of where we are headed in terms of future economic prospects. Whether you are currently a full-time student or are already in the workforce, an understanding of the context of organizations is a critical part of any intelligent person's portfolio. The aim of the upcoming chapters is to shed more light on the environment of organizations and to consider the implications for the future of organizations. What are the prospects for business, and what are the challenges we must confront? No organization operates in a vacuum, so the real world surrounding the organization must be addressed.

Indeed, within each external and internal force there are many factors that can positively or negatively impact business, as seen in Exhibits 1.7 and 1.8.

---

[31] Norton Rose Group. (2012, March). *Global anti-corruption developments: Annual review 2011*, p. 18. Retrieved from www.nortonrosefulbright.com/files/download-the-anti-corruption-annual-review-2011-65076.pdf.

Exhibit 1.7 The External Forces Framework: Considerations for Analysis

External Force	Examples
Economic	

a. State of the economy	• Is the economy growing or slowing down?
	• What stage of the business cycle is the economy in?
	  ○ expansionary (slow, moderate, high growth)
	  ○ peak
	  ○ contractionary (recession)
	  ○ trough
	• How is the economy affecting business? Are businesses expanding operations or downsizing?

b. Interest rates	• What are the lending interest rates?
	  ○ Are they low, moderate, or high?
	• How are interest rates affecting business?
	  ○ low interest rates = lower financing costs
	  ○ high interest rates = higher financing costs

c. Currency rate	• What is the domestic currency rate compared to other countries?
	• Is the currency rate appreciating or depreciating?
	• How is the currency rate affecting business?
	  ○ If the domestic currency is appreciating,
	    ■ = more expensive for foreign countries to buy Canadian goods (exports)
	    ■ = less expensive for Canadians to buy foreign goods (imports)
	  ○ If the foreign currency is appreciating,
	    ■ = more expensive for Canadians to buy foreign goods (imports)
	    ■ = less expensive for foreign countries to buy Canadian goods (exports)

d. Unemployment rate	• What is the unemployment rate?
	• How is the unemployment rate affecting business?
	  ○ low unemployment = more people working = increased spending power
	  ○ high unemployment = less people working = decreased spending power

e. Inflation rate	• What is the inflation rate?
	• How is inflation affecting business?
	  ○ low inflation = price level increasing at a slow pace
	  ○ high inflation = price level increasing at a rapid pace

f. National debt	• What is the national debt? • Is a country's debt so high that it is creating economic instability in the country?
Competitive	

a. Type of competition	• What type of competition exists in your industry?
	  ○ perfect competition
	  ○ monopoly
	  ○ oligopoly
	  ○ monopolistic competition

b. Phase of the industry in industry life-cycle model	• What phase of the industry life-cycle model is your industry in?
	  ○ introduction
	  ○ growth
	  ○ mature
	  ○ decline

External Force	Examples
c. Intra-industry competition	• How competitive is your industry? (Low, moderate, or high?) • How large is your company compared to your competitors? • Does your company dominate the industry? • Did your company create an industry standard? • Who are your competitors? • How many competitors do you have? • Do you have domestic and foreign competition? • What opportunities and threats exist in your industry that can affect your company being more competitive or less competitive?

Technological

a. Type of technology	• What types of technology are used in your company's industry?
	• How is technology impacting or changing business?
	  ◦ Work approaches
	    ■ Videoconferencing versus in-person meetings
	    ■ Tablets versus desktop computers
	  ◦ Equipment
	    ■ Manufacturing assembly line
	    ■ Special computer-aided tools
	  ◦ Electronics
	    ■ Smartphones, tablets, robotics, etc.
	  ◦ Telecommunications
	    ■ Internet, phone service, etc.
	  ◦ Processing systems
	    ■ Computers, data processing systems, etc.

Political/Legal

a. Country stability	• Are there wars, natural disasters, national debt, civil unrest, or other issues that threaten the government and businesses being able to function?
b. Laws and regulations	• How do municipal, provincial, federal, or international laws and regulations affect business operations, projects, and activities?
c. Taxes	• What taxes does your organization have to pay? For example, corporate tax, property tax, sales tax, land transfer tax, tariffs on imported goods, etc.
d. Trade relationships	• How is a country's trade relationship with another country affecting business? • Is there a free trade agreement (e.g., NAFTA) or trade barriers (e.g., quotas and tariffs)? • Does the relationship protect domestic business or open up the market to foreign competition?

(continued)

Exhibit 1.7 The External Forces Framework: Considerations for Analysis *(continued)*

External Force	Examples
e. Environmental fees	• Are there environment fees that businesses need to collect and remit? For example, are there recycling fees on designated electronic products or garbage collection fees?
f. Business incentives	• What incentives does the government give businesses to encourage them to operate in a particular region, create jobs, increase profitability, or increase competitiveness? • For example, in Canada, the Scientific Research and Experimental Development (SR&ED) tax credit for eligible companies encourages research and innovation; subsidies (e.g., free cash or loans by government) also support certain industries.
g. Crown corporations	• Are there certain industries the government has control over that affect how your business operates and competes? (For example, the Liquor Control Board of Ontario (LCBO), Canada Post, etc.)
h. Deregulation/ privatization	• Are there certain industries the government is releasing control over that may affect how your business operates and competes?
Societal	
a. Societal customs, attitudes, values, ethics	• What does society think about certain issues (the environment, foreign-made goods, workers' rights, health and safety issues, etc.)? • What demands are consumers requiring businesses to adhere to that are driven by values, customs, attitudes, and ethics? (Corporate social responsibility, fair reporting, sustainability, etc.)
b. Demographics	• Is the majority of the population young or old? • How is the age of the population affecting consumer spending and demand for certain products and services? • How are demographics affecting or changing business?
c. Consumer preferences	• What products and services are customers preferring and willing to pay for? • Are consumer preferences changing? If so, why? • How are consumers' changing tastes affecting business?
Global	

Includes all of the forces described above in an international context.

a. Political	• Are political issues and events in foreign countries affecting how domestic companies do business? (Country stability, laws, taxes, trade relationships, etc.)
b. Economic	• How are foreign economic conditions affecting domestic businesses? (e.g., Will the debt problems of Europe affect the economy in Canada and the global economy?)
c. Technological	• How do foreign technological innovations affect competition for Canadian firms? (e.g., iPhone technology versus BlackBerry technology?)
d. Societal	• How do Canadian societal values, attitudes, and expectations affect business operations in other countries? • How do foreign societal values, attitudes, and expectations affect businesses in Canada?
e. Competitive	• How do foreign companies impact how domestic firms operate and compete?

Exhibit 1.8 The Internal Forces Framework: Considerations for Analysis

Internal Forces	Examples
1. People	
a. Employment relationship (responsibilities toward labour)	
i. Labour relationship • employee or contractor	• Are you hiring employees or contractors?
ii. Legal compliance • Canadian Charter of Rights and Freedoms • human rights laws • employment equity legislation	• Are you abiding by all employment-related laws?
iii. Work perspective • neoclassical perspective • managerial perspective • industrial pluralist perspective • critical perspective	• What is your perspective on the governance of work?
b. Leadership and managing people	
i. Classical • Frederick Taylor • Henri Foyal • Max Weber ii. Behavioural • Elton Mayo • Mary Parker Follet • Chester Barnard • modern behavioural science iii. Contingency theory • size • technology • environmental uncertainty • individual differences iv. Modern behavioural science	• What management approach is best suited to manage people in your organization and in your industry?
2. Strategy	
a. Business-level strategies	
i. Cost leadership • efficient-scale facilities • cost reduction on overhead, marginal customer accounts, R&D, marketing, general administration, etc. ii. Product differentiation • product features • links functions • location	• How should a company compete in a given market?

(continued)

Internal Forces	Examples

• product mix
• links with other firms
• service
iii. Focus
  • a particular buyer group
  • a segment of the product line
  • a narrow geographic market	

b. Corporate-level strategies

Types of diversification	
• related • unrelated • vertical integration • backward integration • forward integration	• What businesses or markets should a firm compete in? • How should these businesses or markets be managed so they create synergies?
Michael Porter's Five Forces Model	

i. Threat of new entrants
  • economies of scale
  • capital requirements
  • switching costs
  • access to distribution channels
  • cost disadvantages independent of scale
ii. Bargaining power of suppliers
iii. Bargaining power of customers
  • switching costs
  • undifferentiated products
  • importance of incumbents' products to buyers
  • the number of incumbents relative to the number of buyers
iv. Threat of substitutes
v. Threat of existing rivalry
  • lack of differentiation or switching costs
  • numerous or equally balanced competitors
  • high exit barriers
	• What is the state of the industry?
	• How competitive is the industry?
	• How easy or difficult is it going to be to compete and be successful?

The VRIO Model	
• value • rareness • imitability • organization	• How strong is the company compared to its competitors? • Are your company's resources, products, and services more valuable, rare, difficult to imitate, or better managed?
SWOT Analysis	
• strengths • weaknesses • opportunities • threats	• What are the internal and external forces affecting the company? • What are the company's strengths, weaknesses, opportunities, and threats?

Internal Forces	Examples
3. Structure	

a. Mechanistic
  • narrow division of labour
  • centralized decision making
  • narrow span of control
  • high formalization
b. Organic
  • wide division of labour
  • decentralized decision making
  • wide span of control
  • low formalization
c. Contingency theory
  • strategy
  • size
  • technology
  • environment
	• What structure will best suit your organization?
	• Do you need to be cost efficient or innovative?
	• Is your company in a new industry or a mature one?

CHAPTER LEARNING TOOLS

Key Terms

attribute 16

Big Six 15

branch plant 24

change 5

competitive advantage 16

competitive forces 8

economic forces 8

external stakeholders 7

general environment 7

global forces 9

globalization 9

gross domestic product (GDP) 13

labour 5

leadership 4

knowledge workers 21

mixed system 25

organizational learning 12

political forces 10

societal forces 10

specific or task environment 7

strategy 4

structure 6

sustainability 11

technological forces 9

triple bottom line 11

Multiple-Choice Questions

Select the *best* answer for each of the following questions. Solutions are located in the back of your textbook.

1. The internal challenges of business consist of all of the following *except*
   a. labour
   b. unions
   c. leadership
   d. structure

2. An organizational structure involves
   a. a pattern of relationships between individuals in various roles or positions
   b. a formal hierarchy of authority
   c. rules and procedures
   d. all of the above

3. Outside the organization, challenges that exist include all of the following *except*
   a. political forces
   b. strategic forces
   c. competitive forces
   d. societal forces

4. The general environment involves
   a. strategic forces
   b. labour forces
   c. economic forces
   d. structure forces

5. An example of an external stakeholder is a(n)
   a. creditor
   b. employee union
   c. customer
   d. all of the above

6. The availability of telework is primarily the result of
   a. societal forces
   b. political forces
   c. competitive forces
   d. technological forces

7. All of the following belong to the specific environment *except* a
   a. customer   b. city government
   c. newly formed union   d. political force

8. An example of a component of the general environment is the
   a. political force   b. economic force
   c. environmental force d. both a and b

9. Globalization can be defined as
   a. the integration of world economies
   b. the process of creating and negotiating trade agreements
   c. the globalization of markets
   d. both a and c

10. Changing consumer tastes is an example of the
    a. technological force   b. societal force
    c. economic force   d. competitive force

11. The "invisible hand" to ensure the market works effectively is also known as
    a. competition
    b. economic forces
    c. government policies and regulations
    d. all of the above

12. Organizational learning involves
    a. adapting to the environment
    b. learning from the organization's people
    c. contributing to the learning of the wider community
    d. all of the above

13. A worker with specialized education, skills, and training is sometimes called a
    a. high school graduate b. knowledge worker
    c. professional   d. both b and c

14. Canada's exports to the United States make up approximately ____ of its total exports.
    a. 30%   b. 50%
    c. 75%   d. 10%

15. Canada's economic system has been described as a
    a. free market system   b. mixed system
    c. socialist system   d. communist system

Discussion Questions

1. Identify and explain four internal challenges for business.
2. Describe the difference between the general environment and the specific environment.
3. Identify and describe the six external challenges for business.
4. Provide five examples of an external stakeholder.
5. How can the political force influence business?
6. How can the societal force influence business?
7. Compare and contrast competitive force and technological force. How do they relate to one another?
8. Why is organizational learning important to a company's success?
9. How is the resource industry impacting Canada's economy?
10. Does Canada have a competitive advantage?

CONCEPT APPLICATION   FACEBOOK: WHEN YOUR FRIENDS ARE WORTH A BILLION!

By September 2012, Facebook had accomplished a major milestone: It had reached 1 billion users worldwide. Put another way, one seventh of the world's population has a Facebook account. Since Facebook was first launched in 2004, critics have doubted whether Mark Zuckerberg, a 21-year-old Harvard dropout, could make any money by providing a free networking service on the Internet. After all, Facebook began in a Harvard dorm room and became successful because of the exclusivity it offered. It was a network built for just college students; therefore, a certain amount of privacy was already built in.

Although Facebook has typically earned only a fraction of its principal rival, Google, the company took in an impressive $5 billion in revenue in 2012 (one tenth of what Google earned). How did Facebook get to be so rich?

The vast majority of Facebook's revenues comes from advertising. What is so appealing to advertisers? It's simple—they can tailor ads for each user based on all the personal information a user is willing to share. In addition, Facebook allows advertisers to target users' friends, who are more likely to respond favourably to an ad when they know that their friend has endorsed that brand or simply "checked in" at a store.

If you've used Facebook you'll know that advertisements appear on the border of the screen. Information is gathered about you from your "likes" and your activity on

AP Photo/Paul Sakuma

the site. This information is used to tailor advertisements for you whenever you visit the site. The obvious question is, "So what?" How effective are these tailored ads for the advertiser? There is something called a click-through rate, or CTR, which is the number of times a user clicks on an ad for every 1 million times it's seen. What is the CTR rate for Facebook? It is about 400—that is, about 400 users are clicking ads for every 1 million page views. This is much lower than many other websites, so why bother paying to advertise on Facebook? The answer is because Facebook generates high traffic and offers a powerful venue for ads. Even if most users don't click on the ads, brand awareness will be built.

Another source of revenue for Facebook is through online games supplied by companies like Zynga. These games have attracted millions of users who pay real money for in-game items. Supplier companies like Zynga earn their revenue though these in-game purchases, and Facebook gets a percentage of the profits.

Today, some observers call Zuckerberg a genius with a little bit of luck, but many critics argue that Facebook is simply a virtual space that doesn't have anything to sell except information about its customers.

Facebook's leadership team, however, sees things differently. The average age of its executives is under 45, and Facebook recently increased its global workforce to over 4,600—still a lean company for its revenue size.

Since the company went public in May 2012, the share price dropped from US$38 to less than US$20,[32] leading shareholders to question whether the company can continue to grow. Some disgruntled shareholders have even filed lawsuits against Facebook, questioning the validity of its initial public offering (IPO) valuation. But how do you grow a company that already has a billion customers?

Keeping members interested and coming back is critical to maintaining market share. Certainly, clicking "like" or "poke" was interesting at the beginning, but like all technology features, these, too, get outdated fast.

---

[32] Vance, A. (2012, October 4). Facebook: The making of 1 billion users. *Businessweek*. Retrieved from www.businessweek.com/articles/2012-10-04/facebook-the-making-of-1-billion-users; Lee, D. (2012, October 5). Facebook surpasses one billion users as it tempts new markets. *BBC News*. Retrieved from www.bbc.co.uk/news/technology-19816709

Case Continued >

Unlike other tech companies, Facebook doesn't do controlled testing of its technologies. According to a *Businessweek* article,

> engineers race to put up new features, see if they work, and make tweeks to fix them if they don't. Even trainees who haven't finished their six-week indoctrination program are asked to work on the live site . . . [however], the learn on-the-go philosophy regularly blows up in Zuckerberg's face. He and his team periodically revamp Facebook's privacy policy, triggering a predictable chain reaction: consumer outrage, company walkback, adjusted policy, re-release, lessened outrage, and so forth until the furor dies down. . . . [But], these iterations are apt to leave lasting damage to Facebook's reputation.[33]

So far, Facebook has tried to minimize this. In fact, Facebook has slowly started charging customers for one service (sending messages to new people, or "nonfriends"), but the social networking site doesn't want to lose customers to similar companies such as Google+, Twitter, and LinkedIn.[34]

In addition, gaining new regular members is no easy task. Privacy concerns are still a big issue for many users. Many parents of young teens are either monitoring or limiting their children's social media usage because of cyberbullying, privacy, and other safety and security concerns. And corporations are using Facebook to do background checks on potential new employees. Certainly, there have been numerous newspaper stories of people being fired for their inappropriate photos, status updates, and other public activity on Facebook.[35]

So where do Facebook's next 1 billion members come from? Indeed, growth in North America and Europe has started to level off. According to CNN Money, "less than 20% of Facebook's users live in the U.S. and Canada, but those users account for 48% of advertising revenue that Facebook took in last quarter."[36] Zuckerberg is hoping this will change, but there are still challenges ahead. Facebook has been unable to prosper in one of the world's largest markets, China, because of government censor restrictions. Instead, China's 1.3 billion citizens use local social media sites such as Sina Weibo, Renren, and Tencent.[37]

Russia is another market where local sites are still the choice for its users. VKontakte is one Russian network with over 100 million users, compared to Facebook's mere 7 million users in the same region.[38]

---

[33] Vance, 2012.

[34] Shaughnessy, H. (2013, April 8). Facebook extends charging for messages. Great move! *Forbes*. Retrieved from www.forbes.com/sites/haydnshaughnessy/2013/04/08/facebook-extends-charging-and-that-is-good.

[35] Ramirez, A. (2010, May 28). What Facebook learned from Apple and what we can learn from Facebook. *Executive Street*. Retrieved from http://blog.vistage.com/business-innovation/what-facebook-learned-from-apple-and-what-we-can-learn-from-facebook

[36] Smith, A., Segall, L., & Cowley, S. (2012, October 4). Facebook reaches one billion users. *CNN* Money. Retrieved from http://money.cnn.com/2012/10/04/technology/facebook-billion-users/index.html

[37] Smith, Segall, & Cowley, 2012.

[38] Lee, 2012.

Given these challenges, how is Facebook trying to change? In 2013, Facebook significantly increased its mobile ad presence, which earned close to $1 billion in mobile ad revenue. The company also recently entered the mobile phone market itself by introducing its first smartphone, the HTC First. While Zuckerberg was attempting to build a better mobile experience, he recognized that an increasing number of Facebook users access the site from their mobile phones and tablets, where ads need to be targeted.[39] "We're picking these big investments because I think these are important areas for us to focus on," said Zuckerberg.[40]

David Ebersman, Facebook's chief financial officer, explained, "We're pleased with our progress in product development and with our financial results as well. Mobile has the opportunity to be huge for Facebook if we execute well and continue to attract mobile users and develop valuable mobile monetization products."[41]

What else is Facebook doing right? It is still the top choice among business users as well. According to one survey, Facebook is still the preferred platform among 85% of social media professionals.[42]

Since social networking is a relatively new industry, many organizations are still learning how Facebook and other social media sites can best achieve their goals. Clearly, Facebook is also being used to advertise products, organize protests, and provide awareness on social issues—and now it is selling products, too. Academics of different disciplines are closely watching how social media is beginning to change life in North America as we know it. "It's really humbling to get a billion people to do anything," Zuckerberg says.[43]

Questions

1. What elements of the external and internal environment do you think contributed to Facebook's success?

2. Which elements of the external and internal environment are beginning to create challenges for Facebook?

3. Which force must Facebook work the hardest to address to continue to prosper? Why?

---

[39] Metz, R. (2013, April 10). The first Facebook phone: A little too much information. *MIT Technology Review*. April 10, 2013. Retrieved from www.technologyreview.com/news/513566/the-first-facebook-phone-a-little-too-much-information

[40] Womack, B. (2013, May 2). Facebook revenue exceeds estimates on mobile advertising. *Bloomberg*. www.bloomberg.com/news/print/2013-05-01/facebook-revenue-exceeds-estimates-on-mobile-advertising.html

[41] Womack, 2013.

[42] Shaughnessy, H. (2012, October 4). Facebook's 1 Billion Users: Why the Sky is Still the Limit. *Forbes*. Retrieved from www.forbes.com/sites/haydnshaughnessy/2012/10/04/facebooks-1-billion-users-why-the-sky-is-still-the-limit

[43] Vance, 2012.

Chapter 2

The Employee–Employer Relationship

What Responsibilities Do Bosses Have to Their Employees?

Konstantin Chagin/Shutterstock

Learning Objectives

After studying this chapter, you should be able to

1. Discuss the meaning and significance of *employment* and explain how it differs from other forms of work arrangements.

2. Explain the difference between the standard employment and the nonstandard employment relationship.

3. Identify and explain the main perspectives that shape debates about the appropriate role of markets, management, unions, and legislation.

4. Explain how we balance the interests of employers and employees when employment relationships are terminated.

5. Identify and explain the business responsibilities and opportunities within Canada's diverse labour force environment.

Canada's society and its economy can be significantly influenced by how work and employment are organized. This chapter examines the nature of work, employment and the labour-management relationship. Workers are interested in maximizing the income they receive from the sale of their labour, whereas businesses usually desire to maximize profit. These two objectives can clash, creating conflicts that can have negative effects on productivity and profits. In our examination of the labour relationship, we will consider perspectives that shape debates about how that relationship should be governed. Should businesses and workers be free to negotiate conditions of work, or should the government closely monitor and influence those conditions? We will also identify the obligations that organizations have to diverse members of the labour force.

THE BUSINESS WORLD

Is Working for Free Illegal?

Would you work for free to gain work experience? Many Canadian students who are trying to secure a job in their chosen career would answer "yes." Anya Oberdorf is one graduate who took two unpaid internships with different employers in the hopes of getting a full-time job in the publishing industry. While she gained valuable experience, she wasn't offered a permanent role. "My experience has been really frustrating," said the Toronto graduate. "I can't afford a third internship, but I don't want to sit around at home either."[1] Certainly, students have bills to pay such as rent, groceries, and student loan payments. But how do you pay your bills when you can't find a job?

A group of University of Toronto students have gone to Ontario's Minister of Labour to end a growing practice of unpaid internships in Ontario and across the country. While the legal interpretation is more complex, an *internship* is generally referred to as on-the-job training with an employer to provide an individual with practical work experience. The University of Toronto Students' Union (UTSU) argues that approximately 300,000 entry-level positions are being illegally misclassified as internships, trainee positions, or nonemployee work so that employers can avoid paying recent graduates for their hard work.

Indeed, very little is known about internships. The Ministry of Labour doesn't regulate or keep statistics about interns or internship programs, as such. "You won't find the word 'intern' in our employment laws at all. It's an industry term," said David Doorey, employment law professor at York University.[2] The Ministry of Labour does not track by job type, but rather by the type of contravent of the Employment Standards Act, 2000 (e.g. overtime pay, vacation pay/time, severance, etc.) Many observers, however, agree that students working for free is nothing new. While volunteer work in nonprofit organizations has helped students gain experience, many lawyers argue internships are different.

While providing students with work experience is clearly beneficial, the increasing number of unpaid internships can have a negative effect on the economy. Unpaid work can drive wages down and lead to higher unemployment levels. Currently, graduates face an 18% unemployment rate—more than double the national average. Unpaid work also means interns cannot pay down their student debt, collect unemployment insurance, or contribute to the Canada Pension Plan. With an estimated 300,000 unpaid interns working in Canada, this also means less consumer spending. The problem is that students need work experience, but employers don't always have the resources to hire them.

Proponents of internships argue that a bridge is needed between textbook knowledge and real-life experience, and internships help meet this missing component. While charitable institutions offer volunteer opportunities, this does not necessarily help students gain meaningful experience in their field of study.

Lauren Friese, founder of TalentEgg, a website that helps students find jobs, believes that students should be careful when accusing an employer of illegal activity, especially since students benefit from these programs: "Without internships—whether they're paid

---

[1] Oved, M. (2013, March 5). Unpaid internships: The most precarious work of all. *Toronto Star.* Retrieved from www.thestar.com/news/gta/2013/03/05/unpaid_internships_the_most_precarious_work_of_all.html.

[2] Oved, 2013.

or unpaid . . . there is absolutely no way for those young people to get the experience they need to find that first meaningful career."[3]

Provincial labour laws vary across the country, making the issue even more complex. Moreover, internships are not well-defined or regulated, leading to legal loopholes that allow employers to take advantage of students who are desperate to find meaningful work.

HootSuite, a Vancouver social media company, was recently criticized over its internship practices because it did not comply with British Columbia's Employment Standards Act. In British Columbia, the law defines *internship* and *practicum* differently. An internship is "on-the-job training offered by an employer to provide a person with practical experience." A practicum, on the other hand, involves a formal education process and does not have to be paid.[4]

Ryan Holmes, Hootsuite's CEO, quickly responded to the growing online complaints: "Recently, I learned about some concerns that a few of our internship job postings may not be in compliance with the local laws," Holmes wrote. "I appreciate those who have taken the time to bring this to our attention and we will immediately review this internally . . . When we created the internship program, I believed we were doing the right thing by offering the opportunity for young people to add experience to their résumé and join a Vancouver success story."[5]

Certainly, the practice of internships is growing at a time when many employers are also increasingly hiring temporary and contract workers in Canada because of increasing costs and other competitive pressures. A report by the Law Commission of Ontario indicated that existing laws do not adequately protect unpaid workers.

The U of T student group contends that the province's Employment Standards Act (ESA) "disfranchises students, trainees, interns, and young workers by either partially or completely exempting them from employment standard protections."[6] Other provinces have similar issues.

Today, there is no clear definition of a legal or illegal intern. "I can't say definitely on whether an intern is or is not an employee, and therefore covered by the *Employment Standards Act*, An investigation would have to be conducted in order to gather the facts of a particular situation. An Employment Standards Officer would also have to review the exemptions and special rules in order to determine if any applied. The ESA establishes conditions that must be met in order for an individual to be considered a non-employee "trainee" or a co-op student who is exempt from the Act. Only an Employment Standards Officer can determine whether the ESA applies in a given situation. The Ministry of Labour's website offers the following Information Sheet entitled: "*Are Unpaid Internships Legal in Ontario?*".

The Ministry of Labour is committed to ensuring fairness and protecting young workers. The fact that you are called an "intern" does not determine whether or not you are entitled to the protections of the Employment Standards Act, 2000 (ESA), including the minimum wage.

Here's what you need to know: generally, if you perform work for another person or a company or other organization and you are not in business for yourself, you would be considered to be an employee, and therefore entitled to ESA rights such as the minimum

---

[3] Freeman, S. (2013, April 18). Unpaid internships: U of T students' group calls for ban, says 300,000 illegal interns working in Canada. *Huffington Post*. Retrieved from www.huffingtonpost.ca/2013/04/18/unpaid-internships-ban-canada_n_3103664.html.

[4] Hager, M. (2013, April 8). HootSuite faces online backlash over unpaid internships. *Vancouver Sun*. Retrieved from www.vancouversun.com/HootSuite+faces+online+backlash+over+unpaid+internships/8209279/story.html. Reprinted by permission.

[5] Hager, 2013.

[6] Freeman, 2013.

wage. There are some exceptions, but they are very limited, and the fact that you are called an intern is not relevant.

One such circumstance where a person can work as an intern for no pay concerns a person receiving training, but it has very restrictive conditions. If an employer provides an intern with training in skills that are used by the employer's employees, the intern will generally also be considered to be an employee for purposes of the ESA unless all of the conditions below are met:

1. The training is similar to that which is given in a vocational school.

2. The training is for the benefit of the intern. You receive some benefit from the training, such as new knowledge or skills.

3. The employer derives little, if any, benefit from the activity of the intern while he or she is being trained.

4. Your training doesn't take someone else's job.

5. Your employer isn't promising you a job at the end of your training.

6. You have been told that you will not be paid for your time.[7]

Another exception concerns college and university programs. The ESA does not apply to an individual who performs work under a program approved by a college of applied arts and technology or a university. This exception exists to encourage employers to provide students enrolled in a college or university program with practical training to complement their classroom learning.

If someone performing work as an unpaid intern is unsure of whether he or she is excluded from the ESA, he or she should call the Employment Standards Information Centre toll-free at 1-800-531-5551 for further information.

Note: For the most current version of this Information Sheet please visit the Ontario Ministry of Labour website at www.labour.gov.on.ca.

"It may be time for governments to consider introducing a permit system," says Doorey. "This would allow the government to verify that internships are not being used as a method to obtain free labour." Nav Bhandal, a labour and employment lawyer, says it is difficult to interpret what the law means since there are few cases of student interns suing for wages. Furthermore, students who need work experience and a job reference for future employment don't want to file complaints.[8]

THE LABOUR ENVIRONMENT AND CANADIAN SOCIETY

Objective 1 Discuss the meaning and significance of *employment* and explain how it differs from other forms of work arrangements.

In modern industrial societies, most people depend on income from the sale of their labour to survive. As demonstrated in the discussion of internships in The Business World vignette, work is also a central means by which wealth is distributed in a capitalist economy. It is also an important aspect of personal self-identity and self-worth in many societies—our jobs

---

[7] Langille, A. (2012, July 30). The legality of unpaid internships in Ontario. First Reference Talks. http://blog.firstreference.com/2012/07/30/the-legality-of-unpaid-internships-in-ontario/#axzz2S437oNu9. Reprinted with permission.

[8] Oved, 2013.

employment A relationship between an employer and an employee involving an exchange of labour power (work) for something of value, such as wages or benefits.

employment contract A contract that defines the terms and conditions of a contractual relationship between an employer and an employee. The contract may include reference to services to be performed, working hours, compensation, and other work-related obligations of the employer and the employee.

employee A person hired by an employer to perform work according to the terms of an employment contract.

independent contractors Independent contractors or the self-employed provide labour services in exchange for compensation. They run their own businesses rather than serving as an employee for another organization or person.

partners Individuals who share part ownership in a business. There can be two or more partners in a partnership.

temporary placement organization A business that helps match workers looking for jobs with businesses that require temporary help. Also called an employment agency.

volunteer An unpaid individual who performs services for an organization voluntarily. A volunteer is not an employee under the law.

intern A worker who receives on-the-job training at a workplace. The internship may or may not be a formal requirement of an educational program and can be paid or unpaid. Whether an intern is considered an "employee" and is therefore entitled to legal entitlements available to employees in Canada, such as a minimum wage, depends on how a province's employment standards laws define an employee. Some unpaid internships are unlawful, while others are not.

help define who we are and how others perceive us. For these reasons, the way in which a society manages the labour relationship tells us a lot about that society's values and beliefs.

The nature of work varies over time and space. The labour environment in Canada differs from those in many economically developing countries and from those that existed a generation ago. For example, as we will discuss later in this chapter, Canada's labour force is substantially more diverse than in the past. This creates both challenges and opportunities for Canadian businesses and also for Canadian policymakers, whose job it is to develop policies that will promote efficient business and job growth while also protecting workers and promoting the sustainable distribution of wealth necessary for a healthy society and economy. The range of options policymakers perceive as sensible to create or maintain this complex balance is influenced by their perspective on work and the role of markets and government regulation of business. We will discuss these various perspectives below.

First, we need to understand what we mean by *work* and *employment* in the Canadian context.

Distinguishing Work and Employment

Since the 20th century, the dominant model of organizing work has been employment. **Employment** is a form of work in which a person (an *employee*) is dependent on and mostly subservient to an *employer*. In an employment relationship, the employer is assumed to have control over the methods of production, the unilateral authority to decide what and how much to produce, and the right to direct when, where, and how the employee is required to perform his or her job. The employment relationship is governed by an **employment contract**, which may set out specific rules, obligations, and rights applicable to the employer and employee and is usually enforceable in a court of law, just like other contracts are. At the core of the employment relationship is a basic exchange: **Employees** sell their labour in exchange for compensation, usually in the form of wages and perhaps benefits of some sort. Employment can be full-time or part-time and indefinite in duration or for a fixed period of time—for example, it can last 50 years, or a few hours.

The Employment Contract   However, employment is just one of many ways that work can be organized. There are many people who work but who are not employed. For example, **independent contractors** or the self-employed are not "employees." They still provide labour services in exchange for compensation, but they are running their own business rather than serving as an employee for another business or person. Some people are **partners** in a business rather than employees. Partners also sell their labour, but they are part owners of the business and not its employees. Partners and independent contractors earn *revenues*, not wages. Others obtain work through **temporary placement organizations**, which assign them to work for some other business. Whether these "temp" workers are employees, and if they are who employs them, can be complex questions to answer. Others are categorized as unpaid **volunteers** or **interns** to distinguish their situation from employment. See the discussion in Talking Business 2.1.

Whether a work arrangement is characterized as employment or as some other form of business arrangement has significant implications in Canada. That is because many legal rights and entitlements are tied to the existence of an employment relationship. For example, Canadian governments have enacted a considerable amount of legislation to regulate employment based on the theory that employees require government protection

Are Unpaid Interns "Employees"?

Are unpaid interns illegal in Canada? The answer is surprisingly complicated, because governments are trying to balance a variety of competing policy interests.

On the one hand, employers could easily exploit a law that permitted them to simply call people interns and thereby avoid employment standards laws. Also, unpaid interns could replace real jobs, which is not good for the economy. On the other hand, the state wants young people to gain work experience, and some employers who would not otherwise provide workers with experience to develop skills might allow interns to gain some experience by hanging around the workplace if they don't have to pay them. Therefore, the state is trying to write a law that protects against the first two "bad" aspects of internships while permitting the third "good" aspect. Try writing a law that does that!

You have to start with the question of whether the interns are "employees" under the employment standards legislation, since only "employees" are covered by the Employment Standards Act (ESA). Section 3(5) of the Ontario ESA excludes from the Act, "an individual who performs work under a program approved by a college of applied arts and technology or a university." So that's easy: If the internship is part of a higher education co-op program, then the Act does not apply.

Then things get more complicated. The Ontario ESA defines an "employee" (in section 1(1)) as follows:

"employee" includes,

a. a person . . . who performs work for an employer for wages,

b. a person who supplies services to an employer for wages,

c. a person who receives training from a person who is an employer, as set out in subsection (2) . . .

Subsection (2) then says (with my comments added):

(2) For the purposes of clause (c) of the definition of "employee" in subsection (1), an individual receiving training from a person who is an employer is an employee of that person if the skill in which the individual is being trained is a skill used by the person's employees, unless all of the following conditions are met (note that all of these conditions must be met):

1. The training is similar to that which is given in a vocational school.

[What do you think a "vocational" school means? Well, it almost certainly does NOT include getting coffee, answering phones, and running errands for some idiot who thinks an "intern" means "personal slave." Do you know any colleges that teach "coffee making" or "errand running"?]

2. The training is for the benefit of the individual.

3. The person providing the training derives little, if any, benefit from the activity of the individual while he or she is being trained.

[So, numbers 2 and 3 together mean that the purpose of the internship/training is to provide a benefit for the intern, but not the person/entity providing the training. Thus, if the person does "real" work, that the employer would need to have hired people [to] do, then the intern begins to look a lot like an "employee."]

4. The individual does not displace employees of the person providing the training.

[This clearly catches an employer who lays-off an employee and gives their work to an "intern." If that is done, the intern is an "employee." Does "displace" also cover an employer who uses an intern instead of a hiring a new "employee"?]

5. The individual is not accorded a right to become an employee of the person providing the training.

[This creates an incentive for employers to tell employees that they will NEVER get hired into a real job. Is that a good policy? It also means that when the possibility exists for the intern to be hired at the end of the intern period, the person is an "employee."]

6. The individual is advised that he or she will receive no remuneration for the time that he or she spends in training.

[This seems to mean that if an intern is paid anything, then she is an "employee" under the ESA. An intern is someone who is paid "no remuneration."]

As you can see, whether or not an "intern" is an "employee" under the Ontario ESA depends on all of the circumstances as applied to these criteria. The rules would

(continued)

because of their vulnerability to the employer. Employment standards legislation is one example. It entitles employees to a minimum wage, overtime pay, mandatory time off and holiday pay, and notice of termination among other benefits. None of these entitlements apply unless the arrangement is characterized as employment. Similarly, human rights laws prohibit discrimination in employment relationships, and access to unemployment insurance, public pension schemes, and workers' compensation benefits are often contingent upon a worker having been employed for a period of time prior to making their claim for benefits. Tax systems also treat employees and nonemployees differently—nonemployees can deduct business expenses from their taxable income, whereas employees cannot.

From a business perspective, there may be advantages to using workers who are not employees of the business. A business that uses independent contractors or temporary placement workers may avoid employment standards laws or the requirement to pay insurance premiums to workers' compensation systems, for instance. An employer must usually provide their employees with notice of termination in Canada before they can end an employment relationship. By not *employing* workers, businesses can avoid this potentially costly requirement and adjust more quickly and with less cost to economic downturns.

On the other hand, there may be business benefits associated with the employment relationship as well. According to human resource management literature, employers can maximize worker effectiveness by designing workplace reward systems that recognize and promote loyalty and commitment. One way to do this is to promise workers job security while granting them good pay and benefits. Employers can benefit from having long-service employees who acquire knowledge and skills in the performance of their jobs. The employment relationship may be more likely to foster worker commitment than a model in which workers answer to another employer or work for themselves. Businesses need to weigh these factors when deciding whether to arrange their labour force needs by using employees or retaining independent contractors or businesses to perform the work needed.

What Is an Employee?

What distinguishes an employee from an independent contractor? This is a legal question, and it is answered by courts and administrative tribunals tasked with interpreting employment-related statutes. Factors that are considered in deciding whether someone is an employee or an independent contractor include the following:

- *Degree of control:* Independent contractors can *usually* determine the hours they work and the manner in which the work is performed, and can usually hire other people to perform the work. An employee, on the other hand, is *usually* told when and how to do the work and is subject to supervision of some sort.

- *Degree of economic risk:* An independent contractor assumes the risk of nonpayment of bills by customers, loss of customers, as well as the potential benefit of profits. An employee is *usually* paid their wages even if a customer does not pay their bills (the risk of nonpayment is the employers'), but they also do not *usually* share directly in profits.

- *Degree to which the worker performs an essential service for an organization:* A person who performs an integral task for an organization is more likely to be perceived as an employee than someone who performs a task that is peripheral to the organization's business. For example, a chemist is more likely to be perceived as an employee of a chemical company than a person retained to mow the company's grass once a month.

- *Degree to which the organization provides the necessary tools:* Independent contractors are more likely to own their own tools, whereas employees are more likely to have the tools provided to them by their employer.

A court or tribunal may consider one or more of these factors in determining whether someone is an employee or not. At its core is a basic question: Does the worker look more like a person who is in business for herself or for someone else?

The fact that a contract might say that a person is "not an employee" will not be binding on a court or tribunal. Courts look past that contract language and consider the above factors. Why do you think this is so? The answer is that courts are concerned about workers being taken advantage of by employers. Courts know that employers most often write work contracts, and workers often just sign on the dotted line. If employers could just include a sentence in every contract saying that the worker is "not an employee," then it would be very easy to avoid all of the rules and laws that are designed to protect employees because of their economic vulnerability. Whether these laws are actually necessary to protect employees, and whether they help or harm businesses, the economy, and society, are issues that have been debated for as long as people have been paid to perform work.

From Standard to Nonstandard Employment Relationships

Objective 2 Explain the difference between the standard employment and the nonstandard employment relationship.

The period from approximately the 1930s to the 1980s was the golden age for the employment relationship in Canada. During that period, the **standard employment relationship (SER)** dominated the economic landscape. The SER is characterized by regular, full-time hours at a single employer, often spanning an entire working career. Employees working under an SER receive periodic pay raises and their employers usually provide health benefits and pension plans. The SER functions in the shadow of an extensive array of government regulation that guides the relationship and is underpinned by a strong social security net that provides protection to employees whose employment ends for one reason or another. For example, an employee who is laid off due to lack of work is entitled to unemployment insurance benefits, and an employee injured at work is entitled to workers' compensation benefits. Unemployment and workers' compensation benefits are funded by mandatory employer contributions.

Since the 1980s, however, the SER has been disintegrating as the dominant form of work. Large segments of the working population in Canada today work under arrangements that are frequently described as **nonstandard employment (NSE)**. NSE is less stable and is characterized by part time, temporary, or variable working hours; lower pay; fewer employer-provided benefits; shorter job tenure; and no access to collective bargaining. A 2009 study of Canadian

standard employment relationship (SER) A form of employment relationship characterized by regular, full-time hours at a single employer, often spanning an entire working career. Employees working under an SER usually receive periodic pay raises, and their employers usually provide health benefits and pension plans.

nonstandard employment (NSE) A less stable form of employment than the SER that is characterized by part-time, temporary, or variable working hours; lower pay; fewer employer-provided benefits; shorter job tenure; and is usually non-unionized.

labour standards found that NSE accounts for about 32% of the Canadian workforce. Many of these workers are young, recent entrants into the labour force. This trend toward NSE means that young people graduating from university today are far less likely to experience the sort of stable, predictable employment patterns that were the norm for earlier generations.

Many other workers are being characterized as independent contractors, sometimes at their own request, but often at the behest of businesses seeking to benefit from the financial savings and legal flexibility associated with eliminating "employees." The shift from standard employment to "self-employment" is a major contributor to growing **income inequality** in Canada, since self-employed workers tend to be lower paid, have fewer employer-paid benefits, have less job security, and are not entitled to the many social protections (unemployment insurance, workers' compensation) or guarantees (minimum wage, overtime pay, paid holidays) available only to people who are or were "employees."

Workers employed under NSE arrangements and low-income workers who are treated as independent contractors are often described as **vulnerable or precarious workers**. They live on the cusp of poverty and are unable to save or plan for the future because their source of income is always on the verge of disappearing.

income inequality The unequal distribution of wealth to individuals or households in an economy.

vulnerable or precarious workers Individuals who perform work in a nonstandard employment relationship. They are always at risk of unemployment since their jobs are insecure, and because their pay is low they live on the cusp of poverty.

Objective 3 Identify and explain the main perspectives that shape debates about the appropriate role of markets, management, unions, and legislation.

Perspectives on Work and Government Policy

Whether this shift toward NSE and "self-employment" is cause for concern is a matter of substantial debate. Certainly businesses can benefit in terms of lower labour costs and greater managerial flexibility. That can help profitability, which in turn could make Canada an attractive place for corporations to invest. However, the OECD has noted that the growth in NSE and self-employment is also a significant cause of growing income inequality in Canada.[9] Some workers benefit from this shift, but it appears that many more do not.

This points to a familiar problem in labour policy debates. Practices and policies that may benefit employers and businesses are not always good for workers, the economy, or society more generally. High profits and dividends are almost always treated as positives in business literature. But if they are derived from poor treatment of workers, including low wages, few health benefits, and dangerous working conditions, then are high profits and dividends benefiting society?

Consider an example involving Walmart, the world's most profitable corporation. According to the *Fortune* 500 rank of American corporations, Walmart's 2010 profits were US$14.3 billion. However, Walmart has also found itself on the losing end of numerous legal actions alleging illegal treatment of employees, such as stealing wages from workers and denying legally mandated breaks and rests. In Canada, Walmart has been found in violation of labour laws in its attempt to stop employees from exercising their legal right to join unions.

AP Photo/J Pat Carter

[9] OECD. (2011). *An overview of growing income inequalities in OECD countries: Main findings.* Retrieved from www. oecd.org/els/soc/49499779.pdf.

Do the illegal actions by Walmart against its employees taint its impressive record of big profits? Should governments impose more or less rules on business to influence how workers are treated? If they impose more rules, will this make the climate less friendly for businesses, causing them to hire fewer workers?

How to balance the interests of business in maximizing profits and shareholder dividends, on the one hand, with the interests of workers in securing a decent level of income and security, on the other hand, has been a subject of debate since the beginning of large-scale economic activity. These debates have been informed by a variety of perspectives that vary on such fundamental issues as

- the role and effectiveness of markets
- the role of bargaining power in the employment relationship
- the role of management, and the human resources function in particular
- the role of unions and collective bargaining

The range of responses to work-related issues that is deemed prudent depends on which of these perspectives dominates in a society at any particular moment in time. Four perspectives in particular have shaped debates about the governance of work in Canada: the neoclassical, managerial, industrial pluralist, and critical perspectives.

Neoclassical Perspective
The **neoclassical perspective** argues that **competitive markets** are the best means of organizing complex economies and societies. The forces of supply and demand, if left to operate freely with limited state interference, will ensure optimal assignment of skills and expertise throughout the economy as well as the fairest distribution of wealth. This is because people and businesses are motivated by self-interest. Therefore, they will make decisions that maximize their personal interests and avoid situations that do not. Provided people have adequate information to recognize what is in their best interests and are free to make choices, the **invisible hand of the market** will guide actors toward economic and social prosperity. Neoclassicists assume that labour markets are perfectly competitive, or close to it, and therefore believe that if they left undisturbed by government intervention and unions they will produce the optimal market outcomes.

Adam Smith used the "invisible hand" metaphor in his book *The Wealth of Nations*, published in 1776. Smith argued that, by pursuing their own self-interest, individuals "are led by an invisible hand" to promote the greater public interest, even if that is not their intention. Modern-day adherents to the neoclassical perspective share Smith's recipe for governments: The state should focus on ensuring a legal system is in place to protect property rights, enforce contracts, and prohibit anti-competitive practices, but otherwise should keep taxes low and government administration and regulation to a minimum.

Neoclassicists perceive the labour relationship as simply another form of free exchange between informed and free actors. Therefore, Canadian governments—indeed, governments around the world—are misguided in their attempts to "protect workers" through regulation such as minimum wages, overtime pay, human rights laws, health and safety rules, and laws that permit or even encourage unionization and collective bargaining. Neoclassicists argue that none of these laws are necessary to protect workers, and in fact they do more harm than good.

To see why, consider the example of the **minimum wage**. Imagine that an employer offers an employee $4 per hour and that the employee is prepared to accept that wage rate.

neoclassical perspective One view of how the economy should function. It contends that competitive markets are the best means of organizing complex economies and societies. The forces of supply and demand, if left to operate freely with limited government interference, will ensure optimal assignment of skills and expertise throughout the economy as well as the fairest distribution of wealth.

competitive markets Markets in which there are a sufficient number of participants competing for the same goods, services, and customers. Market forces tend to fix prices at a point where the supply of a good or service equals the demand for that good or service.

invisible hand of the market Adam Smith used the "invisible hand" metaphor in his book *The Wealth of Nations*, published in 1776. Smith argued that, by pursuing their own self-interest, individuals "are led by an invisible hand" to promote the greater public interest, even if that is not their intention.

minimum wage An employment standards law that mandates the minimum hourly wage that must be paid to an employee. Each province sets its own minimum wage.

However, the government passes a minimum wage law prohibiting employers from paying less than the minimum wage. The Neoclassicist position is that this law will have negative effects on the economy that will ultimately harm low-wage workers. By artificially raising the wage rate above the "market rate" ($4 per hour in our example), the minimum wage law will cause employers to hire fewer workers, to replace workers with machinery, or to pack up and move the work to another location that does not have a minimum wage. If none of these options is available, the employer will pass on the additional costs to consumers in higher product prices, and if that is not possible the company may be forced into bankruptcy or close down altogether. In any case, the economy suffers, and the harm will be felt most by the low-wage workers who the minimum wage laws were intended to help.

Neoclassicists are also not concerned about working conditions being too low in the absence of worker protection legislation. They believe that the invisible hand of the market will ensure this does not happen. A business that offers less than the market wage rate will be unable to attract or retain qualified workers, and therefore will either have to raise their offer to attract workers or will be driven out of business. Since workers are assumed by neoclassicists to be knowledgeable about other job possibilities and to be free and mobile—able to move from job to job as better opportunities arise—market forces will ensure that wages and working conditions remain close to that point at which labour supply equals labour demand (the equilibrium market rate). Any attempt by governments to intervene in this process of free bargaining by employers and workers will disturb these market-clearing processes, producing harmful effects.

Managerial Perspective

The **managerial perspective** is closely related to modern human resource management. It shares a belief with the neoclassical perspective that government intervention in the governance of work and employment should be minimal. However, managerialists put their faith in enlightened management practices rather than in the "invisible hand" of the marketplace. They argue that employers and employees, businesses and workers, share a common interest: They both want the business to be successful. Managerialists argue that workers who are treated decently and with respect will be the most productive workers, and that the most successful businesses will be those that provide good wages, benefits, and good working conditions. Therefore, businesses will look out for employees' concerns because it is in their economic interests to do so.

In the managerialist perspective, employment standards and employment regulation should be kept to a minimum since these laws inject rigidity into the work relationship and impose unnecessary costs on employers. If laws are necessary to deal with the worst types of employers—those who do not perceive the wisdom in treating workers decently—the legal standards should be set at a low level and be flexible enough to not punish "good" employers. Unions and collective bargaining are an unnecessary impediment to managerial prerogative and flexibility in the managerialist perspective, and should not be promoted by governments. Since it is in the interest of management to treat workers fairly, there is no need for workers to look to unions for protection. Indeed, mangerialists argue that the decision of workers to support unionization reflects a failure of management to address employee needs through progressive human resource management policies (see Exhibit 2.1).

Industrial Pluralist Perspective

The **industrial pluralist perspective** views the work relationship very differently than both neoclassicists and managerialists. They emphasize the imbalance of power between workers and employers and the value to society and economies of striking a reasonable balance between the *efficiency* concerns of employers and the *equity*

In recent years there has been increasing interest in unionization among coffee shops such as Starbucks and others. Like most businesses, Starbucks would prefer to avoid unionization of its employees. In the United States controversy erupted over the firing of a New York Starbucks employee in 2011 allegedly because she had attempted to join a union (Industrial Workers of the World). In Canada, workers at several Starbucks outlets were represented by the Canadian Auto Workers for a period of time. However, the union's drive to organize the chain stalled and by 2007, all of the unionized stores had become "decertified."

Traditionally, the restaurant and food services industry has been among the most challenging sectors to unionize. The low level of union penetration of the food-service sector is due to a number of factors including the fact that this is a highly competitive industry, and employers believe unionization will pose a threat to their profits. In addition, the labour force is typically part-time, with high turnover, and so many of these workers don't have enough commitment to the job to tolerate any tensions that arise over efforts to start a union. As workers stay in their jobs longer it will become increasingly important for businesses like Starbucks to ensure these employees are feeling satisfied with their working conditions or run the risk of facing unionization.

concerns of workers. For the pluralist, the relationship between a business/employer and a worker/employee involves the bearer of power on the one hand, and subordination on the other hand. In most cases, workers lack the necessary **bargaining power** to engage in meaningful bargaining about conditions of employment, with the result being that the business purchasing their labour can set the working terms unilaterally. This is problematic because workers, unlike bricks and staples, are human beings, and society has an interest in promoting environments in which humans do not feel disenfranchised or exploited.

In contrast with neoclassicists and managerialists, pluralists support an **activist government** that intervenes in the work relationship to promote decent working conditions and worker "voice" in the determination of those conditions. Pluralists support minimum employment standards to ensure decent working conditions because they reject the neoclassical belief that market forces alone will produce a fair balance between equity and efficiency concerns.

Most importantly, pluralists believe that the most effective way to ensure worker voice and to promote a healthy distribution of wealth throughout the economy is to promote collective bargaining and unionization. **Collective bargaining**, including a legal right to withhold labour (a strike), empowers workers by putting them on a more equal footing as they bargain for the sale of their labour. This ensures that workers receive a reasonable share of the economic pie produced by their labour, a result that benefits the economy (by fuelling consumption) and society (by producing a decent standard of living). Therefore, pluralists support laws that protect the right of workers to join unions, to engage in collective bargaining, and to strike if necessary to apply pressure on their employers to agree to better working conditions (see Exhibit 2.2).

Pluralists reject the neoclassical claim that labour markets are perfectly competitive, or even nearly so. For example, they argue that in the real world, workers usually lack information about new jobs, so they are ill equipped to assess the true value of their labour during the initial bargaining process. Workers also lack information about alternative job opportunities, contrary to the assumptions of the neoclassical model. Even if they have that information, in practice people do not move from job to job with the mobility and ease that the neoclassical model assumes. Workers will often remain at a workplace for years, even if there are better job opportunities elsewhere. Behavioural economists describe this effect as **bounded rationality**—the recognition that humans often do not make decisions that would maximize their personal utility because they either lack the necessary information to assess the various options or lack the capacity to assess the information they have.

Exhibit 2.1 Would you like a union with that coffee?

bargaining power The amount of power workers have to determine their conditions of employment with their employer, such as wages, hours, training, vacation time, health and safety measures, and other factors.

activist government A government that intervenes in the employment relationship by passing laws that restrict freedom of contract, such as employment standards, human rights, health and safety, and employment equity laws.

collective bargaining A process of negotiation measures between a group of employees (through a union) and an employer (or group of employers) leading to a collective agreement that applies to the entire group of employees.

bounded rationality The idea that humans often do not make decisions that would maximize their personal utility because they either lack the necessary information to assess the various options or lack the capacity to assess the information they have.

Pluralists argue that collective bargaining is valuable because it promotes two important outcomes:

Democracy and voice: It introduces a form of democracy into the workplace by giving workers the tools and power to participate directly in the development and enforcement of workplace rules and practices.

Distributive Fairness: It empowers workers to bargain for a larger share of the economic pie than is possible in the alternative system in which individual employees bargain for the sale of their labour. This encourages a stronger middle class and lesser income inequality, which according to the pluralists facilitates a healthier economy and more stable society.

Exhibit 2.2 The Benefits of Collective Bargaining

critical perspective A perspective that believes the interests of labour (workers) and capital (the owners and managers of economic organizations) are irreconcilably in conflict. The objective of capital is to extract from labour maximum effort and control at minimal cost. Since workers depend on capital for their basic needs in a capitalist system, and there are almost always more workers than jobs, labour is inherently disadvantaged and subject to exploitation at the hands of the more powerful capitalists.

In short, people are far more complex and unpredictable than their depiction in the neoclassical model. Pluralists argue that since the assumptions on which that model is based do not hold true in the real world, it is inappropriate to base real-life public policies on neoclassical ideas. Pluralists also reject the managerialist claim that progressive human resource management policies and the supposed economic benefits derived from them will protect the interests of workers. For example, pluralists argue that the shift toward NSE, discussed earlier, which is contributing to the growth in economic inequality and fall in workers' real wages in Canada, is a trend being pushed and implemented by human resource management professionals. Unions, not management, are the institution that fights against these trends in favour of more secure, higher-paying jobs (see Talking Business 2.2).

Critical Perspective The focus of the **critical perspective** is the inherently exploitive nature of the capitalist system. This perspective draws its inspiration from Marxist theory. It argues that the interests of labour (workers) and capital (the owners and managers of economic organizations) are irreconcilably in conflict. The objective of capital is to extract from labour maximum effort and control at minimal cost. Since workers depend on capital for their basic needs in a capitalist system, and there are almost always more workers than jobs, labour is inherently disadvantaged and subject to exploitation at the hands of the more powerful capitalists.

The critical perspective posits that employment regulation and collective bargaining are at best only marginally useful in protecting workers from this exploitation. In fact, these measures can actually be harmful to worker interests insofar as they can blind workers to their exploitation and distract them from the more important objective of building class consciousness, which will be necessary to challenge the capitalist model and replace it with a more egalitarian model. From the critical perspective, the managerialist perspective glorifies the manipulation of labour by capital in an attempt to mask the inherent conflict between labour and capital. The neoclassical model is dismissed as a faulty theory based on nonsensical assumptions that have no basis in reality. Moreover, neoclassicists ignore the central fact that the "market" itself is a construct developed by capitalists and supportive politicians to serve the interests of capital.

THE LABOUR CONTEXT IN CANADA: WHERE ARE WE NOW?

Which of these perspectives dominates public policy in Canada today? The best answer is probably that all of them play some role in shaping the debates about how best to organize and structure the labour relationship. Certainly, in the period running from the end of World War II until about the 1980s, the industrial pluralist perspective was highly influential. Governments across the country, from all of the major political parties, supported

The State of Canadian Unions—Down but Not Out

Employees who are covered by a collective agreement or a union contract earn higher wages than employees who are not. In 2012, the average hourly wage for unionized employees was $27.36, compared to $22.25 for non-unionized employees. However, after adjusting for variances by occupation, education, and experience, the union wage premium has declined in recent decades to less than 8 per cent—nonetheless, a clear benefit still flows to unionized workers.

Despite this advantage, the proportion of workers covered by a collective agreement has been slowly trending downward in Canada over the last twenty years. Union coverage now sits at 31 percent, down from close to 34 percent in 1997.

In order for union membership to grow, the labour movement must find a way to make strides in organizing some industries that have traditionally remained elusive—such as the services, agriculture, and financial sectors. And, as business continues to boom in the resources sector, companies in the mining and oil and gas sector may present opportunities to expand.

The first bold step taken by the labour movement has been the merger of the Canadian Auto Workers (CAW) and the Communications, Energy and Paperworkers Union of Canada (CEP). The merged entity will be Canada's largest private-sector union, representing roughly 300,000 workers right out of the gate. The new conglomerate will not only have more clout thanks to its larger size, but will be better able to focus its resources to support organizing efforts. The union leadership plans to grow the union—to about double its current membership—in relatively short order and will devote 10 per cent of its revenue to these activities. Membership may be expanded to include students, retirees, and the unemployed, demonstrating its commitment to move beyond the limits of the traditional union model. The impact could be significant.

Unions know they need to adapt to the new realities of the Canadian landscape—the economy will grow only slowly over the medium term, technological change will continue at a rapid pace and international competition will intensify. This will make gains at the bargaining table increasingly difficult. In the public sector, concessions are likely as governments grapple with budget deficits and growing levels of debt. In response, unions will need to be creative in growing their membership base to secure their social and political power but also their financial future. So, while unions may be down, don't count them out quite yet.

Source: Excerpted from Thorpe, K. (2013, January 31). The state of Canadian Unions—down but not out. The Conference Board of Canada. Retrieved from www.conferenceboard.ca/topics/humanresource/commentaries/13-01-31/the_state_of_canadian_unions%E2%80%94down_but_not_out.aspx. Reprinted with permission.

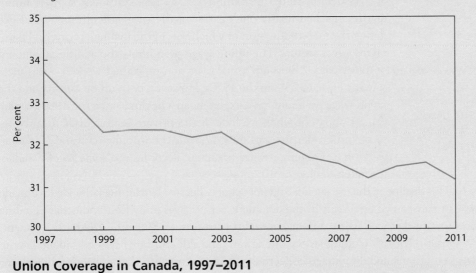

Union Coverage in Canada, 1997–2011

strong labour laws that facilitated and encouraged workers to join unions and engage in collective bargaining.

These laws remain in place. For example, Canadian employers are prohibited by **labour relations statutes**, such as the Ontario Labour Relations Act, from discriminating against employees who try to organize a union or who support unions. These statutes also require

labour relations statutes Laws that govern labour issues in a particular province. In Canada, each province has the power to enact its own labour laws.

Exhibit 2.3 Union Density in Canada, 1921–2010

Year	Union Density (percentage of nonagricultural workers who are union members)
1921	16
1930	13.1
1940	16.3
1945	24.2
1951	28.4
1958	34.2
1960	32.3
1965	29.7
1970	33.6
1975	35.6
1980	35.7
1985	36.4
1990	36.2
1995	34.3
2000	31.9
2005	30.7
2009	29.9
2010	29.6

Source: Godard, J. (2010). *Industrial relations, the economy, and society* (4th ed.), pp. 77–78. Concord, ON: Captus Press; Human Resources and Skills Development Canada. (2010). Union membership in Canada. Retrieved from www4.hrsdc.gc.ca/.3ndic.1t.4r@-eng.jsp?iid=17.

family income A historical term used to describe the amount of money working men were able to bring home to support their spouses and children. Today, *household income* is used to describe the total amount of income brought in by all members of a household or place of residence.

union density A measure of the percentage of employees who are members of a union out of the total employees in the labour market.

union wage premium The additional amount of wages paid to unionized over non-unionized workers.

employers to engage in collective bargaining with unions that have been certified by the government as the representative of a group of the employer's employees. Unions get certified when they can demonstrate that a majority of the employees want union representation. Once this happens, the government orders the employer to bargain "in good faith" with the union toward reaching a collective agreement. If no agreement is reached, labour relations laws permit employees to go on strike to put pressure on the employer to improve its offer and prohibit employers from firing the employees for doing so. The law also permits employers to lockout the employees, thereby denying them their pay.

For much of the 20th century, the Canadian economy was dominated by large manufacturing workplaces (steel, automakers) and the extractive (mining, oil and gas) and forestry industries. The SER dominated in these industries, which were staffed primarily by men. Canadian governments during the postwar period sought to encourage an economy in which working men were able to earn a **"family income"** sufficient to support their spouses and children. This was the ideal Canadian family around which public policies were designed. Promoting collective bargaining in heavy industry was considered a sensible way to protect the ideal: Working men were encouraged to join unions, and through collective bargaining they would bargain for stable, long-term employment and wages and benefits sufficient to support a family and fuel a consumer economy. Women, who worked primarily either in the home or in service-sector jobs, were considered secondary income earners and less important from a public policy perspective.

As demonstrated in Exhibit 2.3, with government support **union density** reached nearly one quarter of the (nonagricultural) workforce during the mid-1980s, most of which was in the manufacturing and natural resources sectors. The **union wage premium**—the additional amount of wages paid to non-unionized over non-unionized workers—was measured at close to 25% in the 1970s. However, both union density and the union wage premium have experienced a decline since the 1980s, which is most apparent when we look at the private sector. In 2010, private-sector union density was only 17.5% of the nonagricultural Canadian workforce. The union wage premium, according to some recent studies, has fallen to close to 10%.

This decline in the prevalence and impact of collective bargaining coincided with, and was in part caused by, a shift in the dominant perspectives away from industrial pluralism and toward the neoclassical and managerialist perspectives. Since the 1990s, governments in Ontario, British Columbia, Saskatchewan, and Alberta have revised labour laws to weaken unions and discourage collective bargaining, arguing that collective bargaining discourages businesses from investing in Canada. Recently, the federal government has been prohibiting workers from going on strike. This turn against unions and collective bargaining is closely aligned with the neoclassical perspective and the belief that markets operate most efficiently without collective bargaining and with little employment regulation.

Economic globalization has also influenced the debate about how best to organize work in Canada. Greater mobility of capital and industry has contributed to a shift in the composition of the Canadian economy. Many manufacturing workplaces have moved to lower-wage countries, and many of the new jobs being created are in the service sector.

Are Unions Relevant in Canada Today?

The past decade has seen organized labour decline as a share of the Canadian workforce. Between 1997 and 2011, union density in Canada fell approximately 1.7 per cent from 30.9 per cent to about 29.2 per cent. The overall decline in union density would have been greater but for the fact that the highly-unionized public sector continued to represent a large share of total employment. More than 70 per cent of the broader public sector is unionized—which includes government departments, agencies, and Crown corporations, along with publicly funded schools, hospitals, and other institutions.

In contrast, union density in the private sector now sits at an all time low of 15.9 per cent. This decline is due, in part, to legislative changes restricting union certification processes but also changes in the economy including the "hollowing-out" of the manufacturing sector.

Union density is not a flawless measure of labour's influence in terms of bargaining power and wage setting. Collectively-bargained agreements can serve as a standard against which other non-unionized organizations set wages and benefits in order to remain competitive. As union density declines, however, the degree to which it serves as the benchmark also diminishes.

The changing demographic profile of the population is also undermining the role and importance of unions. Baby boomers, who are beginning to exit the workforce, can more easily relate to the success of the labour movement in achieving gains around pay equity for women, racial equality, and improved working conditions. Many members of the younger generation—call them Millennials or Generation Y—hold negative views about the relevance of labour unions. This generation has grown up in a society where many of these battles were already won. Therefore, many younger workers fail to see the benefits of belonging to a union. In fact, seniority rules can be impediments to younger workers getting coveted day shifts and vacation time during summer months.

Unions have historically played an active role lobbying on issues affecting working Canadians. Labour's influence has produced public policy improvements in workplace health and safety in the workplace, pension benefits, wellness, and literacy, to name just a few areas. However, labour's ability to exert pressure on behalf of workers will undoubtedly be impacted by a declining base of members and the resulting loss of union dues. Even though union density is on the wane, organized labour can continue to have a positive impact on government policy—particularly if they focus on issues that have broader public appeal.

Source: Excerpted from Thorpe, K. (2011, November 9). *Are unions relevant in Canada today?* The Conference Board of Canada. Retrieved from www.conferenceboard.ca/topics/humanresource/commentaries/11-11-09/are_unions_relevant_in_canada_today.aspx. Reprinted with permission.

Governments must wrestle with how to balance their desire to create a "business-friendly" climate while also ensuring that good jobs are created. This challenge has been rendered more difficult by the increased ability for businesses to move from one jurisdiction to another. The fear is that if labour costs rise too high, or laws make control of labour to rigid, businesses will avoid Canada or leave. In this way, globalization can be said to create downward pressure on employment-related laws and practices (see Talking Business 2.3).

DISMISSING EMPLOYEES

Unemployment rates measure the percentage of adults in the labour market who are actively seeking employment. Exhibit 2.4 shows how those rates have varied over a 35-year period. In 2012, the unemployment rate was between 7% and 7.5%. Avoiding high rates of unemployment is one of the great challenges of governments. High, sustained unemployment imposes high costs on economies and societies.

For example, workers who lose their job often need to access public resources, such as unemployment insurance or welfare benefits. People who are not earning money are not paying taxes, so government revenues used to fund essential public services decrease. The

Objective 4 Explain how we balance the interests of employers and employees when employment relationships are terminated.

unemployment rate The percentage of adults in the labour market without employment who are actively seeking employment.

Exhibit 2.4
Unemployment Rates in
Canada

Source: Statistics Canada.
(2012). Labour force survey
estimates (LFS), supplementary
unemployment rates by sex
and age group, annual, CAN-
SIM Table 282-0086. Ottawa,
ON: Statistics Canada.

unemployed also have less money to spend in the economy, and our economy depends in large measure on Canadians buying things. Unemployment also imposes other social costs, including higher incidence of depression, alcohol and drug dependency, and poor child nutrition. When a community suffers large numbers of job losses at one time, such as when a factory closes, there are negative spillover effects throughout the entire community.

Therefore, governments have an interest in discouraging unemployment and job losses. On the other hand, employers sometimes need to respond to changes in their economic situation by downsizing the labour force. If the survival of the business requires shedding labour costs, then employers should be permitted to do this with as little complication and cost as possible. An important challenge for business and government alike is to find an appropriate balance between permitting flexibility in work practices while also protecting the welfare of workers. The most obvious point when these interests come into conflict is at the end of the employment relationship.

Rules and programs have emerged over time that attempt to balance the interests of business in being able to downsize and the interests of workers and the community in avoiding unemployment. These rules come in a variety of forms. Here we will briefly discuss three of them: (1) court-made common law rules; (2) employment standards notice requirements; and (3) unemployment insurance benefits.

Common Law Rules Requiring Notice of Termination

common law of the employment contract All of the rules of interpretation of employment contracts applied by judges over the years, as recorded in legal decisions.

All non-union employees in Canada have an employment contract with their employer. Sometimes the contract is written, but if it is not then the parties have a verbal contract. Disputes about what an employment contract says or how it should apply in a given situation are resolved by judges in courts of laws. Over time, a large body of decisions by judges interpreting employment contracts have been released and recorded in law books and, more recently, on electronic websites. This body of case law is known as the **common law of the employment contract**.

reasonable notice The amount of time in advance that employers must inform employees that their services are no longer necessary and their employment contract is ending. How much notice is "reasonable" is decided by judges and depends on a number of factors, including the length of the employee's service, the employee's age, and the type of work the employee performed.

One rule that judges created and that forms part of the common law of the employment contract is a requirement for employers to provide employees with **reasonable notice** of the termination of the employment contract. How much notice is "reasonable" is decided by judges and depends on a number of factors, including the length of the employee's service, the employee's age, and the type of work the employee performed. For long-service employees, the notice period required can be as much as one to two years. The notice can be working notice, or pay in lieu of notice, meaning that the employer can just pay the employee their wages for the period of notice without requiring the employee to actually work. This requirement for employers to give reasonable notice helps employees transition from one job to the next.

Statutory Minimum Notice of Termination

If an employer fails to provide the employee with reasonable notice, the employee can sue the employer in court to recover it. However, this is costly and takes a lot of time, so most workers do not bother. To provide a less expensive, quicker, and more informal means of ensuring employees receive some notice of their termination, governments have imposed notice requirements. Employment standards statutes in Canada include **mandatory minimum statutory notice** provisions. For example, in Ontario the Employment Standards Act requires employers to provide the following minimum periods of notice of termination:

mandatory minimum statutory notice The minimum job termination notice employers must give their employees. It is found in employment standards statutes and varies from province to province.

1. At least one week before the termination if the employee's period of employment is less than one year

2. At least two weeks before the termination if the employee's period of employment is one year or more and fewer than three years

3. At least three weeks before the termination if the employee's period of employment is three years or more and fewer than four years

4. At least four weeks before the termination if the employee's period of employment is four years or more and fewer than five years

5. At least five weeks before the termination if the employee's period of employment is five years or more and fewer than six years

6. At least six weeks before the termination if the employee's period of employment is six years or more and fewer than seven years

7. At least seven weeks before the termination if the employee's period of employment is seven years or more and fewer than eight years

8. At least eight weeks before the termination if the employee's period of employment is eight years or more[10]

The amount of notice is higher if 50 or more employees are terminated in a four-week period. While the statutory minimum notice is usually less than the common law period of reasonable notice assessed by judges, the employee does not need to sue the employer in court to recover it. An employment standards complaint to recover statutory minimum notice can be filed by completing a form online, at which point the government will investigate and order the employer to comply with the statute.

Both reasonable notice and statutory minimum notice are intended to provide employees with a cushion—a period of time to plan for their job loss and to look for another job. These requirements impose costs on employers. However, they are justified on the basis that job losses impose costs on society and employees, some of which should be borne by employers. This is a different approach than that used in the United States, where employment contracts can be terminated at any time with no notice. That model is known as **"at will" employment** and is highly influenced by the neoclassical perspective. The US approach assumes that if employees

"at will" employment A concept used in US labour law that allows employers to terminate employees without any notice for any reason. At-will employment does not exist in Canada.

---

[10] Ontario Ministry of Labour. (2013). *Your guide to the Employment Standards Act, 2000*, p. 81. Retrieved from www.labour.gov.on.ca/english/es/pdf/es_guide.pdf.

value notice of termination, they will bargain a contract term requiring it. In Canada, our courts and governments have imposed a notice requirement, recognizing that most employees will not know that they should bargain for one or will lack the bargaining power to do so.

Unemployment Insurance Programs

unemployment insurance program A federal government program that requires employers and employees to make contributions into an unemployment insurance fund. To access benefits, unemployed individuals must satisfy a series of conditions, including having paid into the fund for a specified period of time and actively searching for employment. The amount of benefits payable are based on a percentage of the employee's prior earnings up to a maximum amount, and benefits last for only a fixed period of time (usually several weeks) and vary according to the level of unemployment in the region where the worker lives.

Another way that we attempt to reduce the cost to workers and society associated with job losses in Canada is through **unemployment insurance programs**. The unemployment insurance program operated by the federal government first appeared in 1940. Today, the program is administered under the Employment Insurance Act. The model requires employers and employees to make contributions into an unemployment insurance fund. To access benefits, unemployed individuals must satisfy a series of conditions, including having paid into the fund for a specified period of time and actively searching for employment. The amount of benefits payable are based on a percentage of the employee's prior earnings up to a maximum amount, and benefits last for only a fixed period of time (usually several weeks).

The unemployment insurance program provides a measure of security to some Canadian workers who lose their jobs. However, the model has been criticized on a number of fronts. Supporters of a strong insurance program point out that less than 50% of unemployed people in Canada qualify for benefits because of the strict qualifying criteria; they want the criteria to be loosened so that more people can receive the benefits they contribute to. Others are critical of unemployment insurance plans because they believe that they discourage people from working. These critics call for the elimination of unemployment benefits altogether, or at least for lower benefit levels and even more stringent eligibility requirements.

CURRENT ISSUES IN THE WORKPLACE: MANAGING WORKFORCE DIVERSITY

Objective 5 Identify and explain the business responsibilities and opportunities within Canada's diverse labour force environment.

Canadian businesses operate within a diverse society. The Canadian population reflects a multitude of cultures and demographic backgrounds. For example, recent census figures provided by Statistics Canada show that over 5 million Canadian citizens were foreign-born, comprising nearly 20% of the total population. This diversity is increasingly reflected in the Canadian labour pool. Immigrants who came to Canada in the 1990s have accounted for approximately 70% of the total growth of the labour force in recent years. Women also comprise a significant component of the Canadian labour force and account for about half of both the employed workforce and all union members. Visible minorities and people with disabilities, together with women, make up over 60% of Canada's labour force.

Diversity in our workforce is also reflected in the growing presence of older workers. At the start of the 21st century, Canadians between the ages of 37 and 55 made up about 47% of the labour force, but by 2011 half of these workers were 55 or over. Consequently, it is clear that organizations must attend to the rights of a diverse group of individuals.

Protecting Diversity and Guarding against Discrimination in Canadian Law

If the Canadian economy is to flourish, businesses must be encouraged to tap the considerable potential of Canada's diverse population. However, how best to achieve this is the source of much debate.

For politicians, the question arises as to whether it is appropriate to use legislation to address these challenges, and if so, what sorts of laws to deploy for this purpose. Neoclassicists reject the need for legal intervention to address discrimination in the labour market. They argue that market forces will punish employers who select employees based on factors unrelated to productivity (such as skin colour, sex, disability, or ethnic origin) and reward employers who ignore those irrelevant factors. In the "long run" these market forces will drive discriminatory employers to alter their behaviour or else put them out of business.

However, that is not a position that Canadian governments have accepted. In fact, there is extensive regulation intended to break down barriers to employment that confront Canada's diverse labour force. In this section, we will consider three types of laws that address discrimination in the labour relationship: (1) the Charter of Rights and Freedoms; (2) human rights legislation; and (3) employment equity legislation.

Canadian Charter of Rights and Freedoms

The **Charter of Rights and Freedoms** forms part of Canada's Constitution. It governs the relationship between governments and citizens by protecting fundamental rights and freedoms of Canadians against state interference, including the following:

- fundamental freedoms of speech, press, assembly, association, and religion
- democratic rights
- mobility rights regarding the right to move freely from province to province for the purposes of residence or employment
- legal rights, which provide standard procedural rights in criminal proceedings
- equality rights, which guarantee no discrimination by law on grounds of race, ethnic origin, colour, religion, sex, age, or mental and physical ability
- language rights

The Charter applies only to government action. Governments can act in two ways: as an employer and as lawmakers. Therefore, in the labour context, the Charter is applicable directly to governments as employers and to all laws passed by governments.

For example, if the Government of Ontario paid its female employees less than its male employees for the same work, that would be in violation of the Charter's protection of equality rights based on sex. However, if it were a private corporation that was paying its female employees less than its male employees, such as McDonald's, the Charter would not apply because McDonald's is not the government. Employees of McDonald's could still file a complaint under a human rights statute (see the discussion that follows). All laws passed by a government must be consistent with the rights and freedoms guaranteed in the Charter. For example, if a government passed a law that granted special privileges to Christian workers, that law would violate Section 15 of the Charter, which protects Canadians from discrimination by the government on the basis of religion.

Equality rights are not the only part of the Charter that can affect the employment relationship. There has been a considerable number of Charter cases in recent years exploring the

© GoodMood Photo/Fotolia

Charter of Rights and Freedoms A part of the Canadian Constitution that governs the relationship between governments and citizens by protecting fundamental rights and freedoms of Canadians against state interference.

meaning of "freedom of association," which is protected by Section 2(d) of the Charter. Courts have ruled that freedom of association guarantees workers the right to form and join unions and to engage in collective bargaining. That means laws that restrict the right of workers to engage in these activities could be, and sometimes have been, struck down as illegal. In 2012, unions launched Charter complaints challenging laws that prohibited Air Canada and Canada Post employees from going on strike. If the unions are successful in those complaints, the ability of governments to pass laws that ban strikes would be curtailed.

A law that violates a right or freedom found in the Charter might nevertheless be "saved" if a court finds that the violation is justified "in a free and democratic society" because the harm caused by the limitation on rights and freedoms is outweighed by the benefits produced by the challenged law. This exception appears in Section 1 of the Charter. For example, in 1990 the Supreme Court of Canada ruled that laws permitting forced or "mandatory retirement" of workers who reach the age of 65 violated the Section 15 guarantee of protection against age discrimination. However, the court then ruled that the laws were "saved" by Section 1, because retiring people at age 65 created necessary job opportunities for young people, among other reasons, and the retired workers had access to pension plans.

If a law violates the Charter and is not "saved" by Section 1, then a court can order that the law is no longer in effect. That is because the Charter supercedes all other laws.

Human Rights Laws   While the Charter does not apply to private-sector businesses, human rights laws do. Those laws typically prohibit discrimination in employment based on certain **prohibited grounds**. For example, in the Canadian Human Rights Act, which applies to businesses governed by federal laws (about 10% of Canadian employees are governed by laws made in Ottawa), prohibits discrimination in employment on the following grounds:

■ race	■ marital status
■ colour	■ family status
■ national or ethnic origin	■ physical or mental disability (including dependence on alcohol or drugs)
■ religion	
■ age	■ pardoned criminal conviction
■ sex (including pregnancy and childbearing)	■ sexual orientation

The Canadian Human Rights Act and each of the provincial human rights codes govern human rights issues and provide detailed procedures for investigation and resolution. An employee who feels they employer has discriminated against them on a prohibited ground may file a complaint with the appropriate human rights tribunal and seek a remedy, including lost wages and reinstatement if they have been dismissed for discriminatory reasons. The prohibitions on discrimination in employment apply throughout the life of the employment relationship, including hiring, terms of employment, and dismissal.

Provincial human rights legislation, which governs most Canadian businesses, include similar though not identical prohibited grounds. For example, in Manitoba it is unlawful for an employer to discriminate on the basis of political belief, but that prohibited ground is not included in either the Ontario Human Rights Code or the Canadian Human Rights Act. Recently, Ontario added the new ground of gender identity and gender expression to

prohibited grounds Those grounds listed in human rights statutes. Discrimination is prohibited in employment on the prohibited grounds only. Prohibited grounds vary from province to province, but all include common grounds such as race, colour, ethnicity, religion, age, disability, sex, and sexual orientation.

the list of prohibited grounds, making it the first province to do so. Which grounds to protect, and how to apply those grounds to employment situations, can be controversial.

Indeed, employers who are proactive in understanding the law and its application can benefit from diversity, as seen in Talking Business 2.4.

TALKING BUSINESS 2.4

Organizations Seeing the Light about Faith at Work

Religion may still be an off-limits topic for some people, but organizations can't afford to ignore the subject. . . .

First, religious accommodation is a legal requirement; it is not about endorsing a specific belief system: Deb Volberg Pagnotta, a legal human rights expert, told the CIWE [Council on Inclusive Work Environments] that federal and provincial human rights laws prohibit discrimination in the workplace based on religion. For example, under the Ontario Human Rights Code, employers are required to accommodate employees who are unable to work certain days for religious reasons, unless the employer can demonstrate that it would cause it undue hardship to do so. In addition to religious leave, employers may be asked to consider requests related to issues such as dress code flexibility and breaks for religious observance or prayer.

However, Nouman Ashraf, Director of the Anti-Racism and Cultural Diversity Office at the University of Toronto, emphasized that "accommodating and celebrating spiritual traditions and holidays does not constitute an endorsement of a specific belief system, just as supporting women or those with different levels of ability and sexual preferences does not translate into a corporate statement of preferential treatment."

Second, faith is not too personal for the workplace: Some organizations are hesitant to visibly support religious diversity because faith is "too private." Consequently, they respond reactively to religious requests rather than proactively supporting faith at work. Yet organizations have grown to support diversity related to grounds such as sexual orientation that were once also considered private or personal. Today, leading organizations recognize that, for many employees, faith is an essential aspect of their identities and an integral part of who they are. Respectfully acknowledging their faith is fundamental to engaging the whole person.

Third, culture and faith are not one and the same: Many organizations assume that religious diversity is addressed under cultural diversity policies and training. Nadir Shirazi, President of Multifacet Diversity Solutions, stressed that religious affiliation is not synonymous with culture; therefore, training in religious diversity is required, particularly as the workplace becomes increasingly multicultural and global. In addition, some workers choose religions or belief systems outside of their cultural and family traditions. Nadir noted that organizations also need to be aware that even people who share the same faith will practice it in different ways.

Fourth, acknowledging religious diversity can benefit the company: The Ford Motor Company, viewed by many as a leader in supporting faith diversity, connects its faith-based efforts to its business goals. Dan Dunnigan, Chair of Ford's Interfaith Network, told the council how Ford's faith-friendly initiatives have helped the company attract and retain valued employees. He noted how one Ford employee summed up the benefits: "My faith is the foundation of who I am as a human being. It is deeply important to me and guides how I choose to live my life, the quality of my work, [and] everything I do, and the company honours and embraces that."

There are also opportunities for organizations to encourage employee faith groups to get involved in community activities, such as food drives, violence prevention programs, and green initiatives. Supporting their efforts can further an organization's corporate social responsibility goals.

Senior management support and a strong diversity policy that is aligned with business values and goals are prerequisites for creating a faith-inclusive environment. Effective faith diversity strategies are proactive and go beyond the requirements of compliance; they are designed to help the organization value, strengthen, and respect religious differences. A study by the Society for Human Resource Management found that employee morale, retention, and loyalty are the factors most positively affected when companies grant religious accommodations to workers. By embracing religious diversity, employers can leverage the unique talents, knowledge, and backgrounds of their workers to gain a competitive advantage during this turbulent economic time.

Source: Excerpted from Zettel, K. (Winter 2009). Organizations seeing the light about faith at work. *InsideEdge.* Retrieved from www.conferenceboard.ca/insideedge/q12009/q109-organizations-seeing-the-light.aspx. Reprinted with permission from The Conference Board of Canada.

All Canadian human rights legislation prohibits employers from discriminating on the basis of physical and mental disability. When a disabled worker is unable to perform all of the essential duties of a job, these laws impose on employers a **duty to accommodate** the employee's disability with the aim of enabling the worker to perform the job. This might mean providing the employee with special tools to help with lifting, to build ramps or elevators, or to change schedules to give disabled workers more frequent breaks, among other changes. Changes need to be made up to the point that they would cause **undue hardship**, which is an onerous standard for employers to meet. The duty to accommodate applies to other prohibited grounds too, including religion. For example, employers have been ordered to give employees time off work to observe religious holidays that fall on regular work days.

Employment Equity Legislation   A significant portion of our valued labour pool is derived from members of **designated groups** whose participation in the workplace contributes to the success of an organization. With regard to past discrimination, there are four groups in particular that traditionally have not received equitable treatment in employment: women, Aboriginal peoples, visible minorities, and people with disabilities. Exhibit 2.5 identifies their relative presence in the population and the labour pool. These groups represent approximately 60% of the total workforce. They have faced significant obstacles related to their status in the labour force, including high unemployment, occupational segregation, pay inequities, and limited opportunities for career advancement.

The federal government introduced the Employment Equity Act in 1986 to break down barriers for these four designated groups. Before looking at how that legislation works, consider the following background on the designated groups.

Women   Traditionally, women have been segregated in occupations that are accorded both lower status and lower pay. According to a 2003 report by Statistics Canada (based on 2001 census data), while women represented 44.8% of the total workforce, they were clearly not equally represented across occupations. For example, women have been underrepresented in such areas as semiprofessional occupations, management and board positions, supervisors in crafts and trades, and sales and service personnel. The failure of women to achieve higher-level corporate positions has been attributed to a variety of sources, including lack of mentoring opportunities, lack of female role models, stereotyping and preconceptions of women's roles and abilities, exclusion from informal networks of communication, and failure of senior leaders to assume accountability for women's advancement.

In a report commissioned by the Women's Executive Network (WXN) in Canada, the majority of women executives surveyed believe they have to work twice as hard as men to achieve success. Respondents also indicated that they continuously find themselves hitting

Exhibit 2.5
Representation of Designated Groups in the Labour Force

	Representation in the Canadian Population	Representation in the Workforce
Women	50.85%	44.8%
Aboriginal peoples	3.3	1.6
People with disabilities	12.4	2.3
Members of visible minorities	13.4	11.7

Source: Courtesy of Statistics Canada, Table 282-0002. Retrieved from www.statcan.ca/english/Pgdb/labor20a.htm.

the "glass ceiling" and are not accepted into the executive-level culture, which includes participation in "the boys club." The findings also revealed a concern that women continue to face more barriers to career advancement than men with the same qualifications and are often presented with fewer opportunities. Among the greatest career barriers identified was the "the lack of comfort on the part of men in dealing with women on a professional level." Gender-based stereotyping was also indicated as a career barrier. In addition, many respondents felt that they are paid less than men with similar qualifications and they receive less credit and recognition for accomplishments (see Talking Business 2.5).

TALKING BUSINESS 2.5

He Says, She Says: Gender Gap Persists in Attitudes toward Women's Advancement in the Workplace

Attitudes about advancing women into senior management roles are still polarized along gender lines. Men in senior executive positions appear to be the least concerned about increasing the number of women in the top ranks of organizations.

Yet the stagnating advancement of women to senior positions in recent decades may be due to more than the attitudes of men. *Women in Leadership: Perceptions and Priorities for Change* finds that a gap in opportunities between women and men emerges early in their respective careers—at the first level of management. Compared to men, women are less likely to feel they can obtain line management responsibilities, creating an experience gap at the earliest stages of their management careers.

Further, both women and men were of the view that leadership development and human resource management programs were not serving their intended purposes—identifying and developing the next generation of leadership candidates.

"Gender diversity in senior management is a strategic and cultural issue within organizations. Our research shows that barriers to women's advancement exist throughout organizations, but the responsibility starts at the very top—with the board of directors and the existing senior management," said Ian Cullwick, Vice-President, Leadership and Human Resources.

"It will take more than neutrality on the part of senior male executives to bring about significant improvement in the advancement of women within organizations."

Numerous studies have shown that organizations improve their bottom lines when they have more women in senior management positions.

Leadership opportunities, motivations and abilities are three factors that are crucial to women's advancement. In the research, a fourth factor has emerged as even more crucial—

attitudes. These attitudes can have a huge influence on the other factors. Eighty-six (86) per cent of women believe there is still a glass ceiling. While 68 per cent of women managers think that the organizations are still run by an "old-boys club", only 43 per cent of men agree.

This finding shows in the survey results when upper-level female managers indicated that they have the same aspirations as their male counterparts to reach senior management. Women in first-level management, however, appeared less ambitious to reach senior levels of the organization than men.

"Paradoxically, we may need more female leaders before we can increase the number of women in senior management," said Donna Burnett-Vachon, Associate Director, Leadership and Human Resources.

Most women (and men, for that matter) ranked formal Talent Management programs at the bottom of the list in terms of having an impact on their careers. Further, mentors for women were more likely [to] have a lower organizational rank than men, and women were more likely than men to look outside their organizations for mentors.

"To advance, women need not just mentors, but sponsors—senior leaders who can advocate for them and help to open up career opportunities, often in an informal way. However, women are less likely than men to have sponsors as they work their way up the ranks," said Burnett-Vachon.

Based on a core focus on changing philosophies and values, recommendations for change fall into three categories, which together make up an integrated approach to promoting the advancement of women in organizations:

- Governance: Make women's advancement a formal governance and performance priority for the board; ensure that policies, practices and measures are both in place

(continued)

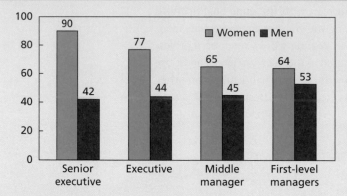

Support for Increasing the Number of Women in Senior Management, by Gender and Level

Note: Data represent the percentage of respondents who strongly agree/agree with the statement "Organizations should try to increase the numbers of women in their senior ranks," *n* = 430.

and consistently applied; communicate the business case for advancing women throughout the organization.

- Leadership development: Engage senior leaders to identify emerging women leaders; ensure there are senior women role models in the organization; provide high-potential and emerging women leaders with strategic assignments.

- Human Resources Management: Identify actual or perceived barriers to career development; seek out high-potential women from the earliest career stages and provide meaningful support; regularly review talent management practices and educate supervisors and managers on such processes; provide more family-friendly

policies and encourage all employees (men and women) to take advantage of them.

Some Canadian organizations do follow best practices and get exceptional results, but they are not the norm. Without the involvement of top leaders who champion, monitor, and measure organizational progress, the number of women in the senior leadership ranks will not increase dramatically any time soon.

The report is based on a national survey of 876 women and men, along with in-depth interviews with 29 women (15 who have reached C-suite levels and 14 emerging leaders). Overall, 43 per cent of male managers and 68 per cent of female managers agree that organizations should try to increase the number of women in senior management. Male senior executives were the least likely of all management groups to agree that there is a need to increase the number of women in leadership roles. The vast majority of female senior executives (90 per cent) agreed or strongly agreed that organizations should try to increase the number of women in their senior ranks. But only 42 per cent of men agreed with that sentiment.

Source: Brent Dowdall, (2013, May 15). *He Says, She Says: Gender Gap Persists in Attitudes Toward Women's Advancement in the Workplace.* Reprinted with permission from The Conference Board of Canada. Retrieved from www.conferenceboard.ca/press/newsrelease/13-05-15/he_says_she_says_gender_gap_persists_in_attitudes_toward_women_s_advancement_in_the_workplace.aspx.

Aboriginal Peoples Aboriginals make up about 3.3% of the population. They represent one of the fastest growing populations in Canada but remain vastly underrepresented in the workforce, with their unemployment rate hovering at the 20% range. Researchers have estimated that the Aboriginal population "baby boom" will result in 350,000 Aboriginal people reaching working age by the next few years, and this underscores the growing need for Canada to absorb more Aboriginal people into its workforce. However, as researcher Stelios Loizedes of The Conference Board of Canada observed:

> A major difficulty in achieving this goal is that most of this large cohort of Native Canadians coming of working age will have insufficient education and limited job experience, restricting their ability to compete for jobs. . . . Native communities and the private and public sectors will have to implement creative solutions to narrow the education and employment gaps.[11]

---

[11] Loizides, S. (2003, December 15). Aboriginal baby boom a challenge for employment prospects. *Canadian HR Reporter, 16*(22), 10.

The educational challenge has proven to be a significant barrier, with Aboriginal populations experiencing a high school dropout rate of 70%. In addition, the lack of job experience and language and cultural barriers have made the plight of this group often appear bleak.

Another barrier to improved employment is the geographical distribution of the Aboriginal community. Employment opportunities on or near Aboriginal reserves are limited. In addition, while over half of the Aboriginal population live in the four Western provinces, these provinces account for a relatively small percentage of the total jobs in Canada, compared to Quebec and Ontario. Sadly, in many urban contexts, Aboriginal workers have typically been largely segregated in low-wage, unstable employment.

Among the biggest barriers faced by the Aboriginal community may be perception—with many Aboriginal Canadians feeling that they do not "fit" with the corporate environment. As David Brown observed:

> That's a problem for both the First Nations community and corporate Canada to address. Aboriginal Canadians have been prevented from playing a part in the modern corporate world for so long that many now feel that exclusion is normal.[12]

Aboriginal Canadians, however, have the potential ability to meet Canada's labour shortages, as seen in Talking Business 2.6.

TALKING BUSINESS 2.6

Aboriginal Workers: Integral to Canada's Ongoing Competitiveness and Performance

In the coming years, Canada's economy is unlikely to have enough workers with the right skills to meet its labour market needs. Our workforce is aging at an accelerating rate, and the fertility levels of the Canadian population are below replacement levels. Canada's Aboriginal population—including Métis, Inuit, and First Nations—can play an important role in helping meet Canada's current and future labour market needs.

The Aboriginal population is the fastest growing population in Canada, and is also much younger than the non-Aboriginal population. Between 1996 and 2006, Canada's Aboriginal population grew by 45 per cent while Canada's non-Aboriginal population grew by just 8 per cent. In 2006, 39.8 per cent of Aboriginals were under the age of twenty, compared to only 24.1 per cent of non-Aboriginals.

Yet, Canada's Aboriginal population continues to be underutilized within the workforce. In 2006, the unemployment rate for non-Aboriginals was 5.2 per cent, compared with unemployment rates of 19 per cent for Inuit, 16.3 per cent for

First Nations, and 8.4 per cent for Métis. Why do Aboriginal employment levels lag behind those of Canada's non-Aboriginal population? . . .

One reason for the lagging employment levels of [the] Aboriginal population is lower educational attainment. Some Aboriginal workers lack the educational qualifications they need to succeed in the labour force—such as postsecondary education, or skills such as literacy and numeracy. The educational shortfall compared to the Canadian average is striking. The 2006 Census notes that just 8 per cent of Aboriginals have a university degree compared to 23 per cent of non-Aboriginals. And 34 per cent of Aboriginals aged 25 to 64 have not completed high school compared to 15 percent of non-Aboriginals in Canada. However, Aboriginals are also more likely to be unemployed than non-Aboriginals with the same level of education. What else might explain the underutilization of Canada's Métis, Inuit, and First Nations within the labour force?

(continued)

---

[12] Brown, D. (2003, December 15). Overcoming sense of exclusion is key to making inroads in mainstream jobs. *Canadian HR Reporter, 16*(22). 9.

Our initial findings suggest that Aboriginal workers often lack much-needed work experience, or formal documentation of their work experiences and skills, required to gain entry to good jobs. As well, some Aboriginals, particularly those in remote areas, lack access to transportation to get to work. Others are reluctant to leave their communities for a job for an extended period, contributing further to their underutilization. Negative stereotypes may also make it difficult for Aboriginals to gain employment, and may make it difficult for them to succeed in some work environments.

The challenges facing Aboriginal people will need to be overcome in order to reduce Canada's labour shortages. The solutions will not be easy or quick: engaging Métis, Inuit, and First Nations people more fully in Canadian workplaces will take some time.

Source: Excerpted from Edge, J. (2012, February 1). Aboriginal workers: Integral to Canada's ongoing competitiveness and performance. Reprinted with permission from The Conference Board of Canada. Retrieved from www.conferenceboard.ca/topics/education/commentaries/12-02-01/aboriginal_workers_integral_to_canada_s_ongoing_competitiveness_and_performance.aspx.

Individuals with Disabilities   Individuals with disabilities have faced a variety of employment obstacles. Typically, this group has experienced a higher unemployment rate compared to the national average. Among the challenges faced are attitudinal barriers in the workplace, physical demands unrelated to the job requirements, and inadequate access to technical and human support systems.

The Canadian Healthcare Network, a national nonprofit web-based health information service, clearly notes the importance of acknowledging this segment of the population and of the labour pool:

> In the coming decades, people with a disability will comprise a larger percentage of the population in Canada than ever before. The math is pretty straightforward. As the baby boom generation grows older, the overall age of the population will increase. And because the incidence of disabilities is strongly correlated to age, these numbers will rise together. The degree of accessibility available to this aging population will play a key role in determining their level of health or of hardship, just as it plays a critical role in the daily lives of the more than four million people currently living with a disability in Canada.[13]

A major challenge faced by people with disabilities is the issue of accessibility. This can entail a variety of obstacles. While physical barriers may be the most visible obstacle to full accessibility, economic barriers, social discrimination, and obstacles to communication can all prevent someone from having equal access to a building, a service, or a job (see Talking Business 2.7).

Visible Minorities   Visible minorities make up a growing segment of the population. In the past decade, almost 70% of the growth in the labour force was accounted for by newcomers who arrived in the 1990s.[14] In addition, as the baby boom generation

---

[13] Canadian Health Network. Retrieved from www.canadian-health-network.ca/servlet/ContentServer?cid=1045848110489&pagename=CHN-RCS%2FPage%2FGTPageTemplate&c=Page&lang=En.

[14] Canadian Labour and Business Centre (n.d.). *CLBC Handbook: Immigration and skill shortages*. Retrieved from www.clbc.ca/files/reports/immigration_handbook.pdf.

Ontario Employers Have a New Tool to Improve Accessibility for People with Disabilities

The Conference Board of Canada in partnership with the Government of Ontario's EnAbling Change program have released a new free resource to help employers make their workplaces more inclusive.

This free resource, *Employers' Toolkit: Making Ontario Workplaces Accessible to People With Disabilities*, is intended to help employers to understand and implement the Employment Standard related to the Accessibility for Ontarians with Disabilities Act (AODA).

"Employers across Ontario will have to implement the Employment Standard over the next five years. This toolkit will help organizations make their workplaces more inclusive. A strong business case exists for creating accessible and inclusive work environments for employees with disabilities," said Ruth Wright, Director, Human Resources Management Research, The Conference Board of Canada.

"The full inclusion of people with disabilities in all aspects of community life and the workplace opens the door to their full participation in the economy as customers, entrepreneurs, and employees. An inclusive work environment is one where everyone is treated with respect and all employees are valued for their contributions."

Labour shortages are looming in Ontario. A 2007 Conference Board report indicated that vacancies in Ontario could reach 190,000 in 2020, and rise to 364,000 by 2025 and to 564,000 by 2030.

According to Statistics Canada, approximately 15.5 per cent of Ontarians had a disability in 2006. And Ontario government data reveal that in 2009, people with disabilities were three times more likely than people without disabilities to be unemployed or out of the labour force.

This toolkit helps employers of all sizes to implement the Employment Standard. It includes:

- Special text boxes that introduce each of the individual sections of the Employment Standard requirements;
- Tips and good practices to promote inclusive practices at all stages of employment;
- Case studies to help employers to see how others have successfully implemented accessible strategies and policies;
- Tips for small businesses that frame the requirements of the Employment Standard according [to] their specific circumstances; and
- Tools and templates that employers can tailor to their own organizations.

Source: Brent Dowdall, (2013, January 23). Ontario employers have a new tool to improve accessibility for people with disabilities. Reprinted with permission from The Conference Board of Canada. Retrieved from www.conferenceboard.ca/press/newsrelease/13-01-23/ontario_employers_have_a_new_tool_to_improve_accessibility_for_people_with_disabilities.aspx.

retires, immigrant workers will play a greater role in the labour pool. It is estimated that sometime between 2011 and 2016, new immigrants will account for 100% of the labour force growth.[15]

Workplace obstacles faced by visible minorities include culturally biased aptitude tests, lack of recognition of foreign credentials, and excessively high language requirements. Recent statistics indicate that while visible minorities are well educated, they experience the highest unemployment rates, with recent estimates at roughly twice as high as that for the Canadian-born population.

A study released by the Canadian Race Relations Foundation indicated that desirable jobs and promotions elude many visible minorities and Aboriginal people who believe

---

[15] Kustec, S. (2012). Appendix A: The importance of immigration to labour force growth. *The role of migrant labour supply in the Canadian labour market.* Citizenship and Immigration Canada. Retrieved from www.cic.gc.ca/english/resources/research/2012-migrant/appa.asp.

that subtle forms of racism permeate the workplace.[16] The report, prepared by Jean Lock Kunz, Anne Milan, and Sylvain Schetagne from the Canadian Council on Social Development (CCSD), examined the experiences of visible minorities and Aboriginal peoples in cities across Canada. Among the findings were the following:

■ Aboriginal peoples, visible minorities, and immigrants to Canada encounter more challenges in finding employment in all regions in Canada.

■ Foreign-born visible minorities experience the greatest difficulty finding desirable work, and only half of those with a university education have high-skilled jobs.

■ Compared to White Canadians, visible minorities and Aboriginals who possess a university education are less likely to hold managerial and professional positions. Among those visible minorities who do hold managerial positions, over 50% are self-employed, compared with only 30% of White Canadians.

■ Higher education appears to yield fewer benefits for minorities and Aboriginals in terms of employment and income. Given the same level of education, White Canadians (both foreign-born and Canadian-born) are three times as likely as Aboriginals and about twice as likely as foreign-born visible minorities to rank among the top 20% of income earners.

The Model of the Employment Equity Act

The Department of Justice defines equity as focusing on treating people fairly by recognizing that different individuals and groups require different measures to ensure fair and comparable results. **Employment equity** was a term developed by Justice Rosalie Abella, commissioner of the Royal Commission on Equality in Employment (1984), to reflect a distinct Canadian process for achieving equality in all areas of employment. In addition, the term was intended to distinguish the process from the US notion of "affirmative action" as well as to move beyond the "equal opportunity" measures that were available in Canada at that time.

According to the commission, "systemic discrimination" was responsible for most of the inequality found in employment. **Systemic discrimination** refers to internal policies, practices, patterns, or biases that tend to disadvantage some groups and favour others. It might not be deliberate, but it has the effect of excluding certain classes of people. For example, if managers of a business hold management meetings and make important business decisions on golf courses or in "men's clubs," they might envision managers as people who like to go to those places. This perception would tend to work against women seeking management positions. If managers believe people educated in Canada are "smarter" than people educated in other countries, then they will tend to give preference to Canadian-educated applicants and employees. Systemic discrimination maintains historical preferences and creates barriers to diversity in workplaces.

employment equity A term that was developed by Justice Rosalie Abella, commissioner of the Royal Commission on Equality in Employment (1984), to describe a model designed to remove systemic barriers that have historically led to underrepresentation in Canada's labour market of people from the four designated groups.

systemic discrimination Internal policies, practices, patterns, or biases that tend to disadvantage some groups and favour others. It might not be deliberate, but it has the effect of excluding certain classes of people.

[16] Kunz, J.L., Milan, A., & Schetagne, S. (2000). *Unequal access: A Canadian profile of racial differences in education, employment and income.* Canadian Race Relations Foundation. Retrieved from http://atwork.settlement.org/downloads/unequal_access.pdf.

To address systemic discrimination, the Employment Equity Act (EEA) was designed as an ongoing planning process used by an employer to accomplish a number of objectives:

- eliminating employment barriers for the four designated groups identified in the Employment Equity Act—women, people with disabilities, Aboriginal people, and members of visible minorities
- redressing past discrimination in employment opportunities and preventing future barriers
- improving access for the designated groups and increasing their distribution throughout all occupations and at all levels
- fostering a climate of equity in the organization
- implementing positive policies and practices to ensure the effects of systemic barriers are eliminated.

Note that the EEA only applies to private-sector employers *under federal jurisdiction* as well as almost all employees of the federal government. This means that it does not apply to the vast majority of private-sector businesses in Canada, which are governed by provincial laws.

The EEA requires employers that have 100 employees or more to implement employment equity and to report on their results. Under the act, the employer must do the following:

- Distribute to employees a questionnaire that allows them to indicate whether they belong to one of the four designated groups.
- Identify jobs in which the percentage of members of designated groups is below their relative representation in the labour market.
- Disseminate information on employment equity to employees, and consult with employee representatives.
- Scrutinize the current employment system to assess whether any barriers exist that may limit the employment opportunities of members of designated groups.
- Generate an employment equity plan directed at promoting an equitable workplace.
- Endeavour to implement the employment equity plan.
- Monitor, assess, and revise the plan in a timely fashion.
- Complete an annual report on the company's employment equity status and activities.

The objective of the EEA is to slowly break down systemic discrimination and thereby build up the composition within the workforce that reflects the diversity of the labour force as a whole. A number of resources are available to employers to help in this endeavour, as outlined in Talking Business 2.8.

More and more businesses have begun to recognize that employment equity is good for business, and Canada continues to strengthen its programs to capitalize on the strength of an increasingly diverse workforce, including immigrants (see Talking Business 2.9). Among the numerous organizations that focus on employee equity is BMO Financial Group. BMO recently received accolades from The Conference Board of Canada for its employment equity and diversity initiatives, including its employee-led diversity action teams, its internal employee assistance program, and its recently launched project to help identify workplace barriers among individuals with disabilities.

Employment Equity Resources

1. *Government of Canada Labour Program:* The Government of Canada's Labour Program website (www. labour.gc.ca/eng/standards_equity/eq/index.shtml) is a national clearinghouse of employment equity technical expertise. Through the site, you can obtain general information on employment equity or access tools and resources for the implementation of employment equity as well as information on legislation and programs.

2. *Employment and Social Development Canada:* This department is mandated with breaking down barriers to equality of opportunity for Canadians. Responsibilities include helping families with children, supporting people with disabilities, and ensuring that seniors can fully participate in their communities. The department provides policies, services, and programs for Canadians who need assistance in overcoming challenges they encounter in their lives and their communities. These resources can be accessed at its website (www.hrsdc. gc.ca/eng/home.shtml).

3. *Human Resources and Skills Development Canada (HRSDC):* HRSDC supports human capital development and labour market development. Among its clients are employees, employers, individuals receiving employment insurance benefits, students, and those who need focused support to participate in the workforce. HRSDC provides federal-level management of labour and homelessness issues and supports students and communities through the Canada Student Loans Program and community economic development initiatives. Visit the website at www.hrsdc.gc.ca/eng/home.shtml.

Immigrants Make Significant Contributions to Innovation

Immigrants can help boost Canada's innovation performance, which has been lagging behind many other developed countries, according to a The Conference Board of Canada report…

"Immigrants tend to be motivated individuals willing to take risks in search of greater opportunities, which should predispose them to be innovative," said Diana MacKay, Director, Education and Health. "At every level we examined—individual, organizational, national and global—immigrants were associated with increased innovation in Canada."

Canada is a consistent below-average performer in its capacity to innovate. Canada ranks 14th out of 17 industrialized countries in the Conference Board's *How Canada Performs* innovation report card.

The report, *Immigrants as Innovators: Boosting Canada's Global Competitiveness*, uses a number of measures to show that countries benefit from welcoming immigrants. For example, in Canada:

• At least 35 per cent of Canada Research Chairs are foreign-born, even though immigrants are just one-fifth of the Canadian population;

• Immigrants to Canada win proportionally more prestigious literary and performing arts awards (immigrants comprise 23 per cent of Giller Prize finalists and 29 per cent of winners; 23 per cent of Governor Generals Performing Arts Award recipients are immigrants);

• Immigration rates affect trade levels between Canada and immigrants' countries of origin. Based on the Conference Board's model of known factors influencing trade, a one percentage point increase in the number of immigrants to Canada can increase the value of imports into Canada by 0.21 per cent, and raise the value of exports by 0.11 per cent;

• Immigrants are a source of diverse knowledge and experience that can increase innovation in Canadian businesses, based on a survey undertaken for this study and a literature review; and,

• Foreign direct investment into Canada is greater from countries that are well represented in Canada through immigration, based on data from the census and from Foreign Affairs and International Trade Canada.

Despite the innovation skills that immigrants bring to Canada, they face obstacles that limit their ability to maximize their contribution as innovators. These include inadequate recognition of international experience and qualifications, failure of employers to tap foreign language skills which could be employed in international markets, and lack of opportunities for newcomers to fully utilize their skills.

Employers can make hiring, integrating, and retaining immigrants effective innovation strategies. Policies and practices available to employers to help immigrants contribute in the labour market include:

- Hiring immigrants at every level of the organization, including leadership roles—Employees tend to be more dedicated to an organization and motivated in their work if they see that the organization is committed to their advancement.

- Matching the organization's workforce to its clientele—Employers who match the diversity of their staff to that of their markets may be better positioned to meet their client's needs.

- Providing encouragement for immigrants to share their views—Managers who actively invite feedback from immigrant employees reap the benefits of hearing diverse points of view, which is essential for innovation.

The research was jointly conducted as part of the CanCompete project and the Leaders' Roundtable on Immigration. CanCompete is a three-year Conference Board program of research and dialogue [that] is designed to help leading decision makers advance Canada on a path of national competitiveness. The Leaders' Roundtable on Immigration brings together key stakeholder groups to address common issues relating to immigration.

Source: Brent Dowdall, (2010, October 15). Immigrants make significant contributions to innovation. Reprinted with permission from The Conference Board of Canada. Retrieved from www.conferenceboard.ca/press/newsrelease/10-10-15/immigrants_make_significant_contributions_to_innovation.aspx.

Many businesses have also stepped up their efforts to assist the Aboriginal community in gaining greater self-sufficiency and participation in the workforce. There are a number of companies that have been actively involved in boosting the presence of Aboriginals in the workplace. Many businesses have proven that they can work with Aboriginal communities, educational institutions, and government to enhance employment prospects for Aboriginals. A typical recruitment method for companies is to offer support for educational institutions, training initiatives, and scholarships for Aboriginal students. For example, 3M Canada contributes to bursaries given through Aboriginal Affairs and Northern Development Canada for Aboriginal students who are pursuing careers in fields related to health care. In addition, recruitment strategies that reach out to Aboriginal communities and organizations are also employed.

Dating back to 1990, the federal government formally recognizes federally regulated companies for achievements in implementing employment equity and addressing the needs of a diverse workforce. Employment equity awards have been given to those organizations deemed to be models in the establishment and implementation of equity practices. The Vision Award is presented to those organizations that exhibit outstanding approaches to the implementation of equity, diversity, and inclusiveness in the workplace. The Certificate of Merit is presented to organizations for their sustained efforts toward attaining a representative workforce.

Recent awards have been presented to such high achievers in equity and diversity as Pelmorex Media Inc., the company that runs the Weather Network. Employee surveys conducted at Pelmorex indicated that more than 90% of employees feel the company highly values equity. This company also offers training on nondiscriminatory interviewing techniques, integrating new employees into the workplace, and accommodation strategies. Interestingly, the company rewards managers for their support of the company's efforts—annual bonuses for managers are linked to promoting equity.

CHAPTER SUMMARY

This chapter has considered the complexities associated with the labour context of business. Societies and economies are influenced dramatically by how work is organized. We discussed how debates about the best way to organize work are long-standing and influenced by perspectives on markets, power, and the role of the state in capitalist societies. The result is a complex web of rules and forces that businesses must learn and adapt to if they are to operate successfully. We looked more closely at some of these rules, including rules and processes relating to unemployment and the loss of work and rules that attempt to address Canada's diverse labour force.

CHAPTER LEARNING TOOLS

Key Terms

activist government 51

"at will" employment 57

bargaining power 51

bounded rationality 51

Charter of Rights and
Freedoms 59

collective bargaining 51

common law of the
employment contract 56

competitive markets 49

critical perspective 52

designated groups 62

duty to accommodate 62

employee 44

employment 44

employment contract 44

employment equity 68

family income 54

income inequality 48

independent
contractors 44

industrial pluralist
perspective 50

intern 44

invisible hand of the
market 49

labour relations
statutes 53

managerial perspective 50

mandatory minimum
statutory notice 57

minimum wage 49

neoclassical
perspective 49

nonstandard employment
(NSE) 47

partners 44

prohibited grounds 60

reasonable notice 56

standard employment
relationship
(SER) 47

systemic discrimination 68

temporary placement
organizations 44

undue hardship 62

unemployment insurance
programs 58

unemployment
rate 55

union density 54

union wage
premium 54

volunteer 44

vulnerable or precarious
workers 48

Multiple-Choice Questions

Select the *best* answer for each of the following multiple choice questions. Solutions are located in the back of your textbook.

1. Which of the following factors are important considerations in deciding whether a worker is an employee or an independent contractor?
   a. Who controls the manner in which work is performed
   b. Who owns the tools used in performing the work
   c. Who assumes the economic risks
   d. All of the above

2. "A legal minimum wage harms businesses and workers alike." This statement is most consistent with which perspective?
   a. Managerial   b. Neoclassical
   c. Industrial pluralist   d. Critical

3. The belief that employers, through enlightened managerial practices, will protect the interests of workers is most consistent with which perspective?
   a. Managerial   b. Industrial pluralist
   c. Neoclassical   d. Critical

4. "Collective bargaining through unions is the best way to address income inequality." This statement is most consistent with which perspective?
   a. Managerial   b. Industrial pluralist
   c. Neoclassical   d. Critical

5. The Canadian Charter of Rights and Freedoms governs
   a. the behaviour of workers
   b. the behaviour of private corporations
   c. the behaviour of governments
   d. both B and C

6. The Canada Human Rights Act prohibits employers from discriminating against employees on the basis of
   a. political opinion   b. weight
   c. physical appearance   d. none of the above

7. An employer in Canada is prohibited from firing an employee because
   a. of the employee's religion
   b. the employee is a union supporter
   c. the employee participated in a legal strike
   d. all the above

8. A union certification
   a. gives a union the legal right to represent employees
   b. requires a union to demonstrate that a majority of employees support the union
   c. requires the employer's approval
   d. all of the above

9. An example of a common law rule applicable to employment contracts is
   a. the requirement for employers to comply with the Employment Standards Act
   b. the requirement for employers to provide employees with reasonable notice of termination
   c. the requirement for employers to collectively bargain in good faith with unions
   d. the requirement for employers to make contributions to the unemployment insurance fund

10. Human rights statutes in Canada
    a. prohibit all forms of discrimination
    b. prohibit some forms of discrimination
    c. impose a duty on employers to accommodate employee disabilities
    d. B and C only

11. An "unpaid intern" under Canadian law is considered to be
    a. an employee
    b. a volunteer
    c. a student
    d. It depends on the unique circumstances of the situation and the provincial law where the intern works.

12. The managerial perspective is closely related to the
    a. human resource management perspective
    b. neoclassical perspective
    c. industrial pluralist perspective
    d. both A and B

13. Industrial pluralists acknowledge that
    a. an imbalance of power exists between employers and workers
    b. strikes are not an effective way for workers to bargain
    c. the market will correct labour issues
    d. none of the above

14. Non-union employees in Canada can have a/an _____ with their employer.
    a. written employment contract
    b. oral employment contract
    c. either A or B
    d. none of the above

15. The Canadian Charter of Rights and Freedoms is
    a. part of Canada's Constitution
    b. a legal document that protects mobility rights
    c. a trade document
    d. both A and B

Discussion Questions

1. Why does the distinction between employment and other forms of work arrangements matter to businesses in Canada?

2. What are some potential benefits and disadvantages to businesses of hiring employees rather than retaining independent contractors?

3. Explain the difference between standard and nonstandard employment.

4. Which of the various perspectives on work and government policy do you most agree with, and why?

5. Identify and describe three approaches used in Canada to protecting employees when their employment is terminated. How do they affect business?

6. Identify and explain three types of laws used in Canada to address worker diversity.

7. What are the four designated groups that are protected in the Employment Equity Act?

8. What factors are affecting union density in Canada?

9. Provide arguments both in favour of and against a strong and generous unemployment insurance program.

10. In what ways has economic globalization affected the labour market and debates over how best to regulate globalization in Canada?

Sue Zheng, 40, immigrated to Canada from Fuzhou, China, in 2006. Like most immigrants, Zheng was happy to come to Canada, start working, and begin a new life for her and her family. But Zheng's experience was not what she expected. To get a job at a manicure salon, Zheng had to pay a $400 deposit. Eager to gain work experience and earn money, Zheng paid the deposit and took the job.

Once she began working, she worked seven days a week, 10 hours a day, for just $25 a day. Zheng decided to quit the job after only two months because of extreme exhaustion. She had no idea about her labour rights until she agreed to participate in a street survey.

"I don't know any English and had no idea what my rights were," she explained in Mandarin during an interview. "Workers don't have a lot of rights where I came from."[17] Since that time, Zheng has been referred to a legal clinic to try to get back her $400 from her former employer and other possible compensation.

According to the Chinese Interagency Network of Greater Toronto, who conducted the survey, Zheng's story of immigrant abuse and exploitation is all too common. "Many of the workers have worked in those kinds of conditions for years and they just don't care about their rights. They just do whatever their bosses order them to do and accept what they pay them. They never challenge," said Wei Sun, a volunteer who conducted the survey.[18]

Indeed, the survey revealed some surprising facts. Of the 119 respondents who agreed to be interviewed, most could only answer about 5 out of the 10 questions correctly. Most people were not familiar with the Employment Standards Act and did not know the current provincial minimum wage. Moreover, 66% of participants were not aware of overtime pay and 64% were not familiar with holiday pay. Only 55% of respondents knew about severance pay as well as proper notice after a probationary period. And most surprising was that only 18% of those interviewed knew the maximum work hours allowed each week.[19]

According to Daniel Yau of the Metro Toronto Chinese and Southeast Asian Legal Clinic, "the problem is newcomers are not familiar with their rights in Canada. They also face the language barrier and don't know the social infrastructure and supports available to them."[20]

"It's shocking in Canada that these people are working 70 hours a week, with an average hourly wage of $4," said Andy Mark of the Chinese Canadian National Council. "It is difficult to find jobs in the mainstream job market. They want to keep their jobs. It's simply about survival."[21]

In 2008, a Chinese-operated automobile parts facility laid off its employees and moved to Mexico. Hui-min Li, a Shanghai immigrant and employee of eight years, was left without $8,000 in severance pay. Li filed a complaint with the Ontario Labour Relations Board and won his case.

---

[17] Keung, N. (2010 July 23). Few aware of labour rights in Toronto's Chinatown. *Toronto Star*. July 23, 2010. Retrieved from www.thestar.com/news/investigations/2010/07/23/few_aware_of_labour_rights_in_torontos_chinatown.html. Reprinted with permission.

[18] Keung, 2010.

[19] Chinese Canadian National Council Toronto Chapter. (2010, July). Chinese workers are not protected by ESA. Retrieved from www.ccnctoronto.ca/?q=zh-hans/node/343.

[20] Keung, 2010.

[21] Keung, 2010.

"It was not unusual for us to work 70 hours a week. We worked from 8 A.M. to 1 A.M. and the boss wouldn't let you go until you finished the work," said Li. "Most people don't have knowledge of their rights. Even if they do, they don't dare to fight for their rights because they are not the type to rock the boat."[22]

© Robert Estall photo agency/Alamy

Chinese workers are not the only workers affected by employer abuse. Migrant workers across Canada face similar issues but are not Canadian residents. Migrant workers are workers who come to Canada to gain temporary employment and then return to their home countries. These workers often fill low-skilled jobs such as seasonal farm workers or live-in caregivers. According to one study, these workers are particularly vulnerable to exploitation since they are not permanent residents and there is little oversight by the government. The report explains "the depths of the violations are degrading. There is a deepening concern that Canada's temporary labour migration programs are entrenching and normalizing a low-wage, low-rights 'guest' workforce."[23]

Former Bank of Canada Governor Mark Carney has recently acknowledged the problem. "One doesn't want an over-reliance on temporary foreign workers for lower-skilled jobs," said Carney. "Relying too much on temporary employees from abroad distorts wage adjustments that lead to Canadians getting better pay and delays changes that make companies more efficient."[24]

Currently, the federal government is looking at changing the Temporary Foreign Worker Program to reduce abuses by businesses. Under the new rules, companies will need to attempt to hire Canadian workers first before hiring temporary, lower-paid foreign workers.[25]

Worker Rights in Ontario	
Minimum hourly wage:	$10.25
Maximum work hours per week:	48 hours without written consent
Overtime pay eligibility:	Over 44 hours
Overtime pay rate:	1.5 times base pay
Paid holidays per year:	Two weeks
Percentage of vacation pay:	4% of annual salary
Note: In certain circumstances, there are some exceptions to the above.	

Why does exploitation continue to exist? Clearly, full-time work is not as easy to come by as it was a couple of decades ago. According to a McMaster University and United Way study, approximately half of Greater Toronto and Hamilton-area workers belong to precarious employment. What is precarious employment? Typically, it consists

[22] Keung, 2010.

[23] Keung, N. (2012, September 17). Abuse of migrant workers endemic in Canada, new study says. *Toronto Star*. Retrieved from www.thestar.com/news/gta/2012/09/17/abuse_of_migrant_workers_endemic_in_canada_new_study_says.html.

[24] Whittington, L. (2013, April 23). Don't let temporary foreign workers drive down wages: Carney. *Toronto Star*. Retrieved from www.thestar.com/business/economy/2013/04/23/foreign_worker_program_must_be_temporary_carney.html.

[25] Whittington, 2013.

Case Continued >

of temporary, contract, part-time, or on-call positions without benefits. While these types of positions are legal, the reduction in permanent, stable, full-time jobs is a potential threat to the economic prosperity of the region and the social health of communities.[26]

According to the university study, it is now more common for many people to work multiple jobs to achieve full-time hours. Every demographic, industry sector, and income level is being affected. With union membership on the decline, so is the protection of workers. The study also found working conditions to be more uncertain and opportunities for job training and development on the decline as well.[27]

Susan McIsaac, president and CEO of the United Way, a researcher in the study, explained that job insecurity is not just about reducing poverty. Employment concerns affect our society in a widespread manner from how we contribute to the economy, care for our children, and socialize with family and friends. Certainly, instability in the workforce creates stress and pressure that have an effect on our self-confidence and level of anxiety. While the study was limited to the Toronto and Hamilton regions, many observers contend a similar pattern may also exist across other parts of Canada.

How can workers be protected from unethical employers? According to Charlotte Yates, dean at the Faculty of Social Sciences at McMaster University, "Raising incomes is an obvious and critical area of focus, but it is not enough. The reality that workers in precarious employment tend to exit and re-enter the labour market much more often than those in permanent employment requires a renewed look at the basic employment standards and protections as well as revamped income security programs."[28]

Clearly the labour market has changed, and labour laws need to catch up to protect workers. It is a time for labour organizations, community groups, businesses, and the government to address how to reduce the negative effects of an unstable labour market. Indeed, uncertainty about employment can become a barrier to deciding on a career, starting a family, or beginning other life plans.

According to the Chinese Canadian National Council, "stopping worker exploitation goes beyond educating the public. It is also the employers' responsibility to treat workers fairly and with respect. A law without reinforcement is futile . . . the Ministry of Labour needs to reinforce the regulations . . . and harsh penalties should be dealt out to offenders."[29]

To enjoy a prosperous future, the university study recommends a renewed public policy framework to support those in precarious employment and to respond to changes in the labour market for the benefit of all workers.

Questions

1. What factors are identified as contributing to the low (and illegal) pay of the workers in this story?

2. How do you think this story would be explained through the lens of each of the four perspectives discussed in this chapter?

3. What, if anything, should be done to improve the working conditions for these workers?

[26] McIsaac, S., & Yates, C. (2013, February 23). Half of Toronto-area workers have fallen into precarious employment: study. *Globe and Mail*. Retrieved from www.theglobeandmail.com/commentary/columnists/half-of-toronto-area-workers-have-fallen-into-precarious-employment-study/article9003680.

[27] McIsaac & Yates, 2013.

[28] McIsaac & Yates, 2013.

[29] Chinese Workers are not protected by ESA. Chinese Canadian National Council. Toronto Chapter. July 2010.

Chapter 3
Managing the Workforce
How Can Business Leaders Best Manage Their Employees?

Edhar/Shutterstock

Organizations that succeed can only do so with the support of their organizational members. In this chapter we will examine the roles of managers and the fundamental philosophies underlying different management styles. You will become familiar with the classical approaches and the behavioural approaches to management. As well, we will consider the significance of building trust in the workplace.

Learning Objectives

After studying this chapter, you should be able to

1. Describe the types of roles managers play within organizations.
2. Identify the underlying philosophies of management within the classical school of thought.
3. Discuss the underlying philosophies of the behavioural school of thought in relation to management.
4. Consider the importance and role of trust in the workplace.

THE BUSINESS WORLD

Learning How to Be an Effective Leader: Lessons from the Executive Roundtable

Leadership skills are widely considered critical to organizational success, and companies that manage to effectively develop leadership capabilities tend to outperform their competitors. Ironically, while the popularity of leadership development programs continues to escalate, organizations still struggle to find programs that deliver solid results—the magic bullet, it seems, has yet to be found.

According to The Conference Board of Canada, the majority of Canadian organizations regard their leadership development practices as "relatively ineffective" and express only "lukewarm support" for them. There are indeed serious questions about whether Canadian organizations have the leadership development systems in place to effectively support their future leadership requirements.[1]

Given the leadership talent gap, it is time to look beyond traditional approaches to leadership development. In this regard, the efforts of such forward-thinking organizations as The Executive Roundtable appear to be moving leadership development forward.

The Executive Roundtable (www.theexecutiveroundtable.ca) is a successful Canadian consulting firm that offers a uniquely different and powerful approach to nurturing and developing leadership talent. Glain Roberts-McCabe, founder and CEO of The Executive Roundtable, developed "The Roundtable for Leaders" program after she noticed that up-and-coming corporate leaders enjoyed expanding their leadership capability through interactions with other leaders of the same level and ambition.

In 2010, Roberts-McCabe launched a 10-month program that featured *peer mentoring*, and today the program is used by an impressive list of corporate clients, including PepsiCo Canada, RBC, Torstar, Maple Leaf Foods, and the Canadian Automobile Association (CAA).

What makes The Executive Roundtable's program different? A third of Canadian organizations already provide mentoring and coaching programs for their managerial-level employees, but such programs are based on the belief that knowledge is best transferred down from more seasoned, or even soon-to-be-retiring, managers to less-experienced employees. In contrast, "The Roundtable for Leaders" has been designed in large part around the concept of having "high potential" managers work in small exclusive groups, led by an executive facilitator, to share and exchange ideas, perspectives, and actionable advice.

Participants meet regularly to discuss key issues and topics relevant to their jobs and stage of career and to provide each other with advice and feedback. The sessions are structured and led by an expert facilitator, who brings additional skills and experiences to the group and to the learning process. The program is offered to large corporate clients as well as to the public, in which case managers from different organizations gather around the table.

The program combines peer mentoring with more traditional one-on-one coaching. It is striking how the program participants perceive the value of peer mentoring differently than that of coaching. The coaching process helped them establish and clarify their short- and long-term goals through challenging questions and personal reflections. In contrast, peer mentoring helped them generate concrete ideas for dealing with specific

---

[1] Kotlyar, I., & Karakowsky, L. (2013). Leading edge leadership development: A lesson from The Executive Roundtable. *HR Edge*. Retrieved from www.theexecutiveroundtable.ca/wp-content/uploads/2013/08/HR-Edge-Article1.pdf.

work challenges, exposed them to different ways of thinking, and provided a sounding board as well as an opportunity for vicarious learning. While some individuals saw more value in peer mentoring and others in coaching, depending on their personal developmental needs, most liked the blended approach of "The Roundtable for Leaders," where peer mentoring and coaching were combined into one program.[2]

Can leadership skills really be acquired effectively from one's peers rather than from those higher up the hierarchy? According to participants in this program, the answer is a resounding "yes!" Participants in "The Roundtable for Leaders" program include everyone from senior managers to directors and vice-presidents at companies from different industries. And these executives are very enthusiastic about their experience. According to one executive, "We liked it so much we convinced Glain to set up an Alumni program and so we stuck together for another year and continued a similar approach."

Based on their accounts, the program facilitates two types of learning outcomes: work related and career related. The former includes enhanced abilities to address various strategic and tactical challenges, deal with subordinates, and make better decisions. Participants describe the value they obtain from being able to receive critical feedback in a supportive, nonthreatening and noncompetitive context—which is a unique opportunity since traditional performance appraisals are notoriously poor at juggling the mentoring function and the performance evaluative function. They also report how much they benefited from the rare opportunity to practise providing coaching advice to others.

The second type of learning outcome can be called career-related learning. Participants describe how their participation in the program elevated their level of aspiration and created a different outlook on their careers. These two types of personal learning appear to be related and mutually reinforcing. As one participant explained, "It's a great opportunity to really make sure that you understand who you are as a leader and as a manager, and how you want to envision yourself and grow."[3]

It appears there are a couple of key elements that make peer mentoring successful. First, the diverse composition of roundtables appears to be critical to the effectiveness of the program. Participants in the program generally represent a range of functional backgrounds—finance, marketing, sales, operations, human resources—thereby contributing a rich variety of expertise and perspectives to group discussions. A common sentiment among participants was the appreciation for being exposed to such diversity of views and experiences, which enhanced their capacity to apply different lenses when analyzing their own situations and expanded the mindset they needed for success in their senior leadership roles. As one participant, a vice-president of a large advertising firm, commented:

> I like that it brings people from different roles together, and we share problems that we all have. [While] the exact problem might not be identical, there are similarities that we face in our various roles, and we explore those together, and what I think is very interesting is that we all tend to have a different approach to how we might solve a different problem, the questions we might ask, and it's very interesting to hear how others provided their objective counsel on what they might do or might not do, and we learn from that. It's very interesting to hear other people's points of view and at the end of the day it causes you to be more thoughtful about how you might approach a similar challenge if you were to face it.[4]

[2] Kotlyar & Karakowsky, 2013.

[3] Kotlyar & Karakowsky, 2013.

[4] Kotlyar & Karakowsky, 2013.

Similarly, a director at a large media company commented that "The perspective the people brought to the table was great, because someone from HR is going to have a different perspective than someone from finance or someone from marketing or operations. It was great to see that cross-section and from different industries."[5]

Second, the quality of the facilitator seems to be another essential ingredient. The role of the facilitator is to establish a sense of trust and confidentiality, which in turn facilitates openness and sharing, and without which the effectiveness of peer mentoring as a leadership development tool would be greatly diminished. The Executive Roundtable employs former senior-level executives who bring their first-hand leadership experiences along with facilitation skills to guide the discussion.

Overall, peer mentoring appears to represent an effective approach to leadership development. Although it is often assumed that "leadership" is best learned from the top, it appears that organizations can acquire unique benefits by having up-and-coming leaders learn from each other. Peer mentoring may become a best practice for more and more organizations seeking to expand their repertoire of leadership development initiatives.

WHY STUDY MANAGEMENT THOUGHT?

Leading and managing people is clearly central to an organization's success in today's context. However, what is the best way to manage people? Are there philosophies of managing?

Regardless of whether we are looking at a small business or a giant corporation, any type of organization must be managed. When we refer to the notion of a *manager*, who are we referring to? A manager can be an individual at any level of the organization. For example, *top management* could include the chief executive officer (CEO) or president along with vice-presidents; *middle managers* could include such figures as departmental or division heads, plant or branch managers, or deans; *supervisors*, or first-line managers, might include department heads, forepersons, or supervisors.

Individuals can take on formal or informal managerial roles. For example, a *team leader* may or may not be formally assigned a managerial role, though that person may have much of the responsibilities of a manager. Regardless of your profession or your role in an organization, no doubt at some point in your career you will be required to apply some sort of management or leadership skills.

The field of management can indeed be systematically studied, and a consideration of it is of benefit to anyone who wishes to understand the philosophies that have guided managers for the past century. In this chapter we will consider the body of knowledge that attempts to identify principles employed by managers in their daily practice. However, before we embark, we need to ask a simple question: What do managers do?

---

[5] Kotlyar & Karakowsky, 2013.

WHAT DO MANAGERS *DO*?

What exactly does it mean to manage? What are the functions or roles of a manager? **Management** has been defined in many ways, including the following:

> "The art of getting things done through people." (Mary Parker Follett)
>
> "Managers give direction to their organizations, provide leadership and decide how to use organizational resources." (Peter Drucker)

To be a little more systematic, management has also been described as

> The process of administering and coordinating resources effectively and efficiently in an effort to achieve the organization's goals.

This last definition needs a little more explanation. The term **efficiency** refers to using the fewest inputs to produce a given level of output. The term **effectiveness** refers to the pursuit and achievement of goals that are appropriate for the organization.

We need to be a little more specific about what exactly it is that managers do. Here's a somewhat more detailed definition:

> Managing includes the process of planning, organizing, leading, and controlling organizational resources in the effort to achieve organizational goals.

Exhibit 3.1 outlines each element of this definition—or what have commonly been considered the four central functions of management: planning, organizing, leading, and controlling.

The Roles Managers Play in Organizations

Henry Mintzberg, a management scholar, conducted an in-depth study of managers in the 1960s. His observations have stuck with us today and seem to present a useful account of the many roles that managers can potentially play. Among the interesting results of his study is the fact that Mintzberg's work contradicted the then-dominant view of the role of managers.

The traditional view of the role of managers was that managers were able to reflect systematically on information before making decisions and that their job was relatively clear and narrow. Mintzberg's study of managers found that managers engaged in a variety of unpatterned short-duration activities, and the constant interruptions suggested that there was little time for systematic reflection. Most important, Mintzberg offered a classification of the various roles that managers play (see Exhibit 3.2). Let's briefly consider each of the roles that Mintzberg identified.

Mintzberg presented 10 roles classified within three broad categories: interpersonal roles, informational roles, and decisional roles. Essentially, these reflect three key areas of managing: developing and managing interpersonal relationships; dealing with the transfer of information; and making decisions.

Objective 1 Describe the types of roles managers play within organizations.

management The process of administering and coordinating resources effectively and efficiently in an effort to achieve the organization's goals.

efficiency Using the fewest inputs to produce a given level of output.

effectiveness The pursuit and achievement of goals that are appropriate for an organization.

Exhibit 3.1 What Managers Do

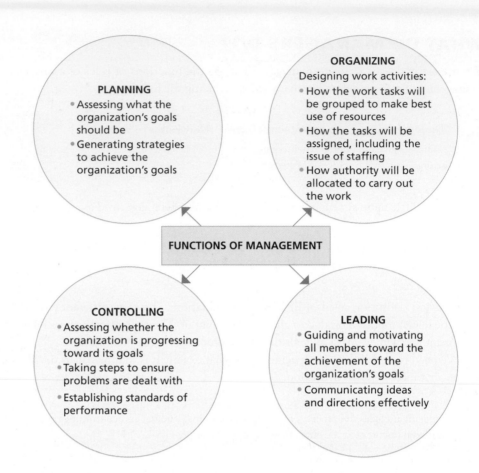

Interpersonal Roles **Interpersonal roles** include those managerial tasks that arise from the manager's formal authority base and involve relationships with either other organizational members or external parties. **Figurehead** roles are typically ceremonial or symbolic in nature. For example, in the role of a figurehead, a supervisor might hand out "employee of the month" awards at a company banquet. In the **leader** role, the manager may serve as a motivator, a communicator, and a coordinator of her subordinates' activities. This might include conducting performance appraisals, offering training to a new recruit, and so on. A final role within the interpersonal grouping is that of **liaison**, which includes those managerial activities that involve developing relationships with members of the organization outside the manager's area of authority. This could include anything from a sales manager's relationship with the production department to a university dean's networking relationship with the city council.

Informational Roles Mintzberg's second broad category of managerial roles, referred to as **informational roles**, reflects the importance of managers as communication

Exhibit 3.2 Roles of Managers

Interpersonal Roles	Informational Roles	Decisional Roles
1. Figurehead	1. Monitor	1. Entrepreneur
2. Leader	2. Disseminator	2. Disturbance Handler
3. Liaison	3. Spokesperson	3. Resource Allocator
		4. Negotiator

sources for the organization—whether this involves gathering or giving out important information to other organizational members or to parties outside the organization.

First, we can consider the manager as a **monitor** of sorts. That is, managers must constantly monitor the internal and external environments of their organization to gather information that is useful for organizational decision making. For example, the marketing manager may be responsible for assessing consumer demand for a newly proposed product.

Second, managers are also **disseminators** of information. That is, they may share or distribute the information that they have gained in their role as monitors. Obviously, managers must ensure that subordinates have all the information they require to perform their job effectively. This might include offering clear information regarding company expectations of performance standards and performance appraisal criteria.

Third, the manager may act as a **spokesperson**. Managers can also transmit information to individuals outside their area of authority. For example, a marketing manager might provide the engineering department with the latest report of consumer preferences regarding product design. Or the company president may report to a government regulatory board regarding the company's environmental policy.

Decisional Roles

Mintzberg's final category is referred to as **decisional roles**, and highlights the fact that managers must process information and act as decision makers. There are four classes of roles described here. First is the notion of the manager as **entrepreneur**. That is, the manager may, for example, develop and initiate new projects. This might include the personnel manager developing a new performance appraisal system, the marketing manager developing a new product, and so on. Generating new projects and new ventures is a highly valued trait among today's managers. Perhaps one of the greatest entrepreneurial leaders in recent times was the late Apple leader, Steve Jobs. For a discussion of his leadership contributions, see Talking Business 3.1.

Managers might also play the role of **disturbance handler**. Dealing with and attempting to resolve conflict can include things such as resolving a dispute between two employees, dealing with a difficult or uncooperative supplier, and so on. The ability to manage conflict effectively can often be a critical role of a manager (see Talking Business 3.2).

A third role that managers can play is that of **resource allocator**, which involves deciding how resources (money, equipment, personnel, time) will be allocated. For example, a department head might decide how to allocate a limited financial budget among the different areas. Deciding how much time the division should invest in a new project is also a decision about resources.

The final decisional role identified by Mintzberg is the manager as **negotiator**. Indeed, numerous research studies have underscored the degree to which managers are engaged in some form of negotiation throughout their activities. Whether this involves negotiating with customers, employees, or other departments, a manager often bargains over issues that affect the operation of his or her department, unit, or organization. For example, the production purchasing manager might negotiate with the supplier in an effort to speed up the supply of raw materials for the company's production department. A personnel manager might negotiate with a representative of the union to resolve a conflict.

monitor One of the three informational roles that managers play (the others being disseminator and spokesperson), where the internal and external environments of the organization are constantly monitored for information useful in decision making.

disseminator One of the three informational roles that managers play (the others being monitor and spokesperson), where the information obtained through monitoring is shared and distributed.

spokesperson One of the three informational roles that managers play (the others being monitor and disseminator), where information is transmitted to individuals outside the manager's area of authority.

decisional roles One of Mintzberg's three broad categories of roles that managers play, where information is processed and decisions made. Includes entrepreneur, disturbance handler, resource allocator, and negotiator.

entrepreneur One of the four decisional roles that managers play (the others being disturbance handler, resource allocator, and negotiator), where the manager develops and initiates new projects.

disturbance handler One of the four decisional roles that managers play (the others being entrepreneur, resource allocator, and negotiator), where the manager deals with and attempts to resolve conflicts, such as dealing with a difficult or uncooperative supplier.

resource allocator One of the four decisional roles that managers play (the others being entrepreneur, disturbance handler, and negotiator), where it is decided how resources such as money, equipment, personnel, and time will be allocated.

negotiator One of the four decisional roles that managers play (the others being entrepreneur, disturbance handler, and resource allocator) involving negotiation in all its forms, whether with customers, employees, or other departments.

The Visionary Leader: Steve Jobs

Reuters/Toshiyuki Aizawa TA/LA

Steve Jobs was an innovative visionary who, at the young age of 56, died of cancer on October 5, 2011, leaving behind a technological giant known as Apple Inc. as well as two other companies that he cofounded, Pixar and NeXT Inc. During his reign, Jobs was considered to be Apple's anchor, driving it to be one of the most valuable companies in the world. His strategy toward his employees, as unorthodox as it was, was the reason why Apple was so successful.

Born on February 24, 1955, Jobs was always a determined individual. Since high school he was distracted by technology and was soon attending lectures at Hewlett-Packard. This quickly got him a job working with Steve Wozniak, his future business partner. Jobs attended Reed College in Portland, Oregon, but dropped out after only a year and began working for Atari as a technician. Jobs received his first shot at strategic leadership upon his return from India. His initial strategy came more out of necessity than forethought when driven by his desire to build Apple.

Together with Steve Wozniak and Ronald Wayne, they created their first Apple computer, along with the initial formation of the company, in the garage of Jobs's parents' house. Shortly after the company went public, generating a value of $1.79 billion. In 1983, Jobs lured John Sculley away from Pepsi-Cola to serve as Apple's CEO, but their different attitudes led to an antagonistic working relationship. As persuasive and charismatic as he was about his goals, Jobs butted heads with a person he previously claimed to be the best thing for Apple. Not only was

Jobs having issues with management, but his task-driven attitude left employees a bit frazzled. Jobs was known for ignoring the feelings of his employees in the workplace, focusing only on getting the best product out quickly. While Jobs reigned there was approximately a 75% turnover rate at Apple. Over time the partners did not see eye to eye, and Sculley held a board meeting to remove Jobs from Apple on May 24, 1985.

At this point in his life, Jobs fully believed getting fired was the best thing for him. Being a strong-willed individual he was determined to keep the momentum of his innovative ideas flowing. Jobs was a religiously task-oriented individual, so without waiting long he developed another computer company called NeXT Inc. in 1985. One of the company's claims to fame was creating a software program called WebObjects, which was later used to create the Apple store and iTunes Store. By the time Jobs had built up NeXT he was considered a leading egomaniac with an aggressive and demanding personality who quickly made *Fortune*'s list of America's Toughest Bosses.

Only one year later, in 1986, Jobs bought The Graphics Group (later renamed Pixar) from Lucasfilm's computer graphics division for the price of $10 million, $5 million of which was given to the company as capital. Pixar became widely popular and to this day is still a very successful company.

A short while after, Jobs became reunited with his brain child when Apple decided to buy NeXT for $429 million, so that by 1997 Jobs was back in his role as CEO of Apple. While settling in, Jobs viewed Apple's new chapter as an opportunity to create large profit margins and turn the company around. He started by cutting many projects and jobs to the point where people were scared of passing him in the hallway. Slowly, through the integration of NeXT's technology into Apple products, the company was able to improve sales significantly. Although considered an irregular practice, as CEO Jobs had over 100 employees reporting to him, regardless of his harsh task-driven ideals. His authoritarian model ensured that he was involved in every step of product design. Jobs even instituted a product-recycling program that greatly appealed to Apple's customers. Since then, Apple has produced many lines of products including the iPod and iMac—products that have found their way into homes and offices around the world.

In October 2003, Jobs was diagnosed with pancreatic cancer. Being the determined individual he was, however, Jobs never slowed down and continued to push new and innovative ideas while convincing his audience that his health was of no concern. In fact, Jobs delayed informing anyone at Apple about his condition, including the board of directors and its shareholders, for as long as he could. However, Jobs never retired his high-involvement tactics, and soon enough employees began to appreciate his state of mind. Debi Coleman, a manufacturing manager for Apple, considered herself lucky to have worked for him (Taggart, 2011). Jobs's leadership strategy was able to "infuse employees with an abiding passion to create groundbreaking products and a belief that they could accomplish what seemed impossible" (Isaacson, 2011). Granted, Jobs's relational tactics seemed questionable, but Jobs was successful in taking an almost bankrupt company and converting it into one of the most valuable in the world. It was not long before Jobs's health caught up with him in August 2011, when he decided to resign as CEO of Apple. Ultimately, his battle ended that October when he passed away.

It would appear that Apple employees over the years began to develop an appreciation for Jobs's leadership style and strategy for product output within the company.

When Apple first opened, its leaders and subordinates questioned Jobs's tactics, which ultimately led to his termination. When he returned to Apple, its employees started to see the value in a visionary who could only describe reality as malleable. Albeit he had moments of bullying, Jobs was able to motivate and instill an ideology in his workers that anything was possible, including achieving true perfection. As one individual who worked with Jobs observed: "Over a million people from all over the world have shared their memories, thoughts, and feelings about Steve. One thing they all have in common . . . is how they've been touched by his passion and creativity" (Apple, n.d.).

Sources: Griggs, B., & CNN. (2011, October 5). Steve Jobs, Apple founder, dies - CNN. Featured Articles from CNN. Retrieved January 29, 2012, from http://articles.cnn.com/2011-10-05/us/us_obit-steve-jobs_1_jobs-and-wozniak-iphone-apple-founder?_s=PM:US; Isaacson, W. (2011). Steve Jobs. New York: Simon & Schuster.; Moisescot, R. (n.d.). Long Bio. all about Steve Jobs. Retrieved February 20, 2012, from http://allaboutstevejobs.com/bio/long/12.html#; Steve Jobs: The Man Who Saved Apple. (2011, November 1). MacWorld, 28,; 14. Retrieved February 29, 2012, from the ProQuest database.; Taggart, J. (2011, November 21). Steve Jobs' Reality Distortion Field: Leadership or Bullying? ChangingWinds. R.

TALKING BUSINESS 3.2

Conflict Management: The Toxic Employee

An interview with Dr. Mitchell Kusy and Dr. Elizabeth Holloway

Dr. Mitchell Kusy and Dr. Elizabeth Holloway are management scholars and practitioners who recently coauthored a book, *Toxic Workplace!* This is the first book to tackle the underlying systems issues that enable a toxic person to create a path of destruction in an organization, pervading others' thoughts and energies, even undermining their sense of well-being. Dr. Kusy and Dr. Holloway's research reveals the warning signs that indicate a serious behavioral problem and identifies how this toxicity spreads with long-term effects on organizational climate.

Dr. Kusy has had over 25 years experience in leadership and organization development. He is a full professor in the Ph.D. program in leadership and change at Antioch University and has written several books on leadership. Dr. Elizabeth Holloway is a full professor and psychologist with over 25 years experience as a practitioner, trainer, and consultant in relational practice with leaders worldwide. She has held faculty appointments at the Universities of California, Utah, Oregon, Wisconsin, and currently at Antioch University. She has written several books, numerous research articles, and consults internationally on topics ranging from mentoring to organizational learning.

Question: In your extremely insightful book, you expose the dynamics of the toxic workplace and provide practitioners with clear guidance on how to deal with this serious problem. The book's rich observations stem from the exhaustive

(continued)

research you conducted with over 400 business leaders, many from the *Fortune* 500 List. I am curious as to how you managed to get so many business leaders to "open up" to you about the "dark side" of their workplaces?

> **Dr. Holloway:** Interestingly, these leaders were more than willing and prepared to share their stories. Many had never talked about it before. For most, I think the interviews we conducted were cathartic. Leaders also are genuinely interested in understanding how to better deal with these kinds of individuals. We know that toxic individuals can cost the company substantially in both human and financial terms. Leaders understandably want solutions.

> **Dr. Kusy:** It came as a complete surprise to us that 94 percent of the respondents in our research reported they had worked with or were currently working with a toxic person. So far, most solutions have been short-sighted—simply firing the person without attention to the effect the toxicity has had on the team, the culture, and the leaders. The fact is, a toxic personality can infect a whole team and potentially bring down a company.

Question: In your experience, how well does the "average" person cope with a toxic colleague or a toxic boss at work?

> **Dr. Kusy:** Although much has been written about the more serious types of personal impairment, such as alcoholism, mental illness, physical aggression, and sexual harassment, the toxic effects of incivility in the workplace are only now being unveiled. People can't sleep, they get sick, their relationships suffer, and they lose the enjoyment of going to work.

> **Dr. Holloway:** The additional danger is that a toxic personality spreads like a virus. Once you have one person who is toxic, other people start to behave badly because they are in survival mode. And once you have a culture of nastiness, then it isn't automatically going to revert back to everyone feeling good. Incivility—backstabbing, gossip, angry outbursts, condescension, and sabotage—can quickly become the norm of operations and with that come costly losses in reputation and productivity.

Question: It's a potentially devastating issue—both to the organization and to the individual—and yet we all know that toxic workplaces persist. For organizations seeking to take action, how difficult is it to identify toxic behavior? It seems like a very broad concept. Does it include things like harassment and bullying?

> **Dr. Holloway:** In general, toxic individuals are those who exhibit counterproductive work behaviors that can debilitate individuals, teams, and even entire organizations. Our research indicates that toxic behaviors can fall below the threshold of bullying or harassing. Toxic behaviors are actually harder for an employer to address formally through a disciplinary process. In fact, one of the key challenges of dealing with toxic behavior is that, ironically, it can slip under the "radar" even though it often exacts a huge toll on employees and corporate profits.

> **Dr. Kusy:** In our research, we discovered three primary categories of toxic behaviors that often fall outside of any written corporate policy. The first is what we refer to as "shaming." This includes the use of humiliation, sarcasm, potshots, or mistake-pointing with the intent of reducing another's self-worth. The second kind of toxic behavior is "passive hostility" which involves the use of passive aggressive behavior with the intent of directing one's anger inappropriately. The third kind is "team sabotage" or meddling with the intent of either establishing a negative power base or making the team less productive.

> **Dr. Holloway:** Surprisingly, while these three behaviors can make work life intolerable, only about 1 percent to 6 percent of victims ever report these behaviors. Toxic employees can gnaw away at their colleagues on an ongoing basis. Yet the target(s) can rarely point a finger to exactly what happened in any particular instance. And when bad behavior stems from the boss, finger pointing may be even less likely. The reality is that toxic people have a predilection toward behaving badly, and when you have people in authority, who work in a team, and they are allowed to be condescending—and they get away with it—their colleagues often feel silenced.

Question: Your research points out that most organizations have gone about battling toxic behavior in the "wrong way"? How so?

> **Dr. Kusy:** In our research, we were interested in how leaders and their teams reacted to the presence of toxic behaviors. Often leaders try to minimize team interactions with the toxic individual, restructure the environment, or remove responsibilities from the toxic individual. In the cases we examined, none of these strategies proved very effective; each was time-consuming, reactive, and left a fragmented team in its wake.

Dr. Holloway: Yes, the typical organizational responses were short-sighted and ineffective. In most situations, we found that everything was directed toward avoiding the influence of the toxic individual. Much of the team's energies may be drained in efforts to manage this person. You can see the damaging effects such reactions have on a fully functioning and efficient team. Not only are good team members leaving but the functional communication or decision-making path also breaks down.

Question: Your book was among the first to identify the underlying systems issues that enable toxic individuals to persist. You identify important supporters of the toxic individual—can you tell us about them?

Dr. Kusy: Toxic systems are particularly resistant to change and are often tolerated for years. In our research, we discovered two roles that create such a toxic system: the "toxic protector" and the "toxic buffer." The toxic protector is the person who unwittingly permits the toxic behavior to continue. Toxic protectors feel compelled to protect the toxic person from negative reviews or termination because they have a special interest in keeping them as a part of their team, often because the toxic person is highly productive or has a special expertise. Toxic protectors typically don't realize that they are putting the team in jeopardy.

Dr. Holloway: Unlike toxic protectors, the "toxic buffer" seems to have a different motivation. Buffers actually recognize that the toxic employee's behavior is detrimental to team functioning. However, they feel that the solution is to serve as a shield or buffer between the toxic person and team members. Unfortunately, despite their good intentions, the buffer is actually enabling the toxic employee to get away with bad behavior. While trying to absorb the toxicity, the buffer will often become emotionally damaged in the process and unwittingly assists in a downward team spiral—a dysfunctional pattern of communication and authority in the team. In this way, both toxic protectors and toxic buffers actually facilitate the enactment of a culture of incivility.

Question: You identify three levels of strategy to combat toxic behavior. Can you briefly tell us about the aim of this approach and how it succeeds where traditional approaches have failed?

Dr. Kusy: Our view is that to effectively address this problem, actions need to occur on three levels: the organization, the team, and the individual. We refer to this as the

Toxic Organization Change System (TOCS). For example, at the organizational level we need to understand what values exist and are being practiced. Most organizations have stated values. But how pronounced are they in your organization? Is one of these values about respect? If not, you have some work to do. First, you'll need to make sure the value of respect (or however you term this value) gets incorporated into a code of professional conduct. Ultimately, this code gets rolled into an organizational policy. It becomes your mantra in creating a culture of respectful engagement. It's not just a nice-to-do; it turns out to have important impacts on the human and financial bottom line.

Dr. Holloway: Part of the large-scale design of the professional conduct code is the establishment of a zero tolerance policy. This policy is important because it provides the context not only for how we live by these values but also for what happens when they are breached. Certainly, due process procedures must be followed when the situation is serious enough to warrant dismissal. However, there are many intermediary actions that can be taken by leaders to turn a culture of disrespect around.

Question: In your experience, how common is it for organizations to integrate a values-based approach with management processes?

Dr. Kusy: What we have found is that most organizations do not have values integrated into their management process. So that is another reason why toxic cultures won't get better quickly. For example, we favor a situation where there is a 60–40 split when it comes to performance reviews. This means 60 percent of the reward is based on task work, and 40 percent on the values work. But in most organizations, it is 90 to 100 percent based on task work. If the values really mean so much within an organization then they need to put their money where their mouths are.

Dr. Holloway: If you change the culture by changing the criteria for the performance appraisal to include things such as interpersonal behavior, then you can start to change some of those unwanted behaviors. Performance management processes are not simply a mandate to monitor and reprimand but a real opportunity to reward interpersonally effective behaviors that uphold your values.

Source: Excerpted from Karakowsky, L. (2011). Workplace detox: Dr. Mitch Kusy and Dr. Elizabeth Holloway shed some light on the dark-side of your workplace. *HR Edge* (Fall), 14–17. Available at www.yorku.ca/laps/shrm/hredge/HR-Edge_issue3.pdf.

Now that we have outlined the notion of managing and the roles managers play, in the next section we will take a more systematic look at how the role of manager is changing. We'll start with the oldest approach, then consider more recent philosophies of managing people in organizations.

MANAGEMENT PHILOSOPHIES

Objective 2 Identify the underlying philosophies of management within the classical school of thought.

If you have ever taken a trip to Disneyland, you will notice the great level of care and professionalism with which Disney employees (referred to as "cast members") conduct their jobs. In fact, Disney even offers management training programs through its "university" for countless other organizations. What is so special about Disney's management approach that has helped it achieve worldwide fame and success? The answer might surprise you: nothing. However, what is rare is its ability to make sure the management philosophies employed are suitable for the nature of their organization. While a lot of what Disney is doing may be common sense, common sense alone won't get you very far when it comes to selecting and implementing a system of managerial practices that is suitable for today's organization.

Clearly, not all organizations are created equal—from the McDonald's of the fast-food industry to the Microsoft of the high-tech world, what works for one organization with regard to management philosophy may be deadly if applied in another environment. So the question is, what are the ranges of management philosophies that exist, and upon what principles are they based? Let's answer these questions as we consider the elements of two fundamentally different schools of management thought: the classical and the behavioural approaches. (See Exhibit 3.3 for a comparison of the two approaches.)

Exhibit 3.3
Management Philosophies

I. Classical Approaches to Managing
1. Scientific Management
2. Administrative Management
3. Bureaucratic Management

II. Behavioural Approaches to Managing
1. The Human Relations Movement
2. Mary Parker Follett and Chester Barnard
3. Modern Behavioural Science and Motivation-Based Perspectives

CLASSICAL APPROACHES TO MANAGEMENT

classical approaches to management The oldest of the formalized perspectives of management, which arose in the late 19th and early 20th centuries during a period of rapid industrialization in the US and European business sectors. Includes scientific, administrative, and bureaucratic management.

The oldest of the formalized perspectives of management has come to be known as the **classical approaches to management**, and it arose during the late 19th and early 20th centuries. This view originated during a time of rapid industrialization in the United States and European business sectors. Three streams that are central components of this school are (1) scientific management, (2) administrative management, and (3) bureaucratic management. We will look at each of these perspectives and attempt to understand the contributions they have made to the field of managing, but first we must consider the environment surrounding the evolution of management thought.

The Social Context

Understanding the social context of late 19th and early 20th centuries sheds light on the logic of the management approaches that were generated during that time.

One of the major driving forces behind the formalization of management thought was the **Industrial Revolution**. While management concepts have been around practically since the dawn of civilization, it was not until the 18th century, as a consequence of the intellectual and scientific accomplishments of the Renaissance period, that the systematic development of management principles and practices began.

The Industrial Revolution, as the name implies, was a major transformation in work processes that began in the 18th century with the replacement of hand production by machine and factory production. For example, a new energy source, the coal-driven steam engine, was created to run the machines. The introduction of new work processes and machinery culminated in the factory system of production that eventually led to mass production processes. Certainly, the factory system brought with it many benefits, including a higher standard of living. It also brought with it extensive changes in management, given that work was no longer conducted in workers' homes, but in factories.

The philosophy that fuelled the Industrial Revolution was the notion of "***laissez faire***," a term used by the economist Adam Smith in his book *The Wealth of Nations*. This term essentially meant that businesses or manufacturers should be free to make and sell what they please and, consequently, reflected the notion that government should not interfere with the economic affairs of business. Businesses should be allowed to pursue their own self-interest. The economic view of labour was a straightforward one—the employer buys the labour, and the employee provides the labour. There was no long-term obligation on either side, which reinforced the notion that employees were not valued. With a great supply of labour and jobs involving little skill, it became clear that all power rested with the employer. It was in such an environment that philosophies like scientific management eventually arose.

Scientific Management

Frederick Taylor (1856–1915) was an American engineer who sought to help American industry deal with the challenges of improving productivity. Keep in mind that in Taylor's time there were no clear concepts of management and worker responsibilities. Taylor thought the problem was a simple one to solve: Improve management practices and you'll improve productivity. So Taylor sought a way to better manage workers.

For most of his working life, Taylor was employed in steel mills, first as a labourer, eventually as a foreman, and ultimately as chief engineer. While working as a foreman at Midvale Steel Company in Philadelphia, and later as a consulting engineer at Pittsburgh's Bethlehem Steel, Taylor observed what he thought were significant inefficiencies in the conduct of work. The results of his observations and studies were eventually reported in a series of papers, *The Principles of Scientific Management*, published in 1911.

What was Taylor's philosophy? Taylor stated the fundamental objective of management as follows: "Securing the maximum prosperity for the employer coupled with the maximum prosperity for each employee."[6] This sounds reasonable; but what, specifically, does it mean and how do you go about achieving that apparently admirable objective? To answer the second question, Taylor believed that the way to improve worker–manager relations was through **scientific management**, which involves at least three central features: compartmentalizing and standardizing the work, supervising the workers, and motivating the workers.

Industrial Revolution A period of time when manufacturing practices developed, between 1760 to 1840, changing the nature of work from manual hand production methods to machine use and mass production.

laissez faire A term meaning that businesses or manufacturers should be free to make and sell what they please and, consequently, reflects the notion that government should not interfere with the economic affairs of business.

scientific management
Frederick Taylor's philosophy that the fundamental objective of management is "securing the maximum prosperity for the employer coupled with the maximum prosperity for each employee" by standardizing and compartmentalizing work practices. This is one of the three central classical approaches to management, the others being the administrative and the bureaucratic.

---

[6] Taylor, F.W. (1911). *The principles of scientific management*. New York, NY: Harper & Brothers.

U. Baumgarten via Getty Images

Compartmentalizing and Standardizing the Work

During Taylor's days with Midvale Steel in Philadelphia, he made some interesting observations of workers whose task it was to shovel coal and iron during the manufacture of pig iron. After carefully analyzing the range of motions involved in shovelling, he decided to experiment with different sizes of shovels and varied the size of the load scooped to minimize fatigue. He also arranged for the workers to have varying work and rest intervals so that he could experiment with recovery rate. Based on his observations and recommendations, the average daily output of workers was tripled, and the number of shovellers required for the job was reduced from 600 to 140![7] The science of shovelling was indeed born, and scientific management was a hit!

Scientific management, or Taylorism, was based on careful observation and measurement to determine the most efficient methods for performing a task. This essentially involves the scientific and systematic study of how work is done to improve the work process. Work can be studied objectively, and tasks can be broken down into their simplest steps. The scientific analysis of jobs required **time and motion studies**, which involved using a movie camera and a stopwatch to closely scrutinize the elements of performing a task. For example, bricklayers could be observed and timed to assess precisely which movements were most efficient for laying bricks.

time and motion studies
In scientific management, the scientific analysis of work, often using a movie camera and a stopwatch to closely scrutinize the elements of performing a task.

compartmentalizing In scientific management, the result of Frederick Taylor's pursuit of the one best method of performing a job, which involves breaking the job down into its most fundamental steps or components. Also called specializing.

standardizing In scientific management, the establishment of clear rules regarding how to perform a job, leaving little or no room for individual discretion, thus assuring consistent performance.

All this was based on Taylor's belief that there is one best method for performing the job—and the job of management is to discover that method, train workers, and ensure that they use the method. This resulted in specializing, or **compartmentalizing**, the job into its basic parts—that is, breaking the job down into its most fundamental steps and, where feasible, allowing workers to perform the most basic tasks. This kept the job simple, made it easy and inexpensive to train workers, and ensured a cheap and ready supply of labour to perform the job. **Standardizing** the work meant that there were clear rules regarding how to perform it, which left little or no room for individual discretion. There is no better way of ensuring consistent performance than through the creation of strict guidelines.

According to Taylor, then, the purpose of managers is to help set proper standards for work performance. Managers must also train the workers in these standards and direct their performance to achieve the most efficient and least fatiguing manner of working. Other responsibilities of management include selecting workers with the abilities that make them the most suitable for the job.

Supervising the Workers

Taylor believed that a manager can't be an expert in everything. He therefore suggested that managers take charge only of their area of expertise. As a first-level supervisor, you should be responsible for workers who perform a common function with which you are familiar. Of course, it is the supervisor or foreman who would do the planning, time motion studies, scheduling, and so on. More generally, what Taylor did was make clear the separation of the mental work of managers from the physical

[7] Taylor, 1911.

work of the labourers. The managers directed workers to do the work in the standardized manner. Keep in mind that Taylor's views arose at a time when American industry had at its disposal a vast supply of labour with a huge segment of new immigrants who, it was felt, were not fully capable of managing themselves.

Taylor's views have been criticized as denigrating employees and treating them as machines. However, Taylor did contribute to the creation of management as a "profession." Think about it: Managers' skills became specific not to the manufacture of the product, but rather to *managing*—that is, coordinating the activities of large numbers of people regardless of the organizational context.

Motivating the Workers

Taylor's philosophy about motivating the workers was quite simple: Money motivates! While that may seem obvious to most of us, Taylor's views were interestingly consistent with the rest of his philosophy. In a sense, Taylor advocated a system that has recently been revisited by many different types of organizations. Taylor believed that compensation must be closely tied to performance. A paycheque for simply "walking through the door" is not motivating. It must be clear in workers' minds that they only get a "good day's pay" for a "good day's work." So a **piece-rate system** was desirable, whereby workers' pay was directly tied to their output. If you produced at a standard level of production, you received a standard rate of pay; if you produced above average, you were paid at a higher rate.

How far-reaching are Taylor's views, and does Taylorism exist today? Scientific management continues to influence the management of work. From the manufacturing sector to the service industry, in many ways this philosophy has guided organizations for much of the past century. For example, consider the teaching profession. Believe it or not, Taylor and the principles of scientific management had a profound impact on the education system. The industrial expansion of the early 20th century demanded a system of mass education that would educate huge numbers of formerly rural people as well as new immigrants. The system required a rapid increase in the number of able and inexpensive teachers. Taylorism facilitated such a transition in the education system. Managers, who were typically male, became the supervisors or principals of the teachers, who were mostly women and less powerful and less well paid. The nature of teaching, too, became subject to the principles of scientific management. Remember the need to break the job down into its simplest components? Teachers were now specialized by grade and by subject; just as manufacturing work became specialized or compartmentalized, the task of teaching became standardized—what you taught and how you taught it were all part of a common plan. Clearly, then, Taylorism was adopted widely in industrial as well as nonindustrial settings. Taylor's ideas also spread beyond North America to Russia, Japan, Germany, and elsewhere.

Taylorism certainly remains alive and well across many different industries. You can probably think of some real-life organizations that are managed according to the principles of scientific management. For example, UPS (United Parcel Service) built its success in the delivery business on the principles of Taylorism. This company designed time and motion studies to ensure that the work of its delivery team is based on maximum efficiency and performed under strict standardized guidelines.

However, there is likely no better example of the modern application of scientific management than McDonald's. The success of McDonald's is obvious and is largely based on the duplication of its services across diverse areas. Their management system has been adopted not only by other fast-food chains but has spread to retail and other industries.

piece-rate system In scientific management, motivating workers by tying compensation to performance according to output, so that a standard level of output produces a standard level of pay, and above-average output produces above-average pay.

McDonald's achieved fame by making the dining experience reliable and predicable for consumers through the application of the principles of scientific management. Standardization guaranteed that customers continually received what they expected—both in the design of the store and in the system. Employee jobs are compartmentalized and standardized: Cooking and customer service are broken down into a series of simple, standardized tasks performed according to strict procedures.

Administrative Management

administrative management
Henri Fayol's philosophy of management, one of the three major classical approaches (the others being scientific and bureaucratic management). It focuses on the principles of division of work, unity of command, subordination of employees' individual interests to the common good, and *esprit de corps*.

A second subschool of the classical perspective of management is closely associated with the work of Henri Fayol (1841–1925). As the name implies, **administrative management** focuses specifically on management and the functions that managers should perform. Fayol, like Taylor, had some compelling views on how organizations should be managed. An engineer for a mining company in France, Fayol applied his principles with much success—and revitalizing an ailing company certainly helped Fayol's management approach gain attention. However, whereas Taylor's work was largely aimed at guiding managers at the lower levels, Fayol's work focused on upper levels of administration. Fayol developed a number of principles of management that he believed could serve as universal principles that could be taught to managers regardless of their specific organizational environment.

Like Taylor, Fayol supported the notion of *division of work:* By breaking work down into its simplest components and assigning these separate elements to workers, the work can be conducted more efficiently and productively. Similarly, Fayol believed that a manager's role is to give orders and to discipline employees. Fayol also advocated the notion of **unity of command**— each employee should report to only one boss to avoid confusion and conflicting instructions. In addition, this authority should be concentrated at the upper levels of the organization.

unity of command In administrative management, avoiding confusion and conflicting instructions by having each employee report to only one boss, preferably in the upper levels of the organization.

Fayol believed that employees should subordinate their individual interests to the common good or general interest of the organization. In other words, the goals of the overall organization must take precedence over any individual interests of employees. Finally, among Fayol's stated principles was the concept of *esprit de corps*—that is, team spirit and harmony should be encouraged among workers to generate organizational cohesiveness and unity.

esprit de corps In administrative management, generating organizational cohesiveness and unity by encouraging team spirit and harmony among workers.

Are Fayol's views still with us? Some of Fayol's assertions have gone out of vogue. For example, in today's environment many organizations do not view centralized decision-making authority as being as efficient as allowing authority to reside at lower levels of the organization. In addition, the rights of workers certainly are no longer subordinated to organizational goals, and considerable attention is placed on satisfying individual interests and needs at work. However, some of Fayol's principles are quite compatible with contemporary management views. For example, Fayol's notion of team spirit is important in many workplaces that are attempting to facilitate team work (see Talking Business 3.3).

Bureaucratic Management

bureaucratic management
One of the classical approaches to management (the others being scientific and administrative management) that focuses more broadly on the organization as a whole and incorporates the ideas of rules and procedures, hierarchy of authority, division of labour, impersonality, and selection and promotion. Associated with Max Weber.

Max Weber (1864–1920) was a German sociologist whose work became most closely affiliated with the school of thought eventually known as **bureaucratic management**. This perspective is broader in its focus than scientific and administrative management in that Weber's focus is on the nature of the organization as a whole. As was the case with Taylor and Fayol, Weber's beliefs came from observations of his environment.

Leading Teams in a New Direction

An Interview with Harvard Business School Professor Todd Pittinsky

Todd L. Pittinsky is a professor of public policy and a core faculty member of Harvard University's Center for Public Leadership at the John F. Kennedy School of Government. He also serves as research director of the Kennedy School's Center for Public Leadership. Dr. Pittinsky earned his B.A. in psychology from Yale University, his M.A. in psychology from Harvard, and his Ph.D. in organizational behaviour from the Harvard Graduate School of Arts and Sciences. Recently profiled in *The Economist* magazine, his research explores positive intergroup attitudes (allophilia) and how leaders can use them to bring groups together.

Question: You have asserted that team leaders often spend too much time on "leading by dividing." What do you mean by that?

Dr. Pittinsky: One of the most common approaches taken by team leaders in many contexts is leading by dividing. History shows us that there is often an ingroup/outgroup leadership trade-off: Leaders solidify their own standing within their groups by stirring up hostility or rivalry with other groups. It's common because it can work: An atmosphere of "us versus them" often can give a leader a boost in status and power. This trade-off occurs in settings as diverse as sports, business, and international relations. (How much team spirit has been stoked up by getting everyone to hate the Yankees, or Microsoft?)

Question: Is the notion of a "common enemy" ("us versus them") necessarily a bad thing for leaders to emphasize? Can't it create greater cohesiveness among team members?

Dr. Pittinsky: The ingroup/outgroup leadership trade-off isn't always intended to cause conflict. In fact, it isn't always intended at all. Intergroup relations may be harmed as a natural consequence of basic leadership techniques. Strong leadership is naturally associated with feelings of group connectedness, which is normally a good thing for a leader to develop. But the more intensely a group feels its own

solidarity, the more "other" everyone else may seem and the easier it can be to end up in conflict with them. It's no accident that revving up a team effort is often called "rallying the troops"—and in the end, what are troops for but to fight? Certainly, intragroup cohesiveness can be achieved by less destructive and more creative means.

Let's consider a real example. We know that the vast majority of corporate merger efforts fail. Why? Culture clash—the leaders fail to effectively integrate members of diverse groups from their respective organizations. Now, I'll bet these groups had great cohesiveness among their own members. However, this intragroup cohesiveness doesn't help bridge the divide across these two solitudes. The new organization fails to gel because the leaders can't wrap their heads around the concept of intergroup leadership. This can apply to any number of diverse contexts: cliques in a school, an acquisition of a smaller company, various ethnic groups living in the same neighborhood, members of a multidisciplinary research team trying to work together, or even countries trying to forge economic partnerships.

Question: What is the alternative to leading by dividing?

Dr. Pittinsky: While it is common for leaders to promote their own leadership at the expense of intergroup relations, it is not universal. There is an alternative style of leadership that resolves the ingroup/outgroup trade-off in a way that lessens the ill will between groups and sometimes even creates good will among groups. I call this *intergroup leadership*. It is leading by uniting. It can require that a leader consider the well-being of people outside his or her formal group and formal responsibility.

Question: What is involved in adopting the intergroup leadership style?

Dr. Pittinsky: In situations ranging from ethnic gang rivalries to corporate turf battles to wars between nations, leaders face the challenge of changing how different groups think and feel about each other. Bringing groups together is important as an end-goal of

(continued)

leadership, but also as a means: leaders require followers, and creating a followership requires bringing together diverse individuals but also diverse subgroups of individuals. This is the general aim of intergroup leadership.

Question: Based on your research, what are some of the specific approaches team leaders employ to demonstrate intergroup leadership?

Dr. Pittinsky: In my research, I have found that there are at least five recurring tactics used by leaders who aim to bring differing groups together. Probably the most fundamental one is promoting personal contact. Often the members of groups in conflict have little to no direct contact with each other. It seems common sense that personal contact between members of different groups could help give each group a better feeling about the other. An example would be to pair the members of two rival gangs to sit together in a classroom with shared desks. Research by social scientists confirms that this is helpful, but with a caveat that is not so obvious. Contact has a much more beneficial effect when it is encouraged and sanctioned by the groups' leaders. The Peace Corps may have had an even greater effect due to John F. Kennedy's stirring public endorsement of it than it would have had as a private project.

Question: Does simply ensuring more contact bring groups closer together?

Dr. Pittinsky: Encouraging contact is one of the tactics a leader can use to encourage good will between groups. But the leader needs to take into account the classic research done by Gordon Allport who argued that fulfilling certain conditions increased the positive effects of contact, including the members of the groups who have contact with each other need to be of equal status; they need to have common goals; they should be cooperating; they need the support of some acknowledged authority. Leaders also need to remember that, while contact is necessary for improving relations between groups, it is far from sufficient. For instance, a famous study took place at a boys' summer camp where two cabins of boys, the "Rattlers" and the "Eagles," had to compete. Even though both groups were in daily contact with one another, the conflict between them actually *increased* rather than decreased.

Whatever good was being done by the contact was being undone by the intense competition.

Question: So how does a leader diffuse the conflict that can arise through competition?

Dr. Pittinsky: Two other measures that would combat such conflict involve promoting common goals and promoting a common identity. First, introducing a common goal to members of different groups can be an incredibly powerful tool for bringing them together. In the situation of the boy's camp mentioned above, the researchers mitigated the competition between the two groups of boys by giving both teams goals they had to work on together. For example, the researchers pretended that the bus carrying the boys back to camp had broken down; both teams had to work together to push the bus back to camp. This tactic led to a complete change in the boys' attitudes toward each other. A real-life example can be found in the former Yugoslavia. During the Cold War, Yugoslavia's multiple ethnic groups held together to achieve a common goal—to remain as free as possible from the influence of both superpowers [the USSR and the United States].

Common goals are particularly effective when groups must negotiate with each other over a limited resource, for example funding or water. In such cases, a common goal helps to foster cooperation between the two groups. Cooperating with members of another group helps people revise their prejudices and—if the cooperation is managed carefully—gives people in different groups a chance to develop trust in each other. When it comes to common goals, more may be better. While one common goal can help reduce negative attitudes and relations, a more permanent reduction can result from a *series of goals* that require cooperation.

Question: How does promoting a common identity further mitigate conflict?

Dr. Pittinsky: Promoting a common identity among the groups turns "us" and "them" into "we." For instance, a governor might emphasize that both Democrats and Republicans in his or her state are, after all, U.S. citizens. Companies with geographically dispersed offices, possibly including various merged or bought-out divisions, often try to promote a single corporate identity. This tactic works when the leaders can clearly and convincingly point out what the two groups have in common so that people can easily see members of the other group as part of their own group. (For example, because U.S. Americans often think of voting as a quintessentially U.S. American act, the sight of Iraqis voting in 2005 tended to make them seem a little more like "one of us.") One can promote a common identity either by (a) emphasizing an identity that is already shared (as in uniting various ethnic groups who all live in the same neighborhood) or by (b) creating a new identity that would include both groups (as Flemings and Walloons were encouraged to become something new—"Belgians").

Question: The final tactic you advocate, promoting *allophilia*, seems to go beyond the traditional notion of just breaking down group stereotypes and prejudices. What is allophilia?

Dr. Pittinsky: It has long been obvious that leaders need to reduce prejudices and negative attitudes toward those who are different in order to improve relations between different groups—ethnic, religious, national, organizational, professional, generational, and so on. Negative attitudes toward others can lead to discrimination, hostility, and even violence. But recent research has shown that reducing negative attitudes is only half the challenge. Leaders also have to create or beef up the positive feelings that members of one group have toward another group. (Such positive feelings are called *allophilia*.) It is these positive attitudes—not the mere absence of negative attitudes—that will motivate acts of good will toward members of other groups. Mere tolerance is not enough. To transform an overgrown lot into a garden, you need to pull the weeds, but you also need to plant flowers. Reducing negative attitudes is picking weeds; promoting allophilia is planting flower seeds.

Promoting positive attitudes and relations among *distinct* groups—appreciating and liking their differences, not merely tolerating or discounting them—is a valuable tactic when it isn't possible to bring groups together under the umbrella of a shared identity. Allophilia promotion, as an intergroup leadership tactic, becomes important too because even when a "we" is successfully forged from an "us" and "them," over time "us" and "them" often reemerge. Instead of making "us" and "them" into "we," promoting allophilia suggests that it is possible to encourage groups to feel appreciation, affection, kinship, comfort, and interest toward others, as others.

Source: Excerpted from Karakowsky, L. (2009). Leading teams in a new direction. *HR Edge* (Fall), 23–26. Available at www.yorku. ca/laps/shrm/hredge/HR-Edge_issue2.pdf.

Weber observed that many 19th-century European organizations were, in a number of ways, very poorly managed. One critical observation was that numerous organizations were managed on a personal basis, with employees guided more by personal loyalties to other individuals' agendas than by professional loyalties to organizational goals. This often resulted in the misuse of resources for personal means.

Weber believed that an alternative organizational structure was required, and this structure would improve the operations of the organization in a number of ways; this was the origin of the notion of the bureaucratic organization. Weber identified several fundamental elements of such an organization, including those in Exhibit 3.4.

What was behind Weber's principles? Consider what is potentially accomplished through these elements. Weber believed that an organization possessing these characteristics could best maintain consistent, dependable, and reliable performance by its members. By having rigid rules and procedures and insisting on conformity to these guidelines, organizations ensure that the goals of the organization are perpetuated and are not dependent on the individuals who populate the organization at any one time.

The impersonality of a bureaucracy was also intended to avoid arbitrary and biased decisions of individuals that might be based on favouritism or personal agendas. Weber wanted to see an organization with a clear administrative structure so that employees

Exhibit 3.4 Characteristics of Bureaucratic Organizations

1. **Rules and procedures:** Organizations require stable, comprehensive, and usually documented rules for administration as well as for just about any organizational activity. All employees are expected to strictly obey these rules and procedures.

2. **Hierarchy of authority:** To ensure accountability among organizational members, fixed positions that are essentially ranked according to the level of power or authority held in the position need to be created so that members with higher positions will supervise those in lower positions. Typically, this means that the organizational chart looks like a pyramid, with the masses of workers at the lower levels while the number of organizational members in higher-level positions are fewer.

3. **Division of labour:** Like Taylor's notion of specialization, Weber acknowledged the usefulness of simplifying the job to achieve greater efficiencies.

4. **Impersonality:** Rules and procedures, not personal agendas, need to govern behaviour so that relationships between organizational members or between the individual and the organization are professional rather than personal. This attempts to avoid such dysfunctional behaviour as favouritism.

5. **Selection and promotion:** Those hired to fill positions will have specialized training and will be hired based on ability rather than on friendship or family ties. Similarly, promotion will be based on job performance rather than on favouritism.

would conform to these rules and regulations and understand that they must answer to their boss for their actions. Without these characteristics, Weber believed that organizational behaviour could be neither reliable nor predictable, and decisions might become arbitrary or biased. The impact of Weber's philosophy is discussed in Talking Business 3.4.

The Classical Approaches in Perspective

The three classical approaches to management (scientific, administrative, and bureaucratic) share a basic philosophy regarding what is required to manage effectively: The job of managers is to plan, control, and direct the actions of their subordinates to obtain the

TALKING BUSINESS 3.4

Is Weber Alive and Well?

Ironically, while Weber's work was based on observations of European organizations, his views (translated into English in the 1940s) had a profound impact on North American organizations. Certainly, we have witnessed the growth of bureaucracies over a good part of the past century. In fact, it is only more recently that we have come to question the utility of the bureaucratic organization with its emphasis on rules and regulations.

Rigid bureaucratic rules work well when the environment is stable—that is, where consumer needs are unchanging, where technology is fixed, and where other environmental factors such as political and social forces are relatively constant. In that type of environment, the

need to have comprehensive rules and regulations governing organizational activity and to ensure that authority rests with well-trained managers makes sense. However, business environments have increasingly undergone rapid change and, consequently, organizations have been moving away from bureaucratic structures and the traditional rules and regulations that might now be outdated.

On the other hand, some of the features of bureaucracies remain as strengths for almost any organization. For example, the notion of applying rules and procedures equally to all individuals across the organization would appear to support fairness and dependable behaviour in organizations.

greatest efficiency from their workers. Scientific management advocated the construction of tasks in a way that minimizes their complexity and emphasized a machine-like approach to managing workers. The administrative management perspective highlighted the view that fundamental principles should guide the role of the manager, regardless of the context. Finally, the belief in the benefits of bureaucracy reflects the view that organizations must be run according to a strict set of rules with a clear hierarchy of authority to ensure accountability and adherence to the rules. Exhibit 3.5 summarizes the classical approaches.

Exhibit 3.5 Classical Approaches to Management

Theorist/Approach	Perspectives on Effective Management

Frederick Taylor
(1856–1915)
 	
Scientific Management
	Standardizing the work
	• Observation and measurement were used to determine the most efficient method (e.g., time and motion studies)
	• Belief that there is one best method for performing a job
	• Jobs are compartmentalized (broken down into small, simple steps)
	• Benefits:
	  ○ easy and inexpensive to train workers
	  ○ cheap and readily available pool of labour
	  ○ clear rules in how to perform the job
	  ○ little to no room for individual discretion
	  ○ consistent job performance
	
	Supervising the workers
	• Managers can only take charge of their area of expertise
	• Managers' mental work should be separated from labourers' physical work
	• Workers are not capable of managing themselves
	
	Motivating the workers
	• Money is the only factor in motivating workers
	• Compensation must be closely tied to performance
	• Piece-rate pay was desirable

Henri Fayol (1841–1925) **Administrative Management**	**Division of work** • Breaking work down into its simplest components and assigning separate tasks to workers • Manager's role is to give orders and discipline workers **Unity of command** • Each employee reports to only one boss to avoid confusion and conflicting instructions *Esprit de corps* • Team spirit and harmony should be encouraged amongst workers to generate organizational cohesiveness and unity **Goals of the company** • Company goals should take precedence over individual interests

(continued)

Exhibit 3.5 Classical Approaches to Management *(continued)*

Theorist/Approach	Perspectives on Effective Management
Max Weber (1864–1920) **Bureaucratic Management**	**Rules and procedures** • Organizations require stable and documented rules **Hierarchy of authority** • Organizations should have fixed positions that are ranked according to their level of power **Division of labour** • Simplifying the job will achieve greater efficiencies **Impersonality** • Rules and procedures, not personal agendas, govern behaviour; the individual and organization are professional, not personal **Selection and promotion** • Hiring will be based on ability, not friendship or family ties; promotion will be based on job performance, not favouritism

But is this the best way to manage? Let's reconsider the context within which this perspective was born. As mentioned, these approaches arose at a time when industry was rapidly expanding and relatively unskilled labour was in abundant supply. These approaches, in fact, all worked quite well from the time of their conception through the Great Depression of the 1930s. But times do change. And over time, the weaknesses of the classical approaches became more and more apparent in some organizations. One major element absent in these approaches is the role of human behaviour—the employee. These approaches assume that the worker will respond passively to his or her designated role in the workplace, and increasingly managers found that this assumption can break down in practice. If management practices are too unreasonable or employees feel mistreated, employees may have a basis to complain. Talking Business 3.5 clearly illustrates that employees' concerns cannot be ignored.

Objective 3 Discuss the underlying philosophies of the behavioural school of thought in relation to management.

BEHAVIOURAL APPROACHES TO MANAGEMENT

What we observed during the early part of the 20th century was that employees were managed pretty much the same way as the company managed their physical or financial resources: as another piece of capital to serve the organization's objectives. Over the course of the 20th century, approaches to managing people changed dramatically. What caused us to change our philosophy of management? The impetus for change arose through a variety of sources. Some of the initiatives came from business itself, some from government, some through union action, and some through broad social changes. Whatever the source, what we witnessed in the second and third decades of the 20th century was the beginning of a more humane way of managing—a recognition of employees not simply as another resource to be managed but as individuals with certain needs that must be addressed.

behavioural approaches to management Managerial perspectives that consider the social or human side of organizations and address the challenges of managing people. Assume that achieving maximum productivity requires understanding the human factor of organizations and creating an environment that permits employees to fulfill social, not only economic, needs.

The **behavioural approaches to management** focus on the nature of the employee and on what factors encourage employees to maximize their effort. Consequently, the

The High Costs of Workplace Harassment

Workplace harassment has been defined as a "course of vexatious comment or conduct that is known, or ought reasonably to be known to be, unwelcome." This may include "hostile or unwanted conduct" and/or "verbal comments, actions or gestures" that affect an employee's "dignity" or "psychological integrity." Four Canadian provinces—Quebec, Saskatchewan, Manitoba, and most recently Ontario—now legally distinguish workplace harassment . . .

For employers the costs associated with harassment include not only the human costs of victimization, but the financial fallouts that result from lost productivity and health costs associated with helping employees recover. This is in addition to the adverse reputational effects that our federal government is currently experiencing as a result of recent media reports of workplace harassment. There are also operational implications for employers, some of which are, in many regions, reinforced by legislation. These include:

- Periodic assessment of the risks associated with psychologically harmful workplace behaviours
- Heightened awareness of the early warning signs and the actions necessary to curb escalation
- The provision of professional assistance service options
- Clear communication of behavioural expectations
- Action plans for prevention, effective intervention, leadership, and response

For both employers and employees alike, an increasing awareness of the working environments in which the risk of harassment is greater is paramount, because both victims and perpetrators are oftentimes otherwise highly performing individuals. Research shows that high-risk working conditions include environments characterized by the following:

- Interpersonal conflicts or incompatible relationships between two or more individuals
- Frequent labour–management disputes
- The perception of mistreatment among individuals
- Abusive supervisory leadership behaviours

Such working conditions are not only acknowledged—as media reports pertaining to the federal public service show—but are oftentimes condoned by organizations. The rise in employee assistance plan (EAP) referrals, third party mediations and interventions, and the increasing use of counseling services in recent years all bear testament to this workplace reality.

Has harassment cost you, as an employee, team member, manager, or employer? The now tarnished sheen coating the federal public service shows the corrosive power and high costs workplace harassment imposes on us all.

Source: Excerpted from Hughes, L. (2011, May 16). The high costs of workplace harassment. The Conference Board of Canada. Retrieved from www.conferenceboard.ca/topics/humanresource/commentaries/11-05-16/the_high_costs_of_workplace_harassment.aspx. Reprinted by permission.

behavioural school ultimately has led to a consideration of what lies beneath the surface. That is, what is the driving force behind our decisions to put effort into our jobs or careers? What factors determine how much "blood, sweat, and tears" employees are willing to expend in work performance?

The behavioural approach to management refers to managerial perspectives that consider the social or human side of organizations and address the challenges of managing human beings. This approach assumes that to achieve maximum productivity requires an understanding of the human factor of organizations and an ability to create an environment that permits employees to fulfill social, as opposed to only economic, needs. The ongoing conflicts observed between management and employees are not necessarily a consequence of purely financial interests. Salary is obviously an important factor in employer–employee relationships. However, employees also require treatment that respects their dignity and work efforts.

As with the classical approach, the school of thought that has come to be known as the behavioural approach is actually composed of a number of different perspectives. In sum, this school of thought calls on managers to consider at least two critical features of organizations:

1. Organizations are designed to produce a good or service efficiently and effectively (a view shared by the classical school).

2. However, unlike the classical school, consideration must also be given to the fact that organizations are *social systems* through which individuals attempt to satisfy their personal and social needs, as well as their economic needs.

We can consider four broad perspectives that make up the behavioural approach: the work of Elton Mayo and the human relations perspective, the assertions of **Mary Parker Follett**, the observations of **Chester Barnard**, and finally another subschool that has been referred to as modern behavioural science.

The Human Relations Movement

Elton Mayo (1880–1949) conducted studies at Western Electric, in Hawthorne, Illinois, around 1924 that drew great attention to the importance of the social dimension of work. Among Mayo's studies was an investigation of the effects of lighting on worker productivity. To test the effects of lighting, Mayo chose one group of workers to be the experimental group—the "guinea pigs," so to speak. A variety of lighting conditions were manipulated. A control group was also used where this group of workers worked under constant lighting conditions. If better lighting improved productivity, then the group of workers working under better lighting conditions should outperform the control group. The results were puzzling, however: The productivity of *both* the control and the experimental group increased. In fact, even when lighting was worsened for the experimental group, their productivity nonetheless increased. How could these results be explained?

Mayo had inadvertently discovered what came to be known as the **Hawthorne effect**. The experimental results (productivity increases) were not, in fact, caused by the intended experimental manipulation (better lighting), but by other factors—here, by "human nature." Specifically, Mayo uncovered that the true source of the productivity increase was the fact that the employees were receiving special attention. That is, all subjects realized that they were the focus of attention for the study, and that in itself increased their motivation to do a good job. Thus, social factors had a greater impact on productivity than actual working conditions did.

The Hawthorne effect had a major impact on management thinking; in fact, it has been viewed as marking the transition from scientific management to the **human relations movement**. This approach focuses on organizations as social systems, not simply as formal structures. It stresses the need for managers to recognize that managing involves social interaction—that "employees are people, too!"

Mary Parker Follett (1868–1933)

Mary Parker Follett was a social philosopher who made a number of significant contributions to the field of management in the first decades of the 20th century. Based on Follett's observations of real-life managers, she identified a number of elements necessary for

---

Mary Parker Follett A social philosopher who made a number of significant contributions to the field of management in the first decades of the 20th century. She focused on coordination, self-management, and collaboration.

Chester Barnard An organizational practitioner who served as president of the New Jersey Bell Telephone company; he was interested in organizational structure, but he considered organizations to be social systems. He focused on communication and authority in management practices.

Hawthorne effect The discovery that productivity can be enhanced by giving employees special attention rather than by simply improving their physical working conditions.

human relations movement One of the schools of behavioural management developed by Elton Mayo, who emphasized that social factors had a greater impact on productivity than actual working conditions. Focuses on organizations as social systems.

effective management. Among the factors she emphasized as critical were coordination, self-management, and collaboration.

First, Follett argued that **coordination** was central to a manager's function. That is, Follett suggested that the manager's job of encouraging workers to maximize their productivity should come about not through force or coercion, but through involvement in coordinating and harmonizing group efforts. This requires managers to be closely involved with subordinates in the daily conduct of their work, rather than simply being people who make and enforce rules.

Second, Follett stressed the importance of **self-management** and **collaboration**. Follett felt that decisions regarding how work is done can often be made by those performing the work, rather than by managers who may not be as familiar with the task. Consequently, subordinates should be involved in the decision-making process in matters that affect their work and how they should perform their work. Moreover, she felt that individuals would much prefer managing themselves than being led by a boss. Managers and workers should view themselves as collaborators or partners.

Follett advocated her views at a time when Taylor was considered the leading management scholar, so Follett's views were largely ignored and have only gained acceptance in more recent times. Some observers suggest that the practice of management for the past 100 years might have looked very different had Follett been given more attention than Taylor.

coordination In behavioural approaches to management, the harmonizing of workers and activities to maximize productivity. Mary Parker Follett argued that management needed to be closely involved with subordinates in the daily conduct of their work, rather than simply being people who made and enforced rules.

self-management In behavioural approaches to management, the action of workers, who perform the work, managing themselves by making decisions regarding how the work is done, rather than by managers who may not be as familiar with the task.

collaboration In behavioural approaches to management, the consequence of managers and workers viewing themselves as collaborators or partners.

Chester Barnard (1886–1961)

Chester Barnard was a practitioner who served as president of New Jersey Bell Telephone Company. Like Weber, he was interested in organizational structure; but unlike Weber, with his impersonal idea of organizations, Barnard considered organizations as social systems. Among Barnard's contributions were his notions of communication and authority. He felt that the two most critical functions of managers were as follows:

1. To establish and maintain a communication system with employees. Barnard felt that organizations, as social systems, required continual communication and cooperation among all members to be effective.

2. To clearly establish the organizational objectives and ensure that all employees are motivated to help attain these objectives.

In terms of the notion of authority, Barnard contradicted the then-popular view of traditional authority, which reflected the notion that those in power have an absolute right to receive compliance from those at lower levels in the hierarchy. Barnard felt that authority of management over subordinates must be earned—that is, workers will only follow orders to the extent that the following conditions are met:

■ They understand what is required.

■ They see how their work relates to organizational goals.

■ They believe that they will gain some benefit from accomplishing these goals.

Fundamentally, Barnard, like Follett, believed that a collaborative approach to management would be most effective for organizations.

Modern Behavioural Science and Motivation-Based Perspectives

Look around your workplace and you will see some individuals who are completely committed to fulfilling the expectations and responsibilities of their employer. Continue looking, and you may also find someone asleep at his or her desk, or maybe surfing the web for interesting vacation sites while the boss's back is turned. What distinguishes these two workers? Is it a personality difference? Is it a difference in work ethic? Is it pay? Is it the boss? Is it the work environment? What variables play a critical role in determining the level of effort or motivation that employees bring to the job? Clearly, this question is critical for any organization aiming to maximize the potential of its workforce.

modern behavioural science The school of thought that consists of sociological, psychological, and anthropological perspectives based on the premise that motivating workers is preferable to controlling them. It has produced an enormous number of theories, including need-based and cognitive-based theories of motivation.

Another category of management theories that should be considered as an important part of the behavioural approach can be referred to as **modern behavioural science**. This school of thought arose largely in the 1950s and continued the systematic study of the human element of organizations. Researchers came from academic backgrounds in sociology, psychology, and anthropology and became known as behavioural scientists and industrial psychologists. One underlying theme of this work is the issue of motivation. That is, rather than considering the primary role of management to be one of control (the classical approach), these theories consider the role of management as one that must foster a motivated workforce. Consequently, the underlying aim of much of this school of thought is to consider factors that influence the motivation of employees—a key issue for many of today's organizations (see Talking Business 3.6). Exhibit 3.6 (on page 105) summarizes the behavioural approaches to management.

THE BEST MANAGEMENT PHILOSOPHY? CONTINGENCY APPROACH

Now that we have considered two very popular schools of management thought, the question is, "Where are we today?" What approaches are guiding leaders in management of organizations today? The approaches described above have both strengths and weaknesses.

contingency approach to management The acknowledgement that there is no one best way to manage and that different conditions and situations require the application of different approaches or techniques. Includes consideration of organization size, environmental uncertainty, routineness of task technology, and individual differences.

Experts agree that there is simply no one best way to manage. Instead, what has been advocated is referred to as the **contingency approach to management**. As the name implies, this approach assumes that the best style of management depends on many contingencies: Different conditions and situations require the application of different approaches or techniques. Essentially, this approach argues that there are few, if any, universal truths governing management techniques. Consequently, contingency management theories continue to examine different factors that dictate different requirements for managing people. For example, how to manage at UPS will differ from managing at Microsoft, which will differ from managing at a local hospital, and so on. This is a central challenge for any manager—fitting their management philosophy to suit the organizational context. Think about the nature of different organizations and the type of work performed and you will begin to see the importance of understanding the contingencies of management.

Here are some of the contingencies that should be taken into account when implementing a management philosophy (see also Exhibit 3.7 on page 106):

1. *Organizational size:* Large organizations with hundreds of employees cannot be managed in the same manner as small organizations with few employees. The need for control and the challenge to achieve it in massive organizations may tend to encourage an

The Myths and Realities of Motivation

© Andres Rodriguez/Fotolia

An Interview with *New York Times* Best-Selling Author Daniel Pink

Daniel H. Pink is the author of several provocative, best-selling books about the changing world of work. One of his recent books, *Drive: The Surprising Truth about What Motivates Us,* explores 50 years of behavioral science to challenge the conventional wisdom about human motivation. *Drive* was a *New York Times, Wall Street Journal, Washington Post,* and *Publishers Weekly* bestseller.

Question: Why did you write *Drive?*

Daniel Pink: After I wrote *A Whole New Mind*—about the shift from "left-brain" abilities to "right-brain" ones—lots of people asked me about how to motivate people to do this sort of work. I didn't have a clue. So I began looking at what turned out to be an absolute treasure trove of research on human motivation. And the answers I found were surprising. Very surprising.

Question: *Drive* has been on the *New York Times* Bestsellers List for close to a year. What do you think has contributed to this book's enormous and enduring popularity?

Daniel Pink: First, thanks for the kind acknowledgment. I'm still surprised—and delighted—that anybody reads what I write! In a sense, timing worked to the book's advantage. After the financial crisis, there was a sense that the old verities were failing us—and people were searching for some new rules, especially those that ran with the grain of human nature rather than against it.

Question: You cover a lot of ground in *Drive*, making accessible an abundance of academic research. As your title indicates, this book does indeed reveal a lot of surprising truths about what motivates us. What was the biggest surprise to you in terms of the research findings?

Daniel Pink: I was surprised by how vast the research was—and by how much of it overturned orthodoxies I didn't even realize were orthodoxies.

Question: What are the biggest mistakes that organizational leaders make in their attempt to generate a highly motivated workforce?

Daniel Pink: They're too simplistic. They believe that getting people to do great work requires simply rewarding the behavior you want and punishing the behavior you don't. But it's far more complicated than that. And most leaders know that even they themselves are motivated by forces beyond carrots and sticks.

Question: When an employee isn't motivated, how much is the organization to blame? How much of the onus should be on the individual? For example, if all of us could successfully match ourselves with our "perfect-fit" job, wouldn't we be intrinsically motivated?

Daniel Pink: That's a tough one. It's obviously a mix between individual attributes and the context in which one is operating. But I think in many ways we've undersold both aspects of the equation. We haven't demanded that individuals go through the sometimes painful process of figuring out what they're good at, what they enjoy doing, and what gives them meaning. Yet, we still take a mostly one-size-fits all approach to managing people—which creates cultures that can be alienating at a human level and inefficient at an economic one.

Question: It would be great to "enrich" every job but it can't always be done. Perhaps many employees, for better or worse, need extrinsic motivation because they

(continued)

are desperately lacking in intrinsic motivation and we can't necessarily provide that. Do you think that is true?

Daniel Pink: Maybe. But I think the calculus works slightly differently. Everybody needs baseline rewards—a decent salary, benefits, etc.—so they're not desperate and insecure. Without that, enduring motivation is tough. But once you cross that threshold, these other forces matter more. Of course, there are some people who don't deliver or who don't have good habits. IMHO, that's learned behavior rather than their natural state. But even so, I'm not against firing people who don't perform. I just don't think you'll get them to perform any better by deploying an endless arsenal of carrots.

Question: We seem to learn in our childhood education the same approach to motivation that most organizations use—a focus on achievement or results (grades/pay) rather than on genuine effort or learning. Isn't that what we keep trying to do as adults—"make the grade"? It's not about learning or improving, it's about achievement. How can we ever change that, particularly in today's highly competitive and volatile business environment?

Daniel Pink: That's another tough one. In some ways, schools are even more rooted in an outdated approach to motivation. Especially here in the US, they're doubling down on external motivators and renewing their emphasis on routines, right answers, and standardization. In a sense, they risk becoming compliance factories. The solutions are difficult, but they begin with understanding. That's why I encourage every parent and policy maker to read the work of (Stanford University psychologist) Carol Dweck. Her work brilliantly shows the difference between performance goals (example: getting a good grade) and learning goals (example: mastering the material). We mistakenly believe that hitting performance goals means students have learned something—but that's just not true. It's why a nominally "good" student like me could have taken French for 6 years and gotten straight A's—and still not be able to speak French. We ought to be emphasizing—and measuring—learning goals, though that's far less convenient for the adults in charge of education.

Question: One of the many insightful observations you make in *Drive* is that, "Most twenty-first century notions of management presume that, in the end, people are pawns

rather than players" (p. 91). Can you speak to that notion a bit? Do you think that belief will ever really change?

Daniel Pink: A lot of the decisions we make in business are rooted in our belief about human nature. Some folks believe that people are fundamentally passive and inert—that their natural state is to not do anything worthwhile and that we need sweet or bitter external rewards to get us to move. The other belief is different—that our nature is to be active and engaged. I side—strongly—with the second view. That's not because I'm a dewy-eyed optimist. It's because I have three children—and I've seen hundreds more. I defy you to find me a two-year-old who's passive and inert—or a four-year-old who's "not" active and engaged. That's our natural state. If people are passive and inert—and, of course, millions and millions are—that's learned behavior, which means it might be susceptible to change.

Question: *Drive* explores a number of "best practices" organizations, in terms of motivation. Which company stood out most in your mind as a role model? Do you think these "best practices" will ever spread across industries?

Daniel Pink: I'm a big fan of Atlassian, the Australian software company—and of one of their practices in particular. Once a quarter, on a Thursday afternoon, the company says to its software developers: "Go work on anything you want—so long as it's part of your regular job." The only thing the company asks is that people show what they've created to the rest of the company in a fun, freewheeling meeting on Friday afternoon. Altlassian calls these FedEx Days (because people have to deliver something overnight.) It turns out that this one day of intense, undiluted autonomy has led to a whole array of fixes for existing software and lots of ideas for new products that had otherwise never emerged. Now these FedEx Days are spreading to lots of other companies, large and small. Atlassian is also doing some cool things to rethink traditional performance reviews and make them useful exercises in feedback rather than the painful kabuki-theater-style encounters they typically are.

Source: Excerpted from Karakowsky, L. (2011). What drives us. *HR Edge* (Fall), 6–9. Available at www.yorku.ca/laps/shrm/hredge/HR-Edge_issue3.pdf.

Exhibit 3.6 Behavioural School of Management

Theorist/Approach	Perspectives on effective management
Elton Mayo (1880–1949) **Human Relations Movement**	**"Hawthorne effect"** • Special attention paid to employees increased productivity • Social factors had a greater impact on productivity than actual working conditions • Managing involves social interaction
Mary Parker Follet (1868–1933)	**Coordination** • Managers must coordinate and harmonize group efforts ○ Managers must be closely involved with subordinates in the daily conduct of their work **Self-management** • Workers should self-manage themselves by making decisions about how they perform their work tasks **Collaboration** • Managers and workers should view themselves as collaborators or partners

Chester Barnard (1886–1961)	**Social systems**
	• Organizations are social systems requiring continuous communication and cooperation among all members
	Communication system
	• Managers must establish and maintain a communication system with employees
	Organizational objectives
	• Managers must establish organizational objectives and ensure employees are motivated to help attain those objectives
	Authority of management
	• Authority over subordinates must be earned, since workers will only follow orders when
	  ○ they understand what is required
	  ○ they see how their work relates to organizational goals
	  ○ they believe they will gain some benefit from accomplishing these goals

Modern Behavioural Science and Motivation-Based Perspectives (1950s–present)	• Management should be more about motivating employees than controlling them • Developed from various disciplines such as sociology, psychology, and anthropology

approach that relies on elements of the classical school, such as the need for rules and regulations and the importance of an administrative hierarchy to ensure control. On the other hand, small, entrepreneurial organizations might function more effectively with a minimal number of rules and regulations.

2. *Routineness of task technology:* Some organizations may require employees to work in an assembly-line fashion, while their work is governed by machinery. Other jobs may not involve any significant level of technology: retail sales or being a bank teller are jobs that do not necessarily require technological expertise. These jobs are more easily subjected

Exhibit 3.7
Contingencies of
Management
Philosophies

```
    ┌─────────────────┐          ┌─────────────────┐
    │       1.        │          │       2.        │
    │  Organizational │          │   Routineness of │
    │      Size       │          │ Task and Technology│
    └─────────────────┘          └─────────────────┘
              │                            │
              ▼                            ▼
    ┌─────────────────────────────────────────────┐
    │     MANAGEMENT PHILOSOPHIES MIX              │
    ├─────────────────────────────────────────────┤
    │        • Classical                          │
    │        • Behavioural                        │
    └─────────────────────────────────────────────┘
              ▲                            ▲
              │                            │
    ┌─────────────────┐          ┌─────────────────┐
    │       4.        │          │       3.        │
    │   Individual    │          │  Environmental  │
    │   Differences   │          │   Uncertainty   │
    └─────────────────┘          └─────────────────┘
```

to routinization, as advocated by Taylor, and there should be strict rules on which such workers can rely. On the other hand, jobs that must continually adapt to changing technology require employees who are equally adaptive. High-tech organizations that employ "knowledge workers" are keenly aware that it is difficult to standardize the jobs of these workers, given the high rate of change within the present technology environment.

3. *Environmental uncertainty:* An organization that exists within a volatile environment must be prepared for continuous change. Change is the antithesis of the classical approaches, which emphasize stability and order. Consequently, organizations functioning in rapidly changing environments are less likely to find extensive application of the classical school useful in managing their workforce.

4. *Individual differences:* In any organization, employees differ with regard to their ability and motivation. Some people function better when given clear guidance—rules and regulations regarding how their job should be performed. Others perform better when the rules governing their performance are minimal. These differences suggest that a blanket application of either the classical or behavioural schools may risk ignoring the fact that the labour force is not homogeneous in terms of responses to the nature of work and management style.

Objective 4 Consider the importance and role of trust in the workplace.

THE CRITICAL IMPORTANCE OF TRUST IN THE WORKPLACE

Globalization has created many new tests for organizations while they are simultaneously dealing with the usual challenges, such as achieving profit and growth targets, creating value, maintaining security, protecting privacy, managing diversity, and managing change. All of these factors have led to organizations today facing a fundamental crisis: Many companies are failing to uphold basic business principles such as leadership and trust. Combine this with the fact that the labour force is rapidly declining while the demise of employee loyalty is rapidly increasing and you can see that there's a problem. Organizations are faced with figuring out how to improve elements that contribute to organizational success. The search for the next successful model to guide managers continues, and in searching for guidance it may be necessary to look in some familiar but largely ignored places.

Many books have been written on successful business models to achieve organizational effectiveness. Traditional management research has largely condemned the military model of leadership and culture as outdated and old-fashioned. The military model conjures up words such as *dictatorship, command and control, chain of command, hierarchy,* and *regimentation,* which are often words associated with the manner in which the military runs its business. However, arguably, the military is the ultimate model for achieving organizational effectiveness based on the importance of trust.

While military leaders might disagree on how to lead, one theme is consistently repeated in discussions with successful military leaders—the central value of trust. Trust is a major component of the successful military ethos or character. Likewise, organizational trust is crucial. Organizations must focus on creating a culture of trust to maximize effectiveness. Most important, trust can provide an organization with a competitive advantage that cannot be easily duplicated. Trust is an integral aspect of the psychological contract that exists between the employee and the employer.

Trust refers to one's perception of the integrity and openness of others, one's comfort with the expected actions of others, one's faith in how others will react, and one's willingness to become vulnerable to the actions of others.[8] Employees want to feel that the organization has their best interests in mind. Although it is now rare to find a worker who remains with one company for his or her entire career, companies are rediscovering the value of loyalty. Organizations cannot build loyalty in the absence of trust (see Talking Business 3.7).

trust One's perception of the integrity and openness of others, one's comfort with the expected actions of others, one's faith in how others will react, and one's willingness to become vulnerable to the actions of others.

TALKING BUSINESS 3.7
How One Canadian Company Earns Trust

At a time when the decline of trust in business is accelerating, one Canadian company has made earning the trust of its stakeholders the cornerstone of its business. A The Conference Board of Canada case study, *The Dalton Company Ltd.: Building on a Foundation of Trust*, describes how this professional building services firm has created a culture of trust and implemented systems to ensure that its values are translated into actions for its stakeholders.

"Trust is not an intangible, 'soft' concept, but a key issue in business today," says Andrew Dalton, CEO of The Dalton Company Ltd. "In a challenging economy, a corporate culture of earning, predicting, and measuring trust will prove critical to any organization's sustainability. If you don't have clear standards, you can't hold people accountable."

Dalton's systems and processes have made it a leader in restoring trust in the construction industry as a whole. Its trust model is based on accountability and leadership. Through this approach, Dalton seeks to understand each customer's purpose, vision, objectives, and limitations early in a project, and monitors how it is meeting these needs throughout the building process.

One key factor for Dalton in building trust is its issue resolution mechanism, which identifies potential solutions to problems as they arise in each project. The process begins with the responsible lead for the project. Known as the

"Yellow," this person reports on the project to the leadership team at Dalton each week. In this process, there is no finger pointing; instead, the team works together to find solutions.

In its Alternative Approach to Building, Dalton positions clients as the priority and focuses on their needs—in Dalton's words, their Definition of Success (DOS). Developing the DOS at the start of a project is an important trust-building exercise, as it creates accountability between clients and employees. While a client typically defines success as a project that is delivered well, on time, and on budget, Dalton delves deeper to understand all of the client's underlying motivations. Once the DOS is established, Dalton measures the performance of its project team based on the client's feedback in relation to the DOS.

While cultivating trust externally is vital, the company also believes strongly in showing and rewarding trust internally: Trust is integrated into hiring practices and Dalton's bonus system. The organization's recruiting process focuses on whether potential employees will fit into the firm's culture, and employees are rewarded for demonstrating trustworthy behaviour.

"You can train skills; I don't think you can train trust," says Andrew Dalton.

Source: Michael Bassett, "Case Study: How One Canadian Company Earns Trust," InsideEdge, The Conference Board of Canada. Reprinted with permission.

---

[8] Sashittal, H.C., Berman, J., & Ilter, S. (1998). Impact of trust on performance evaluations. *Mid-Atlantic Journal of Business*, 34(2), 163.

Research consistently supports the idea that organizational trust has an impact on organizational effectiveness. For example, numerous studies have linked trust with a variety of desirable work behaviours such as organizational citizenship behaviour, performance, intention to turnover, problem solving, level of openness within a top management team, support for authorities, satisfaction, and organizational commitment.[9] Similarly, trust has been linked with better task performance, openness in communication, information sharing, reduced conflict between partners in interorganizational relationships, and better acceptance of organizational decisions and goals.[10]

Equally, the absence of organizational trust can create serious challenges for an organization. Where there is a lack of trust, there will be failings in communication, delegation, empowerment, and quality.[11] A corporate culture of mistrust causes employees to focus on survival and self-preservation by pursuing defensive values such as control, power, expediency, and manipulation, which have a negative effect on productivity and morale.[12] Organizations must strive to create a culture of trust. As the military model illustrates, the critical factors needed to create a culture of trust are effective communication, leadership, and human resources practices and programs that establish and reinforce the value of trust.

Organizational trust is of paramount importance in the military setting. There can be no greater context than war where individuals must expose their vulnerability and trust the person beside them. Trust is reinforced through several mechanisms: an open culture, social structures, effective communication mechanisms, leadership, teamwork, and human resource policies and practices. The military reinforces trust through a shared purpose, vision, mission, and ethos. The military believes that trust is formed when people get to know each other on a personal level as well as on a professional basis. Military messes and institutes provide a social structure where common experiences can be shared and where storytelling occurs. Members of the military at all levels of rank and structure interact in this social setting, where members can get to know each other on a personal level. A senior officer (a colonel) commented, "We tend to deal with people that we trust in preference over those who we don't know." Thus, the military provides and supports this social structure for its members.

Trust, Teamwork, and Citizenship

Although the research supports the positive effects of the use of teams, the existence of high-performance teams is considered to be rare. High-performance teams "frequently outperform the teams that produce similar products and services under similar conditions and constraints."[13]

---

[9] Tzafrir, S.S., Harel, G.H., Baruch, B., & Dolan, S.L. (2004). The consequences of emerging HRM practices for employees' trust in their managers. *Personnel Review, 33*(5/6), 628–647; Ferres, N., Connell, J., & Travaglione, A. (2004). Co-worker trust as a social catalyst for constructive employee attitudes. *Journal of Managerial Psychology, 19*(6), 608–622.

[10] Lines, R., Selart, M., Espedal, B., Johansen, S.T. (2005). The production of trust during organizational change. *Journal of Change Management, 5*(2), 221–245.

[11] Erdem, F., Ozen, J., & Atsan, N. (2003). The relationship between trust and team performance. *Work Study, 52*(6/7), 337–340.

[12] Hultman, K. (2004). Let's wipe out systemic mistrust. *Organization Development Journal, 22*(1), 102–106.

[13] Castka, P., Bamber, C.J., Sharp, J.M., & Belohoubek, P. (2001). Factors affecting successful implementation of high performance teams. *Team Performance Management, 7*(7/8), 123–134.

There appears to be a common theme among the research with respect to the effectiveness of teams. The key factors for effective teams include a shared vision, empowerment, and trust among team members. Teamwork creates a community because everyone must accept ownership and responsibility for a project's success or failure.[14] In order for team-based structures to be effective, the organization must provide a culture that supports collaboration and a highly involved workforce. The culture should be based on empowerment, creativity, shared vision, participation, learning ability, trust, and a shared consensus (see Talking Business 3.8).

Teamwork is of paramount importance in the military. Teams are built to succeed in the mission. The mission cannot be accomplished individually, and thus teamwork is a critical part of the military ethos. Teamwork is required to foster the cohesion necessary to

TALKING BUSINESS 3.8

How Teams Learn at Teleflex Canada

Teleflex Canada Ltd. is a Richmond, British Columbia-based company with a reputation as a world leader in the design and manufacture of hydraulic and thermal technology products for industrial and marine use. A recent focus on developing cost effective solutions has resulted in a dramatic expansion of their customer base to include most North American boat and bus manufacturers; many truck-accessory, engine and marine distributors; as well as the United States and Canadian military forces. The Teleflex Canada workforce is over 300 strong and represents diverse cultural backgrounds and ages. Employees must bring together the right mix of skills, experience and technological know-how to cost-effectively design and manufacture products that meet customers' needs.

Learning has always been part of the corporate culture at Teleflex—senior management recognizes the benefits of a well-trained and skilled workforce. Initial training programs included English as a second language (ESL) classes, academic upgrading, and the basic skills of reading, writing and numeracy. However, management soon realized that although employees were participating in training, they were not using their new-found skills in their jobs. Concerned, senior management turned to workplace education consultants for advice. The results led to the complete transformation of training at Teleflex into "Team Time," a model based on the full participation of manufacturing teams working together on real challenges and changing understandings of their work. The Team Time training model evolved into a series of topic-specific modules for learning "lean manufacturing," teamwork and related skills....

At Teleflex, the focus of training is to help production teams solve their respective work challenges. Team Time training modules addressing specific machine or data source issues allow production teams to solve problems using actual workplace tools. These hands-on, real-life activities are well suited for the production team work model at Teleflex.

Training is organized into regular production team meetings, which usually last 60 minutes. Team leaders are responsible for facilitating each module and covering the material. Team leaders must also assemble the required learning materials. There are 15 modules, with new modules being developed continually. Modules cover topics such as the purpose of Team Time training, how Team Time learning works, customer needs, how to add value, and information systems....

Through the Team Time training initiative, the reading, writing and numeracy skills of employees have improved significantly. Specific outcomes of training include the following:

- The training program has influenced the company to present its newsletter and corporate data in "plain language."

- On-time delivery of finished products has increased from 65 to 90 per cent.

- Inventory turnover in a given time period has increased from four times to more than seven times.

- Parts shortages have been significantly reduced.

(continued)

---

[14] Scarnati, J.T. (2001). On becoming a team player. *Team Performance Management*, 7(1/2), 5–10.

One of the greatest accomplishments of the program has been the number of people involved in its development, piloting and maintenance. More than one-third of the workforce at Teleflex had a role in developing Team Time—many more than had been anticipated.

Specific impacts and benefits include the following:

- More effective change management—employees, managers, engineers and production leaders are becoming change agents within the organization.

- Employees are better able to adapt to new products and manufacturing processes.

- Cross-functional communication has improved on the shop floor.

- Smoother job transitions are facilitated through the training.

- Communication skills and problem-solving skills have improved within work teams; and

- The training program scores helped Teleflex Canada achieve a designation as a "Lean Manufacturer" in 2002.

Source: Excerpted from Campbell, A. (2005). Developing a community of employees through team time at Teleflex Canada. The Conference Board of Canada. Retrieved from www.conference-board.ca/temp/23808387-1455-45f7-b817-6f5aea9ade89/129-06_cs_teleflex.pdf.

achieve the organizational mission. The military stresses the importance of the team over the individual, and teamwork is reinforced through doctrine, training, and exercises.

The concept of teamwork can be found throughout military doctrine. Teamwork is one of the main principles of the military ethos. The importance of the mission is understood, and completion of the mission depends on teamwork. The fact that all members share and understand this mission is a key enabler of teamwork. As previously discussed, teamwork is a fundamental component of basic training. Members are placed in small groups and given tasks to execute as a team. Members must work together to achieve the goals established for them. Individual strengths and weaknesses are identified, and members work together to overcome the weaknesses of the individual and capitalize on the strength of the collective team. These types of exercises continue well past basic training and reinforce values such as trust, selflessness, and conscientiousness. These exercises in teamwork build trust through adversity and humility and reinforce selflessness, a sense of belonging and respect for peers. Team-building exercises like the ruck march are a common organizational practice used to reinforce the importance of teams and trust.

Many nonmilitary companies use job descriptions to outline the expected tasks and responsibilities of an employee's position. In essence, each job description is linked to the specific output necessary to accomplish organizational goals and remain effective and competitive. However, it is the actions of employees performed outside of these standardized job descriptions that can have a profound impact on organizational effectiveness. Successful organizations need employees who will do more than what is stated in the job description and extend themselves beyond normal requirements and expectations. Organizational citizenship behaviour describes the actions taken by employees that demonstrate a willingness to go "above and beyond" the duties outlined in their job description.

The fact is, a business that fosters a climate of trust can more effectively reinforce a shared purpose and values. This in turn will encourage members to go above and beyond simply fulfilling their minimal job requirements and instead also become accountable for building and fostering organizational citizenship behaviours.

CHAPTER SUMMARY

We have discussed the nature of managerial roles and considered what the job of a manager entails. This chapter also identified the central schools of management thought that have guided our thinking for over a century. We also considered the elements of managing that contribute to success and how the successful use of these elements depends largely on the presence of trust in the organization.

CHAPTER LEARNING TOOLS

Key Terms

administrative management 92

behavioural approaches to management 98

bureaucratic management 92

Chester Barnard 100

classical approaches to management 88

collaboration 101

compartmentalizing 90

contingency approach to management 102

coordination 101

decisional roles 83

disseminator 83

disturbance handler 83

effectiveness 81

efficiency 81

entrepreneur 83

esprit de corps 92

figurehead 82

Hawthorne effect 100

human relations movement 100

Industrial Revolution 89

informational roles 82

interpersonal roles 82

laissez faire 89

leader 82

liaison 82

management 81

Mary Parker Follett 100

modern behavioural science 102

monitor 83

negotiator 83

piece-rate system 91

resource allocator 83

scientific management 89

self-management 101

spokesperson 83

standardizing 90

time and motion studies 90

trust 107

unity of command 92

Multiple-Choice Questions

Select the *best* answer for each of the following questions. Solutions are located in the back of your textbook.

1. What category of management is a department or division head?
   a. Top management
   b. Middle management
   c. Supervisor or lower-level management
   d. Executive management

2. Efficiency often refers to
   a. delegating tasks to reduce time
   b. using the fewest inputs to produce an output
   c. organizing resources effectively
   d. planning and controlling resources effectively

3. All of the following are central functions of management *except*
   a. changing   b. planning
   c. organizing   d. leading

4. A leader role can be categorized as
   a. an informational role
   b. a decisional role
   c. an interpersonal role
   d. a delegating role

5. A resource allocator is considered to be
   a. an informational role   b. an interpersonal role
   c. a delegating role   d. a decisional role

6. An informational role can include all of the following roles *except*
   a. liaison   b. monitor
   c. disseminator   d. spokesperson

7. In Taylor's perspective on standardizing work, a job should be
   a. broken down into simple parts
   b. easy and inexpensive to train workers
   c. designed with room for individual discretion
   d. both A and B

8. Taylor believed workers were best motivated by
   a. social interaction
   b. a piece-rate system
   c. managers and workers collaborating as partners
   d. fair employment practices

9. The classical school of management is sometimes referred to as an approach that
   a. is machine-like
   b. promotes a clear role for managers
   c. has a clear hierarchy of authority to ensure accountability
   d. all of the above

10. *Esprit de corps* is often referred to as
    a. a military model of management
    b. team spirit and harmony
    c. both A and B
    d. none of the above

11. The Hawthorne effect involves all of the following *except*
    a. employees receiving special attention
    b. the human side of motivating workers
    c. how to decrease productivity
    d. productivity factors on working conditions

12. Mary Parker Follett argued that all of the following were critical to a manager's function *except*
    a. collaboration
    b. coordination
    c. collective negotiation
    d. harmonizing group efforts

13. The contingency approach can involve factors like
    a. organizational size
    b. environmental uncertainty
    c. individual differences
    d. all of the above

14. Chester Barnard believed the most critical functions of managers involved
    a. communication
    b. authority
    c. cooperation
    d. all of the above

15. The behavioural school of management promotes
    a. a piece-rate system
    b. standardization of job tasks
    c. human and social factors to managing people
    d. a hierarchical structure for management

Discussion Questions

1. Define *management* and explain what it means to manage.
2. Discuss the four main functions of management.
3. Compare three roles of management: interpersonal, informational, and decisional roles.
4. Explain and discuss three classical management philosophies.
5. Compare the differences between Taylor's and Fayol's views on management.
6. Explain and discuss three behavioural management philosophies.

7. Compare the differences between Follett's and Barnard's views on managers' key functions.
8. Discuss the military model of management.
9. Discuss the importance of the contingency approach to management.
10. Select a business or organization and explain what style of management you think would work best at that organization and why.

CONCEPT APPLICATION   KICKING HORSE COFFEE

For many years, Kicking Horse Coffee was one of Canada's best kept secrets. However, the word is out, as writer Chris Ryan noted in July of 2013:

> The town of Invermere isn't exactly a specialty-coffee powerhouse. Though its location in eastern British Columbia between the Canadian Rockies and the Purcell Mountains provides plenty of picturesque backdrops . . . [it] boasts only a handful of coffee shops. But one of those is a behemoth. The flagship café for Kicking Horse Coffee serves as home base for the well-established roaster that distributes throughout Canada and much of the Western United States.[15]

---

[15] Ryan, C. (2013, June). Spotlight: Kicking Horse Coffee. *Fresh Cup Magazine*. Retrieved from http://www.kickinghorsecoffee.com/files/2013_06_FreshCup.pdf

If you are not quite convinced of the power of Kicking Horse, consider that by 2012 AC Nielsen ranked Kicking Horse among the top 10 commercial brands in Canada, along with such brands as Folgers, Nabob, and Tim Hortons.[16] And by that time, Kicking Horse was selling 2 million pounds of coffee a year and was carried in many retail stores across the country, from Loblaw to Sobeys to Shoppers Drug Mart, while also making inroads into the United States.

Those of you following the Canadian business press in recent years will have noted the rapid rise of this company. It has been identified in the press as a top organic fair-trade coffee company in Canada. And its reputation is strong. It is known as a company whose brand has been built around quality and consistent character. The CEO, Elana Rosenfeld, was recently ranked among Canada's top female entrepreneurs in *PROFIT Magazine*.[17]

Located in Invermere, British Columbia, Kicking Horse boasts 17 coffee varieties, sells its products worldwide, roasts 4 million pounds of coffee annually, and has achieved about $25 million in annual sales with expected growth each coming year. Rather than opening cafés (like Starbucks), the company focuses on roasting and wholesaling. It is based out of a 60,000-square-foot facility in Invermere, and it operates one flagship café for its local residents.

So how did this coffee powerhouse get started? In 1996, Rosenfeld and her husband, Leo Johnson, decided to buy a local café. From its early days, customer response to Kicking Horse Coffee was strong. Initially, Johnson's contributions were mostly in design and operations, and Rosenfeld focused on sales, marketing, and finance. While competing against much larger businesses, they decided to price their coffee as a premium product and attempted to build a loyal following.[18]

© Spofi-Fotolia.com

For years, Rosenfeld and Johnson would leave Kicking Horse in the capable hands of their employees as they travelled for up to a month at a time to Mexico, Peru, and elsewhere. The aim was to build relationships with farmer co-ops in those countries that have been central to the success of the company.[19] The fact that the heads of Kicking Horse felt comfortable turning over leadership roles to their employees says a lot. It reflects the kind of relationship that Rosenfeld and Johnson established with their employees based on employee autonomy and shared goals.

If you could study the management style of Rosenfeld and Johnson, you might be surprised by their informal and accessible approach. With approximately 40 employees,[20]

[16] Lee, J. (2012, November 28). B.C. entrepreneur celebrates the sweet smell of (Kicking Horse Coffee) success. *Vancouver Sun*. Retrieved from www.vancouversun.com/business/smallbusiness/Vancouver+entrepreneur+celebrates+sweet+smell/7617938/story.html#Comments#ixzz2YaZi9OTh.

[17] Amos, G. (2012, November 30). Kicking Horse Coffee geared to grow. *Columbia Valley Pioneer*. Retrieved from www.columbiavalleypioneer.com/?p=7753.

[18] Lee, J. (2012, November 28).

[19] BDC Consulting. (2011, February 15). How to get the best from your employees. Retrieved from www.bdc.ca/en/advice_centre/articles/Pages/successful_management_tips.aspx.

[20] Kicking Horse Coffee website, www.kickinghorsecoffee.com/en/media/presskit.

Case Continued >

these two business leaders who manage a multimillion dollar business in a relatively "fun" way. They make great efforts to do more than simply manage an efficient workforce.

Management at Kicking Horse considers their employees as key to their success and treats them in a manner that reflects that belief. For example, a major focus is on timely and consistent communication with employees. But these communication efforts are not simply to disseminate information from the "top," but also to gather information from those who work closest with the product.

Rosenfeld and Johnson understand that, given the specialized nature of the roasting work, these employees must maintain a certain level of autonomy. However, like any business, efficiency of production is critical and so measures of performance must also be applied to gauge how the group is performing.

The work is exacting and can be demanding given Kicking Horse's high standards. Consequently, Rosenfeld and Johnson have made every effort to make the culture "fun" and as stress free as possible. Therefore, for example, work practices include things like flexible hours, daily stretch breaks for line workers, and catered monthly meetings as well as official fun days for kayaking, skiing, and holiday celebrations.

Specialized work can easily become tedious and machine like. However, "tedious" is the polar opposite of the culture at Kicking Horse. The culture is much more "laid back" than might be expected for this kind of business, and observers would likely be surprised by the "fun" atmosphere that might seem more suitable to a summer camp than a multimillion-dollar business. Does it work at Kicking Horse, though? It sure does.

In one interview, Rosenfeld commented, "Doing it from the heart is paying off for us . . . Our employees are highly motivated, very productive and usually stay with us a long time."[21]

Over the past 10 years, the company's efforts have paid off. Kicking Horse Coffee has won numerous awards in a variety of categories, including Canada's Top Female Entrepreneurs, Canada's Fastest-Growing Companies, and Biggest BC Businesses Owned by Women to name a few:

2012 Business in Vancouver: Biggest BC businesses Owned by Women

2011 Profit W100: Canada's Top Female Entrepreneurs

2011 Kootenay Business: Top 50 Kootenay Companies

2011 Business in Vancouver: Top 100 Fastest-Growing Companies

2009 Kootenay Business: Top 50 Kootenay Companies

2009 Profit 100: Canada's Fastest-Growing Companies

2008 Profit W100: Canada's Top Female Entrepreneurs

2007 Profit W100: Canada's Top Female Entrepreneurs

2007 Kootenay Business: Top 50 Kootenay Companies

2007 Profit 100: Canada's Fastest-Growing Companies

2006 Profit W100: Canada's Top Female Entrepreneurs

2005 BDC: Ongoing Achievement Elana & Leo

2004 Business in Vancouver: 40 under 40 Elana & Leo

2003 BDC: Young Entrepreneur Award for British Columbia[22]

---

[21] BDC Consulting, 2011.

[22] Kicking Horse Coffee website, www.kickinghorsecoffee.com/en/media/awards.

The ability to nurture an engaged, high-performance workforce is more likely to be found in Kicking Horse's leadership style than in the more traditional "command-and-control" management approaches. Certainly, the performance of Kicking Horse is evidence that they are doing something right. According to a report by BDC Consulting, the company's revenue doubled annually for the first few years and more recently increased by about 15–20% a year. This also allowed for the expansion of plant facilities to 60,000 square feet, along with a café for local residents.[23]

Many management experts embrace the leadership style of Kicking Horse and would advocate the spread of this approach to other organizations. In their discussion of Kicking Horse Coffee, BDC Consulting noted that to attract the best people, the company offers an above-average benefit package that includes competitive wages compared to other coffee retailers. To ensure consistent quality standards, the company monitors performance on a regular basis. According to BDC senior consulting manager Bonnie Elliot, the culture for the company is created at the top. "When you walk into the facilities at Kicking Horse, the way people interact makes it evident that the place is different from a company that is run bureaucratically and autocratically," Elliot says. "The commitment to staff well-being and community is not just talk, but something that the partners live and breathe."[24]

Questions

1. Discuss in detail which elements of the behavioural school are being applied at the Kicking Horse Coffee Company.

2. How might the classical school of management also be applied effectively here?

3. What contingencies might influence the suitability of the management style for Kicking Horse Coffee?

---

[23] BDC Consulting, 2011.
[24] BDC Consulting, 2011.

Chapter 4

Establishing the Structure of a Business

What Does Organizational Design Have to do With Business Success?

© William Perlman/Star Ledger/Corbis

Learning Objectives

After studying this chapter, you should be able to

1. Identify four broad trends in the changing nature of organizational design.
2. Discuss the relevance of metaphors used to describe organizations.
3. Identify the elements of organizational structure.
4. Explain the concept of reengineering.
5. Describe the notion of the virtual organization.
6. Discuss the phenomenon of downsizing and its rationale, methods, and objectives.

Organizations in just about every industrialized nation have been undergoing change. Many companies have reduced the number of levels in their hierarchy, others have undergone a change in their whole business process, while others have simply closed down. The aim of this chapter is to examine some of the approaches that organizations have adopted with regard to structure and design, including reengineering, downsizing, and going virtual. We will also examine the reasons behind these changes and consider more generally the question, "What determines how an organization is designed?"

THE BUSINESS WORLD

How Google Designed Itself for Success

Google has done more than any other business in terms of changing how people find information and conduct business. Traditionally, Google has been associated solely with Internet search. In fact, it still generates most (85%) of its revenue from search-related advertising. However, it has increasingly focused on diverse projects, including Gmail and the Android operating system. Google has shaken up several industries, including smartphones, television, and advertising. In 2013, it reached profits of about US$13 billion and it became the third most valuable corporation in the United States after Apple Inc. and Exxon Mobil Corp. Google continues to take on new and innovative ventures that will likely redefine its core competancies as it continues to evolve.

Google started out as a very modest business launched by two Stanford University graduates, Larry Page and Sergey Brin, who had the simple idea of the Google search engine. They started out with 10 employees working in a garage in Palo Alto, California. However, over a 10-year period, this little company became hugely successful. Google's success was built entirely on innovation. Brand new products, new services, and news ways of conducting business were the means through which Google rose to fame. All this required a strong company culture of innovation. Its most fundamental challenge has always been to generate an environment where new ideas can flourish. Therefore a critical requirement for its organizational structure is to ensure that the network of relationships, the rules governing work, and the administrative framework all support and encourage innovation. Undoubtedly, Google's organizational design has played a central role in the company's culture of innovation.

Larry Page and Sergey Brin knew that their company had to be highly efficient at meeting changing market demands and needed to be continually innovating. So how exactly did Page and Brin decide to design their organizational structure in order to promote innovation? They knew that how they organized the pattern of relationships and authority in their company would have a critical impact on these goals. Consequently, they needed a structure that encouraged the kind of fast and flexible decision making and creativity that Google would need to compete in this industry. They organized their company in a very unconventional way compared to other companies in the industry.

Brin and Page implemented a very flat level of hierarchy whereby top level management was only one level up from lower level employees. Why? Because in traditional, hierarchical structures, authority systems and reporting levels would slow down the decision-making process and any unnecessary delays in bringing new ideas to the market could mean losing out to competitors. So, instead of hierarchal levels, Google was divided up into small teams that worked on individual projects. Team members rotate to take on the role of team leaders with every new project. This is in contrast to other organizations that often establish one team leader who is always in that role. At Google, the role of the manager or team is to help build consensus among team members rather than to "control" or "manage" them in the traditional sense. In this kind of structure, the role of a manager or leader is analogous to that of an editor who relies on a team of journalists to generate decisions based on the team's input.

Another element of the structure of the teams is the actual composition. Google employees are extremely diverse. Consequently, teams might be composed of members with backgrounds that could range from former neurosurgeons to CEOs to marines. The intent of this diversity is to nurture innovation by exposing members to others with diverse backgrounds and perspectives. These teams range from five to ten people depending on the project. The relative small team size also gives the teams more flexibility and speed for decision making. In addition to dividing into these small teams, every six months, a mutual peer evaluation questionnaire is completed by all team members and this leads to a public ranking where natural leaders are identified.

Of course, while teams are central to Google's successful innovation, all this is not to say that there are no other elements of structure or departments at Google. Given the fact that this company has grown so large, it needs a certain degree of departmentation. Google is overseen by a board of directors that directs the company via an executive management group. This group oversees the Engineering, Products, Legal, Finance, and Sales departments. In turn, these departments are each divided into smaller units. For example, the Sales department has branches focused on the Americas, Asia Pacific, Europe, the Middle East, and Africa. However, beyond this traditional-looking structure, Google's organization minimizes power differences and formal authority.

One element central to nurturing innovation is the access to social networks in Google. Brainstorming and collaborating with other employees stimulates a wealth of diverse ideas and information sharing. The ability of people to communicate easily within a larger, diverse group allows continual access to novel information and potential collaborators. How does Google actually implement a network perspective? In his study of Google, Professor David Dubois of *Insead* found that Google expends a lot of organizational effort to empower collaborators and give them more freedom to start projects that matter to them.

Google has always minimized its levels of administrators and over the years as it has grown, it has endeavoured to flatten its organizational hierarchy as much as possible. The fact is, the fewer the levels of hierarchy, the greater becomes the opportunity for employees to interact freely, collaborate, and make their own decisions. This also has the effect of encouraging leaders or experts to arise naturally rather than being held to a specific job title. The other benefit of creating this relatively flat structure is the ability of employees to readily communicate with the operational leadership, which affords the company a tremendous amount of flexibility. As Google grew in size, it became more difficult to manage the flow of new ideas and projects. Consequently, it implemented a schedule of meetings between employees and the company's founders and chief executives where employees can "pitch" new ideas or projects directly to the top executives.

The organizational structure is designed to offer employees extensive freedom in making decisions and trying new ideas. This requires a structure that is not managed by "command and control." The aim is to de-emphasize job titles and power and instead focus on teamwork. Employees need to know that they can take on much decision authority and power over their work. This, too, means that job standardization is a foreign notion to this company. After all, you can't standardize the process of innovation. The decentralized manner of decision making is also reflected across the organization in such functions as hiring decisions, where at least four Google collaborators co-decide on a new hire. In addition to reinforcing the empowered culture, such participative decision-making helps to ensure that new recruits will "fit" within the organizational culture.

Employees are given the autonomy to make changes to a current project or to start their own. Google employees follow something called the 70/20/10 rule. This requires that each employee devotes 70% of every work day to whatever projects are assigned by management, 20% to new projects or ideas related to their core projects, and 10% to any new ideas they want to pursue. Many believe that this rule has driven the development of Google's innovative products and services. This rule is not restricted to one set of employees. A broad range of programmers, salespeople, and even executives are provided with enough "down time" to be creative. While critics might argue that allowing employees the opportunity to work on whatever they want is a waste of time, that is precisely one of the reasons for Google's success. It encourages employees to create innovative products by surrounding them with an open environment. Given the fast-paced environment that Google must compete in, its organizational structure is designed to meet market demands efficiently.

Sources: From: Google, the Network Company: From Theory to Practice, David Dubois, INSEAD Assistant Professor of Marketing | September 11, 2013, INSEAD KNOWLEDGE, 2013, http://knowledge.insead.edu/leadership-management/organisational-behaviour/google-the-network-company-from-theory-to-practice-2602

Thompson, Scott. (n.d.). Google's Business Leadership and Organizational Culture. CHRON. Retrieved from http://smallbusiness.chron.com/googles-business-leadership-organizational-culture-58108.html.

Thomas, Owen. (2013, March 14). There's a Pretty Big Tension in How Larry Page is Running Google. *Business Insider*. Retrieved from http://www.businessinsider.com/how-larry-page-is-running-google-2013-3.

El Akkad, Omar. (2013, October 26). What's next for Google, the most successful Internet company in the world? The Globe and Mail. Retrieved from http://www.theglobeandmail.com/report-on-business/international-business/us-business/growing-plans-inside-googles-expanding-world/article15096740/?page=3.

THE CHANGING NATURE OF ORGANIZATIONS

Objective 1 Identify four broad trends in the changing nature of organizational design.

Everywhere you look, it is obvious that we are a society of organizations. From our hospitals to our schools to our multinational organizations, it is hard to imagine life without organizations. And, for better or worse, those very institutions and organizations that we have grown up with are continuing to undergo dramatic change. To understand what is going on out there, we need to first consider several things. What exactly are organizations? What constitutes the structure or anatomy of an organization? Why do different organizations have different structures? These are among the key questions addressed in this chapter.

We have witnessed tremendous change and turmoil over the past two decades across the organizational landscape. From the massive reductions in the workforces of many well-known organizations like GM and Bell Canada to changes in how organizations are designed and operated, there has been a fundamental rethinking of how organizations should be designed. Organizational theory has been trying to make sense of the revolution we have observed in the organizational world.

Some observers have suggested that what is going on is a shift away from the classical, traditional, bureaucratic model. Recall our discussion in Chapter 3 of perspectives of management and Weber's notion of the bureaucratic organization, which is a central theme in classical management thought. This philosophy of organization design guided many of our organizations for most of the 20th century. The traditional, bureaucratic organizational structure emphasizes factors such as job specialization, a formal hierarchy of authority, a clear system of control, and rules and regulations to guide behaviour.

Why do we need the bureaucratic design? Because it achieves the fundamental goals of organizations: predictability and reliability (rules and standardized jobs ensure workers are

Exhibit 4.1 Goodbye Bureaucracy

Traditional Bureaucracy	Modern Organizations
• Tall/hierarchical	• Flat
• Rigid, rule-oriented	• Fluid
• Buffered from the environment	• Integrated
• Narrow market	• Global

doing what the boss wants) and control (the formal hierarchy ensures that how the work is conducted is clearly controlled). Ironically, these very strengths of the bureaucratic structure can also become weaknesses when the environment changes. For example, increasing competition and demands for better products and services, improved customer service, and more sophisticated processes all suggest that the stability of bureaucracies impedes any chance for innovation. The philosophy of organizational structure that emphasized job specialization, the narrow division of labour, standardization, rules, and the like is simply not suitable to a changing environment.

Believe it or not, the traditional or classical approach to organizational structure, which arose in the time of the Industrial Revolution, dominated our thinking about the nature of organizational design right up until the 1980s. It was not until then that organizations began to realize that the bureaucratic structure needed to be replaced. Most of the shifts in organizational design essentially aimed to move away from the bureaucratic paradigm. The adjectives identified in Exhibit 4.1 best describe the new approaches and the shift away from the bureaucratic design.

Flat Organizations

delayering Flattening organizational hierarchies so that they have a wider span of control; the elimination of hierarchical layers, often involving downsizing.

If there is any consistent pattern in the sweeping changes to corporate architecture, it has been the **delayering** of organizational hierarchies. Tall organizations have narrow spans of control, and flat organizations have wider spans of control. The shift we have observed in organizational redesign has been from the former to the latter. Certainly, one of the most pervasive phenomena to hit the organizational landscape since the 1980s has been downsizing, which often involves flattening the organizational hierarchy (we will address this issue in more detail later in the chapter). It is difficult to read the newspaper without reading some report about an organization flattening its hierarchy through downsizing. For example, Toyota eliminated three of its seven layers of management, and IBM Canada cut its levels from ten to about four in the 1990s, and these trends continue today among many organizations.

Flattening the hierarchy accomplishes a number of things. Among the benefits are increased speed of decision making, since decisions and information take much less time to travel across levels of bureaucracy. This allows organizations to react much faster to the demands of a changing environment. In addition, the delayering of management means that much more responsibility and self-management is coming from the lower levels of the organization, so that employees and those who are closest to serving customers or producing the product are now more involved in the decision-making process.

Fluid Organizations

The bureaucratic organization is obsessed with control, largely through strict adherence to rules and standards for how work is done. Again, think back to our discussion of the purposes of organizational structure. When organizations exist in dynamic environments, being able to adapt to change is critical. Bureaucratic rules tend to impede such adaptiveness, given that rules must be changed to fit new circumstances. The organic organization derives some of its strength from its ability to avoid being bogged down in rules that govern how work must be performed. Later in this chapter we will examine a very fluid or organic form of organization—the virtual organization.

Fluidity or flexibility in the functioning of an organization has been reflected in other ways, such as the notion of *just-in-time inventory*, which emphasizes the ability to generate inventory as needed through flexible manufacturing/supplier relationships and, consequently, to minimize costs. These just-in-time inventory principles have also been applied to the work relationship, where we now have a just-in-time labour pool, so to speak. That is, organizations have recognized that they no longer need to maintain a fixed supply of labour. If revenues at any time are diminishing, the labour pool can also be diminished via downsizing, or built back up when revenues increase. Consequently, in the 1980s and throughout the 1990s we witnessed growth in temporary or contract-based employment. This adds immensely to the fluidity of an organization, since a temporary workforce can be easily adjusted to meet the upswings and downturns of a less predictable environment. This fluidity has, of course, profound implications for individuals within organizations, because it also underscores attitudes toward the permanence or lack of permanence of jobs within the "new" workplace.

Integrated Organizations

The traditional bureaucratic organization advocates clear lines of authority and control. However, the newer organizational designs are less focused on the need for unity of command and clear lines of authority—it is unimportant to maintain distinct boundaries between levels in the hierarchy, between individuals and departments, and between organizational members and individuals external to the organization. In fact, just the opposite is now emphasized, where integrated organizations aim to create more integration among formerly disparate units. For example, the new approaches to organizational design typically focus on teams of workers rather than on individuals. **Cross-functional teams**, work groups that bring together members from various parts of the organization, are becoming increasingly popular.

Typically, work teams are given the power to manage themselves and make decisions without the approval of formal management—hence the name **self-managing work teams**. Thus, GM's Saturn plant brought individuals from the legal department to marketing and to engineering so that they could be involved in the production of the Saturn car. Shell Canada has achieved much success with its use of self-managed teams, as have numerous other companies. **Information sharing** is a big part of the team-based approach—that is, having management give over information that once was solely their domain. This is much more common in today's organization than in the traditional bureaucratic model, where those in power held the information and did not share it with the lower levels.

The integration of units or members within the organization is one major trend. Another trend includes integration of the organization with players outside its boundaries. Organizations are increasingly building closer connections with their external environment. For example, an organization may attempt to establish close relationships with suppliers, integrating them into the manufacturing process and generally creating an interdependent relationship. Other organizations are even creating alliances with other companies to develop new products or services. There are even cross-functional teams that include participants from outside the organization, such as suppliers, distributors, or even competitors.

cross-functional teams Work groups that bring together members from various parts of the organization.

self-managing work teams Teams that are given the power to manage themselves and make decisions without the approval of formal management.

information sharing Workers sharing knowledge with other workers in the organization to help better meet the organization's goals and needs. Information sharing is an important component of the team-based approach.

Atlantic Canada's Overseas Playground?

Gary Corbett/age fotostock/SuperStock

Atlantic Canadian companies can be global players in international trade and supply chains. But they need to find their niches to succeed in this new global economic order.

In response to demand—largely from fast-growing emerging economies—what Atlantic Canada sells, and to whom companies sell, has already begun to change.

But not enough companies are taking full advantage of the range of opportunities these fast-growth markets present. For example, a The Conference Board of Canada study of Nova Scotia's economy showed that although the province is participating in global supply chains, few companies are using other methods—such as selling through foreign affiliates—to enter and succeed in international markets.

While global trade exploded over the past decade, Canada's export volumes flatlined. This is bad news for a region like Atlantic Canada and for Canada as a whole. With small domestic markets, we depend on global opportunities to help bolster our citizens' living standards.

To a large extent, this weak performance reflects with whom we do business. Traditional areas of trade growth have plateaued. Most of our exports are aimed at slow-growth markets, such as the United States.

Meanwhile, we are underexposed to the faster-growing developing markets, notably China, India and Brazil. And fast-growth countries such as China now actively compete with our companies in both the U.S. and Canadian markets.

What we trade has also changed in response to growth in developing markets. Developing-country demand for raw materials has led to a resource boom.

Resources Now Lead Atlantic Canada's Goods Exports

The trend is poised to accelerate. The U.S. will remain Canada's largest export market for the foreseeable future.

But Canada's exports to the U.S., currently about three-quarters of our total, will slip to just over two-thirds in 2025.

In contrast, Canada's share of goods trade with China could expand from 3.6 to almost 7 per cent by 2025. The same goes for other fast-growing markets. We forecast that the share of Canada's exports to India and Brazil will more than double by 2025. Trade with Brazil is also likely to double by 2025.

McCain and Clearwater are two food product companies that have adapted and sold their offerings into fast-growth markets. And companies of all sizes can tap into these opportunities. Small companies, for example, are leading Canada's export growth to markets such as India and Thailand.

To seize more of these opportunities, Atlantic Canada's companies should:

- **Find the "sweet spots."** Atlantic Canada's companies need to tap into pockets of growth and openness within fast-growth markets that align with their areas of strength and expertise. One example is India's demand for and openness towards environmentally-friendly technologies and products.

- **Look beyond the obvious markets.** There are tremendous opportunities in China, India, and Brazil, but a new Conference Board study of Canada's next top markets identifies a list of 24 non-traditional markets that offer both growth potential and are likely to represent important commercial possibilities for Canadian companies. These markets—in Asia, Latin America, the Middle East, Africa, and Eastern Europe—represent far greater growth potential than our traditional markets.

- **Look beyond selling goods.** Atlantic Canada has expertise in financial services, communications services, education services, and a range of other services that fast-growth markets need.

Fast-growth markets have dramatically changed the world economy over the past decade. Companies that find the global "sweet spots" for their products and services will prosper.

Source: Excerpted from Goldfarb, D. (2013, June 17). Atlantic Canada's overseas playground? The Conference Board of Canada. Retrieved from www.conferenceboard.ca/press/speech_oped/13-06-17/atlantic_canada_s_overseas_playground.aspx. Reprinted with permission.

The Japanese term for networking of major enterprises is **keiretsu**. These are loosely affiliated collections of companies and are quite common in industry and banking in Japan.

Of course, not all integration of organizations has been of such a loosely coupled nature. We have also witnessed the trend toward building collections of organizations through mergers and acquisitions, which began in the 1990s and seems to be continuing unabated.

keiretsu The Japanese term for networking of major enterprises—creating loosely affiliated collections of companies. These are quite common in Japanese industry and banking.

Global Organizations

Perhaps the most profound recent trend in the changing nature of organizations is the drive to "go global," which is an issue that will be discussed in detail in a later chapter. Globalization can be considered one of the leading forces behind organizational change since the 1980s and 1990s. Globalization has brought with it many implications, including an increase in competition and greater access to more markets. Industries that were traditionally "protected" by tariffs, such as auto manufacturing, faced intense competition from foreign companies for the first time, and with serious consequences.

Just about every sector of business is no longer insulated from competitors, customers, or suppliers outside of their home country. Consequently, the notion of integration or networking can include relationships with suppliers or even competitors outside local boundaries—even in other countries. An organization may have networks of members across the world. For example, Canadian Company X might be selling a product it had designed in Sweden, engineered in the United States, and manufactured in Japan. In the global marketplace, businesses are also selling to customers all over the world. Consider, for example, Google, whose head office is in Mountain View, California. This is a company that has approximately 70 offices in about 40 different countries. Consequently, it employs a geographic form of departmentalization, with independent divisions operating in Europe, Africa, South America, and the Far East. Just think about the challenges this company faces in terms of responding to the variety of consumer preferences within these different locations. For Google, decentralized decision-making authority is required to permit these divisions to focus on and quickly respond to local market needs. Certainly, for Canadian companies to better compete in the global marketplace, more Canadian companies will need to do the same (see Talking Business 4.1).

THINKING ABOUT ORGANIZATIONS

What Is an Organization?

Objective 2 Discuss the relevance of metaphors used to describe organizations.

What do you think of when you think of an "organization"? We can identify three broad categories of organizations:

1. *public/governmental organizations*, which provide goods and services without necessarily generating a profit

2. *private/nongovernmental organizations*, including voluntary organizations, which offer goods or services without necessarily generating a profit

3. *private organizations*, which produce goods or services with the intent of making a profit for the benefit of their owners or shareholders

Though we can easily observe organizations that operate in these different sectors, we can also identify underlying characteristics that are common to all organizations. In fact, it is useful to consider a fundamental question as a starting point for our examination of the nature of organizations: What is an organization? How do we define it? Nortel, GM, Microsoft, your high school, St. John Ambulance—what do all these entities have in common? Organizations may be large corporations or small nonprofit organizations; they might be housed within a large skyscraper or they could simply be composed of members who are spread across a wide location. What makes them all organizations?

So What Is an Organization?   Given the implications of the systems approach to organization, we can generate the following definition of organizations:

1. *Organizations are social entities:* Clearly, all the examples cited above have at least one common element—they are made up of people! They are entities that have been generated and are maintained by people. They involve some level of human interaction.

2. *Organizations interact with the environment:* Can you think of any organization that is not somehow linked to its external environment? Think about it. An organization obtains inputs from its environment, whether in the form of people, raw materials, technology, or financial capital. All these inputs are transformed by the organization and become outputs: the goods, services, or knowledge that the organization generates.

3. *Organizations are created to achieve goals:* That is, they are goal-directed. Whether it is a profit-making organization or a nonprofit organization, all organizations have some kind of goal or objective that they were designed to achieve.

4. *Organizations possess some sort of structure:* All organizations need some kind of structure to ensure the work is properly allocated and coordinated. Of course, this is not as straightforward as it may at first appear. What do we mean when we say that organizations possess a structure? How are organizations structured? We will address these questions below.

Using Metaphors to Describe Organizations

One helpful method of understanding the nature of organizations is through the use of metaphors. According to Gareth Morgan, a management scholar and author of *Images of Organization*, we can consider the notion of an organization as, essentially, a social construction. That is, we are giving a tangible name to something that we take for granted. Words, names, concepts, ideas, facts, observations, and so on do not so much denote external "things" as conceptions of things activated in the mind. They are not representations of a reality "out there," but as tools for capturing and dealing with what is *perceived* to be "out there."[1] Hence, we understand the usefulness of metaphors. A metaphor is often regarded as no more than a literary and descriptive device for embellishment, but more fundamentally it is a creative form that produces its effect through a crossing of images. A metaphor proceeds through assertions that "subject A is like B and . . . ." Through the processes of comparison between the images of A and B we generate new meaning. The use of metaphors serves to generate an image for studying a subject. Different images of a subject guide and ultimately shape what is seen.

In more practical terms, what are the common features of these things that we call organizations? Why does this label fit a variety of entities, from nonprofit to for-profit

---

[1] Morgan, G. (1986). *Images of organization.* Newbury Park, CA: Sage.

contexts? Metaphors are useful to help us describe and ultimately understand these social constructions. Consider dictionary definitions of the term *organization*. The Oxford English Dictionary has defined it as a term used primarily to describe the action of organizing or the state of being organized, particularly in a biological sense. Also, the term has been considered as referring to an organized body, system, or society. The state of being organized in a biological sense was the basis of the metaphor of arranging or coordinating.

The term *organization* as a depiction of a social institution is relatively new and creates a new meaning through metaphorical extension of older meanings. Ultimately, the importance of the metaphors we use to describe our hospitals, businesses, places of worship, and so on are important because they lead our thinking about the nature of these places, how they should be designed, and how they should function. Let's consider an example of how metaphors guide our thinking in the area of management philosophy.

The Machine or Mechanistic Organizational Structure   In many ways, the different schools of thought with regard to organizational theories arise from insights associated with different metaphors for the study of organizations. Consider, for example, the theories of management discussed in Chapter 3. The classical schools of management thought, including scientific management, administrative management, and bureaucratic management, can be viewed as arising from a specific conceptualization or metaphor of what organizations represent. Arguably, the classical school of management thought is based implicitly on a conception of organizations that employs a **machine metaphor**. Machines are perceived as entities that function in a prescribed, rational manner. They are devised to perform work that leads toward specific goals, structure, and technology. Consequently, some organizational scholars, implicitly drawing on such a conception or metaphor of organizations as machines, emphasize an analysis and design of the formal structure of an organization and its technology. These scholars have explained the purpose of organizations as they would a machine—to function in an orderly, prescribed, and controlled manner. The aim, then, is to design organizations as if they were machines.

Taylor's notion of the "economic man" and Weber's notion of the "faceless bureaucrat" are natural extensions of the principles of the machine metaphor. Scientific management encompasses the notions of control and efficiency—objectives well fitted to a machine metaphor of organizations. Of course, managers or management scholars whose philosophy is based on a machine metaphor will be led by such a metaphor. Consequently, the classical schools focused only on those issues pertinent to this metaphor: rules, regulations, a bureaucratic structure, and so on. Human needs had no relevance in such a metaphor or model.

The Organic Organizational Structure   Of course, management thought has also been affected by other metaphors. For example, the **organism metaphor** encompasses a conception of organizations as systems of mutually connected and dependent parts that share a common life. This metaphor suggests that we can conceive of organizations as living organisms that contain a combination of elements that are differentiated yet integrated, attempting to survive within the context of a wider environment. The open-systems approach of organizations, discussed next, is based on this metaphor. And with regard to management philosophies (see Chapter 3), the behavioural school of management thought is, in fact, based on this metaphor. Consequently, these schools are concerned with sustaining human motivation and treating organizations as social systems.

machine metaphor (of an organization) A metaphor used to describe organizations that function like a machine—that is, in an orderly, prescribed, rational, and controlled manner. The classical school of management viewed organizations as entities devised to perform work that led toward specific goals, structure, and technology.

organism metaphor (of an organization) A metaphor used to describe organizations as systems of mutually connected and dependent parts that share a common life. This metaphor suggests that we can conceive of organizations as living organisms that contain a combination of elements that are differentiated yet integrated, attempting to survive within the context of a wider environment.

Exhibit 4.2 What Does
Organization Mean
to You?

- Organization as a machine
- Organization as a living organism
- Organization as a political system
- Organization as a theatre
- Organization as a sports team
- Organization as a family

Certainly, we can apply myriad metaphors to try to advance our understanding of what organizations really represent. The important point is that the metaphor used implicitly underlies and ultimately guides thinking of how organizations should be designed and managed. Among some of the more popular conceptions of organizations in terms of metaphors are organizations as political systems,[2] organizations as loosely coupled systems,[3] organizations as theatres,[4] or organizations as a collection of cultures[5] (see Exhibit 4.2). No one metaphor can capture the total nature of organizational life. New metaphors can be created for viewing and understanding organizations. Indeed, the very nature of the study of organizations and the field of organizational theory is metaphorical—that is, it is subjective in many ways.

Organizations as Systems Scholars who have studied organizations have generated countless perspectives on the nature of these entities. One useful perspective involves the view of organizations as systems. How might the metaphor of an organization as a "system" guide our understanding with regard to how organizations operate and sustain themselves?

A *system* can de defined as interdependent elements working together to achieve a goal or goals. The interdependence of the elements creates an entity that is more than just the sum of its parts—something is achieved beyond the mere putting together of these separate components. The notion of organizations as systems is intended to guide our understanding of what organizations are all about and how they function and survive.[6] Specifically, the notion of an **open system** asserts that organizations are entities that are embedded in and dependent on exchanges with the environment they operate within. In addition, organizations can be viewed as social systems, with people constituting the basic elements.

Interestingly, there have been times when organizations have been viewed as closed systems, with the belief that how organizations function and survive depends on their ability to remain divorced from their environment. **Closed systems** have been defined as fully self-sufficient entities requiring no interaction with the environment, and this clearly makes this metaphor difficult to find in practice. This guiding metaphor led much organizational thinking to focus on the organization's internal environment with regard to dealing with organizational functioning and survival. At the same time, this approach failed to recognize the role that the external environment can have on the organization's operations.

It was only when the environment became sufficiently volatile and complex that theorists recognized the futility of viewing organizations as closed systems. It became necessary to embrace the open-systems metaphor and further acknowledge the critical importance of the notion that organizations are embedded in their environment (see Exhibit 4.3). This also underscored the importance of further understanding the nature of the organization's external environment.

An organization's environment represents all elements that exist outside the organization and that potentially influence or affect the organization in some way. Clearly,

open systems Entities that are embedded in and dependent on exchanges with the environment within which they operate. The interdependence of elements means that the entity (the organization) is more than the sum of its parts; it interacts with its environment.

closed systems Entities viewed as being fully self-sufficient and thus requiring no interaction with the environment, which is difficult to find in practice.

---

[2] Pfeffer, J., & Salancik, G.R. (1978). *The external control of organizations*. New York, NY: Harper & Row.

[3] Weick, K. (1976). Educational organizations as loosely coupled systems. *Administrative Science Quarterly, 21*, 1–19.

[4] Goffman, E. (1967). *Interaction ritual*. Garden City, NY: Doubleday.

[5] Pondy, L. et al. (Eds.). (1983). *Organizational symbolism*. Greenwich, CT: JAI Press.

[6] Thompson, J.D. (1967). *Organizations in action*. New York, NY: McGraw-Hill; Katz, D., & Kahn, R.L. (1978). *The social psychology of organization* (2nd ed.). New York, NY: Wiley.

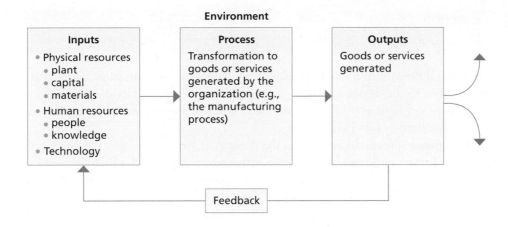

Exhibit 4.3
Organizations as Open Systems

organizations are dependent on the environment for their survival and success. Without obtaining the necessary environmental inputs, whether they are suitable employees or the raw materials for production, organizations cannot function effectively. Similarly, if organizations fail to generate the types of products or services sought by the environment then these organizations will cease to exist. As suggested earlier, organizations are created in response to societal or environmental needs—and ultimately, it is the environment that will determine the organization's fate.

THE ANATOMY OF AN ORGANIZATION

What is organizational structure? The image of an organizational chart might come to mind for some of you. And in fact, the organizational chart is a reflection of the underlying structure of an organization. However, there is a more specific notion of **organizational structure** that we will review in this section: a deliberately planned network or pattern of relationships that exists among individuals in various roles or positions. This includes the formal hierarchy of authority, the distribution or grouping of work (into departments, for example), and the rules or procedures that control and coordinate behaviour in the organization. However, we can also move beyond this definition and attempt to examine more systematically the dimensions along which organizational structure can be described (see Exhibit 4.4).

What Constitutes an Organization's Structure?

Work Specialization   One fundamental question that must be addressed in designing organizational structure is how an organization is going to divide up the work that must be done to achieve organizational goals.

Horizontal differentiation represents the degree of differentiation between horizontal (as opposed to vertical) units of the organization, based on things like the orientation of the members, the nature of their jobs, and their education or training. The greater the number of occupations in an organization that require specialized knowledge and skills, the more complex the organization. One obvious dimension of

Objective 3 Identify the elements of organizational structure.

organizational structure
A deliberately planned network or pattern of relationships that exists among individuals in various roles or positions.

Exhibit 4.4 Four Defining Elements of Organizational Structure

1. Work specialization
2. Centralization
3. Span of control
4. Formalization

horizontal differentiation
The degree of differentiation between horizontal (as opposed to vertical) units of the organization, based on things such as the orientation of the members, the nature of their jobs, and their education or training. Includes job specialization, which is divided into functional and social specialization.

Exhibit 4.5 Job Specialization

FUNCTIONAL	SOCIAL
Division of jobs into simple tasks	Level of professionalism among employees

specialization Also called *division of labour,* refers to the degree to which organizational tasks are subdivided into separate jobs. There are fundamentally two different kinds of specialization: functional and social specialization.

functional specialization The dividing up of jobs into their smallest components so that workers perform simple, specific, and repetitive tasks.

social specialization The specialization of individuals rather than jobs, which is accomplished through employment of professionals whose skills cannot be easily routinized.

centralization The degree to which decision-making authority in an organization is concentrated at the top level.

decentralization The degree to which decision-making authority in an organization is spread to the lower levels.

worker empowerment A move toward shifting greater levels of responsibility back to employees, so that in a sense they are at least partly their own bosses. One popular example of the trend toward less emphasis on one boss is the use of self-managing work teams.

horizontal differentiation is job specialization. The term **specialization**, or *division of labour,* refers to the degree to which organizational tasks are subdivided into separate jobs. There are fundamentally two different kinds of specialization: functional and social specialization (see Exhibit 4.5).

Functional specialization refers to the division of jobs into simple, repetitive tasks. Frederick Taylor's philosophy of scientific management advocated a high degree of job specialization; that is, Taylor argued that to maximize worker efficiency, jobs should be divided up into their smallest components so that workers perform simple, specific, and repetitive tasks. More recently, there has been a dramatic shift in belief regarding the degree of job specialization that should be implemented at work. Approaches to job redesign, like job enrichment, essentially advocate a low degree of job specialization; that is, rather than performing one narrow task, employees in some organizations perform a wide range of tasks. Job enrichment involves providing employees with more challenging and meaningful work largely by allowing them to increase the variety of work they perform and the level of autonomy or freedom they have in performing the work.

Social specialization refers to the specialization of individuals rather than the specialization of jobs. Social specialization is accomplished through the employment of professionals whose skills cannot be easily routinized. For example, an accountant who performs an audit does so through the application of specialized, trained skills. Similarly, engineers, nurses, doctors, and professors are specialized professionals whose skills have been developed in a specific area or specialty.

Centralization   Where does authority rest within the organization? That is, what level in the organizational hierarchy has decision-making authority? This raises the question of centralization and decentralization.

Decision-making power can rest at the top of the organizational hierarchy. For example, if top management makes all the important decisions with little or no input from lower levels of the organization, this would be considered a highly centralized decision-making structure and is known as **centralization**. On the other hand, if decision-making authority is not concentrated at the top level, but rather is spread to the lower levels, this is referred to as **decentralization**.

As with the other elements we have discussed to this point, the 20th century also witnessed great changes in the relative concentration of decision-making authority, Essentially, many organizations chose to move from centralized to more decentralized structures. Largely, this move was intended to make organizations more efficient and faster in their decision-making ability. Centralized organizations typically require longer time frames for decisions to be made. For example, it takes much longer for the head office of a geographically diverse operation to make decisions about its operations in another corner of the world than it would if that operation had authority to make its own decisions.

The notion of **worker empowerment** is a move toward shifting much greater levels of responsibility back to employees, so that in a sense they are at least partly their own bosses. One popular example of the trend toward less emphasis on one boss is the use of self-managing work teams, which we discussed earlier. These are essentially collections of workers who work together on a project or task and largely manage themselves. Some organizations that have employed self-managing teams include GM's Saturn division, Motorola, Frito Lay, Shell, and Microsoft, to name but a few. The need to have one all-powerful boss is no longer considered the best way of designing organizations.

Span of Control   How many levels of management does an organization have? To address this question, we can consider the notion of hierarchy of authority. The hierarchy is very much connected to something called the **span of control**, which refers to the number of employees reporting to a supervisor. Obviously, it can vary from organization to organization, depending on how many subordinates an organization feels a manager can effectively direct.

The span of control is important because it really determines the number of managers and levels there are in the organizational hierarchy, which is referred to as **vertical differentiation**. How does the span of control determine the number of managers and levels? Consider the following examples (and review Exhibit 4.6).

Imagine two organizations with the same total number of seven members, but with different spans of control. In Organization X, there is an average span of control of two employees with three levels of hierarchy (the president, two managers, and four subordinates). In Organization Y, which also has a total of seven members, the span of control is six and there are only two levels in the hierarchy. (This organization might be considered as having one central leader with all employees as one self-managing team who only report to one boss, the president.)

We can describe Organization X as having

- a relatively narrower span of control (two) compared to Organization Y, which has a wider span of control (six).

- a taller hierarchical structure (three levels of hierarchy) compared to Organization Y, which is relatively flatter (two levels of hierarchy). That is, the span of control clearly determines how "flat" or how "tall" an organization is.

In general terms, a narrow span of control tends to reflect a tall organization, while a wide span of control tends to reflect a flat organization. What difference does it make how

span of control The number of employees reporting to a supervisor.

vertical differentiation The number of managers and levels in the organizational hierarchy.

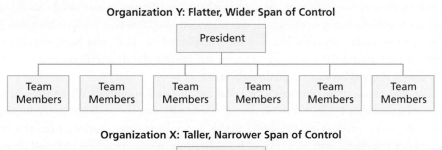

Organization Y: Flatter, Wider Span of Control

Organization X: Taller, Narrower Span of Control

Exhibit 4.6 Span of Control

many subordinates a supervisor oversees? Or how many levels of hierarchy exist within an organization? First, it has been argued that maintaining small or narrow spans of control improves a manager's ability to manage. Think about it—a manager who oversees, say, a handful of employees is much more capable of maintaining close supervision than a manager with a wide span of control who is responsible for a large number of employees. However, there are also downsides to the narrow span of control: It is costly! Why? Quite simply, because it adds layers of management, and more management means more expenses to cover. Second, a narrow span of control (or tall structures) makes vertical communication more time consuming. To see why, again consider what a narrow span of control creates—more levels in the hierarchy, which means that any information that must be transmitted from the top of the hierarchy to the bottom takes longer than it would to communicate if there were fewer levels. One other potential disadvantage of narrow spans of control, or tall structures, is that the close supervision such a system encourages also tends to discourage employee autonomy and self-management.

We have seen changes in the span of control in organizations over the past century. Certainly, the trend in recent years is to widen the span of control or, in other words, flatten the organizational hierarchy. From IBM to Toyota, we have seen significant delayering of organizational hierarchies. Why? This has occurred for most of the reasons cited above: cutting costs and speeding up the communication or decision-making process. Typically, widening the span of control, or flattening the hierarchy, includes spreading decision-making authority down to the lower levels of the organization.

Formalization

formalization The degree to which rules, regulations, procedures, and so on govern how work is performed; the degree of the standardization of jobs in the organization. The greater the degree of formalization, the lower the reliance on individual discretion and the greater the assurance of consistent and reliable performance.

Formalization   To what degree will rules or procedures be used to guide organizational members? The answer to that question is addressed in the notion of formalization. The level of formalization in an organization refers to the degree to which rules, regulations, procedures, and the like govern how work is performed. In other words, **formalization** reflects the degree to which jobs within the organization are standardized. A high level of formalization means highly standardized work—that is, clear rules regarding how the work should be performed. Highly standardized work, or work that is very much rule-directed, suggests that there is little individual discretion in how that work can be performed. In this regard, high formalization is what scientific management advocated in its assertion of standardizing work, which was intended to ensure that performance was consistent and reliable—workers know what is expected of them and how, exactly, they should be performing their jobs. In addition, the greater the degree of formalization, the less reliance there is on individual discretion.

Can you think of any organizations that are highly formalized? Wherever you have an organization that has explicit job descriptions and numerous rules or procedures governing the work process, you've got a highly formalized organization. Like the other elements of structure, attitudes toward formalization in organizations changed dramatically throughout the 20th century. Essentially, what we have witnessed in many organizations is a shift from high formalization and standardization of work practices to less formality. Why? Given the need to adapt to the rapidly changing external environment, organizations have found they must be willing to scrap the old way of doing things in favour of methods that better accommodate the changing demands of their environment, whether the sources of change come from competitors, consumers, technological changes, and so on.

WHAT DETERMINES ORGANIZATIONAL STRUCTURE? A RATIONAL PERSPECTIVE

In broad terms, we can consider why organizations take on different structures, and we can consider sources of influence on organizational design. To simplify our discussion, we can consider the two extreme opposites in terms of the organizational configuration identified previously: the mechanistic organization and the organic organization. Each can be assessed using the four elements of structure (see Exhibit 4.7).

	Mechanistic	Organic
1. Division of labour/work specialization	Narrow	Wide
2. Centralization	Centralized	Decentralized
3. Span of control	Narrow	Wide
4. Formalization	High	Low

Exhibit 4.7 Mechanistic vs. Organic Organizations

Organic organizations and **mechanistic organizations** are polar opposites in structure. Machine bureaucracies, or mechanistic organizations, maintain jobs that are narrow in scope; decision making is centralized at the top of the organizational hierarchy and work is conducted within highly formalized rules and procedures. On the other hand, organic organizations tend to have jobs that are enriched with more variety and task responsibilities; typically, there is a team-based approach rather than a "top-down" approach to authority and decision making is decentralized throughout the organization. The worker is less restricted with fewer rules and regulations. While there are a variety of influences on the design of organizations, perhaps among the most significant sources are strategy, size, technology, and the environment.

organic organizations The extreme opposite from mechanistic organizations in organizational design. Organic organizations tend to have jobs that are enriched with more variety and task responsibilities (wide work specialization); typically, there is a team-based approach rather than a "top-down" approach to authority, and decision making is decentralized throughout the organization. There is a wide span of control. The worker is also less restricted with fewer rules and regulations. These organizations tend to be innovative and flexible.

mechanistic organizations The extreme opposite from organic organizations in organizational design. These organizations are exemplified by the machine bureaucracy. Machine bureaucracies, or mechanistic organizations, maintain jobs that are narrow in scope, decision making is centralized at the top of the organizational hierarchy, there is a narrow span of control, and work is conducted within highly formalized rules and procedures.

Strategy

Clearly, an organization's structure is intended to help achieve its organizational objectives or strategy. In other words, structure should follow strategy. For example, if an organization's central mission is to be innovative, to pursue new product designs or services, then its structure should help achieve that goal. From what we have discussed earlier, the characteristics associated with the organic organization would best suit that objective. Few rules and decentralized decision making encourage flexibility and adaptiveness to environmental demands. And these are, consequently, useful for encouraging innovation. If, on the other hand, efficiency or cost minimization is a central strategy, then the mechanistic organization is the better-suited structure (see Exhibit 4.8).

	Types of Organizational Strategies	
Elements of Structure	**Focus on Innovation**	**Focus on Cost and Efficiency**
1. Division of labour	Wide	Narrow
2. Centralization	Decentralized	Centralized
3. Span of control	Wide	Narrow
4. Formalization	Low	High

Exhibit 4.8 Strategy and Structure

Organizational Size

If you observe the organizational landscape, it is hard not to see some kind of connection between the size of an organization and its structure. In terms of our organic–mechanistic classification, there is a tendency for larger organizations to shift toward a more mechanistic structure—largely because of the need to control and coordinate many employees. When you have masses of employees whose performance must be directed, it would seem beneficial to standardize or routinize the work and ensure there are clear rules and regulations to guide performance. It is difficult to maintain the informality of the organic structure when organizations grow. However, that is not to say that many large organizations do not try to retain an organic structure, even in the face of significant growth. For example, although Microsoft is a large organization, it prides itself on innovation and has attempted to divide itself into manageable units that use team-based approaches and where informality frees up the entrepreneurial spirit. Similarly, Johnson & Johnson prides itself on being a decentralized empire. The top managers are given much decision-making power for their units, and there is a great effort to maintain a flat organizational structure, even though the company itself is quite large (see Exhibit 4.9).

Exhibit 4.9
Organizational Size and Structure

Elements of Structure	Small Organization	Large Organization
1. Division of labour	Wide	Narrow
2. Centralization	Centralized	Decentralized
3. Span of control	Wide	Narrow
4. Formalization	Low	High

Technology

Technology essentially refers to how an organization transforms its inputs, such as financial capital and physical and human resources, into services or products. For example, the assembly-line approach has been used to produce output in the car manufacturing industry.

Among classifications within technology is how routine or nonroutine that technology is. **Routine technology** refers to automated and standardized operations typical of mass production operations, while **nonroutine technology** is not standardized and might include anything from conducting genetic research to making custom-made furniture. As you might have guessed, standardized, mass production technologies are more compatible with mechanistic structures where such standardization or routinization of work is part of the main objective. Nonroutine technologies, on the other hand, are better suited to innovative, organic structures that do not allow formality and rules to govern activity.

routine technology Automated and standardized technology and operations typical of mass production operations.

nonroutine technology Nonstandardized technology. Might include anything from conducting genetic research to making custom furniture.

Environment

Among the main elements we might consider as composing an organization's environment are suppliers, customers, competitors, the government, and the general public. When might an organization's structure be affected by its environment? Again, if we can use a broad classification, you can think of an organization's environment in two broad classes: dynamic or static. **Static environments**, as the name suggests, exhibit little if any change—no new competitors, no new technologies, no government regulatory changes, and so on. In such an environment of certainty, the mechanistic structure would be quite

static environment One of the two broad classifications of environments of organizations (the other being dynamic). The static environment exhibits little if any change.

suitable: It generates rules and methods of performance based on environmental needs and, once established, does not change. A **dynamic environment**, on the other hand, contains much uncertainty and undergoes a lot of change. Clearly, an organic structure is better suited in this situation, given its higher adaptiveness to change. Competition alone has accounted for many of the changes in the environment of a business.

Contingency Theory and the Importance of the Environment

In order to understand why organizations are designed in a certain way, it makes sense to consider the environment within which they operate. There are numerous theories and models that have attempted to identify those factors that determine the structure of organizations. For example, **contingency theory** is a natural outgrowth of **systems theory**,[7] which recognizes that all organizations are open systems that can only survive through continuous and successful interaction with their environment.

What factors influence whether a tall bureaucratic organization or a simple flat structure is suitable? In what contexts does a centralized decision-making structure, as opposed to a decentralized structure, make sense? Contingency theory focuses on the contextual factors that can influence the structure and management of organizations, with a particular emphasis on organizational design. For example, contingency theories seek to answer questions such as, why do some organizations benefit from centralized decision making? Why do some organizations require a high level of formalization with regard to employee job responsibilities?

A central philosophy underlying contingency theory is that there is no one ideal way to organize. That is, there are no universal principles of what constitutes the best form of organization. The optimal organizational structure is dependent on (or contingent on) the nature of its operating environment. Consequently, this implies that managers should seek to achieve a fit or alignment among the major elements of their organization's environment and its internal organizational design. Therefore, while contingency theory suggests that there is no one best way to organize universally, it does assert that there is one best way to organize given a specific type of operating environment or organizational context.

Contingency theory is based on the assumption that organizations are able to adapt to changing environmental conditions. Given the need for organizations to design their structure in reference to their environment, successful organizations must adapt to any changes in that environment via structural change. This also assumes that organizations behave as rational entities that are able and willing to make internal structural changes to achieve compatibility with their environment as a means for survival and success. According to contingency theory, there are a number of specific contingency factors that can influence organizational design. One of the most widely studied factors is the notion of environmental uncertainty.

Environmental uncertainty has been defined as the rate at which market conditions and production technologies change. There is no doubt that environmental uncertainty is an important dimension that varies widely among organizations and industries. For example, some organizations and industries operate within relatively static environments. Other organizations may exist in very dynamic environments, where there are constantly new competitors, rapidly changing technology, new governmental regulations, and so on. Indeed, one example is the digital technology industry, which operates in an uncertain and evolving environment, as seen in Talking Business 4.2.

---

[7] Hall, A.D., & Fagen, R.E. (1956). Definition of system. In *General Systems: The Yearbook of the Society for the Advancement of General Systems Theory: Vol. 1*, 18–28.

dynamic environment One of the two broad classifications of environments of organizations (the other being static). The dynamic environment contains much uncertainty and change.

contingency theory A natural outgrowth of systems theory, which recognizes that all organizations are open systems that can only survive through continuous and successful interaction with their environment. A central philosophy underlying contingency theory is that there is no one ideal way to organize.

systems theory A theory that recognizes that all organizations are open systems that can only survive through continuous and successful interaction with their environment.

environmental uncertainty The rate at which market conditions and production technologies change, producing dynamic or static environments.

Canada's Trade in a Digital World

Shutter_M/Shutterstock

The digital economy can be defined to include all economic activities that the digitization of information permits. This broad definition includes not just digital media-related activities and not just the Internet, but all digital technologies, including mobile technologies. . . .

When we think about this country's global strengths in the digital economy, we typically think about digital activities. But digitization allows us to benefit across all economic activities, rather than just specifically "digital producing" activities. What are Canada's areas of potential strength in using digital technologies to open up global trade opportunities in other areas, including resources, services, and manufacturing?

These "digital-using" areas of potential strength may not be as obvious as, say, digital-producing activities such as creating video games. So a good place to start might be Canada's traditional areas of relative strength. To take what many would consider a "non digital" example, let us start with Canada's relative strength in resource extraction. As previously discussed, digitization now makes it easier to sell services globally and provides the tools to more effectively coordinate global supply chains. This means Canadian businesses can use digital tools to be more effective in global markets in activities such as mining, as well as to more easily sell their resource-related services in global markets.

To build on Canada's existing strengths in the digital economy, Canadian businesses must invest more heavily in digital technologies and Canadian policy-makers must address a wider range of trade barriers.

Canada's banking sector is another area of relative global strength. UNCTAD consistently ranks Canadian banks among the most globalized financial services companies in the world. During the recent global financial crisis, Canadian banks also proved to be among the most resilient. The small number of players in the sector is a benefit. It allows Canadian banks to invest heavily in technologies—such as those for online and mobile banking—and to test these technologies extensively on a large group of customers. (Canadians are relatively heavy users of online banking—they are, in fact, more likely than Americans to adopt it.) Canadian banks can leverage this experience in new markets, where they are already expanding. Similarly, Canada can build on its professional services strengths in other areas in which it has global expertise—such as engineering and waste management services—now that the cost of coordinating such projects globally has fallen dramatically thanks to digital technologies.

A third example is Canada's traditional expertise in making cross-border value chains work, as we have done for decades across the Canada–U.S. border. Canada could become a leader in cross-border logistics, adopting technologies and developing leading-edge practices that allow for better coordination of global value chains.

A final example of a relative strength—one that we do not often view as a strength—is the pre-eminent role smaller businesses play in the Canadian economy. Digitization makes it easier to break down production into smaller tasks and to coordinate these tasks globally. This means that many more opportunities are now available for smaller companies to link themselves into global value chains—even though competition is fiercer. Smaller companies that offer a world-leading product or service may not have been able to tap into global markets before. Now, companies that identify and fill a niche can use digitization to go global more easily. This strength cuts across a range of economic activities. (An upcoming Conference Board report will identify best practices and provide more insight into how smaller businesses are using digital technologies to go global.)

These ideas are only the tip of the iceberg. In other words, Canada has a lot to offer. But to seize on these and myriad other promising opportunities, Canadian businesses will need to invest more heavily in digital technologies and related skills than they do now. And for Canadian businesses to ensure the secure and wide-ranging access to global markets they need to capitalize on their relative strengths, policy-makers will need to address a wider range of trade barriers than they have in the past.

Trade Barriers in a Digital World

India, the United Arab Emirates, Turkey, and other countries have threatened to ban service for Canadian based Research In Motion's (RIM's) BlackBerry devices within their borders. This is an example of the new types of barriers Canadian and global companies face when buying or selling their products or services in a world that increasingly relies on digital information flows.

A ban—or simply the threat of one—would obviously create a barrier to selling BlackBerry products and services in those coveted, rapidly growing markets. But the repercussions would be much broader. Businesses and individuals have come to rely on access to smart phones, search engines, and other communications tools to conduct their businesses and enter new markets. Threats to ban such tools lead to self-censorship and uncertainty, both of which undermine global trade and investment (not to mention human rights). Banning such tools outright is likely to have an even stronger negative impact on the scope, efficiency, and stability of legitimate global business activities.

To be sure, there can be legitimate privacy or security reasons for countries to filter some types of cross-border data flows. Often, however, barriers to digital data flows are aimed at protecting domestic companies ("digital protectionism") or at clamping down on dissent.

Digital Information Barriers Are Trade Barriers

Yet, typically, neither policy-makers nor members of the public think of barriers to digital information flows as barriers to trade and investment. Historically, Canadian and global trade policy-makers have focused on eliminating tariffs on goods trade, and almost all academic work on trade barriers has related to these tariffs.

Though tariffs have fallen considerably in recent decades, Canadian companies still face them in a number of global markets. And even relatively low tariffs can have significant effects. When each production task is done in a separate country, products cross multiple borders, potentially encountering tariffs at each one.

Canada must work with other countries to address the many non-tariff barriers that Canadian companies face, such as restrictions on foreign investment, barriers to the flow of information and people, and the threat of compromised cybersecurity.

But the ability to digitize information and send it anywhere means we also need to think beyond tariff barriers in our trade and related public policies. The use of digital technologies underpins all global trade and investment today. It has opened up new trade possibilities for digital products, such as music and video games, that are made using digital tools and that "travel" electronically. It has made it possible to trade virtual items, such as clothing and accessories, in virtual worlds. But it has also revolutionized the way physical goods are made and how they are tracked on their way to their customers. It has increased the ability to trade services globally, and it has made it easier to coordinate trade, investment, and information flows across global value chains.

Source: Excerpted from Goldfarb, D. (2011, April). Canada's trade in a digital world. The Conference Board of Canada. Retrieved from www.conferenceboard.ca/reports/briefings/tradingdigitally/pg2.aspx. Reprinted with permission.

Researchers by the names of Burns and Stalker were among the first, back in the 1960s, to systematically study the influence of the environment on organizational structure.[8] Among their studies was a comparison of organizations existing in two fundamentally different environments: one set of firms operated within a dynamic, changing industry; another set operated in a stable, established industry. The researchers found that there were a number of significant structural differences in these two sets of organizations (see Exhibit 4.10). In essence, the results of this research suggested that an organization's structure is contingent on the type of environment within which the organization operates.

Lessons for Managers   The contingency approach presents some important lessons for managers. Among these is the need for managers to take great caution in the way they interpret

---

[8] Burns, T., & Stalker, G.M. (1961). *The management of innovation.* London, UK: Tavistock.

Exhibit 4.10 Dynamic vs. Static Industry

Organizational Characteristics	Static Industry	Dynamic Industry
Rules and procedures	• Reliance on formal rules and procedures to carry out most organizational activities	• Relatively fewer rules
Decision making	• Highly centralized	• More decentralized
Levels of administration or supervisory control	• Greater number of levels	• Fewer levels

the organization's environment. Managers must accurately define those environmental factors that have a significant impact on their organizations to generate a suitable organizational structure—one capable of responding to environmental demands and the characteristics for which it was designed. By the mid-1980s, managers found that their assumptions about the environment largely no longer held. Organizational characteristics regarding the different kinds of hierarchies, organizational practices, and strategies developed in the past were suddenly incapable of dealing with changes in the organizational environment.

REENGINEERING

Objective 4 Explain the concept of reengineering.

A management consultant by the name of James Champy was asked to observe the operations of an insurance company in an effort to improve its efficiency.[9] Among his observations, Champy discovered that it took 24 days to obtain a policy after the client purchased it. Champy was curious to understand what work was done on these insurance policies during the 24 days it took to reach the purchaser. After following the trail of these policies, Champy found that only about 10 minutes of work was actually performed on these policies during that 24-day period. The additional time arose because the policies were transferred through 14 different departments. Was this necessary? Champy discovered that while there was no real need for policies to travel through this long and winding road, it nevertheless had become a tradition: "This is how we do things here." There had been no assessment, however, of whether this method was still necessary.

reengineering The fundamental rethinking and radical redesign of business processes to achieve dramatic improvements in measures of performance. It often advocates the collection of individual tasks into a greater number of whole jobs.

James Champy and one of his colleagues, Michael Hammer, engaged in many more observations of different types of organizations. They advocated a rethinking of organizational design, detailed in their best-selling book *Reengineering the Corporation*. **Reengineering** became one of the hottest business buzzwords of the 1990s, but what exactly is it? Fundamentally, reengineering asks the question, if I were creating this company today—if I could start over given what I know and current technology—what would it look like? A more systematic definition includes the following elements:

> The fundamental rethinking and radical redesigning of business processes to achieve dramatic improvements in measures of performance (cost, quality, service, speed).[10]

---

[9] Hammer, M., & Champy, J. (1993). *Reengineering the corporation: A manifesto for business revolution.* New York, NY: HarperCollins.

[10] Hammer & Champy, 1993.

In examining the definition of reengineering, we can understand its essence and its basic contributions to organizational design. Let's consider each element of this definition:

1. *Fundamental rethinking of the organization's structure and functions:* Reengineering involves a critical examination of the traditional method of structuring work. An organization will examine how it performs its functions to assess whether this method does indeed make the most sense. This examination of work processes is done with a focus on how to best serve customer needs. Two fundamental questions that any reengineering effort must ask are "How do we improve quality of our product/service?" and "How can we reduce costs?" One central aim is to eliminate any company practice that is not adding value to the process of generating a product or service for the customer. The notion of focusing on the company's "core competencies" implies that the aim is to concentrate on what the company does best and eliminate unnecessary functions or practices.

2. *Radical redesign of organization processes and structure:* The thrust of reengineering is to "reinvent" the organization according to the current objectives. Hammer and Champy suggested that a lot of organizations that claim they are making changes to become more efficient are really just trying to do "worthless tasks" more efficiently. What reengineering advocates is a "quantum leap." However, it is important to note that while the radical redesign of an organization is the fundamental rationale behind reengineering, it is difficult to achieve in practice.

Accomplishing the goal of redesign typically involves organizing around process rather than around functions. For much of the 20th century, beliefs about organizing focused on work specialization—compartmentalizing jobs into the simplest elements—therefore ensuring work was standardized (as advocated by scientific management and Weber's notion of bureaucracy). Reengineering advocates the collection of individual tasks into more whole jobs. This relates to the distinction between process and functions. It is reflected in the notion of moving away from a focus on specialized tasks to a focus on process. Consider an example offered by Hammer and Champy, the case of a credit agency, in Talking Business 4.3.

TALKING BUSINESS 4.3

The Credit Agency

An organization found that the task of processing a credit application was extremely slow and inefficient, taking anywhere from six days to two weeks to complete. After a credit request was received by phone it was recorded on a piece of paper. This paper was then passed along to credit checkers, pricers (who determined what interest rate to charge), and many other individuals who performed single, compartmentalized tasks. Credit applications typically were bounced around to different areas before they were properly completed. After much scrutiny, it was discovered that the time actually required to complete such an application shouldn't take more than 90 minutes! Consequently, it was time to reengineer—to "scrap" the traditional method organized around specialized, compartmentalized tasks and redesign the work around the process of completing a credit application. This did not require numerous specialists, but simply a few generalists. That is, one person could process an entire application without passing it on to others. So this work was reengineered, resulting in a decrease in the application time, an enormous increase in the number of applications processed, and fewer employees required to do the job.[11]

---

[11] Hammer & Champy, 1993.

This illustration reflects the notion of organizing around process—in other words, designing the organization in a way that considers the actual jobs that need to be performed. This is in contrast to a blanket approach to organizational design that would simply advocate the creation of different departments that jobs will be organized in. Often the bureaucratic structure becomes preoccupied with administrative levels of hierarchy, rules, and regulations. What reengineering advocates is to move away from a preoccupation with organizing work based on tasks, jobs, departments, and administrative levels of hierarchy, and instead to focus on processes—the activities required to transform inputs into outputs.

With regard to the nature of the job, reengineering also advocates combining several jobs into one. This, too, was reflected in the credit agency example in Talking Business 4.3. This is akin to the notion of job enrichment—that is, enriching the responsibility and challenge of jobs by allowing workers to do more of the task rather than one narrow, highly specialized piece of the work. Certainly technology has helped facilitate the integration of jobs and the ability of fewer people to perform a greater variety of tasks. In fact, it has been observed that among the leading factors contributing to the proliferation of reengineering activity in the early 1990s were advances in information technology. Technologies, including shared databases, client-server architecture, and imaging, could be efficiently applied to facilitate processes that cross different functional departments.[12]

The above suggests that reengineering may result in the view that work can be performed efficiently with fewer employees. Typically, reengineering means *cutting* the size of the workforce and often involves flattening the organizational hierarchy. Examples abound, including organizations like PepsiCo North America, which cut seven layers of its hierarchy to four in order to focus on designing itself around serving customers rather than simply maintaining a hierarchical bureaucracy. This also presents a major challenge for organizations attempting to reengineer, though: the threat of job loss for many employees. Management scholar Varun Grover recently observed the following:

> Perhaps the biggest challenge associated with the success of the reengineering phenomenon may be that of selling such a major change to the employees of the organization and getting them to "buy into" the strategic changes that must be undertaken for the firm to survive and prosper. [See Talking Business 4.4.] For example, outsourcing activities that don't contribute to core competencies or technology to other firms that can perform them better may be a legitimate outcome of a good reengineering effort. It would lead to work-force reduction, but only with the purpose of making the firm leaner and more responsive. Time-based competition and the creation of "agile" corporations may not even be possible without such changes in work-force size and composition. As companies emphasize the notion of capturing and leveraging "knowledge" as a source of value, a broader focus on process change management may perhaps be the only way to avoid skill obsolescence of employees and encourage horizontal career paths. The extent to which top-level management can sell such a vision of change and its impact on the employees will determine whether the reengineering phenomenon fulfills its true potential.[13]

---

[12] Grover, V., Kettinger, W.J., & Teng, J.T.C. (2000). Business process change in the 21st century. *Business and Economic Review, 46*(2), 14–18.

[13] Grover, V. (1999). From business reengineering to business process change management: A longitudinal study of trends and practices. *IEEE Transactions on Engineering Management, 46*(1), 45.

Former Outsourcer Describes How Job Destruction Works

© 06photo/Fotolia

These are the confessions of an outsourcer. She has spent more than a decade helping some of Canada's biggest financial institutions shed workers and replace them with low-wage help.

She has made a good living doing this. But she now thinks that contracting out middle-class jobs—the very practice she aided—is short-sighted and morally wrong.

"What kind of world do we want?" she asks. "We are not building a future for kids."

She doesn't want her name used, so I shall call her Arlene. Her story jibes with others I have heard since the furor over the Royal Bank's decision to outsource high-tech workers to India broke.

A highly trained, university-educated professional, Arlene has been at the centre of the action. She is frustrated by the media coverage of the RBC affair. She says those who focus on Ottawa's foreign temporary worker program miss the point.

The big banks she has worked for under contract don't bring in temporary foreign workers to take Canadian jobs. Rather they send those jobs abroad through what they call "preferred vendors," such as the India-based outsourcing firm iGate.

True, these preferred vendors may temporarily import foreign managers to organize the job drain. But typically, such managers do not stay long.

More to the point, the lower-paid foreigners who will eventually do the actual work rarely, if ever, set foot in Canada.

Arlene says any outsourcing scheme begins with the institution's senior management. Usually, she says, the aim is to transfer about 60 percent of the affected jobs—often in back-shop areas like information technology—to India where wages are a fraction of those paid in Canada.

The remaining 40 percent, which generally require more local support, are outsourced to third-party firms in Canada. They in turn, subcontract the jobs to individual Canadians.

The aim here, Arlene says, is to not only to save the bank money but ensure that it is legally insulated from those who work for it.

Technically, those Canadians doing outsourced work are viewed as self-employed. That means that the bank no longer has to pay statutory benefits such as Canada Pension Plan premiums.

In most cases, subcontracts with Canadian workers are renewed for up to two years. Then, in order to maintain the fiction that they are not real bank employees, they are let go. After a few weeks, they are rehired on another set of short-term contracts.

"It's sad," says Arlene. "Really and truly sad. If you're on contract you have no security. You do exactly what you're told or you're gone. You look the wrong way at someone and you're gone. If you even question someone, you're gone."

Foreign outsourcing works slightly differently.

In this case, the financial institution will hire not only someone like Arlene but a foreign preferred vendor like iGate. "We work side by side in the bank," she says.

Her job might involve bundling the tasks to be outsourced. Her foreign counterpart then arranges with his home office in, say, India to have its low-wage employees do the tasks.

The foreign outsourcer might use Canadians from its Toronto office to manage what corporations euphemistically call "the transition." Or it might bring in employees from abroad under one of several visa arrangements permitted by Ottawa.

(continued)

Typically, any foreigners brought in are tasked not with doing the work being outsourced but with learning how to train others who are already abroad to do that work.

In that sense, they are not replacing qualified Canadian workers. They are merely executing a job-killing decision already made by the bank.

The corporate world has invented various phrases to describe this drive to cheap labour. Some versions are referred to as "organizational redevelopment." Others are called "process reengineering."

In most cases, employees about to be fired are compelled to explain how their jobs work so that cheaper workers can take over. Arlene recalls one instance where senior directors broke down in tears as they spelled out how best they could be replaced.

"One was a single mother," she recalls. "Another had two kids . . . usually they get rid of the directors first before outsourcing the entire unit."

Typically, she says, employees are instructed to explain their work processes before they receive their pink slips. This causes less fuss.

In the Royal Bank case, information technology professionals were given notice before being required to detail their jobs to RBC's Indian partner. That led some to complain publicly.

"Perhaps bad planning," says Arlene.

The former outsourcer says she now thinks outsourcing is monstrous. She says she left the field because she couldn't bear it any more. She says she has seen too much damage up close.

She says outsourcing, either domestically or abroad, is destroying the dreams of young Canadians. She has a child of her own. She wants government to crack down on companies that, just to make a buck, deliberately kill good jobs. Her words spill out. "This isn't my Canada," she says. "It's not fair. It's like that television show *Survivor*."

Source: Excerpted from Walkom, T. (2013, April 12). Former outsourcer describes how job destruction works. *Toronto Star*. Retrieved from www.thestar.com/news/canada/2013/04/12/former_outsourcer_describes_how_rbcstyle_job_destruction_works_walkom.html. Reprinted with permission from the Toronto Star.

Objective 5 Describe the notion of the virtual organization.

virtual organization An organization that attempts to maximize its fluidity, flatness, and integratedness with the environment. Outsourcing, networking, and shedding noncore functions are three ways organizations can become more virtual.

TOWARD A VIRTUAL ORGANIZATION

If downsizing has become one of the most feared business buzzwords in recent years, a much more benevolent yet popular buzzword is the **virtual organization**. How does an organization become virtual? And equally important, why would an organization want to become virtual? The virtual organization underscores how far we have come from the traditional notion of organizations. According to our old philosophy, the bureaucratic structure is typically large. The virtual organization, on the other hand, is not dependent on size for its functions. In fact, the virtual organization attempts to maximize its fluidity, flatness, and integratedness with the environment—that is, building on many of the structural trends we identified earlier. Let's consider the ways a virtual organization attempts to achieve these characteristics.

Outsourcing

outsourcing Hiring external organizations to perform certain noncore activities of the company. May be employed by corporations engaged in downsizing.

Outsourcing (or contracting out) involves hiring external organizations to conduct work in certain functions of the company. For example, payroll, accounting, and legal work can be assigned to outsourced staff. The organization typically will retain its core functions or competencies—that is, those areas that it is in business to conduct. In other words, it sticks to what it does best and outsources functions that it doesn't wish to focus on. Outsourcing can also be useful for small businesses or startups that do not have time to devote to administrative tasks but rather need to focus on their core activities and to grow their business.

While the buzzword *outsourcing* may seem relatively recent, the practice of outsourcing has, in fact, been with us for many years. Consider the extensive list of "suppliers" of expertise to industry—lawyers, public accountants, independent insurance adjusters, contractors, appraisers, health care professionals, and independent medical specialists. Perhaps what is more recent is the trend toward building businesses with a consideration of which activities are required "in-house" and which functions can simply be outsourced. For example, CIBC outsourced a major portion of its human resource administrative functions to Electronic Data Systems (EDS). The move is consistent with the philosophy of outsourcing: shedding business activities that do not reflect the organization's core competencies. Obviously, managing human resource functions, such as payroll or pension plans, are not part of CIBC's core competencies. These functions can be outsourced to a company whose core competency is in such areas, like EDS. CIBC gains by having an expert company deal with these functions, and at the same time the company has cut costs through the elimination of almost half of its human resources department.[14]

A good example of the potential benefits and, often, the necessity of outsourcing is found in the popular trend of outsourcing the payroll function. There are a variety of reasons for choosing to outsource the payroll function, including dealing with increased human resource demands that may be caused by employee population growth, mergers, acquisitions, spinoffs, consolidations, and downsizing.

In general, the power of outsourcing has been embraced across many diverse industries. A *Businessweek* article underscored this growing phenomenon:

> You likely have never heard of HTC, Flextronics or Cellon. However, these companies design some very famous products. They represent the new trend in outsourcing—outsourcing innovation! Companies such as Dell, Motorola, and Philips are purchasing complete designs from Asian developers, making minor adjustments to their own specifications, and putting their own brand names on the label. This type of outsourcing may also involve "off shoring"—relying on different regions of the world to provide this expertise.
>
> Why is this trend occurring? Companies gain tremendous cost savings from this type of outsourcing. The outsourcing of manufacturing, technological support, and back-office work is not the only way to cut costs. Now, even outsourcing core competencies such as innovation can make financial sense! However, it also raises some risks. Who "owns" the final innovation? That's one reason why Apple Computer, for example, insists on developing its major products "in-house." On the other hand, companies such as Nokia no longer insist on developing everything itself. Because of the complexities of changing technologies, outsourcing may permit Nokia to focus on other areas while deferring to innovators for assistance on some projects.[15]

However, if outsourced products, services, and processes do not provide the quality expected by consumers, then the company's reputation may suffer as a result, as seen in Talking Business 4.5.

---

[14] Brown, D. (2001, June 4). CIBC HR department halved as non-strategic roles outsources. *Canadian HR Reporter, 14*(11), 1.

[15] Based on Engardlo, P., & Elnhorn, B., with Kripaiani, M. in Bangalore, Reinhardt, A. in Cannes, Nussbaum, B. in Somers, N.Y., and Burrows, P. in San Mateo, California, (2005, March 21). Outsourcing innovation. *Businessweek* [New York]. Retrieved from www.businessweek.com/stories/2005-03-20/outsourcing-innovation.

Out-of-Control Outsourcing Ruined Boeing's Beautiful Dreamliner

The latest Boeing 787 Dreamliner problem—the planes were grounded after a battery fire on two Japanese airline flights—is just another blow to the airline industry but it is the one I and other potential passengers take most personally.

Air travel has become little more than a series of affronts to one's dignity, so the idea of a fuel-conserving lighter plane that could fly longer distances with better interior air and bigger windows, look, it was a dream, get over it.

It does seem as though Boeing, which launched its dream scheme in 2004, hedged its bets, outsourcing the design, engineering and manufacture of the plane, as is the modern way. James Surowiecki, the *New Yorker*'s sturdy reliable economics reporter—no dreamer he—has traced Boeing's disastrous decision to outsource most of the work to 50 different companies—yes, 50—to the bad marriage Boeing made with McDonnell Douglas in 1997.

Essentially, he wrote, Boeing was the wild-eyed dreamer and McDonnell Douglas was Mr. Cautious, which meant that they compromised on a queen-sized bed, so to speak. They outsourced to such a degree that it was more trouble to keep track of the sub- and sub-sub-contractors than just to have done the thing in-house in the first place.

The timeline of the Dreamliner's problems reads like a thriller plot—you may well say I am easily entertained—but it's perhaps more of a Greek tragedy. Christopher Tang and Joshua Zimmerman's crisply written UCLA study, *Managing New Product Development and Supply Chain Risks: The Boeing 787 Case*, reveals Boeing's crush on outsourcing.

Normally firms gather parts from suppliers and build a product. Boeing devised a three-tier system of suppliers before the bits even reached it for assembly, the study says. The jigsaw map of the plane looks like something devised by the UN, the wing sections alone coming from six companies in four nations.

The initial rationale for planetwide sourcing sounded plausible. So did preventing delays by refusing to pay suppliers until the first 787 reached customers. But there were technical problems with things like the composite materials that replaced the aluminum normally used for planes. They made the plane wonderfully light but lightning strikes were initially a worry, the study reported.

Then came Boeing's risk. Just-in-time delivery, that gift to the trucking industry and to Walmart, doesn't work perfectly. Why would it? Humans don't meet deadlines. Almost no managers were sufficiently gifted to track and discipline the vast supply chain, the study said. Boeing's workforce, terrified of layoffs, went on strike. Customers began backing out.

I won't recount what the study reported Boeing did to even out the risk because it starts to read like a history of the doomed 1910 Scott expedition to the South Pole. Boeing was calm and brave, buying up the weakest suppliers, hiring a new manager and CEO, giving staff a raise and edgy customers interim airplanes.

But discovering that lithium-ion batteries tend to overheat? That's like Scott's fatal decision to go with ponies instead of sled dogs.

There is a splendid 20/20 clarity in the study's sad little sentence, "Boeing should have chosen the right people for the job at the outset." Sometimes I think the secret of hiring is that people are either intelligent or they're not, whatever the job is.

Surowiecki says exciting new products always have flaws and we should have expected trouble. He is wrong. It's not that we have no tolerance for mistakes in airplanes, but that we have no tolerance for ending up in a fireball catapulting to earth.

Outsourcing the outsourced has a cost: it overstretches the link between parts and the final product. It's a risk British consumers took when they bought cheap burgers made from meat outsourced all over Europe, which turned out to be horse, not beef. And now they're retching.

Consumers paid a price in quality when they demanded cheap airfares. They worshipped the god of cheap and Boeing tried to please them.

The 787 delays, plus the new merger between American and US Airways, will mean higher U.S. domestic airfares and rightly so. We'll fly less often but more happily.

Source: Excerpted from Mallick, H. (2013, February 25). Out-of-control outsourcing ruined Boeing's beautiful Dreamliner: Mallick. *Toronto Star*. Retrieved from www.thestar.com/opinion/editorialopinion/2013/02/25/outofcontrol_outsourcing_ruined_boeings_beautiful_dreamliner_mallick.html. Reprinted with permission from the Toronto Star.

Networking

We have increasingly been observing organizations limiting themselves to fewer activities in which they have expertise and assigning specialists to handle all other functions. This is also associated with the notion of integrated or networked organizations that we identified earlier. Through **networking**, organizations can engage in cooperative relationships with suppliers, distributors, or competitors. The aim is to improve their efficiency and flexibility in meeting new consumer needs. For example, a close relationship with a distributor might offer the supplier company more information about the changing needs of customers. The Japanese version of networked organizations called *keiretsu* could, in fact, really be considered the first form of the virtual organization.

networking Organizations engaging in cooperative relationships with suppliers, distributors, or competitors with the aim of improving efficiency and flexibility in meeting consumer needs. The Japanese version is called *keiretsu*.

Typically, a *keiretsu* involves a large bank or financial institution, a large industrial organization, and a number of smaller firms, where the integrated network of relationships allows the large industrial organization to produce the product with financial assistance from the bank. The role of the smaller firms may be to supply parts to the manufacturer, conduct research, or perhaps distribute the final product. What we observe in virtual organizations are only those activities that are central—they are kept in-house, so to speak, and all other functions are outsourced to separate companies or individuals who are typically coordinated by a small head office. Or, each company is simply involved in some kind of network where each brings its own expertise to the collection of companies.

Shedding Noncore Functions

The outsourcing aspect, again, is a central feature of the virtual organization. Clearly, organizations can become more "virtual" by shedding some of their noncore functions and outsourcing these to affiliated organizations. Companies that use information technology (IT) need to become as flexible as the virtual organizations, given the rapidly changing face of technology and its applications. For organizations whose core competency is not IT or all its elements, there is much to be gained from partnering with other organizations in the virtual sense. A growing number of IT departments are considering outsourcing models to address all or part of their needs. "Small component" or discrete outsourcing service providers include such specialized offerings as storage and web hosting. Application management has become a high-growth area in outsourcing service markets in Canada. Those seeking such services have a range to choose from for outsourcing, including desktop or infrastructure services to various business functions. Network management can be outsourced, along with backup and recovery as well as data centre services.

A virtual organization might be composed of simply a small group of business executives who form the core of the organization. Their responsibility is to oversee and coordinate the activities that might be done in-house as well as those functions that are outsourced—which might involve coordinating relationships among the companies that develop, manufacture, market, and sell their products. Many more companies have found that they can become quite profitable without actually having to own their entire operation. Certainly, the traditional bureaucracy is structured so that production occurs in company-owned plants, research and development are conducted by in-house experts, and sales and marketing are performed by the company's own sales and marketing department. This is not the case for the virtual organization, which doesn't believe you need to own everything. For example, Dell Computer owns no plants and simply assembles computers from parts whose manufacture has been outsourced. Similarly, Apple Computer subcontracted the manufacture of its first Notebook to Sony as a means to speed up entry into the market. Companies like Nike and Reebok have achieved success by focusing on what they do best—designing and marketing their products. They outsource almost all their footwear manufacturing to outside suppliers. Obviously, the virtual organization doesn't just outsource the peripheral function of the company; it outsources whatever costs less to outsource than to do in-house.

There are a number of *gains* potentially achieved by going virtual:

1. *The cost savings are significant:* A virtual organization does not need to own its own plants, nor employ its own research and development teams, nor hire its own sales staff. This means the virtual organization also doesn't need to hire the extra staff to support all these functions—such as personnel specialists, company lawyers, accountants, and so on. The virtual organization can outsource most of these functions and focus on what it does best. So there is little if any administrative overhead, so to speak, because work activities are largely contracted. Cost savings arise in areas such as training, purchasing of work-related tools, benefits, downtime, and educational requirements. All these requirements are typically obtained with the arrival of the external or "outsourced" experts.

2. *The virtual organization is a great alternative for entrepreneurs:* Individuals seeking to start up a new business or venture may face huge startup costs. The network of arrangements within a virtual organization can exploit the expertise of different companies while not requiring the initiator of the business to buy everything and start a business from scratch.

3. *For a mature company, going virtual can be a fast way to develop and market new products:* Relying on the expertise of partners means that no huge investment is required to enter a new product or service territory.

4. *Virtual organizations are fast and flexible:* For example, the flexible arrangements of those parties involved can be of a temporary nature to produce a good or service; resources can be quickly arranged and rearranged to meet changing demands and best serve customers; management isn't getting bogged down in peripheral functions, but is simply focusing on central functions.

Among the *risks and challenges* of becoming virtual are the following:

1. *Giving up the notion of control:* Control has traditionally been a key goal of any organization. The structure of the bureaucratic organization is fundamentally based on the notion of control—control through standardization of work, control through hierarchy of authority, control through rules and regulations, control through clear division of labour. However, the virtual organization doesn't provide such control. Think of it—how can you monitor all activity when it may not even be occurring within the walls of one building? Among the fears of going virtual and outsourcing is that we are "hollowing out" the organization and making it extremely dependent on external sources. The employees are not all yours; outsourcing to independent contractors doesn't carry with it the same level of control as staffing your own employees to do the work. Difficulties in control can occur particularly when a variety of subcontractors are involved in the work. This lack of control may also generate a lack of control over costs—once a company becomes dependent on a supplier, it may be unable to refuse an increase in the supplier's prices.

2. *Lack of employee loyalty:* If your organization is largely composed of temporary workers and subcontractors, who is really committed to perpetuating the goals of the company?

Can a virtual organization really develop a sense of identity or culture that is the "glue" that binds everyone to a common purpose? This is an issue that virtual organizations must deal with. In fact, turnover in many virtual organizations tends to be high because employees are committed only to the task for which they are hired. In addition, employees may be working under temporary contractual arrangements and could be dismissed in favour of another contractor.

3. *Potential to sacrifice competitive learning opportunities*: Outsourcing involves the strategic decision to "let go" of some aspect of the organization—the decision could be to permit the manufacture of the footwear to occur elsewhere, as in the case of Nike, while retaining the core competencies (such as the marketing function). The question is whether there is a danger in "letting go" of functions that may currently appear peripheral, but could become important functions of the organization should the strategy change in the future. Clearly, if a function is outsourced, the experience or learning of this function as a skill is lost to the internal organization. Is there an inherent danger in such a situation? That is, is there a danger in outsourcing, given the risk of losing key skills that could be needed for future competitiveness?

DOWNSIZING

Objective 6 Discuss the phenomenon of downsizing and its rationale, methods, and objectives.

In terms of business buzzwords, probably the most dreaded buzzword of the 1990s was the term *downsizing*. While the 1990s have been referred to as the "lean, mean 90s," the trend toward leanness via downsizing has not gone away in the new millennium. In recent years, thousands of workers across Canada have been losing their jobs.

In broad terms, **downsizing** refers to the planned reduction in the breadth of an organization's operations. Typically, it entails terminating relatively large numbers of employees or decreasing the number of products or services the organization provides. It seems that if you think of just about any large corporation, it has likely experienced some kind of downsizing: from AT&T to Bell Canada to Air Canada to IBM to General Motors to Nortel—all have experienced massive cuts in their workforce.

downsizing The planned reduction in breadth of an organization's operations, typically involving terminating relatively large numbers of employees or decreasing the number of products or services the organization provides.

Consequently, most of us associate downsizing with the reduction of the workforce. However, we can be more specific, given that organizations can downsize in a variety of ways. For example, does reducing an organization's ownership of assets amount to downsizing? Does a reduction in the number of employees constitute downsizing?

> One definition of downsizing that has been offered is "downsizing is a set of activities undertaken on the part of management and designed to improve organizational efficiency, productivity, and/or competitiveness. It represents a strategy implemented by managers that affects the size of the firm's work force and its work processes."[16]

workforce reduction A short-term strategy that is aimed at reducing the number of employees through attrition, early retirement, voluntary severance package, layoffs, or terminations.

Based on this definition, there are three fundamental types of strategies for downsizing: workforce reduction, work redesign, and systematic change. **Workforce reduction**

---

[16] Cameron, K. (1994). Strategies for successful organizational downsizing. *Human Resource Management*, 33(2), 192.

typically involves a short-term strategy that is aimed at reducing the number of employees through such programs as attrition, early retirement, voluntary severance packages, layoffs, or terminations. Downsizing approaches have largely been directed at workforce reduction rather than the more detailed and longer-term strategies of job redesign and systematic change.[17] For a recent example of downsizing, see Talking Business 4.6.

TALKING BUSINESS 4.6

Loblaw Cuts 700 Head Office Jobs

The decision by Loblaw Companies Limited to chop 700 jobs from the payroll in administration and at head office in Brampton . . . was met with mixed reviews from analysts and investors.

After the announcement, shares rose 84 cents and closed at $34.72.

Loblaw has been upgrading its supply chain technology and infrastructure and while the job cuts may reflect greater efficiencies, Perry Caicco, managing director, CIBC World Markets, warned investors against applying the savings directly to the company's bottom line.

"Notwithstanding that these job cuts probably reflect a demand from the parent company to generate some return on the outsized capital spending on systems, it is highly unlikely that these actions will directly boost earnings," wrote Caicco in a note to investors on Tuesday.

"The recent history of the company suggests that some of these job cuts will be replaced by equally expensive outsourcing, and that the company will struggle to re-assign eliminated roles in a productive fashion. In other words, we believe the risk of poor head office execution and service to stores will be high for at least 12 months."

Caicco said some portion of the cuts will likely reduce expenses, a necessity in light of the surge in growth in the grocery sector in Canada.

Walmart is in the midst of adding 4.6-million square feet of retail space to operations in Canada. More than half of the projects will involve supercentres providing a full range of groceries.

The family-owned Longo's is also expanding in carefully selected prime locations in the GTA.

Loblaw Companies Limited is Canada's largest food retailer, with more than 1,000 corporate and franchised stores, including Loblaws, Zehrs, T&T, Fortinos, Provigo, No Frills and the Real Canadian Superstore. The company employs about 138,000 full- and part-time workers.

© Helen Sessions/Alamy

In the past 12 months, Loblaw has opened 14 new stores across Canada, creating 2,000 new jobs.

The investment in infrastructure at Loblaw—trimming 250 separate systems down to something manageable—began in 2009.

"It's a huge job, particularly when you've got to keep the old systems running to keep doing business. It's like changing the engine on a car while the engine is still running," said retail analyst Ed Strapagiel.

"This year, 2012, is when most of their system conversion takes place. There will likely be teething pains, so add a few months to work the bugs out. I think most professional stock analysts understand this. I think they think Loblaw is doing the right thing, but they would prefer to see it go faster."

Kenric Tyghe, an analyst with Raymond James Securities told Bloomberg news he viewed the move positively.

"With their new systems capabilities, certain HR requirements are now redundant and hence the job cuts," he said.

Vicente Trius, president, Loblaw Companies Ltd., broke the news to employees this morning, according to Loblaw spokesperson Julija Hunter.

---

[17] Cameron, 1994, 189–211.

The changes will take effect starting Tuesday and should be complete within three weeks. The company expects to take a one-time estimated $60 million charge in the fourth quarter as a result.

"We feel really confident in our direction," Hunter said, adding that the job reductions will make the company more competitive, eliminate duplications and allow the firm to focus more on the customer experience.

"We're managing costs where it makes sense."

The transition will not be fully in place until the end of 2014.

Loblaw is a subsidiary of George Weston Ltd., which is sitting on $3.6-billion in cash. A spokesman for George Weston Ltd. said in September that the cash will be used in part to refresh its North American bakeries and Canadian Loblaw stores.

It's also looking to make acquisitions.

Loblaw saw its profit drop 22 per cent in the first quarter of 2012. Second quarter net earnings per common share were 57 cents, down almost 19 per cent compared to the same period in 2011.

Source: Excerpted from Kopun, F. (2012, October 16). Loblaw cuts 700 Toronto head office jobs. *Toronto Star*. www.thestar.com/business/2012/10/16/loblaw_cuts_700_toronto_head_office_jobs.html. Reprinted with permission from the Toronto Star.

Now that we've looked at definitions of downsizing, we can more clearly identify the common approaches to downsizing. That is, we can be more specific about what exactly an organizational downsizing may entail. This will allow us to briefly identify the potential benefits as well as pitfalls of an organizational downsizing.

Methods of Downsizing

Management scholar Martin Evans has provided a summary of the forms of downsizing where he also identified the potential benefits and consequences of the different approaches to it.[18] The most common forms of downsizing include any one or a combination of the following strategies (the pros and cons of each of these approaches are shown in Exhibit 4.11 on next page):

1. *Across-the-board cutbacks:* Cutting a fixed percentage of the workforce across all departments or units.

2. *Early retirement and voluntary severance:* Asking those nearing retirement to take early retirement voluntarily as opposed to being forced to leave. Typically, this is the first stage in a downsizing process.

3. *Delayering by cutting a level or levels of the organization:* Terminating or reassigning middle managers who are not being replaced, thereby flattening the organizational hierarchy by removing horizontal slices.

4. *Contracting out work (or outsourcing):* Laying off staff in areas that perform specialized functions and contracting out this work to agencies that can staff those areas with temporary workers. Types of activities that are typically contracted out include payroll, data entry, public relations, and clerical work as opposed to the core activities of the organization.

5. *Dropping product lines:* Discontinuing some programs or product lines provided by the organization.

[18] Evans, M.G., Gunz, H.P., & Jalland, R.M. (1997). Implications of organizational downsizing for managerial careers. *Canadian Journal of Administrative Sciences, 14*, 359–371.

Exhibit 4.11 Potential Benefits and Risks of Downsizing

Potential Benefits	
1. Across-the-board cuts	"Shares the pain," spreading it across the organization—all levels are equally affected.
2. Early retirement and voluntary severance	Concentrates the terminations among those who are willing to leave.
	May help achieve the reduced cost objective by encouraging the more senior and more highly paid staff to leave.
3. Delayering	Because the organization is cut horizontally, all areas are equally affected and the "pain" is shared across all departments.
	To the extent that decentralized decision making is desired, this approach allows the shift of responsibility to the lower and perhaps more-appropriate levels in the organization.
4. Contracting out	Immediate costs savings.
5. Dropping product lines	Decide what areas may not be productive to continue to maintain.
	A closer connection to long-term strategic planning compared to other approaches.
	Concentrates the disruption in one or a few business units as opposed to the entire organization.
Potential Risks	
1. Across-the-board cuts	Efficient parts of the organization are hurt. This form of downsizing ignores how well or how poorly the units are managed.
	Typically conducted when there is no strategic plan—it simply cuts staff throughout the organization.
2. Early retirement and voluntary severance	Not necessarily guided by a strategic plan.
	Encourages voluntary exits from all parts of the organization.
	"Loss of corporate memory"—that is, a company may lose highly experienced, valued members who have been an intrinsic part of what the organization is all about.
3. Delayering	A loss of corporate memory with the removal of middle managers. There may also be an overload of responsibility to top management, who may now need to fill the role of some middle management as well.
	There may be significant costs attached to the transition from a taller organization to a flatter one because lower-level employees must be trained to take on additional roles and responsibilities.
4. Contracting out	Difficulties of dealing with the new suppliers and avoiding future cost increases.
	The general loss of control over these temporary workers.
5. Dropping product lines	Pain is concentrated and not shared across the entire organization—a few people will carry the burden of this type of downsizing.

Consequences of Downsizing

The strategy of downsizing that started in the mid-1980s has now become commonplace. In the early stages, downsizing strategies were viewed as a panacea for the ills of organizations, providing organizations with a method of cost reduction, productivity, and profitability improvement and, consequently, a higher competitive ability. Unfortunately, there is vast evidence that the anticipated benefits of corporate downsizing have largely failed to materialize. It is of interest to reconsider the anticipated benefits of downsizing and in what way these benefits have not been realized.

As the Wyatt report and numerous other studies have indicated, there are a host of benefits that organizations feel they can achieve through downsizing, including reduced bureaucracy, lower overhead costs, improved decision making, improvements in productivity, and a stronger ability to innovate.[19] But does downsizing contribute to a better "bottom line"? That is, does this activity enhance the organization's financial performance? There is research evidence that suggests that a downsizing or layoff announcement often leads to a drop in the organization's share price, particularly if that announcement was related to financial concerns or a massive and permanent cutback of employees.[20] There is also evidence to suggest that investors respond negatively to layoff announcements.[21]

Does downsizing improve organizational performance as measured by return on assets and common shares? There is research evidence indicating that organizations that engaged in an employee downsizing (that is, terminated at least 5% of the workforce combined with little change in plant and equipment costs) did not outperform other organizations in their industry.[22] Similarly, a CSC Index survey found that less than 33% of all downsizing initiatives had achieved their anticipated productivity or profitability goals.

In a large-scale study conducted in Canada, data were collected from 1,907 Canadian organizations with at least 75 employees. This study examined how a permanent workforce reduction affects employer efficiency, employee satisfaction, and employee–employer relations. The findings indicated that a permanent workforce reduction was associated with negative consequences. This echoes the findings in the United States and elsewhere and underscores the consistent failure of downsizing to live up to its expectations.[23]

Added to the lacklustre results of downsizing is the wealth of evidence of the costs of downsizing in terms of human consequences. Needless to say, those individuals who are victims of a downsizing can be subjected to intense psychological trauma. However, there is ample research evidence to indicate that the *survivors* of a downsizing may also experience trauma. According to numerous studies, survivors of a downsizing typically report greater levels of stress, burnout, reduced self-confidence and self-esteem, and lower job satisfaction.[24] Studies have also found that a downsizing can have adverse effects on employee commitment to the organization, their performance, their ability to serve customer and client needs, and reduced morale and trust.[25] See Talking Business 4.7.

---

[19] Wyatt Group. (1993). *Best practices in corporate restructuring.* Washington, DC: The Wyatt Company.

[20] Worrell, D., Davidson, W., & Sharma, V. (1991). Layoff announcements and stockholder wealth. *Academy of Management Journal, 34*, 662–678.

[21] Lee, P. (1997). A comparative analysis of layoff announcements and stock price reactions in the United States and Japan. *Strategic Management Journal, 18*, 879–894.

[22] Cascio, W. (1993). Downsizing? What do we know? What have we learned? *Academy of Management Executive, 7*, 95–100.

[23] Wagar, T.H. (1998). Exploring the consequences of workforce reduction. *Canadian Journal of Administrative Sciences, 15*(4), 300–309.

[24] Mone, M. (2006). Relationships between self-concepts, aspirations, emotional responses, and intent to leave a downsizing organization. *Human Resource Management, 33*, 281–298; Ryan, L., & Macky, K. (1998) Downsizing organizations: Uses, outcomes and strategies. *Asia Pacific Journal of Human Resources, 36*, 29–45.

[25] Tomasko, J.A. (1990). *Downsizing: Reshaping the corporation of the future.* New York, NY: AMACON; Cascio, 1993; Brockner, J. (1988). The effects of work layoff on survivors: Research, theory, and practice. *Research in Organizational Behaviour, 10*(1), 213–256; Brockner, J., et al. (1994). Interactive effects of procedural justice and outcome negativity on victims and survivors of job loss. *Academy of Management Journal, 37*, 397–409; Sutton, R.I., & D'Aunno, T. (1989). Decreasing organizational size: Untangling the effects of money and people. *Academy of Management Review, 14*, 194–212; McLellan, K., & Marcolin, B. (1994). Information technology outsourcing. *Business Quarterly, 59*, 95–104.

What Every Leader Should Know about Survivor Syndrome

While restructuring and downsizing are often critical components of business strategy for the short-term, these actions can lead to longer-term engagement challenges. Studies have indicated that downsizing has a significantly negative impact on work attitudes, and that the impact varies over time. Downsizing and layoffs are frequently viewed by employees as a break in the presumed employer–employee contract, and those remaining employed at downsized companies often suffer from low morale, reduced commitment, and lack of trust and loyalty. These behaviors are indicative of a phenomenon called "survivor syndrome." . . .

What Is "Survivor Syndrome"?

Survivor syndrome refers to a marked decrease in motivation, engagement, and productivity of employees that remain at the company as a result of downsizing and workforce reductions.

- **Motivation** This is the combination of forces that energizes individuals to perform and behave in certain ways. "Intrinsic motivation" refers to the internal forces (e.g., personal satisfaction) that drive an employee to perform an action; while "extrinsic motivation" refers to the external forces (e.g., salary) that drive an employee to perform an action.

- **Employee Engagement** A heightened emotional and intellectual connection that an employee has for his/her job, organization, manager, or co-workers that, in turn, influences him/her to apply additional discretionary effort to his/her work.

- **Productivity** At the individual level, productivity is measured by actual output divided by potential output over a period of time. More simply stated, individual productivity is the amount of work completed relative to the amount of time engaged in a task and the total time an employee has devoted to completing the task. . . .

To survive corporate downsizing, companies can leverage existing "people strategies" and provide tools to support motivation, productivity, engagement, and the performance of the business over the longer-term. In particular:

- **Internal communication** Provide employees with information related to the company's status, progress, and strategic direction; and solicit employee ideas and opinions via open forums and one-to-one settings (e.g., staff meetings, blogs, brown bag lunches, strategy planning groups, etc.). Encourage line-managers to reinforce communication messages coming from [the] top of the company.

- **Learning opportunities** Provide additional training to employees who have assumed new or added responsibilities so that they can be more effective in their roles. Train line-managers in ways to communicate effectively with employees under times of uncertainty, crisis, and change. Motivate employees to seek out opportunities to improve their skills and contribute to the organization.

- **Staff development initiatives** Offer one-to-one career counseling to those employees whose roles/positions are at risk for becoming obsolete or employees who are seeking advancement opportunities in the future. Provide employees with (and encourage them to use) multiple outlets for stress management, e.g., social/wellness breaks, yoga classes, flexible work schedules, vacation time, etc.

Ultimately, the ability to survive a downsizing will depend not only on the processes that are used to execute the downsizing, but also on the level of commitment the management team has to reengaging employees at all levels.

Source: Excerpted from Creary, S.J., & Rosner, L. (2009). What every leader should know about survivor syndrome. The Conference Board of Canada. Reprinted with permission. Retrieved from www.conferenceboard.ca/temp/ac8225af-e12d-4087-acc3-b51e4933e59d/a-0307-09-ea.pdf.

Why Has Downsizing Failed to Achieve Anticipated Results?

If the cost reduction results are inconsistent and there is no evidence that productivity, profitability, and competitiveness improve as a result of downsizing, what is going wrong? There are at least three fundamental issues that have been repeatedly linked with the failure of downsizing. These issues reflect shortcomings in the planning for and execution of organizational downsizings rather than an outright condemnation of the practice itself.

1. *Lack of strategic planning:* Many downsizings have not been guided by a long-range strategic plan, but rather have been a short-term response to environmental pressures. The poor performance of downsizing has been associated with the tendency of downsizing programs to be hastily formulated and not linked with the organization's strategic plans.[26] While downsizing is by no means going away, by the end of the 1990s organizations were looking more critically at downsizing as a method of organizational change, and many reconsidered its role without the broader framework of organizational planning. Moreover, there has been a growing sentiment that downsizing by itself provides no answers for organizational ills without a strategic plan.

2. *Lack of concern for, and involvement with, employees:* Many downsizings do not involve those who are affected in the planning stages. That is, those in charge of the downsizing do not expect to get objective feedback or advice from those who will potentially be terminated, and so many employees are cut off from the actual planning of the organizational downsizing. It is important to note that the adverse effects of a downsizing may be mitigated through suitable communication of the downsizing to employees,[27] employee participation in the planning of the downsizing, a thorough analysis of tasks and perceived employee support from the organization,[28] as well as advanced planning and coordination of outplacement services.[29] Attention needs to be given to both the terminated employees and those remaining. However, research evidence has suggested that insufficient attention has been given to the survivors of a downsizing.

3. *Careless removal of corporate memory:* Downsizings can eliminate individuals who are a central part of the organization's knowledge base—the notion of **corporate memory**. While intangible, the cost of corporate memory loss to an organization can be significant. This can go beyond simply losing the expertise of a valued, experienced employee. This significance has been expressed by many observers:

> Downsizing devastates social networks. When a person is laid off, an entire personal network of internal and external relationships is lost as well. Downsizing destroys informal bridges between departments, disrupts the information grapevine, severs ties with customers, and eliminates the friendships that bond people to the workplace.[30]

corporate memory The knowledge of individuals who are a central part of an organization's knowledge base. If they are eliminated by downsizing there is a significant loss of informal bridges, business relationships, customer ties, friendship ties, and so on that bond people together in the workplace.

It has also been suggested that the loss of corporate memory can be particularly devastating to the organization's ability to innovate.

---

[26] Cascio, 1993; Cameron, 1994.

[27] Wanberg, C., Bunce, L., & Gavin, M. (1999). Perceived fairness of layoffs among individuals who have been laid off: A longitudinal study. *Personnel Psychology, 52,* 59–84.

[28] Armstrong-Stassen, M. (2008). Downsizing the federal government: A longitudinal study of managers' reactions. *Canadian Journal of Administrative Sciences, 15,* 310–321.

[29] Havlovic, S., Bouthillette, F., van der Wal, R. (2009). Coping with downsizing and job loss: Lessons from the Shaughnessy Hospital closure. *Canadian Journal of Administrative Sciences, 15,* 322–332.

[30] Baker, W.E. (1996). Bloodletting and downsizing executive excellence. *Provo, 13*(5), 20.

For better or worse, downsizings continue to reshape the corporate landscape; and, given that they are unlikely to disappear in the near future, one can only hope that they will be planned carefully to bring about some of the improvements for which they are intended. To this point, the results of downsizing do not appear to be largely positive for many organizations, and yet we have witnessed the pervasive acceptance of downsizing as a legitimate organizational practice.

The question naturally arises: Why have so many organizations agreed to adopt a practice that is not proven to be effective? If there is no significant proof that downsizing offers the results organizations are struggling to achieve, why do companies continue to downsize? In order to make sense of why organizations engage in restructuring themselves, it is useful to consider why organizations adopt such trends as downsizing. In terms of a rational explanation, the evidence is weak. Consequently, researchers have also considered nonrational approaches to explaining the phenomenon of downsizing. This requires an understanding of how nonrationality can influence organizational structure.

Downsizing as a Nonrational Approach to Organizational Structure

How can organizational structure be nonrational? A perspective of organizations called **institutionalization theory** argues that organizations are driven to incorporate practices and procedures defined by current concepts of work and those accepted or institutionalized in society. Institutional acts, or the rules that govern organizational activity, are simply taken-for-granted means of "getting things done." They represent shared norms or expectations within or across industries. These rules dominate thinking about how organizations should be designed. The implications are that accepted norms or rules, rather than a set of rational reasons based on clearly identifiable and measurable objectives, can encourage the creation or maintenance of organizational structures and processes. Institutional rules have little to do with efficiency, but they give organizations that conform to them a sense of legitimacy. That is, organizations can have elements embedded in their structure that are simply taken-for-granted ways of doing things—which may not, in fact, be accomplishing any specific organizational goals.

According to institutional theory, organizations may conform to institutionalized beliefs as a means to achieve legitimacy, resources, and survival capabilities. The shared beliefs provide order through their institutionalization into organizational procedures and their direct influence on the behaviour of individuals. Consider such diverse organizations as IBM, Ben & Jerry's, McDonald's, Procter & Gamble, and Bell Canada. All these organizations have risen within society. They have gained success and longevity through their ability to adapt their operations to the needs of society. Specifically, the organization becomes filled with various cultural forces: for example, political rules, occupational groups, and professional knowledge. In other words, as these organizations have grown, they have instituted acceptable ways of conducting business.

The ideas generated from institutional theory draw attention to the notion of the forces that act on an organization and encourage the adoption and maintenance of those activities that are viewed as legitimate. This perspective suggests that organizational structures and processes can arise not simply because of rational objectives for control and coordination, but because of adherence to nonrational (but institutional or socially

institutionalization theory
The theory that organizations are driven to incorporate practices and procedures defined by current concepts of work and those accepted or institutionalized by society. Taken-for-granted means of "getting things done" and, as such, not necessarily rational.

accepted) rules. Meyer and Scott described a "continuum"—from organizations dominated by technical criteria (manufacturing organizations) to those dominated by institutional criteria (schools).[31] What we have seen since the mid-1980s is a questioning of many of the fundamental institutional rules governing how organizations should be designed. In other words, at one time the machine bureaucracy was the socially accepted structure for most organizations. Recently, this rule has been called into question, and increasingly the phenomena of reengineering, downsizing, and going virtual seem to be the established trend in organizational design.

The continued use of downsizing by organizations, even though it has not lived up to its reputation, appears to be nonrational. Organizations do not, in fact, always act purely rationally. Institutional theory asserts that organizational structures and policies can become institutionalized and persist even when they are no longer efficient.[32] This theory emphasizes the fact that an organization's functions can become established or embedded in social networks. These functions, whether they are how organizations are designed or simply how they behave, are affected by the pressures of conformity and legitimacy, which arise from the organization's environment.[33] Meyer and Rowan defined *institutionalization* as "the processes by which social processes, obligations, or actualities come to take on a rule-like status in social thought and action."[34]

The notion of downsizing has come to represent more than a reduction in an organization's workforce. It has come to reflect a longer-term organizational evolution. Numerous organizations by the 1990s felt obligated to downsize given the intrinsic connection between being "lean and mean" and being highly competitive. Institutional theorists offer some insight, suggesting that the spread of corporate downsizing has been facilitated through conforming to institutional rules that define legitimate structures and management practices, copying the actions of industry leaders, and responding to the legitimization of downsizing practices as accepted management practices via the media and popular press.[35]

But why do organizations persist in conforming to the "rules" of downsizing? Addressing this question can be accomplished through addressing the question of why organizations conform to institutional rules. At least three social factors have been cited: constraining, cloning, and learning. We will briefly consider each factor to get a better understanding of how they influence adherence to the institutional rule of downsizing. In this regard, we can understand how these factors can make organizations follow rules or ideas that are not necessarily rational.

Constraining Forces   **Constraining forces** represent those practices that come to define what are perceived as legitimate management structures and activities and that

constraining forces Practices that come to define what are perceived as legitimate management structures and activities and that, consequently, place pressure on organizations to conform to these institutional roles.

---

[31] Meyer, J. W., & Scott, R. (1983). *Organizational environments: Ritual and rationality.* Beverly Hills, CA: Sage Publications.

[32] DiMaggio, P., & Powell, W. (1983). The iron cage revisited: Institutional isomorphism and collective rationality in organizational fields. *American Sociological Review, 48*(2), 147–160; Meyer, J., & Rowan, B. (1977). Institutionalized organizations: Formal structure as myth and ceremony. *American Journal of Sociology, 83*(2), 440–463.

[33] DiMaggio & Powell, 1983.

[34] Meyer & Rowan, 1977.

[35] DiMaggio & Powell, 1983; McKinley, W., Sanchez, C., & Schick, A. (1995). Organizational downsizing: Constraining, cloning, and learning. *Academy of Management Executive, 9*(3), 32–41.

consequently place pressure on organizations to conform to these institutional rules. An example given involves the relationship between large US corporations and the stock market.[36] Interestingly, studies have found that layoff announcements made by large corporations that were undergoing restructuring and consolidation were followed by increases in share prices. In other words, we have seen the tendency for public reactions to downsizings to be favourable—the notion of becoming "leaner and meaner" has become an accepted business strategy, and one that is apparently favoured by shareholders. Consequently, since the markets respond positively to such news, organizations have become constrained to perceive downsizing as a positive strategy and one that should be sought. Of more interest is the finding that this constraining force was found to be even stronger when executives' compensation packages and bonuses were linked to share values.

Cloning Forces

cloning forces Pressure on organizations to imitate the behaviour of industry leaders. "Jumping on the bandwagon," or "keeping up with the corporate Joneses."

Cloning forces are pressure for organizations to imitate the behaviours of industry leaders. Revisiting the downsizing example, some observers have suggested that organizations have been "jumping on the bandwagon." That is, many organizations downsize to demonstrate they are in tune with modern business trends, and consequently downsizing has been viewed as a way of "keeping up with the corporate Joneses."[37] This action represents a clear reduction in rationality—that is, a move away from objectively defined criteria for downsizing and toward strict adherence to institutional rules. It has also been found that downsizing among industry members is more likely to occur when industry leaders downsize. The risks of failure are obvious given that this approach lacks a careful evaluation of the costs and benefits of this strategy.

Learning Forces

learning forces Lessons that result from institutionalized management practices and that are taught to future managers and business leaders in the course of their formal education.

Learning forces are the result of institutionalized management practices. The lessons we teach future managers and businesses leaders are embedded in the courses taught in universities and professional associations. As an example of the biases generated in business schools, researchers like McKinley and his colleagues point out the case of cost accounting techniques used in business strategy education.[38] From a purely cost accounting perspective, the practice of outsourcing appears infinitely superior to maintaining a full-time workforce. Specifically, the method of allocating overhead costs clearly draws attention to the cost efficiencies gained by outsourcing; and by definition, those units remaining as a permanent fixture for the organization appear more costly. According to McKinley, this perceived cost reduction gained from outsourcing increases the preference to outsource and can consequently become the driving force for a series of outsourcings and downsizings. This, then, is an example of how an emphasis on certain approaches toward business strategy that are spread through business education can come to play a role in rationalizing downsizing as a legitimate activity.

---

[36] McKinley, Sanchez, & Schick, 1995.

[37] Evans, M.G., Gunz, H.P., & Jalland, R.M. (1997). Implications of organizational downsizing for managerial careers. *Canadian Journal of Administrative Sciences, 14,* 359–371.

[38] McKinley, Sanchez, & Schick, 1995.

CHAPTER SUMMARY

You will remember that contingency theory asserts that organizations continually adapt to "fit" the environment. This implies that organizations will respond to changes in economic and environmental conditions by looking for alternatives to the traditional hierarchical organizational structure. Recent years have been marked by increasing threats to the survival of many organizations stemming from sources such as technological change, global competition, and the emergence of a knowledge-based economy. And in response to these threats, many organizations have attempted to redesign and initiate fundamental changes in their organizational forms and management practices. According to many observers, the accumulation of changes in the organizational environment has demanded a shift in thinking with regard to organizational design. This shift has involved the movement away from the traditional, large, rigid, bureaucratic structure. Current practices now include reengineering, outsourcing, going virtual, and downsizing.

CHAPTER LEARNING TOOLS

Key Terms

centralization 128

cloning forces 154

closed systems 126

constraining forces 153

contingency theory 133

corporate memory 151

cross-functional teams 121

decentralization 128

delayering 120

downsizing 145

dynamic environment 133

environmental uncertainty 133

formalization 130

functional specialization 128

horizontal differentiation 127

information sharing 121

institutionalization theory 152

keiretsu 123

learning forces 154

machine metaphor (of an organization) 125

mechanistic organizations 131

networking 143

nonroutine technology 132

open systems 126

organic organizations 131

organism metaphor (of an organization) 125

organizational structure 127

outsourcing 140

reengineering 136

routine technology 132

self-managing work teams 121

social specialization 128

span of control 129

specialization 128

static environment 132

systems theory 133

vertical differentiation 129

virtual organization 140

worker empowerment 128

workforce reduction 145

Multiple-Choice Questions

Select the *best* answer for each of the following questions. Solutions are located in the back of your textbook.

1. A traditional bureaucracy is often
   a. rule-oriented
   b. tall/hierarchical
   c. buffered from the environment
   d. all of the above

2. *Keiretsu* means
   a. networking of major enterprises
   b. globalization
   c. modern bureaucracy
   d. self-managing work teams

3. An organization is
   a. a social entity
   b. goal-directed
   c. both A and B
   d. none of the above

4. The "machine metaphor" refers to
   a. organizations that function in a rational manner
   b. the behavioural school of thought
   c. both A and B
   d. none of the above

5. Closed systems require
   a. ongoing interaction with their environment
   b. no interaction with their environment
   c. dependence on exchanges with the environment
   d. some interaction with their environment

6. Division of labour refers to
   a. the degree of which tasks are divided into separate jobs
   b. diversity within organizations
   c. both A and B
   d. none of the above

7. Social specialization is
   a. the specialization of individuals
   b. the specialization of jobs
   c. when jobs are routinized
   d. both A and B

8. Two levels of job specialization are
   a. top and bottom
   b. manager and staff level
   c. professional and blue-collar
   d. functional and social

9. When decision making rests at the top of the organization, it is said to be
   a. compromised   b. decentralized
   c. centralized   d. both A and C

10. A wide span of control reflects a
   a. flat organization
   b. tall organization

   c. wide organization
   d. narrow organization

11. A high level of formalization means work
   a. is highly standardized
   b. has clear rules on how it is to be performed
   c. is flexible and not standardized
   d. both A and B

12. Google's flexible work arrangements and push for creativity make Google's structure more likely to be
   a. mechanistic
   b. organic
   c. highly formalized
   d. centralized

13. Custom-made furniture or genetic research is work that typically uses
   a. nonroutine technology
   b. routine technology
   c. assembly-line technology
   d. formalized technology

14. An environment that undergoes much change or uncertainty is said to be a(n)
   a. dynamic environment
   b. static environment
   c. adaptive environment
   d. resistant environment

15. Reengineering often involves
   a. a rethinking of the organization's structure and functions
   b. a radical redesign of the organization's processes and structure
   c. the goal to achieve dramatic improvements
   d. all of the above

Discussion Questions

1. Explain the differences between a traditional bureaucracy and a modern organization.

2. Describe three broad categories of organizations.

3. Provide a definition of an organization and explain four characteristics of what an organization is.

4. Compare and contrast mechanistic and organic organizations.

5. Compare and contrast open systems and closed systems.

6. What are four defining elements of organizational structure?

7. What characteristics determine organizational structure?

8. Why is contingency theory important in studying organizations?

9. What are the benefits and challenges of having a virtual organization?

10. Discuss the potential benefits and risks of downsizing.

CONCEPT APPLICATION   PIXAR: NO MICKEY MOUSE ORGANIZATION!

In 1995, a little company called Pixar presented the world with the very first fully computer-animated movie. It was called *Toy Story* and it received both critical acclaim and $29 million in box-office receipts. Since that time Pixar has become one of the most successful animation studios in movie history.

Behind every amazing creation there is an even greater creator: Dr. Ed Catmull. Ed Catmull, with a vast education in the field of computer sciences and a passion for animation, revolutionized the way films are made. Not only has Pixar broken ground in the field of computer graphics and animation but it has also proven itself to be an exemplary organization.

Step by step Catmull built his empire. In the beginning there were the commercials and short films that would eventually get the attention of the former head of Disney's animation unit, Peter Schneider. Taken with the creative ability and talent seen in the ads and short films by John Lasseter, a ground-breaking animator, Disney sponsored a full-length feature by Pixar, including expenses and even some production people. Schneider saw this as a worthwhile and low-risk investment. The hard work obviously paid off because, just as Schneider predicted, the backing of a full-length feature proved to be a wise choice as *Toy Story* and its followup, *A Bug's Life*, went above and beyond what anyone could have hoped for. And these were just a preview of the blockbusters that Pixar would produce shortly after, such as *Finding Nemo* and *The Incredibles*.

Ed Catmull's vast array of talents was responsible for the creation of such a strong animation studio. Making animated films, particularly the 3-D computer-generated kind, is more like software design than it is live-action filmmaking. Cartoon editing takes place simultaneously with the storyboard process. As the script is mapped out into scenes that are then drawn and animated, the cartoons and individual scenes are fine tuned. For example, Nemo, the loveable clownfish, may have stripes added or removed from his scaly orange skin. This collaborative editing is comparable to the way programmers optimize features in a piece of software. Differences between live-action films and animated ones lie in their procedural organization.

An animated film benefits from having the same team work together many times, and collaboration is a must. By way of collaboration and the freedom to be flexible, computer animation studios already possess inherent qualities necessary for a successful corporation. According to Catmull, it is important to allow risk taking to unleash creativity:

> Well, the first thing to note is that we're supposed to be taking risks, so we don't think of risk management as trying to minimize risk. That's actually the way to prevent creativity. Rather, it's to do risky things, and then when they go in some unpredicted path, to be able to respond to it. So our job as managers is to create not only a community but a way that that community works together, so they can solve the problems that are coming up that are unforeseen. If you've got the good community, they will solve these problems. So for us, it's clear, it's building the community and putting elements in place so that community is vibrant and healthy.[39]

---

[39] HBR IdeaCast. (2008, August 28). Pixar and collective creativity. *HBR Blog Network, Pixar and Collective Creativity.* Retrieved from http://blogs.hbr.org/ideacast/2008/08/harvard-business-ideacast-109.html.

Case Continued >

Catmull's Pixar creation consists largely of just three equal groups that are consistently working together to achieve the organization's impressive goals. To begin with, there is the technology development group, which is generally responsible for the supply of computer-graphics tools. The creative development group conceives of and animates the stories and characters. And the production group coordinates the entire filmmaking process. Aside from the crucial aspect of communication and collaboration, the freedom given to each group to work directly with one another and avoid going through higher-ups was almost ground-breaking at the time. This, in effect, attracted organizations such as the US Navy to send their organizational experts into Pixar and take notes on how to improve their own organizations.

Animated films have always used technology, even in Disney's earlier days. Today, artists' easels have been replaced by computers, and Pixar has a small army of employees whose jobs consist of ambitiously inventing and innovating technology to improve the appeal and increase efficiency throughout the company. In its consistent efforts to develop, Pixar has created a motivational flow and balance between art and technology, where creativity in art provokes advances in technology, and advances in technology inspire the art.[40]

Questions

1. Do you think that Pixar most closely resembles an organic or a mechanistic structure? Why?

2. Describe the nature of Pixar's "contingencies" and explain how they influence the suitability of Pixar's structure.

3. How could Pixar be redesigned as a virtual organization?

---

[40] Based on Schlender, B. (2004, November 15). The man who built Pixar's incredible innovation machine. *Fortune, 150*(10), 206–210.

Chapter 5
Business Strategy
How Do Businesses Generate a Successful Strategy?

Bloomberg via Getty Images

The ability to respond effectively to the business environment is the fundamental challenge of strategic management. How does a business create and sustain its competitive advantage? One of the fundamental internal forces that organizations must address is the issue of strategy. This chapter examines the nature and role of strategic management and the challenges it presents. We will also explore the importance of understanding the nature of an organization's specific industry.

Learning Objectives

After studying this chapter, you should be able to

1. Describe the nature of strategic management.
2. Identify key forces in determining an industry's structure.
3. Describe how organizational resources and capabilities affect firm performance.
4. Describe three generic business strategies.
5. Explain the nature of corporate strategy.

THE BUSINESS WORLD

Tim Hortons: Is Its Strategy "Always Fresh"?

Did you know that coffee is the second most consumed beverage in Canada, next to water, for individuals 25 years of age or older? Clearly that is a fact that Tim Hortons is very well aware of.

As of 2013, Tim Hortons was the largest publicly traded restaurant chain in Canada and among the largest in North America. From 2007 through 2011, total revenues rose at an annual rate of 8.7%, and earnings per share grew by 13.2%.[1] It has also commanded about 80% of the $3 billion "away-from-home" coffee market in Canada.[2] That is a lot of coffee!

Tim Hortons certainly has a heavy presence in Canada. There are more than 3,000 Tim Hortons restaurants across the country. Among areas for potential expansion are Quebec and Western Canada, which may well permit Tim Hortons to soon reach its goal of 4,000 restaurants. It also has over 700 locations in the United States, and in recent years it has attempted to initiate overseas markets, including the Middle East.[3]

According to marketing experts, Tim Hortons's success is based on the ability of its restaurants to be efficient, dependable (that is, always open), places for community-based conversations (particularly in small towns), friendly, and of course value conscious.[4] In addition to regular restaurants, Tim Hortons locations can also be found in shopping malls, highway outlets, universities, and hospitals. And in some locations there is also a 24-hour drive-thru service. In 1995, Tim Hortons merged with Wendy's International, Inc., giving momentum to the expansion of Tim Hortons in the United States. The Canadian operations are 95% franchise owned, and the company is working toward implementing that strategy in the United States as expansion progresses.

The Tim Hortons chain was first established in 1964 in Hamilton, Ontario. With its humble beginnings of offering only two products (coffee and donuts), the menu has expanded considerably over the years. Way back in 1976, Tim Hortons unveiled its biggest change in the chain's product focus—the hugely successful Timbit (a bite-sized donut hole). Growth through the 1980s brought about more new product introductions, including muffins (1981), cakes (1981), pies (1982), croissants (1983), cookies (1984), and soups and chili (1985). Yet more variety followed in the 1990s with the introduction of sandwiches, flavoured cappuccino (1997), café mocha (1999), and iced cappuccino (1999). While the 2000s saw yet more menu expansion, the company's biggest attraction

[1] Heinzl, J. (2013, January 11). Why I'll buy Tim Hortons as other investors bail. *Globe and Mail*. Retrieved from www.theglobeandmail.com/globe-investor/investor-community/trading-shots/why-ill-buy-tim-hortons-as-other-investors-bail/article7177472.

[2] Tedesco, T. (2013, February 25). Rivals' attack on Tim Hortons in morning market forces menu shakeup. *Financial Post*. Retrieved from http://business.financialpost.com/2013/02/25/rivals-attack-of-tim-hortons-in-morning-market-forces-shakeup/.

[3] Keith, D. (2013, January 8). Falling out of love with Tim Hortons. *Globe and Mail*. Retrieved from www.theglobeandmail.com/globe-investor/investor-community/trading-shots/falling-out-of-love-with-tim-hortons/article7001460.

[4] Blackshaw, P. (2008, July 14). What Starbucks can learn from a Canadian competitor. *Ad Age Digital*. Retrieved from http://adage.com/article/digital-columns/starbucks-learn-a-canadian-competitor/129607.

continues to be its coffee. And Tim Hortons also continues to grow its sales and profits by expanding into such premium offerings as lattes and panini sandwiches.[5]

Tim Hortons has been a Canadian icon for years (ranking right up there with hockey and maple syrup). However, while its brand resonates strongly among Canadian consumers, skeptics still question its future prosperity. As Theresa Tedesco bluntly stated in the *Financial Post*:

> For the first time in its history, Tim Hortons is facing stiff competition from rivals—mostly Americans accustomed to grinding ground wars in the quick-serve restaurant business—with deep pockets who are aggressively contending for a slice of the profitable morning market.[6]

Clearly, the coffee industry has never been so fierce.

McDonald's, the US fast-food giant, has been spending $1 billion in recent years to establish and renovate 1,400 McCafés in Canada. For the past few years, McDonald's has been moving steadily into Tim Hortons's domain since it began offering free cups of coffee at selected times in its newly renovated stores, which are beginning to resemble a neighbourhood café.[7]

Similarly, Starbucks has added over 100 cafés recently. In fact, in 2012 Starbucks announced plans to open its first coffee shop in a rather unlikely location—a South Carolina funeral home. While there are significantly more Tim Hortons locations in Canada compared to Starbucks, almost all of Canada's major cities have a few neighbourhoods with more Starbucks than Tim Hortons. However, once you move outside of the urban core, Tim Hortons still tends to be the favourite.

Tim Hortons remains a formidable force in this industry. Its iconic "Roll Up the Rim to Win" contest continues to resonate with Canadians every year. As competition further intensifies, it will be interesting to see how Tim Hortons responds. And competitors in the coffee industry are everywhere, it seems. While, Starbucks, Second Cup, and Timothy's are coffeehouses that directly compete with Tim Hortons, other less direct competitors also exist. There are the basic convenience stores such as 7-Eleven or gas station outlets such as On the Run, which also conveniently sell you coffee when you are on the go.

According to *Financial Post* writer Theresa Tedesco:

> Feeling the squeeze from rivals, and facing a new breed of consumer demanding value-for-money products but willing to pay more for small luxuries, Tim Hortons is at a crossroad . . . The challenge will be to entice a new, younger generation of customers . . . Thus, the menu additions: grilled panini, breakfast sandwiches, healthy wraps, espresso-based specialty coffees (café lattes and cappuccinos), blended beverages and smoothies . . . Preferably, the 18 to 24 age crowd who are more inclined to pay for expensive non-coffee blended beverages and healthier food choices, and are less likely to nurse the same cup of brewed coffee for hours.[8]

---

[5] Tim Hortons. (n.d.). The history of Tim Hortons. Retrieved from www.timhortons.com/us/en/about/media-history.html.

[6] Tedesco, 2013.

[7] Tedesco, 2013.

[8] Tedesco, 2013.

So if you are Tim Hortons, what do you do to retain your customers and attract more? Some Tim Hortons restaurants instituted wireless services to attract more customers. The company also super-sized its coffee cups, appealing to those who need that extra caffeine fix. Some drive-thrus have been renovated to process more vehicles in less time. In a typical Tim Hortons restaurant, you can now can buy its fresh ground coffee in tins or purchase other items like specially branded mugs. Indeed, there is more required in this industry then just selling a cup of coffee.

The increasing pressure from rivals is forcing Tim Hortons to revisit its traditional strategy that helped it generate profits for decades. For example, it recently shook up its corporate ranks with dozens of its 2,000 corporate staff being terminated. It also recently began decentralizing functions to prepare for international growth. Given that McDonald's spent $1 billion renovating its Canadian restaurants, Tim Hortons followed suit by increasing its renovation efforts and doubling the number of stores being remodelled.

In Canada, Tim Hortons can surely build upon its brand recognition. According to James Cowan of *Maclean's* magazine,

> It took 27 years for Tim Hortons to open its first 500 outlets. Over that time, the brand built an emotional connection with Canadians, supporting charities, backing amateur hockey teams and serving as the default community centre for many small towns. Perhaps most importantly, the brand was unabashedly patriotic, from its hockey rink-laden advertising to its support of Canadian troops in Afghanistan. Underneath the folksy, homespun image is a finely calibrated brand identity, one that's earned notice from both *Ad Age* magazine and the Reputation Institute.[9]

But this Canadian identity is meaningless in the United States and other international markets. Tim Hortons's expansion into the United States has not been as successful as it hoped. The company needs help in developing an effective strategy to expand further to gain new customers in other markets.

In 2010, Tim Hortons was forced to close 36 stores in the New England region. And in 2012, only 22 new coffee shops were opened in the United States. Can Tim Hortons remain a low-cost coffee shop, or is differentiating its product further the way to go? The coffee industry is still a hot market in Canada. Will consumers keep "rolling up the rim"? If Tim Hortons can keep its strategy as fresh as its coffee, then the answer is a resounding yes!

WHAT IS STRATEGIC MANAGEMENT?

Objective 1 Describe the nature of strategic management.

strategic management
An ongoing process that requires managers of a firm to constantly analyze their external and internal environments, make decisions about what kinds of strategies they should pursue, implement the strategies, and evaluate the outcomes to make any changes, if necessary, in order to create and sustain its competitive advantages.

Strategic management consists of the analysis, decisions, implementations, and evaluations a firm undertakes to create and sustain its competitive advantages. As such, strategic management can be an ongoing process where managers of a firm constantly analyze their external and internal environments, make decisions about what kinds of strategies they should pursue, implement the strategies, and evaluate the outcomes to make any changes if necessary. The ongoing process of strategic management is critical to firm performance and survival in that an effective process of strategic management can allow a firm to sustain its competitive advantage, which in turn enhances its performance and chances of survival.

[9] Cowan, J. (2013, February 20). Why Tim Hortons can't rroll into the United States. *Maclean's Magazine*. Reprinted with permission from Maclean's Magazine.

But what is strategy? Most can agree that much of the success of Walmart, Canadian Tire, or other highly profitable corporations can be attributed in part to the strategies these firms have pursued. However, there is no consensus on how to actually define the concept of a firm's strategy. Some definitions are long and complex; others are deceptively simple. Throughout this chapter, *strategy* is defined as the plans made or the actions taken in an effort to help an organization obtain its intended purposes. Such a definition corresponds with our definition of strategic management, where managers assess their external and internal environments to plan and take actions to pursue organizational goals, either short term or long term. Putting both strategy and strategic management together, a firm can be viewed as a goal-directed entity. By and large, the goals of most publicly traded firms are normally to maximize shareholder returns through various means.

Although strategy is goal-directed, it can sometimes unintentionally evolve with either the internal or external environment. Henry Mintzberg argues that, due to the unpredictability of environments, managers in organizations cannot thoroughly plan out any strategy that would achieve the long-term goals of their firms. As such, some strategies would never be carried out, and managers would pursue strategies that they had not planned at the beginning of the strategic management process. For example, a number of years ago, the SARS outbreak in Canada led firms in the hospitality industry to pursue many different strategies to win back tourists, including cutting prices and seeking financial and nonfinancial supports from provincial governments. The unexpected outbreak forced managers in these firms to change their strategies in response to a decline in their performance. Another example is Microsoft's entry to the Internet browser market (with Internet Explorer), which was not planned by its top management team—it was an idea forwarded by one of its software engineers.

In the next two sections we will survey different approaches to strategy analysis, which is often the first stage of strategic management. Throughout this chapter, we will discuss different types of strategies and how to implement the strategies that are identified in the early stages of the strategic management process.

ANALYZING THE EXTERNAL ENVIRONMENT

Objective 2 Identify key forces in determining an industry's structure.

In this section, we will be focusing on five major groups associated with an industry's external environment. Before we look at each group in depth, however, we first need to define industry. Although **industry** has been defined in many different ways, the definition used throughout this chapter is a group of organizations that share similar resource requirements. The resource requirements range from raw materials to labour to technology to customers. For example, Air Canada, WestJet, Porter Airlines, and Air Transat operate in the airline industry, where the four airline carriers share similar technology (aircrafts), labour (flight attendants), and customers (people who prefer air transportation). FedEx and UPS, however, are not in the airline industry because the customers those two companies serve are different from those of Air Canada, WestJet, Porter Airlines, and Air Transat, even though all of them share similar technology (aircrafts).

industry A group of organizations that share similar resource requirements, including raw materials, labour, technology, and customers.

The Five-Forces Model

How can we systematically analyze the industry environment? Michael Porter drew upon research from industrial organization economics to propose a powerful, prescriptive model

Exhibit 5.1 Forces Driving Competition within an Industry

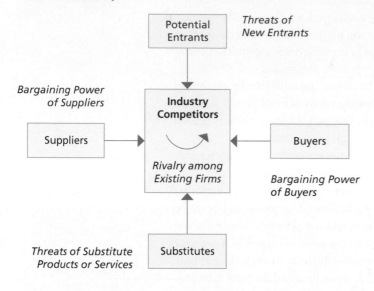

known as the **five-forces model,**[10] which allows us to systematically assess the industry environment. The thrust of the model is that the relationships between these five forces and the incumbent firms (those already in the market) determine the attractiveness of the industry environment, which in turn helps us make strategic decisions about how to achieve organizational goals or to find a position in the industry where we can best defend ourselves against competition. The five forces include threats of new entrants, bargaining power of suppliers, bargaining power of customers, threats of substitute products or services, and rivalry among existing firms (see Exhibit 5.1). These forces can either independently or jointly affect the attractiveness of the industry. Let's examine each force in more detail.

Threats of New Entrants
New entrants can take two basic forms: new startups and diversification of existing firms in other industries. Regardless, the entrants bring new capacities, desire to gain market share, and substantial resources and capabilities. Prices can be bid down or incumbents' costs inflated as a result, reducing profitability. As such, the new entrants may impose significant threats to incumbents. Thus, incumbents need to consider how to create entry barriers to deter potential new entrants. There are five major sources of entry barriers from the potential new entrants' point of view.

five-forces model A prescriptive model developed by Michael Porter (1980) that allows for the systematic assessment of the industry environment. The five forces include the threats of new entrants, the bargaining power of suppliers, the bargaining power of the buyers, the threats of substitutes, and rivalry among existing firms.

economies of scale Spreading the costs of production over the number of units produced, which can provide incumbent firms with cost advantages that create a barrier to entry for new entrants.

Economies of Scale Economies of scale refer to spreading the costs of production over the number of units produced. The cost of a product per unit declines as the number of units per period increases. From the new entrants' point of view, the entry barrier is increased (and the threat of new entrants is reduced) when incumbents enjoy the benefits of economies of scale. Economies of scale can provide the incumbents with cost advantages to compete with new entrants on the price, if necessary. Global companies, for example, that sell their goods in various countries often achieve economies of scale because of the high volume of products they produce. The food industry is one example that is becoming increasingly global, as seen in Talking Business 5.1.

Capital Requirements For some industries, such as the airline and mining industries, the required capital to establish a new firm is significant. Accordingly, the level of required capital for entering certain industries creates barriers for potential new entrants. Thus, the threat of new entrants is reduced as the level of required capital increases.

switching costs The costs, both monetary and psychological, associated with changing from one supplier to another from a buyer's perspective.

Switching Costs Switching costs refer to the costs (monetary or psychological) associated with changing from one supplier to another from the buyer's perspective. When the switching costs are minimal, customers can easily switch buying products from one firm to another. This creates an opportunity for potential new entrants because they can easily acquire customers from incumbents. Thus, the threat of new entrants increases (or the barrier to new entrants decreases) as the switching costs decrease.

---

[10] Porter, M.E. (1980). *Competitive Strategy*. New York, NY: Free Press.

Changes in Global Food Sector Call for Canadian Food Strategy

Food is in demand like never before—and today much of the world can afford what Canada produces.

The food sector is facing a dramatic shift in its customer base as globalization, population patterns, and demographics reshape where food companies will find growth opportunities in the coming decades.

All of the features of globalization—integration, competition, innovation, specialization and economies of scale—affect the food sector. But the food sector is not uniformly or equally integrated into the global economy. With rising international trade in food, nations face competing pressures to open their markets and go global themselves, or protect their domestic markets.

Canada's Good Fortune

Human history has often been driven by food and famine. Fortunately, Canada is a food-rich country—it has almost always been able to produce more food than it needs, and famine has been virtually unknown. Moreover, the food Canadians eat is relatively inexpensive. The share of income Canadians allocate to food has steadily declined: today it is among the lowest in the developed world.

Dramatic increases in commodity prices in 2007–08, and again in 2010, illustrate Canada's good fortune. Analysis by UBS has found that Canada is among the countries likely to suffer the least from higher food prices. Over the course of 2008, food prices in Canada increased by an average of 3.9 per cent versus the previous year. Europeans saw food prices rise 7.1 per cent, while Americans paid 5.9 per cent more and China's food prices rose a full 22 per cent.

Food Companies Are Global Players

The past 10 years have seen an increased consolidation across the food sector. Today, some of the largest companies in the world are involved in the food business. The activities of these globally active companies affect international supply chains and the operation of food economies around the world.

The Canadian food sector is also increasingly global. Globally oriented food companies from Canada are increasing their global reach in three key ways:

- investing in or buying facilities around the world,
- investing in their domestic facilities to capture global economies of scale, and
- extending their supply chains to allow them to source products and resources around the world.

However, our relatively small, slow-growing population means that the potential for domestic growth is limited. Companies seeking to expand must either seize domestic market share or focus on growing their businesses through exports. The latter presents the greatest opportunity. Canada's food sector exports are worth over $38 billion annually—with the potential to go much higher as global demand continues to surge. Over half go to the United States, with Japan, China, Europe, and Mexico rounding out the top five food export destinations.

Apart from protected supply-managed industries, Canada's food sector is highly integrated into the global market. Between 1999 and 2008, Canada's export share of world food trade was consistently around 5.5 per cent. During these years, Canada was the fourth-largest food exporter in the world after the U.S., the European Union, and Brazil.

Significant growth in the food sector of emerging economies, including China and Brazil—along with major reforms in food exporting countries such as Australia and New Zealand—are creating competitive advantages in these countries. The ability and willingness of the Canadian food sector to invest in global integration will significantly determine whether Canadian firms can compete on a global scale.

The canola industry provides a good example of an agrifood industry scaled to service both domestic and global markets. According to the Canola Council of Canada, the canola industry in Canada includes over 50,000 canola growers and 13 processing plants in five provinces. The canola industry was created through the effective commercialization and adoption of a new crop developed through scientific research carried out in Canada. The lesson from canola is that there is room in the other parts of the food sector for profitable corporate innovation, scale, and

(continued)

growth. If they set out to target global markets, Canadian industries can successfully compete in global markets by creating efficient and profitable businesses: Canadian food firms can be world leaders.

Beyond entering markets, however, Canada does not appear to have a strategic overall goal for its food sector. In contrast to countries like the United Kingdom, Brazil, and Australia, there have been limited efforts to craft a national plan for the food sector. Rather, Canada's food sector operates in crop- or sector-specific silos.

The food sector is in a unique position. On the one hand, aspects of food are highly integrated and involve complex relationships and supply chains around the world. On the other, aspects of the sector are intensely rooted in local communities.

If well managed, Canada's agricultural land will continue to keep it a food-rich country through food grown and processed in the country. What is needed to grow the sector is a Canadian Food Strategy that places a premium on enhancing opportunities for trade created through our food exports and the diversity of foods imported to Canada.

Source: Excerpted from Bloom, M. (2012, June 20). Changes in global food sector call for Canadian food strategy. Reprinted with permission from The Conference Board of Canada. Retrieved from www.conferenceboard.ca/press/speech_oped/12-06-20/changes_in_global_food_sector_call_for_canadian_food_strategy.aspx.

Access to Distribution Channels   Accessibility to distribution channels can be an entry barrier for potential new entrants. In the situation where incumbents control most of the distribution channels, potential entrants would find it difficult to distribute their products or services, which in turn defers new entry. Accordingly, the threat of new entrants decreases (or the barrier to new entrants increases) as accessibility to distribution channels decreases.

Cost Disadvantages Independent of Scale   The prior four sources are primarily associated with economic factors. However, sometimes advantages that some incumbents hold over potential entrants are independent of economic factors. Such advantages include governmental policies, legal protection (patents and trademarks), and proprietary products. These advantages create barriers for potential new entrants, which defer their entries.

bargaining power of suppliers
The power held by firms, organizations, and individuals that provide raw materials, technologies, or skills to incumbents in an industry. Suppliers can exert power by demanding better prices or threatening to reduce the quality of purchase goods or services.

Bargaining Power of Suppliers   When considering the **bargaining power of suppliers**, our focus is on the firms, organizations, and individuals that provide raw materials, technologies, or skills to incumbents in an industry. Suppliers can exert bargaining power over incumbents by demanding better prices or threatening to reduce the quality of purchased goods or services. Therefore, the power suppliers hold directly impacts industry profitability as well as the incumbents' performance.

There are two major factors contributing to suppliers' power in relation to incumbents in an industry. The first one is how critical the resources are to the incumbents that the supplier holds. Quite often, when the raw materials suppliers provide are critical to incumbents in an industry, the suppliers are in a good position to demand better prices. The second factor is the number of suppliers available relative to the number of incumbents in an industry. Specifically, when the number of suppliers relative to the number of incumbents is low, the incumbents compete against each other for the relatively small number of suppliers. As such, this gives suppliers power in that they have opportunities to negotiate better prices among incumbents. These two factors can independently contribute to supplier powers—and suppliers will have the highest power when these factors couple together.

Looking at the personal computer manufacturing industry, for example, there are many incumbents, like Dell, Hewlett-Packard, IBM, and others. However, there are only two major firms, Intel and AMD, that supply the processor chips. Thus, the suppliers hold significant bargaining power over computer manufacturers because the processor chips are critical components of personal computers, and there are only two firms that supply this key component.

Bargaining Power of Buyers   When we consider the **bargaining power of buyers**, our attention focuses on the power held by individuals or organizations that purchase incumbents' products or services. Buyers can affect industry performance by demanding lower prices, demanding better quality or services, or playing incumbents against one another. These actions can erode industry profitability as well as firm performance. There are many factors contributing to buyer power in relation to incumbents in an industry, some of which are outlined here.

Switching Costs   Similar to the role of switching costs in the threat of new entrants, the bargaining power of buyers increases as switching costs decrease. Specifically, when buyers can easily switch incumbents with little cost in terms of products or services, the incumbents would have little power over the buyers to enhance their performance.

Undifferentiated Products   Relatedly, when incumbents provide similar products or services to buyers, they would not be in a good position to negotiate with the buyers. Undifferentiated products allow buyers to find alternatives from other incumbents. This situation can also provide an opportunity for buyers to play incumbents against each other to get a better price, quality, or service.

Importance of Incumbents' Products to Buyers   Similar to our discussion on bargaining power of suppliers, when products or services that incumbents offer are important or critical to buyers, the power of buyers would be diminished.

The Number of Incumbents Relative to the Number of Buyers   The bargaining power of buyers could be diminished when there are relatively few incumbents offering the products or services that the buyers need, since the buyers do not have many alternatives to choose from.

Looking at grocery retailers in Canada, for instance, Loblaw, Metro, Sobey's, and others are the key players in the industry. They are the buyers in relation to the grocery producers. The grocery producers do not hold significant bargaining power over these retailers because the number of producers is relatively high compared to the number of retailers, the switching costs for retailers are minimal, and the degree of differentiation among producers is relatively low. As such, the retailers enjoy significant bargaining power over the grocery producers.

Threats of Substitutes   All firms in an industry often compete with other firms in different industries, where the firms provide substitute products or services with similar purposes. For example, the traditional form of newspapers faces substitutes that include the Internet, radio stations, television stations, and so on. Such substitutes would gain newspaper subscribers and advertising revenues that might have belonged to the newspaper industry. As such, they threaten the profitability of the newspaper industry as a whole.

Rivalry among Existing Firms   The final force that affects industry structure is rivalry. The rivalry among incumbents in an industry can take many different forms.

bargaining power of buyers
The power held by individuals or organizations that purchase incumbents' products or services. Buyers can exert power by demanding lower prices, demanding better quality or services, or playing incumbents against one another.

For example, Canadian insurance providers compete against each other by using different strategic actions, including cutting prices, providing new insurance products, improving operational efficiency, advertising, and through mergers and acquisitions. More broadly, rivalry can be intensified by several interacting factors.

Lack of Differentiation or Switching Costs   When products are not significantly differentiated or switching costs are minimal, customer choices are often based on price and service. Under this situation, incumbents may experience pressure to launch more strategic actions in an attempt to attract more customers or keep existing customers by enhancing the company's short-term performance. Accordingly, the rivalry among incumbents is intensified.

Numerous or Equally Balanced Competitors   When there are many incumbents in an industry, the likelihood of mavericks is great. Some firms may believe that they can initiate strategic action without being noticed. As such, their strategic action intensifies the rivalry among incumbents. In addition, the rivalry between firms tends to be highest when the firms are similar in size and resources because they often target similar market niches and share similar resource requirements.

High Exit Barriers   **Exit barriers** refer to economic, strategic, and emotional factors that keep firms competing even though they may be earning low or negative returns on their investments. Examples of exit barriers include visible fixed costs, specialized assets, escalating commitment of management, and government and social pressures.

exit barriers The economic, strategic, and emotional factors that keep firms competing even though they may be earning low or negative returns on their investments.

Overall, the five-forces model provides managers with an assessment of the industry structure to help get some sense of industry attractiveness. Specifically, from the potential entrant's point of view, the five-forces model helps it understand the potential competitive environment of the industry and to make the entry decision. From the incumbent's point of view, the model helps managers assess their position in the industry relative to their rivals. Sometimes, it also provides an overall picture of industry attractiveness to allow managers to make any exit decisions.

Limitations of the Five-Forces Model   Each model has its limitations, however. Although the five-forces model offers a powerful tool for managers to examine an industry's attractiveness, it exhibits some shortcomings. First, the model does not explicitly take the roles of technological change and governmental regulations and how these affect the power relationships between forces into consideration.

Second, the focus of this model is primarily on the power relationships between each force at a given point in time. As such, it may have limited implications for future strategic decision making.

Finally, the model assumes that all incumbents experience the same power relationship with each force. However, incumbents differ in terms of their resources and firm size, which can give them more or less power in influencing their suppliers or customers.

Given the above limitations, to gain a precise assessment of an industry, managers need to use the model with great caution. Specifically, they need to anticipate the effects of technological change, governmental regulations, and industry trends on industry structure and their firm's position in the industry (see Talking Business 5.2).

Foresight and Innovation: Today's Science Fiction, Tomorrow's Reality?

Inspiration and creativity are key ingredients in the innovation process. In many ways, you need to be able to envision what your future customer is going to need if you want to create a successful innovation. To understand the needs of future customers, many organizations are turning to foresight and other futures-related techniques.

Foresight does not aim to predict the future. It utilizes a combination of emerging trends and drivers, as well as some creativity in visualising how these trends and drivers interact, to create plausible alternate futures. The resulting process can generate insights into future needs and demands, creating a competitive advantage for innovative organizations.

There are a variety of ways of presenting these alternate futures, with scenarios being one of the most popular choices. The power of the narrative around a scenario is that it makes it easier for us to visualise the future and the potential customer needs in a given scenario. It is this power of the future narrative that Intel is using to drive innovation.

Intel is the sponsor of the Tomorrow Project, which aims to "explore our possible futures through fact-based, science-based fiction". They have published a series of short stories about the future, looking at potential futures we want as well as those we may wish to avoid. The project has engaged science fiction authors as well as engineers amongst others, to provide their visions of the future. They have also partnered with Arc, *New Scientist* magazine's futures publication, "so that we can have a conversation about the future and these conversations make dramatic changes". These products are generating rich pictures about the future and what it could look and feel like.

Intel employs a resident Futurist, Brian David Johnson, whose role is to help it understand the future and the products it will need for tomorrow's consumer. As part of this effort, Intel also stumbled onto another insight about technology innovation—the need to understand what people will want from technology in the future. Competition from companies like ARM has brought on the realization that simply having a faster or technically superior chip is not enough. Success for future products will be dependent on making sure that they meet future customer needs. Intel uses highly trained cultural anthropologists and ethnographers to build an understanding of the future state of culture in addition to technological trends. They are building pictures of how people use technology in the future to understand how their marketplace could evolve. In combination, the science fiction narratives and cultural understanding are being used to provide actionable technical innovation strategies for the company.

Intel is one of a growing number of organizations harnessing the power of foresight to envision the future and use it as a platform for driving innovation. This approach has even been used by a number of governments across the world, such as the United Kingdom and Singapore. This combination of foresight and cultural awareness provides some very useful tools for understanding the needs of the customer of the future and generating competitive advantage through successful innovation.

Source: Excerpted from Kabilan, S. (2013, April 15). Foresight and innovation: Today's science fiction, tomorrow's reality? Reprinted with permission from The Conference Board of Canada. Retrieved from www.conferenceboard.ca/commentaries/technologyinnovation/default/13-04-15/foresight_and_innovation_today_s_science_fiction_tomorrow_s_reality.aspx.

ANALYZING THE INTERNAL ENVIRONMENT

After discussing how to analyze the industry environment, let's look at strategy analysis from another viewpoint—the internal environment. Indeed, research shows that the effects of the industry environment on firm performance are smaller than those of a firm's internal environment. Furthermore, if we look at all firms in an industry, we will see that some firms are doing much better than others. This implies that how managers organize firm resources and capabilities plays a critical role in firm performance and survival. In order for managers to effectively do this, they need to know what kinds of resources and capabilities the firm has in the

Objective 3 Describe how organizational resources and capabilities affect firm performance.

VRIO model A model that examines an individual firm's value, rareness, imitability, and organization to determine its relative strengths in comparison to its competitors in the industry.

first place. Jay Barney provides a prescriptive **VRIO model** (value, rareness, imitability, organization) that can help managers examine the resources and capabilities in a systematic way.[11] Before we discuss the model, we will first talk about what resources and capabilities are.

A firm's **resources and capabilities** include all of the financial, physical, human, and organizational assets used by the firm to develop, manufacture, and deliver products or services to its customers. **Financial resources** include debt, equity, retained earnings, and so forth. **Physical resources** include the machines, production facilities, and buildings firms use in their operations. **Human resources** include all the experience, knowledge, judgment, risk-taking propensity, and wisdom of individuals associated with a firm. **Organizational resources** include the history, relationships, trust, and organizational culture that permeates a firm, along with a firm's formal reporting structure, management control systems, and compensation policies.

The VRIO Model

Jay Barney suggests that managers need to look inside their firms for competitive advantage. That is, for a firm to achieve high performance, managers need to look at their resources and capabilities and examine four important questions: (1) the question of value (V); (2) the question of rareness (R); (3) the question of imitability (1); and (4) the question of organization (0).

The Question of Value
Managers need to ask if their firm's resources and capabilities add any value to the market that would allow them to capture market share or enhance profitability, either through exploiting emerging opportunities or neutralizing threats. Some firms do have such resources and capabilities. For example, Starbucks, a global coffee chain, attracts customers by providing high-quality coffee in a relaxing coffeehouse atmosphere. Its capability in customizing coffee to a customer's specific tastes allows the firm to charge higher prices and to keep customers coming back. How much customization is there? For starters, Starbucks offers customers various types of milk: whole milk, 2%, and skim. There are caffeinated and decaffeinated coffees—and you can add a shot of vanilla to your coffee or top it off with whip cream, caramel, cocoa, or cinnamon. Whether you take your coffee "to go" or have it "to stay," Starbucks prides itself on a consistent customer experience no matter which location you visit.

The Question of Rareness
Although valuable resources and capabilities help firms survive, those resources and capabilities need to be rare. In other words, they will have to be controlled by only a small number of firms for the firms to obtain competitive advantage. Thus, managers need to assess if their valuable resources and capabilities are unique among their competitors. For example, for many years Walmart's skills in developing and using point-of-purchase data collection to control inventory gave it a competitive advantage over its competitors, like Kmart, a firm that has not had access to this timely information technology. Thus, during those years, Walmart's capability to control inventory gave the company its competitive edge over its major competitor, Kmart.

The Question of Imitability
Valuable and rare resources and capabilities can provide firms with competitive advantage; however, how long the advantage lasts depends on how *quickly* imitation could occur. When imitation occurs, it diminishes the

---

[11] Barney, J.B. (1991). Firm resources and sustained competitive advantage. *Journal of Management, 19,* 99–120.

Groupon

Established in 2008, Groupon is now one of the fastest growing Internet firms in the United States with a presence in more than 160 North American cities and in 48 countries around the world.

Based in Chicago, Groupon began with a simple and unique business model. The company sends daily messages by email to its 142 million subscribers offering discounts on products and services ranging from 50% to 90% off regular prices. Deals include restaurants, spa treatments, haircuts, fitness classes, and much more. The deals are called "groupons" because when a business offers a product or service at a deep discount, after a certain number of customers agree to buy the product "the group is on." In other words, the deal is activated when a minimum volume of orders is achieved. Subscribers can also refer a friend by email to help encourage purchases and achieve the minimum order. Afterward, customers make a secured, online payment and print out a coupon that they take to the store to redeem their product or service. There is usually a time limit to make the purchase, or the offer expires and you lose the deal.

The business model is unique in that it allows local, small businesses like Utopia Café in Toronto to get exposure to a large market quickly. Since Groupon usually takes a 50% cut of each deal, the offer is not always profitable to the promoter, but companies benefit from the increase in new customers.

The founder, a laid-back 29-year-old music major from Northwestern University, is said to be the next Mark Zuckerberg, tapping into the billion-dollar online advertising market. This Groupon mania began during an economic recession when people were eager to save money and were looking for coupons. As customers signed up for email notifications, Groupon's customer base grew larger and larger.

The one problem with the Groupon business model is that anyone can replicate it—it isn't difficult to create a website, after all. There are already 200 copycat sites in the United States, with LivingSocial being its main competitor. Overseas, there are also over 500 competitors, including 100 in China alone. In Canada, the websites RedFlagDeals.com and Koopon.ca are also trying to cash in on the profits.

Another problem with the model is that promoters can sometimes make too many sales too quickly, and the demand for the product (or service) can exceed the supply. This has frustrated customers who had to wait long periods of time for their goods after making their payment well in advance.

How successful the company will be is the question everyone is asking. As hundreds of businesses compete, Groupon will need to adapt to market changes rapidly, both domestically and internationally.

degree of rareness, which may further erode the value of the resources and capabilities. Thus, managers need to ask themselves if their resources and capabilities are difficult to imitate, and then determine how to create barriers for imitation. For example, a pharmaceutical company that invents a new drug can obtain a patent and create a temporary barrier to prevent other firms from imitating its product. In many other industries, this is not possible. Groupon is an Internet company that has had many competitors imitate its model, as seen in Talking Business 5.3.

The Question of Organization The last question managers have to consider is whether their firms can be organized in effective and efficient ways to exploit their valuable, rare, and difficult-to-imitate resources and capabilities to maximize their potentials. How a firm is organized is critical to firm success. Quite often, firms with valuable resources and capabilities experience a decline in performance because they do not have appropriate organizational structure and design, compensation policies, or organizational culture to exploit their resources and capabilities. In our discussion of organizational structure (Chapter 4), we observed that different organizations will be affected by different factors or forces. These factors are essentially contingencies to which their structure must adopt.

Exhibit 5.2 VRIO Model

	Question of Value	Question of Rareness	Question of Imitability	Question of Organization	Competitive Advantage
A particular set of resources and capabilities	In favour of the firm	In favour of the firm	In favour of the firm	In favour of the firm	Sustainable competitive advantage
A particular set of resources and capabilities	In favour of the firm	In favour of the firm	Not in favour of the firm	In favour of the firm	Temporary competitive advantage
A particular set of resources and capabilities	In favour of the firm	Not in favour of the firm	In favour of the firm	In favour of the firm	Temporary competitive advantage

These four questions provide managers with important guidelines to assess their competitive advantage relative to their competitors. If the answers to these questions are all in their firm's favour, then the firm will have sustainable competitive advantage over competitors (see Exhibit 5.2). If any of the answers to these questions are not in their firm's favour, then the firm would only have a temporary advantage over competitors. In this situation, the firm's performance may be threatened by the competitors at any time in the near future. Managers will have to act quickly to develop or acquire new resources or capabilities that help them create sustainable competitive advantage.

SWOT Analysis

At this point, we have discussed two basic and important models that managers can apply to assess their firm's position in the competitive environment: the five-forces model and the VRIO model. To some extent, these two models complement and supplement each other to tell us about where opportunities and threats are situated in the external environment and how good or bad we are in terms of the resources and capabilities we have. In other words, the conclusions of analyses from these two models can be summarized by **SWOT analysis** (strengths, weaknesses, opportunities, and threats). The logic behind SWOT analysis (see Exhibit 5.3) is that firms that strategically use their internal strengths to exploit environmental opportunities and neutralize environmental threats while avoiding internal weaknesses are more likely to increase market share, sales, and profitability than other firms.

Specifically, managers could use the VRIO analysis to identify what kinds of resources and capabilities their firm currently has that provide sustainable competitive advantage and where the firm's weaknesses are. Managers could also examine the trends of general environments and analyze industry structure (by using the five-forces model) to assess opportunities and threats in the external environment. As such, the conclusion from the SWOT analysis can provide insights for managers into strategy formulation for the future.

For example, Starbucks realized that high-quality coffee beans are sensitive to environmental conditions (the weather, for example) and that the coffee-bean suppliers have great

SWOT analysis An analysis of the strengths and weaknesses of an organization and of external opportunities and threats it is exposed to. The strategic planning team can use this information to reexamine the organization's mission statement to capitalize on opportunities and reduce threats.

Exhibit 5.3 SWOT Analysis

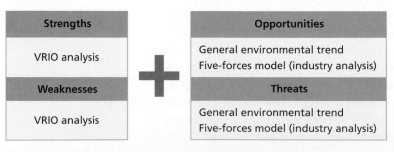

Strengths
VRIO analysis
Weaknesses
VRIO analysis

Opportunities
General environmental trend Five-forces model (industry analysis)
Threats
General environmental trend Five-forces model (industry analysis)

power over specialty coffee retailers because the coffee beans are critical inputs for the retailers. Starbucks used its capability in effective supply chain management to neutralize the threats imposed by specialty coffee-bean suppliers by diversifying its suppliers and through precise inventory control. At one point, the number of Starbucks's suppliers reached over 1,500 worldwide. In addition, Starbucks understood that its brand reputation and image are valuable, rare, and costly to imitate in the industry. It quickly harvested its brand reputation and image through entering international markets and selling its coffee in grocery stores. As such, Starbucks has enjoyed enormous success for quite a long period of time.

The recent Google mania is another example. Google used its strengths in search engines and operating systems design to compete in the highly competitive computer industry. It identified the opportunities situated in the Internet search engine market and the personal computer operating systems market by analyzing the weaknesses of incumbents' products. Google then used its capabilities in product design to capture the opportunities, which in turn gave it great success and challenged Microsoft's market positions in these two markets.

Both Starbucks and Google clearly understood how to use their sustainable competitive advantage (that is, their strengths) to capture opportunities in the marketplace or to neutralize the threats embedded in the industry environment. As such, both firms captured a significant portion of market share in their respective industries.

DIFFERENT LEVELS OF STRATEGIES

Objective 4 Describe three generic business strategies.

To this point, we have discussed how managers can perform strategic analysis to identify opportunities and threats situated in their industry environment and strengths and weaknesses embedded within their firms. In addition, managers need to know whether or not their strengths are sustainable for long-term performance. In this section, we will discuss what kinds of strategies managers can pursue given the opportunities, threats, strengths, and weaknesses they have identified.

Conceptually, we can categorize strategies into two levels: business and corporate levels. Business-level strategy is the strategy a firm uses to compete in a given market. As such, which market a firm intends to operate in is a given. Corporate-level strategy is about how a firm allocates its resources in different markets to create synergy to achieve its organizational goals.

business-level strategy A strategy a firm uses to compete in a given market. Three business-level strategies are cost leadership, product differentiation, and focus.

cost leadership strategy A business-level strategy that aims to reduce economic costs below that of all competitors to gain a competitive advantage. The strategy often requires aggressive construction of efficient-scale facilities, vigorous pursuit of cost reductions from experience, tight cost and overhead control, avoidance of marginal customer accounts, and cost minimization in areas like R&D, service, sales, marketing and advertising, and general administration.

Business-Level Strategy

There are three **business-level strategies** that have been widely discussed in the literature and have sometimes been called *generic business strategies*. These are cost leadership, product differentiation, and focus (see Exhibit 5.4).

Cost Leadership
The purpose of a **cost leadership strategy** is to gain competitive advantages by reducing economic costs below that of all competitors. It often requires aggressive construction of efficient-scale facilities, vigorous pursuit of cost reductions from experience, tight cost and overhead control, avoidance of marginal customer accounts, and cost minimization in areas like R&D, service, sales, marketing and adverting, general administration, and so on. Accordingly, a great deal of managerial attention to cost control is necessary to achieve this leadership position.

Exhibit 5.4 Three Generic Strategies

Target Markets	Generic Strategies
Industry wide	Cost leadership
Industry wide	Differentiation
Particular market segment/buyer group	Focus

There are three sources of cost leadership: (1) economies of scale, where firms can increase their production volume to reduce marginal costs; (2) learning curve economies, where firms can reduce marginal costs by experience, such as learning by doing and decreasing defects of products or services; and (3) access to low-cost factors of productions, such as raw materials, labour, location, and so on. Although each of these sources could be relatively easily imitated by competitors, a combination of these three can make imitation difficult, which in turn gives firms competitive advantages.

There are two major advantages associated with cost leadership. First, being a cost leader gives a firm the highest profit margins in the industry, which allows it to obtain abnormal returns, at least for the short term. The second advantage is that it gives firms flexibility in response to pressures coming from the five forces in the industry environment. This is particularly critical in situations where an industry becomes less attractive to competitors. More specifically, when competition among firms moves toward price competition, like what happens in mature industries, a firm with a cost leadership strategy would likely survive the competition because the firm can reduce its price and still obtain positive profit margins. Such a firm can also absorb increases in costs of raw materials when suppliers charge higher prices; its competitors might not be able to absorb the higher prices, so they may have to transfer the costs to customers. As such, the firm would be able to win its competitors' customers over by charging lower prices. Furthermore, in a situation where buyers demand lower prices, the cost-leader firm could more flexibly respond to customers' demands by reducing its price to maintain or even expand its customer base. Finally, the threat of new entrants would be lower for the cost-leader firm. Since the firm has advantages of economies of scale, learning-curve economies, and access to low-cost production factors, the new entrants are unlikely to be able to charge the same price as the firm does. Accordingly, the new entrants are not likely to pose an immediate threat to the firm in terms of its short-term performance.

Numerous firms have pursued cost-leadership strategies. For example, Walmart, a retail giant, is famous for having the lowest prices in the marketplace. If you look at Walmart closely, you will find that it not only has the lowest prices in the marketplace, but is also the cost leader in the retail industry. Walmart obtains economies of scale by purchasing a high volume of products and services. It also locates its stores in areas where the rent is not expensive. Furthermore, Walmart uses state-of-the-art information technology to monitor its inventory, thereby reducing inventory costs. Although these are small activities by themselves, the cumulative cost savings are huge. Most important, the organization of these small activities makes it difficult for competitors to imitate Walmart's operation.

Recently in Canada, Dollarama has been successful in competing with a cost-leadership strategy, as seen in Talking Business 5.4.

Product Differentiation   A **product differentiation** strategy is about a firm's attempt to gain competitive advantages by increasing the perceived value of its products or services relative to that of other firms' products or services. The other firms can be either competitors in the same industry or firms from other industries. For example, Starbucks provides high-quality specialty coffees as well as high-quality store design to differentiate itself from Tim Hortons and Country Style. As such, Starbucks is able to charge high-price premiums to customers given the value created.

Firms can create value for their products or services to differentiate themselves from other firms in many ways, including product features, links between functions, location,

product differentiation strategy A business-level strategy whereby a firm attempts to gain a competitive advantage by increasing the perceived value of its products or services relative to that of other firms' products or services.

Dollarama Cashing in on Penny-Pinching Canadians

Toronto Star via Getty Images

Dollarama reported record results Friday capping a year in which analysts say Canada's largest dollar-store operator expanded smartly and cashed in on penny-pinching customers.

For the quarter ending Feb. 3, the Montreal-based company reported a profit of $77.1 million, beating expectations. The company earned a profit of $63.6 [million] in the same quarter a year earlier.

During the past year, 81 new stores were opened and Dollarama Inc. CEO Larry Rossy said Friday the company isn't finished growing yet.

"Dollarama completed a very successful fiscal year," Rossy told analysts in a conference call in which the company said it will up its quarterly dividend by 27 per cent.

The chain now has 785 stores but Rossy wants to expand further, including in the GTA and downtown Toronto, Vancouver and Montreal.

"Based on our current real estate pipeline, 75 to 80 new store openings seem to be a realistic objective for fiscal 2014," Rossy said, later adding the company "may want" some shuttered Bargain Shop locations.

Analyst Neil Linsdell, a special situations analyst with Industrial Alliance Securities, said Dollarama is a "machine" that's dominating the dollar-store market in Canada.

In the fourth quarter this year, the company said sales were $561.9 million, increasing 19.9 per cent compared to the same quarter last year, when there was an extra week.

Canadians' appetite for bargains has grown in the past year, Linsdell said. He noted there's less of a stigma attached to discount shopping than in the past.

"For Dollarama and for Target and everybody like that, it really seems to be a function of the economy, everybody's much more concerned," said Linsdell.

"People are concerned about their jobs, consumer confidence is lower."

Linsdell said Dollarama has found a "sweet spot" in the discount world, offering items for as much as $3 but keeping prices low enough that consumers see them in a different category to stores like U.S. discount retailer Target, which expanded into Canada this year.

Although it's "too premature" to really know, he said the results are "so far so good." When Wal-Mart has taken over Zellers locations near Dollarama locations, it has improved traffic for Rossy's company, he said.

As well as expanding its locations, Dollarama has been modernizing its stores in recent years, introducing point-of-sale scanning and use of UPC codes, as well as accepting debit transactions.

Keeping better track of its sales as well as its expansion has helped increase profits, said Canaccord Genuity consumer products analyst Derek Dley.

He said he doesn't expect Canadians to stop looking for discounts at dollar and discount stores, even in prosperous times.

"I can't imagine the economy turns and people are willing to go back to paying $4 for wrapping paper instead of a dollar," Dley said. "It's a very good business model."

Source: Excerpted from Mills, C. (2013, April 12). Dollarama cashing in on penny-pinching Canadians. *Toronto Star.* Retrieved from www.thestar.com/business/2013/04/12/dollarama_cashing_in_on_pennypinching_canadians.print.html. Reprinted by permission of the Toronto Star.

Dollarama Gets Rolling on (Slightly) Higher Prices

WWD reported in April that credit card data shows luxury consumers are very comfortable shopping the other end of the price scale. In the U.S., 25 per cent of

Nordstrom shoppers also shop at the Dollar Tree, Leon Nicholas, director of retail insights at Kantar Retail, told WWD.

(continued)

Consumer psychologist Kit Yarrow has described it as "an anticachet around being wealthy."

"In Canada, Dollarama is a destination retailer for seasonal items, party items, kitchenware and stationary, regardless of income," says [Dollarama CFO Michael] Ross.

In February 2009 the company began rolling out items priced $1.25–$2. The move boosted traffic and sales. According to the financial results released Wednesday, about 51 per cent of the company's sales were from items costing more than a dollar, compared with 44 per cent a year before.

Ross says Dollarama has no plans to expand into the U.S., where Dollar Tree Inc. reported record first quarter earnings in March.

Dollar Tree operates about 4,350 stores in the U.S. Dollar Tree Canada operates 99 stores primarily in the west and Ontario after purchasing 86 stores from Vancouver-based Dollar Giant last year.

"Dollar Tree is a far larger operation overall, but Dollarama should continue to dominate in Canada for some time. Dollarama has 7.5 times the number of locations in this country,

and is still growing, as compared to Dollar Tree. It will take years for Dollar Tree to catch up," said Ed Strapagiel, executive vice-president of Kubas Primedia.

"There isn't anything sacred about the $1 price point at a dollar store. The early concept was 'everything for a dollar,' but this was an obvious gimmick and has since been abandoned. What a dollar store stands for now is the cheapest practical solution for very basic products. This concept can be maintained even when the price is sometimes $3."

Competition from other retailers—Walmart announced this year it would be bulking up on dollar items—doesn't worry Ross. Dollaramas located near Walmart stores do better business.

"Customers don't have to walk 100,000 square feet to find those low-priced items. They go into the store and it's wall-to-wall, but the race track is only 10,000 square feet."

Source: Excerpted from Kopun, F. (2012, June 14). Dollarama gets rolling on (slightly) higher prices. *Toronto Star*. Retrieved from www.thestar.com/business/2012/06/14/dollarama_gets_rolling_on_slightly_higher_prices.print.html.

product mix, links with other firms, and service (see Exhibit 5.5 for examples). However, managers need to keep in mind that the existence of product differentiation, in the end, is always a matter of customer perception. Sometimes, products sold by two different firms may be very similar, but if customers believe the first is more valuable than the second, then the first product has a differentiation advantage. Therefore, the firm with that product may be able to charge a higher price than the other firm.

For firms that obtain competitive advantages by pursuing product differentiation, they are often in good positions to defend themselves against the pressures from the five forces. More specifically, the threats of new entrants and substitutes for the firms would be lower than for others since the firms have imposed switching costs for their customers. In a situation where suppliers apply pressure to increase the prices of raw materials, the firms could transfer the increased costs to the customers as long as the new prices do not exceed the value the firms create. When rivalry among firms becomes fierce, the firms would be unlikely to get trapped in a price competition since the value they provide could protect them from the price wars.

Exhibit 5.5 Examples of Product Differentiation

Ways to Create Value	Examples
Product features	Apple's Mac vs. PC
Links between functions	Traditional televisions vs. televisions with DVD players
Location	Pusateri's (a high-end grocery chain) locates its stores in expensive neighbourhoods
Product mix	McDonald's combo, including burger, soft drink, and fries
Links with other firms	American Express credit card links with Air Miles
Services	Staples's next-business-day delivery service

That being said, managers who intend to pursue a strategy of product differentiation need to consider if the value they are going to create is sustainable, at least for a certain period of time. For example, as you'll see in Talking Business 5.5, FROGBOX is a Vancouver company that believes its service is differentiated from the rest.

As we discussed in the previous section, to achieve abnormal returns firms need to obtain sustainable competitive advantages. Therefore, managers need to think about how to create value that is rare and difficult to imitate or substitute. For example, Apple successfully created an MP3 player, the iPod, and then sold nearly 2 million of them in a relatively short period of time. Although Apple's success invited imitation from Creative, Sony, iRiver, Samsung, and others, Apple has built up its brand loyalty through its product differentiation (unique product designs). Even though these competitors offered MP3 players with different functions and lower prices, the differences in price and functionality did not significantly attract customers' attention. As a result, Apple could continue to harvest its iPod's success.

Focus   While cost leadership and product differentiation are oriented to broad markets, a **focus strategy** targets a particular buyer group, a segment of the product line, or a geographic market. Specifically, the focus strategy rests on the premise that a firm is able to compete

focus strategy A business-level strategy that targets a particular buyer group, a segment of the product line, or a geographic market. Specifically, the focus strategy rests on the premise that a firm is able to compete efficiently or effectively by targeting a particular narrow market. The firm can thus achieve either differentiation by better meeting the needs of a particular buyer group or lower costs in serving this group or both. Accordingly, the firm may potentially earn above-normal returns by adopting either a focused low-cost strategy or a focused differentiation strategy.

TALKING BUSINESS 5.5

FROGBOX: a sustainable franchising success

In 2008, FROGBOX began with one truck, one employee, and one mission: to rent reusable moving boxes as a green alternative to cardboard ones. Today, FROGBOX has 22 locations and expects to expand to 150 cities across North America in the next couple of years.

According to *Forbes* magazine, FROGBOX is one of the most innovative, sustainable, and promising franchise opportunities. In 2011, *Forbes* ranked FROGBOX on its list of America's Most Promising Companies.

Founder and president Doug Burgoyne originally set up FROGBOX in the Vancouver area as a small company, but now Burgoyne has opened franchise opportunities and hopes to expand his business in the next five years. Less than 10 years old, the company has found a unique niche, serving movers with rentable bins instead of throw away cardboard boxes. FROGBOX's business model is simple. According to Burgoyne, the company has expanded as the result of three reasons: "Happy customers, happy employees and a positive bottomline."[12] While the company doesn't provide moving services, it will drop off green plastic containers at your home or office and pick them up when you are done. The convenience makes sense for a lot of consumers and the environmental impact is reduced too. According to Burgoyne, "Pitching in to protect the environment is a big part of what we do and beyond that, we're actually achieving our goal of changing consumers' minds in terms of what they think about the moving industry. We're making a difference in the market and on planet Earth. In my mind, it doesn't get much greater than that."[13]

Of course, customer service has to be exceptional in order to get referrals and grow the business. "It's really about wanting our customers to have a great experience," Burgoyne explains. "Great service can be as simple as a delivery person calling to let a client know that he is stuck in traffic and will be arriving a little later than expected."[14]

(continued)

---

[12] On the path to greatness. October 2010. http://www.makeitbusiness.com/frogbox-on-the-path-to-greatness/.

[13] On the path to greatness. October 2010. http://www.makeitbusiness.com/frogbox-on-the-path-to-greatness/.

[14] On the path to greatness. October 2010. http://www.makeitbusiness.com/frogbox-on-the-path-to-greatness/.

The company now has over 12 employees, a proven business model, and ongoing growth potential. Burgoyne is hoping to change people's view on the moving industry, which in the past has not had the greatest reputation. According to Burgoyne, for most people moving is often a difficult and unpleasant event. From packing to hiring the right mover, moving can be a real nightmare.

How did Burgoyne get into the rentable moving bin business? According to Burgoyne, at the time, he was at a crossroads in his career. He could have accepted a promotion in the telecommunications industry or take a risk on a business idea he had thought of, and listen to his gut. While he had some business experience, he knew starting a business from the ground up would require a lot of work and a bit of luck. "My professional background ranges from physiotherapy to high-tech sales. I earned an MBA from the University of Western Ontario . . . but starting a business from scratch was something new to me," he explains. "I knew I needed to team up with someone who had those types of skills."[15]

Burgoyne eventually did find that person, but prefers to keep his partner silent. His partner has been instrumental in the company's strategy and expansion. "We spent eight months researching the idea and talking about the brand," Burgoyne remembers. "Before we went full throttle, we wanted to make sure we were crystal clear on what value the business was, how we were going to grow it, and that it would be scalable from the ground up."[16]

Marketing the business name, logo, and mission was important too. Currently, FROGBOX provides customers with reusable totes and wardrobes as well as recycled packaging material. And of course, the company donates a portion of its sales to special wildlife programs. In B.C., they include the Vancouver Aquarium's Oregon Spotted Frog Recovery and BC Frog programs. The company has also partnered with Climate Smart to help other businesses implement sustainable practices such as reducing, reusing, and recycling to control or counteract greenhouse gas emissions.

According to *Ottawa Life*, "the success of FROGBOX reflects an increasingly environmentally conscious society. Put simply, Canadian consumers are thinking outside the box and demanding alternatives to wasteful practices."[17]

While most cardboard boxes can only be used twice, "frog boxes" can be used and reused about 400 times before they need to be recycled.

Ottawa Life explains, "Even if cardboard boxes are recycled, they will have to be reprocessed before being used again, making the carbon footprint that much larger than simply reusing."[18]

"We want to run the company in every way we can with the lowest environmental footprint," says Burgoyne. "We believe that we can be a successful business and do what is right for the environment—both at the same time."[19]

By 2010, Burgoyne appeared on CBC's television program *Dragon's Den*, pitching his idea to a panel of investors for further capital. He won their approval and obtained two new partners: Jim Treliving of Boston Pizza and Brett Wilson of Canoe Financial. Together they invested $200,000 cash for 25% equity in the business.

According to the *Globe and Mail*, "to help manage the growth, the company has designed a computer system that can be expanded as new franchises come on board. For a monthly fee, franchises share online systems for ordering, scheduling and billing, as well as a website that can be customized for each market."[20]

Clearly, the business model is working. Recently, FROGBOX achieved the BC Green Business Award and is on its way to expanding in further markets.

---

[15] On the path to greatness. October 2010. http://www.makeitbusiness.com/frogbox-on-the-path-to-greatness/.

[16] On the path to greatness. October 2010. http://www.makeitbusiness.com/frogbox-on-the-path-to-greatness/.

[17] Frogbox: an Alternative to the Traditional Cardboard Moving Box. Ottawa Life. November 16, 2011. http://www.ottawalife.com/2011/11/frogbox-an-alternative-to-the-traditional-cardboard-moving-box/.

[18] Frogbox: an Alternative to the Traditional Cardboard Moving Box. Ottawa Life. November 16, 2011. http://www.ottawalife.com/2011/11/frogbox-an-alternative-to-the-traditional-cardboard-moving-box/.

[19] On the path to greatness. October 2010. http://www.makeitbusiness.com/frogbox-on-the-path-to-greatness/.

[20] Frogbox springs to franchising success with a green idea. September 6, 2012. *The Globe and Mail.* http://www.theglobeandmail.com/report-on-business/small-business/sb-tools/sb-how-to/start-or-buy-a-business/frogbox-springs-to-franchising-success-with-a-green-idea/article642006/.

efficiently or effectively by targeting a particular narrow market. The firm thus can achieve either differentiation by better meeting the needs of a particular buyer group or lower costs in serving this group or both. Accordingly, the firm may potentially earn above-normal returns by adopting either a focused low-cost strategy or a focused differentiation strategy.

For example, before 2003, WestJet's strategy was an example of a focused low-cost strategy. WestJet primarily served the markets in Western Canada, such as British Columbia and Alberta. The company also focused on achieving cost advantages in which it emphasized reducing costs through all value chain activities. IKEA is another example of a focused low-cost strategy adopter, where it targets the buyers, including young families and frequent movers, and it is able to sell knockdown furniture with low pricing through its efficient value chain management. Companies like Godiva chocolates, Häagen-Dazs, and Hugo Boss employ differentiation-based focused strategies targeted at upscale buyers wanting products and services with world-class attributes. These firms focus on the high-income buyers and differentiate their products from other firms in terms of quality. As such, they are able to achieve high performance.

Corporate-Level Strategy

Objective 5 Explain the nature of corporate strategy.

In contrast to the business-level strategy that describes how to compete in a given market, **corporate-level strategy** addresses two related challenges: (1) what businesses or markets a firm should compete in; and (2) how these businesses or markets can be managed to create synergy. In other words, the issues managers deal with concern determining which markets their firms should diversify into in an attempt to create maximum synergies that will allow them to achieve high performance (see Talking Business 5.6). These are critical issues for managers, because continuing to grow in a single market has become very difficult in today's business world, and the globalization trend also presents new market opportunities. Successfully managing diversification can give a firm enormous profitability and competitive advantage. In this section, we will discuss motives of diversification, types of diversification, and the means of diversifying.

corporate-level strategy A strategy a firm uses to determine what businesses or markets it should compete in, and how these businesses or markets can be managed to create synergy.

First we need to define diversification. **Diversification** refers to a situation where a firm operates in more than one market simultaneously. The market can take many different forms. For example, Rogers operates in three major markets: the cable television provider, cellular phone service provider, and Internet service provider markets. RBC, CIBC, Scotiabank, BMO, and TD Canada Trust have all diversified into international markets. Most large Canadian insurance companies are highly diversified in terms of their insurance products and where they sell their products. In fact, if we look at the top 300 corporations in the *Financial Post* 1000, we will find that the majority of the 300 corporations are highly diversified.

diversification A corporate-level strategy where a firm operates in more than one market simultaneously.

Motives for Diversification Why are the majority of the top Canadian corporations highly diversified? More generally, why do firms pursue diversification? There are many motives driving managers to pursue diversification. We can group these motives into two major categories: intrafirm and interfirm dynamics.

The motives derived from **intrafirm dynamics** include growth and managerial self-interests. At some point, firms operating in single markets will face difficulties to grow beyond a certain point even if they have a sustainable competitive advantage. The difficulties may come from market saturation or intense competition within the markets they operate in. Accordingly, diversifying to new markets provides them with opportunities to sustain growth and increase revenue. By diversifying into new markets, firms have

intrafirm dynamics A motive for diversification that can include growth and managerial self-interests.

American Airlines Merges with US Airways

In March 2013, American Airlines won approval in bankruptcy court to merge with US Airways. The merger created the world's biggest airline, with a combined 6,700 daily flights and approximately $40 billion in annual sales. Doug Parker, CEO of US Airways, will lead the new company into the future.

The new company, which will keep the American Airlines name, is hoping to create $1 billion in annual synergies of which 90% will come from additional revenues. The two companies currently employ about 94,000 employees; however, some positions will be cut.

The airline industry has faced numerous challenges over the past two decades, such as the 9/11 terrorist attacks, the 2008 financial crisis, the ongoing recession, and increasing security and fuel costs—all of which have forced airlines to increase fares and reduce expenses to stay afloat.

The merger means that the number of major US airlines will be reduced to four. These include the new American, United, Delta, and Southwest Airlines. With fewer competitors in the marketplace, many analysts predict customers will eventually pay more.

"For consumers, in general, any merger in any industry is not great news, because it reduces the number of options," said Ambarish Chandra, Rotman School of Management economics professor (Lu, 2013).

"The problem is because there have been so many mergers, we are losing whatever little competition we have left in this industry . . . It is true that airlines were losing money, but now we're seeing almost the complete reversal—we're seeing much higher fares, and airlines balance sheets are generally quite solid now," Chandra said (Lu, 2013).

In Canada, a similar trend is occurring. In 2012, WestJet earned a profit of $242.4 million and Air Canada earned a profit of $131 million.

Clearly, mergers are creating synergies that help with profits.

According to York University business professor Fred Lazar, the US airline merger partly represents three global alliances where frequent flyers place their loyalties. "This was inevitable," he said. "As long as you have three major global alliances, you were going to end up with three major carriers in the U.S." (Lu, 2013).

"They will have to make a choice. Are the points more important than price?" Lazar said (Lu, 2013). According to Vanessa Lu of the *Toronto Star*:

> Air Canada is part of the Star Alliance program that includes United, Lufthansa and Singapore Airlines. Delta belongs to the SkyTeam that includes KLM, Air France and Areomexico. US Airways is part of the Star Alliance, but after the merger would join the oneworld program that includes American Airlines, British Airways, Qantas and Japan Airlines. The incentive to fly on US Airways for Air Canada's Aeroplan members to collect points would be eliminated, and those frequent flyers may choose United instead.

The merged company will have other challenges ahead before synergies can be achieved. Operations will need to be combined, IT systems configured, and lots of negotiations with unions to agree on seniority of its employees. All of this takes time. But in the long run shareholders hope synergies will help profits and a stronger, more efficient company will emerge.

Sources: Associated Press. (2013, February 14). World's biggest airline: US Airways, American announce $11 billion merger. Retrieved from http://profit.ndtv.com/news/international-business/article-worlds-biggest-airline-us-airways-american-announce-11-bn-merger-317923; Cousineau, S. (2013, February 15). Why newly merged airlines rarely avoid heavy turbulence. *Globe and Mail*. Retrieved from http://www.the-globeandmail.com/globe-investor/why-newly-merged-airlines-rarely-avoid-heavy-turbulence/article8758328; Lu, V. (2013, February 12). American, US Airways merger to bring higher fares. *Toronto Star*. Retrieved from www.thestar.com/business/2013/02/12/american_us_airways_merger_to_bring_higher_fares.html. Reprinted with permission.; Mayerowitz, S. (2013, March 27). Bankruptcy judge signs off on American–US Airways deal. *USA Today*. Retrieved from http://www.usatoday.com/story/travel/flights/2013/03/27/judge-indicates-support-for-american-us-airways-deal/2025303.

opportunities to share related activities, which in turn achieve economies of scope and increase profitability and revenue. **Economies of scope** refer to situations where the total costs for serving two markets or producing products for two markets are less than the costs for serving or producing them alone. Such cost savings may derive from sharing production facilities, personnel, or marketing activities. In addition to benefits from economies of scope through sharing activities, diversification allows firms to leverage their core resources and capabilities to explore growth opportunities in new markets.

For example, Bell Canada, competing in the cellular phone and Internet service provider markets, provides retailing services through its retail stores, where customers can purchase both cellular phone products and Internet bundles. By combining both its products in a single store, Bell Canada saves the costs associated with physical facilities and duplicated personnel. Second Cup diversified into different markets in the specialty coffee industry by using its core capability—producing high-quality flavoured coffee—to sell its coffee both through its coffeehouses and other distribution channels (such as selling it in Harvey's and Swiss Chalet restaurants).

The motive of growth rests on the assumption that CEOs and top executives are rational human beings—that is, they act in the best interests of shareholders to maximize long-term shareholder value. In the real business world, however, that assumption is tenuous. Quite often, CEOs and top executives act in their own self-interest. Specifically, there are huge incentives for executives to increase the size of their firm, and many of these are hardly consistent with increasing shareholder wealth. In particular, when executive compensation is based on the firm's short-term performance, executives are likely to pursue diversification in an attempt to boost their compensation at the cost of putting the firm in a vulnerable position in the long term.

The motives driven from **interfirm dynamics** include market power enhancement, response to competition, and imitation. When a firm pursues diversification and related diversification (which is discussed in the next section), the firm can increase its market power within the industry it operates in. In this case, market power can come from increases in market share or revenue. As such, the firm can be in a better position to negotiate better prices or higher quality with its suppliers due to higher volume of purchases. The firm therefore has more leverage to compete against its competitors.

Similarly, diversifying into different markets can be due to the intense competition a firm experiences. When competition within an industry intensifies, a firm can either diversify into related markets or pursue vertical integration (which will be discussed shortly). Diversifying into related markets allows the firm to sustain growth or enhance revenue. Pursuing vertical integration provides a means for the firm to secure and control its raw materials or distribution channels.

Finally, diversification can be driven by interfirm imitation that can be independent of economic motives (for example, growth, profitability, securing supply). Research has shown that firms are likely to adopt the diversification strategy when highly successful firms, large firms, or comparable firms have adopted the strategy; even if the other firms pursuing diversification have experienced poor performance. Such imitation can lead to dangerous positions in that diversification may not be consistent with either short-term or long-term objectives. Eventually, it could destroy the firm in the marketplace.

Types of Diversification

There are three major types of diversification: related, unrelated, and vertical integration. **Related diversification** refers to situations where a firm

economies of scope The situation where the total costs for serving two markets or producing products for two markets are less than the costs for serving them or producing them alone.

interfirm dynamics A motive for diversification that includes market power enhancement, a response to competition, and imitation.

related diversification A type of diversification that refers to situations where a firm expands its core businesses or markets into related businesses or markets. Such an expansion usually involves horizontal integration across different business or market domains. It enables a firm to benefit from economies of scope and enjoy greater revenues if the businesses attain higher levels of sales growth combined than either firm could attain independently.

Mmaxer/Shutterstock

expands its core businesses or markets into related businesses or markets. Such an expansion usually involves horizontal integration across different business or market domains. It enables a firm to benefit from economies of scope and enjoy greater revenues if these businesses attain higher levels of sales growth combined than either firm could attain independently. By diversifying into related markets, a firm can create synergies through sharing activities (for example, production facilities, distribution channels, sales representatives) and leverage its resources and capabilities. Related diversification also potentially gives a firm greater market power to compete against its competitors and greater bargaining power over its suppliers and customers.

The recent announcement of Lowe's entry to Canada is an example of related diversification. Lowe's is a home renovation components retailer. It is a market leader in the US home renovation market and has a reputation of excellent service and product quality. By entering the Canadian market, Lowe's creates synergies for its own firm through leveraging its resources and capabilities. Its bargaining power over suppliers is also enhanced in that its potential high volume of purchases would enable it to demand lower prices or higher quality from its suppliers. Similarly, one of the core capabilities embedded in Procter & Gamble (P&G) is marketing competence. Many times, P&G has successfully used its marketing competence to promote different but related products to increase customer loyalty and also increase customers' psychological switching costs, which in turn give P&G more bargaining power with customers and helps increase its revenues. Rogers Communications Inc., which has traditionally operated in the telecommunications industry, uses a similar approach and continues to diversify into new businesses, such as its efforts to start a bank and focus on credit and payment services.

unrelated diversification A type of diversification where a firm diversifies into a new market that is not similar to its current market(s). This kind of diversification tends to provide little synergies for a firm, given that there are few opportunities for sharing activities or leveraging resources and capabilities. Firms pursuing this strategy tend to have the synergies created (or believe that the synergies will be created) through corporate office's management skills.

The second type of diversification is **unrelated diversification**, where a firm diversifies into a new market that is not similar to its current market(s). This kind of diversification tends to provide little synergies for a firm, given that there are few opportunities for sharing activities or leveraging resources and capabilities. An extreme example of such diversification is holding companies. Onex Corporation, one of the biggest holding companies in Canada, is involved in different industries, ranging from electronics manufacturing to health care insurance to consumer care products to transportation and logistics. Why do firms pursue unrelated diversification? Firms pursuing this strategy tend to have the synergies created (or believe that the synergies will be created) through corporate office's management skills. Loblaw is one example. Recently, the Canadian grocery chain diversified into the mobile phone business to penetrate a new market unrelated to its food business (see Talking Business 5.7).

Specifically, management skills in restructuring and financial controls allow a corporation to potentially maximize financial returns of each business unit and the corporation as a whole. When a particular business unit no longer provides financial returns to the corporation, it would be divested by the corporation to ensure the corporation maintains its overall profitability.

vertical integration A type of diversification that refers to an extension or expansion of firm value chain activities by integrating preceding or successive productive processes.

The final type of diversification is **vertical integration**. Vertical integration refers to an extension or expansion of firm value chain activities by integrating preceding or successive productive processes (see Exhibit 5.6). That is, the firm incorporates more processes toward

Loblaw Gets into the Mobile Phone Market

In the past couple of years, Loblaw announced it would enter the mobile phone market by setting up 200 full service phone stores within its grocery store businesses across Canada. The 80-square-foot shops would carry both smartphones and tablets to appeal to its existing customers.[21]

Currently, many Loblaw stores already have self-serve mobile phone kiosks with 27 mobile models, mainly offering prepaid plans.[22]

According to Maria Forlini, senior vice-president of PC Services, The Mobile Shop [would] ease the way Canadians shop for mobile devices. "By offering our customers great choice, convenience and trusted objective advice we're confident The Mobile Shop will provide consumers with the best wireless shopping experience in Canada," said Forlini.[23]

While some phone stores may try to push a certain brand name, the Loblaw representative will serve as an advisor to pick out the right phone and plan for the customer. The stores will also offer monthly, subscription-based plans from selected carriers such as Rogers and Bell.[24]

Loblaw is not the first nonphone company to enter this growing market. Some Shoppers Drug Mart and Canadian Tire stores have already entered this business too. By 2013, Loblaw took the next step and decided to offer its own mobile phone contracts as well.[25]

Loblaw hopes to leverage its phone market growth based on the 14 million customers who pass through its 1,000 stores every week.[26]

In 2013, comScore, a research firm, released a report on the Canadian digital industry and its promising future. The report indicated that only 62% of Canadians owned a smartphone, which means there is still a lot of market potential. Since last year, wireless subscribers also increased by 10% to just over 22 million Canadians. According to the report, users are relying on their smartphones for a variety of activities. For example, users are requiring more data for mobile TV, videos, social networking, mobile banking, and shopping online.[27]

Clearly, Loblaw has experience outside the grocery business already. Many Loblaw stores offer pharmacy services, home kitchen products, a photo lab, and a clothing line for adults and children called Joe Fresh. Loblaw also owns and manages PC Financial, the online banking service with selected kiosks inside many of its stores. The question is, can Loblaw provide another retail service that many of us have come to rely on? Since Loblaw has faced increasing competition in the grocery business by bigger global players such as Walmart and more recently Target, it hopes its diversification strategy will make it a larger, more competitive business. Certainly, the smartphone market continues to be profitable for many different types of retailers across Canada, and will likely remain profitable for some time in the future.

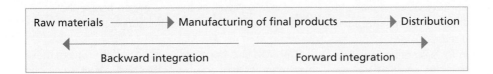

Exhibit 5.6 Two Types of Vertical Integration

[21] http://www.canadiangrocer.com/top-stories/loblaw-gets-into-mobile-phone-market-10015.

[22] http://www.canadiangrocer.com/top-stories/loblaw-gets-into-mobile-phone-market-10015.

[23] http://www.canadiangrocer.com/top-stories/loblaw-gets-into-mobile-phone-market-10015.

[24] http://www.canadiangrocer.com/top-stories/loblaw-gets-into-mobile-phone-market-10015.

[25] http://www.thestar.com/business/personal_finance/spending_saving/2013/06/19/loblaws_pc_mobile_unveils_mobile_phone_contracts.print.html.

[26] http://www.canadiangrocer.com/top-stories/loblaw-gets-into-mobile-phone-market-10015.

[27] http://mobilesyrup.com/2013/03/04/comscore-android-now-has-40-smartphone-market-share-in-canada/.

the source of raw materials (**backward integration**) or toward the ultimate customers (**forward integration**). For example, instead of selling its products through grocery stores, M&M Meat Shops has its own retail stores to serve its customers. Ben & Jerry's sells its ice cream products both through its own retail stores and through Loblaw, Sobeys, and other supermarkets.

Clearly, vertical integration can be a viable strategy for many firms. It provides firms with benefits that include securing raw materials or distribution channels, protecting and controlling valuable assets, and reducing dependence on suppliers or distributors. By absorbing preceding or successive processes into a firm, the firm has better control over prices and quality. Sometimes it can also increase the firm's profit margins, especially when suppliers' or distributors' markets are highly profitable. Most important, the firm would have control in terms of its overall strategic direction. Apple has certainly achieved this in opening its own retail stores.

Since 2005, when Apple opened its first retail store in Canada at Yorkdale Mall (Toronto), customers have been able to receive a complete Apple experience. Such a forward integration enables Apple to have better control over its customer service and to secure and enhance its market position in the highly competitive personal computer market. Similarly, in 2013 Starbucks bought its first coffee farm—an example of backward integration—as seen in Talking Business 5.8.

That said, there are risks associated with vertical integration. One of the major risks is increasing administrative costs associated with managing a more complex set of activities. As a firm absorbing new activities into its internal structure, the complexity of administration further increases. The increases in complexity can come from additional

TALKING BUSINESS 5.8

Starbucks Buys Its First Coffee Farm in Costa Rica

Starbucks has always been known for its friendly, relaxing atmosphere and great coffee, but now Starbucks is broadening its business into something different—farming. In 2013, the Seattle-based coffee chain announced its purchase of a 600-acre plot in Costa Rica, where it plans to grow its own coffee beans, cultivate new varieties, and test crops against plant-related diseases.

While Starbucks is well-known for promoting Fair-Trade coffee and supporting farmers in the coffee industry, the move for Starbucks to own its own raw materials (instead of buying them) may signal a new direction for the company. In the past 40 years, Starbucks has spent approximately $70 million to support coffee farmers in places such as Cameroon and Nicaragua as part of its corporate social responsibility efforts.

Its new farm is located on the slopes of the Poás Volcano, which has a broad range of altitudes and temperatures. The company hopes to develop hybrid coffees without any genetic modification techniques. In a press release, company CEO Howard Schultz stated:

This investment, and the cumulative impact it will have when combined with programs we have put into place over the last forty years, will support the resiliency of coffee farmers and their families as well as the one million people that represent our collective coffee supply chain.

Starbucks also hopes to improve coffee crops to make them more resilient against coffee rust, a disease caused by a fungus called *Hemileia vastatrix*. Currently, a record outbreak threatens more than half of the crops across Central America and may reduce the expected harvest by half.

Sources: Quotes and information from Tepper, R. (2013, March 21). Starbucks to start first farm in Costa Rica to cultivate new types of coffee beans. *Huffington Post.* Retrieved from www.huffingtonpost.com/2013/03/21/starbucks-farm-costa-rica_n_2924436.html?view=print&comm_ref=false;http://news.starbucks.com/article_display.cfm?article_id=762.

physical facilities; coordination between units, departments, or divisions; monitoring employees; and so on. Accordingly, carefully managing vertical integration is needed.

Means to Diversify   There are many ways to achieve diversification, either related or unrelated. Each way has its own advantages and disadvantages. The first is diversification through internal development. For example, Microsoft entered the video game market through its internal development of the Xbox, while Sony and Apple opened their own retail stores to compete in the retailing sectors. Through internal development, firms have full control over the process of diversification and solely capture the potential revenue and profitability.

That said, internal development has two major disadvantages. First, quite often diversifying into new markets requires significant resource commitment. If firms do not have slack resources, then they might find it difficult to pursue internal development for diversification. Furthermore, internal development also requires time to develop the capability unique to the new markets. When the time window for the new market opportunity is narrow, firms might miss the opportunity (after already developing the capability) to compete in the new market. The second disadvantage is the risk associated with diversification. While internal development allows firms to solely absorb the potential returns, it also implies that the firms have to bear all of the risk associated with diversification.

The second way to achieve diversification is through mergers and acquisitions. In general, **mergers** refer to two firms coming together to create a new firm with a new identity. **Acquisitions** refer to a firm acquiring the majority of shares in another firm. In some cases, the acquired firm will become a division of the acquiring firm. In other cases, the acquired firm still operates independently or retains their brand or firm identity. For example, Johnson & Johnson, one of the leading pharmaceutical and consumer care companies, has pursued many acquisitions in the past decade (including ALZA Corporation, Tibotec-Virco, 3-Dimensional Pharmaceuticals, and Egea Biosciences). One of its acquisitions was Neutrogena, which retained its brand identity. In fact, acquisition has been viewed as one of Johnson & Johnson's capabilities. Through its acquisition experience, Johnson & Johnson has developed specific capabilities to handle issues associated with acquisitions.

Mergers and acquisitions have been one of the most popular ways to diversify into new markets or to enhance market power. In addition to providing means for firms to increase market power and acquire new capabilities, they can also help two merged firms save enormous costs, thus increasing their profit margins, like what Swiss commodities trader Glencore expected in its merger with mining company Xstrata. The number of mergers and acquisitions in Canada has typically been over 1,000 in each year since 2000. According to a recent survey, Canadian CEOs still prefer this method to allow their companies to grow.

Mergers and acquisitions certainly provide firms with quick access to new resources and capabilities to compete in the new markets. They also allow the firms to increase market power or market share in a relatively short period of time. However, mergers and acquisitions share the same disadvantages as internal development—risk in the new market. Moreover, mergers and acquisitions have their own unique disadvantages or challenges. In 2013, this was true of the Loblaws–Shoppers Drug Mart merger, as seen in Talking Business 5.9. Quite often, managers face significant challenges in bringing two firms together into one in terms of administrative issues and organizational culture. Failure in managing the processes of mergers and acquisitions can create significant employee turnover and can erode firm performance.

merger A way to achieve diversification, when two firms come together to create a new firm with a new identity.

acquisition A way to achieve diversification, when a firm acquires the majority of shares in another firm.

Understanding the Deal: Shoppers Drug Mart and Loblaw

It's a deal that would join two of Canada's biggest retailers: Canadian supermarket chain Loblaw Companies Ltd. wants to acquire Shoppers Drug Mart for $12.4 billion in cash and stock.

U of T News asked marketing professor David Soberman from the University of Toronto's Rotman School of Management to reflect on the deal and what it could mean for the Canadian retail landscape.

We recently saw Sobeys acquire Safeway; and now Loblaw with Shoppers. Are these transactions more beneficial to the acquiring or acquired companies?

The real point here is that the acquired company and the acquirer still exist; that is Shoppers Drug Mart and Loblaw will continue to exist as a stand-alone organization that has a lot of brand equity and notoriety with Canadian consumers. But often times a merger—at least from the perception of the buyer and the seller—can unlock new value that wasn't possible before when the organizations operated independently.

So is it a win-win for both sides?

It's hard to tell if it's a win-win for both sides. Clearly the argument of Loblaw and people from Shoppers Drug Mart is that it will be, because it will unlock efficiencies that will not be there if the firms do not merge. As you know, many Shoppers Drug Marts have substantial grocery/convenience sections in their stores where people can go after-hours to buy various things they need. So there's a real opportunity there for Loblaw to gain added distribution for its President's Choice products.

How does this change the retail landscape in Canada?

One of the things it does do is create a greater degree of concentration. The only caveat I would suggest—to contrast with the Sobeys–Safeway deal—is that these are deals between firms that operate in quite different sectors (groceries vs. pharmaceuticals). While we sometimes worry about excessive market power, generally when organizations are operating in different sectors, the degree to which a merger can create less competition is much more limited.

What does this mean for consumers?

Shoppers Drug Mart will continue to operate in very much the way it has before, in the sense that their Optimum program and Life brand will continue. Similarly in Loblaw, they will continue pursuing their strategies with quality prevalent private label products under the President's Choice brand.

What we're seeing now is that the things we eat and the way we eat them can actually have a big effect on your health. In that regard, both brands have a similar objective. And there you may see some opportunities for synergy between Shoppers Drug Mart and Loblaw because these were always perceived as very different sectors. This might offer opportunities for the combined organizations to do something in the future that is quite creative.

What will regulators (the Competition Bureau) need to look at before this deal goes through?

One of the things they'll need to look at is the degree to which these firms compete with each other. If you have a merger between two firms, but they don't compete with each other, then it really doesn't affect or reduce competition in any significant way. For the most part people go to Shoppers Drug Mart or Loblaw with different shopping experiences in mind, so the degree to which there's overlap would seem to need to be quite limited. This would then suggest that the Competition Bureau would have little concern.

Why is Loblaw paying such a significant premium (27 per cent) for Shoppers?

One reason is that Shoppers is a very well respected brand. It's got a very strong equity with Canadian consumers, and for that reason it's very attractive.

Secondly, Shoppers Drug Mart has actually demonstrated the ability to be very innovative with the sorts of things that it does. They are very real pioneers in terms of developing higher quality private label products that you see in the healthcare and beauty and household categories. Furthermore, their Optimum Program has gained real traction with Canadian consumers and people wait for the days when they can get double or triple points.

That sort of loyalty and commitment is something which is worth money—it may not be reflected in the stock price, but it's reflected in the acquisition price.

Are we seeing a general trend towards stores which don't just sell one product?

Absolutely, what you see is the traditional categories breaking down. Traditionally people went to Loblaw for groceries. But the first thing we saw was the addition of

The third way to achieve diversification is through strategic alliances. **Strategic alliances** refer to two or more firms or organizations working together to achieve certain common goals. Strategic alliances can take various forms and serve various purposes. The three major forms of strategic alliances are nonequity alliances, equity alliances, and joint ventures. **Nonequity alliances** refer to the participating firms working together based on contractual agreements. **Equity alliances** refer to one firm having partial ownership in the other firm and the two firms working together to pursue common goals. Finally, **joint ventures** refer to two or more firms contributing certain resources to form an independent entity. The purposes of strategic alliances can range from marketing activities, to manufacturing production, to distribution arrangements, to research and development.

Generally, strategic alliances provide firms with quick access to new resources and capabilities contributed by alliance partners. As such, strategic alliances can be less costly and less of a resource commitment. Firms also share risks associated with diversification with alliance partners. On the other hand, firms will have to share potential revenue or profits with alliance partners. Furthermore, there are some specific risks associated with strategic alliances, especially surrounding partner selection. Since alliance partners play a key role in the success of strategic alliances, firms need to carefully select the partners to achieve their purposes in pursuit of diversification. Quite often, firms choose the wrong partners because of the following: (1) the firms misperceive the partners' resources and capabilities; (2) the partners misrepresent their resources and capabilities; and (3) the partners behave solely based on their own interests. Altogether, these could significantly impair the strategic alliance, which ultimately fails to achieve the common purposes.

strategic alliance A way to achieve diversification by two or more organizations working together to achieve certain common goals. Strategic alliances can take various forms and serve various purposes. Three major forms of strategic alliances are nonequity alliances, equity alliances, and joint ventures.

nonequity alliance A form of strategic alliance that involves an arrangement between two or more companies that work together based on contractual agreements.

equity alliance A form of strategic alliance that involves an arrangement between two or more firms where one firm has partial ownership in the other firm and the two firms work together to pursue common goals.

joint venture A form of strategic alliance that involves an arrangement between two or more companies joining to produce a product or service together, or to collaborate in the research, development, or marketing of that product or service.

CHAPTER SUMMARY

How to develop strategy is a critical task that managers face. Managers need to constantly assess both the internal and external environments to formulate appropriate strategy to sustain their firm performance and survival. In this chapter, we discussed two models that help managers effectively assess the environment—Michael Porter's five-forces model and Jay Barney's VRIO model. In using these models, managers can identify opportunities and threats in the external environment as well as strengths and weaknesses embedded within their firms. Business-level strategy focuses on how to compete in a given market, including a cost leadership strategy, product differentiation, and a focus strategy. Corporate-level strategy emphasizes creating synergies through diversification, such as related and unrelated diversifications and vertical integration.

CHAPTER LEARNING TOOLS

Key Terms

acquisition 185

backward integration 184

bargaining power of
buyers 167

bargaining power of
suppliers 166

business-level
strategy 173

corporate-level
strategy 179

cost leadership
strategy 173

diversification 179

economies of scale 164

economies of scope 181

equity alliance 187

exit barriers 168

financial resources 170

five-forces model 164

focus strategy 177

forward integration 184

human resources 170

industry 163

interfirm dynamics 181

intrafirm dynamics 179

joint venture 187

merger 185

nonequity alliance 187

organizational
resources 170

physical resources 170

product differentiation
strategy 174

related
diversification 181

resources and
capabilities 170

strategic alliance 187

strategic
management 162

switching costs 164

SWOT analysis 172

unrelated
diversification 182

vertical integration 182

VRIO model 169

Multiple-Choice Questions

Select the *best* answer for each of the following questions. Solutions are located in the back of your textbook.

1. An industry can share similar resource requirements, such as
   a. raw materials
   b. labour
   c. technology
   d. all of the above

2. Michael Porter designed the following model:
   a. VRIO model
   b. Five-forces model
   c. Seven external forces
   d. SWOT analysis

3. Spreading production costs over the number of units produced is called
   a. economies of scale
   b. economies of scope
   c. an internal strategy
   d. none of the above

4. A threat of a new entrant is high when
   a. capital costs are low
   b. switching costs are minimal
   c. capital costs are high
   d. both A and B

5. The bargaining power of customers is high when
   a. products are differentiated
   b. switching costs are high
   c. the brand is important to the buyer
   d. products are undifferentiated

6. A substitute product of coffee is
   a. tea
   b. bread
   c. a muffin
   d. candy

7. An exit barrier can be
   a. visible fixed costs
   b. specialized assets
   c. employees
   d. both A and B

8. A limitation of the five-forces model is that the model
   a. does not consider the role of technological change
   b. does not consider government regulations
   c. does not consider the different sizes of companies within the industry
   d. all of the above

9. The VRIO model is based on an analysis of several factors, including
   a. value
   b. rareness
   c. innovation
   d. both A and B

10. Which of the following encompasses both the VRIO model and the five-forces model?
    a. Seven external forces
    b. SWOT analysis
    c. Michael Porter model
    d. None of the above

11. A focus strategy is an example of a
    a. corporate-level strategy
    b. broad-market strategy
    c. business-level strategy
    d. diversification strategy

12. Manager self-interest and growth can be called
    a. a growth strategy
    b. interfirm dynamics
    c. intrafirm dynamics
    d. economies of scope

13. A company uses corporate office management skills when it pursues
    a. related diversification
    b. vertical integration
    c. unrelated diversification
    d. none of the above

14. A benefit of backward integration is
    a. a company can secure raw materials
    b. there is less reliance on suppliers
    c. a company can control quality and price
    d. all of the above

15. An equity alliance involves
    a. partial ownership in another firm
    b. two or more firms working together to achieve common goals
    c. a strategic alliance
    d. all of the above

Discussion Questions

1. Explain Michael Porter's five-forces model.

2. What are the limitations of the five-forces model?

3. Identify four key elements of the VRIO model and explain their importance.

4. Describe the components of a SWOT analysis.

5. What is the difference between a business-level strategy and a corporate-level strategy?

6. Provide six ways a product can be differentiated.

7. Identify and explain the two major motives for diversification.

8. Compare and contrast three major types of diversification.

9. Explain three ways a company can achieve diversification.

10. Explain the difference between economies of scale and economies of scope.

CONCEPT APPLICATION   LULULEMON: FOR THE LOVE OF YOGA

If you invested in Lululemon in 2007 at $2 share, your investment would have more than quadrupled. The shares have since risen to as high as $81, and investors are still optimistic about the company's future. The Canadian athletic clothing retailer has a lot to be proud of. What started off as a humble Vancouver company in 1998 has risen to a billion-dollar multinational with over 200 stores across North America, Europe, and Asia.[28]

Lululemon athletica has been called the "Nike for Women."[29] In an already competitive sports retail market, how did this small yoga company rise to such greatness?

Two Canadian marketing academics agree that Lululemon offers something unique: a high-quality product for yoga enthusiasts.

"Lots of people can make a good product, but this is [a] product really specially designed for stretch, fabric, and the age of people who do yoga," explained Alan Middleton, marketing professor at York University's Schulich School of Business.[30]

---

[28] Alini, E. (2011, January 27). Lululemon love affair. *Maclean's*. Retrieved from http://www2.macleans.ca/2011/01/27/lululemon-love-affair.

[29] *The Week* staff. (2012, March 26). How did Lululemon become a $10 billion yoga empire? *The Week*. Retrieved from http://theweek.com/article/index/226020/how-did-lululemon-become-a-10-billion-yoga-empire.

[30] Tucker, E. (2012, December 6). Why is Lululemon so successful? *Global News*. Retrieved from http://globalnews.ca/news/316659/why-is-lululemon-so-successful.

Case Continued >

According to Michael Mulvey, University of Ottawa marketing professor, Lululemon's product is known for its superior design and high quality. Mulvey also credits its sales staff, called "educators," for their focus on the customer. Mulvey explained that its customer service is superior and appeals to the target market. Since Lululemon is not selling an undifferentiated product to the mass market, it is not a traditional mass-market retailer.[31]

Beyond a quality product, interest in the company has grown through the use of social media. The yoga community is a well-connected demographic, says Mulvey. "In where they put stores, in how they linked into local yoga clubs where their stores were . . . and them being engaged in the whole promotion of yoga," he explained. "They've got a very nice niche."[32]

Clearly, strong community ties have resulted in less advertising costs. "We don't do ads," says Nina Gardner, Lululemon's community relations manager. "All of our marketing is done word-of-mouth and grassroots. The only place you'll see ads is in *Yoga Journal* and *Runners World*, two national publications."[33]

Lululemon, of course, is not just selling yoga clothes, it's also selling a lifestyle. You can it see in its stores and its slogans. On a typical Saturday afternoon, its employees are busy helping customers and community building. According to Timothy Taylor of the *Globe and Mail*, in stores you'll see a unique shopping experience. Taylor explains that customers, mostly women, are called "guests," ranging in age from young teenagers to senior citizens. In fact, it is not just about yoga pants. The youthful staff are modelling wraps and toques and advertising product features, and customers are comparing fabrics.[34]

CEO Christine Day argues that yoga isn't just an exercise. It represents a broader trend to take better care of yourself and live a healthier lifestyle. According to Day, Lululemon is "part of, and contributing to a bigger macro-trend that affects consumers from their early teens to their 70s. Investing in your health will pay big dividends for individuals and society . . . elevating the world from mediocrity to greatness."[35]

Part of this lifestyle is also seen in its slogans such as "Friends are more important than money" and "Dance, sing, floss and travel."

Strategically, the company has also done something else differently. The company uses a "scarcity model," keeping inventory supplies low. According to Day, this creates fanatical shoppers who return frequently to the store.[36] Few sales are offered, which means customers must buy products at regular price. Typically, yoga pants range from $75 to $128, when similar products can be found at Old Navy or the Gap for under $30.[37]

The company's reputation for quality and authenticity is one of the reasons customers keep coming back. Marina Strauss of the *Globe and Mail* refers to the clothes as

[31] Tucker, 2012.

[32] Tucker, 2012.

[33] Carter, L. (2013, March 20). Lululemon expands and finds balance with menswear. *Medill Reports Chicago*. Retrieved from http://news.medill.northwestern.edu/chicago/news.aspx?id=219239.

[34] Taylor, T. (2011, November 24). CEO of the year: Christine Day of Lululemon. *Globe and Mail*. Retrieved from www.theglobeandmail.com/report-on-business/rob-magazine/ceo-of-the-year-christine-day-of-lululemon/article4252293/.

[35] Taylor, 2011.

[36] *The Week* Staff, 2012.

[37] *The Week* Staff, 2012.

"aesthetically pleasing, functional—and pricier." Day calls it the "Apple Model." The company keeps improving its clothing features and fabrics, and customers show their appreciation through their ongoing loyalty.[38]

Clearly, Lululemon is focused on its customers and their love of yoga. In recent years, this ancient Hindu custom has become a popular trend in Canada and around the world. Indeed, the practice of yoga is on the rise. The number of people that engage in some form of yoga has risen to over 20 million in the United States alone. It is evident that Lululemon has been able to appeal to this growing market.

Certainly, the value and popularity of the brand is growing. In 2012, the company was ranked the 7th most popular Canadian brand by Interbrand in its biannual *Best Canadian Brands* report.[39]

The company is also unique in how it treats its employees. Often referred to as "educators," Lululemon employees receive special training to ensure professional-quality service for their customers. After their first employment anniversary, staff receive a "learning library" that includes books such as *The Seven Habits of Highly Effective People*, *The Phoenix Seminar: Psychology of Achievement*, and Landmark Forum Seminars.

What's next for Lululemon? The company has started to expand into traditional apparel as well as swim and surf clothes to appeal to a larger customer base. In fact, in 2013 Lululemon decided to develop a men's clothing line to appeal to both runners and male yogis. "They have moved from being strictly yoga to a lot of running stuff, which sort of broadens the appeal," says consultant Maureen Atkinson. "From the point of view of men, it becomes more acceptable to be in a store that focuses on running instead of (just) yoga."[40]

Retail consultant Howard Davidowitz agrees. "Yoga is recognized not only by women," Davidowitz said. "If you call health clubs, more men are attending yoga classes. Men are going to show up with their wives and their girlfriends to shop now. [I'd] say 90 percent of their business is women's wear. If they can add 10 percent for men . . . I look at it as a very strong market for them."[41]

The greater challenge is keeping the company's "aura of virtue" and "specialness" while appealing to the mass population. After all, investors are demanding growth.[42]

According to David Ian Gray, a retail strategist, "the specialness of a brand is hard to sustain when you see it on every street corner or, in this case, on every other woman in your yoga class or in the elementary school playground when you pick up your kids. That sense of being part of a haloed community starts to dissipate when the group has grown so big that it encompasses almost everybody—which is exactly what happened mid-90s to the Gap, or mid-2000s to Starbucks."[43]

---

[38] *The Week* Staff, 2012.

[39] Shaw, H. (2012, June 7). Why all the angst about Lululemon? *Financial Post*. Retrieved from http://business.financialpost.com/2012/06/07/why-all-the-angst-about-lululemon.

[40] Carter, 2013.

[41] Carter, 2013.

[42] Taylor, 2011.

[43] Taylor, 2011.

Case Continued >

Has Lululemon made any mistakes? Some analysts believe the yoga giant could have made even greater sales if it was better at matching supply with demand. The question is, can Lululemon now expand beyond yoga wear and be successful with aiming its products at the mass market? Many say, why not? "Is this a powerhouse company? My answer is yes," Davidowitz said. "Will it be five years from now? Yes, because they're so dominant and so recognizable. They've established themselves as the headquarters for yoga wear in the United States."[44]

Certainly, other retailers have tried to tap into the yoga market. Under Armour, Nike, Adidas, Victoria's Secret, and American Eagle are a few companies that have sold yoga wear. But so far, they haven't captured Lululemon's market share. It seems that Lululemon is doing something special; and for now, it's going to keep on doing it.

There is a saying: "Do what you love and the money will come"—for Lululemon, it's the love of yoga.

Questions

1. Analyze the yoga clothing industry using Michael Porter's five-forces model.

2. Conduct a VRIO analysis of Lululemon.

3. Discuss which of the three kinds of business-level strategies you think Lululemon is employing or should employ.

---

[44] Carter, 2013.

Chapter 6
Economic Forces
Oh Canada, What is Your Economy Like?

Bernhard Richter/Shutterstock

How much do you know about the economic environment within which businesses operate? In this chapter, we will examine a number of economic variables that can influence business and the overall economy. Topics such as economic growth, stability, and employment are economic goals discussed.

Learning Objectives

After studying this chapter, you should be able to

1. Define the elements of an economic environment.
2. Describe four types of economic systems.
3. Compare four types of competition.
4. Discuss how economic elements can affect business.
5. Explain the different types of unemployment.

THE BUSINESS WORLD

Canadians on the Move

If you couldn't get a job in the province where you lived, would you move elsewhere? That is a question many students are asking themselves as they try to obtain employment in a tight job market.

Kieran Thomas, a recent graduate, secured a job in Alberta's prosperous oil and gas industry. It wasn't his first choice, but he's glad he has a job. In 2009, Thomas graduated from the University of Waterloo with an undergraduate degree in engineering. At that time, it was one of the weakest job markets in decades, and Thomas soon realized that getting his dream job close to home wasn't going to happen.[1]

The Montreal student considers himself lucky, though. When he took a co-op program and worked for six terms (three of them in Alberta), his work experience helped him secure a job. "There were little to no jobs in Ontario or Quebec for new grad engineers, and the ones that were available were not very interesting and had very low starting salaries," Thomas, 27, said. "Most of my friends ended up going back to school for a master's degree to wait out the poor job market."[2]

Thomas is not alone in moving to another province for work. According to Statistics Canada, last year over 300,000 Canadians moved provinces to obtain work, attend school, or just have a new start. Stats Canada also cited Alberta as the most poplar province to go to, whereas Ontario was the most poplar province to leave. While the highest movement across provinces occurred during the 1970s and 1980s, the numbers are beginning to pick up again.[3]

The primary reason why people migrate is economic, although language, age, geography and other factors also play a role.[4] On average, men who migrate to another province increase their wages by 15%, whereas women increase their wages by 12%. Although the increase in wages is significant, only about 20% of Canadians are usually willing to change provinces.[5]

"I moved to a town of 3,500 people . . . knowing absolutely no one," Thomas said. "Leaving my friends and family was probably the hardest part."[6]

Another challenge is that some workers are employed in regulated occupations whereby their qualifications may not be recognized in other provinces. These labour barriers affect approximately 10% of the workforce, or 2 million Canadians. The teaching profession is one example. A K–12 teacher trained and certified in Ontario cannot automatically teach in British Columbia. First, a teacher must be in good standing with the Ontario College of Teachers and apply for a "basic certification" from the British Columbia College of Teachers. Then, a further certification test is required to receive full professional certification.[7]

---

[1] Chittley, J. (2013, April 12). More Canadians on the move for better opportunities in other provinces. *Daily Brew*. Retrieved from http://ca.news.yahoo.com/blogs/dailybrew/more-canadians-move-better-opportunities-other-provinces-182507138.html.

[2] Chittley, 2013.

[3] Chittley, 2013.

[4] Gauthier, P. (2011, January 27). *Interprovincial migration: Where are Canadians headed? TD Special Report*. Retrieved from www.td.com/document/PDF/economics/special/td-economics-special-pg0111-migration.pdf.

[5] Chittley, 2013.

[6] Chittley, 2013.

[7] Gauthier, 2011.

According to the Government of Canada,

> Most Canadians are able to work in their chosen occupation anywhere in Canada. Some workers, however, are employed in regulated occupations, certified or licensed by provincial or territorial authorities. Although many occupations enjoy a high degree of consistency in the requirements for a specific job, workers have encountered barriers when they move from one jurisdiction to another because of differences in certification requirements.[8]

How is the government trying to reduce labour mobility issues?

> The Government of Canada is [trying to reduce] unnecessary barriers to labour mobility and [is trying to promote] an open, efficient and stable domestic labour market, which is essential to Canada's economic prosperity. The free movement of workers contributes to sustaining economic growth, innovation, productivity and the improvement of Canada's overall competitiveness. To achieve this goal, the Government of Canada collaborates with the provinces and territories, regulators and stakeholders to strengthen a pan-Canadian approach to labour mobility. The federal government, with the provinces and territories, has signed the Agreement on Internal Trade (AIT), a trade agreement designed to reduce and eliminate barriers to the free movement of goods, services, investment and labour within Canada, and to establish an open, efficient and stable domestic market.[9]

Clearly, interprovincial migration is an important economic issue since it influences provincial demographics. People entering and leaving a province not only alter its size, but this movement also changes a province's demographic characteristics according to age, earnings, and so on, which subsequently affects economic growth.[10]

Which provinces are the easiest to find employment in? Jobs are growing in Alberta and Saskatchewan mainly because of the oil and gas sectors. In November 2012, Alberta created over 10,000 jobs and maintained the lowest unemployment rate in Canada.[11] Newfoundland and Labrador (NL), on the other hand, has had one of the most challenging job markets. For the period ending August 2012, Statistics Canada reported that NL had 12.4 job seekers for every job, whereas Alberta only had 1.7 job seekers.[12] Indeed, high unemployment in the eastern provinces is one motivating factor for residents to consider opportunities in the west.

Michael Hann, an associate professor at the University of New Brunswick, has found that native New Brunswickers who had moved to other provinces within Canada were economically better off than before they left. These expatriates were more likely to own a business, have a university education, and earn more than $100,000 a year.[13] While not everyone wants a job in the resource sector, the west continues to be a major draw for many Canadians.

---

[8] Agreement on Internal Trade. (n.d.). Labour mobility coordinating group. Retrieved from www.ait-aci.ca/index_en/labour.htm.

[9] Labour Mobility. Human Resources and Skills Development Canada. http://www.hrsdc.gc.ca/eng/jobs/credential_recognition/labour_mobility.shtml.

[10] Gauthier, 2011.

[11] Mah, B. (2012, December 7). Alberta's job market keeps booming. *Edmonton Journal*. Retrieved from www.edmontonjournal.com/business/Edmonton+among+cities+with+lowest+unemployment+rate+Canada/7667170/story.html.

[12] *Huffington Post Canada*. (2012, November 24). Best provinces in Canada to find a job: StatsCan vacancy survey shows where to seek work. Retrieved from www.huffingtonpost.ca/2012/11/24/best-provinces-to-find-a-job_n_2176078.html.

[13] Campbell, D. (2011, December 14). Maritimes needs its workers to come back up "the road." *Globe and Mail*. Retrieved from www.theglobeandmail.com/report-on-business/economy/economy-lab/maritimes-needs-its-workers-to-come-back-up-the-road/article620015.

According to a *Globe and Mail* article, Alberta's oil industry needs more than a thousand engineers, as well as several thousand tradespeople such as welders, pipe fitters, and carpenters.[14] The problem for many employers is that they can't fill these jobs. Why not? Many Canadians find it too expensive to move or too difficult to leave family ties.[15]

For many adults with families and aging parents, relocation becomes hard to do. This holds true even with company downsizings. In 2012, Honeywell laid off about 60 factory workers to shift production to lower-cost facilities in Hungary, China, and Mexico. But the fact is that most of these unemployed workers will likely stay in the same province. "I have to take care of my father—he's 82," says Brendan Andrews, a machine operator in Ontario.[16]

How do companies then fill vacancies when people are unwilling or unavailable to move? A growing number of employers are turning to places outside of Canada in their job search efforts, including Ireland, Eastern Europe, South Africa, and the United States. Clearly, there is a mismatch of skills in the labour market, even as unemployment levels are rising in other parts of the country.

"What we're finding is most of our companies have already recruited across Canada. And they still are not finding the numbers they need. So, while there may be unemployed people in Ontario, Quebec, or Eastern Canada—they aren't moving here," said Mike Wo, executive director of the Edmonton Economic Development Corporation.[17]

More recently, the highest unemployment rates have been in Ontario, Quebec, and New Brunswick. For instance, in 2012 Ontario and the eastern provinces had unemployment numbers around 7.8% and upwards; whereas in oil-rich provinces such as Alberta, unemployment remained low at only 4.9%. It is not that Canada does not have any jobs—it is that workers have the wrong skills in the wrong locations. In order for Canada to complete globally, the country needs to fill gaps in skills and labour shortages.[18]

According to a *Globe and Mail* article, most economists agree that the mobility of labour is essential to a prosperous economy over time. If one province is struggling and another is thriving, restricting labour movement will cause inefficient labour markets and lower overall economic performance.[19]

The cross-provincial migration of Canadians also has implications for government service demands and tax revenues. According to a TD report, "while an inflow of individuals dependent on government transfers may reduce some government spending pressure, many of these transfers (e.g. Employment Insurance) are federal rather than provincial. Moreover, any government saving would be more than offset by an inflow of higher-income individuals, which can seriously erode a government's tax base over time."[20]

Certainly, in the short-term, making it easier for Canadians to move between provinces is an important step in reducing structural unemployment and keeping Canadians working. But for Canada to prosper in the longer term, we also need policies to promote economic growth across all regions of the country.

---

[14] Grant, T. (2012, June 12). Stuck in place: Canada's mobility problem. *Globe and Mail*. Retrieved from www.theglobeandmail.com/report-on-business/economy/canada-competes/stuck-in-place-canadas-mobility-problem/article4237314.

[15] Grant, 2012.

[16] Grant, 2012.

[17] Grant, 2012.

[18] Grant, 2012.

[19] Campbell, 2011.

[20] Gauthier, P. (2011, January 27). Interprovincial migration: Where are Canadians headed? TD Special Report. Retrieved from www.td.com/document/PDF/economics/special/td-economics-special-pg0111-migration.pdf.

THE ECONOMIC ENVIRONMENT

What is an economic environment? An **economic environment** refers to the economic conditions in which an organization operates. An economic condition or variable can include job growth, consumer confidence, interest rates, and much more. Individuals, businesses, and the government are three key groups that make up an economic environment.

Individuals

Individuals decide how to spend their money and on what. Since money is a limited resource, an individual is forced to make spending choices—from the daily necessities of life such as food, clothing, and dental care, to more luxurious items such as travel and entertainment. Choosing to purchase certain goods and services automatically precludes the possibility of purchasing others instead. This type of decision is sometimes referred to as an **opportunity cost**—the cost of the best foregone alternative. Even a decision to attend university is an economic choice. By pursuing an education, an individual forgoes the option to work full time, to gain experience, and to save money. In other words, the opportunity cost of an education is a regular income, which could be saved and invested to provide even further income. Thus, one economic decision affects another.

Businesses

Businesses also form part of the economic environment. In order for businesses to make a profit, managers have to balance the right combination of inputs that allow for efficiency, productivity, and overall firm growth. These inputs are often referred to as the **five factors of production**, which include natural resources, labour, capital, knowledge, and entrepreneurs (see Exhibit 6.1).

Natural resources include land and raw materials that are found either below or above the ground, such as soil, rocks, minerals, trees, fruits, and vegetables. Raw materials can also include living organisms like fish or agricultural products such as milk and eggs. For Shell Corporation, oil is a raw material that needs to be refined before it becomes inventory and is sold for profit. For the consumer, oil is a good to be purchased and consumed. Similarly, McCain Foods uses potatoes as a raw material to make french fries. Once they are shipped to grocery stores, the french fries become a good available to the consumer for purchase.

Labour refers to workers. These are typically employees who contribute their talents and strengths to create goods and services for the owners of a business. From the floor cleaner to the CEO, each person has a role to play in producing goods and services and in meeting the company's objectives. In 2008, the role of the cleaner became particularly important to Maple

1. Natural resources	Land and raw materials
2. Labour	Workers
3. Capital	Buildings, machinery, tools, and equipment
4. Knowledge	Knowledge workers with specialized education, skills, and experience
5. Entrepreneurs	Individuals who start up businesses

Objective 1 Define the elements of an economic environment.

economic environment The economic conditions in which an organization operates. Key groups that make up an economic environment are individuals, businesses, and the government.

opportunity cost The cost of the best foregone alternative.

five factors of production The five key inputs in an organization, which include natural resources, labour, capital, knowledge, and entrepreneurs.

natural resources One of the five factors of production. Includes land and raw materials that are found either below or above the ground, such as soil, rocks, minerals, vegetables, and so on. Can also include living organisms like fish and agricultural products.

labour One of the five factors of production. Includes all workers in an organization who contribute their talents and strengths to create goods and services.

Exhibit 6.1 Five Factors of Production

Leaf Foods Inc., a Canadian deli-meat manufacturer. The company underwent a massive cleaning campaign to rid its plants of traces of listeria, which had resulted in 22 deaths across Canada and in significant damage to the company's reputation.[21]

Capital includes buildings, machines, tools, and other physical components used in producing goods and services. For example, CIBC uses capital such as buildings, computers, calculators, and safes to operate its financial services business. Money from shareowners, however, is not capital. Money can be used to purchase capital, but money is not capital itself. Money is only an investment, since it cannot create or produce anything on its own to earn income. To see how Tim Hortons uses capital and other factors of production, see Exhibit 6.2.

Knowledge is another factor of production—in fact, it has become the most important factor of production in today's economy.[22] The high-tech industry has created a need for *knowledge workers*: individuals with specialized education, skills, training, and experience. For many companies, knowledge is the key factor in achieving a competitive advantage. Google, Facebook, and Twitter are three Internet companies whose success was built on their employees' knowledge and creative abilities. Today, Google continues this quest for knowledge by allowing its engineers 20% of their work time to pursue personal ideas. By encouraging creativity at work, new knowledge can be developed and people can be empowered to work better.

According to the Organisation for Economic Co-operation and Development (OECD), knowledge is an important driver of productivity and economic development. **Knowledge-based economies**, for example, are economies that involve the production, distribution, and consumption of knowledge and information.[23] Canada's education

capital One of the five factors of production. Includes buildings, machines, tools, and other physical components used in producing goods and services.

knowledge One of the five factors of production. It is captured in the individuals who work for an organization and the specialized education, skills, training, and experience they bring to their role. In today's business environment, it has become the most important factor of production.

knowledge-based economies Economies that involve the production, distribution, and consumption of knowledge and information.

Exhibit 6.2 Tim Hortons's Utilization of the Five Factors of Production

Factor of Production	Example	Use
Natural resources	Land	• To operate business
	Coffee beans	• To make coffee
	Sugar	• To produce donuts
	Milk	• To produce other products
Labour	Workers in a franchise	• Store manager, cashier, sandwich maker, baker, cleaner
	Workers at corporate head office	• Executives, marketing managers, finance managers, other administrative staff
Capital	Buildings	• To house the fast-food restaurant franchises
	Machines	• Cooking equipment to bake donuts, make coffee, etc.
	Tools	• Computers and calculators to keep track of revenues and expenses
Knowledge	Specialized skills	• Individuals who understand the complexities of the coffee bean trade, growing coffee, etc.
Entrepreneur	Franchise owner	• Tim Horton was the original founder, but an individual can own and operate a franchise

---

[21] *CBC News*. (2009, September 11). Listeriosis outbreak timeline. Retrieved from www.cbc.ca/news/health/story/2008/08/26/f-meat-recall-timeline.html.

[22] Gregory, I. (2004). Peter Drucker on knowledge worker productivity. KnowledgeWorkerPerformance.com. Retrieved from www.knowledgeworkerperformance.com/Peter-Drucker-Knowledge-Worker-Productivity.aspx.

[23] OECD. (1996). *The knowledge-based economy*, 7. Retrieved from www.oecd.org/science/sci-tech/1913021.pdf.

According to the Government of Canada, here are some facts that give Canada a people advantage:

- Canada ranks #4 in the OECD for its high school completion rates (86.6% of working-age Canadians have a high school diploma).

- Canada ranks #1 in the OECD for its college completion rates (23.7% of working-age Canadians have graduated from college).

- Canada ranks #7 in the OECD and #2 in the G7 for its university completion rates (24.6% of working-age Canadians have a university degree).

- The World Economic Forum ranks Canada second in a 133-country study on the quality of their management schools.

- Canada leads the G7 when it comes to the availability of qualified engineers in its workforce, according to the IMD.

- Canada is a multicultural country, where one in every five Canadians has a mother tongue other than English or French. The diversity that Canada's workforce enjoys is a key asset to many foreign investors looking for talented workers who quickly adapt to different ways of taking care of business.

- It is particularly important for global firms in services sectors to have highly skilled workers who are familiar with different languages and varying business cultures. Over 4.4 million working-age Canadians speak a language other than English or French. These languages include Chinese, Italian, Spanish, Punjabi, German, Arabic, Portuguese, Korean, Hindi and Japanese.

- Canada offers global companies excellent time-zone advantages. Canada's human resources capabilities, for functions such as customer support and application development, are enhanced because the country shares the same time zones with North and Latin America.

Source: OECD. (2010). Highlights from education at a glance 2010, Figure 1.2, p. 13. Reprinted with permission.

system is an important component to Canada's knowledge-based economy, as described in Talking Business 6.1. Canadian business leaders also recognize the importance of knowledge in being competitive. Vice-chair of the Bank of Montreal, Kevin Lynch, argues

> Competitiveness in the knowledge-based economy is not about the lowest cost but the highest creativity, and this applies to all sectors, from agriculture to forestry to energy to communications to retail. Competitiveness today is about seizing the opportunities in the dynamic emerging economies, with the new products and services that consumers are seeking, and do so more nimbly and more quickly than our global competitors.[24]

Entrepreneurs are individuals who establish a business in the pursuit of profit and to serve a need in society. They are the owners, decision makers, and risk takers of the business. Unlike their employees, entrepreneurs have no guarantee of income in return for their time and effort. While most new businesses struggle to succeed, small businesses are an important part of the Canadian economy, job creation, and future economic growth. Entrepreneurs can introduce new products, ideas, and business models that can change the way we do business.

entrepreneurs One of the five factors of production. Individuals who establish a business in the pursuit of profit and to serve a need in society. They are the owners, decision makers, and risk takers of the business.

---

[24] Lynch, K. (2011, November 23). The keys to competitiveness? Innovation and productivity. *Globe and Mail.* Retrieved from www.theglobeandmail.com/report-on-business/economy/the-keys-to-competitiveness-innovation-and-productivity/article2246856.

Government

Unlike individuals and businesses that make self-serving economic choices, government has a broader role. Government purchases goods and services for the welfare and well-being of both its citizens and its business-community members. The government is also responsible for making laws, regulations, and policies to manage the country's economy.

To guide the economy in the right direction, the government can influence individual choices with tax credits or business decisions with tax incentives. For instance, the federal government encourages individuals to save for their retirement by allowing a tax deduction if they contribute to a Registered Retirement Savings Plan (RRSP). The government can also encourage innovation for the economy to grow. Businesses can receive a Scientific Research and Experimental Development (SR&ED) tax credit if they conduct eligible research and development in Canada.

One challenge for the Canadian government is to ensure qualified and skilled labour is available in the country to support economic growth, which is discussed in Talking Business 6.2.

ANALYZING THE ECONOMY: TWO APPROACHES

microeconomics The study of smaller components of the economy, such as individuals and businesses.

macroeconomics The study of larger economic issues involving the economy as a whole; examples include unemployment, consumption, inflation, gross domestic product, and price levels.

The performance of an economic environment can be analyzed on a micro or a macro level. **Microeconomics** is the study of smaller components of the economy, such as individuals and businesses. For example, microeconomists analyze consumer demand and existing supply. On the other hand, **macroeconomics** is the study of larger economic issues involving the economy as a whole. Macroeconomics is arguably more complex, since it considers data for large groups of people and firms. Examples of macroeconomic issues include unemployment, consumption, inflation, gross domestic product, and price levels. The role of government in the economy is also studied at this level. Economic policies are one way in which a government can influence an economic environment. Governmental economic policies can even extend beyond a country's borders, impacting the world economy, since a country's policies can shape international transactions through trade. Import duties, which tax foreign goods to protect domestic industries, are an example of the way in which governmental policies can influence trade relations with other countries.

Both micro- and macroeconomics provide valuable insight into current economic realities and aid in predicting future economic trends. For example, in 2011 Canadian Tire decided to introduce large appliances such as stoves and refrigerators in selected test stores. Before making this decision, the company would have performed micro- and macroeconomic analyses to look for answers to a number of questions. For example, on a microeconomic level, is there sufficient consumer demand versus the existing supply of large appliances offered by competitors such as Home Depot, Sears, and Future Shop? On a macroeconomic level, what is the state of the economy? Is the economy growing? Are consumers spending money and are employment levels high?

Macroeconomic questions are important ones from a business perspective. One particularly important macroeconomic consideration is the type of economic system within which a business operates.

Growing Gap of Truck Drivers Will Be Costly to Canadian Economy

Tens of thousands of truck drivers are approaching retirement age, but very few young people and immigrants are entering the industry. A new The Conference Board of Canada report concludes that the gap between the supply of drivers and the demand for them—estimated at 25,000 by 2020—could be costly to the Canadian economy.

"The food we eat, the goods that we enjoy and even the homes we live in are in large part delivered by trucks. The inability to meet a huge demand for drivers could be costly for the trucking industry, consumer goods and the Canadian economy," said Vijay Gill, Principal Research Associate.

The trucking industry moves 90 per cent of all consumer products and food within Canada and 60 per cent of trade with the United States, Canada's largest trading partner. It alone accounts for 33 per cent of real gross domestic product (GDP) in the transportation sector. Most of the demand for truck transport services is tied to the manufacturing, retail and wholesale trade industries. Demand for goods and services from retail industries is expected to grow significantly by

2020. The trucking industry's real GDP is expected to increase from $17 billion to $21.4 billion from 2011.

While truck drivers make up nearly 1.5 per cent of the Canadian labour force—approximately 300,000 truck drivers overall—it struggles to attract drivers to the for-hire industry. The for-hire industry is comprised of companies that provide truck transportation services to other companies. Drivers in the for-hire industry are often required to work long hours, over long distances, and with unpredictable schedules.

Participation of young people, ages 15 to 24, has dropped off significantly in the past decade. As a result, the average truck driver's average age has increased from 40 years in 1996 to 44 years in 2006, an average that surpasses that of many comparable occupations.

Source: Excerpted from Dowdall, B. (2013, February 20). Growing gap of truck drivers will be costly to Canadian economy. Reprinted with permission from The Conference Board of Canada. Retrieved from www.conferenceboard.ca/press/newsrelease/13-02-21/growing_gap_of_truck_drivers_will_be_costly_to_canadian_economy.aspx.

Age Cohorts—Truck Drivers vs. Total Labour Force, 2006

TYPES OF ECONOMIC SYSTEMS

Objective 2 Describe four types of economic systems.

What is an economic system? An **economic system** is the way that the five factors of production are managed. For instance, an economic system can have public or private ownership. In public ownership, decisions on production and the allocation of resources are made centrally by the government. Private ownership is the opposite, where individuals can own their

economic system The way that the five factors of production are managed. Can be classified as either public (where the government makes decisions about production and allocation of resources) or private (where individuals can own their own property and make their own decisions). There are four types of economic systems: a market economy, communism, socialism, and a mixed system.

market economy A free market system in which businesses compete with others in a marketplace where supply and demand determine which goods and services will be produced and consumed. Individuals can decide to be either workers for an employer or owners of a business.

own property and make their own decisions. There are four types of economic systems: a market system, a communist system, a socialist system, and a mixed system.

Market Economy

A **market economy**, also referred to as a *capitalist economy* or a *private enterprise system*, is a free market system in which individuals can decide to be employees or owners of their own business. Individuals who establish businesses are "entrepreneurs" and can freely choose which products to produce, distribute, and sell; where to sell them; and what prices to set. In so doing, businesses compete with others in a marketplace where supply and demand determine which goods and services will be produced and consumed.

Market economies offer entrepreneurs certain *rights*—for example, the right to own private property, the right to compete, the right to make their own choices, and the right to make a profit. The right to make a profit is probably the most significant incentive for individuals to take the risks involved in establishing a business.

Competition is one of the most important features of a market economy. Different individuals and groups are able to compete freely for profit. Competition is beneficial for both consumers and for the overall economy, because it allows different products and services to be produced at different prices. When there is more than one seller of a given product, producers are compelled to create a better product or to find a way of lowering costs to satisfy customers. This rivalry leads to more varied products, lower prices, and more efficient production.

There is a trend today for countries to move toward market economies, but the transition is not always simple nor is it quickly realized. The availability of money, capital, and adequate distribution systems can impact the ability of individuals to establish businesses and to market their products to those who want them.

Communism

communism An economic system where the government owns or controls essentially all of a country's economic resources.

Communism is the economic system that once existed under the Soviet Union. Instead of individuals freely deciding which products to produce, the government owned essentially all of the country's resources, and economic decisions were made centrally. The government decided which goods and services were produced and in what quantities. Communism tended to limit an individual's choices, such as the ability to change jobs or to relocate.

Although in theory communism was designed to create economic equality by allocating resources equally to all, the system had many shortcomings. First, the communist government had to guess which goods to produce, since prices were not set by the market. The government also had to estimate supply and demand. When estimates were inaccurate, the result was either a surplus or a shortage of goods. A second shortcoming of communism was that it offered little incentive for people to work hard, to improve goods, or to invent new products. As a result, creativity and innovation, in terms of business, were nonexistent. The third problem with communism was that the government mainly benefited from the earnings. Individuals had little incentive to build a business, since the government took most of the profits. Little business growth meant little to no economic growth.

Today, there are few pure communist economies in the world whereby governments make all of the economic decisions. Cuba and North Korea are two remaining examples of communist systems. Countries such as China and Vietnam are slowly moving toward market economies and are engaging in ongoing trade with the rest of the world.

Socialism

Socialism is an economic system whereby the government has large ownership in or control over major industries essential to the country's economy. Coal mines, transportation, steel mills, health care, banking, and utilities are a few examples. In Europe, for example, the French government has some ownership of the telecom industry.[25]

With significant ownership, the state can influence business goals, types of goods produced, prices, and even workers' rights. How much government ownership is required for a country to be considered socialist? There is no universal agreement. However, most socialist nations are otherwise similar to other countries. Socialist systems, for example, often have democratic governments that protect the rights of citizens.

Although most businesses are privately owned, individuals are heavily taxed so that the government can redistribute profits among its people. In 2013, Sweden's personal income tax rate was 59%, the second highest in the world. Denmark ranked second at 55%.[26] This is high compared to Canada's top personal tax rate of 50%.[27] High taxation is certainly one disadvantage of socialism.

High taxation levels can also be attributed to the high level of services offered by socialist systems, such as health care, education, child care, and unemployment benefits. One advantage socialists believe their system offers is a higher standard of living and more economic stability than other systems. While this could be true, taxes and unemployment are usually higher and levels of innovation lower. Some examples of socialist countries include France, Denmark, and Sweden.

socialism An economic system where the government has large ownership in or control over major industries essential to the country's economy.

Mixed Economy

Canada's economy is considered a **mixed economy** since it uses more than one economic system. While most industries are the work of private enterprise, the Canadian government may be considered partly socialist in its control of certain industries such as Canada Post, utilities (for example, water), and some public lands. In Canada, for example, the provincial governments control and regulate the health care system. Similarly, the Ontario government owns and operates the Liquor Control Board of Ontario (LCBO), which controls the sale of certain types of alcohol.

The government is also involved in taxation and in the allocation of resources for special purposes, such as the assistance of retired individuals on a fixed income. The Canada Pension Plan (CPP), for example, is administered by the government and provides pension income for individuals age 65 and older.

Today, most economies are considered mixed systems since governments usually play some role in managing the economy. In recent years there has been a trend to privatize government-run agencies with the aim of creating competition in the private sector.

mixed economy An economic system where the government (public) and businesses (private) influence the economy.

---

[25] Oak, C. (2013, July 17). The France Telecom Group turns completely Orange. *Shift Thought*. Retrieved from http://digitalmoney.shiftthought.co.uk/the-france-telecom-group-has-turned-completely-orange.

[26] *Malaysian Digest*. (2012, June 19). 10 countries with the highest taxes, 2012–2013. Retrieved from www.malaysiandigest.com/features/56162-10-countries-with-the-highest-taxes-2012-2013.html.

[27] PriceWaterhouseCoopers. (2012). *Tax facts and figures: Canada 2012*. Retrieved from www.pwc.com/en_CA/ca/tax/publications/pwc-tax-facts-figures-2012-en.pdf.

COMPETITION AND THE ECONOMY

Types of Competition in Free Markets

Most economists agree that private-sector competition improves the quality of goods and services available in the market and lowers consumer prices. Although businesses compete in the economic marketplace, not all companies necessarily compete against one another. **Competition** exists when two or more sellers offer the same or similar products or services to consumers. Typically, companies within the same industry, selling a similar product, compete with one another. In Canada, retail competition is becoming fierce as more US stores head north to compete directly with Canadian companies. Canadian Tire, Rona, and Home Hardware now compete against Home Depot and Lowe's. Walmart and Target are also competitors because they sell similar goods. Competition among providers of goods and services can fall under one of four main categories: perfect competition, a monopoly, an oligopoly, and monopolistic competition (see Exhibit 6.3).

competition When two or more sellers offer the same or similar products or services to consumers.

Perfect (or Pure) competition

Perfect or pure competition is, in theory, the ideal form of competition. It is characterized by four traits. First, a large number of buyers and sellers act independently. Second, the product or service is undifferentiated. In other words, the good or service is similar to or the same as other products and services available in the market. In this case, because there is nothing unique or value-added about the product, the lowest price becomes the key decision-making factor for the consumer. Third, with undifferentiated goods, the market determines the price, not the company. The seller is therefore a price taker. And fourth, in perfect competition there are no barriers to entry. **Barriers to entry** are obstacles that may prevent another company from entering a given market. Barriers of entry could include high capital costs (eg. cost of buildings and equipment), government regulations, customer brand loyalties, intellectual properties (eg. patents and trademarks), and high switching costs (eg. contract cancellation penalties). Barriers to entry usually exist under other forms of competition, too.

perfect or pure competition A form of competition where many small and medium firms produce the same product or service and no single seller has the power to influence the price of that product or service.

barriers to entry Obstacles that may prevent another company from entering a given market. Could include high capital costs, government regulations, customer brand loyalties, intellectual property, and high switching costs.

When these four conditions are present, no one firm can become large enough to set prices, control the market, and significantly affect the free market system. What industries are purely competitive? Many agricultural products such as potatoes, apples, and corn are perfectly competitive. Today, however, there are few other products that exist within the conditions of pure competition since most products are slightly differentiated. How are Canadian farmers doing? Let's consider Canada's agricultural industry in Talking Business 6.3.

Exhibit 6.3 Types of Competition

Type of Competition	Barriers to Entry	Number of Sellers	Firm Price Setter	Product Differentiation	Size of Firms
Perfect (or pure)	None	Many (very competitive)	No	None	Small to medium
Monopolistic	Low	Many (very competitive)	No	Small differentiation	Small to large
Oligopoly	High	Few (somewhat competitive)	Yes	Some differentiation	Large
Monopoly	No entry is achievable	One (no competition)	Yes	None	Large

Better Farm Management Separates the Wheat from the Chaff

Despite a perception that large-scale "corporate farming" is taking over Canadian agriculture, Canada's farming sector remains dominated by relatively small-scale, family owned and operated enterprises. And this is unlikely to change significantly anytime soon.

Canada's largest farming businesses—those earning over $1 million in yearly revenues—comprise less than 5 per cent of all farms in the country, and would be considered small or medium sized enterprises in virtually all other economic sectors.

This does not stop farms from being profitable businesses. A new report by the Conference Board—*Seeds for Success: Enhancing Canada's Farming Enterprises*—shows that, since 2000, almost 30 per cent of Canadian farms have had profit margins over 20 per cent each year. Moreover, a quarter of the smallest sized farms in Canada have been in the top profit margin category. On the downside, about 30 per cent of farms lose substantial amounts of money each year, with profit margins of minus-ten per cent or worse.

Why do some farms greatly outperform others? The key is good management. Farmers have abundant new opportunities, but capitalizing on them requires skillful management of farm capital, marketing, business relationships, and human resources. Increasingly, the old ways of doing things no longer guarantee success in the modern farming economy.

For example, managing farm capital becomes more important as the cost of farmland outpaces growth in agricultural incomes. During the second half of 2011 alone, farmland prices across Canada increased by 6.9 per cent. To meet their operational needs, successful farm managers are renting more land, as opposed to purchasing it outright, to avoid excessive debt. They also make investments in other aspects of the business, including state-of-the-art technology, to improve productivity.

Producing good yields, however, is not enough—marketing is also an increasingly important part of being profitable. To earn price premiums, entrepreneurial farm managers are going beyond traditional selling avenues (such as auction markets and marketing boards), and selling directly to consumers, processors, restaurants and retailers, and foreign buyers. Many tap into niche market opportunities, such as organic and "local" food. Other operators are making greater use of financial instruments (such as futures and options) to maximize price potential and hedge against risk.

Managing and fostering business relationships are increasingly vital to farming success: the image of the solitary farmer is at odds with the realities of today's competitive environment. Farmers can accomplish many things working together through business partnerships, agricultural cooperatives, and joint ventures, including cost-sharing, reduced risk, and increased buying power. Among successful farmers, sophisticated knowledge networks (including producer organizations and marketing clubs) supplement the local coffee shop as places for sharing information about new industry developments.

Managing capital, marketing, and relationships takes time and focus. But many farmers are reluctant to hire more employees to do the on-farm labour they love, so that they can spend more time handling business issues. Most operators—more than 70 per cent—also report problems finding general farm workers to fill positions, owing to skills and labour shortages in the industry. Improving employee management training, as well as farm human resources standards and practices, would help attract a new generation of smart, ambitious, and enterprising Canadians to farming. It is critical that farms rival other industries that compete with them for skilled workers.

Farmers who employ good management and business skills have bright futures in a world where demand for food is growing. Many farms will gradually become larger as a result of greater business sophistication and entrepreneurial ambition. But size is not everything. What matters more is how well farms of all sizes are able to improve farm management in a way that enables them to meet rising consumer expectations for high quality, safe, and environmentally friendly foods—and be prosperous as a result.

Source: Excerpted from Stuckey, J. (2013, July 17). Better farm management separates the wheat from the chaff. The Conference Board of Canada. Retrieved from www.conferenceboard.ca/press/speech_oped/13-07-17/better_farm_management_separates_the_wheat_from_the_chaff.aspx.

Monopoly

monopoly A form of competition that occurs when only one company produces a particular product or service in a given market and, as a result, there are no competitors.

A **monopoly** represents the opposite extreme to perfect competition. A monopoly occurs when only one company produces a particular product or service in a given market and, as a result, there are no competitors. As the sole producer, a company is a price setter—it is able to determine the selling price of its products or services. Significant barriers to entry that prevent other firms from competing in the market must be present for a monopoly to exist.

In Canada, three examples of monopolies are Canada Post, the LCBO in Ontario, and Rogers Communications Inc. Daily mail delivery to businesses and households for bills, flyers, and greeting cards is provided only by Canada Post. While courier services do exist, the higher costs do not provide consumers with a practical alternative for their everyday mail needs. The LCBO is also considered a monopoly. For both consumers and businesses, the LCBO is the only place where certain types of liquor are sold, such as whisky, rum, vodka, and gin. Cable television is another type of monopoly. In certain jurisdictions, Rogers Communications Inc. is the only provider of "cable" television service (although there are alternatives, such as satellite television).

The United States also has its share of monopolies. Microsoft's operating system, Windows, has been called a *quasi* monopoly. While it is not the sole operating system in existence, Microsoft Windows accounts for approximately 90% to 95% of the overall market. As the standard for home and business computer applications, the consumer has little choice. For example, if you buy a new personal computer, chances are that the computer comes with Microsoft Windows. Buying an Apple computer may be your only other alternative for a different operating system. SiriusXM is another monopoly, because it is the sole provider of satellite radio in Canada and the United States.

Many professional sports teams are also considered monopolies because there are no other competitors, as seen in Talking Business 6.4.

natural monopoly A type of monopoly that occurs when economic and technical conditions only allow for one efficient producer. An example is water supplied by a municipality.

limited monopoly A type of monopoly that occurs when a company has a patent that protects its product or idea for a limited time period.

patent A form of intellectual property rights whereby a country grants exclusive rights to an inventor to protest his or her product or idea for a limited period of time.

There are other types of monopolies as well. A **natural monopoly**, for example, occurs when economic and technical conditions only allow for one efficient producer. Water supplied by a municipality is considered a natural monopoly. Another kind of monopoly is a **limited monopoly**, which may exist to a company that has a patent. A **patent** is a form of intellectual property rights whereby a country can grant exclusive rights to an inventor to protect his or her product or idea for a limited period of time in exchange for public disclosure in the future. For instance, when a pharmaceutical company develops a new drug, the company can patent it and then sell it exclusively. Once the time on the patent runs out, any company can access information on the drug, develop it, and sell it as a competitor. Subsequently, the monopoly no longer exists.

Oligopoly

oligopoly A form of competition when only a few large producers sell a certain product or service in a given market.

When only a few competitors dominate an industry, an **oligopoly** exists. Commercial aircraft producers such as Boeing and Airbus are two examples of companies in an oligopoly. Oligopolies are also characterized by high barriers to entry such as capital costs. For instance, to establish a plane-manufacturing business, one would require millions if not billions in investment dollars. Oligopolies are price setters and are also characterized by fierce competition. Prices are usually close between companies. With so few firms within an industry, a change in price by one company will likely cause the price to be matched by others in the industry. Automotive, oil, gas, tobacco, and cereal companies are some examples of oligopolies. Canadian banks also meet the definition, as do the big four accounting firms—Deloitte, Ernst & Young, KPMG, and PricewaterhouseCoopers.

Don't Blame Professional Athletes for High Ticket Prices

Photo by Jared Wickerham/Getty Images

How many times have you heard the owner of a professional sports team justify an increase in ticket prices by saying that the team has no choice because players' salaries are escalating? If ticket prices don't increase, the team would lose all of its best players laments the owner. The problem with this statement is that it is dead wrong since ticket price for sporting events are essentially driven by the demand side of the market. Prices for tickets increase simply because the owner feels that people are willing to pay the extra amount. If people aren't willing to pay the higher price then prices will come down.

In setting prices, owners consider a number of factors including substitute forms of entertainment, demographics and possibly the difficulty in travelling to the arena. Most professional sports teams operate in a monopoly situation where there are no other competitors. This provides owners with a high degree of flexibility when setting prices because the team doesn't have to compete with other professional teams in the same sport in the local market. The team's performance and fan interest also plays a role in determining ticket

prices. Tickets to watch the Phoenix Coyotes play hockey are relatively inexpensive because the team is bad every year and there is a lack of interest in hockey in sunny Arizona. Conversely, in hockey-mad southern Ontario ticket prices are exorbitant, even though the Leafs are a weak team.

The clearest example of the lack of relationship between players' salaries and ticket prices is the World Cup of hockey that took place in Canada a few years ago. Ticket prices in Toronto were expensive even though the players were not compensated for their participation in the event. Fans paid the high prices because they were excited about seeing the best Canadian hockey players compete against the best players from other countries. Similarly, ticket prices to watch the Stanley Cup playoffs are more expensive than regular season games because of higher demand. Yet, players are not compensated during the playoffs since the owners no longer pay them after the regular season is finished. Therefore, the owners are in a position to increase prices, due to soaring demand, at the same time that player salaries decline to zero.

The ongoing outrage over high players' salaries is somewhat puzzling. Sports fans are angered when athletes earn millions of dollars per year yet they are pretty apathetic about the fact that some movie stars like Tom Cruise can earn $25 million for one movie. Both professional athletes and movie stars are performers who are paid based on their ability to attract a paying audience. Possibly, fans are up in arms about athletes' salaries because actors are not local performers in the same way that athletes are. Or, more likely, people are simply jealous.

The salaries that professional athletes make and the prices that we pay to watch them play are actually a pretty accurate reflection of the values in our society. Baseball analyst Bill James once noted that baseball players earn more than medical researchers because the public in the United States is much more focused on having a winning team than finding a cure for life-threatening diseases. He is right with this comment—so the next time you get upset when reading about another multi-million dollar contract awarded to an athlete or ticket prices going up again simply look in the mirror. The problem lies with us, not the athletes.

Source: Excerpted from Beckman, K. (2009, September 3). Don't blame professional athletes for high ticket prices. Reprinted with permission from The Conference Board of Canada. Retrieved from www.conferenceboard.ca/economics/hot_eco_topics/default/09-09-03/don_t_blame_professional_athletes_for_high_ticket_prices.aspx.

They are the only four accounting firms that provide accounting, tax, and audit services globally. The majority of North American multinational corporations use one of these firms to audit their international businesses.

Monopolistic Competition
Most other products and services in free market economies fall under a type of competition known as **monopolistic competition**. In monopolistic competition, a large number of companies compete with one another, offering products and services that are differentiated at least in a minor way. Differentiation strategies include branding, style or design, and advertising. Coffee, shampoo, furniture, and fast-food burger restaurants are a few examples.

Let's consider the coffee industry. Who sells coffee in Canada? Tim Hortons, Starbucks, Second Cup, Timothy's, McDonald's, and Coffee Time are some of the bigger competitors. With more time, you could probably think of many other examples. Each of these coffee sellers are differentiated in some way. There are diverse flavours (mild, medium, or dark roast), brand names (Timothy's versus Second Cup), and advertising. Some coffees are advertised as convenient and low cost (Tim Hortons), while other coffees are promoted as premium brands with higher-quality coffee beans (Starbucks).

Exhibit 6.4 summarizes the types of competition in Canada and provides examples of companies in each category of competition.

monopolistic competition
A form of competition where a large number of small and large firms have a similar product or service that is perceived as slightly different from the others due to branding, style or design, and advertising.

Exhibit 6.4 Industry Competition in Canada

Type of Competition	Industry	Examples of Companies in Canada
Perfect competition	Potatoes	Various farmers
	Apples	Various farmers
	Corn	Various farmers
Monopoly	Satellite radio	SiriusXM
Oligopoly	Air travel	Air Canada
		WestJet
	Smartphones	BlackBerry
		Apple
		Samsung
		Nokia
	Cellphone service	Bell
		Rogers
		Telus
		Public Mobile
		Wind Mobile
		Primus
	Global accounting, auditing, and tax services	Deloitte
		Ernst & Young
		PricewaterhouseCoopers
		KPMG
	Books	Indigo
		Amazon

Type of Competition	Industry	Examples of Companies in Canada
Monopolistic	Small hardware tools (screwdrivers, hammers, etc.)	Rona Canadian Tire Home Hardware Home Depot Lowe's Walmart Target
	Groceries	Loblaw Metro Safeway Sobeys Longo's Walmart Costco No Frills Basics Shoppers Drug Mart Dollarama 7-Eleven
	Women's clothing	Joe Fresh Roots Jacob Tristan Reitmans Holt Renfrew Banana Republic Gap Old Navy Sears The Hudson's Bay Walmart Target
	Coffee	Tim Hortons Starbucks Second Cup Timothy's Coffee Time McDonald's 7-Eleven Miscellaneous snack bars Miscellaneous gas stations Miscellaneous restaurants Other independent coffee shops

GOALS OF CANADA'S ECONOMIC SYSTEM

Besides adequate competition, there are other factors that are important to Canada's economy. To achieve a thriving economy, Canada's economic system has three primary goals: economic growth, economic stability, and employment. The following discussion demonstrates these goals and how several economic elements can positively or negatively influence business activity (see Exhibit 6.5).

Exhibit 6.5 Canada's Economic System

Goals of the Economic System	Economic Elements that Influence Business
Economic Growth	• The business cycle • Productivity • Balance of trade • Exchange rates • National debt
Economic Stability	• Inflation • Deflation • Interest rates
Employment	• Employment rates and measures

Economic Growth

Before business managers make decisions, they must first ask how the economy is doing. Is the economy growing, or are there signs that the economy is slowing down? This macroeconomic analysis can affect whether or not a business expands into a new territory, invests in capital, adds a new product line, hires new workers, or downsizes. Economic growth is affected by five factors: the business cycle, productivity, the balance of trade, exchange rates, and the national debt.

business cycle The rise and fall of economic activity over time. There are five stages: expansionary, peak, contraction, trough, and recovery.

expansionary phase A phase in the business life cycle where economic activity is rising.

peak The point in the business life cycle when the economy has reached its highest point, thus marking the end of the expansionary phase and the beginning of the contraction phase.

The Business Cycle The **business cycle** refers to the rise and fall of economic activity over time. Although the economy will grow over the long term, economic growth is usually unstable. Business cycles or economic fluctuations vary in length and severity. Some periods of fluctuation are difficult and long; others are short and mild. Generally, the economy in the long run has an upward slope with ups and downs of varying degrees (see Exhibit 6.6). The five stages of the business cycle are expansionary, peak, contraction, trough, and recovery (see Exhibit 6.7).

The **expansionary phase** is a period when economic activity is rising. Goods are being produced and sold, the workforce is expanding (that is, jobs are being created), demand for goods is increasing, and the price of goods is rising. Typically, this is a positive period for business. Profits are rising, cash flow is steady, and there is an opportunity for some risk taking. The expansionary period can experience a sudden economic boom or slow and steady growth.

Once the economy has reached its highest point, it can be said to have peaked. A **peak** marks the end of the expansionary phase and the beginning of the contraction phase.

A **contraction phase** is characterized by declining economic activity and falling profits. During this phase, managers usually reduce costs, lay off workers, and halt any plans to invest in the company. A **recession** is realized when there are two or more consecutive quarter periods of negative or falling economic activity. The most recent recession occurred in 2008, as seen in Talking Business 6.5 (on page 212). A **depression** is an extreme recession that is characterized by longer economic periods of declining economic activity, high unemployment, and high levels of personal and commercial bankruptcies.

Exhibit 6.6 Long-Term Economic Growth

© maigi/Fotolia

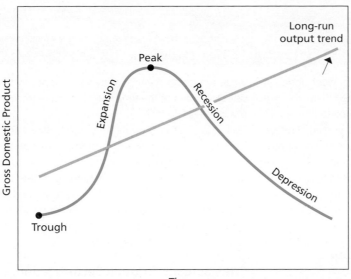

Exhibit 6.7 The Business Cycle

Long-run output trend

Peak

Expansion

Recession

Depression

Trough

Gross Domestic Product

Time

contraction phase A phase in the business life cycle that is characterized by declining economic activity and falling profits.

recession A phase in the business life cycle where there are two or more consecutive quarter periods of negative or falling economic activity.

depression A phase in the business life cycle that is characterized by longer economic periods of declining economic activity, high unemployment, and high levels of personal and commercial bankruptcies. A depression is a severe recession.

trough The point in the business life cycle when the economy has reached its lowest point, thus marking the start of the recovery phase.

recovery phase The phase in the business life cycle that occurs after a trough, where economic activity slowly begins to rise again and the demand for goods and services increases.

gross domestic product (GDP) The total value of a country's output of goods and services produced within a country's borders in a given year.

gross national product (GNP) The value of all final goods and services produced by a national economy inside and outside of the country's borders. (In Canada, this is the the income received in Canada, whether earned in Canada or abroad.)

Real GDP Gross domestic product adjusted to reflect the effects of inflation.

nominal GDP Gross domestic product that is not adjusted for inflation and is measured in current dollars.

A **trough** is the opposite of a peak. A trough is a very low level of economic activity. The **recovery phase** begins after the trough. Here, economic activity slowly begins to rise and the demand for goods and services increases. Firm profits also begin to increase again.

So, how is the economy doing in Canada? Let's take a look in Talking Business 6.6 (on page 213).

Measuring Economic Growth Measuring economic growth accurately is an important function of the government to ensure that the economy is on track. There are two main measures of economic growth: GDP and GNP.

The **gross domestic product (GDP)** is the value of all final goods and services *produced* within a country's borders. In Canada, this includes all goods and services produced by both Canadian and foreign companies physically located in Canada. For example, the value of cars produced by the US Ford Motor Company in Oakville, Ontario, would be included in Canada's GDP.

The **gross national product (GNP)** is the value of all final goods and services produced by a national economy inside and outside of the country's borders. In other words, Canadian GNP measures income *received* in Canada whether earned in Canada or abroad.

What is the difference between GDP and GNP? Let's take a look at the operations of Magellan Aerospace, a Canadian manufacturer with operations in Canada, the United States, and Great Britain. In calculating *Canada's GDP*, one would only include Magellan's Canadian profits that are physically earned in Canada. However, when calculating *Canada's GNP*, one would include profits earned from all Magellan's operations, both in Canada and abroad. When calculating the *US GDP*, one would include only profits from Magellan's US operations. Profits earned in Canada and Great Britain would be outside of the US borders and would not be included in US GDP. As you can see, the calculations can become quite complex.

GDP can also be calculated in different ways. There is real GDP, nominal GDP, and GDP per capita. **Real GDP** is GDP adjusted to reflect the effects of inflation. In other words, real GDP takes out the effect of rising prices. **Nominal GDP**, on the other hand, is not adjusted for inflation and is measured in current dollars. That is, the current price or

The US Subprime Mortgage Crisis and Recession

On September 15, 2008, Lehman Brothers went under. In the two incredible weeks that followed, the Federal Reserve (Fed) and the United States Treasury nationalized the country's two largest mortgage entities, Fannie Mae and Freddie Mac, and took over the world's largest insurance company, AIG. Global capital flows and trade flows spiralled downwards and a vicious cycle of credit withdrawal, halting of investment, weaker growth, and debt impairment took hold. These developments eventually resulted in the first synchronized global recession since the 1940s.

Lehman Collapse a Result, Not a Cause

The dramatic moves by the U.S. government and the Fed were desperately needed; the Lehman bankruptcy led to a panic in global financial markets and an ensuing plunge in equity markets. However, the collapse of Lehman Brothers—while the catalyst for the frightening developments of autumn 2008—did not the cause the crisis. The crisis emerged from decisions made following the mild recession in the U.S. in 2001 caused by the high-tech bust. This recession led the Fed to pursue an accommodative monetary policy and to reduce interest rates sharply. Not surprisingly, low interest rates, which lasted until early 2006, and strong U.S. economic growth led to a surge in home buying that caused house prices to rise sharply.

Suspect Lending Practices

To entice homeowners into the mortgage market, lenders started offering "sub-prime" mortgages. These mortgages had characteristics that appealed to low-income families, including low or zero down payments, long amortization periods, and low "teaser" interest rates that accelerated quickly after the initial year or two of the loan. To push mortgage sales, many unregulated lenders engaged in unscrupulous practices, such as approving loans to borrowers who weren't required to provide proof of employment and income, or didn't possess any assets.

Homes as ATMs

The growing use of home prices to finance increasing consumer spending also contributed to the crisis. Households used the extraordinary run-up in home prices to refinance their debt and used some of the extra cash to buy more goods—boats, cottages, and new consumer electronics—while foregoing savings. Why save money when the prevailing wisdom at the time was that home prices could only go up, never down?

The mix of lax regulation, aggressive and dishonest lenders, naive borrowers, inappropriate policy responses by the Fed, and low household savings eventually led to a housing market meltdown beginning in late 2006 and a severe U.S. recession that just came to an end [in summer 2009]. However, that doesn't explain why some bizarre lending practices in the United States came close to toppling the entire global economy.

Crisis Spreads Through Securitization

Rapid innovation in global financial markets spread the American housing market meltdown to the rest of the world. The surge in U.S. housing prices coincided with the rise of new financial techniques, notably securitization, a process that became quite common in developed countries. Banks bundled the mortgage loans on their books and sold them as securities in secondary markets. These loans became known as mortgage-backed securities (MBS).

MBS were very attractive investments, since on the surface they offered much higher returns than government bonds did. Banks, hedge funds, pension funds, and even municipalities all over the world snapped them up. When home prices started to collapse in the latter half of 2007, a growing number of homeowners were forced into foreclosure, and the securities backed by these mortgages started to default. The bad loans quickly started to erode the balance sheets of financial institutions that had purchased MBS.

Warning Signs

The first sign of trouble came in the summer of 2007, when the market for asset-backed commercial paper in the United States froze. The Fed stepped in and provided liquidity to the market, but this intervention offered only a short respite. The wave of mortgage defaults grew and the balance sheets of certain financial institutions continued to deteriorate. In March 2008, the investment bank Bear Stearns collapsed under the weight of bad debt. Equity markets sank, recovered briefly, then quickly resumed their downward course—culminating in the events of September 2008.

Financial Crisis Causes Global Recession

Credit is a crucial input for both households and firms; once it dried up, both business and consumer confidence plunged. Firms stopped investing and households slashed spending. The combination of tumbling confidence and a loss of credit created the conditions for recession in the United States that quickly spread around the globe. As the global financial crisis gained momentum, it became virtually impossible for the economy to avoid slipping into recession.

Source: Excerpted from Beckman, K. (2010, February 16). What caused the financial crisis and recession? The Conference Board of Canada. *Inside Edge.* Retrieved from www.conferenceboard.ca/insideedge/2010/february-2010/feb16-what-caused-the.aspx.

TALKING BUSINESS 6.6

Canada's World-Class Economy

According to the Canadian Trade Commissioner Service, there are a number of factors that make Canada one of the most welcoming and profitable places in the world for international business and foreign direct investment:

1. Stable and Predictable

The Economist Intelligence Unit considers Canada the best country in the G7 in which to do business over the next five years.

> We've been committed to Canada and investing here for 100 years and our goal is to continue expanding this strong presence for the next 100 years.
>
> —Robert Hardt, President and CEO, Siemens Canada

Canada boasts a diversified economy, a broad resource base and a stable banking and tax environment. Between 2008 and 2011, the country led the G7 with an average real GDP growth rate of 1.0 percent and is now expected to be among the top G7 performers through 2016.

- Canada has the world's tenth-largest economy and second-largest proven reserves of oil, and is the third-largest producer of natural gas.
- Moody's ranks Canada's banking system number one in the world for financial strength. For the sixth consecutive year, the World Economic Forum rates Canada's banking system as the world's soundest. During the global financial crisis, no Canadian bank or insurance company failed or required bailouts.
- More than 100 projects valued at $1 billion or more each, in oil-and-gas, mining and primary metals, have been announced for the 2012–2020 period.

- Canada shares a border and one of the world's largest and most stable commercial relationships with the United States.
- Sailing times from Canada's Atlantic and Pacific deepwater ports are up to two days shorter than from other North American ports.
- Canada's economy was the first among G7 nations to recoup the employment losses recorded during the global recession.

2. Innovative

Canada offers international investors a special blend of innovation capacity across a wide array of industries.

> Canada is one of the world's leaders in mobile-software development. Venture capitalists have started taking note. Google is certainly taking note.
>
> —Chris O'Neill, Managing Director, Google Canada

Canada's predictable, stable fiscal environment ensures that the benefits of innovation can lead to profits over both the short and long terms. The country's efficient innovation system actively involves Canadian research institutions in the development of next-generation products such as electric vehicles, paper phones, wood-based jet fuel, simulation technologies and the new chemicals and plastics that will shape tomorrow's bio-economy.

- Canada is the world's leading country in terms of its integrated approach to driving economic growth through innovation, based on recent research (2012) from the Information Technology and Innovation Foundation (Kansas City) and the Kauffman Foundation (Washington, DC).

(continued)

- In addition to very favourable R&D tax credits and incentives, Canada's appealing environment for leading-edge research is built upon several innovation-supporting policies: effective protection of intellectual-property rights; open competition in domestic market in the deployment of digital information and communications technologies and platforms; transparent government-procurement practices, and openness to high-skill immigration.

- In 2010, IBM, Pratt & Whitney Canada, Ericsson, AMD, Alcatel-Lucent, Sanofi-Aventis group, Pfizer, Glaxosmithkline, Imperial Oil and Novartis were all among Canada's top 25 R&D spenders. In the past five years, these companies have collectively invested more than $10 billion in Canadian R&D.

- In 2011, the OECD ranked Canada number one among G7 countries for higher-education R&D expenditures as a percentage of GDP.

3. Cost Efficient and Profitable

Canada's competitive business costs, low corporate tax rates, successful innovation clusters, efficient transportation infrastructure and ready access to markets enable profitable international investment.

> When it comes to the kind of advanced engineering we do to build high-end products never built before, we've discovered that Canada is actually more cost-effective than China.
>
> —Michael Worry, CEO, Nuvation Engineering

For much of the past decade, the Canadian economy has expanded faster than any other G7 country. While the commodities boom contributed to this growth, sound public policy played an even bigger role. A decade of budget surpluses and debt-reduction initiatives afforded Canada the ability to implement policies to stimulate the economy.

- Today, Canada has the lowest net debt-to-GDP ratio in the G7 and a concrete plan to return to a budget surplus by 2015–16. Canada is well positioned to continue the pro-business strategies that support long-term economic growth and competitiveness, and help the country attract global investors.

- The Economist Intelligence Unit considers Canada the best country in the G7 in which to do business over the next five years.

- Companies operating in Canada can count on fast, reliable access to North American and global markets. Thanks to the North American Free Trade Agreement (NAFTA), companies in Canada have ready access to a massive market (which includes Canada, the US and Mexico) with an annual economic output valued at more than U.S.$16 trillion.

- In the past five years, Canada concluded free-trade agreements with eight countries; negotiations are underway with 50 other countries and regions, including the European Union and India, while early discussions continue with other countries, such as Japan.

Source: Canadian Trade Commissioner Service. (2013). Canada's Advantages. Retrieved from www.international.gc.ca/investors-investisseurs/advantage-avantage/advantage-avantage.aspx?lang=eng.

---

the price right now. Let's say the average cost of one automobile tire in Year 1 is $50 and the average cost of one tire in Year 2 is $55. In addition, 100,000 tires were sold in Year 1 and 100,000 tires were sold in Year 2. Although sales have increased, were there any more tires produced and sold in Year 2? No: There has been no economic growth in the production of tires. Let's calculate this in terms of nominal and real GDP. In Year 1, nominal GDP was $5,000,000 and real GDP was the same at $5,000,000. In Year 2, however, nominal GDP was $5,500,000 ($55 × 100,000) and real GDP was only $5,000,000 ($50 × 100,000). The difference is due to inflation, the rising price level.

GDP per capita is the GDP per person in a country. GDP per capita is calculated by dividing the total GDP by the total population of a country. This figure assists economists and policymakers in assessing the economic well-being of the average person (see Exhibit 6.8).

GDP per capita The gross domestic product per person in a country. Calculated by dividing the total GDP by the total population of a country.

$$\text{GD per Capita} = \frac{\text{Total GDP}}{\text{Total population}}$$

Exhibit 6.8 GDP per Capita

Productivity   Most businesses would like to increase their productivity. **Productivity** measures the level of output versus the level of input in an organization. An **input**, for example, can include materials, labour, or overhead, whereas an **output** is often a finished unit of product (or service) ready to be sold. An organization is said to have improved its productivity when it can produce more outputs with the same number of inputs. Alternatively, an organization can produce the same number of outputs with a reduced number of inputs. When costs are reduced and spread over the total number of units produced, an improvement in productivity has been achieved (see Exhibit 6.9).

Who benefits when productivity is improved? The business benefits by reducing its costs and increasing its net profits. The consumer may also benefit, since prices of products may be reduced. Improving productivity, however, remains a challenge for many countries, including Canada, as seen in Talking Business 6.7.

The Balance of Trade   The **balance of trade** is the value of all the goods and services a country exports minus the value of all the goods and services a country imports. While most trade with Canada involves goods, services have been an important component to the economy, as seen in Talking Business 6.8 (on page 217). Ideally, Canada would like to have

productivity A measure of the level of output versus the level of input in an organization.

input Something a company contributes to creating its products or services, such as materials, labour, or overhead.

output A finished unit of product (or service) ready to be sold.

balance of trade The value of all goods and services a country exports minus the value of goods and services it imports.

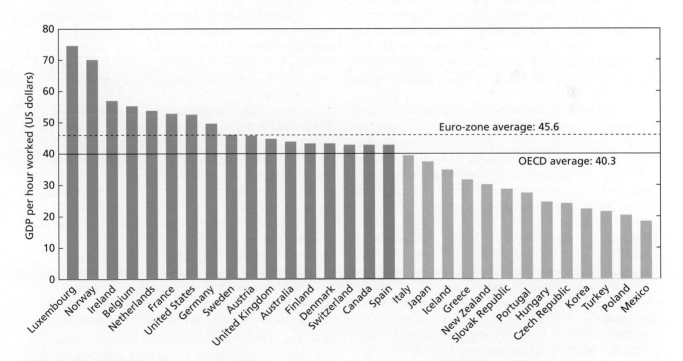

Exhibit 6.9 Productivity in the OECD 2007

Source: OECD productivity levels, 2007. Retrieved from http://en.wikipedia.org/wiki/File:OECD_Productivity_levels_2007.svg.

Canada's Productivity Challenge

We keep hearing about how Canadian business needs to boost productivity to be competitive, and how our workers aren't as productive as some other countries (most notably the United States).

The problem has numerous potential causes, including outdated technology, a somewhat risk-averse culture, low levels of investment in research and development and a lack of commitment to training and development.

In fact, the productivity crisis in the Canadian economy was serious enough to spark a warning from the Organisation for Economic Co-operation and Development (OECD) in 2011 that low productivity is Canada's "great challenge."

Organizations are frequently able to improve productivity and efficiency by fully or partially automating work. In turn, the company can either earn greater profits for its shareholders or pass on cost savings to its customers in the form of lower prices.

Theoretically, this benefits the economy by putting more money into the hands of the company's shareholders or customers. In reality, however, if employees lose their jobs as a result of restructuring, the benefit to the economy is questionable (on the other hand, it may be possible to redeploy displaced workers into more highly skilled roles).

Nevertheless, it's generally advantageous to an organization—and the overall economy—to try to improve productivity.

While the high value of the Canadian dollar has caused some difficulties for Canadian manufacturers, one positive aspect of the higher dollar is employers can better afford investments in high technology equipment and systems manufactured abroad, resulting in productivity improvements. Many experts therefore agree now might be a good time to invest in the infrastructure needed to boost productivity.

A country's productivity is measured by dividing its gross domestic product (GDP) by the total number of hours worked. The U.S., which suffered considerably more than Canada during the last recession, was able to increase productivity while productivity in Canada actually fell.

According to The Conference Board of Canada, this was largely because of the sheer magnitude of job losses south of the border, which were considerably greater in scope than the reduction in GDP, meaning American businesses truly were managing to do more with less. In Canada, there may have been less perceived urgency around the need to boost productivity due to a less severe recession.

However, because Canada weathered the storm of the recent financial crisis better than most countries, Canadian organizations should theoretically be in a better position to invest in technology and infrastructure improvements and employee training and development.

Instead, many businesses decided to hoard their cash reserves rather than making the investments necessary to increase productivity. In fact, both Bank of Canada Governor Mark Carney and federal Finance Minister Jim Flaherty recently warned businesses of the problem of holding excess cash, recommending instead they invest the money or pay it to shareholders as dividends.

Boosting productivity frequently means an organization becomes less reliant on human capital. In theory, at least, automation is supposed to free up workers so they are able to give up routine tasks by enhancing their skills and concentrating on more value-added work. Where this is the case, employees are forced to retrain and enhance their level of skill, frequently resulting in increased wages and improved job satisfaction.

Even if the total amount of human capital required to perform the work decreases, automation can pave the way for enhanced job design initiatives such as job enrichment and job enlargement. In turn, this can help enhance employee engagement by making work more challenging and interesting.

Yet even where total demand for labour doesn't decrease within the organization, it's unlikely there will be absolutely no layoffs. This is because some employees will be resistant to change or may have a difficult time retraining. However, in many cases automation may be the only way an organization or product line can survive in the face of global competition.

The implications for HR are obvious. HR has a role to play in upskilling employees, job and organizational design, change management, redeploying and downsizing employees.

Becoming more productive and competitive won't happen overnight or without a certain amount of pain, but the end result will improve the Canadian economy and increase the level of skill and employability of workers.

Source: Excerpted from Kreissl, B. (2012, September 18). Canada's productivity challenge: How HR can help boost productivity. *HR Reporter.* Retrieved from www.hrreporter.com/blog/hr-policies-practices/postprint/2012/09/18/canadas-productivity-challenge. Reprinted by permission of HR Reporter, 2012.

Canada's Growing but "Invisible" Trade: Services

There is a "hidden" set of exports that account for some of Canada's strongest trade growth: services.

Canada's Newest Export Strengths

You can't drop services on your foot or send them through a pipeline or count them as they cross a border. They also cause less environmental damage. As a result, they get less attention than more visible resources or goods.

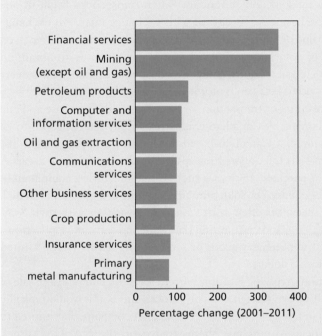

Percentage change (2001–2011)

Services used to be considered "untradeable" in global markets. While true for some services (e.g., haircuts), the ability to digitize information and communicate globally has made it easier to sell services in global markets. Traded services are no longer marginal. While services represent just over one-tenth of Canada's official trade, they represent 40 percent of Canada's trade (and half of global trade) when full supply chains are taken into account. Services make up even more when accounting for Canadian companies that set up offices abroad from which to sell their services.

There are opportunities to sell Canada's services in both traditional markets such as the US and EU, and in fast-growth markets. Take India, for example. A new Conference Board study *The Hottest Prospects for Canadian Companies*

in India, identifies many massive, extremely fast-growing, dynamic service sectors in India that are or are becoming relatively more open to Canadian businesses. Moreover, Canada has global commercial strengths in many of these sectors.

For example, Canadian companies have deep strength in telecommunications, an exploding sector in India. Canada's engineering and architecture companies could tap into India's massive infrastructure needs. And Canada's higher education sector could tap into India's hugely ambitious plans to set up 1,000 universities and 50,000 colleges by 2020. Canada also has deep strengths in energy and autos and could sell its expertise to help India meet its own enormous needs.

To be sure, fast-growth markets such as India that present enormous opportunities to sell services can be some of the world's most challenging places in which to do business. India remains a very closed economy and corruption is pervasive. Despite recent announcements that open up services sectors such as retail, airlines, insurance, and broadcasting to more foreign direct investment, investments in India's services sector are still subject to numerous restrictions.

What is clear is that—while less visible than our resource and goods trade—services are a key trade driver and an important contributor to Canada's living standards. The next generation of Canada's trade agreements—such as the almost complete Canada-EU deal, and the less visible international services negotiations—are starting to address barriers to trade in services. Unlike tariffs or duties on goods, these are more challenging issues such as restrictions on people movements, information flows, or investment.

Policymakers should open doors widely to these hidden trade opportunities. Canadian companies should identify where they have world-leading expertise they could sell in global markets, and walk through those doors.

Source: Excerpted from Goldfarb, D. (2013, May 29). Canada's growing but "invisible" trade: services. Reprinted with permission from The Conference Board of Canada. Retrieved from www.conferenceboard.ca/economics/hot_eco_topics/default/13-05-29/canada_s_growing_but_%E2%80%9Cinvisible%E2%80%9D_trade_services.aspx?pf=true.

a trade surplus instead of a trade deficit. A **trade surplus** occurs when a country exports more goods than it imports. This indicates a positive balance of trade and encourages economic growth. Similarly, a **trade deficit** exists when a country imports more goods than it exports. A trade deficit is problematic because it results in a negative balance of trade, which means more money is leaving the country than is entering the country. Therefore, money is not being reinvested in Canadian productive activities that can help Canada grow and prosper. A negative balance of trade may also indicate that Canada is not making enough of its own goods and is dependent on foreign products.

Exchange Rates

Certainly, trade remains an essential component of Canada's economy. One factor that can affect the cost of trade is exchange rates. In today's competitive marketplace, more firms are doing business outside of their home country—that is, buying and selling goods in different markets and currencies. When transactions begin in one currency and settle in another, businesses must deal with exchange rates. An **exchange rate** or **currency rate** is the value of a foreign currency compared to a home currency or, in other words, the amount of domestic currency that must be given up to obtain an equivalent unit of the foreign currency. Global companies deal with exchange rates every day because their transactions occur between multiple countries.

The most common type of currency transaction for businesses is the purchase and sale of goods and services across borders. A Canadian company can buy foreign goods to be used in its business. For example, a Canadian-based automotive company could buy inventory—such as auto parts—in US dollars from a US firm to manufacture a car. A Canadian company could also purchase an asset—such as manufacturing equipment—from a US firm to help produce goods to be sold. Similarly, services can also be purchased. For example, US technology specialists often assist Canadian businesses with their computer needs by designing, installing, and customizing hardware and software applications. Typically, when a Canadian firm purchases goods or services originating in the United States the firm will be billed in US dollars.

A second type of transaction involving multiple currencies is the purchase and sale of investments. Businesses that invest in foreign company stocks and bonds would typically need to make these purchases in foreign currencies. A Canadian company that wanted to buy shares in Apple would need to purchase shares traded on the NASDAQ stock exchange in US dollars. Similarly, if Apple wanted to buy shares in a Canadian company, Apple would need to purchase them in Canadian dollars.

A third example of a currency transaction is through financial statement translation. A Canadian company conducting sales in the United States—such as through a wholly owned US subsidiary or a sales branch—will have sales in US dollars. If the company's financial statements are in Canadian dollars, there will be an unrealized translation gain or loss when the currency is translated. A financial statement consists of a company's assets, liabilities, and net profits.

Why Can Exchange Rates Be Positive or Negative for Business? The fluctuations of exchange rates can impact a business's profitability and thus expose the company to currency risk. **Currency risk** is the potential risk of financial loss due to transactions in multiple currencies. When can currency risk occur? It depends on the type of transaction (such as a purchase or a sale). However, a rise in the price of a foreign currency means that the home or domestic currency has *depreciated*. Similarly, a decrease in the price of the foreign currency means that the home currency has *appreciated*.

Long-term contracts or business agreements present the greatest risk of currency fluctuation since no one can predict whether a certain currency will appreciate or depreciate in the future. A contract to build an airplane, for example, may require work to be performed over 10 years. Let's consider an example: Boeing, a US plane manufacturer, may enter into an agreement with Air Canada to build an airplane over 10 years. Air Canada agrees to pay US$30 million for the plane when it is completed in 10 years. At the time the order is placed, US$1 buys CDN$0.95. So, according to the *present* exchange rate, the cost of the plane is CDN$28.5 million. However, it is the exchange rate at the *end* of the contract that Air Canada is obligated to pay. If, for example, in 10 years the exchange rate enables the purchase of CDN$1.40 with US$1, the cost of the new plane becomes CDN$42 million—a difference of CDN$13.5 million. If Air Canada were to order 30 new planes, the difference in expected price is CDN$13.5 million × 30 = CDN$405 million. The unexpected increase in cost can impact the company's cash flows, net profits, and even its ability to meet its current and future liabilities with other companies. The company may not even be able to pay.

The National Debt   Most economists will agree that debt is usually not good for an economy. Debt is borrowed money that must be repaid, usually with interest. Unlike consumer debt, which is debt individuals have accumulated from the purchase of goods and services, **national debt**, also known as *federal debt*, is debt accumulated by the government. All local, regional, or national governments can have debt, but a large national debt can be especially problematic for individuals and businesses because this debt can affect the economy as a whole. Indeed, as debt increases, governments have to spend more money (that is, tax dollars) on additional interest costs. Consequently, there is less money to spend on community services such as libraries, health care services, and education. Similarly, there is less money for business subsidies for research and development initiatives.

> **national debt** Debt that is accumulated by the federal government. It can impact businesses because it has an effect on the entire country's economy.

In addition to outstanding debt, many governments also have a current budget deficit. A **budget deficit** is the negative difference between incoming tax revenues (or receipts) and outgoing government expenditures. Like a bank overdraft, a deficit means the cash outflows are greater than the cash inflows in a given period. If a government has a budget deficit, the government must borrow money to pay the amount owing. This new borrowed amount gets added to the outstanding government debt. In Canada, since there are three levels of government, there can be three levels of debt: municipal, provincial, and federal.

> **budget deficit** The negative difference between incoming tax revenues and outgoing government expenditures. Like a bank overdraft, a deficit means the cash outflows are greater than the cash inflows in a given period.

Today, governments around the world are having difficulty preventing budget deficits and paying down their debts. But how much debt is too much? And what impact can debt have on a country and its economy?

Canada's Debt   Canada is a leader among the G7 nations in managing its national debt. The **G7** is a group of seven developed, industrialized countries with large economies that includes France, Germany, the United States, the United Kingdom, Italy, Japan, and Canada. Of the seven, Canada has the lowest debt-to-GDP ratio, estimated at 30%.[28]

> **G7** A group of seven developed, industrialized nations with large economies. Includes France, Germany, the United States, the United Kingdom, Italy, Japan, and Canada.

What is a good debt-to-GDP ratio? The results of a survey of economists, published by the Institute for Research on Public Policy, indicate a manageable federal debt-to-GDP ratio should fall between 20% and 50%.[29] Canada currently falls on the lower end, which is

---

[28] *National Post* staff. (2011, March 21). WTF: The federal budget and 50 years of Canadian debt. *National Post*. Retrieved from http://news.nationalpost.com/2011/03/21/graphic-50-years-of-canadian-debt.

[29] *National Post* staff, 2011.

viewed by many as a good position to be in. Other members of the G7 are in a financial crisis and are seeking alternatives to better manage their governments and their debts. As Greece, Britain, and other nations struggle to address their own debt problems, many countries are turning to Canada to follow its model for debt reduction. Take, for example, George Osborne, Britain's cabinet minister for finance: In 2010, Osborne implemented a plan to reduce government spending by 20%, which was similar to Canada's policy in 1994.[30]

In the early 1990s, the Canadian federal government had a debt crisis of its own. The nation had a budget deficit of approximately 9% of GDP and a federal debt-to-GDP ratio of almost 70%.[31] In 1994, Liberal Prime Minister Jean Chrétien introduced what became known as the "bloodbath budget" and reduced government spending by 20%. The plan worked. By 1997, the federal budget deficit had been eliminated, but some hard choices had to be made. Reductions to social services budgets meant thousands of jobs were lost in the public sector. After three years, however, there were consecutive surpluses, which lasted for almost a decade.[32] Today, some Brits refer to Canada's budget restraints as a "model of brutality," but one that proved successful for the fiscal well-being of its country and its citizens.[33]

According to Kevin Lynch, vice-chair of BMO Financial Group and former deputy minister of finance,

> What has worked [in Canada] is transparently eliminating or reducing programs, with commensurate reductions in budgets and employment, and tacking inefficient tax expenditures, which are no different than ineffective programs. . . . What is needed is a strong commitment to more public-private partnerships, in both infrastructure and service delivery.[34]

But some economists are not as optimistic and have great concerns about Canada's national debt. They argue that the measurement of debt is somewhat subjective, depending on who calculates it and what they include. Canada's gross debt, for example, includes debts of provincial governments but excludes Canada/Quebec Pension Plan accounts. If they were included in the calculation, the debt-to-GDP ratio would be 65%. Similarly, the International Monetary Fund (IMF) calculates Canada's current debt level differently, including unfunded liabilities such as government-sector pension funds, resulting in a debt-to-GDP ratio closer to 80%, which is significantly higher than the OECD's estimate.[35]

So what is the actual amount of Canada's debt? According to the Canadian Taxpayers Federation, Canada's federal debt is over $568 billion dollars[36] and growing. Travelling

[30] Porter, A. (2010, June 6). Britain to emulate Canada's radical solution to tackle debt. *The Telegraph*. Retrieved from www.telegraph.co.uk/news/politics/7807347/Britain-to-emulate-Canadas-radical-solution-to-tackle-debt.html.

[31] McRobie, H. (2010, June 8). George Osborne can't cherry pick from Canada's cuts model. *The Guardian*. Retrieved from www.guardian.co.uk/commentisfree/2010/jun/08/george-osborne-canada-cuts-model.

[32] McRobie, 2010.

[33] Halpern, D., & Myers, J. (2009, May 3). Think tank: A model of brutality Britain can build on. *Sunday Times*. Retrieved from www.timesonline.co.uk/tol/comment/article6210977.ece.

[34] Lynch, K. (2011, January 10). The Canadian way to rein in debt. *Globe and Mail*. Retrieved from www.theglobeandmail.com/news/opinions/opinion/the-canadian-way-to-rein-in-debt/article1862195

[35] *National Post* staff, 2011.

[36] Ross, R. (2011, March 24). Government debts spiralling out of control: Taxpayer's Federation. *The Guardian*. www.theguardian.pe.ca/News/Local/2011-03-24/article-2360653/Government-debts-spiraling-out-of-control%3A-Taxpayers-Federation/1.

around the country, this nonprofit citizens' group uses a debt clock to educate Canadians about their country's growing debt load. After all, debt is not a topic that politicians want to talk about—it doesn't make them popular. When debt levels get too high, the choices for politicians are limited: cut spending, raise taxes, or both. Either way, it means taxpayers have to make difficult sacrifices—reduce their standard of living now or face dire consequences in the future.

The Canadian debt load may be better than most countries, but it still grows by a whopping $1,284 per second, or $111 million per day. On a per capita basis, every Canadian would need to pay the government $16,316 to pay off the current federal debt.[37] Add in the provincial and municipal debts and the amount will be much higher.

In 1996, the debt reached an all-time high of $769 billion after adjusting for inflation.[38] This was the period of Canada's debt crisis. But from 2000 to 2010, Canada's debt declined while the United States's debt doubled. Why the stark contrast? Statistics indicate that Canada paid off about $90 billion of its debt between 1997 and 2008. Although the debt has increased over the past two years, more recent changes have been mainly due to the effects of the global recession.[39] See Exhibit 6.10 for a history of Canada's debt.

How Does the United States Compare?   In August 2011, the US federal debt hit 100% of its GDP, creating a crisis that policymakers had to address.[40] According to DebtClock. org, a US nonprofit organization, the United States's national debt is over $14.6 trillion and growing. In fact, it grows by a staggering $1 million every minute,[41] which means the national debt increases by billions of dollars per day. According to the PEW Center, the US debt increases have been due to a variety of reasons, including recession tax revenue declines (28%), military spending increases (13%), tax reductions implemented by the Bush administration (13%), interest on debt (11%), and other spending (11%).[42] As of September 2013, the US national debt was over $17 trillion and the Canadian national debt was over $616 billion.

Of course, by the time you read this book the Canadian and US national debts will have grown again. See what they are now at www.debtclock.ca and www.usdebtclock.org.

Why Is Debt Bad for the Economy?   Every country has debt, so why does it matter? When debt increases and gets too high, a series of problems can arise. First, a country's credit rating can be lowered, leading to higher borrowing costs and causing a further increase in the debt load, which occurred in the United States. In August 2011, Standard & Poor's, a global credit-rating agency, lowered the United States's credit rating from AAA to AA+ because of a lack of confidence in the government's plan to reduce its debt. While other credit-rating companies did not lower the government's rating, global stock markets took a tumble the following day. Many European countries also face a debt crisis. Greece, Ireland, and Portugal have required significant financial assistance and bailouts from their

---

[37] Ross, 2011.

[38] *National Post* staff, (2011).

[39] Froats, P. (2011, June 18). Chart: Canada vs. U.S. on national debt. *Canadian Business*. Retrieved from www.canadianbusiness.com/article/31335--chart-canada-vs-u-s-on-national-debt.

[40] Milner, B. (2011, August 25). Before new downgrade, decades of economic misery. *Globe and Mail*. Retrieved from http://investdb4.theglobeandmail.com/servlet/story/GAM.20110825.RBJAPANECONO-MYATL/GIStory.

[41] US DebtClock.org. www.usdebtclock.org.

[42] Froats, 2011.

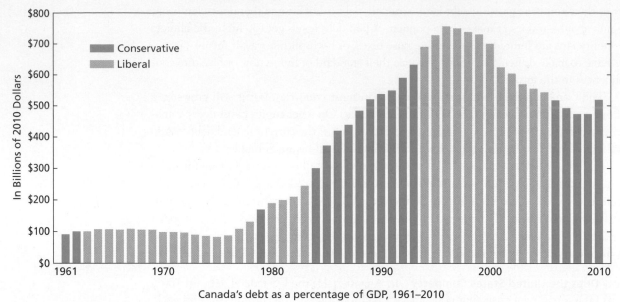

Canada's debt in inflation-adjusted dollars, 1961–2010

Canada's debt as a percentage of GDP, 1961–2010

Exhibit 6.10 History of Canada's debt

Source: MacMahon, Tamsin. "WTF: The federal budget and 50 years of Canadian debt." The National Post. 21 March 2011. Reprinted with permission from Postmedia Network Inc.

European neighbours. In July 2011, Standard & Poor's reduced Greece's credit rating from B to CCC, the lowest-rated country in the world in S&P's rankings.[43]

A second reason why debt is bad for the economy is that government austerity programs are required to reduce the debt. The combination of higher taxes to generate revenue and lower government spending to reduce costs lowers overall demand and, therefore, slows the economy.

[43] Georgiopoulos, G., & Brandimarte, W. (2011, June 13). Greece falls to S&P's lowest rated, default warned. *Reuters.* Retrieved from www.reuters.com/article/2011/06/13/us-greece-ratings-sandp-idUSN1312685920110613.

A third reason is that government will have to spend more time addressing the debt issue than other important issues to the country. The result is a less-efficient use of its resources. Instead of a focus on trade, innovation, or some other value-added activity, a focus on debt reduction means the government has less time and money to spend on more important endeavours.

And finally, according to the doctrine of Ricardian equivalence, increasing government deficits may lead consumers and businesses to believe their taxes will be raised in the future to pay off the growing debt. To prepare for this, consumers and businesses end up saving their money instead of spending it, leading to a worsening of the economic problem.[44]

What if a government cannot repay its debt? The government may need to ask for a loan from another country or the International Monetary Fund (IMF). Greece had to do both. In 2010, $110 billion was granted to Greece as a rescue loan. In 2011, a second bail-out of $109 billion was provided.[45] If there is still no money, the government would essentially become bankrupt and not be able to pay its workers or run its programs. For example, government workers such as teachers, health care providers, or police officers would not get paid; government-paid programs that people rely on—such as pension income received by seniors or unemployment payments for the unemployed—could just stop completely.

How Would You Reduce the Debt?   It seems as if there are no easy solutions for debt reduction. And no one wants to do without government services. How then should a government pay off its rising debt? What services would you be willing to sacrifice or to pay more for? Should we agree to an increase in personal income taxes, sales taxes, or property taxes? Or do we forfeit a government service now to secure a better future for tomorrow? These are certainly difficult questions.

Economic Stability

Clearly, many factors contribute to a stable economy. As we have seen, a trade surplus, low debt, and a high GDP can help improve the economy. **Economic stability** occurs when the amount of money available and the goods and services produced grow at approximately the same rate. Factors that threaten economic stability include inflation, deflation, and unemployment.

economic stability   An economic state that occurs when the amount of money available and the goods and services produced grow at approximately the same rate.

Inflation   Managers are encouraged to reduce costs to increase net profits. However, over time prices generally rise, costs increase, and doing business becomes more expensive. The rise in the price level of goods and services is called **inflation**. *Expected inflation* is the rate at which people believe the price level will rise, whereas *unanticipated inflation* is inflation that people do not expect. *Anticipated inflation* is inflation that has been correctly forecasted.

inflation   The rise in the price level of goods and services.

Inflation is a concern for individuals and businesses since it reduces the **purchasing power of money**; that is, the value of what money can buy. If, for example, a person earns a salary of $30,000 and his rent increases by $100 per month, his purchasing power has decreased by $1,200 even though his salary remains unchanged. Since his expenses have increased, he has less money to spend. Similarly, price increases affect businesses, too.

purchasing power of money
The value of what money can buy. If prices increase, then individuals and businesses have less money to spend on other items.

---

[44] *The Economist.* (2010, June 24). The unkindest cuts. Retrieved from www.economist.com/node/16397086.

[45] Associated Press. (2011, June 25). Greece's credit rating downgraded by Moody's. Retrieved from www.cbc.ca/news/business/story/2011/07/25/business-greece-fininacal-crisis.html.

Inflation means input costs such as labour, materials, and overhead are more expensive and therefore company profits are reduced.

Other types of inflation are demand-pull inflation and cost-push inflation. **Demand-pull inflation** occurs when the demand for goods and services exceeds the supply, which tends to "pull" prices up. When producers can realize higher prices, they produce more goods until demand and supply reach an equilibrium. **Cost-push inflation** results from increases in production costs for businesses such as raw materials and labour expenses. These input costs "push" up the final price of goods and services, thus increasing the price for consumers. Wage increases are the most significant factor in cost-push inflation, since labour is often a business's highest cost.

How Is Inflation Measured?   Statisticians measure inflation by examining price levels and by using price indexes. A **price level** is the average level of prices. A **price index** will show an average change in a group of prices over time. When there is a change in the price level, the inflation rate changes, too (see Exhibit 6.11).

There are different price indices for different baskets of goods. The **consumer price index (CPI)** is a price index that measures commodities commonly purchased by households. Food, clothing, transportation, education, shelter, and recreation are a few of the goods and services that make up the CPI. The **producer price index (PPI)** is the price index that measures the prices of inputs to producers and wholesalers, including finished products for resale, partially finished goods, and raw materials.

Inflation: A Country Comparison   According to Statistics Canada, Canada's CPI rose by 3.1% between June 2010 and June 2011.[46] The main contributors were rising food and gasoline prices. The US CPI was slightly higher at 3.6%.[47] Around the globe, inflation levels continue to vary. Vietnam's prices have increased by 12% since last year, while prices in India and Russia are higher by 8%.[48] Historically, some countries' inflation rates have soared. In the 2000s, Burma had an annual inflation rate of 40% and Iran had an inflation rate of 25%.[49]

Who Is Affected the Most by Inflation?   Generally, people who live on a fixed income, such as senior citizens, are most affected by inflation. For example, if a 70-year-old citizen receives a pension of $1,000 per month in Year 1, and inflation rises by 10% in Year 2, due to rises in prices of food and gasoline that pensioner can buy only 90% of what he or she could have bought in Year 1. Similarly, savers are negatively affected by inflation. Since money is being held, purchasing power is reduced when price levels are rising. For instance, if an individual is saving to buy a home but housing prices are rising, then the person's purchasing power is reduced.

demand-pull inflation A type of inflation that occurs when the demand for goods and services exceeds the supply, which tends to "pull" prices up.

cost-push inflation A type of inflation that occurs when increases in production costs for businesses "push" up the final price that consumers have to pay.

price level The average level of prices.

price index A measure of the average change in a group of prices over time.

consumer price index (CPI) A price index that measures commodities commonly purchased by households, such as food, clothing, transportation, education, shelter, and recreation.

producer price index (PPI) A price index that measures the prices of inputs to producers and wholesalers, including finished products for resale, partially finished goods, and raw materials.

Exhibit 6.11 Inflation Rate Calculation

$$\text{Inflation rate} = \left(\frac{\text{Current year's price level} - \text{Last year's price level}}{\text{Last year's price level}} \right) \times 100$$

[46] Statistics Canada. (2011, July 22). Consumer price index. *The Daily*. Retrieved from www.statcan.gc.ca/daily-quotidien/110722/dq110722a-eng.htm.

[47] Bureau of Labor Statistics. (2011, July 15). Consumer Price Index—June 2011. Retrieved from www.bls.gov/news.release/archives/cpi_07152011.pdf.

[48] Milner, B. (2011, January 14). Global inflation fears reach new heights. *Globe and Mail*. Retrieved from www.theglobeandmail.com/report-on-business/economy/global-inflation-fears-reach-new-heights/article1881500.

[49] *The Economic Times*. (2008, June 19). 10 nations with abnormally high inflation. Retrieved from http://economictimes.indiatimes.com/10-nations-with-abnormally-high-inflation/slideshow/3144922.cms.

Deflation   **Deflation** is the opposite of inflation. Deflation occurs when the price level of goods is falling. Prices can fall for a couple of reasons. First, industrial productivity can increase and cost savings can be passed on to customers in the form of lower prices. On the other hand, customers with high debt may not be able to buy very much, thus reducing demand. Some economists believe deflation can be more problematic than inflation. Since consumers tend to expect prices to fall, they will sometimes stop spending their money altogether, anticipating even lower prices. While falling prices may appear to be good for consumers, falling sales can be damaging to businesses and to the economy. The worst episode of deflation in Canada occurred during the Great Depression of the 1930s. With over 25% unemployment, consumers had little money to spend, demand dropped, and prices fell significantly.

Interest rates   The **Bank of Canada** is Canada's central bank and a Crown corporation of the federal government. Formed in 1934, the Bank of Canada was established to regulate the Canadian banking and financial industry to ensure low inflation, high employment levels, and positive economic growth in the long term.

The interest rates charged by chartered banks such as CIBC, Scotiabank, or TD Canada Trust are influenced by the bank rate established by the Bank of Canada. The **bank rate** is the rate at which the Bank of Canada loans money to financial institutions across the country. When the federal government wants to encourage economic growth, it may reduce the bank rate to encourage banks to borrow more money. When the government wants to do the opposite and slow the economy down, the Bank of Canada can raise the bank rate.

Higher interest rates make it more costly to borrow money; lower interest rates make it cheaper. Therefore, interest rates are relevant to anyone who needs financing. An **interest rate** is a fee charged, usually a percentage, by a lender to a borrower for the use of funds.

Interest rates can affect businesses in two ways. First, interest rates can affect the cost of borrowing (interest expense on mortgages, bank loans, capital investments, and so on). Second, interest rates can affect a customer's ability to buy goods and services. When customers have higher interest costs on mortgages, student loans, bank loans, and credit card debt, they will have less money available to spend on goods and services.

Businesses need to borrow money for a variety of reasons. A business may need cash to meet current or long-term liabilities. This is especially true of seasonal businesses like ski resorts, which have more revenue in the winter months than in the summer months; if money runs out before ski season opens, the business may need a bank loan. Or a company may need to purchase a new asset if one fails, such as a piece of manufacturing equipment. Likewise, a firm may want to expand its operations into new territories and may require money to purchase land and buildings. Similarly, individuals borrow money to meet their own needs. People may need to borrow money to pursue an education or to buy a car to commute to work.

When individuals or businesses borrow money, the interest charged can be at a fixed rate or a variable rate. A **fixed rate** is a permanent interest rate that cannot be changed for the term of the loan. Fixed rates are often higher than variable rates since future interest rates are unknown and banks do not want to lose money should rates increase. Fixed interest rates also reduce risk since they provide some assurance to businesses that their current interest costs will not rise in the future. A **variable rate** is more risky for businesses since variable rates are subject to change. Since interest rates can increase over time, variable rates tend to be lower.

deflation   When the price level of goods is falling; the opposite of inflation.

Bank of Canada   Canada's central bank, which is a Crown corporation of the federal government. It regulates the banking and financial industry to ensure low inflation, high employment levels, and positive long-term economic growth for Canada.

bank rate   The rate at which the Bank of Canada loans money to financial institutions.

interest rate   A fee charged, usually a percentage, by a lender to a borrower for the use of funds.

fixed rate   A permanent interest rate that cannot be changed for the term of a loan. Usually higher than a variable rate.

variable rate   An interest rate that fluctuates over the term of the loan. Since there is more risk for the borrower, variable rates are usually lower than fixed rates.

Employment

Employment is a third goal of Canada's economic system; however, it is not one that is easily achieved. There is always some unemployment, but how much is too much? **Unemployment** occurs when qualified individuals actively looking for work are unable to secure employment. Unemployment can be detrimental to both businesses and the economy. People who are unemployed have less disposable income and often cannot afford basic goods and services.

Employment Rates and Measures The labour force is the total number of people employed and unemployed. The **unemployment rate** is the percentage of people who are unemployed out of the total labour force and who are actively seeking work. New graduates looking for work are an example of unemployed workers included in the unemployment rate, as per Exhibit 6.12. Stay-at-home mothers and retirees would not be included in the unemployment rate because they are not actively seeking employment and therefore are not part of the labour force. Part-time workers, however, are employed and are part of the labour force.

Types of Unemployment What are the various types of unemployment and what are their root causes? **Frictional unemployment** is caused by normal labour market turnover, not a downturn in the economy. New college graduates, mothers looking for work, or anyone looking for his or her first job are a few examples. Employed workers who are laid off also fall under this category. Frictional unemployment is unlikely to disappear, since people are constantly entering and exiting the labour force. The baby boom of the 1950s brought a large number of people into the workforce, creating higher frictional

unemployment A situation that occurs when qualified individuals who are actively looking for work are unable to secure employment.

unemployment rate The percentage of people who are unemployed out of the total labour force and who are actively seeking work.

Objective 5 Explain the different types of unemployment.

frictional unemployment Unemployment that is caused by normal labour market turnover, not a downturn in the economy.

Exhibit 6.12
Unemployment Rate in Canada, 1980–2012

Source: Statistics Canada. (2013, January 4). Labour force characteristics. CANSIM Table 282-0002.

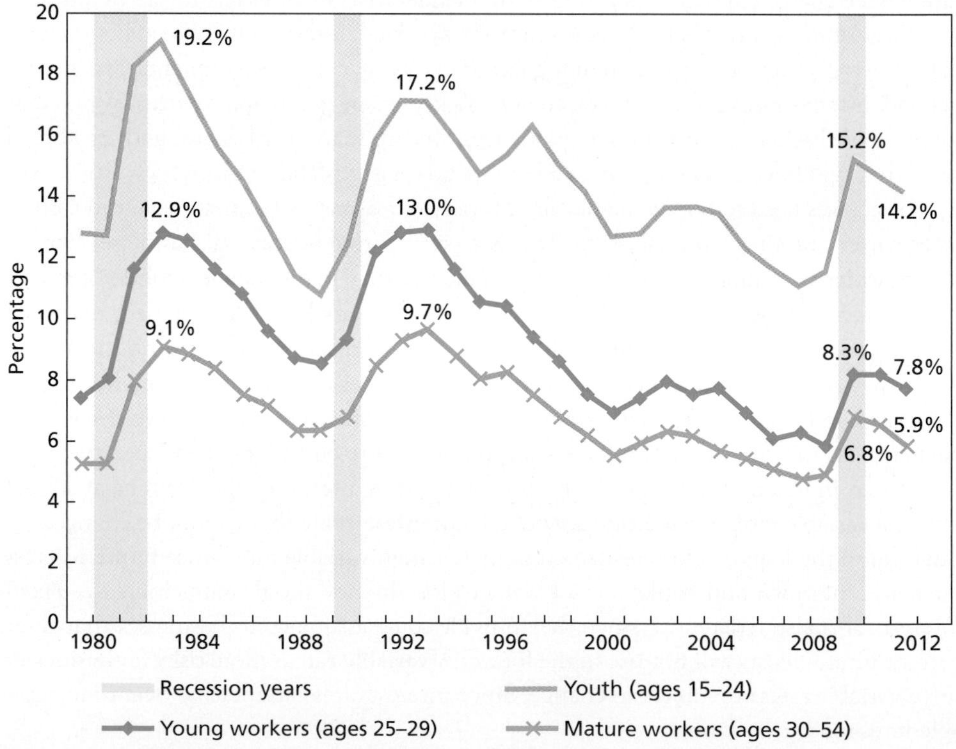

Legend:
- Recession years
- Youth (ages 15–24)
- Young workers (ages 25–29)
- Mature workers (ages 30–54)

unemployment for a period of time. Similarly, when businesses suffer bankruptcy or move to a new location, job losses contribute to frictional unemployment.

Cyclical unemployment, on the other hand, is related to the pace of the economy, or the "business cycle." When the economy slows down or is in a recession, cyclical unemployment is high. Alternatively, when the economy is growing and expanding, cyclical unemployment is low. For instance, auto workers who are laid off during a recession and then hired back months later are individuals who experience cyclical unemployment.

Structural unemployment occurs for two reasons: either the available jobs do not correspond to the skills of the labour force or unemployed individuals do not live in a region where jobs are available. Structural unemployment has also been prevalent where there has been a technological change and old jobs have been discontinued and new jobs created. In the 1980s, typewriters were replaced by personal computers. Those whose job it was to repair typewriters became obsolete and computer administrator jobs were created, requiring a different skill set. Today, with the rise in technological advances, traditional industries such as auto and steel are shrinking and newer industries such as electronics and bioengineering are expanding and creating new jobs. For a recent example of structural unemployment, see Talking Business 6.9.

cyclical unemployment Unemployment caused by changes in the business cycle or pace of the economy. When the economy slows down or is in a recession, cyclical unemployment is high. Alternatively, when the economy is growing and expanding, cyclical unemployment is low.

structural unemployment Unemployment that occurs either because the available jobs do not correspond to the skills of the labour force or unemployed individuals do not live in a region where jobs are available.

TALKING BUSINESS 6.9

Today's High Youth Unemployment: A Solution for Skill Shortages?

Bloomberg via Getty Images

High youth unemployment and growing skill shortages are two important challenges currently facing the labour market. But why not use one problem as the basis of a solution to the other? In a labour market facing growing skill shortages, youth could become an even more valuable source of qualified workers. Current difficulties in finding work are and should send a signal to young people to invest in their own skills. This would help them qualify for a job and contribute to filling the shortages in workers supply, especially among high-skilled occupations.

Canada's economy has been undergoing structural changes over the past two decades and the transition towards a more knowledge-based economy has led to growing demand for a more highly-skilled workforce. Indeed, there are signs that skill shortages are already occurring, especially in the fast-growing parts of the country. The fact that many workers remain unemployed despite the existence of many unfilled positions indicates clear mismatches in the labour market. Employers are thus looking for other means to find qualified workers. Saskatchewan government officials, for example, will participate in a labour recruitment mission to Ireland in March [2012] to support employers looking for potential workers willing to move to the province. And similar support programs to employers were offered by other provinces, even Ontario, where labour markets are relatively slack. While immigration will be an important contributor to labour supply over the long run, other home-grown solutions should complement this approach and training the youth is one of them.

(continued)

Yet even as labour market skills gaps are becoming more evident, employment among those aged 15 to 24 fell significantly as a result of the 2008–09 recession and, even after three years, is showing little signs of recovery. Although Canada's youth unemployment is not as severe as in Europe, where the youth unemployment rate has reached 30 per cent in some countries and exceeded 40 per cent in Spain in 2010, it is still a concern. The youth unemployment rate in Canada climbed from 11.6 per cent in 2008 to 15.2 per cent in 2009, and remained elevated, at 14.2 per cent, in 2011. For young people, the negative consequences are clear in terms of foregone income and lost work experience. But the situation does have a silver lining—it is sending a signal to study, train and acquire skills.

One important reason for the significant fall in youth employment during the recession is that a large number of labour force participants in the 15 to 24 age group have had little training. Young individuals who had not completed a post-secondary program recorded the largest percentage employment declines as a result of the recession, and their employment level remains below pre-recessionary levels; yet employment for those aged 15 to 24 with a post-secondary certificate has recovered to pre-recession levels. And for those with a university degree, employment was 9 per cent higher in 2011 than in 2008. Therefore, the lack of education and training has been a key factor hindering youth employment growth after the recession struck.

As their job prospects became gloomy, many young individuals gave up on looking for a job and left the labour force. Indeed, the labour force participation rate for the 15 to 24 age group has fallen significantly since the 2008–09 recession. Moreover, the participation rate of youth who have not completed a post-secondary educational program posted the sharpest relative decline. If there is an upside, this may reflect the decision by some youths to withdraw from the labour force and to invest in education and training. Tailoring their training to match skills that are in short supply would help alleviate skill shortages. If there were greater communication and coordination between employers and colleges and universities and more skills-specific training programs incorporating co-op and internship opportunities, young Canadians would be in a better position to gain the skills needed to find a job. In Germany, for example, the apprenticeship system combines on-the-job training with formal education, and therefore, allows students to gain concrete work experience while completing their educational program.

Considering youth as potential skilled workers should be a key element of a renewed strategy for tackling skill shortages. Not only is it easier to train and acquire skills at an early age, but the investment in human capital will generate a longer payback period—for the individuals and the economy. With high youth unemployment, now is the right time to strengthen and implement appropriate training strategies. Policy-makers, educational institutions and potential employers should strike while the iron is hot.

Source: Excerpted from Adès, J. (2012, February 29). Today's high youth unemployment: A solution for skill shortages? Reprinted with permission from The Conference Board of Canada. Retrieved from www.conferenceboard.ca/economics/hot_eco_topics/default/ 12-02-29/today_s_high_youth_unemployment_a_solution_for_ skill_shortages.aspx.

---

seasonal unemployment
Unemployment that is caused by the seasonal nature of the job.

Seasonal unemployment is unemployment caused by the seasonal nature of the job. For example, a garden centre may hire workers for the spring and lay them off in the fall. Similarly, a construction company may hire contract workers in the summer and not in the winter. Since Christmas is one of the busiest times of the year for retailers, retail stores are also noted for hiring temporary workers. As you can see, a seasonal job can be created due to special holidays or changes to seasonal weather.

natural rate of unemployment
The total amount of frictional and structural unemployment combined.

The **natural rate of unemployment** is the total amount of frictional and structural unemployment combined. In other words, it is the unemployment that exists when there is no cyclical unemployment.

full employment A situation that occurs when only frictional unemployment exists.

Full employment occurs when only frictional unemployment exists and no structural or cyclical unemployment is present. In this case, the quantity of labour demanded equals the quantity of labour supplied. There will likely always be a certain level of frictional unemployment, since people will always be entering and exiting the workforce.

CHAPTER SUMMARY

The economic environment is certainly a complex one. There are many variables that can influence business and the economy. Changing unemployment rates, inflation rates, and interest rates can pull Canada's economy in different directions. How Canada's economy will perform in the future is something that remains unknown. Certainly, Canada has the potential to build upon its strengths and become an even stronger player in the growing global economy.

CHAPTER LEARNING TOOLS

Key Terms

balance of trade 215
Bank of Canada 225
bank rate 225
barriers to entry 204
budget deficit 219
business cycle 210
capital 198
communism 202
competition 204
consumer price index (CPI) 224
contraction phase 211
cost-push inflation 224
currency risk 218
cyclical unemployment 227
deflation 225
demand-pull inflation 224
depression 211
economic environment 197
economic stability 223

economic system 202
entrepreneurs 199
exchange rate (currency rate) 218
expansionary phase 210
five factors of production 197
fixed rate 225
frictional unemployment 226
full employment 228
G7 219
GDP per capita 214
gross domestic product (GDP) 211
gross national product (GNP) 211
inflation 223
input 215
interest rate 225
knowledge 198
knowledge-based economies 198

labour 197
limited monopoly 206
macroeconomics 200
market economy 202
microeconomics 200
mixed economy 203
monopolistic competition 208
monopoly 206
national debt 219
natural monopoly 206
natural rate of unemployment 228
natural resource 197
nominal GDP 211
oligopoly 206
opportunity cost 197
output 215
patent 206
peak 210
perfect or pure competition 204

price index 224
price level 224
producer price index (PPI) 224
productivity 215
purchasing power of money 223
real GDP 211
recession 211
recovery phase 211
seasonal unemployment 228
socialism 203
structural unemployment 227
trade deficit 218
trade surplus 218
trough 211
unemployment 226
unemployment rate 226
variable rate 225

Multiple-Choice Questions

Select the *best* answer for each of the following questions. Solutions are located in the back of your textbook.

1. All of the following are benefits of a market economy over a communist economy *except*
   a. competition
   b. participation of nonprofit groups
   c. choice
   d. ownership of property

2. All of the following are examples of an oligopolistic industry *except*
   a. cereal companies
   b. airplane manufacturers
   c. coffee shops
   d. auto manufacturers

3. All of the following individuals would be included in the unemployment rate *except*
   a. a worker who has been fired from his job and returns to school full time
   b. a person who was laid off from her job and goes on an extended vacation
   c. a worker who has retired from work and gets a new part-time job
   d. none of the above

4. The consumer price index (CPI) measures all of the following goods *except*
   a. laser eye surgery
   b. personal computers
   c. tools used in a manufacturing plant
   d. fruits and vegetables

5. Deflation can result from
   a. falling prices
   b. industrial productivity increases
   c. high consumer debt
   d. all of the above

6. The US profits from a Canadian company with operations in the United States are included in
   a. Canadian GDP
   b. Canadian GNP
   c. US GDP
   d. both B and C

7. Labour involves
   a. the mental and physical capabilities of people who work for a company
   b. an investor checking her portfolio
   c. both A and B
   d. none of the above

8. The national debt
   a. is the amount of money the government owes to its creditors
   b. can include past budget deficits
   c. both A and B
   d. none of the above

9. Perfect competition exists when
   a. firms are small in size but large in number
   b. prices are set by the market
   c. products are undifferentiated
   d. all the above

10. When Canada's imports are greater than its exports, Canada is said to have
    a. a trade surplus
    b. a trade deficit
    c. an import advantage
    d. an import disadvantage

11. A factor that can contribute to a country's economic success is
    a. strong trading partners
    b. tariffs
    c. unregulated banks
    d. an unskilled labour force

12. Private enterprise requires the presence of all the following *except*
    a. competition
    b. private property
    c. profits
    d. high-quality goods and services

13. An example of a natural monopoly is
    a. an environmental company
    b. a bottled water company
    c. a water utility
    d. both B and C

14. A retail store selling tools and other hardware items is likely an example of
    a. monopolistic competition
    b. an oligopoly
    c. perfect competition
    d. a monopoly

15. Structural unemployment is due to
    a. poor economic times
    b. a lack of the right skills
    c. people entering and exiting the workforce
    d. seasonal conditions

Discussion Questions

1. What is an economic environment?
2. Compare and contrast microeconomics and macroeconomics.
3. Identify and explain four types of economic systems.
4. Identify and explain four types of competition.
5. Discuss three key goals of Canada's economic system.
6. Explain the stages of the business cycle.
7. Identify and discuss different measures of economic growth.
8. Why is debt bad for an economic environment?
9. Describe five types of inflation.
10. Identify and explain the different types of unemployment.

SASKATOON: CANADA'S FASTEST-GROWING ECONOMY

The City of Saskatoon is favoured once again to be one of the fastest-growing economies across Canada, according to a 2013 The Conference Board of Canada report.[50] The report is the Conference Board's annual review of 28 metropolitan areas in Canada.

The expanding job market in Saskatoon is attracting both domestic and foreign applicants, which are growing the housing, retail, and other sectors of the economy. For example, this year Saskatoon's gross domestic product is expected to grow by 3.7%, which is significantly higher than the estimated national average.[51]

How is Saskatoon's economy growing? According to the The Conference Board of Canada, "Saskatoon is benefiting from strong resource development, while healthy population growth is bolstering the housing market." About $10 billion in mining development and expansion has already been invested in the province.[52] Indeed, Saskatchewan has numerous natural resources, such as potash, oil, and uranium.[53]

Tim LeClair, chief executive officer of the Saskatoon Regional Economic Development Authority (SREDA), is also proud of how other sectors are making important contributions to economic growth. "We have to give credit to other sectors of the economy which aren't related to the resource sector, including manufacturing, agriculture, transportation and communication," stated LeClair.[54]

The agriculture sector is a natural strength. Saskatchewan has six different soil zones and over 40% of Canada's arable land. According to the Ministry of Agriculture, the industry produces feed and forage, cereal crops, oilseeds, pulse crops, and some speciality crops.[55]

Saskatchewan has other strengths in agriculture, too. Did you know that Saskatchewan produces the majority of Canada's wild rice? Saskatchewan also produces over 70% of Canada's flax and over 80% of Canada's mustard. And let's not forget that Saskatchewan supplies 5% of the world's exported wheat.[56]

In the manufacturing industry, many local companies are making machinery, wood products, transportation equipment, plastics, and food and beverages. This, in turn, has led 85% of firms to be able to export their goods outside the province, impacting the transportation and distribution industry favourably.[57]

---

[50] Dowdall, B. (2013, February 14). Prairies cities sweep top spots in economic growth in 2013. The Conference Board of Canada. Reprinted by permission. Retrieved from www.conferenceboard.ca/press/newsrelease/13-02-14/prairies_cities_sweep_top_spots_in_economic_growth_in_2013.aspx.

[51] Dowdall, 2013.

[52] Armstrong, J. (2011, October 22). Saskatoon is home to Canada's fastest growing economy. *The StarPhoenix.* Retrieved from http://www2.canada.com/saskatoonstarphoenix/news/business/story.html?id=99a654e8-804d-44c3-98a6-06d014e24b4a. Reprinted by permission.

[53] LeClair, T. (2013, April 8). Why the Saskatoon region is important for China and the world. ConsiderCanada.com. Retrieved from http://considercanada.com/blog/2013/4/8/why-the-saskatoon-region-is-important-for-china-and-the-world.

[54] Armstrong, 2011.

[55] LeClair, 2013.

[56] LeClair, 2013.

[57] Armstrong, 2011.

Case Continued >

"One only has to look at the automotive in Saskatoon. When you see the level of activity here, it's a very basic barometer of the economy," says LeClair. In fact, there is a 12.2% increase in new car and truck sales in the province.[58]

In addition to Saskatoon having the fastest-growing economy, it also ranks as Canada's fastest-growing city. According to Statistics Canada, Saskatoon's population grew by 3%, or 7,200 residents, between 2009 and 2010. Its population is estimated to be 265,300. International immigration into the province is a leading factor for its growth—over 50% of its population increase is due to new families immigrating to Canada. These families are also making Saskatoon one of Canada's youngest cities. Saskatoon's median age is currently 35.4 years, compared to the national median of 39.7 years.[59] This means the majority of its population is of working age.

Clearly, having a large number of working residents translates into lower unemployment rates, and Saskatchewan maintains one of the lowest unemployment rates in the country. According to Statistics Canada, the August 2011 unemployment rate was 4.5%, the lowest in the country. Saskatoon's unemployment rate was slightly higher at 5.1%, but still much lower than the country's 7.3% average.[60]

One reason for the low unemployment rate is the growing number of entrepreneurs. Each year, approximately 1,000 licences are issued to new small businesses. The resource sector is an important employer, too. Mining companies continue to recruit engineers with salaries at $150,000 and up.[61] Good-paying jobs help consumer spending and keep business sales up.

Home construction is also growing fast. In the first six months of 2011, new housing increased by 38%. "Housing is a critical component of the economy," says LeClair. "We have to make sure that we have adequate housing for people to come and take positions in Saskatoon. That's an important part of the equation."[62]

Industrial and commercial construction is of course a direct result of business growth. Vacancy rates for the commercial real estate market are at record lows, including industrial, office, and retail space. Similarly, new office tower construction is on the increase from business expansion.

In the past, Canada's resource sector has gone through "boom and bust" phases. So, can Saskatoon's economy realistically be sustained?

SREDA recognizes that Saskatoon's economy is experiencing significant growth mainly because of the mining industry. "In 15 years, when all of these capital expenditures are done, do we want to go back to the slow growth of the 1980s and start exporting our kids to other provinces again? I was a product of that export market. We want to sustain our economy over the long term. We have to get it right," says LeClair.[63]

To encourage long-term economic growth, SREDA has developed a number of initiatives to address existing challenges faced by business and to encourage a sustainable economy. One project involves analyzing issues facing the region's labour market. "When a company looks at setting up operations in Saskatoon or Regina, the first thing they look at is the labour force. Do we have people to fill those jobs? If you can't answer that question in the affirmative, it becomes very difficult to build a business case."[64]

SREDA is also focusing on bringing global businesses to Saskatoon. "Brazil has two of the world's largest food processing companies. They employ over 130,000 people internationally

---

[58] Armstrong, 2011.

[59] Armstrong, 2011.

[60] Armstrong, 2011.

[61] Armstrong, 2011.

[62] Armstrong, 2011.

[63] Armstrong, 2011.

[64] Armstrong, 2011.

but have no facilities at all in North America. They have no market penetration here, no presence here," says LeClair. "We have the critical mass—the infrastructure, the raw commodities. I met with the Brazilian ambassador and they're willing to open the doors."[65]

Similarly, encouraging entrepreneurship and growing small businesses is important, too. In fact, entrepreneurship is one of the reasons why Saskatoon has the country's fastest-growing economies. "The vast majority of our employment comes out of the entrepreneurial, homegrown companies," says LeClair.[66] One partnership involves IDEALS Inc., an organization designed to support new businesses and reduce potential risks. While 60 to 75% of all new businesses will fail within the first year, business incubator organizations like IDEALS help businesses achieve an 87% success rate.[67]

Investment in research and development and expanding knowledge-based industries is another strategy for continued economic growth. "We have many companies coming from around the world to use our research facilities. There is $2.6 billion worth of research facilities clustered around the university. We'd like to see more companies come to do their research here, and then build their facilities close by."[68] The University of Saskatchewan has developed technologies that have resulted in companies establishing themselves nearby. SED Systems, International Road Dynamics, and Philom Bios are a few examples. Certainly, the potential for more startups or spinoffs exists.[69]

According to LeClair, "information communication technology (ICT) is a critical industry that supports numerous other industries including healthcare, mining, manufacturing and biotechnology. ICT professionals have found Saskatchewan's economy fertile for innovation that only ICT companies can supply."[70]

According to economists at TD Bank, other factors are also needed to sustain economic growth. Skilled labour shortages need to be addressed. Certainly, Canada needs to educate students with the right skills to support a prosperous economy. And keeping taxes low is another challenge to remain competitive. Some economists also believe that Saskatchewan should build upon its resources strength and become a clean energy powerhouse.

"[Clearly,] lots of work needs to be done to build a good commercialization structure. SREDA is part of that discussion," says LeClair. "We started a project last year involving angel tax credits and flow-through share structures that would help support companies that are developing technologies for commercialization. SREDA is part of a very strong working committee and I think we have some broad consensus. Expertise is not the issue. It's the expertise around financing and those kinds of issues that keep a company going. We need to build on that. It's critical."[71]

Questions

1. What economic elements are contributing to Saskatoon's growing economy?

2. What non-economic or other related factors are contributing to Saskatoon's growing economy?

3. What do you think are the most important factors for Saskatoon to sustain long-term economic growth?

---

[65] Armstrong, 2011.

[66] Armstrong, 2011.

[67] Armstrong, 2011.

[68] Armstrong, 2011.

[69] Armstrong, 2011.

[70] LeClair, 2013.

[71] Armstrong, 2011.

Chapter 7
Competitive and Technological Forces
How do Industries Evolve Over Time?

© psdesign1-Fotolia.com

Learning Objectives

After studying this chapter, you should be able to

1. Describe the different stages of the industry life-cycle model, including how competitive forces change and the various success factors for firms in each stage of the life cycle.

2. Identify different types of innovations.

3. Understand the relationship between technological evolution and industry evolution and describe the key features of technology life-cycle models.

4. Describe how technology is changing the workplace.

Why do industry-leading firms sometimes lose their market position to rivals? Why do some entrepreneurial firms fail to survive and grow following early marketplace successes? These questions can be addressed through the study of industry evolution and change. Industries are an essential backdrop for the analysis of how competitive forces affect the viability and performance of organizations. An industry's stage of evolution is a critical determinant of the degree and type of competition faced by organizations.

THE BUSINESS WORLD

From Personal Computers to Newspapers: Technology and Creative Destruction

Joseph Schumpeter (1883–1950) was an Austrian economist and professor at Harvard who wrote much about the evolutionary and cyclical nature of industries. He explained that industries are periodically disrupted by the introduction of revolutionary innovations. In his book *Capitalism, Socialism* and *Democracy*, he coined the now famous expression of creative destruction to explain how innovations can sweep away old technologies, skills, products, ideas, and industries and replace them with new ones.

Many organizations, and indeed entire industries, could benefit by being ever wary of the ability of new technologies to facilitate creative destruction. The personal computer (PC) industry is one example. Technology has facilitated the transition from a *desktop world* to a *mobile world*. In general, PC sales have been in decline for some time now. This, of course, is horrible news for companies like Intel.

Intel, the California-based microchip maker, showed a steady drop in earnings in recent years because of the decreased demand for computer chips alongside the drop in sales of PCs. Consequently, companies like Intel have been forced to expand into other areas, such as phones, tablets, and ultrabooks, to survive. Unfortunately, it appears that Intel's sales of chips for tablets and smartphones may not be sufficient to counter the declining PC revenues.

Intel is not alone in staving off creative destruction in the technology industry. Consider the struggles of Microsoft. Once the icon of stability, Microsoft is also feeling the brunt of the decline in PC sales. As one observer commented,

> For Microsoft and Intel, the day of reckoning is nearer at hand. The two giants still depend on PCs for most of their profits, and sales at both have now declined . . . It's harder to see a good way forward for Microsoft . . . Weak PC sales are squeezing both of the company's cash cows—the Windows operating system and Office software—both of which boast 60 per cent net operating margins.[1]

In addition, according to a recent Bloomberg article, while it has traditionally remained a powerful force with its Windows operating system, Microsoft has been an unimpressive innovator and for many years now has been challenged by Apple, with its own platform.[2] No business is immune from creative destruction.

Regardless of the industry, even the largest, most successful companies can fall victim to changes in technology. For example, the smartphone industry itself has become extremely volatile because of the rapid rate of technological innovation. Consequently, competitors like BlackBerry can be star players one day and casualties the next day. The company, formerly called Research In Motion, rebranded itself as BlackBerry in 2013 to publicly signal a change in the company's vision and approach. However, these and other changes failed to bring about BlackBerry's return to its former "star" role. This is an industry where disruptive change is the norm, and where technological breakthroughs continue to create new winners and losers.

---

[1] Cyran, R. (2013, July 23). Tech giants get taste of their own creative-destruction medicine. *Globe and Mail.* Retrieved from www.theglobeandmail.com/report-on-business/international-business/tech-giants-get-taste-of-their-own-creative-destruction-medicine/article13368796.

[2] Bloomberg. (2012, January 27). Innovate without mercy is the lesson of RIM's BlackBerry. Retrieved from www.bloomberg.com/news/2012-01-27/innovate-without-mercy-is-the-enduring-lesson-of-rim-and-blackberry-view.html.

Perhaps there is no more of a striking example of creative destruction in recent times than that occurring in the newspaper industry. Postmedia Network, Canada's largest metropolitan newspaper chain, has battled increasing losses in recent years, reflecting the speed at which the newspaper market is transforming. The publisher of such titles as the *Ottawa Citizen*, *Calgary Herald*, and *National Post* is not alone in its struggle. The traditional newspaper industry has been dying for several years, thanks to technological innovation. As a recent *Forbes* article stated,

> The first two nails in the local newspapers' coffins have been well reported . . . First, advertising went online. Most classified ads moved to CraigsList.com, and display ads went to Google and Facebook. The second nail was competition for readers from online sources. You don't need a newspaper to read the news. You don't even need to sit at your computer. With a tablet, you can sit in your easy chair with a game on the television and read the news between plays.[3]

While many newspapers have turned to online subscriptions, this has not proven to be much help. As a recent *Globe and Mail* article noted, "the problem for publishers across North America is that digital revenues are not increasing fast enough to make up for the losses in print."[4]

Neil Irwin, writing for the *Washington Post*, succinctly summarized the implications of technological innovation for business and society:

> Manufacturing workers have spent the last generation becoming accustomed to the rise of robots that do their jobs. But the rapid change is quickly enveloping huge chunks of the white-collar workforce . . . This is how economic advancement happens . . . But what is scary is how fast that change is happening . . . For as long as people keep innovating and creating new, better ways of doing things, permanence, in the business world, is always going to be an illusion.[5]

Welcome to the world of creative destruction.

Objective 1 Describe the different stages of the industry life-cycle model, including how competitive forces change and the various success factors for firms in each stage of the life cycle.

THE INDUSTRY LIFE-CYCLE MODEL

This chapter addresses important questions about a business's external environment by taking a macro-level, long-term view of industries and their evolution. Industries, both old and new, are not static and change in dramatic ways over time. It is therefore critical to examine how some of the key competitive forces shape the external environment of organizations.

While it seems obvious to even the most casual observer that the nature and intensity of competition is quite specific to each industry, it is nonetheless remarkable how different industries follow similar and predictable paths in how competitive pressures evolve over

---

[3] Conerly, B. (2013, June 21). The death of newspapers: A third nail in the coffin. *Forbes*. Retrieved from www.forbes.com/sites/billconerly/2013/06/21/the-death-of-newspapers-a-third-nail-in-the-coffin.

[4] Ladurantaye, S. (2013, July 3). Losses mount at Postmedia on anemic print advertising. *Globe and Mail*. Retrieved from www.theglobeandmail.com/report-on-business/postmedia-losses-surge-to-1122-million-in-latest-quarter/article12946673.

[5] Irwin, N. (2013, August 7). The decline of newspapers has been good for everybody else. *Washington Post*. Retrieved from www.washingtonpost.com/blogs/wonkblog/wp/2013/08/07/the-decline-of-newspapers-has-been-good-for-everybody-else.

time. Research in the fields of economics, strategic management, and organization theory has highlighted how virtually all industries evolve along particular trajectories and through specific phases from their early emergence and growth to their eventual maturity and decline.

This is commonly known as the **industry life-cycle model**. Given a long enough period of observation, almost all industries exhibit an inverted U-shaped growth pattern, with the number of organizations rising initially up to a peak, then declining as the industry ages (see Exhibit 7.1). The pace of an industry's evolution along its life cycle is closely related to the evolution of technology within the industry. Technological innovations will often trigger the start of a new life cycle or the creation of an entirely new industry.

It is important to remember that, although based on the marketing theories of product life cycles, the industry life-cycle model describes the evolution of the entire product category and its associated industry, not a single product or firm. The industry life-cycle model divides industry evolution into four distinct phases: introduction, growth, maturity, and decline. According to the model, new industries tend to be highly fragmented (that is, with many small competitors) and characterized by experimentation with novel technologies and business models. This introductory phase sees many entrepreneurial firms enter the industry, hoping to emerge as a market leader.

As the industry coalesces around a particular approach and this dominant model is adopted by customers, suppliers, and other key constituents, the firms whose approach does not conform to the emerging standard exit the industry during a *shakeout*. The widespread diffusion of an industry standard or dominant design is a critical step in facilitating an industry's transition to the growth phase.

Over time, the industry reaches the mature phase, where the market stabilizes and sales grow more slowly. Firms must then become more efficient producers to lower costs and compensate for slower revenue growth. This is often achieved through mergers and acquisitions that result in higher industry concentration. In the decline phase, aggregate sales drop and rivalry further heats up as the industry undergoes greater consolidation through more mergers and the exit of inefficient firms. Exhibit 7.2 shows the typical S-curve pattern of how sales volume grows, stabilizes, and declines as an industry develops.

Understanding which phase of the life cycle an industry is in is critical for effective management at all levels of the organization. The life-cycle phase affects the degree of competition firms face, the type of organizational structure, the kind of strategy used, and the appropriate management approaches needed to survive and grow. The key success factors and sources of competitive advantage for firms are different from one stage of the life cycle to the next. For example, being successful when facing many small entrepreneurial competitors with no clear leader in a fast-growing and technologically innovative market requires a very different approach than being part of a highly concentrated industry with a few large, established incumbents and slow or declining growth. Different types of firms tend to be market leaders at different stages given the difficulties organizations experience when they must adapt to a different environment and make the transition from one type of organizational structure or strategy to another.

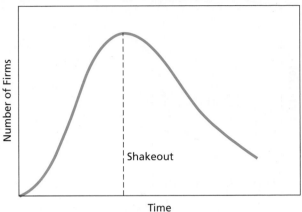

Exhibit 7.1 Industry Growth

industry life-cycle model An inverted U-shaped growth pattern that is seen in almost all industries given a long enough period of observation. The number of organizations rises initially up to a peak, then declines as the industry ages.

Exhibit 7.2 Industry Life Cycle

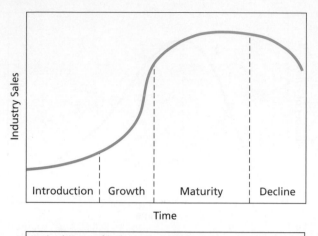

Main drivers of industry evolution:
• Demand growth
• Creation and diffusion of technology and knowledge

While different industries move along the life cycle at different paces, the remarkable regularity of the pattern across a wide spectrum of different industries makes the life-cycle model a powerful tool for managers and entrepreneurs. In addition, the industry life cycle is a complementary approach to Porter's five-forces framework, presented in Chapter 5. The five-forces framework is essentially a static model that provides a valuable snapshot of an industry's attractiveness at a specific point in time. The life-cycle model, however, is inherently dynamic and shows how evolution affects industry structure and thus the forces of rivalry, potential entrants, customer and supplier power, and substitute products described in the Porter model. In conjunction, both models can provide managers with a more complete set of tools for analyzing industries and understanding the forces of competition. We will now examine each of the different phases of the life cycle in greater detail.

The Introduction Phase: Industry Emergence and Creation

introductory phase The first phase in the industry life-cycle model, where many entrepreneurial firms enter the industry, hoping to emerge as a market leader. New industries tend to be highly fragmented (that is, with many small competitors) and characterized by experimentation with novel technologies and business models.

New industries emerge as the result of changes (usually technological or regulatory) that create opportunities for entrepreneurs to leverage novel combinations of resources to develop innovative products, services, or processes. These opportunities are not always exploited immediately, and some remain untapped and unrecognized for many years until someone decides to start a new firm that will take advantage of the resources and create a new market. Some industries are the result of important technological breakthroughs, such as the biotechnology industry that emerged following the discovery of recombinant DNA by scientists Stanley Cohen and Herbert Boyer (see Talking Business 7.1).

Some industries are the outcome of government regulation (or deregulation) that creates markets for new products or services. For example, the Environmental Protection Act and a variety of companion state laws enacted in the United States in 1970 specified guidelines for organizations' behaviour toward the environment. As a result, an industry of consultants, lawyers, lobbyists, and even a market for trading pollution credits through brokers has emerged to enable firms to comply with and adapt to the new legislation. In Canada, the Supreme Court's decision on June 9, 2005, overturned the ban on private health insurance in Quebec. Many analysts regard this ruling as opening the door to the creation of a private health care industry in Canada. Whether this will in fact happen, what this potential industry will look like, and how it will operate remains very unclear at this point.

The early years of an industry are generally a tumultuous period where there is tremendous uncertainty about the future of the market. There is no dominant technology or business model, and it is far from certain that the market will ever grow sufficiently to provide attractive financial returns and growth opportunities. At the same time, this is also a period of unbridled optimism among entrepreneurs jockeying for position as the future of the market unfolds.

Early entrants into an industry tend to be small entrepreneurial firms excited by the prospect and potential growth of a new market. Large, established firms tend to lag behind smaller ones in entering new industries for two reasons. First, a budding market is usually too

The Birth of Biotech

Alexander Raths/Shutterstock

In 1973, Professor Herbert Boyer of the University of California at San Francisco (UCSF) and Professor Stanley Cohen of Stanford University made a breakthrough that essentially gave way to the birth of a new industry—the biotechnology industry. Cohen and Boyer perfected a method for extracting DNA—the blueprint molecules that cells use to make proteins—and combining it with fragments of DNA from another organism.

While this scientific breakthrough was important, it did not itself trigger the birth of a new industry. It was the involvement of an entrepreneur who helped to commercialize this technological innovation that paved the path to an industry. Robert Swanson was a 29-year-old venture capitalist who sought to commercialize a new way of engineering drugs based on splicing DNA from one organism into the genome of another. Together with Boyer, they sketched out their business plan and changed the drug industry forever by creating the field of commercial biotechnology.

Boyer and Swanson incorporated under the name Genentech, and in 1982 the company won FDA approval for the first genetically engineered drug, human insulin. Shortly thereafter, many more entrepreneurial scientists created new biotech companies that developed drugs aimed at treating everything from anemia to cancer. Swanson and Boyer are recognized today as the founding fathers of the multibillion dollar biotech industry.

Source: Based on *Businessweek*. (2004, October 18). Robert Swanson and Herbert Boyer: Giving birth to biotech. Retrieved from www.businessweek.com/stories/2004-10-17/robert-swanson-and-herbert-boyer-giving-birth-to-biotech.

small and risky to justify the entry of large firms burdened with high overhead costs and the need to generate more certain, even if lower, financial returns. Second, older incumbent firms usually have bureaucratic organizational structures that inhibit their ability to move quickly and flexibly into new markets. Smaller and more nimble firms rely on simpler structures and lower startup costs to capture a first-mover advantage. Entrepreneurial startups are inherently more tolerant of ambiguity and risk because they have much less to lose than established firms and are therefore more willing to gamble in the hopes of generating a large payoff.

This introductory phase is one of great technical uncertainty where producers experiment with different and novel combinations in the hopes of discovering a superior approach that will dominate over other firms. Firms are intensely focused on research and development (R&D) activities during this period. This results in a high degree of product innovation with many different versions of products incorporating different features and technologies (see Talking Business 7.2). This also leads to confusion for customers and other stakeholders, which prevents the market from taking off into the growth phase. The types of customers who tend to purchase in the introductory phase of the life cycle are early adopters willing to pay a premium for the privilege of owning a product before most other people, despite its early flaws and glitches. Conservative and price-conscious customers will usually wait until the mature stage before buying.

Despite (and partly because of) the uncertainty inherent in a new industry, the introduction phase of the life cycle is a period of extraordinary creativity and innovation. An industry is rarely as vibrant as in its early years, when hope and optimism fuel the dreams

The Early Years of the Automobile Industry

While it is hard to imagine the modern automobile industry with its few large, established firms as a hotbed of entrepreneurial activity, the early years of the American auto industry were very dynamic and entrepreneurial activity was rampant. Between 1899 and 1923, the industry experienced a large surge of market entrants with over 3,000 recorded attempts at automobile production launched during this period. Many of these firms failed within a year of entering the market, and over 68% exited the industry within two years. While perfectly consistent with the industry life-cycle theory, the sheer abundance and diversity of producers and early designs is quite astonishing in light of today's highly concentrated and standardized industry. Consider, for example, the following early cars and their makers:

- The Roberts Electric was a two-seat electric car powered by two 60-volt motors, one for each rear wheel, and was made in 1897 by C.E. Roberts of Chicago.

- Kent's Pacemaker, a steam-powered car with three rear wheels and a single wheel in front for steering, was made by the Colonial Automobile Co. of Boston from 1899 to 1901.

- The Luxor, a gasoline-powered vehicle that resembled a Roman chariot, was designed by C.R. Harris of Pennsylvania, who never managed to get it into production.

- The Cotta Steam was a steam automobile with four-wheel drive and steering. It was produced in very limited numbers by the Cotta Automobile Co. of Rockford, Illinois, in 1903.

- The Rotary, a gasoline-powered car with a single-cylinder engine and two crankshafts, was made in Boston by the Rotary Motor Vehicle Co. in 1904 and 1905.

- The Pratt was a car with four rear wheels and two front wheels and was powered by a 75-horsepower engine. It was built by Pratt Chuck Works of Frankfurt, New York, in 1907.

- The Menkenns, a three-wheeled car powered by a front-mounted airplane propeller, was made in 1937 by Willie Menkenns of Hillsboro, Oregon.

While many of these designs may seem bizarre today, they highlight the uncertainty faced by the pioneers of the automobile industry. It was far from clear at the turn of the century what basic features the successful car would have. For example, a critical decision involved the type of engine or propulsion system to use. Steam, electric, and gasoline-powered engines were all potential candidates, and many producers used technologies and fuel other than gasoline. In fact, many early analysts believed that steam was a superior technology to power car engines.

Around 1920, however, the dominant design of the automobile had emerged—an all-steel enclosed body mounted on a chassis and a gasoline-powered internal combustion engine. This is the fundamental architecture that remains (save for material innovations in the steel body) unchanged to this day. The adoption of this dominant design for cars was accompanied by the failure of many car manufacturers and a dramatic reduction in the number of new entrants. From a peak of 350 car makers in the United States in 1915, there were fewer than 50 by 1930 and less than 20 by 1940. Today there are only three car makers left in the United States (GM, Ford, and Chrysler), and the global industry is highly concentrated, with 10 manufacturers controlling more than 80% of the worldwide market.

The first cars produced were quite expensive and only the very rich were able to afford them. By 1923, however, 50% of US households owned an automobile. The diffusion of the automobile was accelerated by Henry Ford's introduction of the Model T in 1908 (priced at an affordable $850) and by Ford's development of one of the most significant industrial innovations of the 20th century—the moving assembly line in 1913. This revolutionary process brought the product to the workers rather than having workers moving around a factory to perform tasks. Inspired by Frederick Taylor's principles of specialization and standardization, Ford had workers perform a single repetitive task rather than whole portions of automobile assembly. The new Ford plant in Highland Park, Michigan, produced over 300,000 cars in one year (1914)—more than in the entire history of the company. The increases in productivity allowed Ford to continually drop the price of the Model T to as low as $290 in 1927, making cars truly affordable for the masses and paving the way for the massive changes brought on by the automotive industry we know today.

Sources: Based on Carroll, G.R., & Hannan, M.T. (1995). *Organizations in industry: Strategy, structure & selection.* New York, NY: Oxford University Press; and Constable, G., & Somerville, B. (2003). *A century of innovation: Twenty engineering achievements that transformed our lives.* Washington, DC: Chapter Joseph Henry Press.

of entrepreneurs and inventors. This period is the "gold rush" era of the industry where everyone can still make it big, given that nobody has yet.

In addition to the large upsurge in entrants, new markets are extremely volatile. They may have no clear boundaries, and segments are not well defined. The market shares of the different producers are highly unstable, and many entrants fail shortly after entering. It is nearly impossible to predict which firms will survive and grow, and it is often not all that obvious whether the industry itself will emerge as a viable entity able to sustain a group of producers. While we tend to study only those industries that did develop viable markets because we can observe the entire life cycle, there are numerous examples of industries that began their life cycle with much promise yet never made it past the introductory phase.

In the 1990s, several highly ambitious ventures planning to provide wireless telecommunications and broadband Internet services through satellite networks were launched with much fanfare. Iridium, backed by the wireless firm Motorola, and Teledesic, which was funded by McCaw Cellular and Microsoft owner Bill Gates, were two such ventures, along with Globalstar, ICO, and others. Teledesic planned to blanket the earth's atmosphere with 288 low-earth orbit (LEO) satellites to build an "Internet in the sky." A combination of technical difficulties, financial troubles, mismanagement, and slow customer adoption because of the high cost of satellite communications led to the demise of these ventures and of the emerging satellite communications industry altogether—though not before they had lost billions of dollars in the process (more than $9 billion in Teledesic's case). Iridium filed for bankruptcy in 2001 after having launched 66 satellites into space at a cost of more than $6 billion. An Iridium satellite now hangs in the Smithsonian National Air and Space Museum as a testament to the technological ability (and commercial failure) of this venture.

While some of these firms have emerged from bankruptcy protection in a different form, the satellite communications industry has clearly not lived up to the high expectations of its early pioneers. Perhaps the technology was ahead of its time and it will eventually take off and grow. Nevertheless, this case illustrates that new industries can suffer quite severe growing pains and may never develop into mature industries. There are other industries that are still in the early stages of development and currently struggling to make it into the growth phase.

The Quest for Legitimacy

Organization theorists studying industry emergence and evolution have focused on the institutional and social conditions that affect the changing nature of markets and competitive forces. One of the most important contributions to emerge concerns the concept of the legitimacy of new industries and organizational forms. Marc Suchman, professor of sociology at Brown University, defines organizational legitimacy as "a generalized perception or assumption that the actions of an entity are desirable, proper, or appropriate within some socially constructed system of norms, values, beliefs, and definitions."[6] Other researchers have distinguished between two forms of legitimacy: sociopolitical and cognitive legitimacy.[7] **Sociopolitical legitimacy** refers to the endorsement of an industry, activity, or organizational form by key stakeholders and institutions such as the state and government officials, opinion leaders, or the general public. **Cognitive legitimacy** refers to

sociopolitical legitimacy The endorsement of an industry, activity, or organizational form by key stakeholders and institutions such as the state and government officials, opinion leaders, or the general public.

cognitive legitimacy The level of public knowledge about a new industry and its conformity to established norms and methods reflected in the extent to which it is taken for granted as a desirable and appropriate activity.

---

[6] Suchman, M.C. (1995). Managing legitimacy: Strategic and institutional approaches. *Academy of Management Review, 20*(3), 574.

[7] Aldrich, H. (1999). *Organizations evolving*. Thousand Oaks, CA: Sage Publications; Hannan, M.T., & Carroll, G.R. (1992). *Dynamics of organizational populations: Density, legitimation and competition*. New York, NY: Oxford University Press.

the level of public knowledge about a new industry and its conformity to established norms and methods reflected in the extent to which it is taken for granted as a desirable and appropriate activity (see Talking Business 7.3).

All organizations require legitimacy to acquire the resources they need to survive and grow from external stakeholders. Because organizations must extract resources from their environments, failure to conform to societal and institutionalized norms and beliefs results in a lack of legitimacy that will hinder their ability to recruit employees, obtain financial

and material resources, sell products and services to customers, and so on. There are many reasons why an organization's actions may not be perceived as desirable, proper, or appropriate. Failure to comply with legal rules or the ethical norms of society is one of them, as is pioneering a new type of firm or way of doing business.

Being new, small, unknown, or unrecognized can cause a firm to lack legitimacy because it must prove to outsiders that it does conform to institutional norms. Even in existing industries, startup firms face higher risks of failure than incumbent firms with established track records and relationships with customers, suppliers, and other stakeholders. In entirely new industries, the lack of legitimacy is even more pronounced given how business models and organizational forms are novel and have yet to acquire sufficient legitimacy as desirable and appropriate entities. Entrepreneurs operate in a murky and ambiguous environment where there are few, if any, precedents available to determine what is considered a desirable and appropriate business activity. Stakeholders will therefore question the viability, not only of the specific venture, but of the budding industry itself. Society's lack of understanding, acceptance, and familiarity with the industry leads to even greater difficulties in marshalling resources so that new firms in new industries are even more likely to fail than new firms in established industries (see Talking Business 7.4).

TALKING BUSINESS 7.4

Gray Goo and the Promising Future of the Nanotechnology Industry

Nanotechnology is the science of building electronic circuits and devices from single atoms and molecules. These devices are typically less than 100 nanometres in size (one nanometre equals one-millionth of a millimetre). This burgeoning industry is expected to make significant contributions to the fields of computer storage, semiconductors, biotechnology, manufacturing, and energy. While the concept of nanotechnology was first introduced by physicist Richard Feynman in 1959, advancements truly began to accelerate after Richard Smalley's discovery of carbon nanotubes won the 1996 Nobel Prize in Chemistry. In 2001, following large increases in US government funding for nanotechnology research and the publication of an entire issue of the influential magazine *Scientific American* on the topic, the US National Science Foundation predicted the newly defined "nanotechnology market" would grow to $1 trillion shortly.

These events triggered significant investments by venture capitalists and entrepreneurs in a variety of nanotech startups. According to some scientists, the future of nanotechnology is one of astonishing possibilities, where diseases will be wiped out and we will live for hundreds of years. Envisioned are all kinds of amazing products,

including extraordinarily tiny computers that are very powerful, building materials that withstand earthquakes, advanced systems for drug delivery and custom-tailored pharmaceuticals, as well as the elimination of invasive surgery (because repairs can be made from within the body). Nanosized robots will be injected into the bloodstream and administer a drug directly to an infected cell. Because they are composed of biological elements such as DNA and proteins, the nanobots can easily be removed from the body.

The promise of a technological and industrial revolution of unprecedented magnitude based on the science of nanotechnology rests on many underlying assumptions of technical advances that, while theoretically possible, remain unproven. The emerging industry also has to contend with fears stoked by science fiction films and novels that there are great risks involved with nanotechnology. One of these is that self-replicating nanobots will run amok and devour the earth in three hours, turning it into "gray goo"—a phenomenon called *global ecophagy*. More realistic concerns point to the potential toxicity of certain nanosubstances that are so small they can penetrate cell walls and membranes and disturb the immune system. Nevertheless, the high

(continued)

degree of uncertainty and controversy has not deterred entrepreneurs from entering the fray in the hopes of eventually "cashing in" on the upcoming nanotech revolution.

While there may be intense technological competition between early entrants in an industry, there is also a high degree of collaboration for the greater good through the establishment of trade associations and standards-setting bodies that facilitate the pursuit of industry legitimacy. So-called "institutional entrepreneurs" play a critical role in helping ensure the survival and growth of a fledgling industry by promoting its interests and coordinating efforts to gain institutional support and legitimacy. Linus Torvalds, the Finnish engineer who developed the Linux open source operating system; Jeff Bezos, the founder of Amazon.com; and Richard Smalley and Eric Drexler in the nanotechnology field are among the entrepreneurs who have become advocates and evangelists for the cause of the industry they pioneered in order to mobilize resources and legitimize it in the eyes of society. The collective action strategies pursued by institutional entrepreneurs often bear a striking resemblance to social movements. Successful institutional entrepreneurs are adept at presenting themselves as revolutionaries rebelling against the established order of large corporations, even though most of them actually aspire to grow their organizations and industry to replace the large firms.

In an industry's formative years, intra-industry rivalry is less intense as new organizations collaborate in the pursuit of legitimacy. New markets that have yet to achieve a sufficient degree of acceptance benefit from the endorsement of recognizable players. Smaller startups therefore often welcome the entry of established incumbents into the new market. When a large organization with a known track record enters the new industry, all firms benefit because it acts as an endorsement that signals the industry's viability and attractiveness, which helps it grow. This was the case when IBM entered the personal computer industry, for example, or when Walmart entered the online retail market. When a large and successful retailer like Walmart launches an ecommerce website, this signals to various stakeholders that the new market is important and worthy of Walmart's attention. Walmart's online presence attracts consumers to online shopping as well as attention from the media, the financial community, and other stakeholders, all of which contribute to the establishment of cognitive legitimacy for the ecommerce industry.

To illustrate this idea, contrast the situations of an entrepreneur deciding to start a restaurant and another deciding to start a wireless text message advertising firm. A potential restaurateur does not need to convince external stakeholders of the virtue of the restaurant as a business model. It is a tried and true concept, and we have well-known templates for what they should look like. Everyone the entrepreneur speaks to will know what a restaurant is, how it will operate, and how it will make money: It is taken for granted that customers sit down and make choices from a menu, that food is prepared and served, and that payment is tendered. With minor variations in menu, location, or pricing, virtually all restaurants operate this way and have for hundreds of years. Entrepreneurs who conform to these institutional norms will have an easier time gathering the needed resources for their new venture. While the legitimacy of the individual venture needs to be overcome, the legitimacy of the restaurant industry itself is not an issue.

On the other hand, entrepreneurs launching a wireless text messaging advertising firm will need to explain to stakeholders exactly how the business will operate and generate revenues. They will also need to convince stakeholders of the potential viability of this concept because the text message advertising industry is still so new that, unlike restaurants, there are no institutional norms for how this business should be organized. It is not clear how and to whom ads should be sold and delivered. Will consumers accept them, or find them intrusive and resent them? Is the technology proven? At the organizational level entrepreneurs must establish the legitimacy of their specific venture, and at the industry level they must collectively demonstrate that their novel organizational form or business model is desirable and appropriate.

The Growth Phase: Dominant Designs and Shakeouts

In the introduction stage, the objective is to find the new industry's dominant model and get it accepted and institutionalized; although sales are important and contribute to the purpose, they are subordinate to the main goal of legitimization. As we will discuss, in the industry growth stage, the game becomes all about sales and market share. The growth stage begins when the market converges around a single dominant design or approach. A **dominant design** is defined by Anderson and Tushman as "a single architecture that establishes dominance in a product class."[8] For example, according to the research firm Gartner, Apple's iPad is expected to dominate the tablet industry until at least 2016.

In some cases, technical standards are specified and must be adhered to by all firms wishing to enter the market. When a standard is legally mandated and enforced by a government or standards organization, it is called a ***de jure* standard**. For example, the gauge of a railroad track, a light bulb socket, and an electrical outlet are all based on standards that have been explicitly specified by a standards organization—usually to ensure compatibility. A company wanting to produce light bulbs must make them to the correct specifications or they will be useless to consumers.

A ***de facto* standard**, on the other hand, arises by virtue of common usage and is not officially sanctioned by any authority. It is a standard "in fact" or "in practice," rather than in law. Microsoft Windows is the *de facto* standard for personal computer operating systems because over 90% of the market uses Windows. Software developers must therefore write programs that are compatible with Windows if they want to reach the majority of the market.

As the standard or dominant model spreads across the industry, the producers that persist with a different approach usually exit the industry. This is one of the main causes of industry shakeouts. A **shakeout** in an industry is defined as a large number of exits from the market at the same time as the aggregate output of the industry increases. A large number of failures in a declining market is *not* a shakeout. A shakeout is a natural and healthy—albeit painful—process for an industry as it simply purges and weeds out the weaker competitors. The firms remaining after the shakeout emerge as strong competitors able to scale up production and serve the needs of a growing market.

Nevertheless, there are cases of firms pursuing the path of a proprietary standard not in line with the rest of industry and remaining successful, though on a much smaller scale. Apple Computer, which pioneered the personal computer market, barely survived the industry shakeout by maintaining its small share of loyal customers during the 1980s and 1990s. By not adhering to the Windows standard, Apple effectively restricted its market to small niches of graphic designers, academics, and other consumers dissatisfied with Windows's quasi-monopoly. As Apple's earlier brush with bankruptcy can attest, this is a very risky strategy (Apple has only recently become a technology giant with the iPhone, iPad, and iTunes). A firm must provide a significant benefit for a consumer to be willing to overcome the problems of incompatibility with 90% of the market.

Most other personal computer firms from the early 1980s, such as MITS, Commodore, and Tandy, did not survive. Prior to 1981, when IBM launched the IBM PC and real commercial growth began, the different computer firms all had their own proprietary hardware and software platforms. Most of the exits from the industry occurred between 1987 and 1993. This period coincides with the introduction of Intel's 386 processor in 1986 and the release of Windows 3.0 in 1990, which had graphical interfaces that made computers more

---

growth phase The second phase in the industry life-cycle model that occurs after the industry coalesces around a particular approach and a dominant model. This leads to a shakeout where many firms exit the industry.

dominant design The dominant approach or design established in a product class.

***de jure* standard** A standard that is legally mandated and enforced by a government or standards organization.

***de facto* standard** A standard that arises by virtue of common usage and is not officially sanctioned by any authority. It is a standard "in fact" or "in practice," rather than in law.

shakeout A large number of exits from the market at the same time as the aggregate output of the industry increases; a natural and healthy, though painful, process for an industry to purge and weed out the weaker competitors.

---

[8] Anderson, P.A., & Tushman, M. (1990). Technological discontinuities and dominant designs: A cyclical model of technological change. *Administrative Science Quarterly, 35*, 604–633.

user-friendly. These versions of the Intel X86 line of microprocessors and of the Windows operating system firmly entrenched the so-called Wintel standard, which replaced the IBM PC as the dominant architecture for personal computers. Once this design was institutionalized as the standard, personal computers assembled and sold by clone manufacturers had to conform and include an Intel chip and Windows to be accepted by the market.

When the vast majority of other users have a Wintel PC, few consumers are willing to deviate from the norm. Although there are newer versions of these components, the fundamental architecture of the PC with an Intel central processing unit (CPU) and Windows operating system running application software has remained virtually unchanged for more than 20 years now.

The adoption of a dominant design greatly accelerates the growth rate of new markets. As with automobiles, after about 20 years of industry evolution 50% of US households in 1999 owned a computer. Growth in demand is significantly related to the falling prices for products during the second phase of the life cycle. The diffusion of a dominant industry model allows firms to standardize products and processes, resulting in dramatic cost savings that push prices lower. Standardization creates incentives for other firms to offer complementary products and services, such as software that runs on Windows or gas stations to fuel cars. The development of an industry infrastructure stimulates even more demand for the products in a cycle that leads to growth rates that increase during this stage. Products now appeal to a much wider mass market rather than just early technology adopters or the wealthy. This has proven true in the smartphone industry, where demand for lower-end and lower-priced smartphones keeps increasing (see Talking Business 7.5).

TALKING BUSINESS 7.5

The Smartphone Industry

© Umberto Shtanzman/ Shutterstock

Since their introduction in the late 1990s, smartphones have come to define the way individuals connect to the rest of the world. Mobile phones are an integral part of our lives. Many of us can't imagine coping without our smartphone and consumers often eagerly anticipate the introduction of the next new model. While it may seem like these devices have been around forever, the smartphone industry, in fact, has evolved rapidly over a relatively short period of time. The smartphone's initial attraction was based on that of portability in addition to other features such as accessibility to the internet and personal data such as email. Improvements have continually occurred in such technical specifications as internal processors, battery life, storage capability, screen size, and broadband connectivity. And while the initial focus was on the business segment, this device now has a mainstream appeal.

The ancestor of the smartphone featured such basic capabilities as text messaging, faxing, and emailing, in addition to making phone calls. This device, introduced by IBM in 1994 and called Simon, sold for around $900. It essentially combined the traditional cellphone with a personal data assistant (PDA). Given that it was relatively cumbersome and expensive, it was not successful at capturing a large share of the mobile market. However, it did help ignite the interests of other entrants to this market.

By the mid-nineties market share of the global mobile handset market was controlled by the "Big Three"—Motorola, Ericsson, and Nokia. By the late nineties, competition grew with such new competitors as Siemens, Alcatel, Philips, Mitsubishi, and NEC. The year 1999 saw a significant advancement in the industry with the introduction of the BlackBerry device, which sold for $399, making it more affordable that the Simon. However, this first BlackBerry was simply a two-way pager with email capabilities, not actually a phone. During the late nineties, Nokia also introduced a range of phones that were a cross between a phone and a PDA.

Ericsson was the first brand to coin the term "smartphone," with the release of its GS88 in 1997. In 2000, Ericsson further popularized the "smartphone" with the marketing of its R380 mobile phone. It was a lightweight flip phone that ran the Symbian operating system (which was the dominant smartphone operating system until Android surpassed it in 2011). The year 2002 saw the release of the Palm Treo with its full querty keyboard, as well as the P800 from the recently merged Sony Ericsson, which included new features such as an MP3 player and a colour touchscreen. In that same year, the introduction of the first genuine smartphone can be credited to Research In Motion (RIM). In 2002 it released the BlackBerry 5810, which featured a phone, PDA, email, internet capabilities, a built-in calendar, an address book, and other applications. BlackBerry also focused on providing wireless email access. However, the main shortcoming was the need to connect a headset in order to use it as a phone. Two years later, RIM added full handset-free phone functionality on the BlackBerry 6210 model.

While there was an industry shakeout between 2001 and 2003, by the end of 2004 the industry again saw a high growth rate as consumers were attracted to the new generation of phones with colour displays. Consequently, a new group of competitors arose late in the decade—Apple, HTC, LG, Huawei, and ZTE among others. Most observers view Apple's launch of the iPhone in 2007 as a huge leap forward in the industry. The iPhone was similar to an iPod, except it could also make phone calls, take pictures, and browse the Internet. While Apple was not the first to launch a smartphone, it successfully combined several features in order to offer more than a way to communicate with others. To popular culture, the iPhone became a mobile media centre. In that regard, the iPhone changed the nature of the smartphone market. Up until that time, smartphones were seen more along the lines of something that business people used. Apple entrenched this phone in the minds of countless everyday consumers as a must-have-device.

Google can be credited with the next big change in 2008 as Android phones hit the market and quickly became the dominant mobile operating system. There was not actually one Android phone, but rather a range of models across several companies. In 2010, more Android devices were sold than Apple and Symbian combined. While Apple's operating system (iOS) runs on Apple's own devices, the Android market features intense competition from a large range of devices, including those by Samsung, HTC, LG, and Chinese companies like ZTE and Huawei. In fact,

by 2013, Samsung had achieved 32% of the global smartphone market, followed by Apple, which had only 12%.[9]

According to some, the smartphone concept has peaked in terms of innovation. Critics argue that just as PCs and laptops are based on designs that haven't substantively changed since the 1980s, smartphones are at a stage where most of the revolutionary innovation has already happened. Consistent with this view is the suggestion that new generations of devices won't be as profitable either. Others suggest that there is still room for much growth and innovation. A driving force behind smartphone performance more recently has been the ability to support third party software, and specifically "apps." In fact, this has spawned a whole new industry—the mobile app development industry. That has been a major source of additional revenue for companies like Apple and Google.

Industry experts have observed that the desktop computer market took a little more than 12 years to mature (maturing by about 2008), and the laptop computer market took 10 years (maturing by about 2012). Many of these same experts have suggested that smartphones and tablets are expected to mature in only a few more years. This may be reflected in the trend toward price reductions. As a recent news report observed:

> The dropping asking prices for smartphones caused by low-end market expansion, particularly in China, is putting added pressure on mid-range vendors, while leaving open the question of how long Apple can maintain its premium pricing on the iPhone . . .[10]

Sources: The Bulletin, Is the global smartphone market saturated? By Joe McKendrick on August 25, 2013 http://www.smartplanet.com/blog/bulletin/is-the-global-smartphone-market-saturated/
Every 10 years, a cataclysm kills off most phone brands—the next one is almost here By Tero Kuittinen on Feb 13, 2013 at 11:20 AM, BGR.com http://bgr.com/2013/02/13/smartphone-market-analysis-cycle-crash-325735/
The History of the Smartphone, By Brad McCarty, Tuesday, 6 Dec '11, 06:05 PM, TNW http://thenextweb.com/mobile/2011/12/06/the-history-of-the-smartphone/
How the Cellphone Got 'Smart', Frank berkman, 2012, http://mashable.com/2012/10/15/cellphones-smartphones/

---

[9] (reference: business insider, Steve Kovach, Nov. 14, 2013, http://www.ctpost.com/technology/businessinsider/article/SAMSUNG-Why-We-re-So-Successful-Despite-The-4980767.php)

[10] China drives smartphone growth—and low prices as—Android dominates, Charles Arthur, theguardian.com, Thursday 14 November 2013m, http://www.theguardian.com/technology/2013/nov/14/china-smartphone-android-google-iphone

As output grows further, economies of scale allow producers to generate more cost savings that drive prices even lower. This is another important cause of industry shakeouts. As product prices fall, inefficient producers come under significant competitive pressures and exit. Firms that are unable to match the economies of scale, production process improvements, and lower prices of the most efficient producers will be driven out of the market. Also, high-volume producers can afford to operate with lower profit margins while smaller firms are forced to exit.

Despite fierce competition and many exits, the high growth and reduction in uncertainty attracts many new entrants to the industry. Established firms from other industries that may have lagged behind the startups in entering now see the new industry as either potentially lucrative or threatening to their own assets and markets. They often enter by acquiring a firm already in the market rather than going through the trouble of starting a new division or subsidiary from scratch. Large firms bring tremendous resources to invest in distribution, marketing, and advertising to capture a greater share of the market, as well as expertise in efficient production and the capacity to withstand fierce price competition. This is the case, for example, with many pharmaceutical firms that acquired promising biotech ventures rather than developing their own internal R&D capabilities in biotechnology.

In the introduction phase, product innovation and R&D were critical skills for organizations. After standardization, however, process innovation and sales and marketing become more important. This is a critical difference between the early and middle phases of the life cycle and explains why large firms with greater resources and expertise in production processes and sales and marketing can displace entrepreneurial startups that fail to capture a meaningful first-mover advantage through property rights (patents and trademarks), customer loyalty, or technological leadership. In the early market, organizations were more likely to collaborate to increase aggregate sales and achieve legitimacy. In the growth phase, rivalry is much more intense and firms try to build brand recognition and position themselves for when the market will cease to grow as rapidly.

To see where certain industries fit in the industry life-cycle model, review Exhibit 7.3.

The Maturity Phase: A Critical Transition

mature phase The third phase in the industry life-cycle model, where the market stabilizes and sales grow more slowly. Firms must become more efficient during this stage.

In the mature stage, the third in the life cycle, growth in aggregate demand begins to slow. Markets start to become saturated as there are fewer new adopters to attract and so competition intensifies even more. This can, nevertheless, be a very profitable period for the surviving firms as the industry enters a period of relative stability. For example, between 1980 and 2000, the US beer brewing industry was in a mature phase and was dominated by three large firms that controlled 80% of the market (Anheuser-Busch: 47%; Miller: 23%; and Coors: 10%). Over the 20-year period, market shares were very stable, and no firm gained or lost more than about a single share point in any one year.

Despite the high degree of concentration in mature markets, rivalry is fierce. A single point of market share can mean millions of dollars in revenue, so firms spend large amounts of money on advertising and sometimes enter into damaging price wars to lure customers from the competition. Because technological knowledge has diffused to the far corners of the industry and patents may have expired, firms focus their innovative efforts on incremental improvements to products. This is the era where firms market the "new and improved" versions and 25 different scents and flavours in the hopes of differentiating their products ever so slightly from the competition's. Incremental innovations also

Exhibit 7.3 Competition in Industry

Industry Life-Cycle Model Phases	Industry Examples	Company Examples
Introduction phase	New biotechnology • e.g., TEM liquid-flow holder technology New green technology • e.g., NRGI-ECO technology	• Protochips Inc. • BESTECH
Growth phase	Tablet industry	• Apple • Amazon • Samsung • Microsoft
	Online coupon industry	• Groupon • Dealfind • Wagjag
	Smartphone industry	• Apple • Samsung • Nokia • Google
Maturity phase	Grocery industry	• Loblaw • Metro • Longo's • Safeway • Sobeys • Walmart • Costco
	Automotive industry	• Ford • General Motors • Chrysler • Toyota • Honda • Mazda • Volvo
	Banking industry	• RBC • CIBC • TD Canada Trust • Bank of Montreal • Scotiabank • National Bank
Decline phase	Tobacco industry	• Reynolds • Altria Group • Lorillard

commoditization The process by which a differentiated good becomes undifferentiated in the market. Consumers, thus, become more focused on price, which in turn forces firms to continuously squeeze out more cost savings from their production processes.

provide opportunities to extend the life cycle to delay the inevitable arrival of the decline stage. As consumers accumulate knowledge of the industry and its products over time, they become much more sophisticated and demanding buyers. This influences the industry's trend toward the **commoditization** of its products and makes consumers even more price conscious, which in turn forces firms to continuously squeeze out more cost savings from their production processes (see Talking Business 7.6).

When there is very little product differentiation and consumers have become notoriously fickle, power once held by the manufacturers now shifts to the distribution channel firms that control access to the customer. This is why shelf space is so critical in mature packaged goods markets like laundry detergent. When customers see very little difference between Tide and the competition, they will essentially grab whatever they have access to or what happens to be on sale. Similarly, grocery stores are under continued pressure to keep costs low to maintain their consumer base and to sell their many undifferentiated products.

Retailers who control and allocate shelf space have more bargaining power than they did in earlier phases, where customers would seek out a particular product because it possessed features not shared by others.

TALKING BUSINESS 7.6

The Aging Personal Computer Industry

The personal computer (PC) was the invention that transformed the 1980s. As the demand for typewriters diminished, the PC opened up new opportunities for businesses to be more efficient and productive by changing the way work was performed. And of course, how would we access the Internet? By the 1990s, the Internet (along with the PC) began to be more widely used and businesses found new opportunities to sell their goods and services online. Today the PC has become widely used by businesses, schools, and individuals across the planet. But has there been another change?

Normally, as the school year begins and the demand for computers increases, sales in PCs should be up. But this year, they are unexpectedly down, not just in Canada but worldwide. One analyst found that PC shipments to Western Europe were down by a surprising 19%. Acer, for example, was badly hit, losing over one third of its sales in comparison to last year.

Many analysts agree that the iPad has had an impact on PC sales. For many consumers, the iPad offers just what they need. If you want to browse the Internet, why not browse the net from the comfort of your couch? Not only that, you can also read books, play video games, and much, much more.

According to Oxford, "No one, it seems, is buying anything but iPads. Which is one of the reasons Hewlett-Packard (HP) spectacularly announced . . . that it is selling off its PC business altogether."[11] Gartner, another analyst, explained that along with tablets, future smartphones are expected to become even more capable devices in the future.

Others speculate that lower PC sales may be due to a lack of product innovation. For example, PC users themselves are not finding significant reasons to replace their older models. Other than Windows 8, the more recent operating system by Microsoft, there have not been any new products to enhance the PC-user experience.

Slow growth in the economy is another factor. There has been modest growth in the commercial sector and some significant disruptions. The Japan earthquake in 2010 is one example that affected the PC industry.

Overall, the iPad is slowly starting to change how consumers read, browse the Internet, and play video games. However, there still might be a glimmer of hope for the personal computer. New models of PCs are expected to have thinner designs, longer battery life, and touchscreen features. Innovation may be the key to keeping the PC market alive. Only time will tell.

---

[11] Oxford, A. (2011, August 26). PC sales down, but high end graphics holds steady. *PC Gamer*. Retrieved from www.pcgamer.com/2011/08/26/pc-sales-down-but-high-end-graphics-holds-steady.

Given the scale required to compete efficiently, there is little if any entry at this stage of the life cycle. The sources of competitive advantage for firms reside in process engineering to derive greater manufacturing and production efficiencies and reduce costs even more. This often means outsourcing and shedding activities that can be subcontracted more efficiently. In some industries, production will shift from advanced to developing countries during this stage to benefit from lower labour costs. In terms of the generic competitive strategies described in Chapter 5, whereas differentiation was the favoured approach in the earlier stages, organizations that adopt a cost leadership strategy in mature markets tend to outperform their competitors.

The shift from a dynamic and technologically innovative environment with many small firms to a stable and cost-efficient market with few large rivals also requires a change in the type of organizational structure, as described in Chapter 4. In the high-flying and uncertain early market, entrepreneurial startups need to be innovative, dynamic, and flexible. The organic structure, with its decentralized approach, limited hierarchy, and low formalization, is better suited to the environment of the introduction and early growth phases. In a mature market, where efficiency and cost-cutting matter more than innovation, the mechanistic structure, with its stricter rules, chain of command, and narrow division of labour, is more appropriate. Making the transition from one structure to the next is difficult when organizations have been conditioned to behave a certain way. This is the main reason why few firms are able to remain industry leaders throughout the entire life cycle.

The Decline Phase: Difficult Choices

decline phase The last phase in the industry life-cycle model, where aggregate sales drop and rivalry further heats up.

An industry enters the decline stage when sales begin to fall. Competition may become especially fierce in the decline stage as firms face tough choices regarding the future. It is difficult to predict when this stage will materialize, and the time it takes for industries to reach the decline stage varies widely. Nevertheless, industry sales typically decline as a result of one of the following:

1. *Changes in demographics:* Toward the end of the baby boom in the 1960s, demand for baby food dropped and rivalry among the leading firms—Gerber, Heinz, and Beech-Nut—intensified considerably.

2. *Shifting consumer tastes and needs:* Social trends and health considerations have resulted in declining demand for cigarettes and tobacco products since the 1980s.

3. *Technological substitution:* Word processing software led to the decline of the typewriter industry; online streaming and downloading of movies is replacing DVDs, which replaced VHS cassette tapes as the medium of choice for movies. Sales of DVD players, discs, and movie rentals are therefore declining. (see Talking Business 7.7)

A decline, though, does not necessarily equal the demise or death of the industry, and there are a number of strategic options available to organizations for dealing with a declining market. These choices are often highly dependent on the actions of rivals, however. If many competitors decide to exit the industry and liquidate their assets, this may lead to profitable opportunities for the remaining firms. If other firms merge, however, their increased market power may reduce opportunities for the remaining competitors.

Are Mobile Devices Killing the Video Game Console Industry?

The home video gaming industry has been around for a pretty long time. In May 1972, the first commercial home video game console was created by Magnavox and was called, the Odyssey. Other companies followed suit, including the soon-to-be-famous Atari. Indeed, the 1970's saw an explosion in video games which would eventually replace arcade or game shops. In 1975 Atari made one of the most iconic video games in history, Pong. This company dominated the industry from the late 70's to the early 80's with its Atari 2600 game system. However, it met a formidable foe by the 1980's—Nintendo. In 1985, Nintendo released their home video game console, the Nintendo Entertainment System (NES) along with iconic games to follow like Super Mario Bros, and the Legend of Zelda.[12]

One might consider the early 1990's as a shift from the emergent to the growth phase along with the requisite shakeout of sorts. The Super Nintendo Entertainment System which was launched in 1990 set a standard in the minds of gamers. Consequently, over a dozen other game console makers including Sega were overshadowed and soon forgotten. Sega stuck around for a little while longer with a relatively small market and it presented its final machine, the Dreamcast, toward the end of the 1990's. By the year 2000, only three big players remained to largely "own" the market—Sony, Microsoft and Nintendo.

For decades consoles were the mainstay of the video game industry and the fact is there is still more profits to be had—the global game consoles industry is estimated to reach $16.9 billion by 2018.[13] However, there is also evidence that the popularity of consoles is dwindling. Consoles have seen increased processing power of their machines, enabling greater graphical fidelity in games and more realistic effects. There have been other innovations such as controller free gaming in recent years. Nevertheless, it does seem that this industry is well past the growth stage where radical innovation and rapidly increasing market share characterised the market. If the industry has reached maturity, might it get pushed into decline soon?

So, the question is: Is the video game console industry "past its prime"?

According to a recent article in the Economist:

"At first glance, that seems like an odd question. Video games have never been more popular. The industry is worth around $80 billion worldwide, about the same as the global film industry, and the biggest titles comfortably out earn blockbuster movies. No longer is gaming a pastime for teenaged boys: the average gamer in America is 34, and around two-fifths of players are women. A generation who grew up with games have kept on playing; many now play video games (such as "Lego Star Wars") with their children."[13]

Nonetheless, the increasing popularity of mobile technology like smartphones, as well as Facebook have come to provide games at a lower price and in greater abundance. All this along with free-to-play games disrupted the video-game console industry. Consequently, the emergence of tablets and smartphones as substitutes for game consoles has meant that the industry has taken a downturn during the last five years.[14] As computing hardware, like tablets, become increasingly powerful, mobile and affordable, consoles will likely continue to lose market share to them.

There was a time where consoles reigned supreme over the video game market—but that is no longer the case. Once mobile devices like tablets achieved graphic richness and computing power comparable to consoles, the "tide turned." In terms of trends, new and more powerful tablets come out every year, in contrast to the launch of new consoles which traditionally has been about every seven years.

While critics argue that all this will draw sales away from consoles, which are relatively more expensive and non-portable, supporters of consoles argue that no smartphone screen can match the experience of gaming on a high-powered console attached to a large-screen television. Those supporters believe that with each new generation of consoles sales will once again increase. They believed that the introduction of a new generation of consoles in 2013 would reverse that trend. The question is can the Wii U, PlayStation and Xbox consoles sustain sales in an age of video game mobility?

---

[12] From Pong to DriveClub for PS4: A Brief History of Video Games, August 27, 2013, Jim Donahue, http://guardianlv.com/2013/08/jd-from-pong-to-driveclub-for-ps4-a-brief-history-of-video-games/

[13] The Economist explainshttp://www.economist.com/blogs/economist-explains/2013/05/economist-explains-17, Is it curtains for video-game consoles? May 26th 2013

[14] Mobile Kills the Console But Advances the Gaming Industry, By Kevin Chou, 01.31.13. http://www.wired.com/opinion/2013/01/how-mobile-kills-the-console-but-advances-the-gaming-industry/

Organizations have five basic alternatives in the decline phase:

1. *Maintain a leadership stance:* A **leadership strategy** requires a firm to continue investing in marketing, support, and product development, hoping that competitors will eventually exit the market. Despite declining sales and profit margins, there may still be opportunities to generate above-average returns for firms that remain the industry leaders during this phase.

2. *Pursue a niche strategy:* The objective of a **niche strategy** is to find a specific segment of the industry that may not decline as rapidly as the rest and where the firm can expect to possess some form of competitive advantage to discourage direct competition in the niche. For example, a tobacco firm facing declining cigarette sales may decide to focus exclusively on the more robust cigar market and defend that niche heavily against competitors by investing in marketing and sales support.

   A firm can ultimately choose to switch to a harvest, exit, or consolidation strategy after having pursued a leadership or niche approach; however, the reverse is not true.

3. *Harvest profits:* The **harvesting profits strategy** requires squeezing as much remaining profit as possible from the industry by drastically reducing costs. The firm must eliminate or severely restrict investments in the industry and take advantage of existing strengths to generate incremental sales. This strategy is ultimately followed by the firm's exit from the industry.

4. *Exit early:* The **exit early strategy** allows firms to recover some of their prior investments in the industry by exiting the market early in the decline phase, when assets may still be valuable to others and there is greater uncertainty concerning the speed of the decline. Some firms also choose to exit the industry during the mature phase to truly maximize the value from the sale of its assets. Once decline becomes evident, assets are worth much less to potential buyers, who are in a stronger bargaining position. The risk of exiting so early is that an organization's forecast for decline may prove inaccurate.

   An important point to remember is that just as there are barriers to entering an industry, there are also barriers to exiting a market. A firm may have specialized assets, such as plants and equipment, that cannot be easily redeployed by other businesses. This greatly diminishes their resale value and acts as an exit barrier. Firms may also face high costs due to labour settlements if they exit an industry. The social cost of closing a plant in a region that is economically dependent on the industry can also hinder a smooth exit. Finally, there are nonrational exit barriers linked to the cognitive and emotional barriers that managers face in divestment decisions. Exiting an industry can be perceived as a sign of failure, and managers that have a strong emotional identification and commitment to an industry are understandably reluctant to admit defeat when they have worked hard at being successful.

5. *Consolidate:* A **consolidation strategy** involves acquiring at a reasonable price the best of the remaining firms in the industry. This allows the acquirer to enhance its market power and generate economies of scale and synergies to further reduce costs and make up for declining demand. For example, in the online brokerage industry, sales and profits have declined following the market crash of 2000. Fewer people were trading stocks online, putting pressure on companies like Ameritrade and E-Trade to compensate. While E-Trade responded by entering the growing banking and mortgage markets to diversify its sources of revenue, Ameritrade went on an acquisition binge. Starting with its 2001 acquisition of National Discount Brokers, Ameritrade has devoured several of its smaller competitors: Daytek in 2002; Mydiscountbroker.com and National Brokerage in 2003;

leadership strategy An alternative for firms that are in the decline phase of their industry life cycle whereby the firm continues to invest in marketing, support, and product development, hoping that competitors will eventually exit the market.

niche strategy A strategy whereby the firm focuses on a specific segment of the industry where it can expect to possess some form of competitive advantage.

harvesting profits strategy An alternative for firms that are in the decline phase of their industry life cycle whereby the firm tries to squeeze as much remaining profit as possible from the industry by drastically reducing costs.

exit early strategy An alternative for firms that are in the decline phase of their industry life cycle whereby the firm recovers some of its prior investments by selling off assets to others and exiting the market.

consolidation strategy An alternative for firms that are in the decline phase of their industry life cycle whereby a firm acquires the best of the remaining firms in the market to enhance its market power, to generate economies of scale, and to allow for synergies.

Exhibit 7.4 Characteristics of the Industry Life-Cycle Stages

Market Growth	Slow	Very Rapid	Moderate	Negative
Customers	Affluent, early technology adopters	Niche markets, increasing penetration	Price-conscious mass market, repeat buyers	Late adopters, knowledgeable users, residual segments
Rivalry	Low; technological competition	Increasing; entry and exit; shakeout	Intense; increased concentration; exit	Price wars; exit; mergers and acquisitions; asset liquidation
Critical Functional Areas	Research and development	Sales and marketing	Production and manufacturing	General management and finance
Products	Very wide variety of designs	Standardization	Commoditization	Continued commoditization
Technological Development	Rapid product innovation	Product and process innovation	Incremental innovation	Very little innovation
Organizational Structure	Organic	Organic	Mechanistic	Mechanistic
Generic Strategies	Product differentiation	Product differentiation	Cost leadership	Cost leadership/focus
Key Objectives	Increase awareness; achieve legitimacy; specify dominant design	Create demand; capture market share	Cost efficiency; extend life cycle	Market or niche leadership; cost reduction; consolidation; exit

Bidwell and J.B. Oxford in 2004; and TD Waterhouse for $2.9 billion in 2005. Analysts claimed that the only way for discount brokers to survive the decline in online trading—besides another unlikely stock market bubble—was to merge to generate economies of scale and become more efficient. Ameritrade claimed it would generate more than $500 million in savings by merging its operations with TD Waterhouse.

Exhibit 7.4 shows a summary of the key characteristics of the different industry life-cycle stages.

Objective 2 Identify different types of innovations.

Radical innovations When a new technical process or advancement marks a significant departure from existing practices; they often create a whole new industry (such as automobiles or wireless phones have done). These innovations are often referred to as *discontinuous* because they do not continue to build on the previous technological regime, but instead mark a shift to a completely new technology. An example would be the shift to jet engines in aircrafts, which did not build on the previous propeller-based technology.

INNOVATION AND TECHNOLOGY

Types of Innovation

As our discussion of industry life cycles suggested, technological innovation is a key driver of industry evolution. Radically new innovations or *technological discontinuities* can create entirely new industries such as automobiles or cellphones have done, or seriously disrupt existing ones such as jet engines in the aircraft industry or digital cameras in the photography industry.

Radical innovations: When a new technical process or advancement marks a significant departure from existing practices; they often create a whole new industry (such as automobiles or wireless phones have done). These innovations are often referred to as *discontinuous* because they do not continue to build on the previous technological regime, but instead mark a shift to a completely new technology. An example would be the shift to jet engines in aircrafts, which did not build on the previous propeller-based technology.

Is Canada on the Leading Edge?

© Philippe-Olivier Con/Fotolia

The Conference Board's annual report card, called "How Canada Performs," assesses Canada's relative global performance in the economy, education, the environment, health, innovation, and society. By far our highest recent score was in education, where Canada ranked second and got an "A" grade in 2012, particularly for our K-to-12 education system. But education insiders know that problems are brewing in our post-secondary education system, where our institutions are generally not well-aligned and where there is a wide gap between the knowledge acquired on campus, and the skills needed to succeed in the work place.

In the other categories in "How Canada Performs," our recent rankings were modest to downright mediocre. Similarly, the World Economic Forum's Global Competitive Index for 2012–13 placed Canada a dismal 14th. Perhaps more importantly, Canada's rankings for many of these indicators have been in a slow but steady decline for a number of years, taking us further and further away from that treasured number one position . . .

So what can be done about it? If you want to be the best, you have to be prepared to adopt leading-edge practices and then commit to refining those practices every day through constant innovation. The fundamental message from these generally mediocre and declining grades is that change is required—specifically, that we need to be more innovative, nimble, and unafraid to adapt across Canadian society.

Source: Excerpted from Hodgson, G. (2012, December 20). Hey Canada! Are we really the best at anything—even hockey? Reprinted with permission from The Conference Board of Canada. Retrieved from www.conferenceboard.ca/economics/hot_eco_topics/default/12-12-20/hey_canada_are_we_really_the_best_at_anything%E2%80%94even_hockey.aspx.

Incremental innovations: Making relatively minor improvements or modifications to an existing product or practice in the hopes of differentiating it from the competition. It is also a way to extend the life cycle of the product, delaying the inevitable onset of the decline stage.

How innovative is Canada? Talking Business 7.8 discusses this issue.

Another way to classify innovations relates to the systemic nature of products and how their components interact. Most products can be thought of as a system of components that interact based on an architectural design to achieve a desired purpose. There are thus two aspects of systems here: the type and nature of the components, and how they are organized—the system's architecture. Innovations that involve changes to the product's components but leave the overall configuration of the system relatively intact are called *component or modular innovations*. For example, changes in the materials used in automobile bodies from steel to lighter-weight aluminum composites are component innovations. An innovation that alters the system's architecture or how the components interact and are linked with each other is an *architectural innovation*. Most architectural innovations, however, also require changes in the modules or components. A laptop computer is an architectural innovation given that it changes the standard configuration of a personal computer by making it portable, yet the components—microchip, operating system, keyboard, screen—remain essentially the same. A tablet is another architectural innovation.

Incremental innovations
Making relatively minor improvements or modifications to an existing product or practice in the hopes of differentiating it from the competition. It is also a way to extend the life cycle of the product, delaying the inevitable onset of the decline stage.

Researchers have shown that organizations have a much more difficult time integrating and adapting to architectural innovations compared to modular innovations. Clearly, technology has complex effects on our society, as discussed in Talking Business 7.9.

From an organizational perspective, it is useful to think of innovations in relation to an organization's skills and competencies. Technological innovations that build on a firm's existing knowledge and skills in certain areas are called *competence-enhancing innovations*. Conversely, a *competence-destroying innovation* is one that renders obsolete an organization's technical skills and capabilities. A key point to remember is that whether a technological

TALKING BUSINESS 7.9

The Linked World: How ICT Is Transforming Societies, Cultures, and Economies

Information and communications technology (ICT) is a dominant and pervasive part of modern life. We talk, Tweet, and text on cell phones; work, shop, and entertain ourselves on the Internet. ICT drives corporate growth, the global distribution of jobs, and the value of investments. It spurs innovation and competition and affects our lives—our health, our education, and our personal relationships—in ways unimaginable only a few years ago.

Information and communication technology (ICT) is an umbrella term that includes any communication device or application—including radio, television, cellular phones, computer and network hardware and software, and satellite systems, as well as the various services and applications associated with them, such as video conferencing, social networks, and distance learning. ICT is often considered a general purpose technology. It can be adapted to multiple applications.

ICT Is Everywhere—All the Time

Compared to the development of steam power or the automobile, ICT's growth and diffusion has happened with astounding speed—something that is proving to be a double-edged sword. For example, in the United States, the percentage of households with a broadband connection rose from 4.4 percent in 2000 to 63.5 percent in 2009. In the other G7 countries, the number of broadband subscribers per inhabitant increased by multiples of 5 or more during that period.

ICT's spread is often outpacing our ability to develop new processes, methods, regulations, and organizational structures to take full advantage of technologies—or, in some cases, control them. The interactive connectivity of modern ICT, especially the communications component of ICT, upends established social roles and norms—the analogue to the "creative destruction" it causes in the marketplace.

But, on the whole, when allowed to run its course, ICT is creating more winners than losers across the globe and, in many ways, is leveling the playing field, economically and socially, between advanced and emerging economies and societies.

The Linked World

While much of the attention paid to ICT has been focused on the producers and their products, *The Linked World: How ICT Is Transforming Societies, Cultures, and Economies* examines how technology is reshaping society and, in turn, is being shaped by society.

The result of a two-year global research project led by The Conference Board and underwritten by the Telefónica Foundation, *The Linked World* shows that modern ICT applications contribute significantly to economic growth and innovation, but spread only gradually across economies and geographies. While the benefits and costs to society that ICT generates are not as easy to measure as the economic ones, it is clear that maximizing ICT's net benefits requires strategic and policy commitment and persistence. Complementary essentials to ICT's full use take time to develop—digital books need a convenient e-Reader, educational software needs trained teachers, and e-government services need a technologically adept citizenry. Also, variation in use by age, gender, and social and cultural groups reveals barriers to realizing ICT's full potential that are not easily overcome, but can be guided by a well-developed ICT policy.

Changing W3hat We Do and How We Do It

The impact of technology on economies and societies introduces fundamental changes whose full effects will only be revealed over time. Some examples include:

Economies *Rapid Growth:* ICT use enhances multifactor productivity growth (i.e., the ability of the economy to grow faster than all of its inputs are growing).

Consumer Value: Gains from the switch to ever-faster broadband have hugely benefited consumers because of lower prices for higher quality.

Catching Up: While ICT investment levels are still much higher in advanced countries, emerging countries are rapidly catching up in terms of investment intensity and productivity performance.

Anytime, Anywhere: Businesses have much more geographical flexibility. While distance and transportation costs remain important, ICT plays an increasingly significant role in facilitating globalization and its effects, both negative and positive, for the home country.

Societies *Information Overload:* Decision making (both in business and in personal lives) is more complicated because of the flood of information at an advanced speed—not all of it accurate, but all of it instant.

Who Owns What? Existing structures for ownership and control of knowledge are in flux because of the development of interactive connectivity. Laws regarding intellectual property rights lag behind the technology and its uses.

Who Really Knows Best? Experts' authority can be challenged because of the ready availability of information.

Individuals *See You Soon?* Mobile communication is not eroding social interaction, but, rather, can actually boost face time.

Seller Beware: Consumers are smarter and more discerning with access to specialized information about products and services.

So Who Wants to Know? Formerly personal information can seep into the public domain, raising questions about its ownership and the notion of privacy.

ICT's Impact on Everyday Life

While ICT is growing economies and shrinking the world, it is also having some surprising and sometimes counterintuitive effects on our everyday lives, including:

How We Learn The availability of ICT at home is positively related to learning performance, yet the intensity of ICT use at home is negatively related to learning performance. While ICT use has a positive relationship with student attitudes toward math and science, which contributes positively to performance, there is a negative relationship between computer use at home and reading performance.

ICT availability contributes to use, but insufficient investment in soft infrastructure (teacher skills and organizational changes) can limit its impact. Of the countries studied, only in the United States, where large investments have been made in training teachers in ICT use, is there a positive relationship between ICT use at school and performance in the classroom.

How We Work Advances and investment in ICT will continue to reduce the forces that require large clusters of a firm's and an industry's employment to be in the same physical location. Jobs in occupations that can be performed remotely, such as accounting, computer programming, and reservations, will continue to spread out. While offshoring may result in lower wages or lost jobs in the home country, it can also allow home workers to specialize in more productive tasks and, thus, receive higher pay and boost productivity.

How We Heal The doctor-patient relationship has changed as a result of medical information from the Internet, which has greatly empowered and emancipated patients. Physicians believe that ICT has a neutral impact on diagnosis, causes increased workload, and results in deterioration of the scope of services offered and the doctor-patient relationship. On the other hand, patients value the reduction in waiting times that more efficient scheduling allows.

How We Interact The popularity of social networking sites represents a shift away from online communities organized around common interests toward communities organized around networks of people. And when it comes to an individual's relationship with government, there is a positive spin: citizens' online interactions with government drive a reduction in corruption and improve trust. The young use the Internet more intensively than the old and the most educated more than the least educated. Yet there are significant, unexplained variations across countries in the size of these differences. An "overdose" exposure to online content may lead people (especially children) to expect things instantaneously and to be less creative because they don't need to figure things out for themselves (a "copy and paste" culture.)

Source: Excerpted from The Conference Board of Canada. (2011). Executive summary. *The linked world: How ICT is transforming societies, cultures, and economies.* Reprinted with permission.

discontinuity is competence enhancing or destroying is often a matter of perspective. The same innovation can be competence destroying to one organization and competence enhancing to another, depending on their current knowledge base. Electronic calculators replaced slide rules as the tool of choice for engineers and mathematicians in the 1970s. This discontinuous innovation did not build on the knowledge of making slide rules and forced the largest US slide rule manufacturer, Keuffel & Esser, out of the market. The calculator did, however, build on the electronics capabilities of firms like Hewlett-Packard (HP) and Texas Instruments (TI) that came to dominate the market. The calculator was thus competence destroying for slide rule makers yet competence enhancing for firms like HP and TI.

The Evolution of Technology

Objective 3 Understand the relationship between technological evolution and industry evolution and describe the key features of technology life-cycle models.

creative destruction A term that explains how innovations sweep away old technologies, skills, products, ideas, and industries and replace them with new ones.

Joseph Schumpeter (1883–1950), an Austrian economist and professor at Harvard, was among the first to emphasize the role of technical progress and entrepreneurship as the driving forces of capitalist economies. In his work, he stressed the evolutionary and cyclical nature of industries that were periodically disrupted by the introduction of revolutionary innovations. Certainly, even traditional industries such as health care may benefit from new technologies, as seen in Talking Business 7.10. In his most popular book *Capitalism, Socialism and Democracy*, he coined the colourful and now famous expression of **creative destruction** to explain how innovations swept away old technologies, skills, products, ideas, and industries and replaced them with new ones:

> this process . . . that incessantly revolutionizes the economic structure from within, incessantly destroying the old one, incessantly creating a new one. This process of Creative Destruction is the essential fact about capitalism. It is what capitalism consists in and what every capitalist concern has got to live in.[15]

TALKING BUSINESS 7.10

Embracing Disruption: Lessons from Building the First Quantum Computer

[Many years ago], the September-October issue of *Harvard Business Review* posed the question, "Will Disruptive Innovations Cure Health Care?" In this article, the authors encouraged health care professionals to embrace disruptive technologies that may threaten the status quo but will ultimately raise the quality and performance of the health care system for everyone.

How have Canadian health care professionals succeeded in embracing disruptive innovations since this article was published? Let's consider a disruptive technology that has existed for three decades—the electronic medical record (EMR). The 2012 Commonwealth Fund's International Health Policy Survey of Primary Care Physicians revealed that Canada lags behind other countries in EMR use, with only 56% of doctor's reporting usage in their practices. Clearly, Canada has some catching up to do, especially considering the rate of technological advancement. As new inventions are leveraged to create the next generation of technology, the capability of electronic devices is now growing exponentially.

---

[15] Schumpeter, J. (1942 [1975]). *Capitalism, socialism and democracy*. New York, NY: Harper.

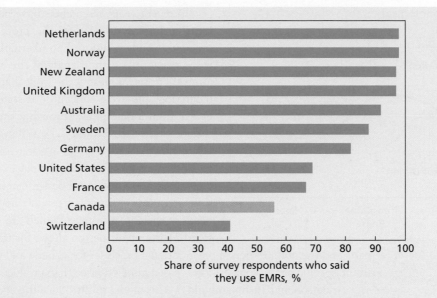

Share of survey respondents who said they use EMRs, %

At a recent meeting of the Centre for the Advancement of Health Innovation, Jeremy Hilton, Vice-President, Processor Development at D-Wave Systems, discussed the potentially disruptive capability of a quantum computer. Quantum computing leverages the most fundamental mechanics of the universe to perform logic operations. This computing model is different from classical computation which adds numbers at blazingly fast speeds. In comparison, quantum computing allows for exponential increases in computing speed. But what does this mean for health care?

For all of the non-physicists in the audience, Mr. Hilton illustrated the potential of quantum computing using a comic book scenario:

Consider the 150 million units of information currently stored in the Library of Congress. An evil villain has hidden a piece of information somewhere in the library that holds the key to stopping his plot for world domination. It is up to you, the hero, to stop the villain from taking over the world. The first solution that comes to mind involves physically searching through each and every item in the library; however, even searching at the rate of one item per second would take you five years. A much faster solution can be devised using the quantum principles of superposition and entanglement. Superposition would allow you to create 150 million copies of yourself, with all searching the library simultaneously. Under the principle of

entanglement, all of those copies can interact with each other and then separate, so that the only copy that finds the information will be left to exist and all the other copies will disappear.

D-Wave is currently investigating the use of quantum computing in understanding protein folding. Mr. Hilton explains "if we could understand the structure of proteins we would know what drugs can interfere with their activity." D-Wave is also developing algorithms that can detect cancer based on x-ray information. This work is complex as machines do not work like a human brain—a machine cannot look at a picture and determine the problem the way that a human can. D-Wave's algorithms work much more similarly to the human brain.

Many health experts believe that in the next five to ten years, quantum computing will radically improve the ability to understand, treat and cure diseases. This technology will have a disruptive impact in numerous fields: machine intelligence, internet, intelligence, data security and many others. There is a need for new and innovative ways to leverage this potential. This can only be achieved, however, if Canadians break with their past performance and embrace disruption.

Source: Excerpted from Lye, J. (2013, January 14). Embracing disruption: Lessons from building the first quantum computer. Reprinted with permission from The Conference Board of Canada. Retrieved from www.conferenceboard.ca/commentaries/healthinnovation/default/13-01-14/embracing_disruption_lessons_from_building_the_first_quantum_computer.aspx.

Exhibit 7.5 Technological Life Cycle

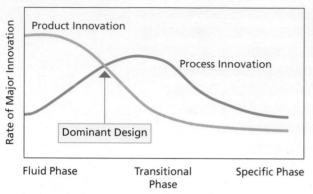

Source: Based on Abernathy, W.J., & Utterback, J.M. (1978). Patterns of industrial innovation. *Technology Review, 80*(7), 40–47.

punctuated equilibrium A pattern that shows, over long periods, that technological discontinuities tend to appear at rare and irregular intervals in industries.

In recent years, researchers have built on Schumpeter's ideas to further understand the process of technological innovation and evolution. The Abernathy-Utterback model, based primarily on their study of the automobile industry, forms the basis for most of the work that has followed on the technology life-cycle concept.[16] It states that technologies evolve from a fluid phase through a transitional phase to a specific phase (see Exhibit 7.5). When a new technology is initially introduced, it is still in a state of flux and there are a lot of technical as well as marketplace uncertainties. As the industry grows, a dominant design emerges and competition shifts from introducing new product features to meeting the needs of specific customers, which are by then well understood. A dominant design allows for the standardization of parts and the optimization of organizational processes for volume and efficiency; therefore, in the specific phase, competition is based more on price than product features.

Anderson and Tushman build on this model to introduce the evolutionary notion of **punctuated equilibrium** to the study of industry evolution.[17] They studied several industries over long periods and showed that technological discontinuities tend to appear at rare and irregular intervals. These discontinuities trigger an *era of ferment*, a period of substantial product-class variation that ends with the emergence of a dominant design. Once a dominant design emerges, future technical progress consists of incremental improvements that elaborate on the standard. The *era of incremental change* (usually coinciding with the industry maturity stage) is a much longer period of relative stability and equilibrium. These long periods of incremental change are punctuated by technological discontinuities, hence the reference to a punctuated equilibrium (see Exhibit 7.6).

Technological Forecasting

One of the problems with the Abernathy-Utterback and Anderson-Tushman models is that, while useful descriptions of technological evolution, they do not help in predicting when a discontinuity will occur. Although it is virtually impossible to accurately predict when a technological discontinuity will appear, we can make more informed analyses of technological trajectories using S-curves. Foster introduced the concept of the S-curve to explain the

Exhibit 7.6 A Cyclical Model of Technological Change

Source: Based on Anderson, P.A., & Tushman, M. (1990). Technological discontinuities and dominant designs: A cyclical model of technological change. *Administrative Science Quarterly, 35,* 604–633.

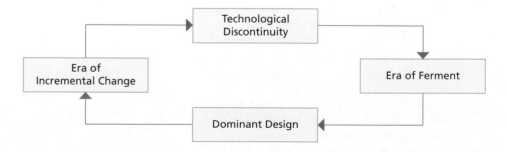

---

[16] Abernathy, W.J., & Utterback, J.M. (1978). Patterns of industrial innovation. Technology Review, 80(7), 40–47; Utterback, J.M. (1994). Mastering the dynamics of innovation. Boston, MA: Harvard Business School Press.

[17] Anderson & Tushman, 1990.

rate of advance of a technology[18] (see Exhibit 7.7). When a new technology emerges, progress starts off slowly, then increases very rapidly as the technology is better understood and firms pour more efforts into research and development. As the physical limits of the technology are reached and the returns to engineering efforts start to decrease, the rate of technical progress begins to diminish. A new technology able to overcome the physical limits of the old one will then trigger a new S-curve so that performance keeps improving with successive generations of S-curves.

Technological progress of the past 30 years in the computer industry has been driven in large part by what has become known as *Moore's law*, after Intel cofounder Gordon Moore. In 1965, Moore predicted that the power and performance of microchips would double every 18 months as a function of semiconductor manufacturers' ability to double the number of transistors on a chip. This prediction has proven fairly accurate, and the rate of technical advance in microprocessor technology has in fact been exponential. These technological achievements are based on a strategy of continually shrinking the size of the transistors on chips so that electrons have less distance to travel, thereby speeding up the processing of data. As circuits get packed closer and closer on chips, however, they begin to overheat and performance suffers. This drop in performance signals that the current microchip technology is reaching the peak of its S-curve as the physical limits to shrinking transistor sizes are reached. In order for semiconductor firms like Intel and AMD to continue to generate performance improvements in line with Moore's law, a new technological discontinuity will have to replace the current strategy of miniaturization.

Several innovations are already in the works. One involves replacing a single high-speed processor with two or three that don't need to be as speedy, linked together on the same chip. A second, even more radical innovation entails stacking circuits in a three-dimensional manner and arranging chip functions vertically rather than in a flat, horizontal design as current chips are configured. This technique promises to generate dramatic performance gains—some claim quantum leaps—and even reduce power consumption. Even though these innovations will require overhauling all the software running on chips and devising new methods for chip design and assembly, they may ultimately allow manufacturers to make the jump to the next technological S-curve and resume the phenomenal progress of Moore's law.

Exhibit 7.7 Foster's Technological S-Curve

Source: Based on Chistensen, C.M. (1992). "Exploring the Limits of the Technology S-Curve". *Production and Operations Management (1).* Reprinted by permission of John Wiley and Sons, Hoboken, NJ.

TECHNOLOGY AND THE CHANGING WORKPLACE

Objective 4 Describe how technology is changing the workplace.

The relationship of employees and organizations has been undergoing tremendous change and will continue to do so. Many years ago in his book entitled *The End of Work*, Jeremy Rifkin talked about how the nature of work itself is changing. That is, the nature of work or the type of work we will perform in the future may be dramatically different from what we did for most of the 20th century. It is argued that the job itself is becoming an artifact, and the task of organizations is to create the "post-job" organization.

---

[18] Foster, R. (1986). The S-curve: A new forecasting tool. In *Innovation: The attacker's advantage* (pp. 88–111). New York, NY: Summit Books, Simon and Schuster.

How will the job disappear, and why should organizations shift away from jobs? Though this sounds mystifying, much of this can be understood in the context within which we have explained many of the changes to organizational design. To clarify, we are not actually referring to disappearing jobs in terms of the number of jobs lost or job losses in certain industries, but rather the very notion of the job itself is becoming outdated. In the future people will continue to work, but not within the familiar envelopes that we call jobs. And in fact, many organizations are already becoming "de-jobbed" (see Talking Business 7.11).

Rifkin argues that what we think of as a "job" is really a social artifact. That is, it is based on an idea that emerged in the late 19th century to package the work that needed to be done in the growing factories and bureaucracies of industrialized societies. Before that time, people worked just as hard, but at shifting clusters of tasks, depending on the needs of the day. In a sense, Taylor and scientific management helped build our concept of jobs as compartmentalized, specialized tasks that we are trained to perform. However, the conditions that created this notion of the job have changed dramatically over 200 years: Mass production and large bureaucratic organizations are vanishing.

Technology allows us to automate the assembly line, so masses of unskilled labour are much less needed. Large firms are also outsourcing much of their activities. So, given that the conditions under which jobs were created have changed, we are redefining not just organizational structure, but also how work should be performed—not in the traditional jobs that led our thinking for most of the 20th century.

TALKING BUSINESS 7.11

Will Technology Replace Middle-Class Jobs?

Technological change has led to restructuring of US labour markets and the loss of bargaining power for some workers, especially those in lower skilled jobs.

The fact that technological change reduces the demand for low-skilled workers is nothing new—remember the telephone operators who were replaced by electronic switchboards. However, the impact of technological change has moved up the income ladder in recent years. The automation of routine jobs is no longer simply a problem for low-skilled workers—technology now affects workers in the middle class with medium skills as well. For instance, computer programs are capable of reviewing case law and legal precedent more efficiently than humans, which has lowered the demand for legal clerks. The analysis of X-rays by technicians can be outsourced to India and the growing use of pattern-recognition software implies that eventually, these jobs may be completely computerized—which will boost productivity in health care.

Technology and outsourcing helps explain why the incomes of low- and middle-class families have stagnated over the past few decades, but it doesn't adequately address the issue of why pay for the super-rich CEOs has soared so much in the past 10 to 15 years. One possible explanation could be the increasing use of stock options since the early 1990s. Ironically, legislation passed by Congress in 1993 may have inadvertently contributed to the rise of stock option compensation for CEOs. This law limited the tax deductibility of any compensation above $1 million in the form of standard salary and bonus pay. As a consequence, companies started to increase the portion of CEO pay in stock options. This factor, combined with surging profitability at the time, has resulted in astronomical pay in the tens of millions of dollars for CEOs. Many CEOs now make even more money than professional athletes!

Unfortunately, the long-term trend in sluggish income growth for middle- and lower-class families is not going away anytime soon. Globalization has increased the supply of low-skilled workers in the world economy, depressing wages of similar workers in the United States. The impact of technological change on the incomes of medium-skilled workers will continue. What should young people do to counteract these forces and succeed in an ultra-competitive global labour market? The answer is simple: Get as much education as possible.

Source: Kip Beckman, "Is Income Inequality a Fact of Life in the U.S. Economy?" (February 06, 2012). The Conference Board of Canada. Reprinted with permission.

It is understandable that with so much change occurring around us the very nature of the type of work we perform within these organizations must also somehow be changing! For example, in place of full-time jobs, we are seeing more and more temporary and part-time work situations. That is simply one manifestation of a greater underlying change: The fact is, organizations are essentially moving away from a structure built for the performance of jobs into simply a field of work needing to be done. In other words, specialization or division of labour encouraged us to become pre-occupied with filling jobs and positions rather than simply focusing on performing the work that needs to be done.

In a relatively stable environment, rigid jobs are fine for performing the work; however, the increasingly dynamic nature of our environment seems to almost continuously require new skills and new combinations of work; a philosophy that is wedded to a "jobs mentality" is simply too slow to adapt. This is the new, post-job world. The acceleration of disruptive innovations will continue to shape our workplace and the evolution of industries. See Exhibit 7.8 for a summary of major innovations throughout history.

Exhibit 7.8 A History of Innovations

Year	Innovation
1023	Paper money first printed in China
1800	The battery is invented by Count Alessandro
1814	First steam locomotive invented by George Stephenson
1829	The typewriter is invented by W.A. Burt
1861	The bicycle is invented by Ernest Michaux
1876	The telephone is invented by Alexander Graham Bell
1902	The air conditioner is invented by Willis Carrier
1959	The microchip is invented by Jack Kilby and Robert Noyce
1965	The compact disc is invented by James Russell
1972	The word processor is invented
1979	The cellphone is invented
1981	The first IBM personal computer is invented
1984	The Apple Macintosh computer is invented
1991	The World Wide Web is invented
1995	The DVD is invented
1998	Google is started by Larry Page and Sergey Brin
1999	The first smartphone (BlackBerry) is invented
2001	The iPod is invented
2004	Facebook is created

Source: Compiled from Stringer, L. (2010). *The green workplace* (pp. 204–205). New York, NY: Palrave Macmillam.

CHAPTER SUMMARY

Competitive processes evolve in a remarkably predictable manner in most industries. Understanding what to expect and what drives evolution along the life cycle of an industry is critical for managers needing to steer their organizations through turbulent times. In this chapter, we identified the major phases and milestones that mark an industry's evolutionary path from introduction and growth to maturity and decline. At each stage of the industry life cycle, the skills and capabilities needed to survive and grow change in significant ways. We examined the nature of these changes as competition evolves in markets that go from fragmented and fast-growing to concentrated and declining. We considered the role played by technological innovation in shaping industry evolution. This chapter also examined different models for the evolution of technology and predicting the path of technological progress.

CHAPTER LEARNING TOOLS

Key Terms

cognitive legitimacy 241

commoditization 250

consolidation strategy 253

creative destruction 258

de facto standard 245

de jure standard 245

decline phase 251

dominant design 245

exit early strategy 253

growth phase 245

harvesting profits
  strategy 253

incremental innovations
  255

industry life-cycle
  model 237

Multiple-Choice Questions

Select the *best* answer for each of the following questions. Solutions are located in the back of your textbook.

1. Over the long run, almost all industries exhibit
   a. an upward sloping curve
   b. an inverted U-shape growth pattern
   c. a downward sloping growth pattern
   d. none of the above

2. The industry life-cycle model has _____ distinct phases.
   a. one   b. two
   c. three   d. four

3. The mature phase is characterized by
   a. slower growth   b. higher growth
   c. rapid growth   d. negative growth

4. Newer industries can have
   a. high fragmentation   b. experimental technology
   c. novel business models d. all of the above

5. The main drivers of industry evolution are
   a. demand growth
   b. creation and diffusion of technology and knowledge
   c. both A and B
   d. none of the above

6. Firms are intensely focused on R&D in which stage?
   a. Introductory   b. Growth
   c. Maturity   d. Decline

7. In which stage are customers more willing to pay a premium for the product?
   a. Decline   b. Maturity
   c. Growth   d. Introduction

8. The endorsement of an industry by a government is sometimes referred to as
   a. cognitive legitimacy   b. sociopolitical legitimacy
   c. both A and B   d. none of the above

9. Cognitive legitimacy refers to
   a. a management thinking process
   b. a level of public knowledge about a new industry
   c. a competitive context model
   d. none of the above

10. A standard that is legally mandated and enforced by a government is sometimes called a
    a. *de facto* standard   b. *de jure* standard
    c. government standard   d. quality assurance standard

11. A large number of exits from the market is called
    a. a decline in market share
    b. a downsizing strategy
    c. a shakeout
    d. an industry meltdown

12. A high degree of concentration and fierce rivalry occurs in the _____ of the industry life-cycle model.
    a. introductory phase   b. growth phase
    c. mature phase   d. decline phase

13. A change in demographics can trigger the _____ of the industry life-cycle model.
    a. introductory phase   b. growth phase
    c. mature phase   d. decline phase

14. In the decline stage, an option to deal with falling sales is to
    a. maintain a leadership stance
    b. pursue a niche strategy
    c. harvest profits
    d. all of the above

15. The smartphone industry is in the _____ phase.
    a. introductory   b. growth
    c. mature   d. decline

Discussion Questions

1. Identify and explain the four phases of the industry life-cycle model.

2. Explain the difference between sociopolitical legitimacy and cognitive legitimacy.

3. Compare and contrast a *de jure* standard with a *de facto* standard.

4. Identify one industry in the introductory phase and support your answer with theoretical references.

5. Identify three industries that are in the growth phase and support your answer with theoretical references.

6. Identify three industries that are in the mature phase and support your answer with theoretical references.

7. Identify three industries that are in the decline phase and support your answer with theoretical references.

8. A decline in sales can be triggered by three causes. What are these causes?

9. Explain the five options available to organizations to deal with declining sales.

10. What phase of the industry life-cycle model do you think the "sports-card collecting" industry fits into and why?

Coca-Cola's advertising has often conjured up positive images about drinking soda. Over the years, some of the slogans have included "Enjoy Life," "Have a Coke and Smile," and, more recently, polar bears have been drinking Coke, too.

In 2013, the Coca-Cola Company decided to promote its nonsoda beverages as part of a campaign to fight global obesity.[19] Some products showcased are lower- to no-calorie drinks, which include some diet sodas, juices, and bottled water. As part of its campaign, Coke decided to improve calorie labelling and offer smaller portion sizes. New partnerships were formed as well. Coke partnered with school breakfast programs and ParticipAC-TION, an active-living organization, to promote a healthier company image and to remind customers to balance taste and calories with exercise.[20]

Steve Cukrov/Shutterstock

Michael Cohen, professor of marketing at New York University, believes it is a good strategy for Coke. "The pressure comes from the market . . . consumers are more educated about what they put in their bodies," he said. "And there's been a shift toward less sweet tastes."[21]

Critics of the company, such as the Center for Science in the Public Interest (CSPI), a US nonprofit organization focused on promoting health and nutrition, argue that soda drinks have been contributing to obesity in both adults and children. According to CSPI executive director Michael Jacobson, 16% of calories in the average American's diet are from added sugars, and about half of those calories come from beverages like sugary soda pop.[22]

Yale University researchers have similarly found in a study that people tend to eat more calories on days that they also consume sweetened soda drinks. Kelly Brownell, who led the Yale study, argues that the beverage industry is trying to avoid government regulation and new taxes on carbonated soda drinks. "Studies that do not support a relationship between consumption of sugared beverages and health outcomes tend to be conducted by authors supported by the beverage industry," said Brownell, who supports a soda tax.[23]

Today in Canada, almost one third of children are overweight or obese. Similarly, 60% of men and 44% of women are also overweight.[24] Many nutritionists claim that most sodas have empty calories: lots of sugar and no nutritional content.

New York University professor Marion Nestle says there is sufficient proof that sugary pop has contributed to America's obesity epidemic, especially in young children. Nestle stated that pediatricians who diagnose obese children explain that many of their patients consume 1,000 to 2,000 calories every day from carbonated soft drinks alone. "Some

[19] Krashinsky, S. (2013, April 23). New Coke campaign targets obesity worldwide. *Globe and Mail*. Retrieved from www.globeinvestor.com/servlet/WireFeedRedirect?cf=GlobeInvestor/config&vg=BigAdVariableGenerator & date=20130422&archive=rtgam&slug=escenic_11478083.

[20] Krashinsky, 2013.

[21] Krashinsky, 2013.

[22] Boyles, S. (n.d.). Sodas and your health: Risks debated. WebMD. Retrieved from www.webmd.com/diet/features/sodas-and-your-health-risks-debated.

[23] Boyles, n.d.

[24] Krashinsky, 2013.

Case Continued >

children drink sodas all day long," she says. "They are getting all of the calories they need in a day from soft drinks, so it's no wonder they are fat . . . The first thing that anyone should do if they are trying to lose weight is eliminate or cut down on soft drinks."[25]

Certainly, Coke's strategy has raised some concerns. "It's part of their broader campaign to reposition the soft drink industry in the public's mind," said Jacobson. "When you look at their ads, its fun and excitement, and happiness, and being hip and modern. But these companies are selling junk food that causes health problems."[26]

According to the CSPI, in the United States obesity costs $147 billion annually, half which is paid by Medicare and Medicaid. Clearly, health care expenditures could be better spent on unpreventable illnesses; however, curbing obesity is a challenge.

In 2013, New York City Mayor Michael Bloomberg attempted to introduce legislation that would have reduced the maximum size of soft drinks sold in delis and other fast-food outlets to 16 ounces. However, the proposed legislation was turned down by a judge in March. Representatives from the soft drink industry argued that obesity is not just caused by soft drinks, but by a wide range of unhealthy food and lifestyle choices. Many industry analysts argue that in the past decade the soft drink industry has begun to change anyways.

According to *Beverage Digest*, a beverage industry publication, the sales of soda declined for the eighth straight year in a row. While soda companies like Coke, Pepsi, and Dr. Pepper have increased prices to help soda revenues, many industry analysts question if this drop in consumption is here to stay.

In 2012, soda sales volume decreased by 1.2% to 9.17 billion cases. While the drop may seem small, the reduction in profit dollars is significant. US consumption of soda has been declining since 2005, and last year it fell to its lowest level since 1996. On the other hand, energy drink consumption increased significantly. Monster was up 19.1%, Red Bull was up 17%, and Rockstar was up 8%.[27]

The most popular drink, surprisingly, is water. Bottled water is the fastest-growing product in the beverage industry today, studies suggest. Between 2001 and 2011, bottled water consumption rose 56% to 26 gallons per person. During the same time, annual soda consumption fell by 16%.[28]

Due to health concerns over diabetes and obesity, many consumers are turning to healthier products such as juices, coffee, and bottled water to reduce calorie intake and maintain better health. There is a demographic reason for fallen sales as well. Baby boomers (soda's traditional target market) are now aging, and youth are turning to other beverages instead.[29]

Indeed, the soda industry has had to adjust their strategy to ensure continued sales and adequate profit margins. In 2010, Coke and Pepsi spent about $20 billion to acquire their bottling companies in an effort to cut costs and reduce shrinking profit margins.[30]

---

[25] Boyles, n.d.

[26] Krashinsky, 2013.

[27] Broderick, J. (2013, March 25). Soda sales down to lowest level since 1996 despite increase in obesity rate. Counsel & Heal. Retrieved from www.counselheal.com/articles/4527/20130325/soda-sales-down-lowest-level-1996-despite-increase-obesity-rate.htm.

[28] Fottrell, Q. (2013, April 15). 10 things Coke, Pepsi and soda industry won't say. *Wall Street Journal*. Retrieved from www.marketwatch.com/story/10-things-the-soda-business-wont-tell-you-2013-04-12.

[29] Esterl, M. (2013, January 18). Is this the end of the soft-drink era? *Wall Street Journal*. Retrieved from http://online.wsj.com/article/SB10001424127887323783704578245973076636056.html.

[30] Esterl, 2013.

Soda companies have also diversified into other beverages such as sport drinks and fruit juices to counteract lost soda sales.

Last year, PepsiCo invested millions of dollars in advertising after losing market share to Coke. Moreover, soda companies are investing heavily in research and development, working on creating zero- to low-calorie natural sweeteners to best mimic the taste of real sugar in sodas.[31]

What else are soda companies doing? Well, acquisitions are also growing in number. Writer Mike Esterl explains that their newer drinks are growing in popularity, which is leading to rising profits in this segment. Last year, Coke acquired Zico, a coconut water brand, and diversified into US dairy for the first time, purchasing a small stake in the company that owns Core Power, a workout recovery shake. According to Esterl, "sales of PepsiCo's Naked juice brand rose about 25% last year and tea and coffee sold through joint ventures with Lipton and Starbucks are posting healthy growth."[32]

"I think we can all be optimistic about the business we're in," said Sandy Douglas, Coke's global chief customer officer.[33]

Currently, the soda market in North America is dominated by Coke, Pepsi, and Dr. Pepper. Coke has 42% of the market, Pepsi has 28%, and Dr. Pepper has 17%. The remaining 13% is held by smaller companies, including no-name and supermarket brands.[34]

Certainly, Coke is going to be around for many years to come. Despite lower sales, carbonated soft drinks still make up the largest segment of nonalcoholic drinks in the beverage industry at 25%. For Coca-Cola, 60% of its revenue is derived from soda sales. For PepsiCo, the percentage is lower at around 25%.[35]

According to the *Wall Street Journal*, Coke and Pepsi are drawing about 60% and 50% of sales outside of the United States, and the companies continue to grow globally. After all, Coke is one of the world's most recognized global brands. In the United States, the company maintains the top brand in the soft drink industry with Coke and Diet Coke retaining the number one and number two spots. For many North American consumers, Coke is more than just a soda—it is a strong part of their culture and history. It's like the famous 1971 jingle: They'd still "like to buy the world a Coke, and keep it company."

Questions

1. What stage in the industry life-cycle model is the soft drink industry in? Explain and justify your answer.

2. What strategies are available to the soft drink industry for dealing with declining sales? What would you recommend?

3. Do you think the soft drink industry will die? Why or why not?

---

[31] Esterl, 2013.

[32] Esterl, 2013.

[33] Esterl, 2013.

[34] Robinson-Jacobs, K. (2013, March 25). Soda sales fall eighth straight year, posting biggest drop since 2009. *Dallas News*. Retrieved from http://bizbeatblog.dallasnews.com/2013/03/soda-sales-fall-for-eighth-straight-year-see-biggest-drop-since-2009.html.

[35] Esterl, 2013.

Chapter 8
Global Forces
How is Canada Faring in the Global Village?

Reuters/Mark Blinch (Canada)

Learning Objectives

After studying this chapter, you should be able to

1. Identify factors that have encouraged the globalization of business.
2. Describe the central channels or forms of global business activity.
3. Discuss the importance and consequences of multinational and borderless corporations.
4. Explain the purpose of protectionism and its relationship with international trade.
5. Identify the types of regional economic integration.
6. Discuss the implications of NAFTA for Canada and the Canadian business environment.

What are some of the fundamental sources of influence on the decision to engage in global business? In addition to addressing this question, this chapter will identify the different types of global business activity. We will examine one of the central controversies of globalization: the multinational corporation. This chapter will also explain why nations desire, or do not desire, to promote international trade, including an examination of the pros and cons of Canada's free trade agreement with the United States.

THE BUSINESS WORLD

Foreign Outsourcing and RBC

It's been about 30 years since the last television was manufactured in Canada.[1] Why? Well, Canadian competitors could no longer compete with their Japanese counterparts, and so production shut down. In fact, the entire consumer electronics industry in North America met a similar demise. Like other similarly affected industries, the results of shifting production locations have brought good news and bad news for different stakeholders.

The good news was largely for consumers, who acquired less expensive electronic goods. For example, a television costs significantly less today in real terms than it did 30 years ago. The bad news was for Canadians employed in those manufacturing jobs—the people who made all of those electronic goods had to find something else to do. This trend in outsourcing of work has been growing and growing, and not just in the manufacturing sector.

Outsourcing involves hiring external organizations to conduct work in certain functions of an organization. For example, payroll, accounting, and legal work can all be assigned to outsourced staff. The organization typically will retain its core functions or competencies—that is, those areas that it is in business to conduct. When this practice is done using foreign labour it has been referred to as *offshore outsourcing* or *offshoring*.

Companies decide to engage in outsourcing, and offshore outsourcing in particular, for sound financial reasons—namely, huge cost savings. Sometimes they also gain access to staff with specialized skills that may not exist within their own organization. The downside, of course, is the impact on a company's internal labour force.

The classic example of outsourcing is Nike. Nike is well-known for its use of outsourcing on an international basis. Nike has typically entered into contractual arrangements with manufacturers in developing nations to produce its footwear while it focuses largely on marketing its product. In fact, this has been a major underlying source of controversy with regard to businesses "going global"—the fear that relatively higher-paying North American jobs will be lost as businesses decide to outsource manufacturing functions to cheaply paid labour in underdeveloped or developing countries.

Countries can be contracted for the production of finished goods or component parts, and these goods or parts can subsequently be imported to the home country or to other countries for further assembly or sale. However, in recent years outsourcing is not just about outsourcing low-wage manufacturing jobs—it has come to include higher-paid knowledge work as well. Outsourcing of high-tech services has become relativity common. Nonetheless, the number of information technology (IT) jobs allocated to offshore firms is increasing, and consequently it continues to raise public concern about the loss of good-paying Canadian jobs to lower-cost countries. Consider the recent controversy regarding IT outsourcing at RBC.

RBC generated a lot of criticism in 2013 after reports surfaced that it was in the process of contracting out jobs of Canadian employees to lower-paid foreign workers. It was reported that 45 IT employees at RBC Investor Services in Toronto were to be transferred abroad via an arrangement with iGATE, a high-tech company based in Bangalore, India. iGATE also has branch offices in Toronto, Mississauga, and Calgary. The foreign workers

[1] McInnes, C. (2013, April 9). Foreign workers are a threat to Canadian jobs, wherever they live. *Vancouver Sun.* Retrieved from www.vancouversun.com/business/bc2035/foreign+workers+threat+canadian+jobs+wherever+they+live/8218779/story.html.

who had been assigned to take over the RBC positions in Toronto were employed by iGATE, which had a contract to provide IT services to RBC.[2]

RBC did not attempt to hide the fact that it, like its competitors, aims to cut costs where legitimately possible. RBC's plan to cut costs and boost profits (which in 2012 were a record $7.5 billion) was to be partly facilitated by outsourcing some Canadian jobs to iGATE's low-wage Indian operation.

The backlash to this plan stemmed from two sources. First, it became a high-profile case of yet more Canadian jobs being lost, but more salient was the manner in which it occurred. According to a report, iGATE was bringing foreign workers into Canada to be trained by the RBC workers whose jobs they would eventually be taking. After this training the iGATE employees would return home (to India, among other regions) and begin their new job responsibilities.[3]

However, many of these same critics also pointed out that this arrangement was legal under present Canadian law. Specifically, the federal government's Temporary Foreign Worker Program (TFWP) permits companies to bring individuals into Canada on a temporary basis. While this law is controversial, the practices it permits have been occurring at numerous other companies. Consequently critics argue that this program should be stopped. Such critics assert that Canadian immigration policy is designed to encourage skilled workers to come to Canada on a permanent basis, which would strengthen the quality of the workforce, rather than simply come here to train, leave, and take Canadian jobs with them. Although it is considered a violation of government regulations for any company to bring foreign workers into Canada temporarily if it will put Canadian citizens out of work, there appear to be loopholes in the regulations. Hence the opposition to the TFWP.

RBC claimed that it did not violate any government regulations regarding the use of foreign employment, and it also claimed that these workers had specialized skills and that outsourcing was being implemented for cost savings and efficiency.

The public controversy and subsequent scrutiny of RBC's hiring practices led the chief executive officer of RBC to issue an open letter to Canadians, which appeared in national newspapers and was posted on RBC's Media website. It included the following statement:

> First, I want to apologize . . .
>
> Second, we are reviewing . . . a leading corporate citizen.[4]

Journalist Andrew Coyne summed up the situation:

> You can hire people from abroad, even at the cost of Canadian jobs, as long as they stay abroad: it's called outsourcing, and it's a broadly accepted practice. You can also hire people from abroad, if they move here to live. That's called immigration, and is also broadly accepted. If, on the other hand, you hire people who fall between the two—who work here but live abroad—then it's a scandal [paraphrased].[5]

---

[2] Walkom, T. (2013, April 22). Deliberately lax visa rules encouraged RBC outsourcing. *Toronto Star*. Retrieved from www.thestar.com/news/canada/2013/04/09/deliberately_lax_visa_rules_encouraged_rbc_outsourcing_walkom.html.

[3] Greenwood, J. (2013, April 13). RBC takes heat for Ottawa's flawed outsourcing policy: CD Howe expert. *National Post*. Retrieved from http://business.financialpost.com/2013/04/08/rbc-takes-heat-for-ottawas-flawed-outsourcing-policy-cd-howe-expert.

[4] CBC *News*. (2013, April 11). RBC CEO Gord Nixon's open letter. Retrieved from www.cbc.ca/news/canada/story/2013/04/11/rbc-gord-nixon-apology-letter.html.

[5] Coyne, A. (2013, April 10). Andrew Coyne: RBC outsourcing controversy an economic fraud. *National Post*. Retrieved from http://fullcomment.nationalpost.com/2013/04/10/andrew-coyne-rbc-outsourcing-controversy-an-economic-fraud.

WHAT IS GLOBALIZATION?

The Business World vignette highlights the global context of business—one that involves many more players than local businesses and the domestic market. Business in the global context involves many stakeholders, including domestic and foreign competitors, workers, industries, governments, national cultures, and economies. How business is conducted in light of trade agreements and the global arrangements is a key issue for our entire society, and this is a theme we will explore more fully in this chapter.

While you may have heard or read about this popular buzzword, many of you may not be completely familiar with what **globalization** represents and its implications. What is globalization? While there is no one, universal definition, it is useful to consider this concept as a process.

Globalization is a process involving the integration of world economics. The presence of trade blocs reflects the accelerating pace with which nations are integrating their economies. For example, the North American Free Trade Agreement (NAFTA), discussed later in this chapter, is a free trade bloc consisting of Canada, the United States, and Mexico. The European Union (EU) groups 25 countries together into one economic union, while the Asia-Pacific Economic Cooperation (APEC) consists of 21 nations forming a free trade zone around the Pacific Ocean.

Globalization is a process involving the integration of world markets. This reflects the notion that consumer preferences are converging around the world. Whether it is for products made by McDonald's, Sony, Gap, or Nike, organizations are increasingly marketing their goods and services worldwide. Though local modifications may be made to tailor the product to local consumers, there is a push toward global products. On the other side, production is increasingly becoming a global affair. Businesses will set up operations wherever it is least costly to do so.

In sum, the recurrent themes raised in any discussion of globalization tend to include elements of the following:

- Globalization can be considered a process that is expanding the degree and forms of cross-border transactions among people, assets, goods, and services.

- Globalization refers to the growth in direct foreign investment in regions across the world.

- Globalization reflects the shift toward increasing economic interdependence—the process of generating one world economic system or a global economy.

SOURCES ENCOURAGING GLOBAL BUSINESS ACTIVITY

Why have we witnessed a tremendous surge in business activity on an international scale? From giant multinational corporations to small businesses, in recent years the drive toward global business has accelerated. A number of fundamental factors have encouraged the move to "go global." Some factors can be considered **pull factors**, and are the positive outcomes a business would gain from entering the international context. Other factors are **push factors**—these are forces that act upon all businesses to create an environment where competing successfully means competing globally (see Exhibit 8.1 on next page).

© adimas/Fotolia

globalization Although there is no universally agreed-upon definition, it may be considered as a process involving the integration of national economies and the process of generating a single world economic system.

pull factors Positive outcomes a business would gain from entering the global market include the potential for sales growth and the opportunity of obtaining needed resources.

Objective 1 Identify factors that have encouraged the globalization of business.

push factors Forces that act on all businesses to create an environment where competing successfully means competing globally include the forces of competition, the shift toward democracy, the reduction in trade barriers, and improvements in technology.

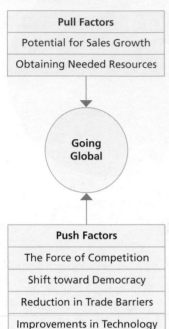

Exhibit 8.1 The Impetus to "Go Global"

| **Pull Factors** |
| Potential for Sales Growth |
| Obtaining Needed Resources |

Going Global

| **Push Factors** |
| The Force of Competition |
| Shift toward Democracy |
| Reduction in Trade Barriers |
| Improvements in Technology |

Pull Factors

Potential for Sales Growth

A fundamental reason for engaging in global operations is to help a business expand its markets. Increased sales are typically the central aim behind a company's expansion into international business. A significant portion of sales among the world's largest firms are generated from outside the home country. For example, US-based specialty coffee chain Starbucks began expanding operations into Europe almost a decade ago (especially in Vienna). The potential for increased sales was clearly a pull factor, but a key question was whether consumers in Europe would be attracted to this American business? Starbucks's aim was to provide a more modern version of the relaxed atmosphere of the Viennese café to attract this new consumer segment.

Clearly, having the world as your market offers almost limitless potential beyond domestic consumers. Having access to foreign consumers may also mitigate the negative effects of domestic downturns in demand for the business's product of service. Consider, for example, the case of Avon Products Inc. This organization faced declining sales in North American markets, largely because of its traditional marketing channel (door-to-door sales), which failed to address the increased entry of women into the workplace and away from the home. On the other hand, Avon was able to successfully transfer its approach globally to over 20 emerging markets, including China, Brazil, South Africa, and Mexico.

Obtaining Needed Resources

Businesses may choose to engage in global business activity to obtain resources that are either unavailable or too costly within the domestic borders. Acquiring foreign imports is a case of obtaining needed resources. It could be the case that a textile manufacturer imports its raw materials from a foreign supplier because these materials are not available locally. As well, the decision to locate businesses or plants in developing or underdeveloped nations may be a means to access inexpensive labour. For example, to access less expensive energy resources, a number of Japanese businesses have located in China, Mexico, and Taiwan, where energy costs are not as high. Both Canadian and US firms continue to expand their operations overseas because they can achieve higher rates of return on their investments, largely due to lower labour costs.

Push Factors

The Force of Competition

Many domestic economies have become inundated with competing products or services. Typically, a business that seeks to grow needs to consider the markets beyond its domestic borders—this is where new and potentially untapped market opportunities still exist. Ironically, domestic economies are increasingly being filled with foreign competitors in many industries. The fact is, a business may find that it must compete against not only domestic competitors, but foreign competitors as well. By default, a business may be *pushed* into becoming a global business by the simple fact that it is forced to compete with a foreign competitor. Moreover, for some businesses it seems foolhardy not to combat the foreign competition by attempting to go after the competitor's market overseas. In other words, the drive to "go global" may be a response to competitors' actions.

In addition, other domestic competitors may be expanding their markets overseas, which creates additional incentive for the business to follow suit. The notion of **first-mover advantage** is a philosophy that underscores the benefits of being among the first to establish strong positions in important world markets. Later entrants into

first-mover advantage The benefits of being among the first to establish strong positions in important world markets.

a foreign market may have more difficulty establishing themselves, and may even be effectively blocked by competitors.

Shift Toward Democracy   The shift toward democracy among many societies that were formerly economically and politically repressed has contributed to the creation of new market opportunities. Numerous totalitarian regimes have been transformed in Eastern Europe and Asia, for example, which has created new economic opportunities for businesses in other parts of the world. Countries like Russia and Poland have shifted toward a more capitalistic and democratic approach. Perhaps one symbol of this acceptance was the success of McDonald's in entering the Russian marketplace years ago. Similarly, there has been a great interest in foreign investment in China since its move toward privatization—reduction in government ownership—in many areas.

Reduction in Trade Barriers   In recent years it has been observed that global business activities have been growing at a faster rate than in previous years and in comparison to growth in domestic business. This acceleration may be largely due to the general push toward freer trade. In fact, probably the most powerful source of influence encouraging increased international business is the reduction in trade and investment restrictions. For example, NAFTA was established as an agreement to remove **trade barriers** between Canada, the United States, and Mexico. This agreement essentially aimed to produce a common market among the members. However, not all Canadian industries compete freely under NAFTA, as seen in Talking Business 8.1. Later in this chapter, we will consider in more detail the nature of NAFTA, as well as a number of other important trade agreements.

trade barriers A government barrier that prevents the free trade of imported goods and services into a country via tariffs, quotas, subsidies, and so on.

TALKING BUSINESS 8.1
Canada's Dairy Industry Under Pressure

smereka/Shutterstock

Though most Canadians drink milk or eat yogurt or cheese, few are aware of the long-standing, complex supply management system that sets milk prices at the farm level and limits milk supply and dairy imports.

More are beginning to notice now. In June 2012, Canada was accepted into Transpacific Partnership trade talks. In exchange for greater access to their markets for all Canadian goods and services, partner countries want access to Canada's long-protected dairy market. (Partner countries will also seek access to other Canadian sectors, as well as changes to other policies, such as Canadian competition policies.)

Canada is also negotiating a trade deal with the European Union. Greater access to Canada's dairy market in return for greater access to the EU market for all goods and services could be part of the deal. Pressure to abandon the long-standing protection of Canada's dairy (as well as poultry and egg) sector from international competition has intensified.

What is clear is that Canada's long-standing policy will need to change—whether marginally, dramatically, or somewhere in between—in response to domestic and international pressures. But why do we have such a policy? How did it come to be, and how has it evolved over time? Does it still help dairy farmers? What are its intended—and unintended—consequences for them?

(continued)

Dairy policy has evolved constantly as the regulated system attempts to adapt to changes in markets, trade, government finances, and technology. A main influencer of milk supply management has been the cost to governments of managing surpluses. This accounted for changes in national milk policy in the late 1960s and in the 1970s, 1980s, and 1990s. More recently, trade pressures have shaped supply management: from competition by imported substitute products such as butter, oil/sugar blends, and, more recently, MPC, as well as from trade challenges to classified pricing schemes for exported product. Improved technology has sharply increased milk production efficiency and scale, and produced new forms of dairy products not anticipated by policymakers in the past.

The system has been buffeted by pressures and challenges and has been constantly changing in response.

Much of Canada's milk supply management regulation goes beyond the necessary, creating unintended costs and burdens to the operation of the system. The challenge for the Canadian dairy industry and policymakers is to retain the elements of supply management that maintain its functions and purpose, while allowing changes in other elements—without being trapped by the system's history.

Source: The Conference Board of Canada. (2012, August). Canada's supply-managed dairy policy: how we got here: Briefing. Retrieved from http://future.aae.wisc.edu/publications/CanadasDairyPolicy.pdf. Reprinted by permission.

Improvements in Technology   Another fundamental source of influence on globalization has been technology. Advancements in technology have more efficiently facilitated cross-border transactions. Innovations in information technology, as well as advances in transportation, have made it increasingly easy to transfer information, products, services, capital, and human resources around the world. Email, the Internet, teleconferencing, faxing, and transatlantic supersonic travel were among the activities that were not available until the late 20th century.

Electronic commerce, or ecommerce, has been relatively free from government control, and this flexibility has contributed to the rate of globalization and the generation of virtual global organizations. Virtual organizations increasingly exist at the global level, where the geographic sources of the product or service and the location of the workforce are unimportant.

Objective 2 Describe the central channels or forms of global business activity.

CHANNELS OF GLOBAL BUSINESS ACTIVITY

There are a variety of ways that organizations engage in global business. While practically any connection a business has with a foreign country essentially constitutes a form of global business, the degree of involvement of a business with a foreign country can vary. In this section we highlight various channels or forms within which businesses operate in the global sense. At a lower level of interconnectedness, a business can simply export or import goods or services to or from other countries. At a somewhat higher level, a company may choose to outsource some aspect of its business operations; it may choose to licence some aspect or perhaps even arrange for franchise operations in foreign territories. Forming a strategic alliance or creating a joint venture with a foreign company requires the business to become more fully entrenched in the global context via directly investing in a foreign country. This can take the form of a merger, acquisition, the creation of a subsidiary, or some other form of direct investment in foreign operations. See Exhibit 8.2 for an overview of all of these channels.

Exporting and Importing

Businesses that engage in international trade are more likely to be involved in importing and exporting than in any other type of global business activity. In addition to selling our goods or services to other countries, Canadian businesses may also purchase goods or services from foreign countries for resale to Canadians. Merchandise exports are tangible goods transferred out of the country, while merchandise imports are goods brought into the country. On the other hand, businesses might deal in service exports or imports of services. For example, banking, insurance, or management services can be performed at an international level. Another type of service export or import can involve the use of a company's assets, including things like patents, trademarks, copyrights, or expertise. The use of such assets constitutes a service rather than the provision of a tangible good and is typically arranged through a licensing agreement. We discuss this channel of global business later on.

Exporting certainly offers additional profitable activity for businesses, and the business opportunities available through exporting are significant. While there are about 30 million potential customers within our Canadian borders, there are over 6 billion potential customers across the world, increasing by about 95 million people annually. Many Canadian businesses have taken advantage of the benefits of exporting. Canada exports over 40% of our production, making us a major trading nation (see Exhibit 8.3 on next page).

According to International Trade Canada,

Exhibit 8.2 Channels of Global Activity

Canada is the most open of the globe's major economies. We are the world's fifth largest exporter and importer—trade is equivalent to more than 70% of our gross domestic product (GDP). Exports account for almost 40% of our economy, and are linked to one-quarter of all Canadian jobs . . . Exports allow Canadian companies to keep generating jobs and remain productive and competitive by selling their goods and services more broadly than in our relatively small domestic market. Imports give our consumers choice and reduce costs, and provide our farmers and manufacturers with inputs and productivity-enhancing technologies. Investment and the movement of people in both directions favour innovation, business and personal growth, and competitiveness. International commerce is the lifeblood of our economy.[6]

---

[6] Government of Canada. (2005). Canada's international policy statement: A role of pride and influence in the world. Retrieved from http://publications.gc.ca/collections/Collection/IT4-8-2005E.pdf.

Exhibit 8.3 Canada's Major Trade Partners, by Country

Canada trades with the world, but its main trading partner is the United States, which accounts for roughly two thirds of trade and the majority of capital moving in and out of Canada.

Source: Data from Statistics Canada & US Census Bureau. Retrieved from www.ic.gc.ca/cis-sic/cis-sic.nsf/IDE/cis-sic22inte.html#int1.

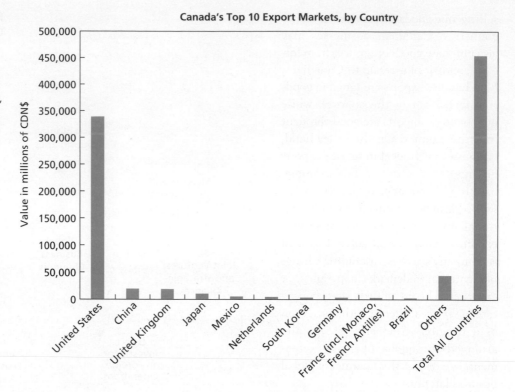

Canada's Top 10 Export Markets, by Country

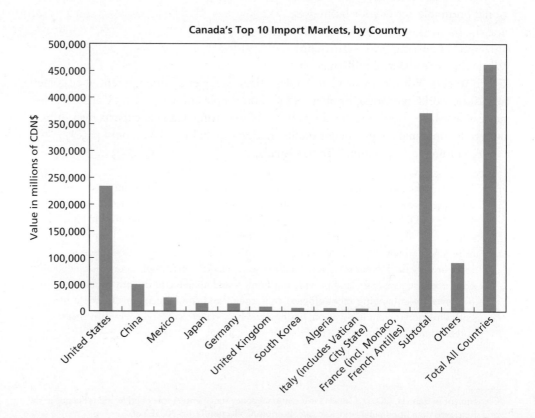

Canada's Top 10 Import Markets, by Country

Statistics Canada reports indicate that Canada is the United States's most important trading partner, and for many years the United States has been Canada's largest trading partner. By the 21st century, the United States accounted for between 75–80% of Canada's total exports. Currently, Canada exports more of its manufacturing output to the United States than it consumes domestically. While Mexico still accounts for a relatively small share of our trade, trade with that country has grown greatly. In recent years, Canada has increased trade with other countries, such as China, as seen in Talking Business 8.2.

TALKING BUSINESS 8.2

Canada's Exports to China: Still Hewers of Wood and Drawers of Water

We all know that the U.S. is Canada's largest trading partner, but do you know who is second? The answer, China, may surprise some. In fact, it's been like that since 2003. What is more, the trade flows are not all one way. Although Canada does run a sizeable merchandise trade deficit of about $30 billion with China that number has been little changed in recent years, as export growth has kept pace with import growth. But note what we're selling; when it comes to trade with China, we largely remain "hewers of wood and drawers of water."

In the past ten years, Canada's exports of goods to China have tripled, from $4 to $13 billion. As a result, China has surpassed Japan to become Canada's third largest export market and is within striking distance of the number two spot, currently held by the United Kingdom. In fact, China would have already surpassed the U.K. if it were not for surging gold prices and a rising volume of gold exports to that country. Gold and silver now account for half of Canada's goods exports to the U.K. by value.

When the surging value of goods exports to countries like the U.K. and China is combined with stagnant exports to the U.S., Canada's export picture is gradually changing.

Today the U.S. is the destination for 75 per cent of Canada's goods exports, compared with a peak of 87 per cent in 2002. In the place of the U.S., other countries have grown in importance. For example, China now accounts for a significant 3.3 per cent of Canadian merchandise exports.

What are we selling to China? Nearly all the major product groupings are either raw materials or partially processed raw materials. Canada's top three exports to China in 2010 were pulp, canola oil and coal. Combined, these three products accounted for nearly one-third of goods exports to China. Our top three non-commodity exports include organic chemicals and resins (both of which are made from petroleum products), and navigational, measuring and control instruments. Combined these three products accounted for about 7 per cent of goods exports to China.

Also, exports of wood products from Canadian sawmills to China have surged over the past two years . . . Nearly all of this wood is being sourced from British Columbia and that's why B.C.'s wood product sales are outperforming every other province this year. The boom in wood exports to China is being driven by robust construction activity in

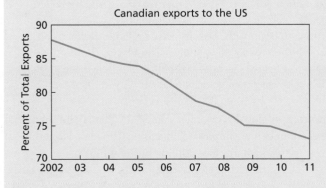

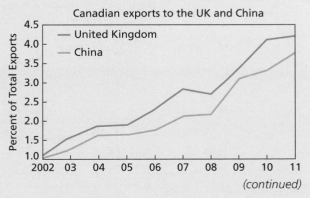

(continued)

China, and reduced access to Russian logs due to the imposition of an export tax by Russia.

If current patterns continue, we could see Canada's role as a supplier of raw materials to the U.S. slowly transition to a supplier to China, much as it did a century ago from the British Empire to the U.S. We would join Australia and others that are already fulfilling this role. This of course is contrary to the often-pronounced desire of policymakers to move the Canadian economy away from its reliance on natural resources. But what if we instead chose to embrace it?

China and to a lesser degree other emerging economies, are driving a global commodities boom that has left few products unaffected by rising demand and prices. Canada has the means to benefit from this boom. We are major global producers of a variety of agricultural, forestry, mineral and energy products, and there is potential for more. For example, Canada has the second largest oil reserves in the world and routinely attracts more mineral exploration dollars than any other country in the world.

As well, our industrial structure is already indirectly linked in many ways to our natural endowments. Perhaps the best example of this is Canada's dominance in mining financing, with approximately one third of global mining capital being raised here and an even larger share of

transactions occurring in Canada. This has substantive secondary effects for industries like accounting, legal services and financial services. Canada could become a global leader in other ways as well, such as pioneering environmentally friendly extraction techniques and providing the services and equipment that are used by the natural resources sector. In other words, the export of commodities could be a critical driver of a diverse array of support technologies and services.

The bottom line is that Canada's success in exporting natural resource-based products to China does not reflect a failure on the part of the Canadian economy or policymakers. Rather, it is a reflection of our endowment of resources and what we are good at doing relative to other countries. Commodity prices are strong thanks to Chinese demand, and we should be doing all we can to harness this opportunity. Rather than trying to break away from our past, we should leverage this strength to expand the list of things for which Canada is regarded as a global leader.

Source: Excerpted from Burt, M. (2011, April 2). Canada's exports to China: Still hewers of wood and drawers of water. Reprinted with permission from The Conference Board of Canada. Retrieved from www.conferenceboard.ca/economics/hot_eco_topics/default/11-08-02/canada_s_exports_to_china_still_hewers_of_wood_and_drawers_of_water.aspx.

Observers have noted that while the bulk of our exports continue to go to the United States, distributing patterns of change have emerged. As a *Maclean's* magazine report noted,

In 1993, 74 per cent of all Canadian exports went to the United States; by 2005, that figure had risen to 84 per cent. And yet . . . even as our U.S.-bound exports have gone up, their profile has been changing, and not for the better: we are becoming more hewers of wood and drawers of water, not less so. We are sending the Americans more and more raw commodities (oil, natural gas, metals and other resources) and a smaller proportion of manufactured goods. Trade in services (everything from call centres to financial services), never strong to begin with, has also seen a relative decline. This trend is particularly worrisome: the services sector now makes up two-thirds of our domestic economy, yet we haven't figured out how to export it. A whole segment of potential export growth and wealth creation is going unfulfilled.[7]

In 2009, the economic downturn in global economies damaged Canada's international trade. However, since that time economies have improved, including Canada's. Nonetheless, Canada must continue to improve its export status (see Talking Business 8.3).

---

[7] Preville, P. (2006, November 27). Exclusive report: How to fix Canada—on the brink. *Maclean's.* Retrieved from www.macleans.ca/business/companies/article.jsp?content=20061127_137129_137129.

What are Canada's New Export Strengths?

A decade ago, Canada's key exports included autos and parts, pulp and paper, electronics and wood products. Today, we export less of all of them. In their stead, exports of oil and gas, mineral products, chemicals, primary metals and food products are growing in importance. Canada has also developed new-found export strength in professional and financial services.

This wholesale change at the top of the list of Canadian exports shows how some of our traditional trade strengths are fading, while we are simultaneously developing new ones. There is every reason to expect this trend to continue.

Canadian policy makers need to adapt to this changing environment. They need to understand and promote our new trade strengths. They must aim to craft trade agreements that will be open to our future trade strengths, including services. And they should focus on helping struggling industries to adjust, rather than protect dwindling markets.

The Conference Board of Canada's recently published report from its Global Commerce Centre, *Walking the Silk Road: Understanding Canada's Changing Trade Patterns,* identifies two broad forces that have driven the shift in export strengths. The first is the growing importance of emerging markets in the world economy. The second flows from changes in the relative prices of goods and services.

In 2001, the 34 members of the Organisation for Economic Co-operation and Development represented 81 per cent of global gross domestic product. In 2011, this club of developed countries held just 66 per cent, an astounding shift in such a short period of time. Led by China, emerging markets have captured a growing share of the global economy, while growth slowed in the United States, the European Union and Japan.

Not surprisingly, emerging markets account for a growing share of Canada's exports, while our trade with the United States has all but stagnated since 2000. And what we export to the rest of the world is very different than what we send to the United States. Products such as minerals, professional and financial services, and agri-food products figure much more prominently in our non-U.S. exports.

Even if volumes of commodity-related exports had remained flat in the past decade, they would have grown in importance because of price trends. And commodity export volumes have risen as Canadian businesses "follow the money"—they are investing in industries that provide the best returns. Since 2001, Statistics Canada's index of raw material prices has risen by 74 per cent, while its price index for manufactured goods has risen by just 15 per cent.

Along with global forces, changes in Canada's export strengths can be attributed to industry-specific factors. On the downside, exports of paper products have plummeted over the past decade as consumers have switched from print to digital media. The housing bust in the United States decimated Canadian exports of wood products.

But exports of mining, oil and gas machinery from Canada nearly tripled over the past decade. Canadian businesses have parlayed their domestic experience and knowledge to take advantage of strong global demand for minerals and energy products. As well, Canadian agri-food production and exports are growing to meet the needs of rising global food demand.

Financial services and insurance also have been key sources of export strength for Canada in recent years. The Canadian banking system is widely considered the safest in the world—the World Economic Forum has ranked it No. 1 for the past five years. Canadian banks have taken advantage of their relative health to make more than 100 acquisitions globally since the economic crisis. Similarly, some of Canada's largest insurance companies are targeting Asia, owing to the region's increasing wealth and underserved insurance market.

This shift in trade patterns needs to be incorporated into Canada's economic and trade policy. Instead of being sheltered, businesses in struggling industries need to adapt to their new competitive environments. Trade missions and promotion should focus on key strengths and new areas of growth. The next generation of Canada's trade agreements should cover a broader spectrum of goods and services. Aligning our economic policies to the new reality of Canada's trade is critical if we are to seize the full potential of the global economy and raise our living standards at home.

Source: Excerpted from Burt, M. (2013, February 21). Canada competes: Guess what Canada's new export strengths are. Reprinted with permission from The Conference Board of Canada. Retrieved from www.conferenceboard.ca/press/speech_oped/13-02-25/canada_competes_guess_what_canada_s_new_export_strengths_are.aspx?pf=true.

Outsourcing/Offshoring

outsourcing Hiring external organizations to conduct work in certain functions of the company.

As you may recall, **outsourcing** involves hiring external organizations to conduct work in certain functions of the company. So, for example, payroll, accounting, and legal work can be assigned to outsourced staff. The organization typically will retain its core functions or competencies—that is, those areas that it is in business to conduct. Nike is well-known for its use of outsourcing on an international basis. Nike has typically entered into contractual arrangements with manufacturers in developing nations to produce its footwear while it focuses largely on marketing its product. In fact, this has been a major underlying source of controversy with regard to businesses "going global"—the fear that relatively higher-paying North American jobs will be lost as businesses decide to outsource manufacturing functions to cheaply paid labour in developing countries.

For example, Taiwanese engineers offer innovative solutions for customers seeking design and manufacturing outsourcing. In fact, Taiwan has become so strong in this field that some observers suggest that it is really the Taiwanese who are outsourcing the marketing and branding of their products to the rest of the world. Taiwan has developed dramatically from the poor and lowly provider of components and assembled machines to that of a leading innovator in the electronics industry. Currently, its companies are increasingly expert at original design, and they typically dominate manufacturing in central categories such as notebook computers. Taiwan's success has been attributed to several sources, including its lower pay scales. For example, its engineering costs are approximately one third that of comparable services in the United States. However, many observers are quick to point out that Taiwan's strength is not simply based on cheap labour but on its entrepreneurial culture combined with effective government involvement. Taiwan has grown from a provider of cheap labour and products to one of the most talented sources of high-tech expertise in the world.

Countries can be contracted for the production of finished goods or component parts, and these goods or parts can subsequently be imported to the home country or to other countries for further assembly or sale.

India is one example cited as a major offshore or outsourced location. As observed by one writer,

> Globalization has played a significant role in India's rise as an economic force. It is also the foundation behind the country's success in the outsourcing industry . . . One of the biggest beneficiaries of this "openness" is the outsourcing industry. Today, no company with outsourcing plans does not have India on its laundry list. India was able to achieve self-sufficiency not by closing its doors to the world. Rather, it spread the word across the world of how easy it is to do business in India.[8]

Licensing and Franchising Arrangements

licensing agreement An arrangement whereby the owner of a product or process is paid a fee or royalty from another company in return for granting them permission to produce or distribute the product or process.

The **licensing agreement** is an arrangement whereby the owner of a product or process is paid a fee or royalty from another company in return for granting them permission to produce or distribute the product or process. How could this be a type of global business activity?

---

[8] *Offshore Outsourcing World.* (2004, February 26). Spotlight India: Globalization. Retrieved from www.enterblog.com/200402060508.php.

For example, a Canadian company might grant a foreign company permission to produce its product; or conversely, perhaps a Canadian company wishes to distribute a foreign-made product in Canada and requires a licensing agreement.

Why might a business enter into licensing agreements? Essentially, companies that don't wish to set up actual production or marketing operations overseas can let the foreign business conduct these activities and simply collect royalties. Whether it is for licensing fees or for management consulting services between two companies from different countries, the fees paid to foreign firms in return for the performance of a service would constitute service imports. Fees earned by businesses through providing such services would constitute service exports.

Franchising shares some of the advantages of licensing, in that both are relatively lower risk forms of global business. Franchising is, of course, a common type of business activity in Canada and elsewhere. This becomes a global business activity when the franchises are scattered in different locations around the world. While franchising is discussed elsewhere in this book, it is sufficient to note here that franchising involves drafting a contract between a supplier (franchisor) and a dealer (franchisee) that stipulates how the supplier's product or service will be sold. The **franchisee** is the dealer (usually the owner of a small business), who is permitted to sell the goods/services of the **franchisor** (the supplier) in exchange for some payment (for example, a flat fee, future royalties/commissions, future advertising fees). Probably one of the best-known international franchises is McDonald's, which licenses its trademark, its fast-food products, and its operating principles to franchisees worldwide in return for an initial fee and ongoing royalties. In return, McDonald's franchises receive the benefit of McDonald's reputation and its management and marketing expertise (See Exhibit 8.4).

Direct Investment in Foreign Operations

Foreign direct investment (FDI) involves the purchase of physical assets or an amount of share ownership in a company from another country to gain a measure of management control. Capital can be invested in factories, inventories and capital goods, or other assets. **Control** of a company can be achieved without necessarily owning a 100%, or even a 51%, interest. A direct investment can be done through acquisition of an already existing business in the host country or through a startup built "from scratch," so to speak.

The choice may be dependent on a number of factors, including the availability of suitable businesses in the host country. If a suitable business already exists in the host country, it may prove more efficient to invest in it than to start up a business there from scratch. It is no surprise that the vast majority (about 90%) of all FDI stems from developed countries,

franchising A method of distribution or marketing where a parent company (the franchisor) grants to another individual or company (the franchisee) the legal right to sell its products or services, with exclusive rights to a particular area or location.

franchisee The dealer in a franchising arrangement, who is permitted to sell the goods/services of the franchisor in exchange for some payment.

franchisor The supplier in a franchising arrangement, who permits a franchisee to sell its goods/services in exchange for some payment.

foreign direct investment (FDI) The purchase of physical assets or an amount of share ownership in a company from another country to gain a measure of management control.

control Typically achieved when a company or individual owns greater than 50% of the shares of another company. However, it can sometimes be achieved by other factors, such as management influence.

Exhibit 8.4 The Power of the Global Franchise

Franchising has proven to be one of the best marketing and expansion methods ever created. And while American franchises may be seen by a few as symbols of American greed, the majority still associates franchise brands with business success and economic development—even hope—worldwide. Why the popularity of international franchising? . . . More than simply liking the concepts, these franchisees desire the advantages U.S. franchises provide. "The consumer perception gives the international franchisee a better base to start with, as many American brands enjoy universal brand recognition."[9]

---

[9] *Entrepreneur Magazine*. *Entrepreneur's* top global franchises for 2004. Retrieved from www.microsoft.com/small-business/resources/startups/franchisetop_global_franchises.mspx.

given that business in these countries will more likely have sufficient resources to invest overseas. Foreign direct investment in Canada is the second highest in the G7 as a share of GDP. What helps a country gain foreign direct investment? This is discussed in Talking Business 8.4. In addition, Canadian investments abroad are the third largest in the G7 as a share of GDP. (See Exhibit 8.5 for an illustration of foreign direct investment in Canada and Canada's direct investment abroad.)

Throughout the 1990s, we observed a growth in foreign ownership in the Canadian business context. Toward the end of the 1990s, foreign firms controlled about 22% of assets in Canada, which is a modest growth from 20.5% in 1994. By 2007, foreign-controlled firms accounted for about 30% of all corporate operating revenues.

Why would businesses wish to engage in foreign direct investment? Controlling companies can obtain access to a larger market or needed resources via the FDI. Earlier in the process of globalization, direct investment was, in a sense, a substitute for trade. That is, while companies traded commodities that they had in abundance or that they could produce more competitively, they would also directly invest in countries where they needed to secure their source of raw materials or to manufacture their products inside the domestic market and thereby avoid tariffs or other import barriers. More recently, however, with the liberalization of trade, foreign investment exists alongside trade. This is clearly seen in the fact that about one third of world trade is conducted between members of the same organizations—that is, between a parent company and its subsidiary, and between two subsidiaries of the same company. For example, a foreign subsidiary may require resources or supplies from the home country and, consequently, will import them.

Consequently, although FDI increases in a country, employment levels do not necessarily rise because of this increased investment. For example, mergers often result in the consolidation and elimination of some common functions: This can entail layoffs and, therefore, reduced employment levels. This relates to a more general concern about FDI:

TALKING BUSINESS 8.4

What Helps a Country Obtain Foreign Direct Investment?

When firms look for a country to invest in, part of their location choice is based on certain national characteristics . . . These characteristics include market size, geography, and language. But other determinants can at least be partially influenced by cities. The firm Copenhagen Economics lists eight regional policy factors, supported by empirical analysis, that can help boost FDI attraction:

1. a highly educated workforce (skill effect)
2. a high level of spending on R&D (innovation effect)
3. penetration of new technologies (particularly information and communications technology)
4. strong regional clusters (industry specialization effect)

5. infrastructure and accessibility (access effect)
6. a well-functioning investment promotion agency
7. regional economic strategies
8. FDI incentives.

To this list we add another regional policy factor that could boost FDI attraction: immigration. A 2009 paper by economist Hisham Foad argued that immigration to a country eventually leads to increased inward FDI.

This list of policy factors is also consistent with the broader national determinants of FDI identified in [the table below], particularly in the physical infrastructure, labour markets, and innovation categories, as well as foreign investment promotion.

Broad Variable Categories for Determinants of FDI

Category	Variables	Government Influence
Economic gravity relationships	• Geographical proximity • Common language and culture	No influence
Macroeconomic conditions	• Market size and market size growth • Inflation rate • Exchange rate stability • Productivity and productivity growth	National level
Institutional infrastructure	• Socio-political stability • Protection of property rights • Government efficiency	All levels
Physical infra-structure	• Transportation • Electricity • Telecommunications	All levels

Category	Variables	Government Influence
Openness	• Investment restrictions • Foreign ownership restrictions • Foreign investment promotion agencies • Trade-to-GDP ratio	All levels
Financial markets	• Interest rates • Liquid stock markets	National level
Labour markets	• Unit labour costs • Skill endowment/education	National and provincial levels
Innovation	• R&D activeness	National and provincial levels
Taxes	• Corporate tax rate • Other taxes	All levels

Source: Excerpted from Arcand, A. (2012, May). *The role of Canada's major cities in attracting foreign direct investment.* Reprinted with permission from The Conference Board of Canada, 60 pages.

Exhibit 8.5 Canada's Foreign Direct Investment Position

Source: Statistics Canada, Foreign direct investment, 2012. Reproduced and distributed on an "as is" basis with the permission of Statistics Canada.

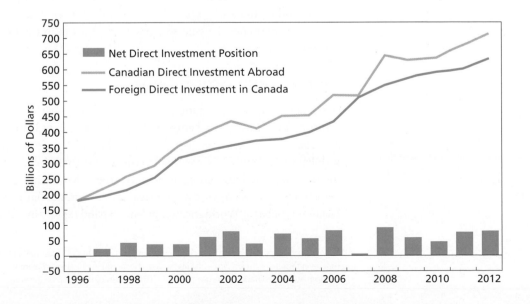

Does it benefit or harm the host country? That question continues to be debated. According to the recent report entitled *Canada's State of Trade* (2010),

> FDI provides benefits to Canadian firms through the transfer of knowledge, technology and skills, and increased trade related to the investment, all of which enhance Canada's productivity and competitiveness. FDI is also one of the ways in which Canadian companies can integrate into global value chains.[10]

Joint Ventures and Strategic Alliances

joint venture A form of strategic alliance that involves an arrangement between two or more companies joining to produce a product or service together, or to collaborate in the research, development, or marketing of that product or service.

A **joint venture** involves an arrangement between two or more companies from different countries to produce a product or service together, or to collaborate in the research, development, or marketing of a product or service. This relationship has also been referred to as a **strategic alliance**. These organizations develop an arrangement whereby they share managerial control over a specific venture, such as seeking to develop a new technology, gaining access to a new market, and so on. For example, Sony Ericsson is a mobile phone maker that is a joint venture between Ericsson of Sweden and Sony of Japan.

strategic alliance A way to achieve diversification by two or more organizations working together to achieve certain common goals. Strategic alliances can take various forms and serve various purposes.

Strategic alliances often aim to extend or enhance the core competencies of the businesses involved, obtain access to the expertise of another organization, and generate new market opportunities for all parties involved. The level of ownership and specific responsibilities can be unique to each particular joint venture created among the partners. It has been observed that a high number of international joint ventures have failed largely because of the inability of the partners to find a proper "fit" in their approaches and managerial styles. As in any relationship among partners, "fit" must be given special attention, particularly when the partners are culturally diverse.

A typical arrangement may exist between a multinational corporation (MNC) and a local partner, since this facilitates the MNC's quick entry into a new foreign market through the joint venture with an already established local business. Consequently, the international joint venture has proven to be an efficient way of entering foreign markets rapidly and easing entry where local requirements have been implemented with regard to a degree of domestic ownership and participation in the production or distribution of the good or service.

Mergers and Acquisitions

merger A way to achieve diversification, when two firms come together to create a new firm with a new identity.

A Canadian-owned company could actually merge with a foreign-owned company and create a new jointly owned enterprise that operates in at least two countries. This is called a **merger**. The newspapers have been littered with reports of mergers and acquisitions on a global scale. It makes sense that, to the extent that globalization is a process of increasing the connectedness among economies, there is a further consolidation of markets and companies. For example, the Montreal-based commercial printing and book-publishing business Quebecor World Inc. was able to expand rapidly in Latin America largely through

---

[10] Foreign Affairs, Trade and Development Canada. (2010). VI: Overview of Canada's investment performance. In *Canada's state of trade: Trade and investment update, 2010.* Retrieved from www.international.gc.ca/economist-economiste/performance/state-point/state_2010_point/2010_6.aspx?lang=eng.

acquisitions and partnerships with local companies in Argentina, Chile, and Peru. Similarly, foreign companies can expand into Canada and establish a North American presence. In 2012, for example, the largest grain handler in Canada, Viterra, was acquired by Glencore, a Swiss-based company, in a $6.1 billion deal.

For the past several decades, the majority of foreign takeovers of large Canadian firms have required a review by the federal government. In order for large companies to merge, the federal government determines if there is a "net benefit" to Canada. Although the Investment Canada Act does not specifically define "net benefit," there are a number of factors that are taken into account. These include the overall effect of the takeover on Canadian employment, technology development, productivity, competition, and national policies.

Why do such mergers occur? A number of factors typically generate the drive to merge, including the goal of obtaining new markets for the business and the desire to obtain new knowledge and expertise in an industry. The notion of achieving economics of scale in production may also influence the decision to merge. Companies that merge on a global scale may be doing so to generate world-scale volume in a more cost-effective way. Specifically, economies of scale in production are obtained when higher levels of output spread fixed costs (overhead, plant, equipment, and so on) over more produced units and, consequently, reduce the per-unit cost. Thus, mergers sometimes give companies the ability to achieve cost efficiency through larger-scale production that is made possible through the creation of a bigger organization. Mergers have occurred frequently in Canada over the past decade, as seen in Talking Business 8.5.

TALKING BUSINESS 8.5

Is Canada Being "Hollowed Out" by Foreign Takeovers? Putting Mergers and Acquisitions in Historical Perspective

Public concerns that Canada is "up for sale" were fuelled by a series of high-profile mergers and acquisitions (M&As) in the 2006–07 period, involving such national icons as the Hudson's Bay Company, Fairmont Hotels, Inco, Falconbridge, and Alcan.

Recent Conference Board analysis shows that these takeovers are an exception to Canada's longer-term investment trend. Canadian companies have actually been more active in M&A activity abroad over the past decade and a half than foreign companies have been in Canada. Mostly smaller in value, these takeovers attracted less attention (although they also involved some mega-deals—notably the acquisition of Reuters Group by Thomson Corp., which was the largest takeover of a foreign company in Canadian history).

Why the recent spike in large and expensive Canadian acquisitions? Analysis shows a strong link between M&A activity and record corporate profits in the US and Canada, as well as with lower interest rates. The spike may also be part of a global phenomenon. In an era when China, India, Brazil, and others have emerged as major exporters and destinations for FDI, many companies need to expand in size in order to become more efficient and be able to compete against these lower-cost economies.

M&A activity in Canada is highly cyclical and is expected to slow over the near term due to tightening US lending standards, a stronger Canadian dollar, and slower growth in US corporate profitability. Given growing global competitiveness, however, the long-term trend for M&A is likely in an upward direction.

Source: Is Canada Being "Hollowed Out" by Foreign Takeovers?* Re-energizing Canada's International Trade – report By: The Conference Board of Canada February 2010, page 19. Reprinted with permission from The Conference Board of Canada.

Establishment of Subsidiaries

Another well-known type of global business activity is the creation of **subsidiaries** or branch operations in foreign countries through which the enterprises can produce or market goods and services. Where possible, a business may choose to maintain total control of its product or service by either establishing a wholly owned subsidiary or by purchasing an existing firm in the host country. **Acquisitions** of local companies have become increasingly popular. These types of acquisitions allow efficient entry into a market with already well-known products and distribution networks. On the other hand, establishing a subsidiary from scratch in the host country may also be a viable option. For example, shortly following the import quota placed on Japanese cars in the 1980s, Japanese-based car manufacturers set up operations in North America and captured an even greater segment of the consumer market. Toyota, Honda, and Nissan are among the companies that have successfully employed this strategy.

What are the benefits of such types of global arrangements? If the foreign country is a high source of sales for the enterprise, it may make sense to establish a presence in that country to be more responsive to local consumer needs. Among the risks is the fact that much more is at stake when the company has invested in a wholly owned subsidiary—including the time, effort, and expense they have invested to create this operation. Subsidiaries may face the threat of political instability, as evidenced in the past in places like China or South Africa. Subsidiaries may also face adverse environments that might turn hostile toward foreign ownership. For example, Toyota's presence in Canada has not been without controversy. In recent years Toyota's Canadian subsidiary argued that it was being unfairly slapped with import tariffs on parts, making it more difficult to compete with North American–based car manufacturers. Acquiring a Canadian business effectively transforms it into a "subsidiary" of the acquiring company.

THE MULTINATIONAL CORPORATION

In terms of global types of business activity, the multinational corporation is a type of global business that has been receiving increasing attention, for better or worse. What is a multinational corporation, and why are we seeing its presence increasing across the globe? Observers have noted that such corporations are breaking down borders among countries and creating, in essence, borderless corporations. What are the implications of multinationals in terms of the costs and benefits they bring to the countries in which they set up business? We will address these questions in this section.

The first place to start is to offer a definition. What exactly are multinational corporations, and in what way are they "global businesses"? A **global business** is a business that engages directly in some form of international business activity, including such activities as exporting, importing, or international production. A business that has direct investments (whether in the form of marketing or manufacturing facilities) in at least two different countries is specifically referred to as a **multinational corporation (MNC)**. In other words, multinational organizations, or MNCs, are business enterprises that control assets, factories, and so on that are either operated as branch offices or affiliates in two or more foreign countries. An MNC generates products or services through its affiliates in several countries, and it maintains control over the operations of those affiliates and manages from a global perspective. MNCs may also be referred to as *global companies* when they operate in myriad countries across the world.

Typically, MNCs are very large organizations and, in terms of their relative role in the world setting, it has been estimated that the 600 largest MNCs account for about one quarter of the activity of the world's economies. Technically, it may be more accurate to refer to such organizations as MNEs (enterprises), given that such organizations could, in fact, possess partnership status, for example, rather than being incorporated—a business can be multinational without being a corporation per se. Further, MNEs can be divided between those businesses that are globally integrated and those that are multidomestic. *Globally integrated companies* are companies that integrate their geographically diverse operations through decisions centralized at head office. Consequently, all areas might be given the task of developing and selling a single global product; or perhaps each region is contributing to the manufacture of a certain product. A *multidomestic company*, on the other hand, permits its geographically diverse components to operate relatively autonomously.

So who, exactly, creates these organizations? Most MNCs have headquarters in developed countries—the *home* country. More specifically, over half of the MNCs have headquarters in the United States. France, Germany, the United Kingdom, and Japan are among the other countries that are home to headquarters for most of the remaining MNCs. MNCs maintain branch plants or subsidiaries in two or more foreign countries; these are the *host* countries, and they are either developed or developing countries (which are sometimes referred to as *Third World* countries; see Talking Business 8.6).

One example of a well-known Canadian MNC is Bombardier, which is very much a part of the global market. This company has operations that include transportation equipment and aircraft production. While its head office is in Montreal, nearly 90% of its sales are in markets outside of Canada. It has production facilities in locations including Canada, the United States, France, and Austria, and it markets products on five different continents.

The Borderless Corporation

Anthony Spaeth commented in a *Time Magazine* article, "The machinery of globalization is already integrating financial systems, dismantling territorial frontiers and bringing

---

TALKING BUSINESS 8.6

What's the Third World?

With regard to the globalization debate, it is useful to note that the term *Third World* was originally intended to describe the poor or developing nations of the world. In contrast, the First and Second Worlds were composed of the advanced or industrialized countries. The developed worlds were viewed as including the United States, Canada, and most of the countries of Eastern and Western Europe, as well as Australia, New Zealand, and Japan. Within the broad territory described as the Third World there are countries that are developing either rapidly (for example, Brazil, Hong Kong, Singapore, South Africa, South Korea, and Taiwan) or modestly (including many countries in Africa, Asia, and Latin America, in addition to India, Indonesia, Malaysia, and China) and others that have remained underdeveloped (for example, Somalia, Sudan, sub-Saharan Africa).

According to recent estimates, the Third World contributes most to the world's population growth but is able to provide only about 20% of the world's economic production. A major controversy with regard to global business revolves around the fate of these underdeveloped nations: Will they be purely exploited for the economic gain of MNCs, or will they benefit from the presence of increased industry?

people closer together."[11] This comment is perhaps best illustrated in the new term for MNCs—*borderless corporations*.

borderless corporation or transnational corporation (TNC) A multinational corporation that is not linked with one specific home country. Such an enterprise thus has no clear nationality.

The term **borderless corporation** refers to the increasing ability of MNCs to ignore international boundaries and set up business just about anywhere. In fact, more and more MNCs are taking on the appearance of borderless corporations. Many of today's organizations that operate globally are, perhaps, less accurately referred to as MNCs than as TNCs, or **transnational corporations**, and in fact these two terms are often used interchangeably. The term *TNC* as well as the term *borderless corporation* is also being applied to MNCs given the increasing tendency of not simply setting up branch plants in foreign countries but of organizing management, investment, production, and distribution as if the world were one country.

The term *multinational* is a bit inaccurate, given that many of these companies do not claim any specific nationality but, in fact, gear their planning and decision making to global markets. For example, goods could be designed in one country, raw materials obtained from a second country, manufactured in a third country, and shipped to consumers in a fourth country. Consequently, top management can be composed of international members, reflecting the international composition of the organization. The headquarters of MNCs can often be quite irrelevant. For example, while Nestlé is headquartered in Switzerland, fewer than 5,000 of its over 200,000 workforce actually work in the home country. Nestlé has manufacturing facilities in over 50 countries and owns suppliers and distributors all over the world. Other similar examples of borderless or stateless corporations would include Coca-Cola, which although headquartered in the United States operates independent facilities around the world. In fact, Coca-Cola has seen the bulk of its profits generated in the Pacific region and Eastern Europe rather than the United States, as have companies like General Motors. Other companies are equally transnational and almost borderless: Philips, Nissan, and Canada's Northern Telecom (Nortel), which has increasingly moved beyond the title of being a "Canadian business" (see Talking Business 8.7).

TALKING BUSINESS 8.7

Think Global, Act Local

There is no better way of serving the needs of a geographically diverse market than by locating in the different geographical regions. This is reflected in the well-known motto among today's MNCs: "Think global, act local!" It has been suggested that many MNCs, such as Coca-Cola, Sony, Motorola, and Nestlé, have decentralized decision making among their geographically dispersed locations. For example, in IBM each subsidiary has its own local management, its own culture, and its own unique market focus. What this does is ensure that, for example, a Canadian client of IBM Canada sees the company as, indeed, IBM Canada, and not simply as a subsidiary of another US MNC.

This same philosophy is increasingly being employed by just about every MNC. Consider Nestlé, which is headquartered in Switzerland, yet seems to many to be a US company. Consider also the car industry—is a Ford car an American car? Well, not exactly, if you can imagine that it might be assembled in Brazil with parts from Europe and the United States. Like many other MNCs, in the new global economy the idea is to think global but act local. Regardless of where they operate, MNCs aim to reflect the local market tastes.

---

[11] Spaeth, A. (1998, April 13). Get rich quick. *Time Magazine*. Retrieved from http://content.time.com/time/magazine/article/0,9171,988175,00.html.

The term *borderless corporation* as opposed to *multinational* emphasizes the notion that an enterprise can be a global company without any clear nationality. Often, the company has international ownership and international management. Headquarters do not necessarily belong to one home country.

Borderless companies are very mobile across borders with regard to the transfer of financial capital, materials, and other resources. They set up business where it is profitable, rather than creating a branch plant whose head office is in another corner of the world. Decision making is local and decentralized. This underscores their focus on addressing the local needs of the market within which they operate.

Reduction in trade barriers is said to give rise to borderless corporations. However, borderless corporations can be equally effective in circumventing any trade barriers. Borderless corporations typically pledge no allegiance to any country or location—business is simply set up wherever profits can be maximized. Consequently, countries refusing to conduct trade with another country may not view a borderless corporation as a problem.

Currently the rapid rise of these MNCs (or TNCs or borderless corporations) is raising many questions and concerns. For example, at a time when many countries are concerned with their competitiveness in the international market and their status in terms of trade, should we be concerned with who is generating the bulk of our exports? Does it matter what a company's nationality is, as long as it is providing jobs? Which government, and whose set of rules, will govern the behaviour of MNCs or borderless corporations? Critics view the globalization of business as bringing with it as many threats as it does opportunities (see Exhibit 8.6).

Exhibit 8.6
The Potential Benefits and Threats of MNCs

Potential Benefits

- Encourages economic development
- Offers management expertise
- Introduces new technologies
- Provides financial support to underdeveloped regions of the world
- Creates employment
- Encourages international trade through a company's access to different markets; it is relatively easy to produce goods in one country and distribute them in another country through a subsidiary or foreign affiliate
- Brings different countries closer together
- Facilitates global cooperation and worldwide economic development

Potential Threats

- MNCs do not have any particular allegiance or commitment to their host country.
- Profits made by an MNC do not necessarily remain within the host country but may be transferred out to other locations depending on where the MNC feels the funds are most needed.
- Decision making and other key functions of MNCs may be highly centralized in the home country, so that even though other operations are performed in the host country, they do not necessarily include things like research and development or strategic planning.
- There is difficulty in the ability to control and hold MNCs accountable, which can create serious ethical concerns for the host country.

Sergey Nivens/Shutterstock

Objective 4 Explain the purpose of protectionism and its relationship with international trade.

international trade Trade that involves the purchase, sale, or exchange of goods or services across countries.

domestic trade Trade that involves the purchase, sale, or exchange of goods between provinces, cities, or regions within the same country.

free trade The trade of goods and services in open markets where a level playing field is created for businesses in one country to compete fairly against businesses in other countries. Government intervention is therefore kept at a minimum.

mercantilism The trade theory that dominated economic thinking for the 15th, 16th, and 17th centuries, where a country's wealth was believed to be a matter of its holdings of treasure, especially gold; the economic policy of accumulating wealth through trade surpluses.

INTERNATIONAL TRADE

The globalization of business may be a relatively new buzzword, but one of its fundamental forms has been around for a long time: the notion of international trade. **International trade** essentially involves the purchase, sale, or exchange of goods or services across countries. This can be distinguished from **domestic trade**, which involves trade between provinces, cities, or regions within a country.

Certainly, the trend of globalization has included the gradual reduction in trade barriers among many nations as a means to promote greater international trade. You have probably heard about free trade agreements and the debates surrounding them, but perhaps you are not very familiar with the issues. What are the implications of promoting freer trade across nations, and what are the implications of barriers to trade?

In order to understand some of the critical implications of free trade, it is useful to first consider the nature of international trade. Why might countries want to trade? Why might countries want to engage in protectionism? In this section we will consider a brief history with regard to the issue of international trade.

The Logic of Trade

One fundamental argument is that since some countries can produce certain goods or services more efficiently than others, global efficiency and hence wealth can be improved through free trade. Clearly, it is not advantageous for citizens of a country to be forced to buy an inferior-quality, higher-priced domestic good if they can purchase a superior, lower-priced foreign-produced import. Consistent with this view is the belief that trade should be permitted to continue according to market forces and not artificially restricted through trade barriers. Freer trade would allow countries to trade as they deemed appropriate, rather than trying to produce all goods domestically. Consequently, each country can specialize or focus on producing those goods or services in which it maintains an absolute advantage, and simply trade with other countries to obtain goods or services that are required but not produced by domestic suppliers.

Free trade is based on the objective of open markets, where a level playing field is created for businesses in one country to compete fairly against businesses in other countries for the sale of their products or services. The aim reflects the fundamental principles of comparative advantage. Each country expects to take advantage of each other's strengths, and thereby be permitted to focus on their own strengths. In simplistic terms, it is relatively inefficient for Canada to try to grow coffee beans or bananas, given the climate. Rather than wasting effort and money on unproductive tasks, these items can be imported from countries more suited to such endeavours, while Canadians can focus their efforts in areas where they can produce relatively more efficiently.

Mercantilism

The trade theory underlying economic thinking from the period ranging from about 1500 to 1800 is referred to as **mercantilism**. Specifically, the fundamental view was that a country's wealth depended on its holdings of treasure, typically in the form of gold. Mercantilism, essentially, is the economic policy of accumulating this financial wealth through trade surpluses. **Trade surpluses** come about when a country's exports exceed its imports and, consequently, more money is entering the country (from foreign consumers buying these exports) than is leaving the country (from domestic consumers buying foreign imports). This policy was particularly popular in Europe from about the late 1500s to the late 1700s, with the most dominant mercantilist nations including Britain, France, Spain, and the Netherlands.

Countries implemented this policy of mercantilism in a number of ways. Foremost, the government would intervene to ensure a trade surplus by imposing tariffs or quotas, or by outright banning some foreign imported commodities. Typically, the governments would also subsidize domestic industries to encourage growth in their exports. Another strategy employed was colonization: acquiring less developed regions around the world as sources of inexpensive raw materials (such as sugar, cotton, rubber, tobacco). These colonies would also serve as markets for finished products. Trade between mercantilist countries and their colonies resulted in large profits, given that the colonies typically were paid little for their raw materials but were forced to pay high prices to purchase the final products. Obviously, the colonial powers benefited to the detriment of the colonies. In addition, mercantilist countries aimed to become as self-sufficient as possible with regard to domestic production of goods and services. This also served to minimize reliance on foreign imports.

Given this brief historical description, it is easy to see why countries today that endeavour to maintain a trade surplus and expand their wealth at the expense of other countries are accused of practising mercantilism or neo-mercantilism. Japan has often been viewed as a mercantilist country because of its typically high trade surplus with a number of industrial nations, including the United States.

trade surplus When a country's exports exceed its imports, so that more money enters the country than leaves it. Also referred to as a positive balance of trade.

Trade Protectionism

Essentially, **trade protectionism** is about protecting a country's domestic economy and businesses through restriction on imports. Why might imports be a threat to a country's businesses and economy? Two fundamental reasons can be considered:

1. Low-priced foreign goods that enter the country could compete with goods already produced here and, in effect, take business away from domestic producers. The ultimate consequence may be loss of sales and loss of jobs for domestic industries that are unable to compete with these lower-priced imports.

2. A country that imports more than it exports will have a negative balance of trade, or a **trade deficit**, which often results in more money flowing out of the country (to buy the imported goods) than flowing in (for our exports).

Among the best-known government responses to address these potential risks are the imposition of tariffs and import quotas. A **tariff** is essentially a tax placed on goods entering a country. Specifically, protective tariffs are intended to raise the price of imported products to ensure that they are not less expensive than domestically produced goods. This, of course, discourages domestic consumers from buying these foreign imports by making them more expensive to purchase. Indeed, when tariffs are reduced or eliminated, global competition may negatively affect some domestic industries more than others, as seen in Talking Business 8.8.

trade protectionism Protecting a country's domestic economy and businesses by restricting imports to prevent domestic producers from losing business to producers of low-priced foreign goods, and to prevent a trade deficit, where more money leaves the country than enters it because imports exceed exports.

trade deficit When a country imports more than it exports to the degree that the value of its imports exceeds the value of its exports.

tariff A tax on imported goods traditionally employed with the intent to ensure that they are not less expensive than domestically produced goods.

Made in Canada: How Globalization Has Hit the Canadian Apparel Industry

The unusual mission statement for the fledgling Canadian-Made Apparel company is written on a board overlooking sewing machines and computerized fabric cutters. It's nothing more than a date and time—Feb. 21, 2013, 1 p.m.

At precisely that moment, in this very same factory, the owners of John Forsyth Shirt Co. Ltd. told 110 employees that a century of shirt-making would come to an end. The company, established in 1903, was closing its factory—the latest victim of a Canadian-made garment industry decimated by globalization and, in Forsyth's case, government decisions.

At its most idealistic, globalization is a business model for a world where market forces put everyone on the same development path to affluence and democracy. At its worst, it's a model for exploitation and corporate conquistadors. In between is a large area where public policy, corporate decisions and consumer attitudes shape a theory often marketed as a force of nature.

"Globalization is about making choices," says Suzanne Berger, a leading researcher of the business model at the Massachusetts Institute of Technology.

The former employees of John Forsyth know that only too well.

The Cambridge factory had been struggling for years. Competition was fierce. The retail price of a Forsyth dress shirt runs from $70 to $125. Shirts made in places like Bangladesh sell for as little as $10 at huge retailers like Walmart. And demand wasn't going Forsyth's way.

"People want cheap shirts," says Forsyth's co-owner, Oliver Morante.

A decade ago the factory had 500 employees making 1.3 million shirts. That dwindled to 110 people working reduced hours to make 500,000. . . .

The death blow came when the federal government cancelled "duty remission programs." In place since 1988, they allowed apparel companies that manufacture in Canada to import some clothing from abroad duty free.

For Forsyth, a Mississauga-based company that imports 75 per cent of its shirts from China and Bangladesh—those sell for $25—it meant the loss of almost $2 million annually. It was money used to partly offset the higher labour costs, compared to offshore rivals, of its Cambridge factory.

"Those are the types of programs the government needs to keep in place if it wants to have any semblance of domestic manufacturing," Morante says.

Seventy Canadian companies benefitted from the $15-million remission programs. The finance ministry says some of them no longer manufactured in Canada while others were selling their remission allocation to companies that don't produce here. . . .

The finance ministry points to other initiatives to help the apparel industry, including removing tariffs on imported equipment. They didn't benefit Forsyth. . . .

"I'm really angry with the government," [Ina Stagl, a Forsyth employee] adds. "They gave millions to the car companies and nothing to us."

Only three shirt-making factories remain in Canada, [one run by Rick Droppo, the former manager at Forsyth who is trying to reopen the factory] and two in Quebec. Droppo is convinced he can make a go of it. And the workers are fully behind him.

In theory, globalization is the process toward a single world economy—a time when the price of labour, capital and goods and services will be the same everywhere. We, of course, are far from that.

The world's economy was more globalized between 1870 and 1914, notes Berger, an MIT political science professor. The price of commodities and labour converged as people moved freely across borders and new technology—from steamships to trans-Atlantic communication cables—fuelled trade.

The First World War brought it to an end. Immigration controls and tariffs went up.

"Globalization is somewhat reversible because governments still have the power to block things at their borders," says Berger, author of *How We Compete: What Companies Around the World Are Doing to Make It in Today's Global Economy*.

In Canada's apparel industry, quotas limited the amount of goods imported from individual countries. When the quota of Chinese imports was filled, Canadian importers shifted to goods from Korea, then Mauritius and so on.

"The structure of the industry was built on the backs of these quota arrangements, which forced you into very mobile sourcing scenarios," says Bob Kirke, executive director of the Canadian Apparel Federation, which represents 300 manufacturers, importers and retailers.

"Canadian companies became experts at moving goods all over the world."

It was training for the next round of globalization, which kicked off in the early 1980s. The corporate model until then was vertical integration—research and development, design, manufacturing and after-sales service were all done under the same corporate roof.

The 1980s saw what Berger describes as a "tectonic shift." Wall Street pushed a leaner, "asset-light" model. Labour-intensive manufacturing arms were often the first to be severed. The reward was higher stock prices. . . .

Unionized jobs largely responsible for expanding a postwar middle class began to disappear. In Canada since the late 1990s, the result is rising income inequality, challenging governments with a series of social policy choices, including how to redistribute wealth.

In the garment industry, clout shifted from manufacturers to big retailers like Walmart. They developed their own brands. Consumers got hooked on "fast fashion," discarding clothes with every new style. Accessing cheaply manufactured garments became a priority.

Government policies obliged. The NAFTA free trade deal between Canada, the U.S. and Mexico happened in 1984. In 2003, Canada removed all tariffs and quotas from 49 "least developed countries," including Bangladesh. Two years later,

as part of its commitment to the World Trade Organization, Canada removed all quotas on textiles and apparel imports—a move that had been signalled for a decade.

To no one's surprise, manufacturing jobs moved to low-wage countries, first Korea and China, and when wages began climbing there, increasingly to places like Bangladesh. Montreal-based Gildan Activewear Inc., with $1.95 billion in 2012 sales, has most of its manufacturing in Latin America and the Caribbean.

The number of Canadians making clothes declined from 94,260 in 2001 to 19,340 in 2010, according to Statistics Canada. (When administrative jobs are included, the total number declined from 106,226 to 25,670.) About half of the industry is based in Quebec; less than 30 per cent is in Ontario.

GDP in the clothing manufacturing sector declined from $3.6 billion in 2002 to $1.4 billion in 2011. The domestic market share of clothes made in Canada dropped from 40 per cent in 2004 to 23 per cent in 2008.

"It's fashionable to say, 'Buy Canadian,' as long as someone else buys it and not me," Droppo says, giving his take on the attitude of consumers who make low price a priority. . . .

Source: Excerpted from Contenta, S. (2013, May 27). Made in Canada: How globalization has hit the Canadian apparel industry. *Toronto Star.* Retrieved from www.thestar.com/news/insight/2013/05/27/made_in_canada_how_globalization_has_hit_the_canadian_apparel_industry.html. Reprinted with permission.

Another common form of trade barrier or restriction is the **import quota**, which limits the amount of a product that can be imported. The reasons for this restriction are the same: to help ensure that domestic producers retain an adequate share of consumer demand for this product. For example, in the 1980s both the US and Canadian governments were concerned with the growing popularity of Japanese-made cars in Canada and the United States. These cars were higher quality and less expensive than the "Big Three" North American car manufacturers. After pressure from the automakers, both the US and Canadian governments negotiated deals with the Japanese government and the Japanese automakers to "voluntarily" restrict the number of vehicles they would export to Canada and the United States for the following three years. Ironically, this strategy was short-lived, given that Japanese automakers eventually built auto plants in Canada and the United States and achieved an even greater share of the North American market.

import quota A limitation on the amount of a product that can be imported to ensure that domestic producers retain an adequate share of consumer demand for their product.

What's Wrong with Mercantilism and Protectionism?

A trade surplus, as opposed to a trade deficit, certainly seems like a desirable aim, and is, in many respects, a benefit for any nation. The issue, though, is whether a policy of mercantilism is feasible, given its dependence on restricting foreign imports. Perhaps the most significant criticism of mercantilism is that the central assumption upon which this policy is largely based is inherently flawed. Mercantilism assumes that trade involves a **zero-sum gain**—that is, the

zero-sum game The assumption of mercantilism that the world's wealth is a fixed amount, so that a nation can only increase its share by forcing other nations to reduce their share.

Restrictions on imports can be self-defeating, given that other countries will act in a similar manner and reduce their imports. Consider the case of Canada, where a large portion of our raw materials are exported. Can it restrict imports from countries who are similarly purchasing our exports?

The Great Depression of the 1930s was largely caused by the protectionist policy passed by the US government at that time. The government placed tariffs on many goods entering the United States in order to protect US industry. However, the result was that many other countries raised their tariffs and caused a sharp drop in US exports and, in fact, hurt trade among almost all countries.

world's wealth is a fixed pie, and a nation can only increase its share of the pie by forcing other nations to reduce their shares of the pie. Based on this logic, one can understand the drive to minimize imports while maximizing exports. The flaw in this logic, however, is readily apparent. The practice creates a "one-way street" of trade, so to speak. That is, a mercantilist country aims to maximize the goods and services it sells to other countries, yet it expects to restrict the goods and services that these same countries attempt to sell to it. Even in the time of colonialism, the policy was ultimately self-defeating: Colonies that received little payment for their raw material exports could not accumulate sufficient wealth to afford the high-priced imports that the mercantilists offered (see Talking Business 8.9).

Promoting International Trade

World Trade Organization (WTO) An international organization created to develop and administer agreed-upon rules for world trade and discourage protectionist laws that restrict international trade.

General Agreement on Tariffs and Trade (GATT) An agreement among approximately 100 countries to reduce the level of tariffs on a worldwide basis.

International Monetary Fund (IMF) An international organization established after World War II to provide short-term assistance in the form of low-interest loans to countries conducting international trade and in need of financial help.

World Bank An international organization that provides long-term loans to countries for economic development projects. Typically, the World Bank will borrow funds from more developed countries and offer low-interest loans to underdeveloped nations.

Whether it is tariffs or quotas or other forms of protectionism, we have seen a gradual lifting of trade restrictions as part of the wave of globalization. Most countries are endeavouring to eliminate trade barriers altogether.

One of the most ambitious programs designed to encourage free trade was established back in 1948 with the founding of the **General Agreement on Tariffs and Trade (GATT)**, which was an agreement among approximately 100 countries to reduce the level of tariffs on a worldwide basis. And it did encourage a gradual reduction in trade barriers. In 1995 the **World Trade Organization (WTO)**, in effect, took over the management of the global trade system from GATT. Its mandate is essentially to develop and administer agreed-upon rules for world trade and discourage protectionist laws that restrict international trade.

Other organizations exist whose purpose is also to assist nations or the global economy. For example, the **International Monetary Fund (IMF)** was established after World War II to provide short-term assistance in the form of low-interest loans to countries conducting international trade and in need of financial help. The **World Bank** was established at the same time to provide long-term loans to countries for economic development projects. Typically, the World Bank will borrow funds from the more developed countries and offer low-interest loans to underdeveloped nations. So both of these organizations, by assisting less prosperous nations, help to facilitate trade and investment between countries.

Countries themselves have been pursuing trading blocs and other forms of economic integration as part of the general thrust toward a more integrated world economy. This means opening doors to more foreign competition as well as more foreign ownership. This issue of economic integration is discussed below.

FACILITATING GLOBAL BUSINESS: REGIONAL ECONOMIC INTEGRATION

Regional economic integration means bringing different countries closer together by reducing or eliminating obstacles to the international movement of capital, labour, and products or services. A collection of countries within such an integrated region is typically referred to as a **regional trading bloc**. Why do countries endeavour to integrate? It is, largely, a logical conclusion to maximizing the benefits of international trade, as discussed earlier, with regard to greater availability of products, lower prices, and increased efficiency or productivity. Trading blocs increase international trade and investment, with the central aim of improving their economies and living standards for their citizens.

Regional integration can occur at different levels of intensity, so to speak. These include, from the lowest to the highest levels of integration, free trade areas, customs unions, common markets, and economic unions. It is worthwhile to briefly examine each form.

1. **Free trade area**: This form of economic integration involves the removal of tariffs and nontariff trade barriers (that is, subsidies and quotas) on international trade in goods and services among the member countries. Given that this form involves the lowest degree of regional economic integration, there is greater member autonomy with regard to such issues as how it chooses to deal with nonmembers and what types of barriers it should construct against nonmember countries. Examples of this form are NAFTA and APEC, both of which are discussed later in this chapter.

2. **Customs union**: This form of economic integration involves the removal of trade barriers on international trade in goods and services among the member countries. However, given that this form involves a somewhat greater degree of economic integration, there is less member autonomy with regard to such issues as how it chooses to deal with nonmembers and what types of barriers it should construct against nonmember countries. Members will typically generate a uniform policy regarding treatment of nonmembers.

   One example of this type of integration is the Mercosur customs union, which is a major trade group in South America. This customs union was established in 1991, and its partners include Argentina, Brazil, Uruguay, and Paraguay; it grants associate status to Chile and Bolivia. By 1996 the members had eliminated tariffs on goods accounting for 90% of trade between the member countries and eventually largely abolished trade barriers. In 1995 Mercosur implemented a common external tariff, which makes it a more highly integrated trading bloc than NAFTA. These countries represent an attractive market for foreign companies because of the large population and high proportion of middle-class consumers. However, tariffs for nonmembers have ranged from 16% to 32% and, consequently, have made it challenging for outsiders. Countries like Canada and the United States are awaiting further agreements like the FTAA (the Free Trade Area of the Americas) that would allow greater access to the Latin American markets for North American exports.

3. **Common market**: This form of economic integration builds on the elements of the two previous forms, including the removal of trade barriers and the implementation of a common trade policy regarding nonmembers. In addition, members of a common

---

Objective 5 Identify the types of regional economic integration.

regional economic integration Bringing different countries closer together by reducing or eliminating obstacles to the international movement of capital, labour, and products or services.

regional trading bloc A collection of countries within an integrated economic region.

free trade area The lowest degree of regional economic integration, where tariffs and nontariff trade barriers on international trade in goods and services among the member countries are removed.

customs union Economic integration with the removal of trade barriers in goods and services among the member countries. A greater degree of integration than free trade areas, but with less member autonomy in how nonmember countries are dealt with.

common market Economic integration that goes beyond free trade areas and customs unions and includes, for example, freer flow of labour and capital across members' borders and a common trade policy regarding nonmembers.

market will typically also generate a freer flow of labour and capital across their borders. Given the requirement of cooperation in economic and labour policy, this level of economic integration is more difficult to achieve than the previous two levels. The European Union is one such example of a common market arrangement.

economic union A higher level of economic integration than a common market, with harmonization of fiscal, monetary, and tax policies and often a common currency. There is comparably very little member autonomy.

4. **Economic union**: This form of economic integration builds on the previous three forms and, in addition, involves a coordination of economic policies among the member countries. It requires a higher level of integration than a common market because it involves the harmonization of fiscal, monetary, and tax policies. In addition, it often includes the creation of a common currency. Consequently, member countries in such an arrangement maintain much less autonomy compared to the lesser forms of economic integration. In the following discussion of the EU, it can be noted that the members are moving toward greater integration of economic and political policies, which would essentially move them closer to a genuine economic union.

A significant portion of total world trade occurs within three regional trading blocs, also referred to as the triad market of North America, Europe, and Asia. Given the importance of these trading blocs, it is worthwhile to highlight each. Following is a relatively brief description of the trading blocs in Europe and Asia, followed by a lengthier discussion of NAFTA and its implications for the Canadian business environment.

European Union (EU)

European Union (EU) A common market with a single currency and a free flow of money, people, products, and services within its member countries.

In 1992, 12 nations of Europe established a common market called the European Community (EC) and in 1994, after adding several new members, it became known as the **European Union (EU)**. The European Union is a common market with a single currency and a free flow of money, people, products, and services within its member countries. Currently, there are 27 member states within the EU, with some members also adopting a common currency (the euro) and monetary policy. The members include Austria, Belgium, Denmark, Germany, Greece, Ireland, Italy, Portugal, and the United Kingdom, among others. In total, the EU is currently the largest integrated common market in the world, with approximately 500 million consumers.

Common market is a term that refers to a group of countries that remove all tariff and non-tariff barriers to trade. Indeed, the aim of the EU is to create a borderless Europe, so to speak. In fact, the bulk of the advanced regions of Europe exist in essentially one giant market, with the free movement of goods and services as well as people and financial capital. Businesses that operate outside the boundaries of the EU can achieve the benefits of membership if they have a subsidiary in at least one member country. For example, US-based companies like 3M, Hewlett-Packard, and GE have already established a European presence and consequently enjoy the same benefits as businesses who are part of the member European countries. Those not yet established in Europe are developing strategies to exploit this large market.

The EU can be a double-edged sword for nonmembers. It can generate protectionist policies for its members, like tariffs or quotas, to bar the United States or Japan from entry, for example. On the other hand, the EU could also create opportunities for nonmembers—for example, it comprises a huge market for North American exports. A number of US-based companies have chosen to engage in joint ventures with European-based companies as a means of obtaining some kind of presence in the European market.

Does this common market matter to Canada? It certainly does. The EU is one of Canada's most important trading partners. Clearly, this large market cannot be ignored. Aside from the United States, five of Canada's top ten export markets are in Europe. Consequently, observers view Europe as a potentially strong market for Canadian goods if tariff and nontariff barriers can be reduced. In addition, many critics feel that there is currently too high a reliance on one market (the United States) for Canadian exports and increased trade with other markets is preferable.

Asian Trading Bloc

Another region of growing importance to Canada has been the Asia-Pacific region. This region has a total population of about 2 billion people—approximately twice that of the European community. In addition to the drive for greater economic integration and free trade in Europe and North and South America, Asia has also sought to create trading blocs. Singapore, Hong Kong, Taiwan, and South Korea (also referred to as the Four Tigers), together with the relatively dominant partner, Japan, have grown to become an increasingly integrated economic region.

Asean   The **Association of Southeast Asian Nations (ASEAN)** was established in 1967 and became the first major free trade bloc in Asia. Its aim was to promote greater cooperation in areas such as industry and trade among the members, including Singapore, Malaysia, Indonesia, Thailand, Vietnam, the Philippines, Brunei, Cambodia, Laos, and Myanmar. At the same time, member countries are protected by trade barriers from nonmembers.

Association of Southeast Asian Nations (ASEAN) The first major free trade bloc in Asia. It aimed to promote greater cooperation in areas such as industry and trade among its members. At the same time, member countries were protected by trade barriers from nonmembers.

There is a move to create a greater East Asian trade and economic grouping, consisting of the ASEAN countries plus Japan, China, and South Korea.[12] The process of creating a trading bloc has been slower in Asia partly because, unlike NAFTA and the EU, there is a wide disparity between the economic infrastructures and the GDPs of Japan, South Korea, and China. While disparities exist among members in the EU, they are not as great. For example, a number of current EU members, like Portugal and Greece, have remained economically behind such members as Germany, France, and the UK. In North America, although much of Mexico's southern region lives in essentially Third World conditions, the disparities in the economics of China, South Korea, and Japan are much greater. All of this contributes to a greater difficulty in integrating the regions for trade purposes.

Apec   The Asia-Pacific region has also set out to facilitate greater economic cooperation and freer trade through the establishment of the **Asia-Pacific Economic Cooperation (APEC)**, formed in 1989. Among the members of APEC are the People's Republic of China, Hong Kong, Japan, Indonesia, Malaysia, South Korea, Canada, and the United States, to name some of the 21 members. It is viewed as a significant economic force, given that its members generate over 50% of the world's output and about 50% of its merchandise trade. APEC was established to promote economic cooperation among members in the areas of trade and investment. Its relatively diverse mix of countries is, in effect, an effort to counter the narrower regionalism of such arrangements as the EU and NAFTA. In fact, APEC includes three of the traditionally largest

Asia-Pacific Economic Cooperation (APEC) A trading bloc formed in 1989. Among the members are the People's Republic of China, Hong Kong, Japan, Indonesia, Malaysia, South Korea, Canada, and the United States, to name a few of the 21 members.

---

[12] Sterling, H. (2011, March 13). Is free trade a realistic option for East Asia? *National Post.*

economies—the United States, China, and Japan. NAFTA was included in APEC largely as a means to forge stronger economic links between North America and Asia.

How important is APEC to Canada? Canada's central aim in joining APEC was to expand trade opportunities with the region. This region has a total population of about 2 billion people—approximately twice that of the European community. This represents a large market for Canadian exports. Next to the United States, Japan has been one of Canada's largest trading partners, and Japan, along with other member nations, represents a high potential as consumers for our exports. The suggestion is not necessarily to decrease the level of trade and investment that Canada has established with the United States, but rather to pursue similar levels of access to other major regions like Asia. According to one observer, in this century globalization is likely to be dominated by Asian countries rather than North American ones as China and India increase their investments in education and research activities, advancing their own multinationals and expanding their economic potential. This means that Canada's capacity to play the global role that Canadians aspire to will depend on many factors, including creating and allocating the resources that allow it to do so. Canada has to be an economic, social, and environmental success at home. In particular, Canada has to make the transition to a knowledge-based society, with a high level of literacy and capacity for innovation.[13]

Objective 6 Discuss the implications of NAFTA for Canada and the Canadian business environment.

Free Trade Agreement (FTA) An agreement established in 1989 between Canada and the United States to remove trade barriers and to produce a common market between the countries.

North American Free Trade Agreement (NAFTA) An agreement established in 1994 between Canada, the United States, and Mexico to remove trade barriers and to produce a common market between the countries. The agreement replaced the FTA from 1989.

North American Trading Bloc and NAFTA

The **Free Trade Agreement (FTA)** came into effect January 1, 1989, and was largely aimed at reducing, and eventually eliminating, tariff barriers on almost all goods and services traded between Canada and the United States, as well as at further facilitating cross-country investments. Among the other provisions of the agreements are rules regarding government subsidies, the imposition of countervailing duties, standards of health and safety, and the environment. Essentially, for Canadian exporters this agreement offered better access to the huge American market for Canadian goods and services.

In 1994, the **North American Free Trade Agreement (NAFTA)** was established, which was an agreement to remove trade barriers between Canada, the United States, and Mexico. This agreement, which replaced the FTA, essentially aimed to produce a common market among the members. There has been much written regarding the impact that NAFTA has had on the three member countries. Before we identify some of the major arguments supporting or condemning free trade, let's consider some of the areas that have been impacted by this free trade agreement: trade, employment and business, culture, competitiveness, and the consumer (see Exhibit 8.7).

NAFTA's Impact on Trade   Advocates of free trade have this to say about NAFTA's impact on trade:

■ NAFTA achieved its most fundamental objective: to increase the level of trade between Canada and the United States. Canada and US trade increased by about 75% since the establishment of the FTA. Of course, the United States continues to

---

[13] Crane, D. (2005). *Canada in a shifting world*. Foreign Affairs Canada. Retrieved from www.dfait-maeci.gc.ca/canada-magazine/01-title-en.asp.

be Canada's major trading partner, accounting for almost 80% of Canada's total trade.

- Canada's merchandise trade with the United States increased by 80% in the first five years of NAFTA, and Canada's trade with Mexico increased by 65%, reaching $271.5 billion and $1.4 billion, respectively, in 1998.

- One measure of the relative significance of trade to a country is to observe the volume of an economy's trade relative to its total output (percentage of GDP). Exports of Canadian goods to the United States were approximately 17% of GDP in the 1980s, prior to NAFTA. With the implementation of NAFTA, exports and imports grew significantly over the period from 1990 to 1999. Specifically, as a proportion of GDP, exports grew from 25.7% to 43.2%, while imports grew from 25.7% to 40.3%. In contrast, for the 10 years prior to the FTA, exports and imports as a proportion of GDP were practically constant. Total Canada–US trade in both goods and services rose from $425 billion in 1995 to $700 billion in 1999.

- The Government of Canada website has underscored what it views as many positive consequences of NAFTA, including the following:

Exhibit 8.7 The Impact of NAFTA

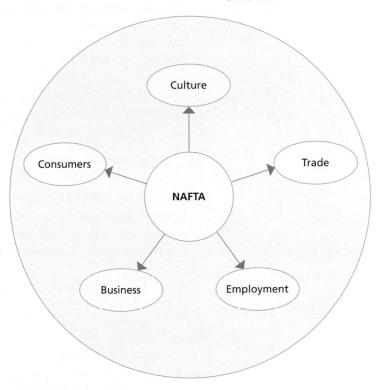

NAFTA has helped transform the three economies while creating synergies that go far beyond economic prosperity. As with any trade liberalization initiative or other economic change, NAFTA affected some sectors positively and others adversely, but there is little doubt that on the whole, the agreement produced real net benefits for workers and consumers of the three countries . . . some 70 million passengers cross the US-Canada border each year (twice the population of Canada), along with 7 million commercial trucks, and 1.3 million rail containers. Since NAFTAs implementation in 1994, total merchandise trade between the US and Canada has grown by over 120%, and when you include trade in services, the growth has been closer to 140%. US trade with Mexico has shown even more significant growth (nearly tripled) over the same period. United States exports to Canada and Mexico have surged 85% from $142 billion to $263 billion in the same period, significantly higher than the 41% increase of United States exports to the rest of the world![14]

[14] Government of Canada. Retrieved from www.dfait-maeci.gc.ca/can-am/menu-en.asp?act=v&did=2890&mid=46&cat=2132&typ=1.

Critics of free trade have this to say about NAFTA's impact on trade:

- Any trade improvements witnessed over the past decade may be more attributable to Canada's then relatively low dollar than due to the results of NAFTA. The fact that for years the US dollar was stronger than the Canadian dollar may have been a stronger help for Canadian exports. As one writer observed,

> Much has been made of Canada's NAFTA-driven trade success, but the reality does not live up to the hype. Canada's merchandise trade surplus with the U.S. is less than meets the eye . . . a federal Industry Department study found that by far the largest factor—accounting for 90% of the 1990s export surge—was the low Canadian dollar.[15]

- While the quantity of Canada–US trade itself may have improved, there have not been any improvements in the quality or nature of Canada's export patterns. As noted earlier, Canada had been far too reliant on exporting of raw materials ("low-technology exports"), in relatively unprocessed form, to the United States. More "added-value," "higher-tech" exports need to be generated so that we can become stronger in more valuable types of exports and engage in more research and development to do so. As one critic indicated,

> Although there was an increase in some high-tech sectors, notably telecommunications and aerospace, the trade deficit in high-tech products remains high . . . and Canada's poor record in private sector R&D persists. Relative to GDP, Canada's exports of higher value-added products—including autos, machinery and equipment, and consumer goods—have fallen by one-quarter since 1999 . . .[16]

- NAFTA has encouraged us to become too dependent on trade with the United States. This point is driven home by observations such as the following:

> Meanwhile, outside NAFTA, the world economy has undergone a vast metamorphosis. China has grown into a trading giant. India is becoming a global leader in the services trade. The European Union is bringing growth to once-perennial underperformers such as eastern Europe and Spain; the latter's economy has grown to roughly the same size as Canada's. The United States has made a higher priority of trading bilaterally with emerging players, and some of their trade agreements may prove more comprehensive than NAFTA, putting Canada's preferred status in the United States at risk. Indeed, China will soon supplant us as America's top trading partner.[17]

---

[15] Campbell, B. (2006, July 1). NAFTA's broken promises. *The CCPA Monitor*. Retrieved from www.policyalternatives.ca/publications/monitor/july-2006-naftas-broken-promises.

[16] Campbell, 2006.

[17] Preville, 2006.

- We need to expand trade with other nations rather than relying solely on NAFTA. NAFTA may have caused Canada to become too complacent in the global market. Consequently, many observers note the need for Canada to put more effort into establishing strong trade ties with other countries. As Philip Preville commented in his *Maclean's* report,

> Our share of global exports and investment to China has actually been on the decline, and we are no longer among China's top 10 trading partners . . . Trade policy should be geared towards facilitating exports of services, and also importing components to reduce the cost of goods manufactured in Canada—a way of making China's manufacturing prowess work for us. [The Conference Board of Canada] also recommends pursuing trade with India and other emerging nations in Asia and Latin America, as well as renewing relationships with old partners in Europe and Japan.[18]

NAFTA's Impact on Canadian Employment and Business   NAFTA's impact on employment and wages has not been clearly determined to date. Different groups have offered different information as to whether jobs have been lost or created as a result of free trade. The key controversy surrounding NAFTA is the issue of jobs. Does open trade and increasing foreign presence in a country result in job creation or job loss? If countries allow products or services to freely enter their borders, what happens to the domestic producers of such products or services?

Advocates of free trade have this to say about NAFTA's impact on Canadian employment and business:

- Foreign competition forces domestic businesses to improve their operations and improve their products and services.
- Protecting domestic business amounts to discouraging competitiveness and innovation and, ultimately, will lead to job losses, given the inability to remain competitive in world markets.
- Free trade encourages countries to abort inefficient operations and focus on the relatively stronger commodities or services in which they have a competitive or comparative advantage.

Critics of free trade have this to say about NAFTA's impact on Canadian employment and business:

- Many Canadian manufacturers cannot compete with US imports and are forced out of business.
- Job losses arise from US companies deciding to shut down their Canadian subsidiaries and exporting their tariff-free goods to Canada.
- Many manufacturing jobs are lost to Mexico, given that country's relatively cheaper labour and, hence, lower-priced goods.

---

[18] Preville, 2006.

> Free trade was sold as a solution to Canada's persistent unemployment problem. Though there are other factors at play, the record does not bear this out. Average unemployment during the last 15 years has remained about the same as the average rate during the previous 15 years. Nor has the promise of increased employment quality—high skill, high-wage jobs—under free trade materialized. On the contrary, displaced workers in the trade sectors have moved to lower-skill, lower-wage jobs in the services sector. Precarious forms of employment (part-time, temporary, and self-employment) have also increased . . .[19]

NAFTA's Impact on Canadian Culture   Advocates of free trade have this to say about NAFTA's impact on Canadian culture:

- The agreement is not signing away Canada's cultural heritage any more than the European Union forced European nations to lose their individual cultures.

- According to Statistics Canada, Canadian cultural exports exceed $4.5 billion, and more royalty money for music is coming into Canada than is leaving.

Critics of free trade have this to say about NAFTA's impact on Canadian culture:

- Free trade will encourage the destruction of a unique Canadian culture.

- Increasing foreign domination of the Canadian economy will transform Canada into a pure economic subsidiary of the United States.

- Publishing and broadcasting industries are threatened by American competitors and the increasing presence of American-based media.

- The presence of the United States in areas like the Canadian entertainment industry would pose a serious threat to the transmission of Canadian culture.

NAFTA's Impact on Canadian Competitiveness and the Canadian Consumer   Advocates of free trade have this to say about NAFTA's impact on Canada's competitiveness and the Canadian consumer:

- One of the central objectives of the FTA was to encourage Canadian businesses to become more competitive through exposure to greater competition from American business.

- Canadian consumers are given more choice and are exposed to competitive products with free trade. That is, they will have access to potentially less expensive goods or services—whether they come from the United States or from increasingly competitive Canadian businesses.

- Canadian companies that require inputs from US businesses can now obtain them more cheaply and pass these savings on to the consumer.

- Canada cannot afford to ignore the US market. If Canadian companies wish to become more competitive, they also need to serve a larger market—and the United States certainly offers a huge market for Canadian goods. Free trade gives Canada greater access to selling goods and services to this market through the reduction of trade barriers.

---

[19] Campbell, 2006.

Critics of free trade have this to say about NAFTA's impact on Canada's competitiveness and the Canadian consumer:

■ NAFTA has not encouraged any increase in productivity. Canadians have been unable to match US productivity rates for the past 20 years, and have produced at rates that are equal to about 80% of the output of workers in the United States.

■ NAFTA has not reduced the productivity gap between Canada and the United States:

> As for the productivity gap with the US that was, according to proponents, supposed to narrow under free trade, it has instead widened. Canadian labour productivity (GDP per hour worked) rose steadily in relation to US productivity during the 1960s and 1970s, peaking at 92% of the US level in 1984. Thereafter, it slid to 89% in 1989 and by 2005 had fallen to just 82% of US productivity—below where it was in 1961.[20]

■ Our good record of exports has come about largely because the relatively low value of the Canadian dollar has made our goods cheaper in the past. In other words, it is not that we were producing cost-efficient goods, but rather it is an artificial reduction in the value of our dollar that has made them cheaper in foreign markets. Consequently, a higher Canadian dollar results in decreased export. What is needed, arguably, is real improvements in productivity coming from things like updating equipment, retraining workers, and building competitiveness.

Where Is Canada Headed?

NAFTA, like other trade agreements, facilitates globalization—the mobility of resources across borders, the freer flow of goods and services, increases in foreign investment, and the growing interdependence of economies. Such instruments bring potential benefits and threats. While many observers see dangers in the outcomes of freer trade, only time will tell whether Canada ultimately gains or loses.

Grappling with NAFTA   Though it has been about two decades since NAFTA has been in effect, its members are still struggling to understand and deal with a number of controversies that NAFTA has presented. For many critics, the benefits of NAFTA accrue largely to corporations rather than to individuals. As one observer comments,

> the North American Free Trade Agreement was sold to the people of the United States, Mexico and Canada as a simple treaty eliminating tariffs on goods crossing the three countries' borders. But NAFTA is much more: It is the constitution of an emerging continental economy that recognizes one citizen—the business corporation. It gives corporations extraordinary protections from government policies that might limit future profits, and extraordinary rights to force the privatization of virtually all civilian public services. Disputes are settled by secret tribunals of experts, many of whom are employed privately as corporate lawyers and consultants. At the same time, NAFTA excludes protections for workers, the environment and the public that are part of the social contract established through long political struggle in each of the countries.[21]

---

[20] Campbell, 2006.

[21] Faux, J. (2004, February 2). NAFTA at 10. *The Nation*. Retrieved from www.thenation.com/article/nafta-10#axzz2eRmdybFW.

The concern that the rights of corporations are paramount in NAFTA is clearly illustrated in the growing number of lawsuits aimed at governments accused of discriminating against foreign-owned corporations. Specifically, this controversy largely stemmed from one section of NAFTA legislation referred to as Chapter 11. Chapter 11 of NAFTA asserts that foreign corporations are permitted to sue the federal government for compensation if that government's legislation, policy, or the delivery of public services interferes with present or future profits of the foreign corporation.

CHAPTER SUMMARY

There is little doubt that the phenomenon of globalization will have profound effects on businesses and societies across the world. In this chapter we tried to make sense of this phenomenon—what it entails and what its implications are. Specifically, we considered why organizations may "go global," and we identified the different types of global business activity. We examined the significance of multinational and borderless corporations. We also considered why nations desire, or do not desire, to promote international trade, including an examination of the pros and cons of Canada's free trade agreement with the United States. Is all this good or bad? That is, will the trend toward an increasingly integrated world economy benefit societies, or generate greater harm? What are the challenges and opportunities for managers in the global workplace? It is hoped that the material in this chapter has encouraged you to think more critically about these questions.

CHAPTER LEARNING TOOLS

Key Terms

acquisition 286
Asia-Pacific Economic Cooperation (APEC) 297
Association of Southeast Asian Nations (ASEAN) 297
borderless corporation 288
common market 295
control 281
customs union 295
domestic trade 290
economic union 296
European Union (EU) 296

first-mover advantage 272
foreign direct investment (FDI) 281
franchisee 281
franchising 281
franchisor 281
free trade 290
Free Trade Agreement (FTA) 298
free trade area 295
General Agreement on Tariffs and Trade (GATT) 294
global business 286
globalization 271
import quota 293

International Monetary Fund (IMF) 294
international trade 290
joint venture 284
licensing agreement 280
mercantilism 290
merger 284
multinational corporation (MNC) 286
North American Free Trade Agreement (NAFTA) 298
outsourcing 280
pull factors 271
push factors 271
regional economic integration 295

regional trading bloc 295
strategic alliance 284
subsidiaries 286
tariff 291
trade barriers 273
trade deficit 291
trade protectionism 291
trade surplus 291
transnational corporation (TNC) 288
World Bank 294
World Trade Organization (WTO) 294
zero-sum gain 293

Multiple-Choice Questions

Select the *best* answer for each of the following questions. Solutions are located in the back of your textbook.

1. Globalization can be referred to as a process involving
   a. the integration of world economies
   b. the integration of world markets
   c. expanding the degree and forms of cross-border transactions
   d. all of the above

2. Going global can be encouraged by
   a. pull factors　　　b. push factors
   c. cross-border tariffs　　d. both A and B

3. In expanding globally, potential for global sales growth is a
   a. pull factor　　　b. push factor
   c. both A and B　　d. none of the above

4. In expanding globally, all of the following are examples of push factors *except*
   a. the force of competition
   b. the shift toward democracy
   c. reduction in trade barriers
   d. obtaining needed resources

5. The first-mover advantage is a philosophy that involves
   a. being the first Canadian company to export goods to an established market
   b. being the first to import goods from a supplier overseas
   c. being the first to establish a strong market position
   d. being the first to change your company's competitive strategy to meet market needs

6. An example of a trade barrier is
   a. a tariff　　　b. a trade agreement
   c. an export quota　　d. both A and C

7. A business can go global by conducting global business activity in the form of
   a. licensing and franchising
   b. joint ventures and strategic alliances
   c. outsourcing to overseas companies
   d. all of the above

8. A franchisee is
   a. the owner of a small business
   b. the dealer
   c. the supplier who receives royalties
   d. both A and B

9. Control of a company can occur with
   a. 100% ownership
   b. less than 50% interest
   c. 50% ownership
   d. all of the above

10. A reason for a business to engage in FDI is to gain
    a. access to a smaller market
    b. needed resources
    c. better trade relations
    d. none of the above

11. A strategic network is a relationship involving a
    a. merger　　　b. subsidiary
    c. joint venture　　d. industry association

12. Economies of scale can be a benefit of a
    a. strategic network　　b. subsidiary
    c. merger　　　d. licensing agreement

13. To gain access to new knowledge or expertise, a company could
    a. create a subsidiary
    b. outsource its payroll department overseas
    c. acquire a new company
    d. license a business to a franchisee

14. A borderless corporation is sometimes referred to as a(n)
    a. MNC　　　b. TNC
    c. subsidiary　　d. both A and B

15. A potential threat of a multinational corporation is that
    a. decision making is centralized
    b. economic development is encouraged
    c. management expertise is shared
    d. rare technologies are shared

Discussion Questions

1. Discuss globalization and compare its many definitions.
2. Describe the differences between pull and push factors.
3. Identify and describe the seven channels of global business activity.
4. What is a multinational corporation (MNC)?
5. What are the potential benefits and risks of an MNC?
6. Explain the meaning of a trade barrier and provide two examples.
7. Contrast the difference between a trade surplus and a trade deficit.
8. Explain regional economic integration and provide five levels of intensity.
9. What is a trade agreement? Provide three examples.
10. What are some arguments for and against the North American Free Trade Agreement (NAFTA)?

Numerous foreign takeovers of prominent Canadian companies have occurred over the past decade. Among the more high-profile takeovers have been Swiss-based Glencore International PLC acquiring Viterra Inc., a Regina-based agribusiness, in 2012; Brazilian mining company Vale acquiring Toronto-based Inco, the world's second-largest nickel producer, in 2007; UK's Rio Tinto purchasing mining and aluminum company Alcan in 2007; Swiss company Xstrata taking over Toronto-based copper and nickel mining company Falconbridge in 2006; U.S. Steel Corp. acquiring Canadian steelmaker Stelco in 2007; graphics chipmaker ATI Technologies based in Markham, Ontario, being acquired by US company Advanced Micro Devices in 2006; and the Caterpillar Inc. takeover of locomotive builder Electro-Motive in London, Ontario, in 2010.[22]

Why would businesses wish to engage in foreign direct investment? Foreign direct investment (FDI) involves the purchase of physical assets or an amount of ownership in a company from another country to gain a measure of management control. A direct investment can be done through acquisition of an already existing business in the host country or through a startup built "from scratch," so to speak. The choice may be dependent on a number of factors, including the availability of suitable businesses in the host country.

A relatively recent foreign acquisition in Canada involved the Calgary-based oil and gas producer Nexen Inc., Canada's 12th largest energy company. In 2013, Nexen was purchased for about $15 billion by the China National Offshore Oil Company (CNOOC), which is owned by the Chinese government. This made Nexen into a wholly owned subsidiary of CNOOC.

Why did this Chinese state-owned company choose Canadian Nexen as a target of its takeover bid? In 2013, Canada was ranked as having the world's third-largest oil reserves, after Saudi Arabia and Venezuela.[23] The leaders of large consuming nations such as China have been seeking to maintain continued access to this natural resource in order to keep their economies growing. Given that China is the biggest energy consumer in the world and the second-biggest consumer of oil, its aim has been to attempt to acquire these resource assets.

Why would Canada be interested in permitting a foreign takeover of important businesses such as one in the petroleum industry? Canada has a large reserve of natural resources, but a relatively smaller population and economy. Consequently, Canada is concerned about finding long-term, stable markets for its products given that developing and selling more of its natural resources boosts economic prosperity. Clearly, having China as a long-term customer guarantees a solid market for Canada's resources. Added to that is that fact that CNOOC has the financial resources to accelerate development of Nexen's oil sands, and thereby can boost investment and tax revenues in Canada.[24]

---

[22] *CBC News*. (2012, July 23). 7 foreign takeovers that shook up Canadian business. Retrieved from www.cbc.ca/news/business/story/2012/07/23/foreign-takeovers-canada-nexen.html.

[23] Perkowski, J. (2012, July 25). Why Nexen is different: The politics of supply. *Forbes*. Retrieved from www.forbes.com/sites/jackperkowski/2012/07/25/why-nexen-is-different-the-politics-of-supply.

[24] Perkowski, 2012.

The foreign acquisition of Nexen had to be approved by the federal government, which needed to consider whether the takeover would be of "net benefit" to Canada. The proposed buyout needed to be carefully considered by the Canadian government since there were a number of potential issues at stake. It was felt that the purchase would positivity impact business relations with Beijing, and potentially contribute to Canada's future energy strategy. Allowing the purchase means more Chinese investment in Canada and boosting oil sands production—both of which are economic benefits to Canada.[25]

On the other hand, as critics suggested, the takeover could trigger a transfer of Canada's control of our natural resources to foreign interests. Petroleum resources are very important to Canada. Some critics argue that given China's poor human rights and environmental records, the deal with CNOOC should be rejected. An editorial in the *Globe and Mail* made some cautionary notes on that topic:

> Nothing can change the fact that CNOOC is led by a Communist dictatorship with a patchy human rights record. . . . Of course, CNOOC plans to run its operation as a commercial enterprise, not as a political arm of Beijing.[26]

Prime Minister Harper asserted that such strategic partnerships would not prevent the Canadian government from standing up for human rights issues in China and that environmental responsibilities must be monitored. In addition, supporters of the acquisition point out that expanding business ties to China will be crucially important to Canada given that China is fast becoming the world's top economic power. This connection can help maintain the strength of Canada's export-based economy and compensate for potentially lower trade with the United States.[27]

Among the other considerations for government approval of the takeover was the willingness of CNOOC to retain all incumbent Nexen employees. To that end, the company agreed that Calgary would serve as its headquarters for North and Central American operations. As well, CNOOC promised to acquire a listing on the Toronto Stock Exchange and sustain Nexen's social responsibility efforts globally. Given that CNOOC is a government-owned agency, the Canadian government also required a commitment from the Beijing government for better investment access for Canadian businesses in China.[28]

Critics of this deal warned that it could trigger more takeovers whereby other foreign governments are encouraged to take over Canadian natural resources. Consequently, while the federal government of Canada approved the controversial acquisition, it put in place regulation that would largely preclude future takeovers of Canadian energy firms by state-owned foreign companies. This means that while Nexen is no longer Canadian owned, the deal did not create a precedent for China or other foreign governments to

---

[25] Whittington, L. (2012, September 29). Nexen takeover decision a crossroads for Canada and China. *Toronto Star*. Retrieved from www.thestar.com/news/canada/2012/09/29/nexen_takeover_decision_a_crossroads_for_canada_and_china.html.

[26] Editorial. (2012, July 23). Nexen takeover must be good for Canada. *Globe and Mail*. Retrieved from www.theglobeandmail.com/commentary/editorials/nexen-takeover-must-be-good-for-canada/article4436664.

[27] Whittington, 2012.

[28] Whittington, 2012.

Case Continued >

have guaranteed growing shares in Canada's energy wealth, thereby protecting future Canadian interests.[29]

The decision to allow the takeover avoided harming Canada's trade and investment prospects with the world's emerging economic power. At the same time, the decision to not permit future takeovers of the same kind prevent the "hollowing out" of the petroleum industry in Canada since it would have allowed takeovers among other oil sands producers like Suncor, Cenovus, or Canadian Natural Resources Ltd. And this serves as a protective measure against losing control over an important and strategic natural resource for Canada. In fact, it led to the updating of Canada's Investment Act to preclude foreign state-owned enterprises from purchasing Canadian oil producers in all but "exceptional circumstances."[30]

Questions

1. How does this case reflect themes of globalization?
2. How are the following parties potentially affected by this takeover? Discuss both the potential benefits and negative consequences that each may experience as a result.
   a. CNOOC
   b. Nexen
   c. Canadian employment
   d. The Canadian economy
   e. Canadian competitors in this industry
   f. Global competitors in this industry
3. "The Canadian government should protect Canadian business from both foreign competition and takeovers." Discuss the merits of this statement in the context of this case.

[29] Goar, C. (2012, December 13). Stephen Harper made the right decision on Nexen takeover. *Toronto Star.* Retrieved from www.thestar.com/opinion/editorialopinion/2012/12/13/goar_stephen_harper_made_the_right_decision_on_nexen_takeover.html.

[30] Whittington, 2012.

Chapter 9
Political Forces
Where Would Canadian Business be Without Our Government?

© Convery flowers/Alamy

Should the Canadian government take a more active role in the welfare of Canadian industry? The traditional relationship between government and business is clearly undergoing change. In this chapter, we will examine how government can intervene in business activity while fulfilling its role as both guardian of society and guardian of business. We will consider current and critically important trends regarding the shift toward reduced government involvement in the business sector. Specific attention will be paid to the issues of deregulation and privatization.

Learning Objectives

After studying this chapter, you should be able to

1. Describe the fundamental nature of the Canadian business enterprise system.
2. Describe how government in Canada is structured.
3. Discuss the government's role as a guardian of society and how this impacts its relationship to business.
4. Identify the purpose of Crown corporations.
5. Explain the notion of government as guardian of the private business sector.
6. Discuss government's role with regard to global business.
7. Describe the objectives and consequences of deregulation and privatization.

THE BUSINESS WORLD

Japan's Toyota and Canada's Subsidies

Should governments be funding private business? Does it matter if those businesses are Canadian owned or foreign owned? The answer to these often-asked questions is . . . well, there is no clear answer.

Governments at all levels can provide assistance for businesses in the form of grants, loans, and subsidies. Between 1983 and 2012, the federal department Industry Canada spent $13.7 billion on grants and loans to businesses, with the majority of these loans remaining unpaid in 2013.[1] The government may be more likely to offer assistance to those industries "in need" that are also deemed to be of particular importance. For example, recipients of government aid have included Canada's big banks, which received billions in support from the federal government and the Bank of Canada during the 2008–2009 financial crisis.[2] While the financial aid was repaid in full, observers suggested that had these public funds not been made available, it could have been disastrous for them. In addition, industries with leading-edge technology, those providing highly skilled jobs, and those that are oriented toward exports may be among the more likely recipients of government aid.

The federal and provincial governments also provide financial incentives in an effort to dissuade companies from moving their operations outside of Canada. For example, the federal government gave Pratt & Whitney Canada an $11 million loan to encourage the company to retain the development of a new aircraft component within Canada. More recently, Pratt & Whitney received a $300 million government loan for research and development.[3] Kellogg, a US cereal manufacturer with operations in Canada, received $4.5 million from the Ontario provincial government to help establish an advanced new production line that would make its Belleville manufacturing plant among the most technologically advanced in Kellogg's worldwide operations.

The auto industry has been a major recipient of government subsidies. This is an important industry in Canada, given that it contributes 1.5% to our gross domestic product directly, and even more when the related industries that it benefits are included. It is therefore important to our continued economic strength. In that vein, in 2012 the Ontario and federal governments announced that they would give Japan's Toyota Motor Corporation up to $34 million to build a hybrid car factory in Cambridge, Ontario. This is in addition to the government's pledge to give $250 million more to its auto subsidy program, formally known as the Automotive Innovation Fund.[4]

The $34 million subsidy is referred to as a "repayable contribution," which is a loan for which the recipient is expected to repay all or part of the amount or on which the government expects to receive a financial return. The government felt that encouraging Toyota to build a hybrid car in Canada would help create high-quality, well-paying jobs for Canadians. In fact, Toyota announced that it would hire about 400 employees as part

[1] Goar, C. (2012, September 12). Corporate welfare flourishes in lean times. *Toronto Star*. Retrieved from www.thestar.com/opinion/editorialopinion/2012/09/13/corporate_welfare_flourishes_in_lean_times.html.

[2] Canadian Press. (2012, April 30). Canadian banks got millions in support, report says. *Globe and Mail*. Retrieved from www.theglobeandmail.com/globe-investor/canadian-banks-got-billions-in-support-report-says/article4103645.

[3] Weston, G. (2010, December 13). Pratt & Whitney deal not quite as advertised. *CBC News*. Retrieved from www.cbc.ca/news/politics/story/2010/12/13/f-weston-pratt-whitney.html.

[4] Based on *CBC News*. (2013, January 23). Toyota gets government funding to build hybrid car in Canada. Retrieved from www.cbc.ca/news/business/story/2013/01/23/pol-harper-toyota.html.

of a plan to increase Lexus RX production by 30,000 vehicles to 104,000, including 15,000 RX450h sport utilities.[5]

Toyota itself will invest $125 million toward the new assembly line to increase production of Lexus luxury cars, including a utility model with a hybrid gasoline-electric engine. These Toyotas were intended to be the first modern hybrid cars produced in Canada. Overall, the expansion will raise Toyota's annual production capacity in Canada to 500,000 vehicles.[6]

Part of the government's aim in offering assistance is to encourage innovation. In fact, in 2012 the federal government renewed a subsidy program first established in 2008 to stimulate research and innovation in Canada's automotive industry. This program requires that manufacturers invest some of their own money before applying for funding targeted at specific research and development projects. The subsidy program aims at offering an incentive to automakers to maintain their plants in Canada and thereby protect domestic jobs.[7]

Critics of government subsidies disparagingly refer to them as "corporate welfare" or "corporate handouts." According to a report by the Fraser Institute, there is little evidence that such government assistance to business actually leads to widespread economic growth or job creation.[8] This casts doubt on the value of funding the auto industry. Opponents of government assistance also argue that the industry should be left to fend for itself. Subsidies often take the form of low-interest-rate loans or outright gifts, so donor governments rarely have any influence over a company's future hiring plans. In the case of the 2009 auto bailout, the Canadian and US governments required shares in the companies they helped. However, they insisted they wouldn't use this equity to influence corporate direction. In other words, often these kinds of government assistance don't come with any guarantees—whether in the form of future job creation or profitability. This has led some observers, like journalist Thomas Walkom, to comment, "So now we're paying for Toyota to build hybrid vehicles in Ontario. Good for us. It will probably result in some new jobs. These jobs may even last for a while. Or at least until some other government offers Toyota a better deal."[9]

On the other hand, advocates of subsidies argue that Canada needs to do more to assist automakers in Canada. In this global world, many believe that Canada needs to compete with other countries to attract business and therefore jobs to this country. The argument is that there is no guarantee that production will remain in Canada if Toyota or any other business gets more government support from other countries to locate there. This has led some observers, include *Globe and Mail* journalist Barrie McKenna, to make comments like the following:

> Canada is a player, but increasingly it is a bit player . . . This country is losing the subsidies game to richer and more aggressive rivals . . . And it's no longer about creating new jobs. It's about salvaging a shrinking global presence. Unless governments find a way to get foreign auto makers to commit to staying in Canada for the long haul, it will be money wasted.[10]

---

[5] *CBC News*, 2013.

[6] *CBC News*, 2013.

[7] *CBC News*, 2013.

[8] Milke, M. (2012, September). Corporate welfare bargains at Industry Canada. *Fraser Alert*. Fraser Institute. Retrieved from www.fraserinstitute.org/default.aspx.

[9] Walkom, T. (2013, January 23). Toyota latest winner from Canada's corporate socialism: Walkom. *Toronto Star*. Retrieved from www.thestar.com/news/canada/2013/01/23/toyota_latest_winner_from_canadas_corporate_socialism_walkom.html.

[10] McKenna, B. (2013, January 13). Canada has become a bit player in the game of auto subsidies. *Globe and Mail*. Retrieved from www.theglobeandmail.com/report-on-business/economy/canada-competes/canada-has-become-a-bit-player-in-the-game-of-auto-subsidies/article7306109.

Other observers suggest that subsidies won't help and may be wasted on what is already a shrinking industry in Canada. For example, Mexico appears to have contributed to the weakened state of the Canadian auto industry. In 2013, the world's automakers announced investments of US$11 billion in Mexico, compared with $2.3 billion in Canada. Why has Mexico attracted so much more investment? According to many industry officials, factors such as the increase in the value of the Canadian dollar, the significantly lower wages in Mexico, and Mexico's position as a gateway to developing markets in South America are among the reasons for this dramatic shift.[11]

Objective 1 Describe the fundamental nature of the Canadian business enterprise system.

THE CANADIAN BUSINESS ENTERPRISE SYSTEM: FUNDAMENTAL FEATURES

"The Business World" vignette highlights the importance of understanding the boundaries of what constitutes a legitimate relationship between business and government. What role should government play in business?

Historically, the government has played a critical role in the Canadian economy. From our very beginning as a nation, the government has taken responsibility for the success of business. It is useful to briefly consider the nature of our economic or business enterprise system, within which all businesses operate. The Canadian economic system has been described as a **mixed system**. This refers to the notion that while we possess a capitalist economy, the government nonetheless plays an important role.

All developed countries have some sort of economic or **business enterprise system** that essentially determines the following:

mixed system An economic system that involves a capitalist economy with an important government role. Most economies today are considered mixed systems.

business enterprise system The system all developed countries possess that determines what goods and services are distributed to society and how those goods and services are produced and distributed. The decisions may be made by government or by business or both.

1. what goods and services are produced and distributed to society

2. how the goods and services are produced and distributed to society

What kind of business enterprise system we have determines how or by whom these decisions are made. For example, the two decisions above might be made purely by business, or they might be determined by government, or perhaps by a combination of the two. To understand the basis of our Canadian business enterprise system, it is necessary to understand the nature of capitalist economic systems. So let's briefly explain what capitalism is.

capitalism An economic system based on the rights of the individual, the rights of private property, and competition and minimal government interference.

Capitalism is a type of economic system that is based on a number of fundamental principles:

1. *Rights of the individual:* The notion of capitalism is based on the view that it is the individual who takes precedence in society, as opposed to institutions or the overall society. This implies that individuals have every right to pursue their own self-interest, which includes seeking to make profits from business enterprises. The notion

[11] Keenan, G. (2013, April 12). Lagging investment a threat to Canadian auto industry. *Globe and Mail*. Retrieved from www.theglobeandmail.com/report-on-business/economy/lagging-investment-a-threat-to-canadian-auto-industry/article11167942/?page=all.

of the individual as the most important element of society is not entirely representative of the ideology present in Canadian society. There are limits placed on individuals' right to pursue their self-interest. Government regulations enforce rules that affect how business owners conduct their affairs. For example, government guidelines regarding job candidate selection criteria may affect who is hired for a job and may place emphasis on certain groups in society over others.

2. *Rights of private property:* As opposed to state ownership, capitalism asserts that individuals have the right to own land, labour, and capital. In Canada, certainly, individuals are permitted to own their means of production, whether it is land, labour, or capital. However, because there has been an uneven distribution of wealth in society, the government has intervened in a number of ways. For example, taxation is one approach that can be partly aimed at redistributing wealth among members of society. Other examples include the fact that much of the natural resources in Canada have been retained by federal or provincial governments. The government may also decide to nationalize certain products or services that it deems to be on national interest—for example, government control of health care.

3. *Competition:* Capitalism advocates competition. The belief is that sufficient competition among business enterprises will ensure that business provides the goods and services required by society at a fair cost. Competition is the **"invisible hand of the market"** (in the words of economist Adam Smith) that ensures the market works in this manner. In Canada, the notion of perfect competition does not exist in practice—there is no guarantee that an adequate supply of competitors exists across all industries.

4. *The role of government:* The view of government is reflected in the French term ***laissez faire***, which means "let people do as they choose." This suggests minimal government interference in the business enterprise system. This notion of capitalism has also been referred to as the **free enterprise system**, reflecting the notion of the right to private ownership of property, competition, and restricted government involvement.

Of course, the polar opposite of capitalism is another economic system referred to as communism. Whereas the capitalist system allows individuals or businesses to choose how to allocate resources, the communist system places this responsibility in the hands of the government.

There really are no societies today that are either purely capitalist or purely communist. In Canada, government does intervene in the affairs of business—business is not left entirely to conduct its own affairs. When Canada first came into existence as a country, the federal government was granted the power to "regulate trade and commerce." And the fact is, throughout our history, the government has played a major role in fostering industrial development and continues to provide significant support to the business sector.

CANADIAN GOVERNMENT STRUCTURE AND ROLES

How is Canada's government structured, and what role does it play in relation to business? The government of Canada is organized into three levels: federal, provincial/territorial, and municipal. Each level has unique responsibilities that govern individuals and business; however, some powers may overlap or be shared (see Exhibit 9.1).

invisible hand of the market Adam Smith used the "invisible hand" metaphor in his book *The Wealth of Nations*, published in 1776. Smith argued that, by pursuing their own self-interest, individuals "are led by an invisible hand" to promote the greater public interest, even if that is not their intention.

laissez faire A term meaning that businesses or manufacturers should be free to make and sell what they please and, consequently, reflects the notion that government should not interfere with the economic affairs of business.

free enterprise system Another term for *laissez faire,* or the capitalist notion that the government should not interfere too much in business affairs.

Objective 2 Describe how government in Canada is structured.

Exhibit 9.1 Government
Activities

Level of Government	Leadership Position	Examples of Activities by Level	Examples of Shared Activities
Federal (national)	Prime Minister	• banking • bankruptcy law • copyright law • criminal law • currency • drug approvals • employment insurance • First Nations • fishing • foreign relations • immigration • national defence • postal service • shipping • trade regulations	• agriculture and food (fed. and prov.) • natural resources and the environment (fed. and prov.) • personal tax (fed. and prov.) • corporate tax (fed. and prov.) • transportation (fed. and prov.) • justice (all) • police (all) • licensing/permits (prov. and mun.)
Provincial (regional)	Premier	• education • health care • labour law • property law	
Municipal (city/town/local)	Mayor or Reeve	• fire protection • food safety • land use planning • libraries • local road repair and maintenance • public transit • sewage • snow removal • waste collection • water	

Levels of Government

federal level of government The highest level of government that governs all Canadian citizens, residents, and others across Canada.

Federal   The **federal level of government** is the highest level of government and applies to all Canadians. Generally, federal responsibilities are very wide. Some roles include national defence, criminal law, bankruptcy law, postal service, foreign policy, currency, First Nations, banking, and immigration. The federal government is led by the prime minister of Canada, who is elected by Canadian voters. There are many federal departments; however, two departments that all businesses deal with are the Canada Revenue Agency and Canada Post. The Canada Revenue Agency (CRA), for example, is the federal department that administers income tax collection from corporations and individuals. Canada Post Corporation, on the other hand, is a federal Crown corporation that provides mail delivery service across Canada.

Provincial and Territorial

The **provincial level of government** is more regional in nature and only affects those citizens and residents who reside in a particular province. Provincial responsibilities include highways, transportation, education, and health care. Since each provincial government is a separate and unique jurisdiction, provinces can have laws and regulations that differ from other provinces. In Ontario, for example, the provincial government owns and controls the sale of distilled spirits through the Liquor Control Board of Ontario (LCBO), a provincial Crown corporation. In Alberta, however, the provincial government does not own or control the sale of alcohol but only regulates it.[12] The leader of the provincial government is called the premier and is elected by citizens who reside in that province.

The territories are run differently than a province. A commissioner, instead of a premier, is federally appointed to run a territory. Therefore, Canadians do not vote to elect a territorial leader. The three Canadian territories are the Northwest Territories, Yukon, and Nunavut.

provincial level of government A regional level of government in Canada that only affects those citizens and residents who reside in a particular province.

Municipal

The **municipal level of government** is the lowest level of government. A municipal government can govern a city or a smaller community, such as a town, village, or parish. In Canada, there are over 4,000 municipal governments.[13] A municipal government can be viewed as a subdivision of the province, since provinces were granted the power over municipal institutions under section 92 of the Constitution Act of 1867.[14] The leader of a municipality has autonomy and decentralized decision-making power to make laws over his or her jurisdiction; however, in some cases laws can be subject to change by the province. Some municipal responsibilities can include police services, fire protection, land planning, sewage, public transportation, garbage collection, and library services. The leader of a city is called a mayor. However, a leader of a rural area may be called a reeve.

municipal level of government The lowest level of government in Canada that governs a city or smaller community, such as a town, village, or parish.

While each level of government has unique responsibilities, certain roles may be shared. The administration of justice is a good example. While municipalities are responsible for police services, there is also provincial police and of course the Royal Canadian Mounted Police (RCMP) at the federal level. Taxation is another shared role. While property taxes are administered and collected by municipalities, provincial and federal governments administer and collect income and sales taxes.

How does the government affect industry? If you are a restaurant owner, you will likely be affected by the government in a number of ways. You may need to apply for a liquor licence, to comply with food and safety regulations, to understand garbage and recycling procedures, and to remit taxes. You may even need to comply with trade regulations if you need to import specialty food items. In other words, you can be impacted by all levels of government. On the other hand, if you are a financial institution, you will likely be most affected by banking regulations at the federal level.

---

[12] Jazairi, N. (1994). The impact of privatizing the Liquor Control Board of Ontario. Report prepared for the Ontario Liquor Boards Employees' Union. Retrieved from www.yorku.ca/nuri/lcbo.htm.

[13] Guy, J. (2010). *People, politics and government: A Canadian perspective* (7th ed., p. 21). Toronto, ON: Pearson Canada.

[14] Guy, 2010, 21.

Exhibit 9.2 Structure of the Federal Government

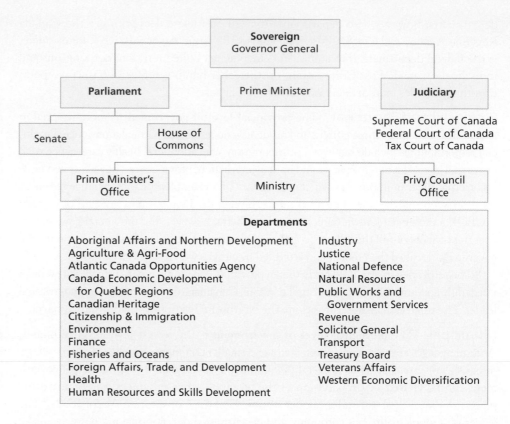

Are there certain industries that are not affected by the government? No—every business is impacted by government in some way. Newer industries, however, such as selling coupons online (for example, Groupon.com), may not be subject to as many laws and regulations. But as issues or concerns arise about the industry, new rules are developed and passed into law. These laws can exist under any level of government. Let's take a closer look at the structure of the federal level of government (see Exhibit 9.2).

Federal Government Structure

Governor General The holder of executive authority in Canada's government. This person typically plays a passive administrative role and usually follows the advice of the prime minister, but he or she must sign bills before they become law.

prime minister The head of the Canadian government; elected by Canadian voters.

Prime Minister's Office (PMO) The office that assists the prime minister with daily activities.

The federal government consists of a Governor General, prime minister, Parliament (Senate and House of Commons), and judiciary.

Governor General Under the Constitution Act of 1867, executive authority was originally vested in the Queen; however, in 1977 the **Governor General** was delegated this authority. The Governor General typically plays a passive administrative role and usually follows the advice of the prime minister (PM). While Canadians elect the prime minister to lead the country, the Governor General appoints the PM and swears him or her into office. The Governor General also signs bills before they become law.[15]

Prime Minister The **prime minister** is the leader of Canada and is typically the person who the public and the media hold accountable when something goes wrong, regardless if the PM holds responsibility for that function. The PM is assisted by the Prime Minister's Office, the Privy Council Office, and the various federal government ministries. The **Prime Minister's Office**

---

[15] Guy, 2010, 141.

(PMO) is the office that assists the PM with daily activities, such as answering mail, writing speeches, making appointments, and maintaining good public relations. The **Privy Council Office (PCO)**, on the other hand, serves as an important policy-advising agency.[16] **Ministries** or *departments* help the PM run the country by specializing in various functions such as health, fisheries, justice, and national defence. When the PM is elected, he or she appoints members to his or her Cabinet. Each **Cabinet** member is then assigned a government ministry or department to oversee.[17]

Rambleon/Shutterstock

Parliament   Parliament consists of the House of Commons and the Senate. The most important role of the **House of Commons** is the passage of legislation. Typically, a bill is proposed to the House of Commons, where it is discussed, debated, and amended if necessary. If the bill is satisfactory and approved, the bill is then introduced to the Senate. If approved by the **Senate**, the bill is presented to the Governor General to sign and enact into law.[18] Other roles of the House of Commons involve questioning the current government's policies and allowing Members of Parliament (MPs) to make speeches on important issues.[19] The House of Commons also includes the prime minister's Cabinet.[20]

Judiciary   The federal judiciary represents the court system dealing with federal matters. Three federal courts are the Tax Court of Canada (lowest level), the Federal Court of Canada, and the Supreme Court of Canada (highest level). The judicial function also exists at the provincial level for provincial matters.[21]

As you can see, the structure of the federal government is quite complex. While the prime minister formerly leads the country, a business is more likely to deal with a government department or ministry. Similarly, each provincial and municipal government will have departments related to the activities that it governs.

GOVERNMENT AS GUARDIAN OF SOCIETY

How often do companies have to deal with the government? And what key roles does the government play in relation to business? This will likely depend on the industry and the nature of a company's activities. However, three key roles the government plays are as the tax collector, the business owner, or the regulator, all of which will be discussed in this section. Exhibit 9.3 summarizes the variety of ways government can influence business activity.

The Tax Collector Role

The government plays many roles in relation to business. The most obvious role, and perhaps the least popular one, is that of government as tax collector, whether it is at the federal, provincial, or municipal level. There are two broad forms of taxes: revenue taxes

Privy Council Office (PCO) An important policy-advising agency that serves the prime minister.

ministries (federal) The various departments of the federal government that specialize in various functions (for example, health, fisheries, justice, national defence). Each ministry is headed by a Cabinet minister.

Cabinet Members of Parliament who are appointed by the prime minister to oversee an assigned government ministry or department.

House of Commons The lower house of Parliament, where Members of Parliament (MPs) sit to discuss, debate, and amend bills to pass legislation.

Senate The upper house of Parliament, where a bill is passed after it has been approved by the House of Commons. If approved by the Senate, the bill is passed to the Governor General to sign and enact into law.

Objective 3 Discuss the government's role as a guardian of society and how this impacts its relationship to business.

---

[16] Guy, 2010, 147.

[17] Guy, 2010, 146.

[18] Guy, 2010, 178.

[19] The Canada Page. (n.d.). The government of Canada. Retrieved from www.thecanadapage.org/Government.htm.

[20] Guy, 2010, 173.

[21] Guy, 2010, 231.

Exhibit 9.3
The Government's
Guardian Roles

Government as Guardian of Society	Government as Guardian of Business

• Collecting taxes from businesses
• Acting as business owners
• Regulating the business sector
• Safeguarding Canadian interests in the global context
	• Spending money on private business
	• Assisting private businesses
	  ○ Bailouts
	  ○ Subsidies
	• Safeguarding Canadian business in the global context

revenue taxes One of two broad forms of taxes, the other being restrictive or regulatory taxes. This money is collected to help fund government services and programs and includes individual income taxes, corporate income tax, property tax, and sales tax.

and regulatory or restrictive taxes. The intent of **revenue taxes** is to collect money to help fund government services and programs. They include *individual income taxes* as well as *corporate income tax*, along with property tax and sales tax. Individual income taxes have provided the largest source of revenue for the federal and provincial governments. Individual income tax is levied on the income of individuals or on the net profits of proprietorships and partnerships. Corporate income tax has provided the second largest source of revenue for the federal government. Corporations are taxed on their net profit at a combined federal and provincial rate that can vary among provinces and that is subject to change based on government policy. Government policy may include an agenda of manipulating taxation to stimulate government investment or to raise more revenues.

Sales taxes are an important source of revenue for most provinces, as well as for the federal government. This tax is paid through retail stores, which act as collection agents when they sell their goods to consumers. The goods and services tax (GST) that came into effect in 1991 provides substantial funds to the federal government. It is a value-added tax—a tax that is paid at each step of the manufacturing process. Consider, for example, a producer that buys raw materials from a supplier; the GST is charged by the supplier. The producer may then work on the raw materials and produce a part for sale to a manufacturer, who is then charged GST on that purchase. Everyone involved in the goods or services production pays GST, but only the final consumer cannot pass the tax on to another party.

The harmonized sales tax (HST) is another form of sales tax. This type of value-added sales tax combines the federal GST with provincial sales tax (PST). There are only five provinces that mandate the HST: Ontario, New Brunswick, Newfoundland and Labrador, Nova Scotia, and Prince Edward Island. The benefit of this one-system, harmonized tax is a reduction in administrative costs for businesses and the government.

Finally, another well-known form of taxation is *property taxes*, which is the largest revenue source for municipal governments. The revenue gained from this form of tax is typically used to fund the operating costs of the municipal government and the services that it provides.

restrictive or regulatory taxes One of two broad forms of taxes, the other being revenue taxes. This form of taxation consists of two types: excise taxes and customs duties or tariffs. Excise taxes are applied to goods and services that the government wants to restrict the purchase of.

As mentioned earlier, the second broad form of taxation is referred to as **restrictive or regulatory taxes**. There are two main types of regulatory taxes: excise taxes and customs duties or tariffs. *Restrictive taxes* are primarily aimed at controlling or curbing the use of specific products or services, such as sugary soft drinks, which may contribute to obesity and higher health care costs, as seen in Talking Business 9.1. *Excise taxes* typically are applied to goods or services that the government desires to restrict, such as products deemed to be potentially harmful (including tobacco and alcohol products). Excise taxes have been used as a deterrent to potential excesses—in fact, back in 1976, the federal government actually levied an additional tax on gasoline to discourage overuse to help conserve what was then a product in very

Should Pop Drinkers Pay More?

Desperate times require desperate measures—and for U.S. state and local governments, many of which are mandated by law to run balanced budgets, these are certainly desperate times. To close gaping budget deficits, some states are considering legalizing marijuana and collecting taxes on its sale. Other states are looking to build more casinos, and this is happening even in states where the governors are vehemently opposed to generating revenue from gambling.

Another idea to raise revenues is the establishing of a special tax on soft drinks. . . . During the discussions on health-care reform, a tax on soft drinks was put forward as a way of helping to pay for the overhaul of the entire system.

Economists generally support taxing consumption rather than income, due to the fact that consumption taxes do less to discourage savings, investment, and, ultimately, economic growth. For this reason, many economists support the introduction of a broad-based consumption tax in the United States. The tax would be similar to Canada's GST, which is a form of a value-added tax (VAT). At this point, however, support for a VAT remains confined to economists—most members of Congress and the general public are not in favour of a consumption tax, despite the fact that it could raise billions of dollars in revenue.

While a tax on a specific good, such as soft drinks, may be more politically acceptable than a VAT, it does raise some important issues. For instance, is it justifiable to single out certain products for higher rates of taxation? Economists advise taxing certain consumer goods at a higher rate because of what are called "negative externalities." These occur when an economic activity—such as the consumption of certain goods—has an adverse effect on other people. Harvard economics professor Gregory Mankiw provides the example of additional taxes on gasoline, which he argues are justifiable due to the negative externalities that arise from driving. When you go for a drive, the roads become more congested and it takes longer for other drivers to get to their destinations. As well, the chance of a car accident increases, which can affect other drivers and innocent bystanders. The gasoline that you burn also contributes to global warming. A high tax on gasoline encourages consumers to internalize these negative externalities and take into account the negative effects they are having on other drivers—and to act accordingly. Studies suggest that U.S. taxes on gasoline would need to be over $2 per gallon if all negative externalities were taken into account.

Attempting to apply the economic logic behind gasoline taxes and the pricing of negative externalities to soft drinks or other consumer goods is less straight forward. Some proponents of "sin" taxes on alcohol and cigarettes argue that the consumption of these products imposes negative externalities on the rest of us, since higher smoking- and alcohol-related diseases increase health-care costs for everyone, in the form of rising insurance premiums and higher taxes (due to the need by governments for higher revenues to recover the costs). There is, however, a counterpoint to this argument—heavy drinkers and smokers frequently die earlier and, as a result, collect less in Social Security payments and old age pensions.

Professor Mankiw points to an entirely different economic rationale for justifying the taxation of soft drinks. When people buy a can of pop, they actually impose a negative externality on future versions of themselves. Someone enjoying a soft drink today may have to pay the price in terms of poorer health in the future. Taxes on soft drinks, the consumption of which has (very) short-term benefits but long-term costs, essentially make us take into account the effects on our health as we age.

Of course, this line of thinking gets into some difficult philosophical questions. Should society use the power of government to protect us from our own lack of willpower to curtail drinking pop? And once government decides to start taxing products that are deemed bad for us, where do we draw the line? Higher taxes on soft drinks may encourage us to live healthier lifestyles, but should we also then tax chocolate bars and french fries? Should people who eat lots of fruits and vegetables or play tennis regularly receive a subsidy? Taking the logic even further, should people who watch mind-numbing reality TV shows pay higher taxes, while those who improve their brain function by reading Tolstoy or economics textbooks receive a subsidy?

These are obviously difficult questions to answer. In any case, in their search for more revenues, governments today may not be concerned whether higher taxes on soft drinks meet economists' lofty theoretical considerations. The fact is, demand is highly inelastic for many consumers—people like soft drinks and will likely keep drinking them even if taxes rise sharply. Look for taxes on soft drinks and other similar goods and services to increase, a development that likely won't be confined to the United States.

Source: Excerpted from Beckman, K. (2010, July 6). Should pop drinkers pay more? The Conference Board of Canada. Retrieved from www.conferenceboard.ca/economics/hot_eco_topics/default/10-07-06/should_pop_drinkers_pay_more.aspx. Reprinted with permission.

short supply. Whatever the source, excise taxes are, essentially, selective sales taxes. Tariffs are also a form of restrictive tax, the purpose of which is detailed in Chapter 8.

The Business Owner Role: Crown Corporations

Objective 4 Identify the purpose of Crown corporations.

Crown corporation A federal or provincial-run government agency, also called a public enterprise, that is accountable to Parliament for its operations through a minister. Examples include Canada Post (federal) and the Liquor Control Board of Ontario (provincial).

What is a Crown corporation? A **Crown corporation** or public enterprise is an organization accountable to Parliament for its operations through a minister. Crown corporations may be federal (for example, Canada Post, the Canadian Broadcasting Corporation [CBC]) or provincial (for example, the Liquor Control Board of Ontario [LCBO]).

Whether federal or provincial, why are Crown corporations established? Governments establish Crown corporations for a number of reasons:

- *To implement public policy that includes protecting or safeguarding national interests:* For example, federal Crown corporations such as Air Canada and Petro-Canada helped facilitate government policy in the area of cross-Canada transportation and Canadian ownership in the domestic oil industry.

- *To protect industries deemed to be vital to the economy:* The Canadian Radio Broadcasting Commission was established by the Canadian government in 1932 to administer a national broadcasting service to prevent Canadian broadcasting becoming inundated with material originating in the United States. Similarly, this was a reason for taking control of the Canadian National Railway (CNR). The CNR originated in 1919 to "safeguard the government's large investment in the railways" and "to protect Canada's image in foreign capital markets."[22] While few municipal governments have traditionally held significant corporate holdings, they have been owners of public transit systems, recreational centres, and other facilities that are intended to enhance the quality of life in society.

- *To provide special services that could not otherwise be made available by private business:* For example, Trans-Canada Airlines (Air Canada) was established in the 1930s after observing that no private business was willing or able to provide domestic air services. Consider also the Bank of Canada. The Bank of Canada, created in 1935, was established to first serve as a control agent for the chartered banks—for example, requiring the banks to report regularly on their operations and to hold deposit reserves with the Bank of Canada. Second, the Bank of Canada is responsible for developing monetary policy and regulating monetary operations in Canada. Another example is Canada Post. Canada Post provides affordable daily delivery of mail such as bills, flyers, and birthday cards, but struggles to remain profitable (see Talking Business 9.2).

- *To nationalize industries that are considered to be "natural monopolies," including the generation and distribution of electricity:* It is not hard to imagine that in the early days of Canadian society the private sector was too small to undertake the creation of a national electricity supply grid. On the other hand, government was capable of raising the necessary capital, and consequently it took on the establishment of public utilities, including things like water supply, sewage treatment plants, and electricity-generating plants in addition to road construction and the like. In some cases, there were companies capable of building their own private utilities, which then became subject to government regulation, as we will discuss later.

---

[22] Legislative Assembly of New Brunswick, Legislative Committees. (n.d.). Looking back. Retrieved from www.gnb.ca/legis/business/committees/previous/reports-e/electricityfuture/look-e.asp.

Canada Post Faces Billion–Dollar Operating Loss by 2020

Technology is having a dramatic impact on how Canadians use postal services, and the resulting decline in mail volume is projected to push Canada Post to an annual operating loss of $1 billion by 2020.

A The Conference Board of Canada report, *The Future of Postal Service in Canada*, looks at how the needs and expectations of Canadian households and businesses are evolving, and assesses a range of options that could enable Canada's postal service to remain self-sustaining in the digital age.

"Canadians recognize that the way they use mail is changing, but haven't yet fully understood how severely that is affecting Canada Post's business model," said David Stewart-Patterson, Vice-President, Public Policy.

"E-commerce is boosting demand for parcel delivery, but households are sending fewer letters, businesses are encouraging electronic bills, governments are moving to direct deposit, and advertising is moving to the Internet. Canadians must consider what kind of postal service they really need in the years ahead."

The Conference Board study estimates that Canada Post's transaction mail, addressed and unaddressed advertising mail, and publication volumes will decline by more than 25 per cent by 2020. The Canadian experience is not unique—postal services around the world are being forced to deal with the same pressures on traditional mail volumes.

Projected Mail Volume to 2020

Parcel volume in Canada is expected to buck the downward trend and increase by 26 per cent by 2020, due in part to the growth in e-commerce. But this growth will not make up for the corresponding loss in revenue from other lines of business.

Canada Post managed a modest profit in 2012 but that will likely be temporary. While the corporation's Postal Transformation initiative will have a significant impact on its bottom line by boosting productivity and improving efficiency, the Conference Board projects an annual operating loss that will reach about $1 billion by 2020.

No single change to prices or service standards will be sufficient to enable self-sustainability as mail volumes continue to decline. Canada Post could reduce its projected losses significantly by raising prices faster than inflation, but it cannot realistically return to self-sustainability through price increases alone.

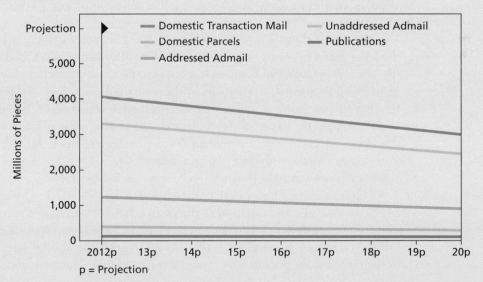

Source: Canada Post Faces Billion Dollar Operating Loss By 2020 April 23, 2013
The Conference Board of Canada

(continued)

The report examined five options for cutting costs:

- Wage restraint;
- Alternate-day delivery for mail (but not parcels);
- Converting Canadian households door-to-door delivery to community mail boxes;
- Further replacement of corporate post offices with franchised postal outlets; and
- Reduced speed of delivery.

Eliminating delivery to the door for urban residential customers would be the option with the largest financial impact, saving a projected $576 million a year. Door-to-door delivery is still the largest single category of delivery method, but two-thirds of Canadian households are now served by delivery to centralized points, group mailboxes, delivery facilities, and rural mailboxes.

Canada Post commissioned The Conference Board of Canada to conduct an independent assessment of the future of postal service in Canada, and to consider potential paths forward.

Source: Excerpted from The Conference Board of Canada. (2013, April 23). Canada Post faces billion dollar operating loss by 2020. Retrieved from www.conferenceboard.ca/press/newsrelease/13-04-23/canada_post_faces_billion_dollar_operating_loss_by_2020.aspx. Reprinted with permission.

Each Crown corporation is a legally distinct entity that is wholly owned by the Crown, and each is managed by a board of directors. The recent range of Crown corporations has been relatively diverse, with corporations operating in a variety of areas of the economy. Naturally, the corporations differ with regard to their public policy purpose, as well as their size and their relative need for government financial support.

Many observers have suggested that, traditionally, there has been a great reliance on Crown corporations in the Canadian context. For example, by the late 1980s there were 53 parent Crown corporations (at the federal level) and 114 wholly owned subsidiaries, employing about 180,000 people and maintaining assets worth approximately $60 billion.[23]

The Liquor Control Board of Ontario (LCBO) is a provincial Crown corporation in the sense that it is owned by the province of Ontario. Technically, it is also an agency of the Ministry of Consumer Services. It receives its purchasing directives from the Management Board Secretariat, and it abides by the same regulations, laws, and trade agreements that govern purchasing for all provincial government departments. For many years, the LCBO has been the largest single retailer (and the largest buyer) of alcoholic beverages in the world. By 2000 it had established five regional warehouses and was supplying 602 stores across Ontario with over 7,000 products.[24]

For examples of other Crown Corporations, see Exhibit 9.4.

The state-owned liquor outlet of the Société des Alcools du Québec receives the same type of praise and criticism as the LCBO. It has been viewed as a well-managed business with excellent customer service. On the other hand, critics also argue that private food retailers would like to be allowed to enter the alcohol sales industry more fully, given that the potential for profits is very lucrative. This sentiment also argues for

---

[23] Legislative Assembly of New Brunswick. (n.d.).

[24] Morrison, C. (n.d.). Beyond booze: Ontario liquor purchasers add entertainment to shopping cart. *Summit Article*. Retrieved from www.summitconnects.com/Articles_Columns/Summit_Articles/2000/1200/1200_Beyond_booze.htm.

Exhibit 9.4 Parent Crown Corporations Grouped by Ministerial Portfolio

Aboriginal Affairs and Northern Development

- Corporation for the Mitigation of Mackenzie Gas Project Impacts
- First Nations Statistical Institute

Agriculture and Agri-Food

- Canadian Dairy Commission
- Farm Credit Canada

Atlantic Canada Opportunities Agency

- Enterprise Cape Breton Corporation

Canadian Heritage and Official Languages

- Canada Council for the Arts
- Canadian Broadcasting Corporation
- Canadian Museum for Human Rights
- Canadian Museum of Civilization
- Canadian Museum of Immigration at Pier 21
- Canadian Museum of Nature
- National Arts Centre Corporation
- National Gallery of Canada
- Science and Technology Museum
- Telefilm Canada

Citizenship, Immigration, and Multiculturalism

- Canadian Race Relations Foundation

Finance

- Bank of Canada
- Canada Deposit Insurance Corporation
- Canada Development Investment Corporation
- Canada Pension Plan Investment Board
- Public-Private Partnerships (PPP) Canada
- Royal Canadian Mint

Fisheries and Oceans

- Fresh Water Fish Marketing Corporation

Foreign Affairs and International Trade

- Canadian Commercial Corporation
- Export Development Canada
- International Development Research Centre
- National Capital Commission

Human Resources and Skills Development

- Canada Employment Insurance Financing Board
- Canada Mortgage and Housing Corporation

Industry

- Business Development Bank of Canada
- Canadian Tourism Commission
- Standards Council of Canada

Natural Resources

- Atomic Energy of Canada Limited

Public Works and Government Services

- Canada Lands Company Limited
- Defence Construction Canada

Transport, Infrastructure, and Communities

- Atlantic Pilotage Authority
- Blue Water Bridge Canada
- Canada Post Corporation
- Canadian Air Transport Security Authority
- Federal Bridge Corporation
- Great Lakes Pilotage Authority
- Laurentian Pilotage Authority
- Marine Atlantic Inc.
- Pacific Pilotage Authority
- Ridley Terminals Inc.
- VIA Rail Canada
- Windsor-Detroit Bridge Authority

Treasury Board

- Public Sector Pension Investment Board

Source: Treasury Board of Canada Secretariat. (2013). Parent Crown corporations grouped by ministerial portfolio (as of June 30, 2013). Retrieved from www.tbs-sct.gc.ca/reports-rapports/cc-se/crown-etat/ccmp-smpm-eng.asp.

privatization—the expansion of private industry into what has traditionally been the domain of the public sector (see Talking Business 9.3).

There are other global examples of state-owned corporations that are struggling to avoid privatization as well as to compete with private businesses. For example, according

Should the LCBO Be Privatized?

© Helen Sessions/Alamy

Considering the prices that Ontarians already pay at LCBO outlets, the recent increases implemented by the provincially owned monopoly are admittedly quite small. For example, as of March 1, about 10 per cent of spirits and three to four per cent of beers saw prices go up five to 50 cents per bottle or case of beer.

For its part, the government-controlled agency says the increases were necessary to set what it calls minimum prices that must be established under its commitment to a "social responsibility mandate."

But there's scant evidence that the increases will result in anyone drinking less. Instead, most people will agree with local consumer Richard White, who recently told *The Windsor Star* the increases are "a lot more like an absolute tax grab if anything."

Certainly, the LCBO likes to boast about its earnings and ever-increasing contributions to the provincial treasury. For

example, on Dec. 23, the LCBO established a one day record for sales of $51 million at the province's 622 liquor stores. That was an increase of $3 million from the previous record of $48 million on Dec. 23, 2010, which was up from $42.5 million on the same day in 2009.

In the most recent fiscal year, the LCBO contributed $1.55 billion to provincial coffers—up $140 million, or 9.9 percent, from the previous year, on record net sales of $4.55 billion.

What's interesting, however, is that the LCBO's record earnings come on the heels of a report from Ontario auditor general Jim McCarter that concluded prices are higher than they should be at the Crown corporation.

Unlike private-sector retailers, who try to find the lowest wholesale prices, McCarter said the LCBO focuses on the price it wants to charge in its stores and then "works backwards." Then suppliers raise or lower the wholesale cost to suit the government-controlled agency.

"Sometimes if suppliers submit significantly lower quotes than the LCBO expects, the LCBO will ask them to raise their wholesale price," according to the auditor general's report.

As McCarter pointed out, this isn't the way the real business world works.

McCarter says the LCBO should be looking at negotiating the best—lowest—price possible with its suppliers. He said this "could result in higher profits for the province while still encouraging responsible consumption."

Source: Excerpted from *Windsor Star.* (2012, March 12). LCBO's monopoly: Time for a debate in the legislature. Retrieved from http://www2.canada.com/windsorstar/news/editorial/story.html?id=700e9cb5-c39b-4c05-9884-e7e178d13063. Reprinted with permission from Postmedia Network Inc.

---

to recent reports, two European post offices are making great efforts to upgrade themselves because their two basic businesses—delivering letters and delivering parcels—are both threatened by email and competition from US market leaders Federal Express and United Parcel Service. At stake is control over Europe's $27-billion fast-growing parcel service. Observers note that Europe's big postal bureaucracies have continued to lose ground and are also losing their domestic letter monopolies because of European Union deregulation.[25] We will discuss the issue of privatization and deregulation in more detail later in this chapter.

---

[25] *Businessweek.* (1999, May 30). Who'll get stomped in Europe's postal wars? Retrieved from www.businessweek.com/stories/1999-05-30/wholl-get-stomped-in-europes-postal-wars-intl-edition.

The Regulator Role

Government economic regulation has been defined as "the imposition of constraints, backed by the authority of a government, that are intended to modify economic behaviour in the private sector significantly."[26] As Exhibit 9.5 indicates, there has been a relatively wide scope for government regulation in business activity: for example, regulation focused on consumer protection, regulation aimed at environmental protection, and regulation regarding the nature of competition. One obvious set of regulations exists to protect the consumer, and the Canadian government has initiated a number of programs designed for consumer protection, many of which are administered by the Office of Consumer Affairs—a body that plays a major role in regulating business in Canada. Among the numerous regulations there is, for example, the Food and Drugs Act, which was designed to protect the public from potential health risks as well as from fraud or deception as it relates to food, drugs, cosmetics, and the like. Similarly, the Hazardous Products Act serves to protect public safety by either banning products because they are deemed dangerous or requiring warning labels on products that might be considered hazardous. Ecological regulations are designed to protect the environment, and include legislation like the Canadian Environmental Protection Act, which creates regulations to limit any dangerous byproducts of industrial production that could be harmful to individuals' health.

government economic regulation The imposition of constraints, backed by the authority of the government, to significantly modify economic behaviour in the private sector. The motive may include protection of the consumer or of the environment, or protection of fair competition among businesses.

Why does the government need to intervene in the functioning of the business enterprise system? Consider the notions of competition and the public interest, which are discussed next.

Imperfect Competition   One fundamental shortcoming in the market system—the presence of imperfect, as opposed to perfect, competition—suggests the need for government involvement. If you recall our earlier discussion of the nature of the business enterprise system, we identified it as a system that essentially determines what goods and services are produced and distributed to society and how those goods and services are produced and distributed. Ideally, such a system produces all the goods and services a society wants at a fair price. In very basic terms, on the demand side, decisions are made by individuals regarding their tastes or preferences for certain goods or services. On the supply side, businesses aim to meet the demands they face. The "invisible hand" of competition transforms these decisions of demand and supply into a system that uses scarce resources in the most efficient manner. In other words, business supply will be responsive to consumer demand. Those products and services that are needed most will demand increased production, while those no longer in demand can only be sold with a drop in price; or, ultimately, businesses that do not serve any demand would go bankrupt. If a resource becomes scarce its price will increase, and this may lead consumers to shift their preferences to a less costly alternative. In this sense, by allowing individuals and businesses to follow self-interest, the market system is responsive to consumer needs and to the capability of the environment. However, the system does not work flawlessly, and in fact there are challenges to the effective functioning of this system. One such challenge is the notion of imperfect competition.

Generally, businesses aim to reduce competition as a means of succeeding and prospering. The fewer the competitors, the more secure a business becomes. Of course, on the consumer side, the ideal scenario is **perfect competition**, where essentially there is an optimal number of

perfect competition A market system where many firms all produce an indistinguishable product or service so that no single producer has the power to affect the price of that product or service.

---

[26] Economic Council of Canada. (1979). *Responsible regulation: An interim report.* Ottawa, ON: Ministry of Supply and Services.

Exhibit 9.5 The Scope of Federal Regulation in Canada, by Sector

Major Federally Regulated Sectors	Scope
Financial, commercial, and government information; regulations affecting business operations in all sectors	• Banking • Financial transactions • Marketplace, trade, and investment • Weights and measures • Incorporation, ownership, investment, competition (e.g., telecommunications), and licensing • Life and health insurance (shared with provinces) • Bankruptcy and insolvency; patents, copyright, and trademarks • GST, HST, excise, T4, T2, payroll, record of employment • Government business surveys • Procurement, contracting (i.e., selling to government) • Temporary foreign workers
Broadcasting, telecommunications, radio frequency spectrum	• Issuing, renewing, and amending broadcasting licences • Decisions on mergers, acquisitions, and changes of ownership in broadcasting • Tariffs and certain agreements for the telecommunications industry • Competition • Licences for international telecommunications services (for incoming and outgoing calls to and from Canada) • Radio frequency spectrum allocation, utilization, and services
Transportation	• Safety, security, and environmental sustainability of air, marine, road, and rail transportation • Interprovincial transportation • Safe and accessible waterways
Environment	• Preserving and enhancing the quality of the natural environment, including water, air, soil, flora, and fauna • Protecting the environment and human health (e.g., toxic substances, species at risk) • Coordinating environmental policies and programs for the federal government • Health and productive aquatic ecosystems • Sustainable fisheries and aquaculture
Food and agriculture	• Food safety, seeds, and marketing • Public health risks associated with the food supply and transmission of animal diseases to humans • Achieving a safe and sustainable plant and animal resource base • Consumer protection and market access based on the application of science and standards • Packaging and labelling

Major Federally Regulated Sectors	Scope
Health	• Drug approvals, product safety, pesticides, and chemicals
	• Approval of the use of products, including biologic, consumer goods, foods, medical devices, natural health products, pesticides, pharmaceuticals, and toxic substances
	• Prevention and reduction of risks to individual health and the overall environment
	• Promotion of healthier lifestyles and help for Canadians to make informed health decisions
Energy and natural resources	• Nuclear energy, pipelines, mines, fisheries, and forestry
	• Responsible development and use of Canada's natural resources and the competitiveness of Canada's resource products
	• Protection of the health, safety, and security of Canadians and the environment related to nuclear energy projects
	• International and interprovincial aspects of the oil, gas, and electric utility industries

Source: Red Tape Reduction Commission. (2011). Fact sheets on federally regulated sectors and federally regulated activities. Retrieved from www.reduceredtape.gc.ca/why-pourquoi/sectors-secteurs-eng.asp.

competitors in any given industry to ensure fair pricing and distribution of the goods or services at the highest possible level of quality. In such a situation, those businesses unable to compete will be replaced by more efficient competitors. **Imperfect competition** occurs when fewer than the optimal number of competitors exist to ensure this type of situation. Where there are an insufficient number of competitors, there is less pressure on businesses to offer the best possible good or service at the lowest possible price. Businesses that are not worried about competition are also not worried about innovating, managing their operations at peak efficiency, improving product/service quality, or offering their product/service at competitive prices. Consequently, inefficient businesses will remain, and consumers will be forced to accept the products or services available at prices dictated by those businesses. Overall, then, society is offered fewer of the goods and services citizens really want. This also leads to a less efficient use of society's resources, particularly compared to perfect competition, where resources are divided among various activities in a manner that generates the optimal combination of goods and services desired by consumers. For example, industries that lack sufficient competition may choose to restrict their output as a means to maintain higher prices, as opposed to the case of perfect competition, where businesses must accept prices determined by the market.

imperfect competition A fundamental shortcoming in the market system that necessitates government involvement. It occurs when fewer than the optimal number of competitors exist to ensure fair pricing and distribution of goods and services at the highest possible level of quality.

With an understanding of the notion of imperfect competition, it is relatively easy to see that the market system itself will not guarantee the best and most efficient use of resources to generate the optimal mix of products and services for consumers at fair prices. Consequently, this is one fundamental rationale for government intervention in business.

The Public Interest   One of the central objectives of government regulation is to protect the public interest. Instead of having to establish its own public enterprise, the government can control the operations of a private enterprise through regulations. Consequently, what we see in some areas of business is government regulation of businesses through commissions, tribunals, agencies, and boards. National regulators include the Canadian Transport Commission, which judges route and rate applications for commercial air and railway companies. In terms of provincial regulatory bodies, like the provincial liquor boards, for example, provincial boards or commissions will assess and judge proposals from private businesses. Liquor boards, for example, are responsible for approving any price changes proposed by breweries within their province. The Canadian Radio-television and Telecommunications Commission (CRTC), under the auspices of the Ministry of Canadian Heritage, regulates the telecommunications industry and its carriers, such as Bell Canada, and its traditional responsibilities have included accepting or refusing requests for rate increases among these carriers.

The government has also established a competition policy to control the nature of competition in the business sector. Earlier, we identified the importance of competition in our economy, given its ability to encourage the production and distribution of goods and services at the lowest possible cost. Consequently, the competition policy set out in the Competition Act is intended to stimulate open competition and eliminate any restrictive business practices with the aim of encouraging maximum production, distribution, and employment opportunities.

We also have government regulation in the area of public utilities, such as an electric power company or a telephone company. The government has regulated these industries because there has traditionally been an absence of competition there. Consequently, the public utilities boards or commission that regulates the industry will monitor the company's performance, as well as assess requests for rate increases and changes in the types of services provided. Consider, for example, the CRTC, which regulates the Canadian broadcasting system, among other things. The CRTC is responsible for issuing broadcasting licences and can require companies seeking such a licence to conform with standards regarding the type or content of programming they will provide. The CRTC's responsibilities extend far beyond broadcasting, however, and also govern the nature of competition in the telecommunications and media industries. For example, in the telecommunications industry, there are regulations regarding the permissible amount of foreign ownership.

In 2010, the Competition Bureau advised the Canadian Real Estate Association to make changes to end its monopoly over the MLS system. The Multiple Listing Service (MLS) was the only centralized service and website that captured all Canadian properties for sale across the country that were listed through a licensed real estate agent. The range of properties included land, homes, cottages, condominiums, and business properties. In the past, the MLS system was a monopoly and unavailable to individuals who wanted to list a property for private sale (without a real estate agent). Once on the Internet, the MLS system became the tool that 90% of buyers used to purchase homes. After much pressure from the Competition Bureau, the Canadian Real Estate Association approved changes to its practices at its annual general meeting, thereby bringing the MLS monopoly to an end. Today, there is the option for an individual to hire a real estate agent to make an MLS listing without the obligation for the agent to also sell your home at an expensive commission. This opens up the market to competition from individuals (private sellers) and others, giving their properties more exposure to a wider group of buyers.

Objective 5 Explain the notion of government as guardian of the private business sector.

GOVERNMENT AS GUARDIAN OF THE PRIVATE BUSINESS SECTOR

Government Assistance to Private Business

In Canada, we have a long history of government involvement in business in the sense of promoting and protecting our industries. For example, tariff and nontariff barriers on imported goods were designed to protect our domestic businesses by making foreign goods more expensive relative to Canadian goods. In fact, we could argue that a large portion of Canada's industrial development is due to protectionism through tariffs first imposed in 1879 by Sir John A. Macdonald's National Policy. Eventually, the government also offered direct incentives for industrial and resource development. Incentive programs were established to encourage managers to conduct business in a manner desired by the government. For example, it may be desirable for managers to invest in new product development, or engage in greater export activities, or locate in an underdeveloped region. Consequently, incentives will be offered, thus influencing managers' decisions to engage in these activities.

© PhotoMan/Fotolia

For example, provincial and municipal governments can encourage new employment opportunities by offering incentives to industry for locating in their areas. The municipal government might offer property tax incentives to attract industry to its jurisdiction, and the provincial government might even offer an outright grant to attract large-scale industry. Governments at all levels have provided both direct and indirect assistance for businesses in the form of grants, loans, information, consulting advice, and bailouts (as discussed below).

The government has offered assistance to those industries deemed to be of particular importance. Industries with leading-edge technology or those providing highly skilled jobs or oriented toward exports might be among the more likely recipients of government aid. The federal and provincial governments have also provided financial incentives in an effort to dissuade companies from moving their operations outside of Canada.

Bailouts   The term **bailout** refers to government assistance given to prevent an organization or industry from financial collapse. That is, a bankrupt (or nearly bankrupt) business (for example, a bank or corporation) is given more "liquidity" to meet its financial obligations. Liquidity refers to cash flow. Typically the business may have a short-term cash flow problem but it possesses sufficient assets. Consequently, the government provides it with funds until it is in a stable financial condition again.

bailout A type of government support to business to prevent an organization or industry from financial collapse, often in the form of a loan or loan guarantee.

A government would usually enter into a bailout if the failing company is very large and whose failure would cause negative repercussions for the economy. Some critics are opposed to government bailouts based on the view that there is a reason the company has failed and therefore it should not be "artificially" sustained. In other words, when the government bails a company out, it can be viewed as overriding the "invisible hand" of the market.

Bailouts may involve a one-time financial contribution to combat significant financial troubles that a business may be experiencing. This financial assistance could take the form of a loan or loan guarantee, for example. Bailouts were relatively common in the 1980s, involving such companies as Dome Petroleum, Chrysler Canada, and Massey Ferguson. By the 1990s, while complete bailouts became rare, the government nevertheless did not refuse to offer some assistance in a bailout arrangement, as evidenced in the 1992 bailout of Algoma Steel, which involved government loan guarantees.

More recently, there have been a number of significant bailouts in Canada and the United States. In 2008, the US government bailed out financial institutions in the midst of a *mortgage crisis*. This industry is an important one for the economy since healthy credit markets are required for a smooth-operating marketplace. Banks use the credit markets to fund their activities. When the credit market is restricted, less money is available for banks to loan to individuals and businesses. This damages economic activities such as home buyers trying to obtain a mortgage. If the banking industry were to collapse, the economy would be in shambles. Consequently, many of the United States's top financial institutions were bailed out, including Citigroup, JPMorgan Chase, Bank of America, Goldman Sachs, and Merrill Lynch. The bailout plan was called the Emergency Economic Stabilization Act of 2008. In total, the US government gave that industry a $700 billion bailout package, which helped to restore liquidity to the financial markets and improve the economy. Other recent bailouts include the US and Canadian government bailout of the auto industry, which is discussed in Talking Business 9.4.

TALKING BUSINESS 9.4

Auto Bailouts: Good or Bad Idea?

For the past decade or so, Chrysler and General Motors (GM) have been experiencing increasing difficulties. Their market shares have declined because they did not produce cars that captured the interest of enough consumers. Chrysler's market share, for example, dropped from about 17% in 1998 to 8.5% in 2009, and its workforce dropped from 17,000 in 2000 to 8,200 in 2009. With the decline in market share came rapidly increasing financial problems, and in April 2009 Chrysler filed for Chapter 11 bankruptcy protection in the United States. During the six weeks Chrysler spent in bankruptcy protection, it shut down its production facilities (the manufacturing plants in Brampton and Windsor were reopened in late June 2009). Chrysler is now controlled by Fiat, a company that is more adept at producing technically advanced small cars.

GM filed for bankruptcy protection in June 2009. Its biggest problem was a $7 billion shortfall in its pension plan. There is only one active GM worker for every six retired workers (at Chrysler, there is one active worker for every two retired workers). After emerging from bankruptcy, GM planned to produce the Volt (a "green" electric car), but doesn't know when it will be profitable.

The US and Canadian governments required GM and Chrysler to come up with a restructuring plan before they would receive any bailout money. In the United States, GM reached an agreement with the United Auto Workers union on a new contract that reduced its costs, but that put pressure on the Canadian Auto Workers union to also reach a new agreement. If they didn't, GM Canada might cease to exist because the government of Canada wouldn't give GM the bailout money it needed to survive. The Canadian government said it had no choice but to get involved in a

bailout once the US government decided to give money to GM and Chrysler. The US government essentially told Canada that if its government didn't help out, GM and Chrysler would leave Canada and all those auto jobs would be lost.

Back in 2008, the federal Ministry of Industry said that the government of Canada would not provide bailouts to auto companies. But in the end, the Canadian government agreed to give GM about $10 billion (the US government gave GM about $50 billion). Both governments then took an ownership percentage of GM (the United States will own 72% of the company and Canada will own 13%). As part of the deal, debt holders traded $27 billion in debt in return for a 15% stake in GM. In return for the bailout money from the Canadian government, GM promised to maintain 16% of its North American production in Canada (that's down from 22% before bankruptcy was declared). GM Canada's workforce will be about 4,400 (it was 20,000 in 2005). The Canadian and US governments also gave bailout money to Chrysler (the United States will now own a 20% stake in Chrysler and the Canadian government will own 2%).

Opponents of the Auto Bailouts

Critics of the auto bailouts have several objections. The first and most fundamental objection is that government should not prop up businesses that are in trouble. If a company is not doing well, it should be allowed to fail. There is an old saying that goes something like this: "Governments are terrible at picking winners, but losers are great at picking governments." The government seems to have forgotten decades of hard lessons that they should not get involved in market-oriented businesses. But now they are involved in the automobile business, and the government is essentially investing money where private citizens would never be willing to put it. Writing in the *National Post*, Terence Corcoran said that ". . . along with Chrysler, GM is sliding through a government-backed reorganization and emerging as part of the same old whining, subsidy-seeking, protectionist, union-locked North American auto industry." He also noted that most of the $10 billion bailout is not going to rebuild the company, but to payoff GM's pension commitments to its workers. He says that Canadian taxpayers are paying to cover pensions of auto workers that the union "extorted" from the auto companies. He estimates that over the last 20 years, Canadian car buyers have paid $10 billion in higher auto costs to cover union workers' contracts and pension entitlements. Many Canadians don't have much of a retirement fund, and they make a lot less than auto workers do, but they are being asked to help bail out the pensions of auto workers.

Second, the GM bailout will cost Canadian taxpayers about $1.4 million for each job that is "saved." That is a very high price to pay for each job. There is also concern that GM will need more bailout money in the future, and the company is therefore a poor choice for a bailout. What's worse, bailouts won't save jobs overall. Rather, they will simply destroy jobs at companies like Toyota and Ford, who didn't get bailouts. Ford will now be saddled with more debt than GM or Chrysler, but Ford shouldn't be punished for not needing bailout money in the first place. Mark Milke, director of research at the Frontier Centre for Public Policy, says that the bailouts for GM and Chrysler are nothing more than a transfer of wealth to companies that consumers have already rejected.

Third, the bailouts in the auto industry will likely lead companies in other industries to request bailouts. For example, the forestry, fisheries, auto parts, and commercial airline industries are all having financial problems. The federal government has already announced $1 billion in aid for the pulp and paper industry so they can invest in technology that will make them more energy efficient and environmentally friendly.

Fourth, there is skepticism that the bailout money will ever be repaid. In 1987, GM's assembly plant in Quebec received $220 million in interest-free government loans. But GM pulled out of the province in 2002 and didn't repay any of the money. If the latest bailout money is not repaid, Canadians will have to bear the burden through higher taxes and/or cuts to public services. Critics are asking why the government is sinking money into two companies that have been steadily losing market share. Peter Coleman, president of the National Citizens Coalition, says that the bailout money will be useless if people don't start buying cars made by Chrysler and GM.

Supporters of the Auto Bailouts

Critics of the bailouts have been very vocal, and their ideas have received a lot of publicity, but there are also defenders of the bailouts. The most fundamental argument in support of bailouts is that they are occasionally necessary when the ups and downs in the economy (oscillations) become so severe that chaos looms. Supporters of bailouts argue that during these times government needs to intervene to reduce the oscillations. They compare the current economic gyrations to the physical gyrations that occurred when the Tacoma Narrows Bridge collapsed. High winds caused oscillations that became progressively more severe until the bridge collapsed in spectacular fashion. Supporters of bailouts argue that governments must stop the oscillations in the economic system before they cause a disaster.

The defenders of bailouts also argue that they are necessary to protect jobs. The view is that it would be disastrous to lose all of those auto worker jobs because the people who have them spend a lot of money on a wide variety of goods and services. If those expenditures stopped, the economy would suffer greatly. A study by the Centre for Spatial Economics found that the failure of any of the Big Three domestic car makers would throw Ontario into a deep recession, and 157,000 jobs would be lost (auto production workers, auto dealers, auto parts suppliers, and professional services that are tied to the auto industry). In addition, GM spent $14 billion in 2007 buying products and services from other Canadian companies, and those other companies employ thousands of additional workers. All those workers spend a lot of money and boost the economy. They also pay a lot of income tax, and the government does not want to lose that revenue.

Source: Excerpted from *Business in the News*, Pearson Canada. Retrieved from www.pearsoned.ca/highered/divisions/blogs/business_inthe_news_griffin_s/archives/00000011.html.

Subsidies   Government assistance to business in the form of subsidies has significant implications in the global business context. **Subsidies** are either cash payments, low-interest loans, or potentially reduced taxes. Specifically, subsidies in the global context are intended to assist domestic industry to compete against foreign businesses, whether in the home country or through exports. One central argument against subsidies, whether in the domestic or

subsidies Government assistance to businesses that are either in the form of cash payments, low-interest loans, or reduced taxes. In a global context, subsidies are meant to assist domestic industry to compete against foreign businesses.

global context, is that businesses should be required to manage their costs without external help, or "handouts," from the government. This is part of the requirement of fair competition, according to the critics. In addition, it is argued that consumers essentially pay for these subsidies. The government collects revenues through income and sales taxes, and it is these funds that are used to help some businesses. The question then becomes "Are subsidies to business an unfair drain on public funds?" There is no clear resolution to this ongoing debate.

From a global perspective, there is a second central criticism aimed at companies that receive subsidies from their local government. The criticism asserts that subsidies are not merely harmless forms of assistance to businesses; rather, they constitute a form of trade barrier, just like tariffs, and they create unfair competition. Take the Ontario government, for example, which gave direct subsidies of over $27 billion to corporations between 1991 and 2009.[27]

One of the highest profile disputes between Canada and the United States has been the softwood lumber dispute. The origins of the dispute can be traced back to 2001 when Canada exported softwood lumber products to the United States (worth about CDN$10 billion). The US lumber industry complained to the US government that Canadian lumber producers were competing in an unfair manner since they received a hidden subsidy from their government. In retaliation for this "unfair trade," the United States imposed countervailing duties averaging 27% on Canadian lumber imports. This had a devastating effect on the Canadian lumber industry, particularly in British Columbia, which accounts for about half of the exports. Many lumber mills had to close, thousands of workers were laid off, and profits crashed.

Why was the Canadian lumber industry accused of receiving government subsidies? This claim, and indeed the basis of this dispute, arose because of the different traditions followed by the two countries. Most US forests are privately owned, and consequently timber prices are set by private contracts or at auction. However, almost all Canadian forests belong to the provincial governments. The Canadian government grants companies long-term cutting rights in return for promises about employment numbers and sustainable forestry, while setting the cutting fees according to market conditions. The US lumber industry feels that the Canadian government has given the Canadian lumber industry an unfair advantage. As of 2006, the dispute was essentially resolved.

Why are subsidies viewed as nontariff trade barriers, and how do they amount to unfair competition? Recently, the WTO has dealt with numerous international cases of allegedly unfair subsidies. The question is, "Why should government subsidies to private industry be considered unfair?" If the government deems it necessary, why shouldn't a domestic business receive some financial assistance? The answers to these questions have been subject to much debate. In the next section, we consider the issue of subsidies in the global context.

Objective 6 Discuss government's role with regard to global business.

GOVERNMENT AS GUARDIAN OF BUSINESS IN THE GLOBAL CONTEXT

The pervasiveness of globalization has demanded that governments reconsider the extent to which they feel obligated to maintain a relationship with the private business sector. In his book *The Lexus and the Olive Tree*, Thomas Friedman asserts that globalization is, in fact, increasing the importance of government while changing the roles that it plays:

---

[27] Milke, M. (2011, December 8). Ontario's corporate welfare bill: $27.7 billion. *Fraser Alert*. Fraser Institute. Retrieved from www.fraserinstitute.org/uploadedFiles/fraser-ca/Content/research-news/research/publications/ontarios-corporate-welfare-bill-27-billion.pdf.

> The ability of an economy to withstand the inevitable ups and downs of the herd depends in large part on the quality of its legal system, financial system and economic management—all matters still under the control of governments and bureaucrats. Chile, Taiwan, Hong Kong and Singapore all survived the economic crises of the 1990s so much better than their neighbors because they had better-quality states running better-quality software and operating systems.[28]

Exhibit 9.6 Government as Guardian of Business in the Global Context

Consequently, while governments may find their role increasingly challenged and in some ways compromised by the onslaught of multinationals and globalization, the need for government involvement may actually be increased in this new, global context. The following section, which is summarized in Exhibit 9.6, offers reasons for government support of Canadian business.

Why Should Government Play the Role of Guardian of Business in the Global Context?

Nurturing Young Industries The notion that government must play a role in nurturing domestic industry was raised earlier in this chapter. The infant-industry argument asserts that government should help a young industry to grow and develop by ensuring that the industry maintains a dominant share of the domestic market until it is

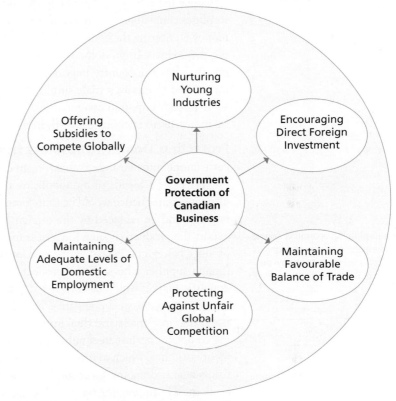

mature enough to compete against foreign companies. Consequently, this philosophy is still applied, particularly among developing countries. The rationale is that the infant industry may be less competitive, particularly because of initially high output costs; however, with maturity the production will become more efficient and protection will no longer be necessary. At least two risks have been associated with this form of government influence:

1. Such protection can discourage domestic industry from increasing competitiveness and engaging in innovation. This is an argument that has been levelled at Canadian business.

2. There is a question as to whether consumers are better or worse off from such practices. Not all Canadian parties want the Canadian steel industry to receive this type of protection from foreign rivals (see the discussion on dumping below). In fact, Canadian purchasers of any good or service arguably would want the lowest-cost supplier to be accessible and, consequently, may not appreciate the protection of an infant industry if it comes at the expense of blocking access to cheaper foreign goods or services.

---

[28] Friedman, T. (1999). *The Lexus and the olive tree*. New York, NY: Farrar Strauss Giroux.

Encouraging Foreign Direct Investment   The action of reducing foreign imports may result in the foreign business directly investing in the target country instead. That is, a foreign company can decide to set up business in the target country if it wishes to gain access to that country's consumer market and it is unable to achieve that with imports. Of course, from the domestic country's viewpoint, this **foreign direct investment** may be desirable if it increases job opportunities, contributes to the growth of industry, and adds to the amount of capital.

foreign direct investment
The purchase of physical assets or an amount of share ownership in a company from another country to gain a measure of management control.

Maintaining a Favourable Balance of Trade   The government may seek to influence the relative status of exports and imports to avoid running a trade deficit. Trade surpluses come about when a country's exports exceed its imports and, consequently, more money is entering the country (from foreign consumers buying these exports) than is leaving the country (from domestic consumers buying foreign imports). A trade deficit is the reverse—when a country imports more than it exports. Traditionally, governments have intervened to ensure a trade surplus by imposing tariffs or quotas or by banning outright some foreign-imported commodities. Typically, governments would also subsidize domestic industries to encourage growth in their exports.

Protecting Domestic Business from Unfair Competition   There is a concern among some businesses that foreign competitors will offer their products at extremely low prices as a means of monopolizing their share of the target country's market. The ultimate consequence would be that domestic producers could potentially be driven out of business and be replaced by the foreign imports. A foreign competitor who manages to export the products at such low prices may be accused of **dumping**—which is pricing the product below cost or below the cost of the target country's product. In other words, a foreign supplier who sells the product at a loss or for less than the price of the seller's domestic market would be considered guilty of dumping.

dumping An accusation against an exporting country of pricing its product below cost or below the cost of the target country's product.

Traditionally, steel companies have been among the most avid users of anti-dumping legislation in Canada and the United States. Hamilton-based Dofasco Inc. lodged a dumping complaint against steel mills in Asia and South America. The aim was to seek government assistance, which in this case resulted in a decision by the Canadian federal government to place anti-dumping tariffs on low-cost imported steel from these foreign suppliers. In total, these anti-dumping tariffs were aimed at blocking the dumping of steel shipments from nine countries. This echoes similar action taken in the United States. Steel producers in both the United States and Canada have blamed the increasing foreign imports of steel for reducing demand for their product domestically and, consequently, reducing product prices and revenue. It is interesting to note that while Canadian steel producers welcome such government intervention, other domestic players are not happy with the implementation of anti-dumping tariffs, which effectively raise the price of these cheaper goods.

Specifically, Western Canadian manufacturers have claimed that the protectionist measures reduce their ability to compete with Ontario steel manufacturers. Many Western steel businesses argued that they will lose access to these cheaper foreign sources and will now be forced to rely on costlier steel sources in Ontario. These businesses argue that they should have access to the lowest-cost sources of steel, whether these sources are from Canada or from foreign producers. In this regard, they are opposed to the government's protectionist policy of imposing anti-dumping tariffs.

Similarly, the Canadian government has protected the dairy industry to protect farmers from foreign competition. However, this may change soon, as seen in Talking Business 9.5.

More Cheese, Please

Africa Studio/Shutterstock

The European Union Trade Commissioner is in Ottawa today to hopefully complete Canada's most significant free trade deal since the Canada–U.S. agreement in the late 1980s.

Negotiators are now getting into the toughest issues, one of which is cheese. Canada applies 200–300 percent tariffs on dairy products and holding an "import quota" is currently the only way to legally import dairy products into Canada duty-free. The EU wants, at a minimum, to increase the amount of cheese it can export to Canada duty-free. Early indications in today's *Globe and Mail* suggest that the Canadian government is prepared to admit more European cheese into this country in return for greater access to EU markets for Canada's beef and pork.

Why wouldn't Canadians welcome more, say, French cheese? Many consumers no doubt would, but cheaper European cheese imports undercut farmer milk prices. So Ottawa has prohibitively high tariffs to keep imports out (see Chart). If Canada allows in more EU cheese imports, it will be hard to sustain farmer milk prices without having to limit production more and more each year. (For those that want to understand how the system works in more detail, see the 2009 Conference Board study *Making Milk*).

Tariffs for Selected Canadian Dairy Products

This trend could erode Canada's long-standing system of dairy supply-management over time, especially if it sets a precedent for other trade negotiations, such as the Transpacific Partnership trade talks which Canada recently joined.

Participants in those talks, such as Australia and the US, have long been pushing for more access to Canada's dairy market.

Opening doors to EU cheese would pose complications. For one, the EU subsidizes its dairy farmers. However, EU subsidies have been cut back, and Canada's dairy farmers also benefit from protection. For another thing, if Canada offers the EU a greater share of imports, it would risk irritating partners in its other trade negotiations such as the TPP.

So, should Canada's policymakers continue to support this policy or should they welcome greater openness, starting with the EU?

All political parties in Canada have traditionally supported supply management (though Liberal leadership candidate Martha Hall Findley has proposed getting rid of it). Recently, Quebec Premier Pauline Marois reiterated how vital supply management was for Quebec in the context of the Canada–EU talks.

To be clear, the policy has largely succeeded at its initial goal: boosting traditionally-low farmer incomes. But a 2012 Conference Board study, *Canada's Supply-Managed Dairy Policy: How Do We Compare?* shows that Canada is the only country among its peers that both maintains dairy supply management policies and has stagnating dairy production. Farmers are unprepared for even a partial opening of Canada's dairy market, and are unable to seize opportunities in fast-growing markets.

Much more than the dairy industry's well-being is at stake. Buyers of dairy products—processors, restaurants, retailers, and consumers—effectively subsidize dairy producers by paying higher prices. The Organisation for Economic Co-operation and Development estimates the subsidy at $175,000 per dairy farm. The poorest in our society—for which dairy products form a larger share of their budget—are the hardest hit.

The existing system has broader effects. Food processors that use higher-priced dairy products have found that they are unable to compete in export markets. And Canadian cheese processors pay at least two times more for their milk compared to those who make other dairy products. The costs are then passed on to restaurateurs and consumers.

Sometimes the incentives created by the system stretch believability. Last year, three men were arrested as part of

(continued)

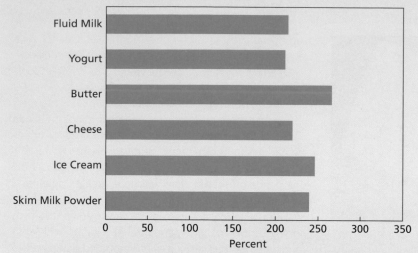

Note: Tariffs are applied to quantities that exceed the import quota.
Import quota is equal to less than 5 percent of Canadian dairy consumption.

a massive cheese-smuggling ring—they allegedly smuggled cheaper U.S. cheese across the border and sold it to Canadian restaurants at a six-figure profit. If this sounds like the plot of a crime drama, it actually is—cross-border cheese-smuggling formed the backdrop for last week's episode of *CSI: NY*.

The EU deal is an opportunity for Canada to embark on reform of a policy that meets neither the interests of the broader public, nor, arguably, even the interests of the dairy sector.

Lowering dairy tariffs, or raising our import quota for dairy from all countries, could allow the industry to gradually adapt to increased competition. At the same time, doors would be opened for Canadian businesses to sell in and from the EU, and to have freer access to the best EU technologies, goods, and services.

Canada should take this opportunity to say "more cheese please."

Source: Excerpted from Goldfarb, D. (2013, February 6). More cheese please. The Conference Board of Canada. Retrieved from www. conferenceboard.ca/economics/hot_eco_topics/default/13-02-06/ more_cheese_please.aspx. Reprinted with permission.

In some cases, the Canadian government is more open to foreign competition. Take Canadian tourism, for instance. The Niagara Parks Commission recently awarded a boat-tour lease to an American company to promote Canadian culture and tourism.

Maintaining Adequate Levels of Domestic Employment   A government knows that society holds it responsible for ensuring that unemployment rates are not high. Imports that come to dominate an industry bring the threat of causing domestic industries to go bankrupt. Consequently, where businesses claim they are under threat of bankruptcy because of foreign competition, the government is forced to consider what action it can take to combat this threat. In the past, the government protected Canadian business and employment from the risk of foreign competition via the implementation of tariffs, as discussed in the previous chapter. Clearly, such an option is complicated by the fact that reducing imports is not necessarily feasible, for reasons described earlier. Protectionist policies are not compatible with the sentiments of free trade, and thus governments are sometimes placed in the unenviable position of balancing the needs of the domestic economy with the need to honour the rules governing global business. A case in point is the issue of government subsidies.

Offering Subsidies to Compete Globally   Whether it is for the purpose of maintaining employment levels or of assisting businesses in the global marketplace, the issue of government subsidies to business has become much more controversial in the context of globalization. Whether it is cash payments, low-interest loans, or tax breaks, such financial assistance is referred to as a subsidy. And in the case of the global context, such subsidies are intended to help domestic industry deal with global competition. In recent years, the World Trade Organization (WTO) has been involved in many international disputes regarding whether a local government has given its domestic industry an unfair advantage through some form of subsidy. The risks of such subsidies, in addition to the potential conflicts they create with regard to facilitating free trade, include the notion that competitive industries should be able to absorb such costs themselves rather than relying on government handouts. Nonetheless, in many countries, governments continue to subsidize certain industries. If Canada does not subsidize the same industry, its domestic industry will be at a disadvantage.

Why Government Should *Not* Play the Role of Guardian of Business

Just as there are arguments for a government stepping in and playing the role of guardian to domestic businesses, there are counterarguments for when it should not, which are summarized in Exhibit 9.7.

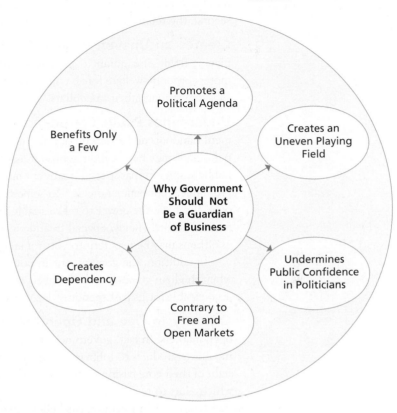

Exhibit 9.7 Government *Not* as Guardian of Business in the Global Context

Promotes a Political Agenda

Government assistance, or **corporate welfare**, often promotes a political agenda instead of a profitable one. What industries should receive government money is a matter of debate and is influenced by political party objectives. Job creation, for example, is one way the government tries to justify handouts and to win citizen votes.[29]

Yet without a focus on profitability, jobs that are created may not be sustained. Subsequently, government can end up wasting its investment on failing companies and industries. Politicians are not investment analysts and cannot easily pick "winners" from "losers." Market decisions should be made by investment specialists who can properly value companies, assess risk, and offer a reasonable rate of return. The Canadian Taxpayers Federation contends

> Corporate welfare decisions are most often made by individuals with little experience in private investing; moreover, decisions are often made in a politically charged environment. As a result, ensuring that taxpayer-financed projects meet geographical, industrial equity, and politically saleable criteria become an end in itself.[30]

corporate welfare A term used to refer to government assistance given to businesses.

---

[29] Williamson, J. (2005, March 13). A corporate welfare primer. The Canadian Taxpayers Association. Retrieved from www.taxpayer.com/commentaries/a-corporate-welfare-primer.

[30] Williamson, 2005.

In certain cases, government assistance can be in the form of a loan. If a company cannot pay its liability back to taxpayers, there is usually no downside to the business: The government bears all risk. Governments are also reluctant to collect business loans for two reasons: First, legal action to enforce loan terms may cause the downfall of a business, and second, the related bad publicity may hurt a political party's chance for reelection.

Creates an Uneven Playing Field   Corporate welfare also creates an uneven playing field—it is unfair to competitor firms who are profitable and successful. Furthermore, corporate welfare forces competitor firms and their employees to pay for competitor subsidies through their tax dollars.[31]

Undermines Public Confidence in Politicians   Why some firms get government handouts and others do not may undermine public confidence in politicians. While politicians may have valid reasons for assisting certain companies and industries, there is public suspicion that special treatment may be due to political connectedness rather than profitable, economic choices.[32] In some cases, it is large corporations that receive handouts who have the power to make sizable political donations, rather than small entrepreneurs with little funds. Special treatment may undermine the democratic process as well, as citizens may be reluctant to vote for any politicians they do not trust.

In addition, the government in power who provided the loan may not be in power when the loan comes due. It then becomes difficult for taxpayers to hold the government accountable for its past spending decisions and political actions.

Contrary to Free and Open Markets   Corporate welfare goes against free and open markets. In fact, government handouts can change a business' priorities from focusing on its products to lobbying for government funds. Subsequently, companies may lose sight of their core business activities.[33] Government assistance may also violate free trade, which aims to remove trade barriers and encourage free markets with little government interference. Many economists believe that when markets are determined by supply and demand, efficient firms will prevail and inefficient ones will fold.

Creates Dependency   Corporate welfare can also encourage companies to become dependent instead of being self-sufficient, thus creating a culture of dependency whereby government handouts are incorporated into budgets as "available funds" instead of as a liability necessary to restructure the company, remove inefficiencies, and create a sustainable business. Corporations may come to expect future free money while remaining ineffective, causing a circular problem that can never be resolved. Moreover, ongoing assistance can lead to higher taxes for everyone, which slows economic growth rather than increasing it.[34]

Benefits Only a Few   Corporate welfare benefits only a few businesses and employees—and arguably, they may not be the most deserving ones. Corporate welfare should not be a public service. Tax dollars should be spent on community services, projects, and social programs that provide the greatest benefit to all taxpayers, such as education, health care, and national defence.[35]

[31] Williamson, 2005.

[32] Williamson, 2005.

[33] Williamson, 2005.

[34] Williamson, 2005.

[35] Williamson, 2005.

SHOULD GOVERNMENT "MIND ITS OWN BUSINESS?"

Objective 7 Describe the objectives and consequences of deregulation and privatization.

Government intervention in the economy has traditionally been greater in Canada than in the United States. For example, government expenditures as a percentage of GDP are typically higher in Canada than in the United States, and public-sector employment in Canada has been as much as 30% greater than the United States. However, Canada has been following the trend of reducing government's involvement in the business sector. Why are we witnessing this reduction in government involvement, and what are the implications of this trend? These questions are addressed in the sections below.

Deregulation

Earlier, we discussed the issue of government regulation. Government regulates the operation of businesses through commissions, tribunals, agencies, and boards. Whatever the form, the government directly regulates about one-third of the economy through more than 600 organizations. However, what we have witnessed since the 1980s is a trend toward deregulation. **Deregulation**, as the name suggests, involves a reduction in the number of laws or regulations affecting business activity. It also suggests a reduction of the powers of government enforcement agencies and other forms of government control or influence.

deregulation A reduction in the number of laws or regulations affecting business activity.

In recent years, the process of deregulation in the Canadian economy seems to have accelerated, particularly in industry sectors such as transportation, telecommunications, financial services, and energy. While the telecommunications sector maintains varying degrees of regulation in different areas, it has seen an increased level of competition through deregulation in areas such as overseas calling, domestic long distance, local telephone service, wireless service, and other services. The Canadian electricity sector has also seen deregulation occurring, particularly in Alberta and Ontario.

We have witnessed economic deregulation among many industries in a number of countries, including airlines, trucking, railroads, financial markets, energy, and telecommunications. At the same time, there has been an increase in regulations that are intended to govern such areas as health and safety and the environment. In order to understand the implications of economic deregulation, it is useful to briefly reconsider why, in fact, there is a need to regulate any industry at all.

Regulation is aimed at correcting market failures and inequities that may arise for a variety of reasons, including the case where insufficient competition exists in an industry. However, just as the market can fail, so can the government policy of deregulation to achieve the goals for which it was intended. While it may be an oversimplification, the significant consequences of deregulation fall into two categories: potential benefit and potential risk.

- The benefit of deregulation for consumers is increased competition arising from the reduction of regulations that have formerly restricted the entry of new competitors.

- The risk of deregulation is consumer exploitation—that is, a reduction in quality of the products or services being offered, increases in consumer fees, or price increases as a result of the reduction in laws governing the industry's operation.

The question is, will deregulation accomplish the central objective of sufficiently loosening constraints to encourage the entry of more competitors? Or will deregulation fail to encourage adequate competition, and will this loosening of constraints instead permit current competitors to abuse the system and exploit consumers in some way?

Research evidence from US-based studies has offered strong support for the benefits of deregulation among a variety of sectors, including railways, trucking, airlines, telecommunications, and financial industries. Comparisons have been made of the US and Canadian railway industries between 1956 and 1974, when the US railway industry was more heavily regulated than the Canadian. While both industries had access to the same technology, productivity growth was much greater in Canada (3.3%) than in the United States (0.5%).[36] Studies have indicated that unit costs in the US trucking industry decreased significantly in the period following deregulation in 1983. Similarly, the airline industry managed to reduce costs by 25% in the period following deregulation.

The US telecommunications industry has also benefited from deregulation, according to recent studies. For example, by 1996 long-distance telephone rates in the United States had dropped by over 70%. A number of studies have also suggested that deregulation encouraged much more innovation, as reflected in the emergence of such profitable services as cellular telephony and voice messaging. It is interesting to note that the concept of cellular phones was discussed as early as the 1950s, and the technology had become available by the early 1970s, yet the Federal Communications Commission did not issue licences until 1983—an illustration of the inhibiting effect of regulations on innovation.

Deregulation in the financial industries, including securities, investment, and banking sectors, has also yielded some positive support from US-based studies with regard to its consequences. For example, it has been estimated that partial deregulation of the banking and savings and loan industry contributed to a 300% increase in productivity, while deregulated brokerage fees resulted in a 25% decrease in rates.[37]

Comparative studies have supported the benefits of deregulation. For example, by 1999, in industries like the airline industry, the United States was clearly maintaining a significantly higher level of deregulation than many European countries. Advocates of deregulation have asserted that the benefits of deregulation were reflected in the fact that European airline fares were about twice as costly as US airfares, while European companies were neither as efficient nor as profitable as the US carriers. Consequently, supporters of deregulation claim that eliminating price and entry restrictions would increase competition and, ultimately, benefit consumers through lower airfares and better service. Comparisons of the relative differences in levels of regulation between Europe and the United States by the late 1990s drew similar conclusions. It was estimated that many European companies were paying about 50% more for their electricity than their US counterparts. For example, the high level of regulation in Germany's electricity market, including the requirement to purchase electricity from regional producers rather than less expensive alternative sources, was viewed as inhibiting efficiency and productivity. In contrast, the UK greatly benefited from energy deregulation with regard to productivity gains, estimated at 70% subsequent to deregulation.

While the findings above certainly point to the potential benefits of deregulation, there is no doubt that support for deregulation is far from universal. While advocates claim that the

---

[36] Caves, D.W., Christensen, L.R., & Swanson, J.A. (1981). Economic performance in regulated and unregulated environments: A comparison of U.S. and Canadian Railroads. *Quarterly Journal of Economics*, 96(4), 559–581.

[37] Pociask, S.B., Fuhr, J.P., & Darby, L.F. (2007, March 20). Insurance regulation: Market or government failure? The American Consumer Institute Center for Citizen Research. Retrieved from www.theamericanconsumer. org/2007/03/20/insurance-regulation-market-or-government-failure.

beneficial impact on consumers and businesses outweighs any costs, opponents suggest the reverse—that the risks of deregulation are too high to enter into this venture. There is likely no area more mixed with regard to the reaction to deregulation than in its impact on developing countries. Nonetheless, there is, again, evidence that is supportive of the policy of deregulation. For example, deregulation in the telecommunications industry among some Latin American countries has greatly encouraged private-sector involvement and led to increased efficiency in services. By the late 1990s, telephone user rates were reduced by about 50% following the deregulation of entry requirements in the long-distance telephone market in Chile. At the same time, studies have pointed out the negative consequences of maintaining regulation in various sectors within developing countries. For example, in the late 1990s Brazil and Argentina's transportation regulations forced businesses to ship largely by road, even though the costs were significantly higher than rail charges.[38]

Example #1: Deregulation in the Transportation Industry   As mentioned earlier, the main objective of government regulation is to protect the public interest. The railroad industry was among the very first to have regulations applied, with a deal made in 1895 between Prime Minister Wilfrid Laurier and the CPR. Essentially, the government promised the CPR the financing it needed to complete a transcontinental line if the CPR would carry wheat produced by western farmers on a regular basis at a negotiated rate. Many years later, the National Transportation Act created the Canadian Transport Commission (in 1970), whose job it was to regulate and control the various means of transportation in Canada, including motor, air, water, and railways, among other things. However, on January 1, 1988, the new Canada Transportation Act came into effect and brought with it a new era of deregulation. What did this new legislation contain, and how did it bring about deregulation in the transportation industry? Well, just consider its impact on the trucking industry.

This act brought with it the passage of the new Motor Vehicle Transport Act. Prior to that time, anyone wanting to enter the trucking business was required to appear before the provincial licensing board and prove there was a public need for their service to get a licence to operate a truck. However, under the new act prospective truckers must simply present proof that they are insurable and can pass some minimal safety criteria. So what is the result of all this? One of the major benefits of the reduction in requirements for new entrants was increased competition: More truckers entered the industry. Shippers gained from a wider choice of trucking services and more competitive rates. Following the passage of this act, shippers could negotiate the level of service and price of any domestic movement with any carrier. Consequently, consumers benefited in terms of reduced costs arising from increased competition in highway carriers. In fact, a central aim of this deregulation was to encourage greater efficiency in Canada's $2 billion transportation market. In a more recent report on the trucking industry in Canada, the following observation was made:

> What has emerged is a new breed of Canadian trucker—one that is more efficient, value-priced, eager to customize to shippers' needs and adept at filling specialized niches in a North American market dominated by huge and efficient American carriers.[39]

---

[38] Guasch, J.L., & Hahn, R.W. (1999). The cost and benefits of regulation: Implications for developing countries. *The World Bank Research Observer, 14*(1), 137–158.

[39] Wasny, G. (1997). A new road for Canadian truckers. *World Trade, 10*(2), 50.

In the related railway shipping industry, recent reports have indicated that shipper rates dropped by 35% since deregulation and were considered the lowest in the world—60% below the international average.[40]

However, there has been a downside for some. With increased competition, some trucking companies have been unable to compete effectively and have gone bankrupt, resulting in the loss of hundreds of jobs. In fact, in 1990 about 130 trucking companies declared bankruptcy—over twice as many as those in the previous year. A major threat has come from US trucking companies, which have lower labour, equipment, and tax costs and, consequently, lower operating costs.

So there are winners and losers in the trend toward deregulation, and the issue of competition lies at the heart of this. Reducing regulations welcomes more entrants and creates more pressure on existing Canadian companies. During the years following deregulation, the Canadian carriers admitted that they were slow to adapt to new technologies such as electronic data interchange, bar coding, and satellite tracking of trailers. For example, by 1997 almost all US truckload tractors were equipped for satellite tracking, while only 50% of Canadian tractors were equipped.[41]

Example #2: Deregulation in the Electricity Industry
The past 10 years or so have seen a great interest in deregulation in the energy sector—specifically in energy supply, with Britain and Scandinavia largely initiating this practice in the early 1990s. Traditionally, electricity costs have been higher in Europe than in North America. After a number of European governments privatized their public utilities, the cost of electricity dropped in those regions. Deregulation also welcomed much more competition, which forced the power companies to become more efficient and improve customer service.

The Canadian government, seemingly drawing on the European experience, decided to initiate privatization and deregulation in the energy sector in Canada, beginning with Alberta in 1995. Unfortunately, the reaction to this transition has been mixed, with some observers criticizing the deregulation process in Alberta's electricity industry and others adding that the purchase of electricity has become more complicated with the advent of deregulation.

Ontario has followed Alberta's lead in electricity deregulation, although it has proceeded somewhat more slowly and, according to some, more cautiously. While advocates of deregulation feel that the benefits of increased competition will ultimately prevail, those opposed to deregulation believe that public ownership should continue to exist for essential services to ensure that all members of society will be guaranteed access to the same service at a reasonable price. As once critic of electricity deregulation argued

> Prior to restructuring and deregulation, the goal of utilities was reliable service at minimum long-term cost. In contrast, the goal of newly restructured organizations in a deregulated environment is short-term profit with little concern for the overall system.[42]

The dangers of deregulation are further addressed in Talking Business 9.6.

---

[40] *Railway Age*. (2001). Deregulations' real winner: The consumer. *Railway Age, 202*(1), 20.

[41] Wasny, 1997.

[42] Campbell, T., Casazza, J., Griffin-Cohen, M., Wilson, J., & Wood, C. (2005, March 1). Another blackout looming: Government inaction could leave millions in the dark again soon. *The Monitor*. Retrieved from www.policyalternatives.ca/publications/monitor/march-2005-another-blackout-looming.

The Dangers of Deregulation

Critics of deregulation argue that removing government control in industries is simply too dangerous given that there is no guarantee that sufficient competition will arise in order to keep businesses from taking advantage of looser restrictions. These critics point to a number of questionable efforts to deregulate, including deregulation in Alberta's electricity sector, and deregulation in Canada's telecommunications and railway industries.

In 1996, Alberta removed government from the power generation business. Rather than a crown corporation running things, the Alberta government deregulated the electricity market in order to welcome a flood of private businesses whose competitive instincts would result in lower power prices. Things didn't go according to plan though. Alberta did not experience a price drop and an improvement in service. The only tangible benefit has been to shift the responsibility and costs of building and managing power plants to the private sector. In that regard, Albertans did benefit from deregulation since the province doesn't have to incur debt to build power plants, while other provinces (that have maintained publicly-owned utilities) have amassed billions in debt. However beyond that benefit, the results were mixed at best, and at worst it has been called a disaster. In addition to high energy rates, the concern is that the private sector cannot sufficiently accommodate the growing electricity needs of Alberta. According to one report, ". . . the market is ill-equipped to foresee and address the unprecedented growth in Alberta's population, industry and overall power demand . . . There are also fears that deregulation could allow power companies to bend the rules."[43] So much for the power of deregulation.

In 2006 Canada deregulated its telecommunications industry with the expectation that it would bring competition, better service, and lower prices. Specifically, this era of deregulation in telecommunications was initiated by a policy decision in December 2006 by the Industry Minister, who ordered the Canadian Radio-television and Telecommunications Commission (CRTC) to rely as much as possible on "market forces" and ensure that regulation was minimally intrusive to business. The results? Not good. Arguably, Canadian consumers are still paying too much for broadband service and getting too little, according to a report from the Public Interest Advocacy Centre, a nonprofit consumer protection organization.[44] In fact, the report asserted that deregulation brought excessive profits for Bell, Telus, and Rogers—Canada's largest telecom companies. In fact, these three companies control 90% of the market so it's hard to argue that deregulation brought more competition and a better world for consumers! While other wireless services were launched in Canada following deregulation, including Wind, Mobilicity, and Public Mobile, none captured any substantial share of the market.

Finally, critics have argued that deregulation was an indirect cause of the horrific disaster in Lac-Mégantic, Quebec, in 2013, where the derailment and subsequent explosion of oil-filled tanker cars destroyed much of the town's central core and killed more than 50 people. How could this be connected to deregulation? Deregulation in the railroad industry occurred beginning in the 1990's. One of the consequences has been a shift to greater self-regulation by the railway companies, who largely carry out their own inspections of processes, equipment, and infrastructure. Critics argue that this has opened the doors to "cutting corners" in safety in order to minimize costs. With less government oversight, companies may be inclined to be less vigilant in such areas as replacing old equipment since this also means more expenses for the company. In addition, when companies focus purely on

(continued)

---

[43] Wingrove, Josh. (2012, March 22). Billions in new power lines and hundreds in monthly bills—the price of a boom for Alberta's power grid. The Globe and Mail. Retrieved from http://www.theglobeandmail.com/news/politics/billions-in-new-power-lines-and-hundreds-in-monthly-bills—the-price-of-a-boom-for-albertas-power-grid/article535421.

[44] Public Interest Advocacy Centre Report by Michael Janigan, 2010; http://www.piac.ca/index.html.

profits, it can create pressures to minimize costs, which often means cutting staff and work schedules. A case in point—the runaway train at Lac-Mégantic was overseen by only a single engineer responsible for 72 cars and five locomotives.

Source: Lampert, Allison. (2013, August 29). Lac-Mégantic: Lack of train staffing, oversight called into question. The Gazette. Retrieved from http://www.montrealgazette.com/news/M%C3%A9gantic+Lack+train+staffing+oversight+called+into+question/8637943/story.html.

CBC News. (2010, Dec. 30). Phone deregulation fails consumers: report. Retrieved from http://www.cbc.ca/news/phone-deregulation-failsconsumers-report-1.967542.

Privatization

privatization Divesting of government involvement in the operation, management, or ownership of business activities, involving transfer of activities or functions from the government to the private sector.

What does privatization mean? In broad terms, **privatization** refers to the divesting of government involvement in the operation, management, and ownership of activities. Typically, privatization involves the transfer of activities or functions from the government to the private sector. Privatization might involve selling off a Crown corporation to the private sector. For example, Air Canada, formerly a Crown corporation, was sold to the private sector in 1988–1989. Also in 1988, the government sold Teleglobe Canada Inc., a handler of overseas satellite calls for the telephone and telecommunications companies, to private business.

Privatization might also involve contracting government jobs to private companies. For example, in some provinces private businesses contracted to manage hospitals and other health care institutions previously managed by government employees. Other services that can be contracted out include garbage collection and road construction. In addition, public institutions have also contracted out services such as data processing and food and janitorial services to private-sector corporations. The closing of some postal stations and the franchising of postal services in retail businesses is yet another example.

In recent years there has been a significant transformation of the organizational landscape across the world, as numerous state-owned monopolies, agencies, and other public organizations have been privatized. Government ownership in areas from airlines to electricity has been sold to either domestic or foreign investors. In fact, over 15,000 enterprises were privatized during the period from 1980 to 1992. By 1997, worldwide privatization proceeds had reached $153 billion.[45]

Privatization has been implemented not only in advanced countries, such as the United States, Canada, the UK, Australia, France, Germany, and Japan, but also in transitional countries such as Poland, Chile, Brazil, Mexico, and Argentina. In addition, developing countries have been implementing privatization—including Nigeria, Tunisia, and Zimbabwe. It is expected that privatization will continue to progress around the world and in most economic sectors over the coming decade.

---

[45] Zahra, S.A., & Hansen, C.D. (2000). Privatization, entrepreneurship, and global competitiveness in the 21st century. *Competition Review, 10*(1), 83–103.

Global privatization accelerated in the 1990s, particularly in Western Europe, with developing countries accounting for about one third of the annual funds raised by privatization. In the economies of Eastern Europe, the transition to private ownership has reflected a particularly significant political transition:

> The development of a large-scale privatization program is also a highly political act. Almost by definition, privatization represents an ideological and symbolic break with a history of state control over a country's productive assets. Nowhere is this symbolism more apparent than in the economies of Eastern Europe and the former Soviet Union, where privatization of state-owned enterprises has come to signal a nation's transition from communism to democratic capitalism. In Russia, the privatization of enormous petroleum (Ltlkoil), natural gas (Gazprom) and telecommunications (Syazinevest) companies represented a fundamental break from socialist state ownership.[46]

Why Do Governments Privatize?   Why have we observed the increased divestiture of government in business activities, including the sale of Crown corporations? What are the reasons for reducing the level of government ownership in business enterprises? Let's consider some of the popular arguments for privatization. See Exhibit 9.8 for a list of some of the Crown corporations in Canada that have been privatized.

Belief in the Power of Competition as a Control Mechanism   Privatization is considered to be an expected outgrowth of the free enterprise system. That is, private enterprise should be allowed to expand into areas that were once monopolized by the government. Moreover, privatization programs are typically guided by the view that the force of market competition is best suited to fostering efficiency and innovation in an industry. This has been a key argument for privatizing the Canadian Broadcasting Corporation (CBC), as costs continue to rise for this federally funded organization.

Specifically, the view is that privatization of a state-owned monopoly will open an industry to competition and, consequently, encourage innovation, growth, and efficiency. Moreover, where privatization opens an industry to foreign competition, this permits consumers to have access to goods or services developed in other parts of the world and will stimulate innovation among domestic firms operating in the industry. In addition, opening an industry to foreign investors may provide access to needed financial and technological resources and create growth in the industry.

Belief that Private Business Can Operate More Efficiently   A second view is that transferring the management of organizations to the private sector will result in increased productivity. Studies conducted in a variety of countries have found evidence that the private production of goods and services is typically more efficient than public production. Why should this be considered true? Well, think back to our discussion of why Crown corporations were established: not for profit, but for a social policy consideration—that is, serving public

Exhibit 9.8 Crown Corporations That Are Now Privatized

Atomic Energy of Canada Limited (commercial division)—2011
Highway 407 (Ontario)—1999
Canadian National Railway—1995
Alberta Liquor Control Board—1993
Nova Scotia Power—1992
Petro-Canada—1991
Potash Corp. (Saskatchewan)—1989
Air Canada—1988
De Havilland Aircraft Co.—1986
Canadair—1986

Source: Stastna, K. (2012, April 1). What are Crown corporations and why do they exist? *CBC News.* Retrieved from http://openmedia.ca/upgradecanada/background. Reprinted by permission of CBC.

---

[46] Megginson, W. (2000). Privatization. *Foreign Policy, 118,* 14.

interests. Consequently, many observers feel that it is difficult for government-owned enterprises to reconcile the social goals of the enterprise with the economic-efficiency goals that must be of concern to any business. Moreover, efficient operation may be difficult given that there are political interests to be considered. Removing the political element of an enterprise allows it to focus on efficiency and avoid potential conflicts of interest.

The Ontario government announced that its main goal for privatization was to improve economic efficiency of the underlying organization, as reflected in reduced prices and improved customer service.

No Longer Need Public Involvement in Some Sectors   Air Canada was established as a Crown corporation at a time when no private company had the resources to develop a transnational airline. Today, there are both domestic and international airlines that are more than capable of conducting such business and, consequently, there is little need for government ownership in the airline industry. Where the enterprise is no longer required by the government to achieve its initial public policy goals, ownership can be handed over to the private sector. If private industry is willing to offer the same product or service in a reliable and cost-effective manner, why not allow it to do so? As we discussed, in Canada's earlier days the creation of Crown corporations was deemed necessary by the "natural monopoly argument" in industries such as public utilities or communications, given that low unit costs of production could be attained only if output was sufficiently high. Consequently, a large government monopoly or a regulated, privately owned monopoly was acceptable, and perhaps even necessary. This argument has weakened in more recent times, when globalization has introduced large worldwide competitors who may be bigger and more efficient than federal or provincial Crown corporations.

Financial Benefits from Selling Government-Owned Assets   Another reason for selling off government-owned enterprises is that the money can be used on other, more needed, areas. Certainly money received from sales of Crown corporations or partial disposition of Crown-owned assets has been applied to government deficit reductions. In addition, opening an industry to private investors may attract an influx of foreign capital.

Maintaining a Crown corporation can be an increasingly costly venture, particularly when high subsidies are made to inefficient state-owned enterprises. Privatization can remove this unnecessary financial burden from the government and taxpayers. For example, in the UK, over US$16.8 billion was raised between 1990 and 1995 through the privatization of two power-generating companies, the 12 regional electricity companies, and the National Grid. Similarly, Argentina raised over US$4 billion through the partial disposition of government-owned electricity assets and cut its level of debt. Here in Canada, the financial incentive for privatizing Ontario Hydro was based on estimates of a corresponding provincial debt reduction of at least CDN$8 billion. As well, the initial public offering of shares in CNR in 1995 was Canada's largest stock market flotation at that time. However, during the 1980s and 1990s, privatizations in Canada were most likely to have been conducted through sales to private businesses rather than public share offerings. Revenues from sales of Canada's 10 largest federal corporations amounted to $7.2 billion in the period between 1986 and 1996. Proceeds to the federal government were over $3.8 billion from the sale of shares in CN and Petro-Canada alone.

Challenges to "Going Private"

Stakeholders and Objectives   Governments in Canada began to privatize their corporate holdings in the mid-1980s for many of the reasons already cited, including efficiency objectives, financial concerns, and the capability of the private sector to fulfill public policy objectives.

It is useful to point out that while these may be objectives of privatization, they are not held equally by all parties affected by a privatization. The objectives of various stakeholders in the privatization of a Crown corporation may be different and potentially conflicting. Consider, for example, the stakeholders affected by the privatization of public utilities, which may include government owners, other government parties (that is, other levels of government), creditors, future shareholders of the organization, unionized and non-unionized employees of the corporation, regulators, taxpayers, consumers, and other existing or potential competitors in the industry.

Employees' Objectives   In effect, the objectives of privatization could all be considered as objectives of the government owners, but some may conflict with elements of the enterprise itself. For example, after initiation of the privatization plan for Ontario Hydro, Hydro's senior management was also agreeable to the province's plan for privatization. In fact, their view was that rapid privatization was necessary to face the increasing competition from the United States and from other provincial utilities in the Ontario electricity market, since deregulation began to open up the market to competition. However, within Hydro there has been much disagreement—culminating in a number of strikes by employees opposed to the government's plans.

A possible cost of privatization is massive layoffs of public employees, particularly in developing and transition countries. For example, the privatization of Argentina's national rail company in 1991 involved laying off almost 80% of the company's total workforce as part of the restructuring. However, numerous studies suggest that aggregate employment remains largely unchanged subsequent to privatization efforts.

The Public's Objectives   Another possible conflict is between the objectives cited and the public's concern for their "protection." For example, in the case of Ontario Hydro, some citizens were concerned that private competitors may be less likely to serve the public's interests than a government-owned enterprise. Consequently, some fear that privatization will bring higher rates and safety concerns.

Other issues may relate to foreign ownership. For example, there were no foreign ownership restrictions placed on the privatization of Canadian National Railway (which involved a public offering of a majority of shares), and consequently 40% of the $2.3 billion share issue was sold outside Canada, largely to US organizations. For some critics, this sale left too much power out of Canadian hands, and there was some question as to whether the newly controlled enterprise would keep Canadian interests high on their agenda. On the other hand, the government did not restrict foreign ownership, given the view that the Canadian market was not large enough to allow for complete privatization in one attempt. There were, however, other restrictions: No investor could own more than 15% of the shares, and CN must remain headquartered in Montreal.

While privatization has been viewed as a means to generate higher levels of entrepreneurship and efficiency in an industry, simply transferring ownership to the private sector does not guarantee efficiency gains. At least one important qualification is the level of competition that exists subsequent to the privatization. For example, critics suggest that although Air Canada was privatized in the late 1980s, clear efficiency gains and benefits to the user did not readily materialize because Air Canada continued to operate in an environment that lacked sufficient competition and, consequently, the airline maintained its monopoly status.

Ironically, the technical responsibilities of the government may increase after privatization, because governments shift from owning and managing individual companies to potentially regulating an entire sector or industry. Critics have asserted that if the government fails to implement effective regulation over the new private-sector owners, then many of the benefits associated with privatization will not materialize. This risk may be most apparent in the case of government transfer of ownership of natural monopolies, such as electricity or gas utilities, to a single private owner who takes over the monopoly. This was a criticism levelled at the British government when a number of utilities were privatized yet monopolistic industries were not consistently restructured to facilitate competition. Consequently, some privatized utility companies continued to operate under monopolistic conditions.

CHAPTER SUMMARY

In this chapter, we noted the shift toward reduced government involvement in the business sector, reflected in the trends toward deregulation and privatization. Observers suggest that what we are witnessing is a marked decrease in government involvement as public preferences shift toward a more purely private market system. It seems that many observers view the decrease in the level of government influence in business as a positive change. However, some believe that there is good reason for advocating a continued and perhaps increased role for government in business.

The question of government involvement in business has been debated for years. Certainly, the trend toward reduced government involvement in terms of deregulation, privatization, and elimination of tariff barriers seems to reflect the ideology that "less government is better." For some, the answer lies in the government's ability to work with industry to develop a long-term industrial strategy to lead the country out of its current problems and ensure a more secure future for working Canadians. Consequently, rather than simply taking a "hands-off" approach, it may be argued that what is required is a clear rethinking of the different types of roles that government can play, or how it may play its current roles in a different manner.

CHAPTER LEARNING TOOLS

Key Terms

bailout 329

business enterprise
    system 312

Cabinet 317

capitalism 312

corporate welfare 337

Crown corporation 320

deregulation 339

dumping 334

federal level
    of government 314

foreign direct
    investment 334

free enterprise
    system 313

government economic
    regulation 325

Governor General 316

House of Commons 317

imperfect
    competition 327

invisible hand of the
    market 313

laissez faire 313

ministries (federal) 317

mixed system 312

municipal level of
    government 315

perfect
    competition 325

prime minister 316

Prime Minister's Office
    (PMO) 316

privatization 344

Privy Council Office
    (PCO) 317

provincial level of
    government 315

restrictive or regulatory
    taxes 318

revenue taxes 318

Senate 317

subsidy 331

Multiple-Choice Questions

Select the *best* answer for each of the following questions. Solutions are located in the back of your textbook.

1. National defence is an activity managed by the _____ level of government.
   a. federal
   b. provincial
   c. municipal
   d. both A and B

2. Capitalism is an economic system that allows all of the following rights *except*
   a. individual rights
   b. private property rights
   c. competition rights
   d. trade rights

3. *Laissez-faire* simply means
   a. fair trade
   b. limited trade
   c. maximum government interference
   d. let people do as they choose

4. Communism is an economic system that allows
   a. the government to control resources
   b. the government to trade on a wide-scale basis
   c. both A and B
   d. none of the above

5. Sales tax is a form of
   a. restrictive taxes
   b. business taxes
   c. excise taxes
   d. revenue taxes

6. An example of a restrictive tax is
   a. an excise tax
   b. customs duties
   c. both A and B
   d. none of the above

7. The largest source of tax revenue for federal and provincial governments is
   a. individual income tax
   b. corporate income tax
   c. sales tax
   d. property tax

8. A Crown corporation may be established for which of the following reasons?
   a. To protect national interests
   b. To protect industries vital to the economy
   c. To provide special services that would otherwise not be available
   d. All of the above

9. The Liquor Control Board of Ontario (LCBO) is an example of
   a. a provincial Crown corporation
   b. a publicly traded corporation
   c. an agency of the Ministry of Consumer Services
   d. both A and C

10. Imperfect competition is a form of competition where
    a. fewer than the optimal number of competitors exist
    b. too many small companies competing exist
    c. too many large companies competing exist
    d. none of the above

11. A bailout is government financial assistance to a business in the form of
    a. tax credits
    b. cash payments
    c. subsidies
    d. all of the above

12. A subsidy is government assistance to a business often in the form of
    a. cash payments
    b. low-interest loans
    c. asset donations
    d. both A and B

13. Government should act as the "guardian of business" in order to
    a. nurture young industries
    b. encourage foreign direct investment
    c. promote strict adherence to trade agreements
    d. both A and B

14. Dumping is
    a. shipping too many exports to one country
    b. an environmental hazard
    c. adding tariffs to imported goods
    d. pricing a product below cost

15. A reduction in the laws over a business activity is sometimes referred to as
    a. deregulation
    b. privatization
    c. legal barrier reduction
    d. corporate lobbying

Discussion Questions

1. Explain the similarities and differences between the three levels of government.

2. Describe the three roles of government: tax collector role, business owner role, and regulatory role.

3. Explain the difference between revenue taxes and restrictive taxes.

4. Explain the reasons why a Crown corporation may be formed.

5. Compare and contrast the difference between perfect competition and imperfect competition.

6. Why should government act as the "guardian of business"?

7. Why should government not act as the "guardian of business"?

8. What is the difference between a bailout and a subsidy?

9. Explain the benefits and risks of deregulation.

10. What is the meaning of privatization, and what are its benefits?

CONCEPT APPLICATION   THE WIRELESS SERVICE INDUSTRY IN CANADA

HelleM/Shutterstock

Oh, Canada, what is wrong with our wireless service industry? Recently, OpenMedia.ca released a report entitled *Time for an Upgrade: Demanding Choice in Canada's Cell Phone Market*, which documented the results of its study of Canadians' experiences with cellphone service. The findings emphasized the existence of systemic mistreatment of cellphone customers by the large telecom providers. The report identified three broad categories of complaints, including disrespectful customer service, cellphone contracts that were overly restrictive to the consumer, and price gouging. In addition, many respondents considered Canadian cellphone service to be inferior compared to that offered in other countries.

Ironically, Canadian consumers pay among the highest cellphone fees in the industrialized world. In addition to the high cost of the service plans, Canadian carriers also impose a 75 cent monthly charge for 911 service—even though the actual cost of that service is closer to 10 cents.[47] Canadian carriers also typically charge among the highest roaming fees in the world. In addition, critics have asserted that Canadian customers must tolerate 36-month contracts, whereas the norm elsewhere is only 24 months, which limits the flexibility of consumers to take advantage of the best deals because they cannot switch easily. Further, trying to end a contract with one company can result in excessive termination fees, and if you do end the contract you are not faced with a lot of alternative choices.

So why is Canada's wireless service industry so dysfunctional? The answer, according to many observers, is simple—we need more competitors in Canada. As of 2013, only three companies—Rogers, Bell, and Telus—possessed a controlling share (about 94%) of the market.[48] And in 2013, these three companies together possessed more than 24 million wireless customers. Competition in the industry is clearly lacking. According to the report by Open Media:

> Canadians have few alternative options because affordable independent cell phone providers cannot effectively reach new customers on a playing-field tilted in favour of these three incumbents. Government policy has allowed the incumbents to entrench and take advantage of their position by acquiring nearly all the wireless spectrum—the infrastructure essential to reaching Canadian customers. Rather than providing a level playing-field and effective safeguards for consumers, just

[47] Geist, M. (2013, March 19). Sorry, Canadian wireless users are still suckers. *The Tyee*. Retrieved from http://thetyee.ca/Mediacheck/2013/03/19/Canadian-Wireless-Suckers.

[48] Anderson, S. (2013, March 6). How long will Canadians put up with mistreatment from cell phone companies? *Toronto Star*. Retrieved from www.thestar.com/opinion/commentary/2013/03/06/how_long_will_canadians_put_up_with_mistreatment_from_cell_phone_companies.html.

three companies are essentially able to regulate the mobile market. There is a serious lack of choice for Canadians, and these incumbents have little incentive to innovate or improve their rates and services, which in turn prevents Canadians from fully realizing the potential benefits of cellular technology. The dysfunctional cell phone market has resulted in poor service, punitively high prices, and acts as a dead weight on the Canadian economy.[49]

So what role can the government play in "fixing" this industry? In 2008 the federal government initiated an ambitious plan to boost competition in the $17-billion mobile phone industry by offering increased access to wireless licences. Smaller new entrants were given an opportunity to enter the market rather than letting the three dominant players snatch up all available licensing.

While the government made "space" for new players, other barriers remained. The fact is, it is not easy to enter the Canadian wireless industry for several reasons. First, the price of entry is still excessive. It requires hundreds of millions, if not billions, of dollars to purchase wireless spectrum, build towers, and lease retail space. Size and budget are important competitive advantages in this industry. Consequently, the relatively younger companies (like Mobilicity, Wind Mobile, and Public Mobile) continue to struggle against the big three players in the industry. In addition, if a newer company is seen as profitable, then it may end up being acquired by a larger firm. For example, Clearnet Communications Inc. was acquired by Telus for $6.6 billion in 2000 after it had accumulated about 2 million subscribers. Microcell Communications similarly was acquired by Rogers for $1.6 billion in 2004.[50]

According to many observers, if Canada wants more competition the government needs to consider reducing barriers to entry such as restrictions on foreign competition and ownership. Canada persists as one of the last developed countries to maintain foreign ownership restrictions in the telecommunications sector. And most agree this restriction has led to inferior service and high costs for the Canadian consumer. There is a consensus that Canada needs more wireless competition if consumers are to benefit, and government restrictions to foreign competition in the wireless industry have impeded any substantial increase in competition.

For example, initially the Canadian Radio-television and Telecommunications Commission prevented Wind Mobile from entering the cellphone market in Canada. It had ruled that Wind wasn't Canadian owned and controlled, given that most of its debt was held by Egyptian-based Orascom (later acquired by Amsterdam-headquartered VimpelCom). However, following a federal Cabinet order that overturned the decision, Wind Mobile launched its business in Canada in 2009. It became the first and strongest of several new companies attempting to gain access to Canada's wireless industry. Wind Mobile was the first new carrier to enter the Canadian wireless industry in many years, and it was followed in 2010 by Mobilicity, Public Mobile, and then Quebecor's

[49] OpenMedia.ca. (n.d.). Background: Canada's dysfunctional cell phone market. *Time for an Upgrade: Demanding change in Canada's cell phone market.* Retrieved from http://openmedia.ca/upgradecanada/background.

[50] Trichur, R., & Marlow, I. (2012, September 6). Canada's newly competitive cellphone market at risk. *Globe and Mail.* Retrieved from http://m.theglobeandmail.com/technology/tech-news/canadas-newly-competitive-cellphone-market-at-risk/article533723/?service=mobile#!.

Case Continued >

Videotron service. These new entrants brought additional choice to the market as well as a number of price wars and subsequent deals for consumers.

So how does a small company like Wind Mobile grow quickly? The answer is by being acquired by a much larger, albeit foreign-owned, organization. Hence, the Canadian government decided to permit full foreign ownership of telecom firms with a market share of 10% or less.[51] This allowed providers like Wind and Mobilicity access to more options for raising the money needed to build their networks. It also means more foreign entrants to the Canadian market.

In a relatively short period of time, Wind became Canada's fourth largest wireless carrier. This made it the first example of a foreign-controlled telecommunications carrier in Canada. The deal was permitted because of the changes made by Industry Canada allowing telecom companies with less than 10% of the market to have no restrictions on foreign investment. On the other hand, foreign ownership limits for large telecom companies like Rogers remained at no more than 33.3% foreign ownership.[52]

Increasingly, the Canadian government has allowed foreign companies to acquire smaller wireless providers (that is, those that currently have less than 10% of the market share). However, in addition to the issue of foreign ownership, smaller competitors are concerned that their presence in Canada may be short lived unless the government ensures fair competition.

These smaller players have helped to reduce prices somewhat, but only time will tell if they will remain and if competition will flourish or die. For example, these newer competitors argue that Industry Canada should better enforce the industry's rules of fair competition, which would include forcing Bell, Telus, and Rogers to share their wireless towers. Clearly, from the issue of foreign ownership to fair competition, this is one industry where the government has a critically important role to play in the affairs of business.

Questions

1. Explain why Canada's foreign-ownership restrictions in the telecommunications sector are a form of "trade protectionism" and how they conflict with the ideals of globalization.

2. By limiting foreign ownership and competition in the telecom industry, the Canadian government is favouring Canadian firms relative to their global rivals. Explain why the federal government should play the role of guardian of these Canadian telecom firms. On the flip side, explain why the government should not protect the existing players from more foreign competition.

3. What are three potential benefits and three potential threats to Canada of more multinational wireless carrier companies coming here?

---

[51] Canadian Press. (2013, January 18). Wind Mobile uses new telecom rules to push for foreign takeover. *CTV News*. Retrieved from www.ctvnews.ca/business/wind-mobile-uses-new-telecom-rules-to-push-for-foreign-takeover-1.1119886#ixzz2RPBX6IKN.

[52] Canadian Press. (2013, January 18). Wind Mobile to become fully foreign owned. *Toronto Star*. Retrieved from www.thestar.com/business/2013/01/18/wind_mobile_to_become_fully_foreign_owned.html.

Chapter 10
Societal Forces
Can Corporations Be Socially Responsible to All Stakeholders?

© Jan Sochor/age fotostock

The purpose of this chapter is to draw attention to the ethical dimension of business and to encourage a more critical understanding of the ethical issues that you will no doubt confront at some point in your career. To this end we will examine models of ethical reasoning in organizations. This chapter also considers what societal roles and responsibilities businesses must address to be successful.

Learning Objectives

After studying this chapter, you should be able to

1. Understand the challenges of defining business ethics.
2. Explain the models for judging the ethics of a decision.
3. Discuss how organizations may contribute to unethical behaviour at work.
4. Define stakeholders and explain why they are important for business to manage.
5. Analyze the debate for and against the relevance of corporate social responsibility.

THE BUSINESS WORLD
The New Blood Diamond: Cellphones

Most of us own cellphones, but few of us have stopped to consider how they are made. Even fewer of us are familiar with a critical component of cellphones—coltan.

Coltan, the short name for columbite-tantalite, is a metallic mineral that is mined mostly in Africa in areas like the Democratic Republic of Congo. In addition to cellphones, coltan is also used in smartphones and other electronic devices like DVD players, computers, video game systems, and so on. Once refined, coltan becomes a heat-resistant powder capable of holding a high electric charge. This is an important element in current flow inside circuit boards. The market for coltan is worth about $2 billion annually. In recent years, the price of coltan has skyrocketed to as high as $600 per kilogram.[1]

Eighty percent of the world's coltan is mined in the Congo. Indeed, coltan mining is a significant economic activity and accounts for 70% of the Congo's revenue.[2] This mineral is mined through a relatively old-fashioned process similar to how gold was mined during the 1800s. Dozens of individuals work together to dig large craters in streambeds. They scrape dirt from the surface to uncover the coltan underground. These workers will use large washtubs to shift around the mud and water until the coltan settles at the bottom. A productive worker can extract one kilogram of coltan a day.

Most of the world's coltan reserves are found specifically in the Congo's war-ravaged Kivu region. That area has been involved in some of the bloodiest conflicts in the world. So far, around 7 million people have died (since 1998) and currently 45,000 die every month from this conflict. In 1998, Rwanda launched an invasion of the Congo, where it seized a third of the country to gain control of Congo's coltan mines. The invasion quickly became profitable for Rwanda given that global demand for coltan is huge. Ironically, this occurred at a time when Sony began to use the mineral in its PlayStations.

In addition to Rwanda, Uganda, Burundi, and their militias are the primary exploiters of coltan in the Congo. Coltan mining has become infamous for financing civil and military conflict. In addition, coltan is mined under terrible working conditions. Men, women, and children are often forced at gunpoint to mine coltan that is then shipped out of the country at huge profits. Child labour in Africa has increased significantly in coltan mines. About 30% of schoolchildren are now forced to work in these mines in the Congo region.

There are also environmental abuses. The same area where coltan is mined also includes the Kahuzi Biega National Park, home to the mountain gorilla. Since coltan mining began, the gorilla population has been reduced by half from 258 to 130. Not only has food been reduced for the gorillas because of land clearing and loss of habitat, mining has also caused some people to become displaced, forcing some civilians to kill gorillas for their meat. Within the Congo, the United Nations has reported that in eight national parks the gorilla population has declined by 90% over the past five years, with only 3,000 gorillas remaining.[3]

---

[1] Delawala, I. (n.d.). What is coltan? *ABC Nightline*. Retrieved from http://abcnews.go.com/Nightline/story?id=128631&page=1.

[2] Najm, F. (2010, October 31). Blood coltan: Is your cell phone soaked in Congolese blood? *The Express Tribune*. Retrieved from http://tribune.com.pk/story/67995/blood-coltan-is-your-cell-phone-soaked-in-congolese-blood.

[3] Cellular-News. (n.d.). Coltan, gorillas, and cellphones. Retrieved from www.cellular-news.com/coltan.

While Rwanda, Uganda, and Burundi have directly exploited coltan, foreign multinational corporations have been indirectly involved in the exploitation of coltan in the Congo, given that the coltan mined by rebels and foreign forces is sold to foreign corporations. The United Nations has asked countries not to purchase coltan from the Congo due to an ongoing civil war that has expanded to surrounding countries. Which corporations buy coltan? Most of the well-known global companies buy it for their products, such as Apple, Nokia, Motorola, Compaq, Alcatel, Dell, IBM, Lucent, and Sony, to name a few.

Right now, there are no clear laws that prevent companies from purchasing products that contain coltan that is mined in these unethical ways. The Canadian government doesn't seem to be able to do much to stop this practice. There is, however, one way the government could improve the situation: force companies to track where their raw materials are coming from for their products. If they find that the materials come from regions where there are human rights violations, then they would have a choice to not buy from them. This would also increase transparency and allow customers to be better informed about the products they are buying.

There is only one problem with the above scenario: It is very expensive to locate where raw materials originate from. So, most companies are not voluntarily doing this. Certainly, it would increase the cost to produce their products. Many powerful retailers such as Walmart and Target have fought against the pressure for companies to identify where their raw materials come from. Tracking a product through the supply chain means suppliers have to keep track of where their raw materials are coming from too. Subsequently, it means a lot of compliance from a lot of different companies.

Major manufacturers of capacitors include Kemet (US), Vishay (US), Kyocera (Japan), NEC/Tokin (Japan), and Samsung (South Korea). However, smelting is dominated by Cabot (US), HC Starck (Germany), and Ningxia (China), which purchase approximately 80% of the ore. While Cabot and Starck agreed they would not purchase Congolese coltan, there is still much ore processed in China.[4]

According to *ABC Nightline*, tracing coltan is challenging:

> The path that coltan takes to get from Central Africa to the world market is a highly convoluted one, with legitimate mining operations often being confused with illegal rebel operations, and vice versa. . . . To be safe, many electronics companies have publicly rejected the use of coltan from anywhere in Central Africa.[5]

Many companies instead are relying on suppliers from Australia. Kemet, the world's largest maker of tantalum capacitors, is one company requiring its suppliers to certify that their coltan is not from Africa, but their efforts may be a little late. Most of the coltan from the Congo is already in cellphones, laptops, and other electronics across the globe.[6]

Would you be willing to pay at least double the price of what you paid for your phone? Clearly, if we want to stop these human rights violations, then that is what we would need to do. This is the ironic dilemma. No one wants people to be abused, but no one wants to pay more for their electronic gadgets either. The evidence to date suggests that most stores (and most consumers) either don't know about coltan or don't care and just want to pay the lowest price possible to obtain their smartphones and other electronic gadgets.

---

[4] Sutherland, E. (2011, April 11). Coltan, the Congo and your cell phone. Research paper, LINK Centre, University of the Witwatersrand.

[5] Delawala, (n.d.).

[6] Delawala, (n.d.).

The Tantalum-Niobium International Study Centre (TIC), an industry organization for producers and consumers of tantalum and niobium, explained that it deplores the illegal activities in coltan mines, but it does not have the power to regulate where producers get their raw materials from.[7]

In 2011, the Organisation for Economic Co-operation and Development (OECD) published recommendations that companies should exercise due diligence when using minerals such as coltan to ensure that their sources are not related to conflicts.[8] While the guidelines are voluntarily and not enforceable, they serve as a first step to reduce the funding of conflicts involving war crimes and human rights violations.

According to one observer,

> It has been argued that the multi-stakeholder approach adopted by the OECD complements traditional command and control systems, which is necessary to address the extra-territorial problems in global supply chains. It is a means by which governments can collectively encourage manufacturers and smelters to address the commercial aspects of the conflicts."[9]

In 2013, human rights issues continue to be addressed, but the underlying problems are not yet resolved. According to US senator Sam Brownback,

> Recent reports state that Rwanda and others are using the war in Congo to continue the exploitation of coltan. Once it is extracted, we are told, it is then sent down to Australia, where it is mixed with Australian coltan—where 20 per cent of the world coltan comes from—before being processed into tantalum. Unfortunately, it is impossible to say with any certainty that the tantalum supply coming out of Australia is conflict-free.[10]

Should consumers protest against cellphone companies to demand transparency in sourcing their raw materials? Perhaps protests instead of lineups are what is needed to continue the dialogue about protecting human rights while also continuing this important industry.

Objective 1 Understand the challenges of defining business ethics.

DEFINING BUSINESS ETHICS

Business ethics is not simply a societal concern—it has increasingly become an organizational issue that demands urgent attention. Managing ethical behaviour in business organizations requires an in-depth understanding of the many factors that contribute to employees' decisions to behave ethically or unethically. Talking Business 10.1 underscores the perceived deterioration of ethics in society as reflected in a lack of trust between the public and organizations.

Before we begin to consider the issue of business ethics, a definition would clearly be helpful. Unfortunately, as numerous writers on business ethics have indicated, defining

---

[7] *Cellular-News*, (n.d.).

[8] OECD. (2013). *OECD due diligence guidance for responsible supply chains of minerals from conflict-affected and high-risk areas*. Retrieved from www.oecd.org/daf/inv/mne/GuidanceEdition2.pdf.

[9] Sutherland, 2011.

[10] Marlow, I., & El Akkad, O. (2010, December 3). Smartphones: Blood stains at our fingertips. *Globe and Mail*. Retrieved from http://m.theglobeandmail.com/technology/smartphones-blood-stains-at-our-fingertips/article13 18713/?service=mobile#!.

High-Level Barriers to Public Trust in Organizations

Our research suggests that there are three high-level impediments to public trust in organizations.

First, changes in the nature of the employee–employer relationship over the last few decades have altered the context for trust in organizations. A variety of factors have made many Canadians feel less secure about their employment. These include automation, computerization, streamlined and "leaner" manufacturing processes, outsourcing, offshoring, demands for increased shareholder returns, difficult economic periods in the 1990s, and the increased competition brought about by globalization. Gone are the days of lifetime employment in exchange for lifelong commitment.

The movement towards a more flexible workforce has had benefits for Canadian corporations, enabling employers to mitigate demand fluctuations and reduce wage and benefit costs. All of this makes for more nimble organizations that are more able to compete in the global marketplace.

However, changes to employment relationships have implications for public trust in organizations. As Francis Fukuyama has noted, corporate-initiated shifts towards leaner production models and a more flexible workforce have not always been accompanied by reciprocal or compensatory benefits for workers. "[Managers] who hope to get loyalty, flexibility and cooperativeness out of their workers without giving anything in return, whether in the form of security, benefits or training, are being exploitative."

Human resource executives who attended a recent The Conference Board of Canada round table on employee trust echoed these sentiments. They noted that corporations were "changing the deal" with their employees, without always adequately discussing the terms of the "new deal," or providing other benefits to compensate for declining employment security. To maintain trust in the context of a shifting social contract between employers and employees, these executives argued that organizations would have to ensure that the terms of the new deal were both fair and effectively communicated to employees.

Second, the information technology revolution has had implications for public trust in organizations. In theory, the increased flow of information in the new "wired" world has broken the mainstream media monopoly on information and empowered ordinary citizens. Numerous examples exist of bloggers exposing political, bureaucratic, corporate or even media wrongdoing. Perhaps most famously, blogs played a pivotal role in bringing to light the fact that a *CBS News* report on U.S. President Bush's National Guard service was based on questionable documentation.

Yet the information revolution's impact on public trust has not necessarily been positive. While blogs or any other media can be used to expose lies, distortions or wrongdoing, they can just as easily be part of crude or sophisticated campaigns to defame, distort or spin. Separating the reliable from the unreliable online can be challenging.

Moreover, several other facets of modern communications further distort issues and complicate the public's ability to assess the trustworthiness of organizations.

One example is the relatively recent phenomenon of 24-hour news channels that rebroadcast the same news throughout the day. News channels' ratings are closely tied to big news events; thus, as one Canadian media expert has noted, "It is in the news channel's interests to always carry big events and to flag them as such for their viewers." This, he argues, has an impact on other forms of news coverage. "[The] news channels are on in every newsroom in the country. In too many cases newspapers seem to decide that because it has been on the news channels for such a long period of time it must be important."

Source: Excerpted from Deloitte. (2005). Rebuilding trust in Canadian organizations. The Conference Board of Canada. Retrieved from www.conferenceboard.ca/temp/da5dbb95-e185-421d-97be-88c926b8aa59/795-05rebuildingtrustrpt.pdf. Reprinted by permission.

business ethics is extremely challenging. However, what we can do is examine what constitutes the topic of business ethics, and we can identify the models that people employ to try to judge what is ethical and what is unethical behaviour. A major weakness of much of the scholarly literature on the topic of business ethics is a failure to adequately define the construct of ethics. Often, ethics has been defined differently by theorists. Some scholars view *ethics* as an inquiry into theories of what is "good and evil" or into what is "right and wrong." Others have quite simply defined ethics as "the study of morality," the right standards of behaviour between parties in a situation,[11] and activities that we should or should not do.[12] **Ethics** is the study of morality or moral judgments, standards, and rules of conduct.[13] The notion of **business ethics** has been considered as comprising the rules, standards, principles, or codes giving guidelines for morally right behaviour in certain contexts.[14]

A situation can have an ethical dimension, where the consequences of an individual's decision affects the interests, welfare, or expectations of others.[15] **Unethical behaviour** has been defined as behaviour that in some way has a harmful effect on others and is "either illegal, or morally unacceptable to the larger community."[16]

Ethical Behaviour as a Social Phenomenon

One central implication in these definitions is that ethical behaviour, by its very nature, occurs within a social context. That is, it is a social phenomenon and, consequently, must be evaluated in terms of the relationships among a potential network of players. The social aspect of ethics is also reflected in theories of ethics, such as Immanuel Kant's **categorical imperative**.[17] Kant asserted that actions, to be moral, must respect others— to function in society, individuals recognize that they must restrict their actions, just as they expect others to restrict theirs.

As many scholars have observed, behaviour, in its abstract interpretation, has no values or ethical component. Therefore, what is defined as ethical or unethical behaviour represents a judgment based on a referent structure. It is further difficult to define what constitutes ethical or unethical behaviour within an organization. In very broad terms, business ethics requires the organization or individual to behave in accordance with some carefully thought-out rules of moral philosophy. While the term itself is not easily definable, one can readily think of examples of activities that could be considered unethical business practices, based on our views of what constitutes ethical or unethical behaviour. For example, types of activity that may be considered unethical behaviour include misrepresenting the worth of a product or a business, engaging in forms of corporate spying, deciding to launch an aircraft that does not meet strict safety requirements, or employee theft.

Certainly, behaviour that is illegal is, by definition, unethical; however, the reverse is not true: What is legal is not necessarily ethical. It is this latter issue that makes the study of business ethics much more compelling. That is, grappling with the "grey areas" of business presents a major challenge. What are the examples of behaviours that might be considered acceptable business practices but might otherwise be considered unethical? Keep in mind that unethical behaviour may be directed against the organization itself, or it may be an activity that is consistent with the organization's goals but inconsistent with commonly accepted ethical principles. Later in this chapter we will identify these types of behaviour.

ethics The study of morality or moral judgments, standards, and rules of conduct.

business ethics The rules, standards, principles, or codes giving guidelines for morally right behaviour in certain contexts.

unethical behaviour Behaviour that in some way has a harmful effect on others and is either illegal or morally unacceptable to the larger community.

categorical imperative The assertion by philosopher Immanuel Kant that moral actions are, by definition, actions that respect others.

---

[11] Runes, D.D. (1964). *Dictionary of philosophy*. Totowa, NJ: Littlefield, Adams and Company.

[12] Beauchamp, T.L., & Bowie, N.E. (1983). *Ethical theory and business*. Englewood Hills, NJ: Prentice Hall.

[13] De George, R.T. (1999). *Business ethics* (5th ed.). Upper Saddle River, NJ: Prentice Hall.

[14] Lewis, P.V. (1985). Defining 'business ethics': Like nailing Jello to a wall. *Journal of Business Ethics 4*(5), 377–383.

[15] Rest, J.R. (1986). *Moral development: Advances in research and theory*. New York, NY: Praeger.

[16] Jones, T.M. (1991). Ethical decision making by individuals in organizations: An issue-contingent model. *Academy of Management Review, 16*(2), 367.

[17] De George, 1999.

Business Ethics as Managing Stakeholder Interests

For the purpose of this chapter, we can consider one of the broader definitions of business ethics. In general terms, we can think of business ethics as the standards, rules, and principles used to judge the rightness or wrongness of behaviour. Mark Pastin, a writer on business ethics, notes that "Managers today manage interests as much or more than they manage people or assets."[18] That is a useful observation from a business ethics perspective. In fact, the workplace can be viewed, in Pastin's terms, as a "tangled web of conflicting interests vying for scarce resources."[19] A manager is required to balance the interests of many different parties: shareholders, employees, customers, creditors, and so on. And a basic issue of business ethics is really all about balancing these interests, many of which may be competing, as seen in Talking Business 10.2.

TALKING BUSINESS 10.2

Lac-Mégantic: Disaster in Quebec

Once a peaceful lakeside town near the Maine border in Quebec, in the summer of 2013 Lac-Mégantic became the site of Canada's deadliest railway disaster, affecting a 1.5-square kilometre area. Rail World Inc. was the parent company of the Montreal, Maine and Atlantic Railway (MMA), which owned the 72-car train that derailed and triggered a series of fatal explosions in the town.

The disaster was preceded by a smaller and otherwise uneventful mishap: The locomotive had caught fire at a station where it was parked just outside of Lac-Mégantic. Fortunately firefighters extinguished the flames, which should have been the end of the story—sadly, it was not.

Shortly after the firefighters and a railway employee left the scene, the driverless train began moving—apparently the train's braking system was insufficient to keep it in place. Reports indicated that a broken piston in the train's engine caused the train to move on its own.[20] MMA chairman Ed Burkhardt admitted to reporters that the train's engineer might have failed to properly secure the brakes after parking the train and leaving for the night.[21]

The runaway train gradually picked up momentum and eventually barreled into the centre of the small town. It derailed, filling the town's sewer system, basements, and local waterways with 6 million litres of crude oil. The resulting explosions flattened the town's centre, killed 47 people, and caused damages in excess of $750 million.[22]

The question on everyone's mind was, how this could have happened?

Was this an unavoidable and blameless tragedy, or was this a case of corporate neglect? Did the MMA train company neglect its fundamental duty to ensure adequate safety for all those potentially impacted by its daily business?

According to transportation safety data, MMA has a long history of accidents in Canada: 129 accidents, including 77 derailments since 2003.[23] Shortly after the Lac-Mégantic disaster, the company initiated a sale of all of its more than 800 kilometres of track that crosses both Canada and the United States.

(continued)

---

[18] Pastin, M. (1986). *The hard problems of management: Gaining an ethics edge*. San Francisco, Jossey-Bass.

[19] Pastin, 1986.

[20] Robertson, G., Giovannetti, J., & Mackrael, K. (2013, September 13). Broken piston blamed for fire that led to Lac-Mégantic disaster. *Globe and Mail*. Retrieved from www.theglobeandmail.com/news/national/broken-piston-blamed-for-fire-that-led-to-lac-megantic-disaster/article14301352.

[21] *CBC News*. (2013, July 10). 50 feared dead in Lac-Mégantic train derailment. Retrieved from www.cbc.ca/news/canada/montreal/50-feared-dead-in-lac-m%C3%A9gantic-train-derailment-1.1327333.

[22] Editorial. (2013, September 29). How long must we wait to get rail safety on track? *Toronto Star*. Retrieved from www.thestar.com/opinion/editorials/2013/09/29/how_long_must_we_wait_to_get_rail_safety_on_track_editorial.html.

[23] *CBC News*, 2013.

In a scathing article for the Huffington Post, author and journalist Wade Rowland made the following comments:

> As completely self-interested machine entities, corporations view risk differently than people do. People see risk in terms of the hazard a product or a practice may pose to the health, safety, and security of themselves, their families, and their communities. For the corporation, risk is assessed in terms of potential damage to the bottom line. Risk-taking is acceptable—and even to be encouraged—up to the point where the potential for financial loss reduces the promise of increased profit to zero . . . The railway industry, despite astronomical growth in the shipment of crude oil by rail over the past few years, has calculated that the added profit to be gained by keeping personnel costs to a bare minimum, and putting off equipment upgrades and rail-bed maintenance as long as possible, is greater than the potential cost of any likely accident . . . Their calculations apparently did not take into account the potential for an accident in the scale of the Lac Mégantic disaster. Oops.[24]

Objective 2 Explain the models for judging the ethics of a decision.

MODELS FOR JUDGING THE ETHICS OF DECISIONS

Employees at all levels invariably face decisions with some kind of ethical dimension. The decision to compromise personal ethics for the sake of organizational objectives can bring devastating results. Consider the situation of Betty Vinson and the iconic case of corruption at WorldCom in the early 21st century:

> Betty Vinson has always kept her life well ordered. . . . In 1996, she took a job as a mid-level accountant at a small long-distance company. Five years later, her solid career took a sudden turn in a very sorry direction. Today Ms. Vinson, 47 years old, is awaiting sentencing on conspiracy and securities-fraud charges. She has begun to prepare her 12-year-old daughter for the possibility that she will go to jail. The long-distance company grew up to be telecom giant WorldCom Inc., which melted down [in 2002] in an [US]$11 billion fraud, the biggest in corporate history. Asked by her bosses there to make false accounting entries, Ms. Vinson balked—and then caved. Over the course of six quarters she continued to make the illegal entries to bolster WorldCom's profits at the request of her superiors. Each time she worried. Each time she hoped it was the last time. At the end of 18 months she had helped falsify at least [US]$3.7 billion in profits.[25]

Notoriety gained through unethical behaviour can be observed in press reports in recent years. For example, a number of years ago one of Canada's most prestigious law schools was shaken with the revelation that law students had lied to prospective employers about the academic grades achieved in their first year of law school. An inquiry launched by the dean of the University of Toronto's Faculty of Law indicated that approximately 30

---

[24] Rowland, W. (2013, July 10). The Lac-Mégantic rail disaster is a corporate crime. *Huffington Post.* Retrieved from www.huffingtonpost.ca/wade-rowland/lacmegantic-corporate-crime_b_3574080.html.

[25] Pulliam, S. (2003, June 23). Over the line: A staffer ordered to commit fraud balked, then caved. *Wall Street Journal,* A1.

of the 170 students were guilty of this offence. All those accused readily admitted that they had lied to prospective employers about grades earned for the purpose of gaining a potential advantage in securing employment. The shock of this offence is reflected in the words of the dean's legal advisor, David Scott: "They are enrolled in a program whose underpinnings depend on scrupulous honesty since, as lawyers, they will be expected to uphold the integrity of our system of justice by their own personal conduct. Honesty, in this context, involves acceptance of responsibility for one's acts."[26]

What guidelines does an individual rely on to grapple with ethical issues in the workplace? Clearly, a greater understanding of the ethical dimension of workplace decisions is required if one hopes to prepare to resolve workplace dilemmas effectively and properly.

The literature on ethics is extensive and exists across a variety of disciplines, including philosophy, anthropology, sociology, and psychology. However, until recently there have been few attempts to apply this theoretical framework to the specific area of business ethics. As Pastin pointed out, the challenge to scholars in the field of business ethics is "to apply what appears to be esoteric, philosophical concepts to the real concerns of business organizations."[27]

Business ethics is typically examined using normative theories—theories of how individuals should ideally behave. There are a variety of ways theories of ethics have been grouped. Among these classifications is the grouping of theories as utilitarian (consequential) or single-rule (non consequential). We can consider two central models that have been used to describe the basis of judging the ethics of organizational decisions:

1. utilitarian, or end-point ethics
2. rule ethics

These two models identify potential methods of resolving conflicting interests within organizations. The models identify the logic or rationale a manager might employ in dealing with organizational issues that possess ethical implications.

End-Point Ethics

A major model of ethics used in the literature is **end-point ethics**. The dominant form of this view was articulated in John Stuart Mills's *Utilitarianism* as a response to the Industrial Revolution. **Utilitarianism** asserts that to determine whether an action is right or wrong, one must assess the likely consequences, including tangible economic outcomes (profit for shareholders) or intangible outcomes, such as happiness or friendship. For example, "What does it mean to be an ethical businessperson?" Utilitarianism posits that an ethical person acts so as to produce the "greatest ratio of good to evil." Consistent with this view, an ethical manager would ensure that owners, employees, and customers all share fairly in the business's gains. Utilitarianism asserts that an action is ethical if it produces, or if it tends to produce, the greatest amount of good for the greatest number of people affected

end-point ethics Assessing the rightness or wrongness of an action by its outcomes. Its modern counterparts are cost-benefit and risk-benefit analysis.

utilitarianism First articulated by John Stuart Mills in response to the Industrial Revolution, a way to determine if an action is right or wrong by assessing the likely consequences of the action, including tangible economic outcomes or intangible outcomes.

---

[26] Morgenson, G. (2001, June 13). Wall Street firm endorse ethics standards for analysts. *New York Times.* Retrieved from www.nytimes.com/2001/06/13/business/wall-street-firms-endorse-ethics-standards-for-analysts. html?n=Top%2fReference%2fTimes%20Topics%2fSubjects%2fF%2fFinances.

[27] Pastin, 1986.

by the action.[28] In other words, actions themselves are neither ethical nor unethical; rather, ethics are judged based on the outcomes of such actions. That is, ethical behaviour is behaviour that results in total benefits or utility exceeding total costs or negative consequences. In this regard, utilitarianism ideally requires an examination of the fairness of the outcomes,[29] given that the consequences experienced by all affected parties ultimately determine whether or not an action is ethical. The "modern" counterparts of end-point ethics are cost-benefit and risk-benefit analyses.

The Consequences of Our Actions In sum, end-point ethics is a model for ethical decision making that states that a person, organization or society should engage in the activity that results in the greatest balance of good over harm for all. In other words, where we have a number of different interests at play, we need to consider what action will benefit most of the parties. The focus is on judging the ethics of an action by considering its outcome for all potentially affected parties. It is not the process of the decision or the behaviour to achieve the outcome that are considered, but the outcome itself. As mentioned, the concept of end-point ethics is also referred to as utilitarianism. Why this strange name? Well, because we are talking about maximizing the utility, or usefulness, of a decision for all stakeholders—those potentially affected by the decision. It is an ethical analysis that considers the relative gains and costs for all parties affected by a decision or action. If the benefits outweigh the costs, then we go ahead with the decision or choose the decision that gives us this outcome.

How do we compare the relative benefit and harm to each stakeholder? That is difficult to answer. In broad terms, we compare the costs and benefits to each stakeholder by considering a number of possible factors, which might include social (how it affects society or the public as a whole), human (psychological or emotional impact), or economic (for example, what is the dollar impact of our decision?) implications.

Limitations Clearly, a major problem with this approach to ethical reasoning lies in the difficulty of estimating and comparing relative benefits and costs to the stakeholders. Consider an example. Many Canadian businesses are increasingly conducting business globally. Should we be concerned if our Canadian businesspeople are conducting business with a foreign country that has a record of human rights violations? For example, the prime minister of Canada has led trade missions to a number of countries with an infamous record of human rights violations to establish business relations. Is this ethical? Let's consider what end-point ethics suggests. Do overall benefits exceed overall harm? There are great potential gains for Canadian businesses by expanding their reach to foreign markets. This means potentially more jobs in Canada and a healthier economy. What harm arises? Those supporting such ventures argue that there is no harm generated and, consequently, they can ethically support such business practices. Those opposed might argue that we might be supporting oppressive regimes. So how do we judge whether there are more benefits than harms arising from such business ventures?

A second fundamental problem with the end-point ethics approach is that, as the name implies, it looks just at the end point, or result, without considering the implications

---

[28] De George, 1999.

[29] Molm, L.D. (). Affect and social exchange: Satisfaction in power-dependence relations. *American Sociological Review*, 56(4), 475–493.

of what it takes to achieve those results. It does not ask us to consider whether or not the manner in which the outcomes were achieved is ethical. This is the notion of the "ends justifying the means." So even if end-point ethics helped generate a solution that resulted in a maximization of the greatest good for all those affected, it ignores what happens "in between" to get to that point or outcome. End-point ethics essentially says, "Start with a consideration of the consequences to judge the ethics of a decision." This involves asking at least two key questions:

1. Who will be significantly affected by this decision?
2. What is the impact of this decision as perceived by each of the affected groups?

In sum, end-point ethics gives managers a tool for analyzing business decisions. This line of thinking basically asks us to consider the following: Who counts most in our decision, and how are they affected by it? However, it doesn't tell us to examine the process or what to do about strategy.

Rule Ethics

A second major method of ethical reasoning is referred to as rule ethics. Deontological theories of ethics (that is, theories of ethics arising from the study of duty) refute the utilitarian assertion that the ethics of an action is based on its outcomes, and suggest instead that the ethics of an action is independent of the outcomes or consequences. **Rule ethics** is essentially the fundamental deontological perspective, which considers actions as ethical or unethical based on their relation to the rules and principles that guide behaviours.[30] Based on this perspective, ethical behaviour is behaviour that can be deemed as morally right regardless of the consequences. In the Western world, for example, Judeo-Christian religious and moral rules or values have played a major role in defining morality in society.[31] Of course, even within Western society, there are a variety of beliefs or rules regarding what is ethical, and society has tended to permit rules to change in many areas of behaviour.

rule ethics Judging actions to be right or wrong according to absolute rules regardless of the consequences. Such rules may be based on religious beliefs, family values, education, experience, and so on.

Right versus Wrong   Rule ethics is the view that there are basic rules that determine the "rightness" or "wrongness" of actions. Stated simply, rule ethics asserts that an individual should do what is required by valid, ethical principles and should not do anything that violates those principles. These are the fundamental notions of right and wrong. Given the diverse nature of society, there is no one clear set of rule ethics that is followed by all individuals. This is, perhaps, one of the central problems in assessing whether behaviour can be deemed ethical—whose rules should apply?

Both utilitarian and rule ethics consider the social aspect of ethics: Unethical behaviour is behaviour that has a harmful effect on others and is "either illegal, or morally unacceptable to the larger community."[32] How do these two models of ethical reasoning

---

[30] Buckley, M.R., Wiese, D.S., & Harvey, M.G. (1998). An investigation into the dimensions of unethical behavior. *Journal of Education for Business, 73*(5), 284–290.

[31] De George, 1999.

[32] Jones, 1991.

operate differently? Let's consider a business issue and see what each model offers with regard to resolving a problem.

Applying the Models: A Scenario

> You are a businessperson trying to win a $22 million contract for your company with a major corporation overseas. You learn that to gain the contract, you need to offer a substantial monetary gift to the CEO of the corporation. What would you do?

This question is one that managers may need to ask themselves as we continue to conduct business on a global scale. And certainly, as many observers have pointed out, attitudes and customs regarding ethical business practices can vary widely among different countries.

From an End-Point Ethics Perspective
From this perspective we could not get any universal agreement as to the ethics of such a practice. Clearly, many countries have no problem with bribery. Reconsider the principles of end-point ethics: Do we achieve the greatest balance of good over harm for all potential stakeholders? First, who gains from a bribe? Well, clearly your company will benefit from getting the deal and, consequently, you will benefit as well. Who is harmed by such a transaction?

You might consider three potential losers:

1. Does the bribe compromise your ability to do business with companies like this one in the future—will the perception of your company be negative?

2. Competent competitors who are otherwise deserving of the contract may lose because they refused to offer this bribe.

3. The bribe might permit inferior products or services to be purchased simply because the supplier bribed those in power to help get the product or service to market. Consequently, consumers may be harmed.

If, indeed, these three stakeholders are harmed in this way as a consequence of our decision, end-point ethics would likely guide us away from such a decision. However, end-point ethics does not necessarily condemn such behaviour as unethical. If the product or service is not inferior—that is, if the bribe helps us conduct business and sell a good product that is fairly priced—then consumers are not harmed. If the CEO will likely receive a bribe from some other supplier, regardless of whether you choose to bribe or not, then end-point ethics suggests that no one is "worse for the wear," so to speak, by having received the bribe. Depending on how it is applied, end-point ethics potentially could justify giving the bribe. Certainly, it does not uniformly condemn such a decision. Rather, the result depends on how rigorously the decision maker has identified all potential stakeholders and how carefully he or she weighed the relative costs and benefits (both tangible and intangible) that arise from this action.

From a Rule Ethics Perspective
What guidance does rule ethics offer us in considering whether or not to bribe the CEO of this foreign corporation to gain the contract? Again, consider what rule ethics says. It says that we should do what our ethical codes or

beliefs tell us to do. Now, in North America at least, there are many organizations that have instituted strict codes of ethics that prohibit giving or accepting gifts of any kind. Perhaps that would be a guiding rule for some decision makers. On the other hand, perhaps an individual's personal or religious beliefs dictate honesty in all aspects of life; this may also serve to act as a rule prohibiting bribery. It may be our belief that no businessperson should pay a bribe to any company official, even though the ethical codes of some other countries do indeed tolerate bribery.

Does rule ethics generate a negative response to the question of gift giving? Once again, this model does not generate universal responses to problems. For example, perhaps we have rules that advocate such gift giving, and these rules guide our behaviour. Do we have any obligations that override our ethical prohibition of bribery? What if your company's survival depended on securing business with this foreign company? What if thousands of jobs would be lost in your company if the business was not obtained, and the only way to obtain it is through a bribe? Could these issues offer compelling reasons to follow a rule that "all is fair in business"? Rule ethics may dictate overriding the general prohibition against bribery because of the greater urgency to protect the company and jobs. Consequently, even rule ethics does not provide a blanket condemnation of bribery. Modern society, it seems, has lost its ability to provide clear rules or guidelines to individuals that will enable them to resolve conflicting interests.

Lessons? What lessons do we learn from an understanding of end-point ethics and rule ethics? Perhaps the greatest value of these models lies in what they demand of us. Both models are inherently flawed: They are limited by the degree of rigour that the user (decision maker) employs in their use. End-point ethics demands that we question the ethics of our actions in the following ways:

- Which stakeholders have we identified, and which have we not identified?
- Have we clearly acknowledged the harm, as well as the benefits, that may arise from our decisions?
- How have we determined the relative importance of each of the stakeholders?
- How have we determined the relative weight of the benefits and harms that will potentially arise from our decisions?

Similarly, rule ethics suggests we need to think more critically about what rules we employ in making decisions:

- Where did the rules that guide our behaviour and choices come from?
- Do we use these rules consistently, or only when it is convenient?
- Do we apply separate sets of rules to govern our professional and our personal lives? Why?

As you can see, the value of considering the models we use to make decisions is in demonstrating the fact that our decisions often have an ethical dimension. Without an understanding of the motivation behind our decisions, we may fall victim to making decisions on purely a business basis, even though they may have ethical implications. The issue of bribery is discussed further in Talking Business 10.3.

The Business of Bribery

© mario beauregard/Fotolia

By Ziv Deutsch

In recent years there has been an outcry by the foreign community about Canada's weak stance against foreign corruption.

Despite Canada's previous efforts to fight global fraud, such as the recently established anti-corruption unit of the RCMP, Canada is still ranked the lowest of all G7 countries in foreign corruption regulation, being described as having little or no enforcement. This is largely because of the tolerance that Canadian firms exhibit toward foreign parties that engage in fraudulent behaviours abroad under the assumption that these were the widely accepted business practices of the international market.

It has taken public outcry over recent bribery scandals involving Canadian firms to cause the federal government to go back and re-examine their own stance on international anti-corruption.

The Canadian government has responded to this criticism of Canada's lax corruption laws by increasing jail time for convicted parties and easing the barriers for conviction, which formerly protected foreign bribery defendants. Canada's historical lack of enforcement on the international stage is also beginning to change.

The RCMP has energetically begun to enforce these new laws, which have in turn caused a dynamic shift in the private sector as companies scramble to put their own anti-corruption policies and training into place. Canada hopes that these changes, both in the severity of charges and the punishment of those convicted of bribery, will help improve our reputation in the international community from negligent regulator to strict enforcer.

One such example of Canada's new strict stance on bribery can be illustrated through the examination of Quebec-based engineering company SNC-Lavalin. SNC-Lavalin and many of its affiliates were recently hit by several sanctions related to bribery by the World Bank. As a result of these sanctions, neither the firm SNC-Lavalin nor any of its affiliates are permitted to bid on or work on any project being run by the World Bank for the next decade. While the implications of these sanctions are not financially massive for the firm, as less than 1% of SNC-Lavalin's potential projects have been taken off the table, the harm done to the company's reputation is extraordinary.

These charges against SNC-Lavalin resulted from the attempted bribery of a Bangladeshi minister to receive a large national engineering job. Originally, SNC-Lavalin was in second place for the project; however, after a high-level company executive and a member of the Bangladeshi cabinet met in private, SNC-Lavalin was moved to the number one position on the list and ultimately received the bridge contract. Interestingly, SNC-Lavalin is no stranger to corruption charges: The former CEO of the company was charged with fraud in late 2012. The firm is also currently involved in scandals in Libya and Algeria, where they are accused of using company resources to illegally secure contracts.

The new management and CEO of SNC-Lavalin have since stated that their goal is to amend their corporate culture and focus on setting ethical business standards for employee conduct and firm governance.

Sources: Douglas Q. (2013, April 12). Reputation-scarring foreign bribery scandals force change upon corporate Canada. *Postmedia*. Retrieved from http://o.canada.com/2013/04/12/reputation-scarring-foreign-bribery-scandals-force-change-upon-corporate-canada; McArthur, G. (2013, April). World Bank locks out SNC-Lavalin over Bangladesh bribery scandal. *Globe and Mail*. Retrieved from www.theglobeandmail.com/report-on-business/world-bank-locks-out-snc-lavalin-over-bangladesh-bribery-scandal/article11349133; CBC News. (2013, April 17). SNC-Lavalin agrees to 10-year ban from World Bank projects. Retrieved from www.cbc.ca/news/business/snc-lavalin-agrees-to-10-year-ban-from-world-bank-projects-1.1316719; Hood, D. (2012, December 13). SNC-Lavalin's problems just beginning. *Canadian Business*. Retrieved from www.canadianbusiness.com/companies-and-industries/snc-lavalin-case-signals-corruption-crackdown-in-canada/?goback=.gde_4485888_member_196511318.

DO ORGANIZATIONS MAKE US UNETHICAL?

Objective 3 Discuss how organizations may contribute to unethical behaviour at work.

The two models of ethical decision making outlined above help give us an understanding of the ways we may resolve conflicting interests in the workplace. Neither model guarantees we will make a sound, ethical decision—that depends on the level of rigour we analyze our choices with and on the impact of our choices. When faced with decisions that involve ethical implications, why might we not "do the right thing"? Why do some individuals choose to engage in unethical behaviour, while others do not?

There are countless theories that attempt to answer that question. Some suggest that self-interest is a major influence on unethical behaviour. For example, based on agency theory, it is argued that when agents (employees) possess more information than principals (employers) and their goals conflict, agents may behave in accordance with their self-interest and, thereby, such individuals may deceive the principal.[33] Other scholars have accused individuals (human agents) of being "pure egoists"[34] whose behaviour typically reflects a desire to maximize their own utility.[35] This sentiment is also expressed in neoclassical economics and social exchange theory, which assert that individuals will engage in unethical behaviour if it is in their best interest to do so.[36] As an example of this self-interest connection, there is some research evidence to suggest that if individuals receive a personal gain or reward from giving a bribe to another party, they are very likely to engage in this form of unethical behaviour.[37]

From a normative perspective, business ethics advocates that individuals should be motivated by more than a complete focus on self-interest.[38] Some scholars have pointed out that a rational, economic focus on self-interest can be irrational—"rational agents approach being psychopathic when their interests are solely in benefit to themselves."[39] Certainly this criticism of self-interest makes sense from a social perspective. We live in societies where cooperation is expected, and a purely economic self-interest focus would prove dysfunctional for society.

For many years researchers have attempted to discern the relative role of the individual's and the organization's characteristics in encouraging unethical behaviour in the workplace—that is, the notion of distinguishing "bad apples or bad barrels."[40]

Managing ethical behaviour in business organizations requires an in-depth understanding of the many factors that contribute to employees' decisions to behave ethically or unethically. One key question that needs to be addressed is, under what conditions will

---

[33] Holmstrom, B. (1979). Moral hazard and observability. *Bell Journal of Economics, 10,* 74–91.

[34] Becker, G. (1976). *The economic approach to human behavior.* Chicago, IL: University of Chicago Press.

[35] Trevino, L.K. (1986). Ethical decision making in organizations: A person-situation interactionist model. *Academy of Management Review, 11*(3), 601–617.

[36] Grover, S.L. (1993). Why professionals lie: The impact of professional role conflict on reporting accuracy. *Organizational Behavior and Human Decision Processing, 55,* 251–272.

[37] Hegarty, W.H., & Sims, H.P. (1978). Some determinants of unethical decision behavior: An experiment. *Journal of Applied Psychology, 63*(4), 451–457.

[38] Pava, M.L. (1998). Religious business ethics and political liberalism: An integrative approach. *Journal of Business Ethics, 17*(15), 1633–1652.

[39] Rawls, J. (1993). *Political liberalism.* New York, NY: Columbia University Press.

[40] Trevino, L.K., & Youngblood, S.A. (1990). Bad apples in bad barrels: A causal analysis of ethical decision making behavior. *Journal of Applied Psychology, 75*(4), 378–385.

individuals, within their roles as employees, engage in behaviour that does not conform with commonly accepted standards of ethical behaviour? In other words, what factors in the workplace might create an environment where unethical behaviour is acceptable? When do employees willingly engage in what would otherwise be considered unacceptable behaviour? For example, why might an individual willingly engage in corporate "spying," or why might an individual willingly misrepresent a product's quality to a customer? The research and theory has acknowledged that organizations can present unique challenges to ethical behaviour for their constituents. Organizational factors play a role in ethical decision making and behaviour at two points: establishing moral intent, and engaging in moral behaviour.

Exhibit 10.1 summarizes the framework adopted to explain the impact of organizational context. The elements that play a critical role in individual ethical behaviour within the organization are culture, organizational decoupling, routinization of work, organizational identity, and work roles. The influence of these factors on behaviour arises through their impact on the following:

- perceptions or recognition of the ethical dimension or ethical implications of the work situation

- critical evaluation of the ethical implications or consequences of work behaviour

- final decision to engage in the behaviour

The elements of this framework are delineated in the following pages.

Exhibit 10.1
Organizational Factors Affecting Decisions to Engage in Ethical or Unethical Behaviour

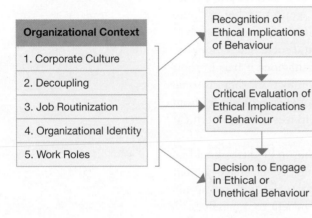

Unethical Behaviour as a Consequence of Corporate Culture

Business morality is essentially a social reality, as opposed to a physical reality, and therefore cannot be fully understood apart from the social system and organizational culture that are conceptualizing it.[41] What is organizational culture, and how can it impact my decision as an employee to engage in ethical or unethical behaviour?

organizational culture A set of shared beliefs regarding how members of the organization should behave and what goals they should seek.

Organizational culture has been defined as the bond or glue that holds an organization together. It encompasses a set of shared beliefs regarding how members of the organization should behave and what goals they should seek. In this sense it is an intangible, abstract component of any organization. There is an IBM culture, a Nortel culture, a McDonald's culture, and a Harvard University culture. Every organization contains some kind of culture. However, when a culture goes bad, it is not easy to fix.

The notion that norms influence ethical behaviour has been suggested for many years. Specifically, organizational culture provides an organizational reality within which ethically relevant actions are discussed, judged, and legitimized. For example, culture,

---

[41] Payne, S.L., & Giacalone, R.A. (1990). Social psychological approaches to the perception of ethical dilemmas. *Human Relations, 43*, 649–665; Trevino, 1986.

through its transmission of organizational beliefs, can provide employees with *legitimate* (sanctioned) or *nonlegitimate* approaches to ethical decision making and behaviour.

Rituals and Myths   Organizational researchers who consider culture to be a system of publicly and collectively accepted meanings also suggest that an organization is filled with organizational "rituals and myths."[42] Organizational rituals and myths contain messages that provide a shared experience and reinforcement of values for members of the organization. Myths specifically contain a narrative of events, often with a "sacred" quality attached. Both rituals and myths play a crucial role in the continuous processes of establishing and maintaining what is legitimate and what is unacceptable in any organizational culture.[43] The "myths" and "rituals" are simply the organization's established products, services, techniques, and policies or rules that employees adopt/conform to.[44]

Organizational myths could be, for example, legends of corporate heroes and their deeds within the organization, which can provide guidance (positive or negative) for employees facing ethical decisions in similar circumstances.[45] This may permit individuals to legitimize their actions in ethical dilemmas.[46] That is, the culture, through its transmission of myths, can provide employees with legitimate (sanctioned) or nonlegitimate approaches to ethical decision making and behaviour.

What's the Connection to Ethics?   How can managers generate a culture that encourages ethical behaviour? It has been suggested that a strong ethical culture can be generated through the areas of selection (choosing employees whose beliefs are consistent with those of the organization), socialization (conveying the organization's goals and norms effectively), and training and mentoring (reinforcing the organization's culture through training and personal role models).[47] Gatewood and Carroll suggest that the **socialization of ethics**, which occurs through a process of internalization of organizational ethical standards, is fundamental to the ethical conduct of organizational members.[48] Other authors have provided similar suggestions for encouraging ethical behaviour in organizations, including the development of corporate ethical codes of conduct,[49] and public discussions of ethical issues through formal meetings.[50] This sense of open confrontation and discussion of ethical concerns must be institutionalized before it can become an effective means of resolving moral conflict.

socialization of ethics The process of conveying the organization's goals and norms to employees so that they internalize organizational ethical standards.

---

[42] Pettigrew, A.M. (1979). On studying organizational cultures. *Administrative Science Quarterly, 24,* 570–581.

[43] Pettigrew, 1979.

[44] Meyer, J., & Rowan, B. (1977). Institutionalized organizations: Formal structure as myth and ceremony. *American Journal of Sociology, 83,* 440–463.

[45] Knouse, S.B., & Giacalone, R.A. (1992). Ethical decision making in business: Behavioral issues and concerns. *Journal of Business Ethics, 11,* 369–377.

[46] Stone, C.D. (1975). The culture of the corporation. In W.M. Hoffman & J.M. Moore (Eds.), *Business ethics* (2nd ed.). New York, NY: McGraw-Hill.

[47] Northcraft, G.B., & Neale, M.A. (1994). *Organizational Behavior.* Chicago, IL: Dryden Press.

[48] Gatewood, R.D., & Carroll, A.B. (1991). Assessment of the ethical performance of organizational members: A conceptual framework. *Academy of Management Review, 16,* 667–690.

[49] Sims, R.R. (1991). The institutionalization of organizational ethics. *Journal of Business Ethics, 10,* 493–511; Brooks, L.J. (1989). Corporate codes of ethics. *Journal of Business Ethics, 8,* 117–129.

[50] Kram, K.E., Yeager, P.C., & Reed, G.E. (1989). Decisions and dilemmas: The ethical dimension in the corporate context. In J.E. Post (Ed.), *Research in Corporate Social Performance and Policy,* Volume 1 (pp. 21–54). Greenwich, CT: JAI Press.

Corporate Codes of Conduct

Corporate **codes of conduct** are one of the most common methods used by the business community to improve ethical conduct. These rules are intended to reflect the general values of society. Codes of ethics are one means of "institutionalizing" ethics in corporations.[51] This involves incorporating ethics formally and explicitly into daily business life.

Ethical codes are necessary because laws cannot prescribe the standard of ethical conduct for all situations.[52] However, it should be noted that many critics have suggested that these codes may become nothing more than "window dressing"—a means of appearing ethical that does not necessarily reflect actual practice. For example, it has been suggested that the lack of reinforcement of ethical behaviour reflected in management's "results orientation" can encourage employees to behave unethically.[53] "Good guys finish last" is the sentiment that propels this attitude in business. In other words, organizations that do not reward ethical behaviour are sending out the message that such behaviour is unnecessary. This can happen regardless of the presence of formal corporate codes of conduct.

Bureaucratic Cultures

Research has supported the notion that the moral atmosphere affects moral reasoning and moral judgment.[54] A number of research studies have attempted to explore this concept within the organizational context. Findings have indicated that when an informal or formal organizational policy was present, ethical behaviour increased and unethical behaviour was deterred.[55] For example, Weber examined the effects of size of the organization on a manager's stage of moral reasoning.[56] The results of Weber's study indicated that managers in smaller organizations appeared to be operating at a higher stage of moral reasoning. Weber suggested several reasons for these findings. Larger organizations often exhibit cultures with more complex bureaucracies and greater control over their employees through rules and regulations. Therefore, managers feeling isolated from the central decision-making authority will tend to rely on more immediate peers or supervisors for support or approval of their behaviour. On the other hand, smaller organizations tend to be less bureaucratic and possess fewer rules to govern employee behaviour. Subsequently, managers in this environment feel a greater sense of control over the decision-making process, along with a greater need to conform with social laws as a means to protect themselves from conflict with other stakeholders (customers, the public, and so on). This reflects a higher stage of cognitive moral development. In other words, a **democratic culture** may encourage members to take responsibility for their actions, while an **authoritative culture** may dictate rules that replace individual discretion, thereby suppressing development of ethical decision making.[57]

---

[51] Weber, J. (1990). Managers' moral reasoning: Assessing their responses to the three moral dilemmas. *Human Relations, 43*, 687–702.

[52] Brooks, 1989.

[53] Baumhart, R.S.J. (1961). How ethical are businessmen? *Harvard Business Review, 39*, 6–31.

[54] Higgins, A., Power, C., & Kohlberg, L. (1984). The relationship of moral atmosphere to judgments of responsibility. In W.M. Kurtines & J.L. Gewirtz (Eds.), *Morality, moral behavior, and moral development* (pp. 74–106). New York, NY: Wiley.

[55] Hegarty, W.H., & Sims, H.P. (1979). Organizational philosophy, policies, and objectives related to unethical decision behavior: A laboratory experiment. *Journal of Applied Psychology, 64*(3), 331–338.

[56] Weber, 1990.

[57] Kohlberg, L. (1969). Stage and sequence: The cognitive developmental approach to socialization. In D.A. Goslin (Ed.), *Handbook of Socialization Theory and Research* (pp. 347–480). Chicago, IL: Rand McNally; Knouse & Giacalone, 1992; Trevino, 1986.

Clearly, our work behaviour is shaped by our company's culture—and bad culture breeds bad behaviour. Behind many a corporate scandal, there lies a horrible corporate culture. Research conducted by the Ethics Resource Centre, a Washington-based nonprofit institution devoted to the advancement of organizational ethics, found that companies with a weak ethical culture experienced more frequent workplace misconduct compared to companies with a strong ethical culture. When top management fails to send a clear message about the principles and values of the company, the default message might be something like, "who cares?"

Fitting in with the culture and becoming a "team player" can be important for career advancement. However, team players need to be aware of the nature of the "team" and its culture. There were many team players in Enron, the Houston utility company that has come to be the poster child of corporate corruption. Research published in the *Journal of Business Ethics* by Sims and Brinkmann indicates that Enron's president and chief executive officer, Jeffrey Skilling, actively cultivated a culture that punished "underachievement" and rewarded unbridled ambition.[58] This kind of culture creates huge pressure to perform and typically leads to ethical compromises.

Unethical Behaviour as a Consequence of Decoupling

Organizations sometimes try to cover up inefficiencies by separating, or decoupling, the behaviour from its evaluation. Specifically, "avoidance," "discretion," and "overlooking" of inefficiencies are acts that maintain the assumption that people are acting in good faith. This encourages confidence in the myths that legitimize an organization's activities. Organizations can protect themselves from public scrutiny by ensuring that any questionable activities are "decoupled" from external evaluation in this sense.[59]

Corporate Language   The notion of decoupling suggests that organizations can conduct themselves in ways that hide activities that would otherwise be considered unacceptable if they were subjected to closer scrutiny. Among the most infamous examples of conformity with organizationally legitimized yet unethical behaviour were the crimes of the Nazi Party during World War II. While a variety of theories have been applied to attempt to explain the atrocities committed by the Nazis, one can consider how the Nazis decoupled behaviour from its evaluation. The use of accepted or legitimized symbols or practices can help to decouple actual activity from evaluation of that activity. For example, the use of euphemisms by the Nazi perpetrators decoupled actual behaviour from evaluation of that behaviour—the victims were not murdered, according to Nazi language, they were "selected." This language provided a sense of legitimacy to what would otherwise be viewed as inhuman behaviour. The ability to decouple deeds from evaluation or scrutiny supported the notion that legitimized beliefs, perpetuated through the use of symbolic language, could help maintain conformity and allegiance to a brutal cause.

Meyer and Rowan argue that to maintain external legitimacy, organizations adopt commonly accepted rules on the surface and incorporate them into their structure.[60] However,

---

[58] Sims, R.R., & Brinkmann, J. (2003). Enron ethics (or: Culture matters more than codes). *Journal of Business Ethics, 45*, 243–256.

[59] Zucker, L.G. (). Institutionalization as a mechanism of cultural persistence. *American Sociological Review, 42*(2), 726–742; Meyer & Rowan, 1977.

[60] Meyer & Rowan, 1977.

these rules may, in effect, be unrelated to how the activities are really conducted. The selective use of language to label various work practices is one method of disguising the unethical implications of workplace behaviour. For example, the unethical practice of corporate spying may be symbolically legitimized (to the organization and its employees) as a form of market analysis—a term that gives a sense of legitimacy to what would otherwise be considered an unethical business practice. This use of corporate language or labels can decouple the behaviour from moral evaluation of the behaviour. Consequently, this suggests that employees will be encouraged to engage in unethical behaviour where that behaviour has been legitimized as accepted business practice and where behaviour and evaluation of that behaviour are decoupled.

The business lexicon is filled with all kinds of buzzwords for the multitude of tasks that we may be asked to carry out at work. In their article published in the *Academy of Management Executive* (a publication produced by a leading international organization of management academics and practitioners), Anand, Ashforth, and Joshi suggest that organizations are sometimes guilty of using euphemisms to help disguise otherwise "illegitimate" workplace behaviour.[61] For example, the term *pretexting* is a polite way of describing the act of acquiring personal information through fraudulent means. This euphemism went relatively unnoticed until recently, when it garnered much unwanted attention at Hewlett-Packard. In 2005, then-CEO Patricia Dunn hired an outside security firm to investigate the source of leaks of confidential HP information to the media. The investigators employed pretexting—gaining confidential information using illicit methods, including impersonation. At the time of HP's investigation, the legality of pretexting was murky at best (it has since been designated as illegal by the US Congress). Regardless of this "innocent-sounding" label, pretexting ultimately cost Dunn her job, and it cost HP $14.5 million in legal penalties to settle a civil suit brought by the attorney general of California for violating the state's identity theft statute.[62]

Unethical Behaviour as a Consequence of Work Routinization

McDonald's is the most famous example of routinized work—work that is governed strictly by rules and regulations, as scientific management advocates. However, McDonald's is not the only organization dependent on routinized work practices; in fact, to a degree, most jobs have some element of routinization. A number of scholars have recognized the pervasive existence of routinized work practices, or habitual routines, in organizations. This phenomenon has been described as concrete behaviour that is not governed by rational deliberation but, rather, by routinized performance programs.[63]

The notion of adopting routinized performance programs as accepted ways of doing work can be thought of in terms of institutionalizing behaviour on the job. For example, consider the airline pilot who follows clear procedures with regard to flying the plane, or the auditor who follows strict guidelines with regard to performing an audit. Clearly, both

---

[61] Anand, V., Ashforth, B.E., & Joshi, M. (2004). Business as usual: The acceptance and perpetuation of corruption in organizations. *Academy of Management Executive, 18*(2), 39–53.

[62] Associated Press. (2006, December 8). HP settles pretexting scandal with fines. *Redmond Magazine*. Retrieved from http://redmondmag.com/articles/2006/12/08/hp-settles-pretexting-scandal-with-fines.aspx.

[63] March, J.G., & Simon, H.A. (1958). *Organizations*. New York, NY: Wiley.

these jobs require a high degree of professional judgment or discretion. However, both also rely on some standards and commonly accepted methods for performing the work, also referred to as **habitual routines**. Gersick and Hackman suggest that behavioural norms that evolve in groups pressure individuals to adhere to habitual routines.[64] That is, once a routine has been established in a group, the behaviours involved in executing the routine will submit to normative control. Management scholars have suggested that once a behaviour is accepted as a legitimate means of accomplishing the work, its actual effects (efficiency or otherwise) are not readily questioned.

habitual routines Commonly accepted methods for performing a task with, potentially, both functional and dysfunctional consequences. For example, once a behaviour is accepted as a legitimate means of accomplishing the work, its actual effects (efficiency or otherwise) are not readily questioned.

Habitual Routines   The legitimization of acceptable behaviour can extend to the actual job itself—how the work is performed. The organization may generate routinized work procedures that are viewed as legitimate since they follow an acceptable set of rules. For example, following the written guidelines of conducting an audit is viewed as a legitimate method of auditing. The proliferation of technical guidelines to govern work methods enhances the perceived legitimacy of the work. However, in actuality, these routinized work methods may be neither the most efficient nor the most effective way of conducting the work.

Gersick and Hackman identify both functional and dysfunctional consequences of routinized or habitual behaviour.[65] A major advantage of habitual routines is that they save time and energy, since they don't require active management; in this respect, they should improve efficiency. How much of our work constitutes simply "going through the motions"—that is, the portion of our work that does not demand constant mental scrutiny but rather can be performed with minimal attention to detail? Among the disadvantages identified were the tendency for routines to permit a misinterpretation of the situation to occur. That is, if a group fails to recognize a novel stimulus situation or changes that occur to familiar situations, then invoking a habitual routine will be inappropriate.

What is the impact of such habitual routines on ethical behaviour in organizations? The everyday patterns of work can create blind spots when it comes to identifying the ethical implications of our actions. Gersick and Hackman assert that, over time, we develop a set of patterns or routines in dealing with the responsibilities of our job. One consequence of this is a reduction in the level of scrutiny of the moral implications of our everyday work decisions.[66] Remember, for example, the Firestone-Ford debacle a number of years back? Over 200 traffic deaths were blamed on defective Firestone tires (many sold with the Ford Explorer). In 2000, Firestone recalled 14.4 million of their tires—but only after 88 people died, and long after an overseas recall had begun (in 1993). Critics have suggested that the decision to avoid a North American recall reflects the common corporate practice of placing shareholders' interests above all other stakeholder interests.[67]

Ironically, managers who are obsessed with short-term, bottom-line results can often damage the longer-term interests of their company (including corporate goodwill or image). This same kind of thinking might be responsible for the exploitation of foreign populations as "guinea pigs" for the pharmaceutical industry (see Talking Business 10.4).

---

[64] Gersick, C.J.G., & Hackman, J.R. (1990). Habitual routines in task-performing groups. *Organizational Behavior and Human Decision Processes, 47*, 65–97.

[65] Gersick & Hackman, 1990.

[66] Gersick & Hackman, 1990.

[67] Verschoor, C. (2000). Legal compliance and ethical blunders at Ford/Firestone. *Strategic Finance, 82*(4).

The Global Pharmaceutical Industry and Human Guinea Pigs

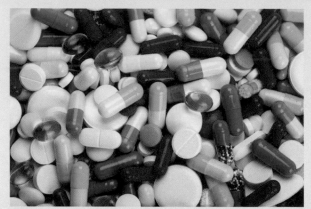

Nomad_Soul/Shutterstock

In a picture perfect world, everyone would have access to the necessary medications to support health and to fight illness and disease. However, there are many citizens in many countries who simply cannot afford to obtain these necessary drugs. So what happens to citizens of the poorer countries? How do they afford needed medicines? What price are they willing to pay to gain access to needed drugs? Are they subject to exploitation by major pharmaceutical companies?

It seems that poor countries have managed to attract needed medicines in recent years not necessarily through the generosity of pharmaceutical companies, but rather through a growing trend—the need for these companies to find suitable locations to test their drugs.

There is evidence that more than half of all drug trials across the world take place in newly industrialized countries. Why? According to many observers, there are cost advantages for companies to seek participants in drug trials from poorer countries. As asserted in a recent article in Spiegel Online International,

> Not only are the studies cheaper to carry out there, but many participants are thankful that they are being cared for in any way at all. The companies are lured by the prospect that established international standards are less stringently applied than they are in Western Europe, Japan or the United States.

Based on reports, apparently pharmaceutical companies can cut their research costs by about 60% by outsourcing the work, which includes the costs of drug testing. Among those countries targeted are China, Indonesia, and Thailand. In addition, India has become an attractive location for researchers because of the size and genetic diversity of its large population. However, critics also argue that India is popular as a testing ground because of its lax regulations. Is it possible that the same stringencies that apply to testing in Canada might not necessarily apply in India?

Some critics assert that pharmaceutical companies are testing new drugs on individuals who may not always be entirely aware of what they are signing up for. These critics have also suggested that some of this drug testing has been reckless and possibly resulted in the deaths of participants. Individuals tested can range from infants to adults.

Controversy erupted in India when infant deaths arose subsequent to the testing of an anti-hypertensive drug called Valsartan. This medication was produced by the Swiss manufacturer Novartis, which has denied all culpability in the deaths. Novartis argued that the infants in the study had already been seriously ill and may have simply succumbed to their illness.

Ironically, if a drug is proven to be successful, often it is no longer accessible to these test subjects, who simply cannot afford the cost of the drug. Sadly, these individuals' health begins to deteriorate once again because of a lack of proper medication.

It is accepted and acknowledged that in order to create drugs for humans, we must test these drugs on human subjects. However, if a pharmaceutical company is hesitant to test its drugs on subjects from the Western hemisphere and turns to poorer countries instead, perhaps we need to ask ourselves why.

Sources: Kuhrt, N. (2013, May 14). Testing meds: Companies look overseas for cheap subjects. Spiegel Online International. Retrieved from www.spiegel.de/international/world/drug-companies-perform-medical-tests-in-developing-countries-a-899798.html; Buncombe, A., & Lakhani, N. (2011, November 14). Without consent: how drugs companies exploit Indian 'guinea pigs.' *The Independent*. Retrieved from www.independent.co.uk/news/world/asia/without-consent-how-drugs-companies-exploit-indian-guinea-pigs-6261919.html.

Reduction of Critical Thought   A fundamental characteristic of habitual routines—the inability to adapt to change—has important implications for ethical behaviour in the workplace. For example, consider a situation involving an engineer who habitually performs a safety check on the construction standards of a building plan. The engineer performs all the checks in accordance with the professional or legal requirements, while neglecting to consider nonroutine indicators of potential risk in the construction. Certainly, there is an ethical or moral dimension to decisions or practices that can affect the well-being of others: The duty of care in performance that exists beyond strict legal requirements can be considered an ethical concern. In the case of the engineer, strict adherence to habitual routines permits unethical behaviour to occur because of the failure to critically analyze the ethical implications of a workplace behaviour—that is, to consider the welfare of all parties potentially affected by the behaviour.

Unethical Behaviour as a Consequence of Organizational Identity

Robert Jackall has argued that the bureaucratization of organizations has influenced "moral consciousness." According to Jackall, this transformation heralded

> . . . the decline of the old middle class of entrepreneurs, free professionals, and independent businessmen—the traditional carriers of the old Protestant Ethic—and the ascendance of a new middle class of salaried employees whose common characteristic was and is their dependence on the big organization.[68]

According to this view, corporate America destroyed ethical values. The Protestant ethic emphasized the "stewardship" responsibilities associated with the accumulation of wealth. However, as Jackall argues, "the very accumulation of wealth that the old Protestant Ethic made possible gradually stripped away the religious basis of the ethic, especially among the rising middle class that benefited from it." In addition, organizational bureaucracies created their own "internal rules" and "social context" to guide individual conduct:

> Bureaucracy . . . breaks apart the older connection between the meaning of work and salvation. In the bureaucratic world, one's success . . . no longer depends on one's own efforts . . . but on the capriciousness of one's superiors and the market.[69]

Is Bureaucracy to Blame?   Based on this perspective, modern organizations encourage unethical behaviour largely as a result of the demise of the Protestant work ethic through the bureaucratization of organizations. Why blame bureaucracy? Bureaucracies are considered guilty given their characteristics of requiring the subjugation of personal belief systems to the beliefs or goals of the organization. This is reflected in the notion of "working for the boss"—our futures are dependent on our ability to fulfill our organizational responsibilities, regardless of the consequences. To the extent that indi-

---

[68] Jackall, R. (1988). *Moral mazes: The world of corporate managers.* New York, NY: Oxford University Press.
[69] Jackall, 1988.

vidual identities continue to become intrinsically bound up with organizational identities, the ethics of an individual employee may be tied to the ethics of the organization he or she identifies with. To the extent that our personal identity is bound up with our organizational identity, what organizations demand of us may dictate the ethics that we live by.

Social identity theory[70] posits that individuals classify themselves and others into social categories (organizational membership, age, gender, and so on) that are defined by the typical characteristics abstracted from the members. Organizational identification is a specific form of social identification.[71] Individuals can identify with elements of the organization that have been reified—that is, that have become embodiments of the characteristics perceived as typical of its members: "I work for IBM," "I am a lawyer," and so on. These are all statements of identity based on an organization or a profession.

What are the consequences of this process of social or organizational identification? One consequence of social identity is the tendency of the individual to support the values and actions of the group and to internalize the perception of the group as more desirable compared to other groups.[72] Group members can enhance their self-esteem by increasing the desirability associated with their social categories.[73] The consequences of identification with the organization also have implications for ethical behaviour of group members.

The close association between our own personal identity and our organization's identity can lead us to view our workplace through "rose-coloured" glasses. According to Ishmael Akaah, our strong desire to believe in the integrity of our organization can cause us to overlook and even assist in unethical acts performed in the "name of the boss." Consider the case of Betty Vinson. By most accounts, she was a caring mother, devoted employee, and certainly not a crook. She also worked for WorldCom as an accountant and assisted in falsifying the reporting of billions of dollars in profits. According to many investigative press reports, Vinson's acquiescence may have been a result of her belief in the integrity of her superiors, including Scott Sullivan (who was considered to be one of the top chief financial officers in the United States). It may have been difficult for her to believe that any requests coming from such a credible source could actually be fraudulent. What Vinson experienced is not unique—she identified with the best aspects of her company and overlooked the worst.

In the Name of the Boss   When we identify with our organizations, we tend to become less critical of its policies and behaviour. The notion that identification with the organization restricts or discourages evaluations or perceptions that might reflect poorly on the organization has clear ethical implications. Ashforth and Mael suggest that identification can provide a mechanism whereby an individual can continue to believe in the integrity of the organization despite wrongdoing by senior management.[74] Individuals who maintain a strong organizational identity will not critically evaluate their behaviour

[70] Tajfel, H. (1981). *Human groups and social categories: Studies in social psychology*. Cambridge, UK: Cambridge University Press; Tajfel, H., & Turner, J.C. (1985). The social identity theory of intergroup behaviour. In S. Worchel & W.G. Austin (Eds.), *Psychology of intergroup relations* (2nd ed.) (pp. 7–24). Chicago, IL: Nelson Hall.

[71] Ashforth, B.E., & Mael, F. (1989). Social identity theory and the organization. *Academy of Management Review, 14*(1), 20–39.

[72] Turner, J. (1982). Towards a cognitive redefinition of the social group. In H. Tajfel (Ed.), *Social identity and intergroup relations* (pp. 15–40). Cambridge, UK: Cambridge University Press.

[73] Tajfel & Turner, 1985.

[74] Ashforth & Mael, 1989.

on its own merits (that is, the actual consequences), but will instead judge behaviour based on perceptions of the social category to which they belong. For example, a public accountant who identifies strongly with her firm or professional body may avoid critical evaluation of her conduct when she perceives herself as acting on behalf of the firm or professional body, which upholds professional standards.

Indeed, at the extreme, there is research to suggest that employees will engage in unethical behaviour at the request of authority figures.[75] In addition to the influence of authority figures, the research has explored the effects of peers on ethical behaviour. In fact, many researchers have suggested that unethical behaviour is learned in the process of interacting with individuals who are part of intimate personal groups or role sets. That is, employees who have learned through differential association in their role sets to be unethical and have the opportunity to engage in unethical behaviour will be more likely to do so.[76]

Unethical Behaviour as a Consequence of Organizational Roles

Organizational role theory proposes that individuals in organizations occupy positions or roles that involve a set of activities, including interactions with others, that are required or expected as part of the job.[77] Individuals fulfill role requirements based on internalized expectations concerning the responsibilities of the role. Roles have a psychological reality to the individuals occupying them.

The presence of incompatible expectations of attitudes, beliefs, and behaviours inherent in social roles will generate an ambivalence known as *role conflict*.[78] Kahn and colleagues identified several forms of role conflict, including inter-role conflict, which refers to the competing demands of two or more roles that an individual occupies.[79] For example, the demands associated with the role of "employee" may conflict with the demands associated with the role of "family member." How do individuals resolve the inherent conflict of organizationally situated roles or identities? Ashforth and Mael summarized the methods individuals employ to cognitively resolve role conflict, including denying role conflict, compartmentalizing roles or identities, and prioritizing roles.[80] These types of coping mechanisms suggest that individuals do not necessarily engage in a critical, objective evaluation of competing role demands.

organizational role theory The theory that organizational roles have a psychological reality to the individuals occupying them, whereby they fulfill role requirements based on internalized expectations concerning responsibilities of the role.

Role Conflict   What are the implications of organizational roles for the ethical behaviour of individuals occupying those roles? More specifically, what are the implications of these conflict resolution strategies for ethical behaviour? Consider the case of an employee in the role of salesperson who must decide whether the role responsibility of reaching the sales target at all costs should take priority over his role as an honest citizen. Similarly, in

[75] Ricklee, R. (1985, October 31). Ethics in America. *Wall Street Journal*, 3; Milgram, S. (1974). *Obedience to authority*. New York: Harper & Row.

[76] Sutherland, E., & Cressey, D.R. (1970). *Principles of criminology*. Chicago, IL: J.B. Lippincott.

[77] Kahn, et al. (1964). *Organizational stress: Studies in role conflict and ambiguity*. New York, NY: Wiley.

[78] Merton, R.K. (1957). *Social theory and social structure* (2nd ed.). New York, NY: Free Press.

[79] Kahn et al., 1964.

[80] Ashforth & Mael, 1989.

the business of sports, a football player in the role of an "employee" must decide whether the role of winning a game at all costs should take priority over his role as a decent and trustworthy human being. What if something is legal but unethical? Should there be consequences?

The individual may rationalize that he is responsibly fulfilling role obligations, even though the behaviour required to fulfill the role of salesperson might be ethically unsound. Consistent with Ashforth and Mael's summary of responses to role conflict, the individual can resolve the role conflict by compartmentalizing or prioritizing role demands as a means to rationalize the behaviour. That is, the employee can adopt a different set of standards to judge what constitutes appropriate salesperson behaviour as contrasted with appropriate honest citizen behaviour. Essentially, this suggests that ethical conflicts among competing role demands can effectively be ignored by the individual through this cognitive process.

Conflict Resolution   What effect does the organization have on role conflict resolution? How an individual chooses to resolve the multiple role conflicts will depend largely on the organizational context. Returning to the previous discussion, the institutional elements, including culture, identity, decoupling, and routinization, will impact the individual's reactions to role conflicts and demands. For example, if the organizational culture ignores an ethical dimension to role requirements, individuals will not attempt to reconcile their role performance with ethical considerations; if the organization institutionalizes habitual behaviour and suppresses analytical thought, then evaluation of the ethical implications of role responsibilities and role conflicts will similarly be reduced. Clearly, organizational context will significantly influence how an individual resolves role conflict.

Judging the Ethics of Organizations

Earlier in this chapter, we considered two central models of ethical decision making: endpoint ethics and rule ethics. These prove to be useful models for critiquing the ethics of our everyday decisions. Can we judge the ethics of organizations as entities? That is, can we critique the nature of the organizational arrangements under which we function as employees? There is another ethical tool or model that speaks directly to the nature of organizations and the question of the conditions under which organizations adhere to or violate ethical principles. One such tool for considering the ethical dimension of organizational issues is social contract ethics.

social contract ethics This model of ethics posits that the rules by which people live are those that they would agree to live by if given the opportunity to make a choice based on reason or knowledge.

Social Contract Ethics   One version of rule ethics, **social contract ethics**, was articulated by John Locke.[81] This model posits that the rules by which people live are those that they would agree to live by if given the opportunity to make a choice based on reason or knowledge. Locke's idea of the social contract provided a basis for a new model of organizations as networks of contracts. Immanuel Kant added that only rules that apply equally to everyone are ethical.[82]

Taken together, the social contract model of ethical reasoning views the ethical rules that we live by as products of an implicit contract. A social contract is an implicit agreement regarding basic principles of conduct. These social contracts are harboured by the

---

[81] Locke, J. (1690). *Second treatise on civil government*. Cambridge, UK: Cambridge University Press.

[82] Kant, I. (1785 [1993]). *Grounding for the metaphysics of morals*. Trans. J.W. Ellington. Indianapolis, IN: Hackett.

cultures of groups or organizations and by our society. Organizational social contracts represent the ground rules regarding conditions of employment, rewards, and performance expectations. Organizational management researchers have viewed organizations as a web of implicit contracts—every time you enter a new organization you are entering a web of contracts. Of course, the question is, "Are these contracts or ground rules sound?"

A contract is sound if all parties entering into it have entered into it freely and fairly. And fairness involves the notion that, regardless of your position, you would view the contract as equally fair from all perspectives. It is not unbalanced in favour of some interests over others. According to social contract ethics, then, an individual should do what a fair, voluntary contract would dictate—that is, this should be the ethical guide for dealing with any issue. Social contract ethics is essentially about assessing the ethics or fairness of an organizational arrangement—whether we are looking at how people are hired or fired, how they are evaluated, or how they are rewarded, among other things. So any member of an organization attempting to address that test would ask at least three questions: Do I really agree with this contract, or am I just tolerating it? If I occupied a different position in this company, would I accept this contract?

An Example: The Ethics of Downsizing Let's consider a pervasive issue that continues to affect the business landscape: organizational downsizing. What might the social contract model say about the ethics of downsizing? Consider the recent observations of a writer who commented on the "new deal" between workers and the organizations:

> In the old manufacturing economy, blue-collar unemployment always rose and fell in lock step with factory inventories; now a similar thing is happening to the mostly white-collar workers in the sleek offices of the new economy. . . . If this sounds like deja vu all over again, it is . . . [Years ago] companies began getting very explicit in their warnings to employees: Jobs were not for life. Harvard professor Rosabeth Moss Kanter was one of a chorus of academics and consultants arguing that since companies could no longer provide job security, they should do more to give workers "employability security" through training and skills counselling.[83]

We could consider the implicit contract between a number of different parties, but let's just consider the implicit agreements between employer and employee. Many critics have argued that what we have seen with the downsizing phenomenon is a violation of a number of implicit rules existing between employer and employee. No longer is there an implied agreement that you enter a company in your twenties, work hard, and retire some 20 or perhaps 30 years later. Throughout the 1990s we witnessed massive layoffs of employees who felt they had kept their end of the social contract by working hard for their organizations, yet were terminated in an organizational restructuring or downsizing.

This view of a violation of the social contract was expressed in the *Globe and Mail*'s article "One Day You're Family, the Next Day You're Fired." The article recounted the events that preceded the termination of about 300 employees at a Canadian company as part of a downsizing. The article told how the terminated employees were locked out of the building and only permitted back inside to collect their personal belongings, under

---

[83] Morris, B. (2001, July 23). White-collar blues. *Fortune*.

Christy Thompson/Shutterstock

the watchful eyes of security guards who also escorted them out again. These kinds of stories were pervasive throughout the 1990s and, unfortunately, continue today.

What does the future hold? Will we see a decreased or increased emphasis on social responsibility? Well, we have been experiencing much turbulence in the corporate world in recent years. Part of the chaos, including the infamous spread of corporate downsizing, has left many people skeptical of the morality of business. On the other hand, there is a strong belief that business will place increasing emphasis on the recognition of the needs of different stakeholders. That is, many observers believe that more and more businesses will need to place more emphasis on their social responsiveness to maintain legitimacy and acceptance from the community at large. Many industries have yet to fully come to grips with the challenge of increasing social responsibility.

Objective 4 Define stakeholders and explain why they are important for business to manage.

BUSINESS AND SOCIETY

What constitutes socially responsible business behaviour? In addition, should businesses be required to look beyond their profit objectives to help society? Unethical behaviour may be directed against the organization itself, or it may be consistent with the organization's goals but inconsistent with commonly accepted ethical principles. Whether unethical behaviour comes in the form of subtle discrimination against other employees, "padding" expense accounts, paying or accepting bribes, questionable advertising, or other forms of fraudulent activity, there is little doubt that the costs of such behaviour eventually accumulate.

The media has increasingly reported a concern over the erosion of business responsibility, and unethical activities in organizations are estimated to cost industry billions of dollars a year.[84] It seems that much of what has been written in the popular press and reported in the news has tended to reflect poorly on the ethics of business. The recent phenomenon of corporate downsizings and massive layoffs has certainly contributed to the public's dim view of business. Other recurring issues that raise questions about the ethics of business include things such as the misuse of natural resources, too close a relationship with government, not treating employees properly, and corporations being too big and too powerful. All these perceptions, whether accurate or inaccurate, reflect a commonly held view that business and ethics do not go together.

Some scholars have suggested that there is a crisis of confidence in a variety of corporate activities.[85] Perhaps most of the blame for the current distrust of business can be traced to the recent flood of scandals that has permeated the news media reports. If anything has shaken the business–society relationship, it has been the countless headline-grabbing scandals, particularly within the past several years. For many observers, the rapidly expanding list of corporate wrongdoers has all but caused a breach in society's trust for business leaders.

Numerous companies worldwide have undermined public confidence in the integrity of business through their scandalous activities. The list of ethics violations is long and has been attributed to such companies as Enron, WorldCom, Tyco International, Conseco,

---

[84] Jones, D. (1997, April 4–6). Doing the wrong thing: 48% of workers admit to unethical or illegal acts. *USA Today*.
[85] Mahar, M. (1992). Unwelcome legacy: There's still a big unpaid tab for the S and L bailout. *Barron's*, *72*(48), 16.

Adelphia Cable, Global Crossing, Xerox, and HealthSouth. Elsewhere, allegations of fraudulent activities have been levelled at the Dutch food distributor and retailer Royal Ahold, France's Vivendi, Britain's Marconi, SK Corporation in South Korea, and Tokyo Electric Power Company in Japan.

Anyone who has paid attention to news reports understands that Canadian businesses are no less immune to corporate scandal and wrongdoing than any other business sector in the world. Consider the following Canadian "Hall of Shame" candidates:

- Canada earned the distinction of being home to a company that became the first multinational corporation to be fined ($2.2 million) for bribing a government official involved in a World Bank–funded dam project designed to provide water to South Africa. Acres International, an Ontario-based engineering firm, was found guilty of paying a bribe of $266,000 to the former chief executive officer of the Lesotho Highlands Water Project in Africa as a means to obtain a $21.5 million technical assistance contract for a multi-dam construction program.

- The Montreal family-entertainment company Cinar paid a total of $25 million in lawsuits stemming from fraudulent business ventures.

- The Canadian government, together with a number of Canadian businesses, faced charges of corruption stemming from a government advertising and corporate sponsorship program managed by the federal Public Works Department. The auditor general's report indicated that $100 million was paid to a number of communications agencies in the form of fees and commissions, and the program was essentially designed to generate commissions for these companies rather than to produce any benefit for Canadians.

- CIBC agreed to pay a penalty of US$80 million to settle charges of aiding and abetting the Enron accounting fraud.

Whether the business community will be able to adequately respond to society's expectations of greater accountability is largely dependent on the level of attention that businesses afford this issue. And, given the growing attention directed at corporate behaviour, the onus appears to be on business to develop a much better understanding of the status of societal expectations.

Managing the Forces of Business and the Stakeholders of Business

> Life in business organizations was once simpler. . . . The business organization today, especially in the modern corporation, is the institutional centrepiece of a complex society. Our society today consists of many people with a multitude of interests, expectations, and demands as to what major organizations ought to provide to accommodate people's lifestyles. . . . In a society conscious of an always-improving lifestyle, with more groups every day laying claims to their pieces of the good life, business organizations today need to be responsive to individuals and groups they once viewed as powerless and unable to make such claims on them. We call these individuals and groups stakeholders.[86]

---

[86] Karakowsky, L., Carroll, A., & Buchholtz, A. (2005). *Business and society* (p. 66). Toronto, ON: Nelson Thomson.

In order to more fully understand the ethical dimension of business, it is critical to appreciate the concept of *stakeholders*. In fact, the stakeholder concept has become a central idea in understanding the business and society relationship. **Stakeholders** are individuals or groups with whom a business interacts and who have a "stake," or vested interest, in the business. A stake can range from simply an interest in management's actions, to a legal or moral right to be treated a certain way, to a legal claim of ownership at the other extreme.[87]

Traditionally, we observe two broad groups of stakeholders: external and internal. External stakeholders comprise such parties as governments, consumers, and community members. Internal stakeholders can include business owners and employees. The notion here is that stakeholders have legitimate claims on the organization. Consequently, a fundamental responsibility of management is to address and manage the needs of differing stakeholder groups—and not just the most obvious stakeholders, the owners/investors or shareholders of the business. Keep in mind that, just as stakeholders can be affected by the actions or decisions of the business firm, these stakeholders also can influence the organization's actions and decisions. Therefore, the management of stakeholder interests is critical to business success (see Exhibit 10.2).

Exhibit 10.2 External Stakeholders of Business

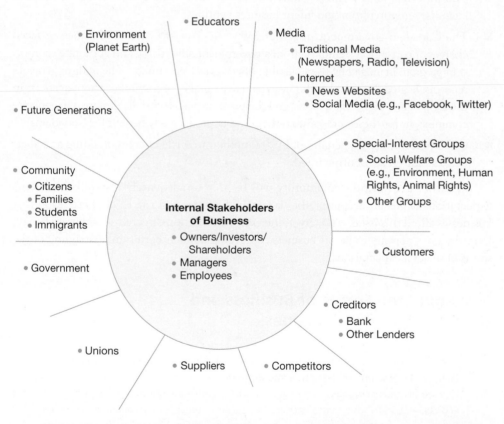

In addition to the owners, investors, and shareholders, other obvious stakeholders include employees and customers, as well as competitors, suppliers, the community, special-interest groups, media, and society in general. Some observers would also view our environment and our future generations as important stakeholders in the activities of business.

---

[87] Karakowsky, Carroll, & Buchholtz, 2005.

The importance of managing diverse stakeholder needs is evident in the following assertion by David Wheeler and Maria Sillanpaa:

> In the future, development of loyal relationships with customers, employees. shareholders, and other stakeholders will become one of the most important determinants of commercial viability and business success. Increasing shareholder value will be best served if your company cultivates the support of all who may influence its importance.[88]

Managing the Challenges of the Societal Force

So what does it take to successfully manage the challenges of the societal force? An organization that adequately addresses the societal force will, by definition, fulfill its responsibilities to its various stakeholders. What is the connection between the societal force and fulfilling the responsibilities to various stakeholder groups? To answer that question we need to understand the concept of corporate social responsibility (CSR), which we discuss next.

CORPORATE SOCIAL RESPONSIBILITY

The historical "ethical yardstick" for businesses has been profit—the "bottom line." Scholars such as economist Milton Friedman argued that the workings of the free and competitive marketplace will "moralize" corporate behaviour.[89] Therefore, businesses need only be concerned with the profit motive, since the "invisible hand" of the free market will produce a "systematic morality." Similarly, John Kenneth Galbraith argued that corporate responsibilities should be purely rational and economic.[90] However, according to Galbraith, it is the regulatory hands of the law and the political process, rather than the invisible hand of the marketplace, that turns these objectives to the "common good."

Both of these views reject the exercise of independent moral judgment by corporations as actors in society. On the other hand, most scholars concerned with the study of business ethics implicitly reject these views and instead argue that it is the responsibility of business organizations to develop a "moral conscience" and exercise ethical judgment or social responsibility.[91]

The term **corporate social responsibility (CSR)** refers to those obligations or responsibilities of an organization that involve going beyond the production of goods or services at a profit and the requirements of competition, legal regulations, or customs. Social responsibility involves an obligation to create policies, make decisions, and engage in actions that are desirable in terms of society's values and objectives.

We can elaborate upon this definition by referring to one of the most commonly cited definitions of CSR. Archie Carroll's four-part definition asserts that the social responsibility

Objective 5 Analyze the debate for and against the relevance of corporate social responsibility.

corporate social responsibility (CSR) Obligations or responsibilities of an organization to go beyond the production of goods or services at a profit, and beyond the requirements of competition, legal regulation, or custom, thus acting in a way desirable in terms of the values and objectives of society. This includes a business's economic, legal, ethical, and philanthropic responsibilities.

[88] Wheeler, D., & Sillanpaa, M. (1997). *The stakeholder corporation: A blueprint for maximizing stakeholder value*. London, UK: Pitman Publishing.

[89] Friedman, M. (1962). *Capitalism and freedom*. Chicago, IL: University of Chicago Press; Friedman, M. (1970, September 13). The social responsibility of business is to increase its profits. *New York Times Magazine*.

[90] Galbraith, J.K. (1958). *The affluent society*. Boston, MA: Houghton Mifflin Company.

[91] Goodpaster, K.E., & Matthews, J.B. (1983). Can a corporation have a conscience? In T.L. Beauchamp & N.E. Bowie (Eds.), *Ethical theory and business*. Englewood Hills, NJ: Prentice Hall.

Exhibit 10.3 The Four Components of CSR

CSR Responsibilities	Societal Expectation	Examples
Economic responsibilities	Society *requires* business to fulfill these responsibilities.	Generate rational business strategy, make profits, minimize costs
Legal responsibilities	Society *requires* business to fulfill these responsibilities.	Honour all relevant laws and regulations governing business activities
Ethical responsibilities	Society *expects* business to fulfill these responsibilities.	Engage in business practices that are in line with what society considers acceptable, fair, and just
Philanthropic responsibilities	Society *desires* business to fulfill these responsibilities.	Engage in activities that help the betterment of society (e.g., volunteerism, charity)

Source: Karakowsky, L., Carroll, A., & Buchholtz, A. (2005). *Business and society*, Exhibit 8.1. Toronto, ON: Thomson Learning Global Rights Group. Reprinted by permission.

economic responsibilities The responsibilities of a company to make profits and minimize costs.

legal responsibilities The responsibilities of businesses to honour all relevant laws and regulations governing business activities.

ethical responsibilities The responsibilities of businesses to engage in business practices that are in line with what society considers acceptable, fair, and just.

philanthropic responsibilities The responsibilities of businesses to engage in activities that help to improve society.

of business encompasses the economic, legal, ethical, and discretionary (philanthropic) expectations that society has of organizations at a given point in time[92] (see Exhibit 10.3).

Carroll's definition indicates that there are issues above economic and legal ones that a business must confront. Obviously, a business must address economic responsibilities—it must generate goods or services that society wants. And further, a business must abide by the laws to fulfill its legal responsibilities. However, this definition suggests that just fulfilling these two areas of concern is insufficient. Ethical responsibilities include the standards or expectations that reflect what the societal stakeholders regard as fair. Finally, business has somewhat voluntary or philanthropic responsibilities that, while not mandatory, do reflect part of the implicit agreement between business and society and can include such activities as corporate donations, volunteerism, and any other kind of voluntary involvement of the business with the community or other stakeholders.[93]

Consider such acts of CSR as those demonstrated by Levi Strauss & Co., which has tried very hard to maintain strict work standards to protect employees in operations in different parts of the world. In addition, the company is consistently lauded for its efforts in the social sphere:

> Besides patching together jeans, Levi Strauss has a long history of funding projects that help patch together groups of people. Project Change, an independent nonprofit originally funded by the Levi Strauss Foundation (and still closely associated with it), combats racism in communities where the company has manufacturing operations. There are now sites in Albuquerque, El Paso, Knoxville, and Valdosta, Ga. In Albuquerque . . . research showed that people of colour were twice as likely as whites to be denied home loans, regardless of their income. Project Change established a Fair Lending Center to help customers comparison-shop among local banks and to encourage banks to lend in poor New Mexico neighbourhoods. In Valdosta, the project talked nine banks into funding mortgages for low-income first-time home buyers.[94]

---

[92] Karakowsky, Carroll, & Buchholtz, 2005.

[93] Karakowsky, Carroll, & Buchholtz, 2005.

[94] Tarpley, N. (2000, July 10). Levi's mends the social fabric. *Fortune.* Reprinted with permission.

This is certainly admirable corporate behaviour, but is it necessary? That is, does Levi Strauss have an ethical obligation as a business to do this? While we applaud the efforts of companies like Canadian Tire, Levi Strauss, Magna, and Southwest Airlines, should we demand such behaviour from all organizations? And more generally, does business have a moral responsibility to us—whether we are employees, customers, creditors, or society in general? These are issues that have been debated for years and that are explored in the following sections.

The CSR Debate

There is much diverse opinion regarding the degree to which business should practise social responsibility. Some argue that, at best, business should have very limited social responsibilities, while others argue that the social responsibilities of business should be extensive. What are the arguments for believing that business should take on extensive social responsibilities, and what is the rationale used by those who believe business should not be required to take on the mantle of social responsibility? Let's consider the cases first against, and then for, social responsibility (see Exhibit 10.4).

Against Social Resonsibility	For Social Responsibility
1. Business is business.	1. Business should conform to societal expectations.
2. Business plays by its own rules.	2. CSR is a practical strategy.
3. Business should not dictate morality.	3. Business must acknowledge its network of shareholders.
4. Organizations cannot be held accountable for their actions.	4. There are long-term benefits to be gained from CSR.
5. High costs are passed to the consumer.	5. Business has the power and resources to do good.

Exhibit 10.4 The CSR Debate

The Case Against CSR

Business Is Business   Probably one of the best-known arguments against social responsibility for business comes from the work of economist Milton Friedman, who argued that profit maximization is the primary purpose of business, and to have any other purpose is not socially responsible! Friedman points out that in a free enterprise, private property system, a manager is an employee of the owners of the business and, consequently, is directly responsible to them. In other words, Friedman and others argue that a business's primary responsibility is to the owners or shareholders. Clearly, owners and shareholders want to maximize profit, and so this should be the business's highest priority.

Similarly, new entrepreneurs often invest their own money in creating companies and sometimes risk their personal life savings. At the start of any business, many would argue that being socially responsible cannot be a priority. Although a product may have much potential, the future success of a business is still unknown. Will customers like the product, buy the product, and rebuy it again and again? Making a profit becomes essential to the business's survival and to the entrepreneur keeping his or her investment. Later on, to expand the business and to get further funding, the business must prove to be well-managed and, of course, be profitable. (See Talking Business 10.5.)

Dragons' Den

On the hit Canadian TV show *Dragons' Den*, the importance of earning a profit is emphasized in each episode. The reality show invites entrepreneurs with new business ideas to showcase their products in front of a panel of successful Canadian businesspeople and to make a case to invest in their company.

The hardest critic on the show is Kevin O'Leary, who always demands, "How is this business going to make me money?" If the business has not made any sales or the product does not appear to be potentially profitable, the panel of investors quickly state their negative opinion and then say: "And for that reason—I'm out!"

The television show is a colourful reminder that investors must be convinced above all that the business will treat their investment with the highest priority. While investors may want the company to "do good," they do not want this to come at the expense of their "hard earned money," so to speak. In fairness to the Dragons, if the business cannot generate profits then no responsibilities are achievable—social or otherwise.

Some have argued that a regard for ethical values in market decisions might lead businesspeople to confuse their economic goals with altruistic goals so that they fail to fulfill the basic business function of operating efficiently. While most scholars in the field advocate one form or another of corporate responsibility, they also acknowledge the difficulty of adopting an ethical corporate objective. Albert Carr argued that no company can be expected to serve the social interest unless its self-interest is also served, either by the expectation of profit or the avoidance of punishment.

Consider the case of Maple Leaf Foods. Here was a national Canadian-based company known for its socially responsible behaviour—including establishing plants in smaller Canadian communities such as Moncton (New Brunswick), Winnipeg (Manitoba), and North Battleford (Saskatchewan). Yet recently it announced that it will close all of these older manufacturing plants to restructure the company, reduce costs, and modernize production of its prepared-meats business. While it plans to open new plants elsewhere, there will be a net job loss of 1,550 positions.[95]

Is it socially responsible for a company to take away jobs that it initially created? On the other hand, given increased competitiveness from larger, more efficient US meat manufacturers gaining market share in Canada, if Maple Leaf does not reduce costs, the company could be put in dire straits. By being more efficient, Maple Leaf can continue its business in the long run and maintain Canadian manufacturing jobs. Is this socially responsible? If you consider Maple Leaf's responsibility to its owners and creditors, they argue that it would have been irresponsible not to close the older plants.

Business Plays by Its Own Rules   This sentiment suggests that business cannot be judged by the same set of rules or standards of moral conduct that we apply outside of business. Carr, in a famous article written for the *Harvard Business Review*, raised the question of whether we should expect business managers to apply the same ethical standards we might apply in our personal lives. Carr suggested that "bluffing" (that is, lying), which may be viewed as an unethical practice in social relations, can be viewed as legitimate behaviour within the boundaries of business activity. Carr compared corporate activity to a poker

---

[95] Mercer, G. (2011, October 19). Maple Leaf Foods closing Kitchener Schneider's plant, 1,200 jobs to be lost. TheRecord.com. Retrieved from www.therecord.com/news/business/article/611727--maple-leaf-foods-closing-kitchener-schneider-s-plant-1-200-jobs-to-be-lost.

game, where ethical standards within the boundaries of the "game" may differ from societal standards.[96] The "players" (business executives), therefore, may engage in activity that is acceptable within the "rules" of business, even though this activity may be viewed as unethical by the public (those outside the "game" of business). Therefore, individuals may employ ethical standards in business that differ from those generally employed in their nonworking lives. That is, where "business bluffing" has been accepted as a form of business conduct, members come to believe in this behaviour as an accepted way of doing business. For example, union and management negotiations are subject to negotiator tendencies to demand more than what might otherwise be equitable as a means of bargaining. Similarly, a company may convince customers that its product is worth significantly more than the cost of producing it as a means to accrue a high profit.

Given this, why should we expect businesses to be good citizens in the same way as individuals? We might expect that a business will try to advertise its product in a manner that suggests it may be of much higher quality than it really is—that's part of the rules of business, which are largely focused on profit maximization and not necessarily on seeking truth in advertising, for example.

But is business a game? Do you accept the notion that business is like a game and should be played by its own rules? Is it acceptable to leave our moral standards at the door, so to speak, when we enter the workplace? Recall the scenario presented earlier in this chapter of the CEO and the gift to achieve the $22 million contract. Would you give the gift? Why or why not? If this is considered a bribe and is therefore unethical, why would you give the gift? The common response is because it is part of the "rules of the game." This is the expectation that, in business, this is a legitimate and commonly accepted practice. However, there is a danger in decoupling behaviour—that is, in avoiding scrutiny of business behaviour. First, it makes an assumption about what is and what is not acceptable in business. In this case, for example, businesses are increasingly frowning upon giving gifts to clients or customers. Consequently, what is acceptable for business and society is not necessarily a stable factor. In addition, for some individuals it is unacceptable to trade off one's ethics in the "line of duty." The question becomes what is acceptable for you.

Business Should Not Dictate Morality Given that business enterprises are fundamentally responsible to the owners or shareholders, their mandate is to maximize profit, which is their area of expertise. They are economic institutions, and they should leave the issue of social policy to the jurisdiction of government. Managers are simply not skilled enough in the area of social policy, so they should not be responsible for carrying out duties of social responsibility. If businesses enter the arena of social policy they are, in effect, expanding their power. How? Well, a corporation that is engaging in extensive social programs is essentially performing a political function in addition to its economic purpose. Some critics suggest that allowing business to have both economic and political power is potentially dangerous. As one critic argued,

> It is no advance for democracy when public policy is "privatized" and corporate boards take it upon themselves to weigh competing social, economic and environmental goals. That is a job for governments, which remain competent to do it if they choose.[97]

[96] Carr, A. (1968). Is business bluffing ethical? *Harvard Business Review, 46,* 127–134.

[97] *The Economist.* (2001, November 17). Curse of the ethical executive. Retrieved from www.economist.com/node/863487.

Consequently, those opposed to businesses venturing into the social sphere for this reason argue that government can simply enforce regulations to ensure that business is socially responsible rather than allowing business to take it upon itself to judge matters of social responsibility.

Organizations Cannot Be Held Accountable   While society may judge somewhat cynically the ethics of "big business," who exactly is to be held accountable for the actions taken by individuals on behalf of their company? It is not always easy to place blame when the entity responsible for an action is not an individual but, rather, a corporation. Many scholars have asserted that rather than observing organizations, it is the corporations' leaders and their constituents whose behaviour must be studied. Following this line of reasoning, Archie Carroll argued that unethical business behaviour is the result of two ethical standards: personal and business. Carroll's research suggests that individuals under pressure compromise their personal standards to achieve the goals of the organization.[98] Similarly, Albert Carr argues that "the ethic of corporate advantage invariably silences and drives out the ethic of individual restraint."[99]

Can we hold organizations responsible for their crimes? For instance, should IBM be somehow held accountable for its alleged involvement in the Holocaust, as reported in Talking Business 10.6? What responsibility do organizations have to ensure their products are not

TALKING BUSINESS 10.6

IBM and Nazi Germany

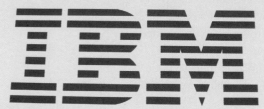
© Andia/Alamy

A book written by Edwin Black, entitled *IBM and the Holocaust,* offers compelling evidence that IBM played an important role in some of the most horrific events of the 1930s and 1940s in Europe. Specifically, IBM's production of hundreds of Hollerith machines, the precursor to the computer, played a central role in the first racial censuses conducted by the Nazis. Beginning in 1933, the Hollerith machine was used by the German government to identify its intended targets. As Black comments in his book,

Nearly every Nazi concentration camp operated a Hollerith Department . . . in some camps . . . as many as two dozen IBM sorters, tabulators and printers were installed . . . [I]t did not matter whether IBM did or did not know exactly which machine was used at which death camp. All that mattered was that the money would be waiting—once the smoke cleared.

The author suggests that IBM's involvement with Nazi Germany helps explain one mystery of the Holocaust—how so many people were killed in so little time. With the knowledge of top IBM management in the United States, IBM's European subsidiaries actually perfected the means for the Nazis to quickly collect census data for its murderous plans. Hitler even awarded IBM chairman Thomas Watson a medal for his company's work.

Source: Based on Black, E. (2001). *IBM and the Holocaust: The strategic alliance between Nazi Germany and America's most powerful corporation.* New York, NY: Crown Publishers, 2(01), p. 375.

---

[98] Carroll, A.B. (1978). Linking business ethics to behavior in organizations. *SAM Advanced Management Journal, 43,* 4–11.

[99] Carr, 1968.

misused? Do businesses have a responsibility not to associate with countries that are violating human rights? Or, on the other hand, should business strategy be guided purely by profits?

High Costs Are Passed to the Customer   Certainly, the additional costs of CSR may limit a company's national competitiveness, since CSR would increase firm costs and require raising prices on goods and services to consumers. In fact, in one survey few consumers wanted to pay more for socially responsible products if there were comparable cheaper versions available. According to one observer,

> Consumers will consistently tell surveys that they are willing to pay more for socially and environmentally superior products. But when they are alone in the shopping aisle and it's just them and their wallet, they rarely fork out more for "green."[100]

Similarly, consumers prefer to donate money to the causes of their own choice, so it does not make sense for businesses to do so:

> when it comes to actually voting with their wallets, consumers prefer not to be directed to do so. They like to contribute individually, to charities they believe in and wish to support as individuals, not as part of a huge pool. They certainly do not expect the for-profit corporations in which they invest to deploy corporate assets for social causes.[101]

Many would argue that CSR is just too expensive and would subsequently lower profits. What does it cost to be socially responsible? A company can set up a CSR department; donate money, goods, or services; donate employee time; sponsor an event; or run a corporate foundation. Typically, larger companies over smaller ones will have a CSR department and engage in more than one CSR activity. Nike, for example, has a CSR department of 135 employees and spends an estimated $25 million annually on CSR-related activities.[102] Nonetheless, Nike continues to be under the watchful eye of human rights groups, and consumer expectations continue to rise.

There are also the costs of a company "doing the right thing"—for example, treating employees fairly, ensuring working conditions meet health and safety standards, and acting in the best interest of the community. But all these efforts cost money and reduce the net profits of the company, which is not in the best interests of shareholders.

The Case for CSR   Now that we have looked at some of the more common sources of support for ignoring social responsibility, let's consider the counterargument. Why should business be concerned with the issue of social responsibility? Why might business be obliged to take on social responsibility? Why should business go beyond its legal requirements or industry standards?

---

[100] Unruh, G. (2011, July 28). No, consumers will not pay more for green. *The CSR Blog, Forbes.* Retrieved from www.forbes.com/sites/csr/2011/07/28/no-consumers-will-not-pay-more-for-green.

[101] Atkins, B. (2011, June 28). Is corporate social responsibility responsible? *Forbes.* Retrieved from www.forbes.com/2006/11/16/leadership-philanthropy-charity-lead-citizen-cx_ba_1128directorship.html.

[102] Palmquist, R. (2010, July 12). Student campaign takes on Nike like never before. *The Huffington Post.* Retrieved from www.huffingtonpost.com/rod-palmquist/student-campaign-takes-on_b_643375.html.

Conform to Societal Expectations   Scholars in the field of business ethics have argued that business and society need not be seen as distinct entities, but rather that business plays a role within society: Fundamentally, businesses are created to serve public needs. It is for this same pragmatic reason that a business will not act in any way that will reduce its legitimacy in the eyes of the public. Given that the very existence of a business enterprise is largely dependent on acceptance by society, there is an obligation not to violate societal beliefs regarding socially responsible behaviour—particularly if such violations would undermine the credibility of an enterprise's role in society. Scholars have suggested that the doctrine of corporate social responsibility can also be understood as part of an effort to reconcile the intentions and results of capitalism. Advocates of corporate social responsibility understand the importance of the profit motive; however, they view this as only part of the social responsibility of business.

Societal expectations, however, can be a challenge for businesses to meet. What is socially responsible is subject to debate. What one person believes is socially responsible may be different from what another person believes is socially responsible. Take, for instance, energy efficient light bulbs, such as compact fluorescent lights (CFLs). Some environmentalists believe CFLs are socially responsible since they conserve energy and are more efficient than traditional incandescent bulbs. CFLs, for example, use one third less energy than incandescent bulbs and can last up to 15 times longer. Other environmentalists, however, argue that CFL bulbs are not socially responsible because they contain mercury and can be toxic if broken or are disposed of in a landfill, which can contaminate fish, water, and food supplies. How much contamination? Since a CFL bulb contains approximately 5 milligrams of mercury, this amount can cause over 22,000 litres of water to become toxic.[103]

Shareholders of major corporations have also shown increased expectations that business behave responsibly. Shareholder proposals permit investors to present issues of concern to corporate management and to other shareholders, who can then vote to support or reject the proposals. For instance, in 2011 investors filed shareholder resolutions with nine oil and gas firms, such as ExxonMobil and Chevron, demanding that the corporations disclose details concerning environmental and regulatory risks connected with natural gas fracking, a process contributing to greenhouse gas emissions. How important are shareholder resolutions? At the onset, they can begin boardroom discussions, which are important in and of themselves; however, over time resolutions can begin a critical mass of support. For many boards, that vital level of support is approximately 30%.[104] Even though shareholder support for CSR activities is on the rise (in 2005, less than 3% of environmental and social resolutions reached the 30% level of support, whereas in 2010 more than 25% did), companies often don't know how to tackle these concerns. As one observer contends, strategies need to be developed that include "increasing social and environmental disclosure through robust sustainability reporting; making sure directors have expertise relevant to environmental and social concerns; [and] using measures that account for environmental performance as well as financial performance."[105]

---

[103] *CBC News*. (2010, December 31). B.C. switches off incandescent bulbs in 2011. Retrieved from www.cbc.ca/news/canada/british-columbia/story/2010/12/31/bc-lightbulb-cfl-incandescent.html.

[104] Sound, S. (2011, May 19). Shareholders bring CSR to the boardroom. *Sustainable Industries*. Retrieved from http://sustainableindustries.com/articles/2011/05/shareholders-bring-csr-boardroom.

[105] Sound, 2011.

Adopt CSR as a Practical Business Strategy   A second, even more pragmatic reason for businesses to be socially responsible is to avoid public criticism or scrutiny that might inadvertently encourage more government involvement or regulation. For example, we have recently witnessed a number of organizations accused of unfair business practices and attempting to create a monopoly. Other organizations, like Nike, have been heavily criticized for shutting down operations in America in favour or setting up business where labour is cheap, and in some cases where sweatshop-like conditions exist among the factories of the foreign contractors. A lack of concern for social responsibility may invite public scrutiny.

The practical side of being socially responsible can be seen in the realm of business–consumer relationships. The notion of exploiting the consumer for profits would be both socially irresponsible and unwise for any business. There are many cases of consumer lawsuits aimed at businesses who lacked responsibility for their treatment of customers. For example, in 2011 Mega Brands agreed to settle a US lawsuit related to a defective magnetic toy sold to consumers. The Montreal-based company agreed to refund consumers their money, set up a children's foundation, and pay up to $3.5 million in legal fees. As part of the foundation, Mega Brands also agreed to make a cash contribution of $100,000 aimed at addressing children's health issues. In 2006, the company reached a settlement of US$13.5 million with 14 families. In one case, a 22-month-old had died from swallowing pieces of a magnetic toy. Since then, the company is still struggling to recover from the product recall issues. While Mega Brands denies any wrongdoing, it has decided to avoid further legal expenses and bad publicity by just settling the matter once and for all.[106]

In a different case, consumers filed a lawsuit against Research In Motion (RIM) for a system-wide failure that led to BlackBerry users having no service for four days in October 2011. The lawsuit accused the company of breach of contract and negligence, which caused thousands of users to not be able to access their email, use instant messaging, or browse the Internet. The lawsuit also claimed that the interruptions prevented business transactions and caused damages such as the loss of income. Although the company had apologized to its millions of BlackBerry users, RIM failed to compensate its customers (through refunds) for the days of no service, leading to more bad publicity.[107] These types of practices bring "unwelcome" public attention and scrutiny to the guilty businesses (see Talking Business 10.7).

Acknowledge Membership in a Broader Network of Stakeholders   As described earlier, stakeholders refer to any individuals or groups who bear some type of risk as a result of the corporation's actions. Stakeholders might have financial, physical, or human stakes in the corporation. Who are the potential stakeholders in business activity? Among the list of stakeholders and the corporation's responsibilities to them, we can include those identified earlier in Exhibit 10.2.

---

[106] Marowits, R. (2011, September 28). Mega Brands turning page on Magnetix mishap with consumer lawsuit settlement. *Canadian Business*. Retrieved from www.canadianbusiness.com/article/48056--mega-brands-turning-page-on-magnetix-mishap-with-consumer-lawsuit-settlement.

[107] Herbst, M. (2011, October 27). RIM hit with consumer lawsuits over BlackBerry outage. Reuters. Retrieved from www.abs-cbnnews.com/business/tech-biz/10/27/11/rim-hit-consumer-lawsuits-over-blackberry-outage.

Corporate Strategy and Long-Term Well Being: Crime Doesn't Pay

The trickle of corporate scandal that seemed to start in the 1980s and rear its head again on occasion in the1990s, seemed to break into an all-out hailstorm by the beginning of the twenty-first century. In 2002, U.S. telecommunications giant WorldCom admitted to perpetrating one of the largest accounting frauds in history. The company had inflated its profits by US$3.8 billion between January 2001 and March 2002. Adelphia Communications Corp. founder John Rigas, along with his two sons, were arrested in 2002 and faced charges of improperly taking US$1 billion from the cable-television giant.[108] Tyco, Parmalat, Merrill Lynch, and Global Crossing were among the other high-profile cases of corporate misdeeds and fraudulent acts in recent years. And, of course, among the most prominent corporate scandals in recent memory was Enron. This energy and trading company was once the U.S.'s seventh largest corporation, with 21 000 employees, and the largest marketer of electricity and natural gas. Enron's downward spiral in 2001 began when the company revealed that it falsified accounting records, including keeping hundreds of millions of dollars of losses off the accounting records. In the third quarter of 2001 alone, Enron had incurred a US$600 million loss, and its bankruptcy (declared on December 2, 2001) was among the largest in U.S. corporate history. In addition to the massive lay-offs, employees lost much of their retirement money since their pension accounts were built around Enron stock—stock that once sold for US$85 a share became worthless.

Like their U.S. counterparts, many Canadian corporate scandals, including Hollinger Inc., Bre-X Minerals Ltd., YBM Magnex International, Livent Inc., and Cinar Corporation "violated the basic tenets of good governance by staffing their boards with insiders, rubber-stamping rich compensation packages and interest-free loans for executives and failing to disclose company financial dealings to investors."[109] In 2003 Conrad Black was forced to step down as chief executive of Hollinger International, the newspaper publisher. The resignation followed accusations that he and other senior Hollinger executives and parent company Hollinger Inc. received millions in unauthorized payments. Allegedly, $32.15 million in payments were made that were not authorized by either the audit committee or the full board of directors of Hollinger. According to many observers, a salient feature of this case was the complicity of the company's board of directors in all this activity and its lack of independence from the CEO.[110]

Lack of board independence also played a central role in the downfall of Parmalat Finanziaria, the Italian dairy and food giant. This company filed for bankruptcy protection in Italy on December 27, 2003, following discovery that huge assets, estimated from US$8–$12 billion were unaccounted for. The alleged financial fraud at Parmalat spans more than a decade. Founder, chairman, and chief executive Calisto Tanzi was fired from the company and board and placed under arrest in 2003. Interestingly, at the time the scandal broke, Parmalat had a particularly poor rating on Institutional Shareholder Service's Global Corporate Governance Quotient, which measures corporations' governance practices against a set of 61 criteria. Parmalat ranked at the bottom of all 69 Italian companies that were rated.

Among some of the other potential stakeholders in a business are suppliers, the government, and society in general—each of whom may also be affected in some way by corporate activity and, consequently, must be considered in conducting business. In any actions a business takes, then, the business should consider the impact on any party that has a stake in its operations—that is affected by its behaviour.

Aside from ethical considerations, there are practical reasons to attend to all stakeholders' interests, even when they conflict: If management focuses on only the concerns of a minority of stakeholders, such as the owners, other stakeholders may withdraw their

---

[108] Joseph McCafferty, "Adelphia Comes Clean," *CFO Magazine* (December 1, 2003).

[109] Nadine Winter, "Fair Pay for Fair Play," *CA Magazine* (Vol. 136, No. 10, December 2003), 34.

[110] Seth Sutel, "Lawyers for Hollinger Lay Out Case Against Conrad Black in Delaware Court," *Canadian Press* (February 18, 2004), http://www.canada.com/search/story.html?id=d9ac2f5d-8e7c-48f7-a2e8-018c07cd6451.

participation in and support for the enterprise and, consequently, harm the business. Thus, to suggest that business need not be socially responsible is to ignore the fact that business enterprises regularly interact with and affect numerous stakeholders.

There are many examples of corporations making a difference in communities through volunteer activities. BlackBerry, for instance, has partnered with Free The Children, an international development charity that helps build schools and provides clean-water projects. In 2011, BlackBerry (then known as Research In Motion) sponsored 50 students to volunteer in Kenya and India to aid communities and promote youth leaders.[111] Tim Hortons, on the other hand, has created its own foundation called the Tim Horton Children's Foundation, which enables disadvantaged children to attend camp. In fact, on one day a year called "Camp Day," Tim Hortons restaurant owners donate all coffee sales to the Tim Horton Children's Foundation. In 2013, Camp Day raised $11.8 million.[112]

Gain Long-Term Benefits from CSR   Advocates of corporate social responsibility suggest that even if an action does not result in immediate benefits for the enterprise, engaging in socially responsible behaviour is wise from a longer-term strategic perspective. This, perhaps, connects to the first point made regarding the relationship of business with society. A business that fosters this relationship will more likely continue to receive acceptance from and be considered legitimate by the public. The notion of building and maintaining goodwill with the public and a positive image are certainly influenced by social responsiveness. For example, Johnson & Johnson, the maker of Tylenol, was faced with major disaster in the 1980s after a number of tragic deaths were found to be the result of poisoned Tylenol capsules. While the cause was later found to be tampering at the retail location, not at the manufacturers' site, Johnson & Johnson took complete, extensive responsibility in withdrawing all their Tylenol capsules from the market (retail value of over $100 million), running television commercials, and establishing telephone hotlines urging the public not to use them. And this also prompted Johnson & Johnson to reintroduce the product in tamper-proof packages. While the company's social responsibility was costly, the company made up for that loss by restoring public confidence in its reputation.

Business Has the Power and Resources to Do "Good"   The ability of corporations to make a positive contribution to their communities has certainly increased. We are living in an era of large, global companies with billion-dollar profits and a customer base that expands across the world. Companies have the power and resources to make the world a better place through their talented workforce and financial resources while still making a profit.

Recently, a US survey revealed some of the most generous corporations in North America. In 2010, the *Chronicle of Philanthropy* reported that Kroger, a Cincinnati-based supermarket operator, donated 10.9% of its pre-tax profits (or US$64 million) to charity, the largest corporate contribution to charitable activities according to percentage of earnings. The *Chronicle of Philanthropy* ranks about 300 of the largest US companies based on their corporate-giving efforts as a percentage of revenue on an annual basis.[113] According to Kroger's vice-president of corporate affairs Lynn Marmer, $40 million of Kroger's cash giving flows through a 15-year-old community rewards program, where shoppers who

[111] Mercer, G. (2011, January 25). RIM sponsoring 50 students to volunteer abroad. *TheRecord.com*. Retrieved from www.therecord.com/print/article/477955.

[112] Tim Hortons Camp Day Raises $9.9 million! newswire.ca June 3, 2011. http://www.newswire.ca/en/story/727203/tim-hortons-camp-day-raises-9-9-million.

[113] Adams, S. (2011, October 21). American companies that give back the most. *Forbes*. Retrieved from www.forbes.com/sites/susanadams/2011/10/21/american-companies-that-give-back-the-most.

carry Kroger loyalty cards name a local charity they want to support. Kroger then gives 2–5% (determined by local stores) of each shopper's bill as a cash contribution to the school, church, or community group chosen by the customer.[114]

There is also another category that the *Chronicle of Philanthropy* ranks of companies who give the most cash as a raw number. Walmart topped the list at US$319 million last year. Given its US$22 billion in pre-tax earnings, Walmart's percentage of charitable giving came to only 1.45% of net profit. Goldman Sachs came in second at US$315 million in cash donations, and Wells Fargo was third at $219 million.[115]

Where do companies like to make a difference, and who benefits the most? In Canada, companies tend to support hospitals and health-related organizations as a preferred choice. Social services and recreational activities are the second most common recipient. The least supported causes by corporations are the environment and animal-protection activities.

Talking Business 10.8 provides some examples of corporations being socially responsible. Do you think these types of behaviours should be mandated as a necessary part of business?

[114] Adams, 2011.

[115] Adams, 2011.

Is Corporate Social Responsibility on the Rise?

The central arguments that support the case against business enterprises taking a more active role in the area of social responsibility were outlined above. So where are we now? That is, how have the views of corporate social responsibility changed over the years? What philosophy are businesses adopting currently with regard to social or moral obligations? According to some observers, we are undergoing a gradual transformation that increasingly involves shaping organizations to reflect higher levels of social responsiveness. There is an increasing push for organizations to balance the profit objective with goals of social responsibility. Three key factors that organizations are being influenced by to become better corporate citizens are social media, corporate disclosure legislation, and CSR rankings.

Social Media   Certainly, social media has given more people the opportunity to voice their opinion and to sway business to be more socially responsible. What is social media? **Social media** are web-based or mobile technologies that allow people to communicate in an interactive way. According to Kaplan and Haenlein, there are six forms of social media: collaborative projects (Wikipedia), blogs (Twitter), social networking sites (Facebook), content communities (YouTube), virtual game worlds ("World of Warcraft"), and virtual social worlds (Second Life).[116] Two widely used social media tools where business is discussed are Facebook and Twitter. With over 1 billion Facebook users and 500 million Twitter users, businesses recognize that public criticism needs to be managed in real time or their reputation may be harmed (see Talking Business 10.9).

> **social media** Web-based or mobile technologies that allow people to communicate in an interactive way.

TALKING BUSINESS 10.9
Social Media Gives Power to Customers

An angry tweet about bad service at a store, restaurant, or airport can easily spiral out of control, especially if other users pile on. Or it can [go] viral, like the "United Breaks Guitars" YouTube video by Halifax singer Dave Carroll. He made a series of music videos after his guitar was broken during a flight. The trilogy was a public relations nightmare for United, but a win for Carroll, boosting his profile as a musician and a speaker on customer service.

Consumers with smart phones mean anything can become public in an instant. That can range from photos of officers at the G20 protests to tweets about a toddler served a margarita at a restaurant chain, to a blog post about a Starbucks barista fired amid a litany of homophobic comments.

"You have to operate your organization as if any employee at any time could be on the six o'clock news," said Wendy Cukier, professor of information technology management at Ryerson University. "It has heightened the consciousness of how important customer service is."

Social media adds a level of transparency and accountability that companies have never seen before, Cukier said. "Not having a social media strategy is no longer an option," she said. . . .

Scott Stratten, Oakville-based author of *UnMarketing: Stop Marketing, Start Engaging*, said people used to put up with bad service because they couldn't be bothered to write a letter or fill out a comment card. Now they don't have to.

"I believe people, in general, aren't naturally aggressive. We're passive in person, but we're aggressive online," he said. "Social media, blogging and Facebook allow us to vent our true feelings, instead of having to confront a driver on the TTC or a waiter." . . .

(continued)

---

[116] Kaplan, A.M., & Haenlein M. (2010). Users of the world, unite! The challenges and opportunities of social media. *Business Horizons, 53*(1), 59–68.

Already scared of messages they can't control, organizations are now dealing with amplified versions, said Stratten.

John Pliniussen, associate professor of Internet marketing at Queen's University, says companies should monitor comments made about them. It doesn't necessarily require a big budget to set up Google alerts that mention a business or product.

"In this day and age, you never close. Customers have a voice 24-7," he said. He doesn't see this feedback as negative. "You want people to complain. You want to know when you have a problem."

Keith McArthur, vice-president of social media for Rogers Communications, leads a small team dedicated to helping customers online—from third-party blogs to creating user forums.

That means dealing with everything from billing inquiries to technical support or questions around policy. While some customers prefer to phone a call centre for help, others like to use social media.

During regular business hours, McArthur said his team's goal is to respond to tweets within an hour.

Danny Brown of Bonsai Interactive Marketing cautions that social media gives a lot of power to consumers, because they can say anything.

Companies should fight fire with fire, but ensure it's done politely and respectfully.

"Respond in public, such as, 'We're sorry you feel that way. It's not what we aspire to. We'll look into it,'" he said. "Answering criticism with politeness, it will put you in a positive way."

Companies probably can't respond to everyone, but try to respond to as many as possible, advised Brown. Also, he said, it's important to realize some chronic complainers will never be satisfied. . . .

Source: Excerpted from Lu, V. (2011, July 12). TTC standoff example of how social media forces firms to rethink service. *Toronto Star.* Retrieved from www.thestar.com/business/2011/07/12/ttc_standoff_example_of_how_social_media_forces_firms_to_rethink_service.print.html. Reprinted with permission from Toronto Star.

In recent years, social media has been used to raise money for causes, to distribute news, to make politicians more responsive, and to talk about everyday issues.[117] In 2011, social media led to the Occupy Wall Street movement, revolutionizing the act of protest and raising awareness about corporate greed and income inequality. Using Twitter, the first protest began in New York City on September 17, 2011. By October, the Occupy movement had grown across 95 cities and 82 countries, including Canada.

Corporate Disclosure Legislation

How corporations govern and oversee their own behaviour has been a central issue in today's business environment. The long list of corporate scandals has drawn attention to this notion of who safeguards the interests of owners and shareholders of large corporations. Recent legislation has attempted to hold organizations more accountable for their behaviour and to offer greater disclosure of their activities to the public.

The aftermath of the huge financial scandals in the early 21st century were the biggest impetus for change, which led to the enactment of such legislation as the 2002 Sarbanes-Oxley Act in the United States and the initiation of similar legislation in Canada. The Sarbanes-Oxley Act was introduced following the flood of accounting scandals at companies such as Enron and WorldCom. The act was aimed at reestablishing corporate accountability and investor confidence. The act's central purpose was to make public companies more accountable by increasing transparency or disclosure in their financial reporting. This required additional regulations governing public company accounting, corporate responsibility, and investor protection. To accomplish this, increased requirements were also placed on CEOs (chief executive officers), CFOs (chief financial officers), and the functions that they oversee.

---

[117] Gelles, D. (2009, September 29). Making sense of Twitter's influence on the corporate world. *Los Angeles Times.* Retrieved from http://articles.latimes.com/2009/sep/28/business/fi-books28.

The significant impact of the Sarbanes-Oxley Act is evident to many observers:

> More than just a buzzword born in the depths of the corporate scandals, good governance has turned into a new way of life for some company gatekeepers. . . . Under the new rule regime, boards find themselves under intense scrutiny. They have fired members who have conflicts of interest, possess thin credentials, or are past their prime. They have hired new directors they believe are beyond reproach, with no skeletons and talents more suited to the job. They have more meetings, more conference calls, and more questions to ask of senior management. They face the challenge of simultaneously beefing up controls to meet new regulatory requirements while remaining active in shaping the company's strategy. They consult more with their lawyers. . . . Boards must now comprise mostly independent directors, which means the individuals must not have any material ties (*a la* Enron) to the company or its management.[118]

While the Sarbanes-Oxley Act itself is not directed at Canadian jurisdictions, it does affect Canadian companies that trade on US stock exchanges, and it has served as an impetus for similar Canadian legislation. The Canadian version of the act was implemented the following year. In April 2003, the Government of Ontario enacted Bill 198 to help protect investors by improving corporate disclosure. It became known as the "Canadian Sarbanes-Oxley Act." In spring 2004, three similar regulations were finalized by the Canadian Securities Administrators and implemented by most provinces across Canada:[119]

- Multilateral Instrument 52-108 Auditor Oversight
- Multilateral Instrument 52-109 Certification of Disclosure in Issuers' Annual and Interim Filings
- Multilateral Instrument 52-110 Audit Committees

The Ontario Securities Commission also presented 18 new corporate governance standards for boards of publicly traded companies. These evolving standards are intended to make corporations more accountable for their behaviour and financial reporting methods.

CSR Rankings   In recent years, companies have also been driven to increase their social responsibility because it improves their public image and brand value. How much social responsibility is required is difficult to determine, but some research groups have published CSR rankings that recognize Canadian companies for their good deeds. Two groups include the Corporate Knights and Jantzi-Sustainalytics.[120]

The rankings, however, are somewhat subjective. Since companies have different CSR programs and goals, businesses can be difficult to compare. For example, in 2010 *Maclean's* CSR rankings included some companies with questionable practices. In the same year that Direct Energy was listed as one of the top 50 socially responsible companies in Canada, a

---

[118] Barnett, M. (2004). The new regime: Corporate reform measures are forcing boards of directors to clean up their act. *U.S. News & World Report*. Retrieved from www.usnews.com/usnews/biztech/articles/040216/16eeboards.htm.

[119] Spector, S. (n.d.). SOX and SOX North, Part 3: The impact of SOX in Canada. PD Net. Retrieved from www.cga-pdnet.org/Non_VerifiableProducts/ArticlePublication/SOX_E/SOX_part_3.pdf.

[120] Jantzi-Sustainalytics. (2010, June 14). Good for business: Corporate social responsibility report 2010. *Maclean's*. Retrieved from www2.macleans.ca/2010/06/14/jantzi-macleans-csr-report-2010.

Canadian newspaper published an article about Direct Energy's unethical sales tactics in selling gas and electricity contracts door to door.[121] Loblaw, on the other hand, won top honours for its social responsibility efforts in 2010 in terms of reducing waste, sustaining seafood, decreasing packaging, and increasing diversity. In 2011, Loblaw ranked fourth, maintaining its high commitment to CSR across Canada. According to one observer,

> Mr. Weston's personal commitment to corporate responsibility has played its part in bolstering the chain's CSR rankings. Since taking the top job almost four years ago, the 37-year-old . . . has focused on putting more discipline into the retailer's social-responsibility efforts. It now releases an annual CSR report.[122]

Outside Canada there are also global CSR rankings. For example, the Ethisphere Institute, a leading international think tank dedicated to bolstering business ethics, produces the "World's Most Ethical Companies" ranking. The Institute reviews nominations from more than 100 companies in 36 industries, and judges them based on codes of ethics, litigation history, how much the company invests in innovation and sustainable business practices, what activities they are involved in that are designed to improve corporate citizenship, and what senior executives, industry peers, suppliers, and customers have to say.[123]

In 2012, the two Canadian companies that made the list were Encana Corporation and Enmax Corporation. Here's what Jeff Paulson, vice-president and associate general counsel and corporate secretary at Encana, had to say about the honour:

> We believe that our environmental, social and corporate governance performance contributes to long-term value for our shareholder and helps us maintain our social license to operate.[124]

With the increase of CSR rankings and company transparency, the demand by stakeholders for more socially responsible companies will certainly continue in the future.

Of course, how business responds to different stakeholders may be represented on a continuum from a purely pragmatic, self-interest approach to a socially responsible approach. The traditional pragmatic approach has been one that focuses on strategies that consider only the objectives of the owners or shareholders. This reflects the notion that the primary orientation of business is to fulfill economic as opposed to social interests. On the other hand, there is a drive to adopt a more socially responsible approach. This approach does not ignore the responsibility of business to owners or shareholders to maximize profits; however, this should not be accomplished at the expense of other stakeholders. Managers are challenged to use ethical principles to guide managerial actions when faced with competing interests among different stakeholders.

---

[121] Roseman, E. (2010, May 15). Don't fall victim to energy fraud at the door. *Toronto Star*. Retrieved from www. thestar.com/business/money911/article/809698--roseman-don-t-fall-victim-to-energy-fraud-at-the-door.

[122] Strauss, M. (2010, June 20). Why Loblaw takes top honours for corporate social responsibility. *Globe and Mail*. Retrieved from www.theglobeandmail.com/report-on-business/careers/management/report-on-corporate-responsibil/article1605337.ece.

[123] 3BL Media. (2012, March 19). Encana ranked among world's most ethical large companies. Retrieved from http://3blmedia.com/theCSRfeed/Encana-Ranked-Among-World%E2%80%99s-Most-Ethical-Large-Companies.

[124] Encana website. (n.d.). Encana ranked among the world's most ethical large companies. Retrieved from www. encana.com/about/awards/2012/ethisphere-ethical.html.

CHAPTER SUMMARY

This chapter attempted to underscore the ethical dimension of organizational decisions and behaviour. How managers balance the different needs of stakeholders demands knowledge of the ethical implications of otherwise typical business decisions. Ethics is central to the managerial task. Management educators have been expanding the realm of management literature to consider the relationship of ethics and management. An understanding of corporate social responsibility of business organizations and their constituents may help create a more productive and trusting relationship between business and society.

CHAPTER LEARNING TOOLS

Key Terms

authoritative culture 370

business ethics 358

categorical imperative 358

codes of conduct 370

corporate social responsibility (CSR) 383

democratic culture 370

economic responsibilities 384

end-point ethics 361

ethical responsibilities 384

ethics 358

habitual routines 373

legal responsibilities 384

organizational culture 368

organizational role theory 377

philanthropic responsibilities 384

rule ethics 363

social contract ethics 378

social identity theory 376

socialization of ethics 369

social media 395

stakeholder 382

unethical behaviour 358

utilitarianism 361

Multiple-Choice Questions

Select the *best* answer for each of the following questions. Solutions are located in the back of your textbook.

1. End-point ethics involves
   a. a focus on the outcome rather than the process
   b. a focus on the process rather than the outcome
   c. the greatest amount of good for the greatest number of people in the end
   d. both A and C

2. Rule ethics asserts that
   a. a person should follow his or her valid principles
   b. it is important to consider what is right and wrong
   c. there are basic principles that consider the "rightness" or "wrongness" of an action
   d. all of the above

3. An organizational factor that may influence an employee to engage in unethical behaviour is
   a. corporate gossip   b. corporate culture
   c. both A and B   d. none of the above

4. An internal stakeholder can be the
   a. owner   b. employee union
   c. both A and B   d. none of the above

5. Caroll's definition of corporate social responsibility involves _____ level(s) of CSR.
   a. one   b. two
   c. three   d. four

6. Although society does not expect business to fulfill these responsibilities, society desires business to fulfill these responsibilities
   a. philanthropic   b. ethical
   c. legal   d. economic

7. An argument in favour of CSR is that
   a. business should not dictate morality
   b. business plays by its own rules
   c. there are long-term benefits to business
   d. organizations cannot be held accountable

8. "Business is business" is an argument against CSR because
   a. the sole focus of business is to make a profit
   b. economic goals should not be mixed with altruistic goals
   c. business is accountable to its shareholders only
   d. all of the above

9. "Business should not dictate morality" is an argument against CSR because
   a. managers are not skilled in CSR
   b. business would become too powerful
   c. social policy should be left to the government
   d. all of the above

10. Business should conform to societal expectations since
    a. customers are too demanding
    b. business was created to serve public needs
    c. the customer is always right
    d. all of the above

11. CSR is a practical business strategy because
    a. CSR avoids public scrutiny
    b. CSR is like a public relations campaign
    c. CSR costs are very low
    d. both A and B

12. A long-term benefit of CSR may be
    a. improved customer loyalty
    b. goodwill
    c. higher costs
    d. both A and B

13. A company's responsibility to shareholders can involve
    a. fair and honest reporting
    b. reasonable profits
    c. a well-developed CSR program
    d. both A and B

14. A company's responsibility to employees can involve
    a. complying to all employment laws
    b. treating employees fairly
    c. improving employee morale
    d. all of the above

15. In the argument against CSR, the person or group who should be accountable for CSR is
    a. the CEO
    b. the shareholders
    c. the manager of a CSR department
    d. difficult to determine

Discussion Questions

1. What is the difference between end-point ethics and rule ethics?

2. What are five organizational factors that can lead employees to engage in unethical behaviour?

3. What is the meaning of a stakeholder?

4. Give some examples of internal stakeholders.

5. Give some examples of external stakeholders.

6. What is the meaning of corporate social responsibility (CSR)? Describe Caroll's four levels of CSR.

7. Provide arguments for businesses engaging in CSR.

8. Provide arguments against businesses engaging in CSR.

9. Explain what factors may influence businesses to be socially responsible.

10. Can companies be both economically responsible and socially responsible? Explain.

CONCEPT APPLICATION JOE FRESH AND THE BANGLADESH TRAGEDY

Joe Fresh was originally launched as a female-only, affordable fashion line in select Loblaw retailers, but has since been launched in over 300 stores across Canada and has expanded to include both men's and children's clothing. Joe Fresh quickly became a major player in Canadian children's apparel retailers in Canada, dominating a large portion of market share. It also recently opened a flagship store on New York's Fifth Avenue and partnered with different retailers across the United States, including JCPenney. No one would have expected this Canadian "rising star" to be immersed in controversy, but that is exactly what happened to it in 2013.

On April 24, 2013, an eight-storey building (the Rana Plaza) collapsed in Savar (an industrial suburb of Dhaka, the capital of Bangladesh), killing 1,127 people in what became the deadliest disaster in the history of the garment industry. The dead were largely factory workers, who were pressured to return to their jobs that day despite knowledge that the building was unsafe. A teenage girl was the last to be found alive after spending over two weeks in the rubble.

© Mark Blinch/Reuters/Corbis

Investigations soon discovered that the building was constructed with substandard materials and with a complete disregard for building codes. According to a government investigation, the Rana Plaza was doomed from the start. It contained illegally built upper floors that housed garment factories and employed thousands of workers. The huge power generators on those upper floors (often used because of regular power failures) literally shook the building when switched on. Though cracks appeared in the building and shook it on April 23, 2013, the factory bosses ignored concerns and ordered workers into the building the next morning. When a generator switched on, the building buckled and collapsed.

In the government's report, the local mayor was also blamed for granting construction approvals. The report recommended charges for the building's owner, Sohel Rana, as well as for the owners of the five garment factories in the building.

This was a horrific tragedy. But what did good companies like Joe Fresh have to do with it?

Bangladesh is the world's second-leading exporter of clothing (behind China). The country has over 5,000 garment factories, and it completes orders for most of the world's top brands and retailers, one of which happens to be the Canadian-based Joe Fresh. Joe Fresh and countless other multinational retailers are attracted to Bangladesh because they have offered the least costly source of garment production; Bangladesh has the lowest wages in the world for garment workers.

Workers in these textile manufacturing companies often have no alternative job opportunities and are forced to work under horrendous conditions with extremely low pay because of financial desperation. Most workers receive the minimum wage for the industry, which is less than $38 a month for full-time work, and are forced into non-unionized jobs with severely restricted workers' rights. Many workers are further threatened or intimidated by local authorities when they try to fight for workers' rights or unions. It is worth mentioning that despite these devastating working conditions, Bangladesh's economy is completely reliant on its textile industry, which accounts for nearly half of its industrial employment in the country and the bulk of the country's merchandise exports—approximately $20 billion a year.

International companies justify the low wages paid to their Bangladeshi employees by arguing that they rely on Bangladesh's minimal labour costs to provide consumers with attractive price points and are forced to adopt offshoring to remain on par with competitors' costs. Interestingly, the actual salary paid to workers in manufacturing makes up a minor component in the overall cost of a product, suggesting that increases in wages would not actually lead to a significant rise in retail prices.

The employment context of Bangladesh differs dramatically from that in Canada or the United States. It is a significantly poorer country. The same rules and regulations

Case Continued >

regarding safety in Canadian factories would be very difficult for a factory in countries like Bangladesh to uphold considering their limited resources. The governments also do not operate in the same way. Many activists believe it is important for companies doing business overseas to be more responsible for ensuring workers' rights are upheld since many governments do not seriously support worker rights. Two years earlier, workers went on strike and were beaten and shot by local police. What were the workers' demands? They wanted a raise from $0.26 to $0.30 per hour.

Low pay is not the only labour problem. Worker hours consistently remain long as well. Often workers are forced to work 13 to 14 hour shifts seven days a week. According to Charles Kernaghan, director at the Institute for Global Labour and Human Rights, in the factory that collapsed, "these workers were mostly young women, and they were ordered into that factory . . . They didn't want to go into work as there were already deep cracks in the walls the day before."[125]

International workers' rights groups have been outraged both with the conditions of work and with the response of the large firms involved with this incident. These international aid groups demand higher wages, access to unions, and governmentally regulated work conditions. Following the collapse, much attention has been directed at steps companies must take to ensure the safety of their workers. These include introducing new programs that would more closely monitor the structural conditions at many of these production facilities to ensure that full safety standards are being met. Sadly, many people feel that this type of disaster was inevitable given that the government cannot be trusted to enforce strict safety standards because of widespread corruption and bribery.

While several companies, including Disney, have stated their intentions to move their operations out of Bangladesh following this disaster, most firms are not budging. Joe Fresh, along with many other brands, will continue to be produced in Bangladesh under the justification that their actions in the country serve as a positive force that fuels the local economy and provides jobs to people living in extreme poverty. As stated by Joe Mimran, cofounder of Joe Fresh, "The apparel industry is at the forefront of every developing country. I believe we can do more good and drive lasting change by staying in Bangladesh."[126]

On top of the obvious ethical and moral concerns involved with such a catastrophe, there is also a large impact on a company's image after receiving such negative media attention. In the case of Joe Fresh, Loblaw, the parent firm, sent several high-ranking members to Bangladesh to try and resolve the situation as quickly as possible. Joe Fresh has promised to compensate the families of workers affected by the accident and provide constant supervision of all aspects of product creation to ensure that Loblaw's values are maintained throughout. It was important for Joe Fresh not only to help the victims of the situation as soon as possible, but also to maintain its public appearance as a compassionate, caring company to its employees and consumers alike.

---

[125] O'Connor, C. (2013, April 30). 'Extreme pricing:' At what cost? Retailer Joe Fresh sends reps to Bangladesh as death toll rises. *Forbes*. Retrieved from www.forbes.com/sites/clareoconnor/2013/04/30/extreme-pricing-at-what-cost-retailer-joe-fresh-sends-reps-to-bangladesh-as-death-toll-rises.

[126] Kopun, F. (2013, May 2). Bangladesh factory collapse: Loblaw to audit structural safety of suppliers' buildings. *Toronto Star*. Retrieved from www.thestar.com/business/2013/05/02/bangladesh_factory_collapse_unions_put_pressure_on_loblaw_joe_fresh.html.

Loblaw made a significant effort to minimize the harm to its brand from the incident with a series of statements, public addresses, and new initiatives that ultimately calmed down the Canadian consumer base and prevented boycotting. In fact, none of the companies that have been tied to such recent disasters in Bangladesh, including Walmart or Joe Fresh, have suffered from any change in consumer purchase behaviour.

Loblaw has revamped its commitment to worker safety; recently it signed a pact along with several other major retailers like H&M promising to create significant improvements to building safety in Bangladesh textile factories. Loblaw stated recently that this pact represents the firm's "belief that active collaboration by retail and manufacturing industries, government and non-governmental organization, is critical to driving effective and lasting change in Bangladesh."[127] The pact constitutes a shift in responsibility for the safety of workers from individualized brand standards to more all-encompassing industry standards. Under these accords, retailers will be responsible for a variety of tasks, including publishing public safety reports, providing safety training for employees, and assuming responsibility for paying for all mandatory repairs and renovations. A new no-tolerance policy that calls for firms to immediately end business relations with any manufacturer that does not abide by these safety standards is also being put in place.

Joe Fresh has made a public commitment to contribute to the welfare of Bangladesh after this terrible tragedy. What can companies like Joe Fresh do to compensate the relatives of the victims? What should they do? While Joe Fresh is making an effort to "do good" and improve safety standards, are these efforts satisfactory and are they "good enough"? Only time will tell.

Questions

1. How is corporate social responsibility (CSR) an issue in this case? In your answer, consider the four levels of CSR.

2. Why should Joe Fresh be expected to act in accordance with societal expectations?

3. What kinds of obligations should companies like Joe Fresh have toward the people in other countries who make its products?

---

[127] Westwood, R. (2013, May 14). Loblaw latest to sign safety pact on Bangledesh factories. *Maclean's*. Retrieved from www2.macleans.ca/2013/05/14/loblaw-latest-to-sign-safety-pact-on-bangladesh-factories.

Chapter 11
The Challenge of Sustainability
Why Does Business Need to Focus on Sustainability?

Mikhail Starodubov/Shutterstock

Learning Objectives

After studying this chapter, you should be able to

1. Define sustainable development.

2. Explain the three components of the triple bottom line (TBL) approach.

3. Discuss the benefits and limitations of using the TBL as a performance tool.

4. Identify and explain four sustainability measures.

5. Explain the business case for implementing sustainable practices.

6. Discuss seven areas in which sustainable practices can be assessed during the product's life.

Have you heard of the term *sustainability*? It is becoming more and more familiar to many businesses in Canada and across the globe. How does sustainability impact business and other organizations? Environmental issues continue to influence businesses in every industry. This chapter examines the importance of sustainability and the benefits and challenges it presents to business. Clearly, for businesses to survive in the long term, sustainable practices are necessary and require managers to understand their economic, social, and environmental components.

THE BUSINESS WORLD

Can Canadian Businesses Afford to Ignore Climate Change?

In June 2013, Calgary and other surrounding communities experienced the worst flood in Alberta's history. Tens of thousands of residents had to leave their homes because of evacuation orders, only to return to find destroyed homes and millions of dollars in damage.

The flood was the result of some unexpected and unusual weather. Besides the rain, there were unexpected wind patterns and two enormous weather systems that had collided together. On June 20, 45 millimetres of rain poured down on the Calgary area. The previous record was set back in 1964 at 35.1 millimetres.[1] According to Stephanie Barsby, a CBC meteorologist, the rain was the result of an odd set of circumstances. "It is unusual to see a system stuck in one place for such an extended period of time," said Barsby.[2]

Was the Alberta flood the result of climate change? Certainly, it may be difficult for climatologists to connect one isolated weather event to global warming. However, scientists agree that climate change is occurring not just in Canada, but around the globe.

The effect of climate change on the environment is slowly starting to occur, and its long-term consequences are expected to be severe. According to the National Roundtable on the Environment and the Economy, climate change will likely cost Canadian taxpayers about $5 billion annually by the year 2020, and up to $43 billion annually by the year 2050.[3] The Roundtable is a group of researchers, academics, and business leaders chosen by the federal government to advise the government on economic and environmental issues.

"Climate change will be expensive for Canada and Canadians," the report stated. "Increasing greenhouse-gas emissions worldwide will exert a growing economic impact on our own country, exacting a rising price from Canadians as climate change impacts occur here at home."[4]

What are the economic impacts of climate change? Severe weather can potentially result in expensive clean-up costs for the government, production delays for businesses, and lost income for individuals. According to Alberta premier Alison Redford, it may take up to 10 years for a full recovery.[5]

---

[1] Davison, J., & Powers, L. (2013, June 22). Why Alberta's floods hit so hard and fast. *CBC News*. Retrieved from www.cbc.ca/news/canada/calgary/story/2013/06/21/f-alberta-floods.html.

[2] Davison & Powers, 2013.

[3] Scoffield, H. (2011, September 29). Climate change will cost Canada $5B yearly by 2020, report shows. *Toronto Star*. The Canadian Press. Reprinted with permission. Retrieved from www.thestar.com/news/canada/2011/09/29/climate_change_will_cost_canada_5b_yearly_by_2020_report_shows.html.

[4] Scoffield, 2011.

[5] Solinsky, K. (2013, June 24). Alison Redford: Alberta flood recovery could take 10 years; $1 billion aid fund approved. *BC Local News*. Retrieved from www.bclocalnews.com/news/212855891.html.

According to the Roundtable report, the warmer weather is expected to impact three key areas: timber, coastal regions, and human health:

> By the 2050s, the effects of warmer weather on forests—pests, forest fires and changes in growth—will cost the lumber industry between $2 billion and $17 billion a year, the report says. The effects will be most dramatic in western Canada. Along the coasts, flooding and changes in sea levels will cost Canada between $1 billion and $8 billion a year within 40 years. Prince Edward Island's coasts are most at risk, but costs will also run high in British Columbia and Nunavut. As for health, the researchers looked at the pressure on city hospitals from illness and death due to hotter temperatures. In Toronto alone, they see $3 million to $8 million more in costs by the 2050s. The report estimates that global warming will lead to between five and 10 additional deaths per 100,000 people per year by 2050.[6]

Some observers contend that the costs have already begun. In the past 25 years, there has been a steady increase in costs resulting from extreme weather events:[7]

2012: Calgary hail, wind storm—$552 million
2011: Calgary wind storm—$225 million
2011: Slave Lake fire—$700 million
2010: Calgary hail storm—$400 million
2005: Alberta flooding—$400 million
1998: Quebec ice storm—$5.4 billion
1997: Manitoba flooding—$3.5 billion
1996: Calgary hail storm—$300 million
1991: Calgary hail storm—$342 million

In order for Canada to potentially reduce these types of costs, the government has to come up with a realistic and achievable plan to reduce greenhouse gas emissions in the future. Climate change will clearly affect our natural resources, our businesses, and the overall economy. Of course, the more pressing issue is how climate change will affect the weather, the environment, and the health of all humans and species on the planet.

Indeed, the right course of action to manage climate change and greenhouse gas emissions is subject to debate. The widespread effects of climate change are complex, and balancing the needs of a country's economy and the demands of its people are ever changing. The following report from The Conference Board of Canada details Canada's greenhouse gas (GHG) emissions and what is being done about them.

How does Canada compare to its peer countries on GHG emissions?

Canada is one of the world's largest per capita GHG emitters. Canada ranks 15th out of 17 OECD countries on GHG emissions per capita and scores a "D" grade. In 2010, Canada's GHG emissions were 20.3 tonnes per capita, significantly higher than the 17-country average of 12.5 tonnes per capita. Canada's per capita GHG emissions were nearly three times greater than Switzerland's, the top performer.

---

[6] Scoffield, 2011.

[7] Kaufman, B. (2013, June 21). Southern Alberta flooding will rack up massive insurance bill, say Canadian underwriters. *Calgary Sun*. Retrieved from www.calgarysun.com/2013/06/21/southern-alberta-flooding-will-rack-up-massive-insurance-bill-say-canadian-underwriters.

While Canada's GHG emissions per capita have fallen since 1990, many other countries have managed to decrease them even more. For example, Germany and the UK reduced their per capita GHG emissions by 27% between 1990 and 2010.

Has Canada reduced GHG emissions?

Despite international commitments to drastically reduce GHGs, Canada has not seen a substantial improvement on its per capita GHG emissions. In 1992, Canada signed the United Nations Framework Convention on Climate Change (UNFCC), under which it committed to stabilizing GHG emissions at 1990 levels by 2000. In 2000, however, Canada's absolute GHG emissions were 22% higher than they had been 10 years earlier.

Canada went on to ratify the Kyoto Protocol in 2002, pledging to reduce GHG emissions to 6% below 1990 levels between 2008 and 2012. As of 2010, however, absolute GHG emissions remained 17% above 1990 levels.

One of the main reasons for the increase has been the growth in exports of petroleum, natural gas, and forest products. These commodities are exported, but the GHG emissions resulting from their production are not. Still, there is significant room for Canada to cut GHG emissions by increasing energy efficiency and using lower-emitting technologies.

To achieve its international commitments, Canada must make substantial GHG reductions now.

REPORT CARD		
GHG Emissions		
	1990s	2000s
Australia	D	D
Austria	A	A
Belgium	B	B
Canada	D	D
Denmark	B	B
Finland	B	B
France	A	A
Germany	B	B
Ireland	C	B
Italy	A	A
Japan	A	A
Netherlands	B	B
Norway	A	A
Sweden	A	A
Switzerland	A	A
U.K.	B	A
U.S.	D	D

Source: The Conference Board of Canada.

Has Canada's relative grade on GHG emissions improved?

No. Canada was a "D" performer in both the 1990s and the 2000s. The report card in the two decades remained the same for all countries except the UK, which moved from a "B" to a "A," and Ireland, which moved from a "C" to a "B."

What contributes most to greenhouse gas emissions in Canada?

The energy sector was responsible for 81% of Canada's total GHG emissions in 2010. Emissions from this sector come from combustion sources (such as electricity and heat generation, and fossil fuel industries), transportation (such as road vehicles), and fugitive sources (generated by oil and natural gas processing and, to a lesser extent, mining). Energy combustion is the largest of these sources, contributing 45% of Canada's total GHG emissions in 2010.

Industrial processes (such as the chemical industry), the waste sector (such as solid waste disposal on land), and agriculture also generate a significant amount of GHG emissions in Canada.

What is being done to reduce greenhouse gas emissions in Canada?

The Canadian federal government recently set a new target of reducing total greenhouse gas emissions by 17% from 2005 levels by 2020. To achieve this goal, it has introduced three major initiatives:

- *Passenger automobile and light truck greenhouse gas emissions regulations:* New emissions standards have been set for 2011–2016 model-year vehicles. The new standards are expected to reduce vehicle emissions from vehicles in these model years by

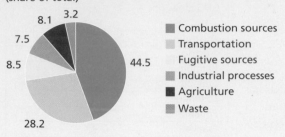

Source of GHG Emissions, Canada, 2010
(share of total)

- 3.2
- 8.1
- 7.5
- 8.5
- 44.5
- 28.2

■ Combustion sources
■ Transportation
■ Fugitive sources
■ Industrial processes
■ Agriculture
■ Waste

25% compared with 2008 models. Over the long term, this could lead to significant reductions in annual emissions from the transport sector. The actual reduction would depend on growth in the vehicle stock, growth in kilometres traveled, and the mix of older vehicles that stay on the road after the new standards take effect. Environment Canada also intends to increase the restrictions for model years 2017 and beyond.

■ *Heavy-duty vehicle emissions regulations:* In April 2012, the government announced new regulations to limit greenhouse gas emissions from heavy-duty vehicles. The aim of the new regulations is to reduce emissions from these vehicles by up to 23% by 2018.[6]

■ *Regulations on coal-fired electricity generation:* In September 2012, final regulations were revealed to reduce emissions from the generation of electricity from coal, beginning in 2015. The proposed regulations will apply stringent performance standards to coal-fired electricity generation facilities.

All of Canada's provincial and territorial governments have also established their own climate action plans with their own targets for reducing GHG emissions. Unfortunately, the lack of coordination among federal and provincial approaches to addressing climate change has reduced the effectiveness and efficiency of GHG reduction policies. Canadians need to get aligned—quickly—on the minimum fundamental requirements of a credible Canadian policy to fight climate change. In the view of The Conference Board of Canada, there are three basic elements to such a policy:

■ being part of a comprehensive global approach

■ providing clarity on attainable targets

■ implementing the optimal mix of market-based policies

Source: Reprinted with permission from The Conference Board of Canada. (2013). Greenhouse gas (GHG) emissions. *How Canada performs: A report card on Canada.* Retrieved from www.conferenceboard.ca/hcp/details/environment/greenhouse-gas-emissions.aspx.

Objective 1 Define sustainable development.

WHAT IS SUSTAINABILITY?

What is sustainability? While there is no one universal definition, one of the first definitions on the topic of sustainability was created in 1987 by former prime minister of Norway Gro Harlem Brundtland. At the United Nations-sponsored World Commission on Environment and Development, Brundtland described **sustainable development** in her report, *Our Common Future,* as "development that meets the needs of the present without compromising the ability of future generations to meet their own needs."[8]

To break it down, there are three components to this definition: development (to progress the economy and society), sustainability (to sustain resources), and people

sustainable development
Development that meets the needs of the present without compromising the ability of future generations to meet their own needs.

---

[8] United Nations General Assembly. (1987). *Report of the World Commission on Environment and Development: Our Common Future.* Retrieved from www.un-documents.net/our-common-future.pdf.

(current and future generations). According to environmental scientist Tim O'Riordon, the concept of sustainable development (SD) can be used by business, emphasizing the development portion, and environmentalists, emphasizing the sustainable portion.[9] How-

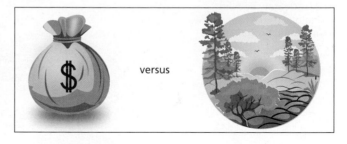

ever, O'Riordon contends that SD is a term that gives priority to business because of the focus on development. Nitin Desai explains that sustainable development is "an attempt essentially at talking in terms of redirecting development and growth, rather than stopping it. Because it recognizes very clearly that you must meet people's needs."[10]

The challenge in understanding this definition is not just the definition itself but the values that underlie it.[11] And what is the dominant priority? Is it economic growth, or environmental protection? Overall, SD represents needs and limits: the needs of business and people, and the resource limitations of the planet.

Traditionally, growing the economy and protecting the environment were looked at as two separate goals, often conflicting with one another (see Exhibit 11.1). For instance, auto manufacturers were looked upon as important contributors to the economy, providing jobs for people and adding to Canada's GDP. Environmentalists, however, insisted that cars contributed to air, water, and land pollution by emitting greenhouse gases and causing climate change. Today, businesses and people recognize the value of gas-efficient cars. And environmentalists are working together with automakers to promote hybrid models.

What was once a radical way of thinking has now become a more understood approach and accepted in the mainstream culture. Business leaders now recognize that society, the economy, and the environment are interrelated systems that have an important impact on one another. One system cannot survive without the others. People require water and air from the environment, and jobs and money from the economy. Similarly, the economy depends on the talents of people and the resources of the earth for development and growth. And the environment requires society and business to maintain its current resources so future generations may enjoy and benefit from its bounty.

Today, SD can be viewed as a long-term approach to balancing the needs of people, while growing the economy and preserving the environment. In a general sense, sustainability involves the relationship between with the three Ps: people, profits, and the planet (also referred to as the three Es: social equity, the economy, and the environment). This accounting framework is the **triple bottom line (TBL)** approach[12] (see Exhibit 11.2). Since this phrase was originally coined by John Elkington in his 1997 book *Cannibals with Forks: The Triple Bottom Line of 21st Century Business*, the model has become the dominant framework for businesses reporting social and environmental performance with

triple bottom line (TBL) An accounting framework that can be voluntarily used by organizations to report performance on social, economic, and environmental results for a project or reporting period.

---

[9] Willard, B. (2010). *The sustainability advantage: Seven business case benefits of a triple bottom line* (p. 146). Gabriola, BC: New Society Publishers.

[10] Dresner, S. (2008). *The principles of sustainability* (2nd ed.) (p. 71). London, UK: Earthscan.

[11] Dresner, 2008, 70.

[12] Willard, 2010, 6.

Exhibit 11.2 The Triple
Bottom Line Framework

Source: Cannibals with
Forks: Triple Bottom Line
of 21st Century by John
Elkington (1997), http://www.
johnelkington.com/.

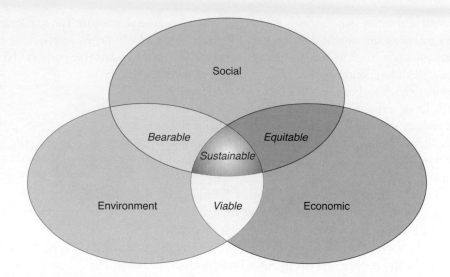

traditional financial results. What does this method entail? And how do the economy, society, and the environment interrelate?

Objective 2 Explain the three
components of the triple bottom
line (TBL) approach.

Economic Factors

While the growth of businesses is necessary for the growth of the economy, the economic category begins with an organization's need for income to survive. Traditional reporting typically focused on a company's financial statements: calculating income, expenses, assets, and liabilities. TBL reporting, however, has a broader approach. It goes beyond the financial statements and can include other indicators to show how a business is performing. Changes to the number of employees, for example, can indicate either job growth or company downsizing. The size of a business, revenue by sector, and research and development costs can also provide other information affecting the company's bottom line and cash flow. The amount of taxes paid is another economic indicator companies can use to show a company's growth or decline.[13]

TBL reporting acknowledges that for a business to be sustainable, a company also needs to be equitable to its employees and respectful to the environment. For instance, an unhappy workforce can lead to lower employee morale, higher employee turnover, and an increase in hiring and training costs. A business also needs to recognize how its methods to make a profit can impact other stakeholders such as the community and even the environment. As some natural resources become scarce and costly, businesses need to find ways to reduce using them or find alternative, more sustainable solutions.

The goal of a sustainable business is to make a profit, to meet the needs of people, and to minimize damage to the environment. Certainly, many organizations are working toward obtaining this balance. In Canada, some Aboriginal businesses have already achieved this goal. With a culture for respecting the earth, Aboriginal sustainable business practices are an extension of their culture and traditional beliefs, as seen in Talking Business 11.1.

---

[13] Slaper, T., & Hall, T. (2011). The triple bottom line: What is it and how does it work? *Indiana Business Review* (Spring). Retrieved from www.ibrc.indiana.edu/ibr/2011/spring/article2.html.

Cree Village Eco Lodge, a Sustainable Travel Destination

In July 2000, Cree Village Eco Lodge opened its doors to Canadian and foreign travellers. It was the first Indigenous owned, sustainable eco lodge in the northern hemisphere.

The facility includes 20 guest rooms that are designed for maximum comfort but minimal impact to the environment, with a 56-seat restaurant modelled on a traditional Cree home. This state-of-the-art building is designed and operated by the MoCreebec people with a focus on Cree traditional values, culture, and ecological sustainability. After five years of meticulous planning before opening, the facility has become a relaxing alterative to southern vacations, while supporting the local economy and protecting the environment.[14]

The facility is one of the more environmentally advanced accommodations facilities across Canada for several reasons. First, there is no air conditioning system in the building. Instead, there are low-noise, high efficiency ceiling fans that circulate the air. Windows and doors face north to take advantage of natural wind conditions and are triple-glazed with low-e argon. The facility was built using sustainable materials. Walls are made from natural cedar and painted with low emissions paints. And the floors are hardwood with some ceramic tile, while natural wool carpeting warms the rooms.[15]

According to the Cree Village Eco Lodge website, "furniture throughout is natural wood and fibres, with details such as birch wood blinds on windows and natural wool bedspreads. Environmental amenities include natural wool carpeting; all organic cotton mattresses, pillows, and sheets; and biodegradable hand soaps and shampoos in dispensers every room."[16]

Guests sometimes describe their experience as living "on the edge of the world." The lodge is surrounded by nature, with plenty of opportunities to explore. Just outside the door is the James Bay sub-artic region and its many nature trails. Tidewater Provincial Park and rugged camping areas are nearby. If you like wildlife, a short boat ride will lead you to beluga whales and fish such as pike and trout. Moose and caribou also habitat the area. If you are a bird-watcher, geese, eagles and migratory birds are also found in the region. And of course, Canadian history is everywhere you look. A short walk away from the lodge are historical buildings and fur trade sites that date back to the 17th century.

Social Factors

Social equity (or the social category) refers to fair and equitable business practices toward employees and the community. What is a fair and equitable business practice? Some examples include fair salaries, a safe workplace, reasonable working hours, and adherence to all employment laws. Respect for diversity and human rights is also an important part of social equity. For companies that outsource some of their business functions to overseas suppliers, a fair business practice would mean not using child labour, even in countries where it may legally be acceptable. Although lower wages are paid, businesses with equitable practices would ensure that workers and their communities are not exploited, harmed, or negatively affected by their business operations. Subsequently, business ethics plays a role in social equity.

In the electronics manufacturing industry, Apple has been criticized for not doing enough to protect overseas workers from unsafe and harsh working conditions. One of its key suppliers, Foxconn, has been accused of forcing employees to work excessive overtime and using dangerous chemicals to produce iPads faster to meet consumer demand. Many advocacy groups contend that for Foxconn to improve working conditions, Apple needs to be willing to pay higher fees to its suppliers so they can make their workplaces safer.

social equity In general terms, fair and equitable business practices toward employees and the community. It involves such things as fair salaries, a safe workplace, reasonable working hours, adherence to employment laws, and respect for diversity and human rights.

---

[14] http://www.creevillage.com/Home.html.

[15] http://www.creevillage.com/Ecolodge.html.

[16] http://www.creevillage.com/Ecolodge.html.

Besides employee welfare, the social category includes a company's commitment to helping the communities it operates in. Charitable donations and volunteer time are two traditional ways an organization can help society. However, many organizations are becoming more involved in meeting specific needs of communities and preserving the long-term sustainability of their businesses. For instance, a company may support education, health care, housing, or other needs that are vital to a community. Let's consider Starbucks and its contributions to social welfare as an example.

In the coffee industry, coffee beans come from many regions in the world, such as South America, Vietnam, and Africa, where poverty and poor economies persist. In recent years, droughts and rising costs have caused hundreds of coffee farmers to go bankrupt. Many coffee companies like Starbucks recognize the importance of farmers making a reasonable living so they can sustain their farms and maintain sufficient coffee supplies in the long run. To achieve this, Starbucks regularly communicates with coffee bean farmers and their local governments to address agricultural, economic, and community issues to ensure the coffee industry will continue to thrive and prosper. Starbucks also pays its farmers a fair price for their coffee beans, which is often referred to as *Fair-Trade coffee*.

Recently, the problem of climate change is creating a new challenge for coffee producers. **Climate change** refers to a change in climate caused by a significant change in weather patterns. A change in weather patterns can be due to natural causes like oceanic processes or unnatural causes like human interference. In order for the industry to be sustainable, Starbucks must continue to be proactive in addressing the needs of both farmers and the environment.

climate change Changes in climate caused by a significant change in weather patterns, either from natural causes like oceanic processes, or unnatural causes like human interference.

Environmental Factors

The environment (or the planet) is the category that refers to the need for sustainable practices that protect our water, land, and air. The environment is what needs to be preserved for future generations to enjoy and for the economy to prosper. What currently threatens the planet? Two key concerns are the depletion of natural resources by overconsumption and the ongoing release of greenhouse gas emissions.

Depletion of Natural Resources The depletion of natural resources by humans is one of the greatest environmental problems that exists today. Human demand for resources is increasing as the earth's population continues to grow. However, the demand for resources is growing 1.5 times faster than the earth has the ability to regenerate them.[17] While the global population exceeds 7 billion people, the United Nations expects the global population to exceed 10 billion by 2050, furthering the need for water, land, and other raw materials.[18]

Water One could argue that water is the most important natural resource on earth. Every living organism relies on water for survival. While the earth is made up of more water than land, not all water is fit or available to drink. Only 3% of the world's water is freshwater, and most of it is frozen in ice or is found deep within the earth (see Exhibit 11.3).

Today, water shortages continue throughout the world due to population growth, pollution, and poor infrastructure.[19] Worldwide, the average person uses 10 gallons

---

[17] Stringer, L. (2010). *The green workplace* (p. 22). New York, NY: Palgrave MacMillan.

[18] Farrell, P.B. (2012, July 24). Water is the new gold, a big commodity bet. *Market Watch, Yahoo Finance.* Retrieved from http://ca.finance.yahoo.com/news/water-gold-big-commodity-bet-040352660.html.

[19] Stringer, 2010, 23.

Exhibit 11.3 Water on the Earth's Surface

Reservoir	Volume (in 1,000 cu km)	% of Total
Atmosphere	13	0.001
Oceans	1,320,000	97.54
Glaciers and ice caps	29,200	1.81
Salt lakes	104	0.007
Freshwater lakes	125	0.009
Rivers	1	0.0000002
Soil moisture	40	0.001
Groundwater	8,350	0.63

Source: Rogers, J.W., & Feiss, P.G. (1999). *People and the earth: Basic issues in the sustainability of resources and environment* (p. 126). Cambridge, UK: Cambridge University Press. Reprinted with permission.

(or approximately 40 litres) of water every day.[20] This includes water for drinking, washing clothes and dishes, and flushing the toilet. But water is needed for more than direct personal use. Worldwide agriculture, for example, accounts for approximately 75% of water consumption, although use by country varies significantly. Industry is also a major user of water to produce goods and services.[21]

Besides the need for drinking water, there is also the need for virtual water. **Virtual water** (also referred to as *embodied water*) is water necessary to produce, process, and transport products for consumption.[22] Let's consider a cup of coffee. A standard or regular-size cup of java requires about 140 litres of water, mostly for growing the coffee plant. According to the Water Footprint Network, this in turn means the world requires approximately 110 billion cubic metres of water annually to enjoy coffee.[23]

virtual water Water necessary to produce, process, and transport products for consumption. Also called embodied water.

Some observers are predicting that water will become the new "gold" of the 21st century. As the demand for water continues to increase, so will its cost. According to a *Market Watch* article, the global market for all water users has an increasing price tag:

Industry needs $28 billion for water equipment and services to all kinds of businesses . . . another $10 billion covers agricultural irrigation . . . another $15 billion in retail products like filters and various heating and cooling systems . . . $170 billion used for waste water, sewage systems, waste-water treatment and water recycling systems . . . and $226 billion for water utilities, treatment plants and distribution systems.[24]

How good is Canada's water, and what challenges are there for its future sustainability? See Talking Business 11.2 to see.

---

[20] Rogers, J.W., & Feiss, P.G. (1999). *People and the earth: Basic issues in the sustainability of resources and environment* (p. 135). Cambridge, UK: Cambridge University Press.

[21] Rogers, & Feiss, 1999, 135.

[22] Stringer, 2010, 24.

[23] Water Footprint Network website (n.d.). Product water footprints: Coffee and tea. Retrieved from www.waterfootprint.org/?page=files/CoffeeTea.

[24] Farrell, 2012.

How Sustainable Is Canada's Water?

silver-john/Shutterstock

Putting Water Quality in Context

The health and well-being of humans and ecosystems depend heavily on the quality of the water resources available. Water is necessary for all biological life. It also supports global food production by providing the fundamental resource upon which agriculture, livestock production, fisheries, and aquaculture depend. Water is also crucial for industrial activity and municipal services.

The main concerns with water quality are the impacts of water pollution (eutrophication, acidification, and toxic contamination) on human health, on the cost of drinking water treatment, and on ecosystems. New waste-water treatment facilities have helped. But pollution from agricultural sources is an issue in many countries, as is the supply of safe drinking water. Policies that promote good water quality are critical to protect aquatic biodiversity and drinking water sources.

How does Canada's Water Quality Compare to that of its Peer Countries?

Canada ranks 4th out of 17 peer OECD counties for water quality and receives an "A" grade for performance. Two Scandinavian countries—Sweden and Norway—together with Austria rank ahead of Canada. Two countries receive "D"s for their overall water quality.

What is Putting Stress on Water Quality in Canada?

Canada's water quality is at risk from poorly treated municipal waste, industrial effluent, and fertilizer run-off from agriculture. Most of the nitrogen and phosphorus released into the environment comes from these three sources. Although toxic effluents are heavily regulated in Canada, release of nutrients into the watershed is common.

Phosphorus and nitrogen are important nutrients in fresh water, but high concentrations can lead to eutrophication—when an excess of nutrients overstimulates plant growth and decreases oxygen supplies, making the water unusable. Eutrophication is a serious water quality issue for the Prairie provinces, southern Ontario, and Quebec. In southern Ontario, nitrogen and phosphorus released from agriculture, municipal sewage, and industrial waste water have hurt the water quality of the Great Lakes and other inland waters. In the Prairies, nutrient concentrations are naturally high in rivers, and intensive agriculture magnifies the problem. British Columbia has fewer eutrophication problems than other provinces. But its heavily populated lower Fraser River Basin has high levels of agricultural runoff and municipal waste-water discharge, resulting in nutrient enrichment. An estimated 90 per cent of the province's municipal waste water is discharged into the lower Fraser River or its tributaries.

What has the Biggest Impact on Canada's Water Quality?

Municipal waste-water discharges are one of the largest sources of pollution in Canadian waters. In 2006, municipal waste-water effluents produced by households, businesses, and industries generated 84 per cent of the water effluents reported under the National Pollutant Release Inventory. Municipal waste water is composed of sanitary sewage and storm water, and can contain grit, debris, suspended solids, disease-causing pathogens, decaying organic wastes, nutrients, and about 200 identified chemicals.

Source: Excerpted from The Conference Board of Canada. (2013). Water quality index. *How Canada performs: A report card on Canada.* Retrieved from www.conferenceboard.ca/hcp/details/environment/water-quality-index.aspx. Reprinted by permission of The Conference Board of Canada.

Raw Materials   Like water, the need for other natural resources is also on the increase. Currently, the average American consumes about five times more stuff than 100 years ago.[25] Just think of all the products you can now buy that your great-grandparents didn't have. Many of us today have the privilege of owning a car, a television, a computer, a tablet, and a smartphone. For every product produced, raw materials are needed to manufacture, market, store, and deliver the final product to the consumer. According to Leigh Stringer, "Total annual material consumption in the United States rose 57% from 1970 to 2000, reaching 6.5 billion metric tons."[26]

Traditionally, Western industrial nations have been the largest consumers of natural resources. According to David Suzuki, "North Americans, Europeans, Japanese, and Australians, who make up 20% of the world's population, are consuming more than 80% of the world's resources."[27] But this reality is changing too. As China and India continue to develop their economies and live more Western lifestyles, their demand for and consumption of natural resources is subsequently rising. Clearly, consuming more and more raw materials is unsustainable in the long term, but are there certain resources that need to be conserved more than others? And what are the effects of their use?

Greenhouse Gas (GHG) Emissions

The human consumption of different forms of energy continues to have one of the largest negative side effects on the planet. While greenhouse gases pollute our air, scientists argue that these emissions are the primary source for climate change; that is, rising temperatures over the earth. According to the David Suzuki Foundation:

> Much like the glass of a greenhouse, gases in our atmosphere sustain life on Earth by trapping the sun's heat. . . . Without naturally-occurring, heat-trapping gases—mainly water vapour, carbon dioxide and methane—Earth would be too cold to sustain life as we know it.
>
> The danger lies in the rapid increase of carbon dioxide and other greenhouse gases that intensify this natural greenhouse effect. . . . Modern human activity—burning fossil fuels, deforestation, intensive agriculture—has added huge quantities of carbon dioxide and other greenhouse gases.
>
> Today's atmosphere contains 32 per cent more carbon dioxide than it did at the start of the industrial era.[28]

Where do greenhouse gas emissions come from? **Greenhouse gas emissions** arise when fossil fuels are burned to make electricity, to heat homes and buildings, to process industrial and commercial activities, to power transportation, and to allow agricultural and other miscellaneous processes (see Exhibit 11.4).

So what is a fossil fuel? A **fossil fuel** is a **nonrenewable resource** that takes millions of years to form. The burning of fossil fuels causes carbon dioxide (CO_2) to be released

greenhouse gas emissions
Gas emissions that result from burning fossil fuels to carry out many of our daily functions in industrialized society, such as to make electricity, to heat homes and buildings, to process industrial and commercial activities, to power transportation, and to allow agricultural and other miscellaneous processes.

fossil fuel A nonrenewable resource that takes millions of years to form. Burning fossil fuels causes carbon dioxide to be released into the atmosphere and causes the earth's surface temperature to rise.

nonrenewable resource
A form of energy that takes millions of years to form.

---

[25] Stringer, 2010, 24.

[26] Stringer, 2010, 25.

[27] Suzuki, D. (2011, November 3). Is seven billion people too many? Retrieved from www.davidsuzuki.org/blogs/science-matters/2011/11/is-seven-billion-people-too-many.

[28] David Suzuki Foundation. (n.d.). Greenhouse gases. Retrieved from www.davidsuzuki.org/issues/climate-change/science/climate-change-basics/greenhouse-gases/?gclid=CJ_ak7ORr7QCFYw-MgoddVoAOQ.

Exhibit 11.4 Sources of Greenhouse Gas Emissions

Activity	Percentage
Electricity	33%
Heating and commercial processes	31%
Transportation	28%
Agriculture and miscellaneous activities	8%
Total	100%

Source: Stringer, L. (2010). *The green workplace* (pp. 33–34). New York, NY: Palgrave MacMillan.

carbon footprint A measurement of the total amount of greenhouse gas emissions from a person, product, event, or organization.

into the atmosphere and causes the earth's average surface temperature to rise. Examples of energy derived from fossil fuels include coal, petroleum (oil or gasoline), and natural gas. An estimated 3.2 billion metric tonnes of carbon is added to the earth's atmosphere annually.[29] A **carbon footprint** measures the total amount of greenhouse gas emissions from a person, product, event, or organization. In recent years, managing our energy needs has created a huge debate. While some forms of energy appear cleaner than others, the process to obtain them has to be considered in whether or not they are truly sustainable in the long term, as seen in Talking Business 11.3.

TALKING BUSINESS 11.3

Fracking Fracas: Pros and Cons of Controversial Gas Extraction Process

Spencer Platt/Getty Images

Injecting a high-pressure mix of water and chemicals deep beneath the ground to free up oil and gas deposits has been in use for more than 60 years.

U.S. President Barack Obama even endorsed the practice in his state of the union address last month. Extracting shale gas will "create jobs and power trucks and factories that are cleaner and cheaper, proving that we don't have to choose between our environment and our economy," he said.

But in recent years the process called hydraulic fracturing—"fracking" for short—has also become a flashpoint for environmental critics.

Why has a long-accepted practice now become such a hot button topic?

Anthony Ingraffea, a professor of engineering at Cornell University, suggests there is confusion about fracking in conventional wells and fracking for natural gas in shale formations.

In fracking for natural gas in shale, a well is drilled both vertically and horizontally. Along that horizontal seam, which can extend for thousands of metres, hundreds of well pads are built to collect the gas. They intersect with

[29] US Energy Information Administration. (2004). What are greenhouse gases? Retrieved from www.eia.gov/oiaf/1605/ggccebro/chapter1.html.

thousands of pockets of gas which are distributed along the shale formation.

To fracture, or open up the shale's pores, as much as 20 million gallons of highly pressurized fracking fluid—made of chemicals, water and sand—are pumped into the well. The shale then opens up and releases the gas, which flows back to the surface. It's occurs on a much bigger scale than conventional fracking.

Conservatively, there are close to 500 wells being hydraulically fractured in shale formations in the U.S. and Canada, said David Burnett, director of technology for the Global Petroleum Research Institute at Texas A&M University.

It's "an oil and gas boom the likes of which we haven't seen since the development of the rotary drilling rig in the 1800s," Burnett said.

Some of the biggest shale gas formations in the U.S. are in Wyoming, Texas, New York (part of which extends into Ontario) and Pennsylvania.

With shale extraction comes what Burnett describes as a "tsunami of people and equipment," which can lead to problems, particularly in a wilderness area.

The environmental risks are higher than in conventional drilling, said Cornell's Ingraffea. Everything from groundwater contamination to a pipeline leak are possible, he said.

The equipment emits pollutants into the air. Fracking fluid, once it returns to the surface, contains chemicals and naturally occurring hazardous materials.

"The biggest controversy is clearly water," said Robert Jackson, professor of environmental sciences at Duke University in North Carolina.

"Hydraulic fracturing takes millions of gallons of water to fracture a single well. Depending on where you are in the country, you may have to pump groundwater or take it from a stream."

There often are no facilities for storing or disposing of the fracking fluid.

"People are worried about the chemicals from the fracturing fluid getting into their drinking water," Jackson said.

A recent U.S. Environmental Protection Agency report found groundwater in an aquifer around Pavillion, Wyoming contained "compounds likely associated with gas production practices, including hydraulic fracturing."

In addition, Ingraffea said, the infrastructure required to maintain these wells—processing equipment, compressor stations, trucks and highways—all bring potential risks. The wells and the pipeline could also fail. According to some studies seen by Ingraffea, at least 5 per cent of all new wells exhibit some kind of failure to contain hydrocarbons.

Climate change is another risk. Methane, a much stronger greenhouse gas than carbon dioxide, is emitted into the atmosphere during the extraction.

The disposal of fracking waste underground also causes earthquakes, Ingraffea said.

"The question is what frequency, what magnitude and what level is deemed acceptable," he said.

There are potentially huge profits for the oil and gas sector, with some of that flowing into government coffers. Towns and communities could also experience a boom in jobs.

The bigger dream? Reducing America's dependence on oil.

"Without (fracking) you can't get the gas out of the ground. There are huge amounts of gas locked up in shale and other formations. These technologies allow you to find and retrieve that gas," said Jackson.

"Our conventional gas supplies are dwindling in North America. These unconventional sources are making up the difference."

Source: Excerpted from Black, D. (2012, February 5). Fracking fracas: Pros and cons of controversial gas extraction process. *Toronto Star.* Retrieved from www.thestar.com/news/world/2012/02/05/fracking_fracas_pros_and_cons_of_controversial_gas_extraction_process.print.html. Reprinted with permission from The Toronto Star.

As temperatures continue to rise, there are many negative effects on the planet and its ecosystems. Icebergs are melting and causing water levels to rise. Animals such as polar bears that normally live on the ice are being forced onto land to look for nontraditional sources of food. Rising temperatures are also causing more drastic weather patterns and more droughts around the world. In Exhibit 11.5, it is clear that CO_2 emissions have increased substantially over the last century.

What improvements can be made? What sustainable resources currently exist? A **sustainable resource** is a resource that can be replenished at the same rate as it is

sustainable resource
A resource that can be replenished at the same rate as it is used. It typically derives from renewable resources or recycled materials.

Exhibit 11.5 CO_2 Emissions over the Past 300 Years

Source: US Energy Information Administration. (2004). What are greenhouse gases? Retrieved from www.eia.gov/oiaf/1605/ggccebro/chapter1.html.

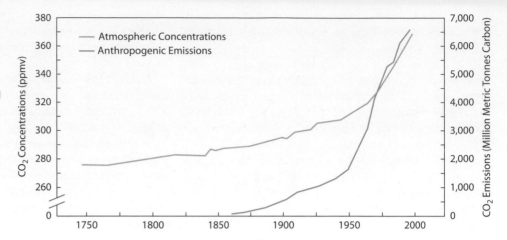

used. It typically derives from renewable resources or recycled materials. Since fossil fuels produce much more carbon emissions than other sources of energy, many governments are encouraging alternative forms of energy to be used to reduce carbon emissions. Some examples include solar energy, wind power, hydropower, and geothermal power.

As you can see, environmental issues can pose unique challenges for business. But what are the benefits and limitations of using the triple bottom line approach?

Objective 3 Discuss the benefits and limitations of using the TBL as a performance tool.

BENEFITS AND LIMITATIONS OF THE TRIPLE BOTTOM LINE FRAMEWORK

The triple bottom line framework is currently the dominant approach for businesses to report their efforts in supporting the economy, satisfying their stakeholders, and protecting the environment. But how does the TBL approach benefit business?

Benefits of the TBL Approach

There are three main benefits to business of using the triple bottom line approach:[30]

1. *Improves transparency:* In addition to financial statement reporting, the TBL allows an organization to voluntarily report its impact on society and the environment. This can improve accountability as the organization provides information on its nonfinancial activities and exposes itself to both public criticism and praise.

2. *Allows flexibility:* The TBL is also a framework any organization can use. Whether you are a corporation, the government, or a nonprofit organization, the framework is general enough for most organizations to easily adopt. An organization of any size or any industry can use the TBL method. It can also be used broadly to assess an organization's overall performance or be applied to an individual project, policy, or geographic area.

---

[30] Slaper, T., & Hall, T. (2011). The triple bottom line: What is it and how does it work? *Indiana Business Review* (Spring). Retrieved from www.ibrc.indiana.edu/ibr/2011/spring/article2.html.

On an annual basis, organizations can use the framework to assess performance, identify necessary changes, and assist in future decision making.

3. *Aims to satisfy more stakeholders:* The approach also recognizes the impact of the organization's actions on all its stakeholders. Stakeholders can include shareowners, employees, the community, and even the environment. As a result, this methodology uses a long-term perspective to improve the impact of an organization's activities on all the people and groups being affected by it.

Limitations of the TBL Approach

Critics argue, however, that TBL reporting is just a marketing tool that highlights achievements over failures. For example, the following three criticisms have been levelled at the TBL approach:[31]

1. *No measurement standards:* Unlike generally accepted accounting principles (GAAP) used in accounting, there are no widely accepted standards or rules for measuring, verifying, or auditing TBL data. The mixture of both quantitative and qualitative data means that there is no common unit of measure that can allow all three categories to be added together to arrive at a net figure. Each component—economic, social, and environmental—is unique. While the economic category can use a dollar-based measure, it can also use additional measures to track other indicators other than profits. For example, job growth and employee turnover are two variables. Similarly, the social and environmental categories have other unique indicators that cannot simply be added together.

2. *Too subjective:* Another limitation of this qualitative method is its subjectivity. The social category, for instance, is subjective and requires more personal judgment than the economic category. For example, what is a positive social action that a company can take to improve the well-being of its employees, the community, and other stakeholders? Is it a monetary donation to a charitable organization, or will a company allowing its employee's to volunteer their time to a worthy cause also suffice? What meets the needs of employees and the community may depend on a variety of factors: The region, the culture, the values, and the expectations of its stakeholders are just a few. Consider the scenarios shown in Exhibit 11.6.

3. *Lack of comparability:* Since the TBL approach is not legally required, not all organizations voluntarily use this approach. For organizations that do use it, each organization has the flexibility to choose what data to collect, measure, and include for reporting purposes. For instance, companies can decide to exclude negative activities and only include positive ones. Cost and time constraints may also create obstacles for some organizations in tracking data. There are no consequences if there is missing data or a lack of information, and there is no legal requirement to have a third-party audit. Other factors such as the size of the organization or the type of industry can affect what indicators organizations decide to use. A construction company, for instance, may use a lot of environmental indicators to track waste and other environmental impacts, whereas a nonprofit health group may have more social indicators aimed at helping people.

---

[31] Slaper & Hall, 2011.

Exhibit 11.6 Social Scenarios Requiring Personal Judgment

Scenario	Questions for Consideration
• A company donates $1 million dollars to a children's hospital, and the following year the same company donates $1 million dollars to an abortion clinic.	• Does it matter who receives the donation? • Do you give credit to the donation amount in the same way? • Does it matter how many people benefit from the social action? • How do you determine what is a benefit?
• An organization has women in over 50% of its management positions; however, the same organization has five separate sexual harassment lawsuits filed by women over the past few years.	• Do you give credit to only the benefits or positive actions toward employees, the community, and other stakeholders? Or do you subtract negative actions as well? How do you measure these actions? • Does it matter how large the organization is? Certainly, your answer may be different if there are only 100 employees versus 100,000.
• A food company allows Canadian employees to volunteer their time at a food shelter one day a month; however, the same company uses unhealthy (but legal) trans fats in all of its food products, which have been linked to obesity and other health issues.	• How do you value a negative social action, even if it does not break the law? • How do you value an action versus an inaction?

Objective 4 Identify and explain four sustainability measures.

MEASURING SUSTAINABILITY

Since the movement toward sustainability is still relatively new, the development of a common standard of global measures is still underway. What are some measures that currently exist, and how can businesses implement more sustainable practices? There are a number of ways to measure sustainable performance changes on a national or global basis, including the Living Planet Index (see Exhibit 11.7), the Ecological Footprint, the Index of Sustainable Economic Welfare, and the Genuine Progress Indicator.

Exhibit 11.7 Sustainability Measures

1. Living Planet Index	3. Index of Sustainable Economic Welfare
2. Ecological Footprint	4. Genuine Progress Indicator

Living Planet Index

Living Planet Index (LPI)
Created by the World Wildlife Fund, this index aims to measure changes to the world's biological diversity.

biological diversity The different forms of life and number of species on earth. It includes people, plants, animals, bacteria, and other living organisms.

The **Living Planet Index (LPI)**, created by the World Wildlife Fund (WWF), aims to measure changes to the world's biological diversity based on over 9,000 populations of more than 2,600 species from around the world.[32] **Biological diversity** refers to the different forms of life and number of species on earth. This includes people, plants, animals, bacteria, and other living organisms. In 2012, the LPI indicated there had been a decline in biodiversity health of approximately 30% since 1970. Tropical areas had suffered the hardest, with a 60% decline in less than 40 years[33] (see Exhibit 11.8).

---

[32] World Wildlife Fund. (2012). *Living Planet Report 2012: Summary*. Retrieved from http://awsassets.panda.org/downloads/lpr_2012_summary_booklet_final.pdf.

[33] World Wildlife Fund, 2012.

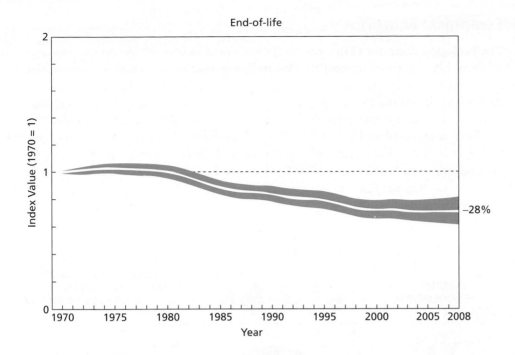

End-of-life

While the LPI only measures a small fraction of the 1.75 million species that have been identified by researchers, the LPI can be used as an informative tool for scientists, policymakers, and the general public to identify trends on where species may be declining the fastest across the globe.

Clearly, human consumption has affected biological diversity and the ecosystems that interact with these life forms. An **ecosystem** is a set of complex relationships among living organisms and their environment. An ecosystem can include trees, plants, water, soil, animals, fish, birds, microorganisms, and people. If one part of the ecosystem is damaged, other parts can be negatively affected too.

So how is the global LPI calculated? According to the WWF, it is an aggregate of two equally weighted indices of vertebrae populations—the tropical and temperate LPIs:

ecosystem A set of complex relationships among all living organisms and their environment.

> The Tropical LPI consists of the terrestrial and freshwater species populations found in the Afrotropical, Indo-Pacific and Neotropical realms and marine species populations from the zone between the Tropics of Cancer and Capricorn. The Temperate LPI includes all terrestrial and freshwater species populations from the Palearctic and Nearctics realms, and marine species north and south of the tropics.[34]

Since the index was developed in 1997, the Institute of Zoology has been working in collaboration with the WWF to improve the index and to identify where humans may be having the most negative impact.

---

[34] World Wildlife Fund. (2010). 2010 Biodiversity Indicators Partnership: Living Planet Index Fact Sheet. Retrieved from http://static.zsl.org/files/1-2-1-living-planet-index-1062.pdf.

Ecological Footprint

The **Ecological Footprint (EP)** measures the amount of biologically productive land and sea area that is required to meet the demands of human consumption for a particular population or country. According to the Global Footprint Network, the EP includes "the areas for producing the resource it consumes, the space for accommodating its buildings and roads, and the ecosystems for absorbing its waste emissions such as carbon dioxide."[35]

Since it was developed in 1990 by William Rees and Mathis Wackernagel at the University of British Columbia, the EP has become a predominant measure of humanity's demand on nature. The World Wildlife Fund measures an Ecological Footprint by considering six subcategories: carbon, grazing land, fishing grounds, built-up land, forest, and cropland (see Exhibit 11.9).

Exhibit 11.9
Components of the Ecological Footprint

Source: Global living planet index. © 2012 World Wildlife Federation (panda.org). Some rights reserved.

THE COMPONENTS OF THE ECOLOGICAL FOOTPRINT

Carbon
Represents the amount of forest land that could sequester CO_2 emissions from the burning of fossil fuels, excluding the fraction absorbed by the oceans that leads to acidification.

Cropland
Represents the amount of cropland used to grow crops for food and fibre for human consumption as well as for animal feed, oil crops, and rubber.

Grazing Land
Represents the amount of grazing land used to raise livestock for meat, dairy, hide, and wool products.

Forest
Represents the amount of forest required to supply timber products, pulp, and fuel wood.

Built-up Land
Represents the amount of land covered by human infrastructure, including transportation, housing, industrial structures, and reservoirs for hydropower.

Fishing Grounds
Calculated from the estimated primary production required to support the fish and seafood caught, based on catch data for marine and freshwater species.

Let's consider Canada and measure its ecological footprint. As a nation that experiences four seasons—fall, winter, spring, and summer—Canada relies on food from both within and outside its borders. Consider your last trip to a grocery store: Your oranges may have come from Florida, your pineapples from Costa Rica, your coffee from Brazil, and your peppers from Mexico. All of this food must be transported to Canada, burning fossil fuels and contributing to climate change. How much energy do you use to heat your home,

---

[35] Global Footprint Network. (n.d.). Footprint basics—overview. Retrieved from www.footprintnetwork.org/en/index.php/GFN/page/footprint_basics_overview.

travel to work, or run your air conditioner, washing machine, and dishwasher? According to the World Wildlife Fund's 2012 *Living Planet Report*, Canada had the eighth-highest ecological footprint per capita, while the United States had the fifth highest.[36] For the earth, this means Canadians are consuming 3.5 times our share of resources faster than the earth has the means to replenish them.[37] See Exhibit 11.10 for the 10 worst country Ecological Footprints and Exhibit 11.11 for the 10 best country Ecological Footprints.

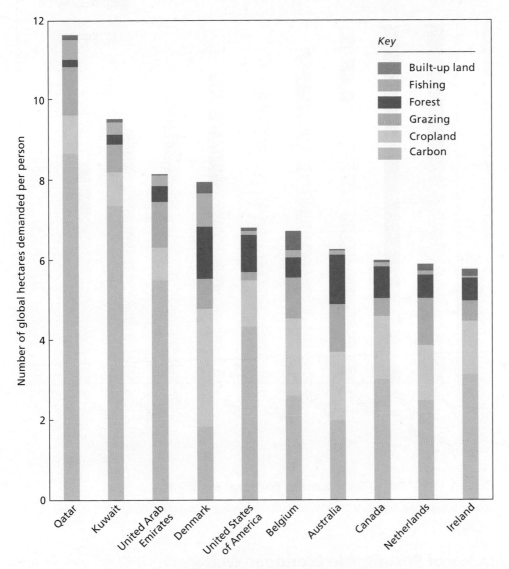

Exhibit 11.10 The 10 Worst Countries' Ecological Footprints

Source: Global living planet index. © 2012 World Wildlife Federation (panda.org). Some rights reserved.

---

[36] World Wildlife Fund, 2012, 8.

[37] WWF Canada. (2012). *Living Planet Report 2012*: Canadians must choose environment and economy for strong future. Retrieved from www.wwf.ca/newsroom/reports/living_planet_report_2012.cfm.

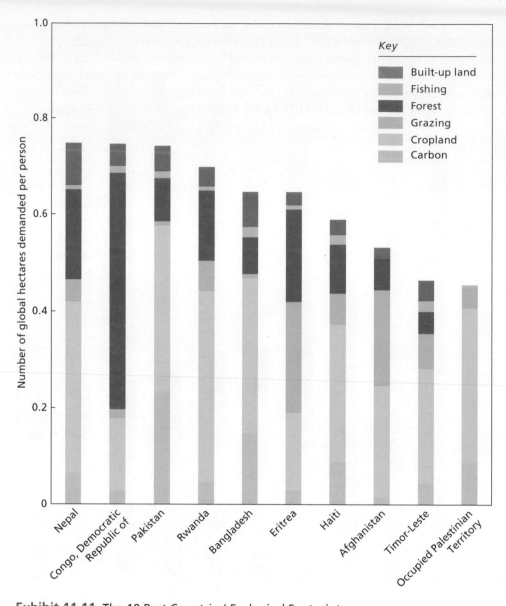

Exhibit 11.11 The 10 Best Countries' Ecological Footprints

Index of Sustainable Economic Welfare

Index of Sustainable Economic Welfare (ISEW) An index that attempts to measure both positive and negative activities that affect a society's well-being.

While the Ecological Footprint indicates how humans have impacted the environment, the Index of Sustainable Economic Welfare (ISEW) focuses on the welfare of a country. Developed in 1989 by Herman Daly and John Cobb,[38] the **Index of Sustainable Economic Welfare (ISEW)** attempts to measure both positive and negative activities that affect a society's

[38] *CBC News*. (2008, June 30). GDP. Retrieved from www.cbc.ca/news/business/story/2008/06/16/f-economy-gdp.html.

well-being. Traditionally, the main economic indicator, gross domestic product (GDP), measures the value of all goods and services produced within a country. While the GDP helps to show changes in economic prosperity, it fails to reflect the social well-being of a nation. The ISEW aims to present both. The ISEW, for example, would add unpaid childcare costs to the index, but subtract water pollution. This dollar-based index goes beyond the measure of GDP by including beneficial activities and harmful effects of economic growth that can negatively affect a population's well-being. Exhibit 11.12 shows how to calculate the ISEW.

ISEW = Personal Expenditure + Public Expenditure (e.g., defence) + Value of Unpaid Work − Private Defence − Value of Environmental Damage

Exhibit 11.12 Index of Sustainable Economic Welfare (ISEW)

Source: Economics Online. (n.d.). Measures of economic welfare. Retrieved from http://economicsonline.co.uk/Global_economics/Measure_of_economic_welfare_MEW.html.

Genuine Progress Indicator

Similar to the ISEW, the **Genuine Progress Indicator (GPI)** is a tool used to measure a country or region's economic growth and social well-being. The GPI includes all variables calculated under the GDP, but subtracts the negative effects of economic growth that cause social harm to a community. The cost of crime, pollution, and resource depletion are a few examples. How does the cost of crime normally increase GDP? Let's consider a family injured in a home break-in. In calculating GDP, lawyer's fees, property damage repairs, and medical fees are treated as forms of revenue; however, since the action does harm to a society, in calculating GPI these revenues are subtracted.

The GPI also considers positive contributions of the family and the community that are not included in the GDP because no money changes hands. For example, the value of housework, volunteer work, and unpaid childcare all contribute to a society's well-being. Under the GPI, these actions are calculated at the approximate market value of hiring someone to do the work.

The GPI indicator helps us understand why a population may feel unhappy or dissatisfied despite economic growth. According to one observer,

> **Genuine Progress Indicator (GPI)** A tool used to measure a country or region's economic growth and social well-being. It includes all variables calculated under the GDP, but subtracts the negative effects of economic growth that cause social harm to a community.

While per capita GDP has more than doubled from 1950 to present, the GPI shows a very different picture. It increased during the 1950s and 1960s, but has declined by roughly 45% since 1970 . . . Specifically, the GPI reveals that much of what economists now consider economic growth, as measured by GDP, is really one of three things: 1) fixing blunders and social decay from the past; 2) borrowing resources from the future; or 3) shifting functions from the community and household realm to that of the monetized economy. The GPI strongly suggests that the costs of the nation's current economic trajectory have begun to outweigh the benefits, leading to growth that is actually uneconomic.[39]

---

[39] Sustainability website. (n.d.). The Genuine Progress Indicator. Retrieved from www.sustainwellbeing.net/gpi.html.

While there is no standard formula for calculating the GPI, it can be a useful tool to assess annual changes to a population's quality of life.

Objective 5 Explain the business case for implementing sustainable practices.

THE BUSINESS CASE FOR IMPLEMENTING SUSTAINABLE PRACTICES

Why should businesses want to be sustainable? What are the motivating factors for business to implement sustainable practices? While the primary goal of a business is to make a profit, sustainable practices can contribute to this goal and help create value on a number of levels. Companies, for example, can reduce costs, reduce risk, and improve public relations.

Reducing Costs

Reducing costs can be achieved in a variety of ways. Whether you are a manufacturer or a retailer, reducing packaging, lowering energy use, and reducing waste can help businesses save money.

Reducing Packaging How many times have you bought a product and thrown away the packaging? Certainly, packaging products to make them more appealing is an important part of marketing, but sometimes not all packaging is necessary and can even create unnecessary costs for a company. Larger packaging can result in higher materials costs, higher shipping costs, and can take up more shelf space in stores. Many companies are reevaluating their packaging, such as Canadian Tire. According to Tyler Elm, vice-president of corporate strategy and business sustainability at Canadian Tire, one of his first sustainability projects was to reduce the packaging of a 14-piece socket set:

> We worked with the vendor to shrink the amount of packaging. It protected the product and it was a more effective storage medium, but . . . we [also] reduced the amount of plastic in that packaging by 55%, [and] we reduced the amount of space that package took up by almost 70%. It took 2.7 fewer ocean containers to ship that product, [and] as a result it saved us over $20,000 in shipping costs. It reduced the product's shipping cost by 15% and it generated about 10 tonnes of greenhouse gas emissions avoidance.[40]

Another common source of packaging is found in take-out food containers. Every day thousands of paper plates, cups, and plastic cutlery end up in garbage bins and then head for landfills. In 2011, one Canadian mall spent $120 million to renovate its food eatery and to change this unsustainable practice. The 900-seat Urban Eatery at the Toronto Eaton Centre offered a modern upgrade to customers, plus a greener dining experience. Customers could now enjoy the option of eating fast food with reusable dishware and cutlery. After eating, customers brought their trays and dirty dishes to one of several return stations. A solid waste compactor also helped reduce waste by over 80%.[41]

---

[40] Morison, O. (2012, August 9). In this job, sustainability is the business plan. *Globe and Mail*. Retrieved from www.theglobeandmail.com/report-on-business/careers/in-this-job-sustainability-is-the-business-plan/article4469921.

[41] *Snap Downtown Toronto*. (2011, October). Cadillac Fairview reveals Eaton Centre's Urban Eatery. Retrieved from www.snapdowntowntoronto.com/index.php?option=com_sngevents&id[]=314083.

Lowering Energy Use   Another way organizations can reduce costs is by lowering energy consumption. When it comes to building design, green facilities lower energy costs and increase market value for building owners. According to McGraw-Hill Construction, green buildings can result in an average reduction in operating costs by 8–9% and increase market values by up to 7.5%.[42] Subsequently, green facilities are more attractive to potential rental tenants since business operating costs can be saved. According to one observer, "building values are expected to increase by 7.5 percent, occupancy by 3.5 percent, rents by 3 percent, and the return on investment 6.6 percent or more for green buildings."[43]

Building owners can also save money. In 2011, Canadian Tire built its first energy-efficient store in Kemptville, Ontario. What did Canadian Tire achieve? The store design was 75% more efficient. For instance, the new store only consumed 9.7 ekWh/sq ft (a unit of energy usage for gas and hydro in kilowatt hours), versus 17.8 in its previous models. One of the design initiatives introduced was a rooftop solar system in 40 of its stores. The energy savings was determined to be equivalent to powering 1,000 homes annually for the next 20 years.[44] New office tower designs are also incorporating greener ways to reduce energy costs. Geothermal energy is one green alternative, which is using the natural heat originating from deep within the earth. A geothermal system can heat offices in the winter and remove heat during the summer. As an alternative to gas and oil, geothermal systems can reduce heating expenses by approximately 44%. There are other benefits, too. Geothermal systems reduce structural requirements, saving building costs. For example, a geothermal furnace eliminates smokestacks and rooftop chillers, opening up roof spaces for rooftop terraces and green roofs. Less piping within the building allows for more floor space and higher ceilings. While geothermal systems are initially a lot more expensive than traditional heating systems, the energy savings pays for the cost in just a few short years. For instance, when Équiterre, a Montreal-based environmental group, moved into a new green office building, the building had a geothermal system. Although the cost of the system was $300,000, the expected energy savings were about $60,000 annually. While subway lines or other infrastructure issues can sometimes prevent a geothermal system from being installed, geothermal systems remain an excellent green alternative to reduce costs for business and reduce harm for the environment.[45]

Reducing Waste   Reducing waste is another way for companies to save money. Let's consider the construction industry, which is known for producing considerable waste. The construction industry is the largest producer of wood waste, accounting for 25–45% of all generated solid waste in North America. Other materials such as concrete, asphalt, bricks, insulation, plumbing, glass, and electrical fixtures make up another 23%.[46]

---

[42] Knowledge@Wharton. (2013, April). Re-energizing aging cities: The green building option. Retrieved from http://knowledge.wharton.upenn.edu/article.cfm?articleid=3245.

[43] Stringer, 2010, 13.

[44] *Digital Journal*. (2011, July 25). Canadian Tire makes stores more sustainable through energy-saving features and solar panels. Retrieved from http://canadasolarforum.com/content.php?332-Canadian-Tire-Makes-Stores-More-Sustainable-Through-Energy-Saving-Features-and-Solar-Panels.

[45] Lanktree, G. (2011, December 5). What lies beneath: Tapping geothermal heat in Montreal. *Globe and Mail*. Retrieved from www.theglobeandmail.com/report-on-business/industry-news/property-report/what-lies-beneath-tapping-geothermal-heat-in-montreal/article4235196.

[46] Johnson, G. (2011, December 9). A growing green gap in the construction waste market. *Globe and Mail*. Retrieved from www.theglobeandmail.com/report-on-business/small-business/sb-growth/sustainability/a-growing-green-gap-in-the-construction-waste-market/article4180610.

Yet more than 50% of all construction materials can be reused or recycled. For example, steel can be melted and made into new steel, old concrete can be turned into gravel, and pieces of drywall can be recycled and reused. How can this be achieved? New construction waste-removal companies are saving the construction industry money and making a profit in this green niche market. Diverting waste from landfills can save companies disposal costs by up to 30% and preserve valuable lumber.[47]

Another incentive for the construction industry to be green is an internationally recognized sustainable building certification system called Leadership in Energy and Environmental Design (LEED). LEED is a rating system that measures green buildings and homes:

> LEED awards up to two points for diverting between 50 to 75 percent of demolition, land clearing, and construction waste from landfills and redirecting recyclables back to the manufacturing process. LEED guidelines allow diversion to include the salvage of materials on-site and the donation of materials to charitable organizations.[48]

Another source of waste, regardless of industry, is corporate office waste. Paper and employee food waste are two examples. In Vancouver, Urban Impact is one office compost service helping companies redirect employee food waste from landfills into nutrient-rich soil. In addition to fruits and vegetables, other waste that can be collected includes spoiled food, coffee grounds and filters, tea bags, waxed paper, and greasy pizza boxes. Urban Impact so far has diverted 100,000 metric tonnes of waste from landfills to environmentally friendly alternatives.[49]

According to a research study by the George Morris Centre, a Guelph-based think tank, about 40% of food in Canada is thrown out rather than consumed. "This inevitably also means that huge amounts of the resources used in food production are used in vain, and that the greenhouse gas emissions caused by production of food that gets lost or wasted are also emitted in vain," the study stated. Globally, the amount of food wasted is estimated at one third or 1.3 billion tonnes per year according to the United Nations Food and Agriculture Organization.[50]

In manufacturing food products, there can also be a lot of waste. In some cases, food waste that ends up in the water system can be problematic and cause environmental damage.

Reducing Risk

Sustainability can also be viewed from a risk management perspective. Businesses can reduce *operational risk* by improving health and safety programs and by taking proactive steps to protect the environment. In 2010, for example, British Petroleum was responsible for one of the worst oil spills in US history, which was caused by an explosion on its Gulf of Mexico oil rig that killed 11 crew members. A series of investigations found that the

---

[47] Johnson, 2011.

[48] Johnson, 2011.

[49] Johnson, G. (2012, March 6). Eco-entrepreneurs put food scraps to work. *Globe and Mail*. Retrieved from www.theglobeandmail.com/report-on-business/small-business/sb-growth/sustainability/eco-entrepreneurs-put-food-scraps-to-work/article551193.

[50] Johnson, 2012.

explosion could have been prevented if proper safety measures had been taken. After paying out billions of dollars in environmental cleanup costs, lost business income, lost wages, and other damages, in 2012 the US Department of Justice fined BP $4.5 billion, the largest criminal penalty in US history.[51]

Companies can also mitigate regulatory risk through self-regulation by encouraging industry members to adhere to certain environmental standards. When companies initiate sustainable practices, government may be less compelled to create new environmental laws if they are not required. In the past 10 years, different levels of government in Canada have introduced new laws requiring businesses to engage in environmental practices.

Most Canadian provincial governments now require businesses to charge and collect electronic recycling fees from customers on designated products. The purpose of the fee is to pay for the collection, recycling, and safe disposal of selected electronic goods. When you buy your next desktop, TV, or printer, check your receipt. Most fees are between $1.00 and $40.00, depending on the device, its size, and the province it is purchased in.[52]

Improving Public Relations

Good public relations may be achieved over the long term by a company providing quality products, offering excellent service, and helping local communities. However, bad customer relations can occur quickly and be damaging to the business's overall brand and reputation. With the speed of information available on the Internet, customers can quickly become aware of a company's wrongdoings.

In the past 10 years, Walmart, the largest global company, has been under more scrutiny for some of its controversial labour practices and perceived image to "do anything for a low price." Walmart was also identified as the largest private user of electricity in the United States. As its image suffered, Walmart needed to address these issues and make some public relations efforts to improve its brand.[53] In its 2012 *Global Responsibility Report*, Walmart reported its achievements toward sustainable practices to its stakeholders. Some of the initiatives included the following:

- implementing a zero-waste program and reducing waste by 80% from all US operations
- increasing locally grown food by 97% (locally grown here means from the same state)
- supporting women's organizations and initiatives by donating $100 million in grants
- saving customers $1 billion by reducing prices on fresh fruits and vegetables and other healthy food items
- using 1.1 billion kilowatt hours (kWh) of renewable energy, making Walmart one of the largest onsite green power generators in the United States[54]

---

[51] Taylor, A. (2012, November 15). BP to pay $4.5 billion in largest criminal payout ever. *Business Insider*. Retrieved from http://finance.yahoo.com/news/bp-set-pay-largest-criminal-140001636.html.

[52] Dell Canada. (n.d.). Canada's recycling laws. Retrieved from http://content.dell.com/ca/en/corp/d/corp-comm/canada-recycling-laws.

[53] Stringer, 2010, 12.

[54] Walmart website. (2012, April 16). Walmart announces significant progress toward ambitious sustainability goals in 2012. *Global Responsibility Report*. Retrieved from http://news.walmart.com/news-archive/investors/walmart-announces-significant-progress-toward-ambitious-sustainability-goals-in-2012-global-responsibility-report-1683331.

At a more local level, in October 2011 the Toronto-Dominion Bank (TD) renovated a branch in London, Ontario, designed to produce as much energy as it uses—that is, a "net-zero energy" building. The renovation included solar panels that would generate over 100,000 kilowatt hours of green electricity:

> TD also installed LED lighting and upgraded its control systems for heating and cooling. In addition, it will renovate the land surrounding the property into a "green energy park" that will include an amphitheatre for community use and a solar electric car charging station for its customers . . . TD is vying for transparency, aiming to show its customers . . . that this building is indeed as advertised.[55]

The value of this public relations initiative has many benefits. Not only does TD brand itself positively as a "green bank," but it can attract loyal customers and talented employees.

So if the results of sustainable practices can lower costs, lower risks, and improve public relations for business, why don't all businesses embrace sustainable practices? What are the obstacles for change?

Obstacles to Change

We already know that the goal of a sustainable business is to make a profit, meet the needs of society, and minimize damage to the environment. Certainly, this is no easy task. The three biggest obstacles to companies becoming more sustainable are time, money, and a lack of knowledge.

Time Running a business in itself is challenging. In order to save on costs, companies usually hire a minimal amount of workers to complete daily tasks. Focusing on core business activities is essential to ensuring quality and satisfying customer demands. In some cases, businesses are unable to spend time on traditional activities such as marketing and training. For example, in a recent survey by Red Rocket Media, 32% of companies indicated "lack the time" as their biggest social media challenge.[56] In another case, one small business owner explained that he does not have the time nor the money to spend on training new employees and needs to hire qualified individuals ready to start on the job:

> I can't afford to develop every worker that I need from scratch. One, that's not my core competency. We're not a school, we're a company. We can't do that well. Two, we can't afford to do that. If we actually had to do that from scratch, even if we could, the jobs would have to go somewhere else, because it's simply not economically tenable to do that.[57]

---

[55] Kelly, E.R. (2011, December 19). The latest shade of green—zero energy use. *Globe and Mail*. Retrieved from www.theglobeandmail.com/report-on-business/industry-news/property-report/the-latest-shade-of-green---zero-energy-use/article4247962.

[56] Ecoconsultancy. (2011, November). 32% of businesses cite 'lack of time' as biggest social media challenge. Retrieved from http://econsultancy.com/ca/press-releases/6031-32-of-businesses-cite-lack-of-time-as-biggest-social-media-challenge.

[57] *60 Minutes*. (2012, November 11). Three million open jobs in U.S., but who's qualified? The following script is from "Three Million Open Jobs" which aired on Nov. 11, 2012. Byron Pitts is the correspondent. David Schneider, producer. Retrieved from www.cbsnews.com/2102-18560_162-57547342.html?tag=contentMain;contentBody.

As you can see, for some businesses available time for implementing sustainable practices is minimal to nonexistent.

Money   Implementing sustainable practices may also require businesses to commit to initial upfront costs that may not be feasible for many. In the example of geothermal energy, it is clear that there are long-term cost benefits, but not all businesses may be able to afford it. Similarly, solar panels and special LED lighting require initial upfront costs that require businesses to either have available cash or available financing. According to one observer, "Solar power is a clean, renewable energy source, yet it makes up less than 1 percent of the power used in the United States. Part of the reason more people aren't using solar energy . . . is the cost."[58]

Lack of Knowledge   Since every industry has its own unique energy and waste issues, implementing sustainable practices cannot always be easily replicated from one business to another. For instance, a food manufacturer will likely have different waste issues than a construction company. In fact, achieving cost-effective sustainable practices requires a cross-disciplinary effort from environmentalists, engineers, and others in assessing and evaluating all business processes, products, and services.

Some managers may not even understand the long-term value of sustainable practices. Like corporate social responsibility, sustainability issues are not normally part of a manager's education, skills, or job training. Nonetheless, many businesses and countries continue to profit from new green technologies. Canadian businesses, however, have been slow to embrace them, as seen in Talking Business 11.4.

TALKING BUSINESS 11.4

Canada Isn't Cleaning Up on Green Technology Exports

2009fotofriends/Shutterstock

Around the world, trade and investment in technologies that reduce greenhouse-gas emissions—such as solar power, energy efficient appliances and hybrid cars—is growing rapidly. Unfortunately, Canadian businesses are largely failing to take advantage of these global opportunities.

Canada's exports of "climate-friendly technologies" did not grow at all between 2002 and 2008, according to new The Conference Board of Canada research. Worse, when we account for inflation, this country's climate-friendly exports fell by 2 per cent annually on average. In short, Canadian businesses have failed to seize new—or even maintain existing—opportunities to sell such technologies globally. Our businesses and individuals have also been relatively slow to import and adopt world-leading technologies from others.

(continued)

[58] Watson, S. (n.d.). Why is solar power still a pay up-front system? How Stuff Works. Retrieved from http://science.howstuffworks.com/environmental/green-science/solar-power-pay-upfront.htm.

Our weak climate-friendly trade performance stands in contrast with exploding global opportunities. While Canadian exports stagnated between 2002 and 2008, and imports grew only slowly, world trade in climate-friendly technologies grew by a massive 10 per cent on average each year.

Europe and Asia are the key drivers of this global trend. For example, Germany is the global leader in selling climate-friendly technologies and the second-largest global buyer of such technologies. Even though it has been in this game for several decades, that country still grew its climate-friendly technology exports by 15 per cent on average over 2002–2008, and grew its imports at a roughly similar rate. Germany's government has made sustained commitments to support the development of climate-friendly technologies.

China, the No. 2 global seller of climate-friendly technologies, grew its exports at a rate of over 40 per cent annually, and its imports at almost 20 per cent annually. Over the past decade, China's government has invested heavily in such technologies, and used its stimulus package to reinforce this stance.

Despite some global policy uncertainty and a lack of mainstream adoption of climate-friendly technologies, the stars seem relatively well aligned for continued rapid global growth. Increasing energy and water costs, coupled with massive environmental problems in the developing world, seem likely to reinforce a growing global consensus on the need to move toward a low-carbon future. According to estimates from Roland Berger Strategy Consultants, clean energy technologies will be the third-largest industrial sector in the world in 2020.

In sum, climate-friendly technologies represent a major economic opportunity for Canada, one that has not been fully exploited. Despite this poor overall global performance, the good news is that Canada does certain things well. Canadian businesses "overtrade"—have global strengths relative to other countries—notably in waste management and energy technologies associated with the country's geography and resource base. And our strengths can lie in specific parts of global supply chains, rather than in an entire supply chain. For example, though we are not overall leaders in solar power, we have strengths in selling parts or components into related global supply chains.

Looking forward, Canada may have future strengths in wave and tidal power, as well as the next generation of biofuels. Potential niches include other energy, mining and telecommunications-related technologies that leverage Canada's resources and geography. We are likely to also have relative global strengths in the associated services.

Canadian businesses will need to determine where in global value chains for climate-friendly technologies they can be world leaders, and which world-leading technologies, parts, and services they should buy from others. A recent article by Evan Osnos in the *New Yorker* sums up the situation well: "No single nation is likely to dominate the clean energy economy. . . . No nation has yet mastered both the invention and the low-cost manufacturing of clean technology. It appears increasingly clear that winners in the new-energy economy will exploit the strengths of each side."

To capitalize on these opportunities, Canadian governments will need to send clear climate policy signals and commit to sustained public investments in research and development in climate-friendly technologies and related services. Governments should also remove both domestic and international barriers to the development of, and trade in, such products and services.

Greater clarity in policy would give businesses incentives to ramp up investment in these areas. Even with some uncertainty, however, businesses should get out ahead of policy makers. They should do so to protect their brand and reputation, to ensure they are an active player when policies catch up, to take advantage of well-established policy signals in other countries, and to establish long-term relationships in global markets.

The growing global market for climate-friendly technologies represents a major long-term opportunity. Now is the time for Canada to seize this opportunity to "clean up."

Source: Excerpted from Goldfarb, D. (2010, March 22). Canada isn't cleaning up on green technology exports. Reprinted with permission from The Conference Board of Canada. Retrieved from www.conferenceboard.ca/press/speech_oped/10-03-23/canada_isn_t_cleaning_up_on_green_technology_exports.aspx?pf=true.

Meanwhile, others may deny that environmental issues exist altogether. Certainly, the unknown consequences of long-term environmental damage may delay some businesses from planning appropriately to sustain their businesses in the future. While most scientists agree that climate change will have a significant, negative impact on all of us, the future effects of climate change are difficult to measure and quantify. Indeed, climate change is a growing global problem that none of us have any experience in. For example, Al Gore's Academy award-winning documentary on climate change, *An Inconvenient Truth*, continues to be questioned despite growing scientific evidence of environmental damage.

IMPLEMENTING SUSTAINABLE PRACTICES

Objective 6 Discuss seven areas in which sustainable practices can be assessed during the product's life.

Where should a manager start to look for sustainable opportunities within his or her own organization? From the beginning to the end of the product's life, the economic, environmental, and social impact of the product needs to be assessed[59] (see Exhibit 11.13). Some questions that may be asked can include the following: What raw materials are required? Are they from renewable or nonrenewable resources? What type of energy is used and how much is consumed in production, distribution, and disposal? What is the impact on the environment? How much waste goes into landfills, and what is the organization's carbon footprint from greenhouse gas emissions? Overall, businesses must *reduce*, *reuse*, and *recycle* in every aspect of their operations. In our analysis, let's assess sustainability at each stage of a product's life. We will consider the food industry in our examples.

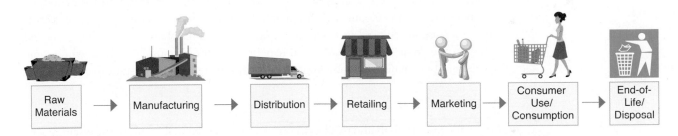

Exhibit 11.13 Sustainability over a Product's Life

Raw Materials

What business or industry are you in and what type of raw materials do you need? How can raw materials be sustained, and what sustainable practices are available? The type of raw materials needed by a business will likely impact what sustainable method can be used. For example, are your raw materials from *renewable* or *nonrenewable resources*?

In the food industry, certainly food as a raw material is a renewable resource. However, some food may be more difficult to grow or harder to obtain. Let's consider fish. Do your vendors get their fish from more sustainable resources, or are your fish products at risk from declining stocks? Some companies recognize the environmental problem of declining fish reserves and are implementing more sustainable practices. For example, in 2012 the World Wildlife Fund (WWF) recognized Loblaw for sourcing almost 100%

---

[59] Laszlo, C., & Zhexembayeva, N. (2011). *Embedded sustainability: The next big competitive advantage* (p. 181). Stanford, CA: Stanford University Press.

of its seafood from sustainable sources. President and CEO of WWF Canada, Gerald Butts, explains,

> Loblaw has developed the most aggressive sustainable seafood commitment in the world. Through its collaboration within the supply chain, investment in education, and stakeholder and government engagement, Loblaw is driving large-scale transformational change.[60]

Achievements of Loblaw include providing customers with more sustainable seafood options, collaborating with industry members, and educating customers through online and in-store events. This means a change in the variety of fish Loblaw currently offers. Instead of many species at risk such as skate, shark, orange roughy, and Chilean sea bass, Loblaw offers eco-friendly alternatives such as Pacific halibut.[61] (See Talking Business 11.5.) Loblaw has also introduced 73 Marine Stewardship Council-certified seafood products, making it the largest retailer of MSC-certified products in Canada.[62] The MSC is a nonprofit agency with a certification program that works with over 200 fisheries across the globe. The MSC focuses on sustainable seafood by considering how seafood is raised and harvested and how businesses can conserve marine life as well as their natural habitats.[63]

How about how other food is grown? For example, did you know that over 70% of the world's water use relates to growing food? According to the Organisation for Economic Co-operation and Development, "sustainable management of water in agriculture is critical to increase agricultural production, ensure water can be shared with other users and maintain the environmental and social benefits of water systems."[64] Indeed, while some raw materials are renewable, ongoing measures may be required to sustain them.

Manufacturing

sustainable manufacturing
Creating manufactured products using processes that are nonpolluting, that conserve energy and natural resources, and that are economically sound and safe for employees, communities, and consumers.

Processing raw materials also requires a consideration of potential harms to the environment and the impact to society at large. What is sustainable manufacturing? **Sustainable manufacturing**, as defined by the US Department of Commerce, is "the creation of manufactured products that use processes that are nonpolluting, conserve energy and natural resources, and are economically sound and safe for employees, communities, and consumers."[65]

How sustainable are your manufacturing processes? In other words, how much *water* and *energy* do you use and how much *waste* comes from the products you produce? Is there opportunity for your factory to *reduce, reuse,* and *recycle*? For instance, energy can be reduced by using less oil, gas, and electricity. According to Industry Canada, there are many lighting options available that can reduce electricity costs for organizations, as well as their effects on global warming:

---

[60] Canada Newswire. (2012, June 26). Loblaw makes progress toward 2013 sustainable seafood commitment. Retrieved from www.newswire.ca/en/story/999141/loblaw-makes-progress-towards-2013-sustainable-seafood-commitment#.

[61] Sampson, S. (2010, February 4). Loblaw guides consumers towards sustainable seafood. *Toronto Star*. Retrieved from www.thestar.com/unassigned/article/760679--loblaw-guides-consumers-towards-sustainable-seafood.

[62] Canada Newswire, 2012.

[63] Fisk, 2010, 150.

[64] OECD. (n.d.) Water use in agriculture. Retrieved from www.oecd.org/environment/wateruseinagriculture.htm.

[65] National Council for Advanced Manufacturing. (n.d.). Sustainable manufacturing. Retrieved from www.nacfam.org/PolicyInitiatives/SustainableManufacturing/tabid/64/Default.aspx.

Leading Change in the Food Sector

©Mark Blinch/Reuters/Corbis

Galen G. Weston is Executive Chairman of Loblaw Companies Limited, Canada's largest food retailer and a leading provider of drugstore, general merchandise, and financial products and services.

Five years ago, Loblaw Companies undertook a renewal plan to ensure the growth and stability of the business well into the future. During that time Mr. Weston has overseen significant improvements in fresh foods, the strengthening and growth of the President's Choice and No Name brands, the emergence of the Joe Fresh brand as one of the country's top fashion brands, and the addition of T&T, Canada's leading Asian supermarket chain to the Loblaw portfolio of banners, positioning it to serve the growing ethnic customer segment.

An advocate of food sustainability and diet as solutions to health-related issues, Mr. Weston has led a range of initiatives that include an industry-leading sustainable seafood policy, the reduction of plastic bag use, the establishment of the Loblaw Companies Limited Chair in Sustainable Food Production at the University of Guelph, and the development of The Conference Board of Canada's Centre for Food in Canada, which aims to develop a framework for a national food strategy. Loblaw is helping to tackle these complex issues in ways that enable it to compete successfully today while preparing for the world of tomorrow. It is a highly strategic, values-based approach to doing business that helps Loblaw serve its customers better and, in so doing, makes Loblaw a higher-performing organization.

In 2010, in concert with Corporate Knights, the *Globe and Mail* recognized Loblaw as the top Corporate Citizen in Canada.

InsideEdge: You are a champion investor in the Conference Board's Centre for Food in Canada. What impact do you hope this project will have on the food sector and the broader economy? Why have you chosen to support the Conference Board's initiative?

Galen G. Weston: My family has been in the business of feeding Canadians for more than 126 years through the Weston Bakery and Loblaw businesses, so—as you can imagine—long-term trends in food are central to what we do. There are a number of long-term challenges facing the food sector. These include the security, safety, and sustainability of our food supply and the impact diet can have on the future health of Canadians. I believe we have an opportunity to develop long-term strategies for dealing with these challenges.

The Conference Board has a strong reputation for thoughtful, well-researched, strategic planning, so it is an entirely appropriate organization to complete this work.

InsideEdge: Do you think that the impact of the food sector on Canada's economy and society is well understood?

Galen G. Weston: From our perspective, there is a great deal of education to be done. The food sector has grown to be one of the top industries in Canada—and, of course, food plays a critical role in our daily lives. The Conference Board's initiative can shine a bright light on the impact of the sector, facilitate a much-needed discussion about its future, and help to lay the groundwork for initiatives to help meet tomorrow's challenges.

InsideEdge: Do you think food is a strategic resource for Canada, given the projected significant increase in the future global demand for food? What do you think this will mean for food companies and retailers in Canada?

Galen G. Weston: Canada is one of the world's great food exporters. One of our challenges will be finding the right balance between ensuring our domestic food supply is secure and sustainable, and continuing to grow a vibrant export business. Ensuring that we have the scale to compete and that we take full advantage of opportunities to add value to food production will be critical to the contribution that the food sector can make to Canada's economy.

(continued)

InsideEdge: How is the Canadian food consumer changing, both in expectations and in diet, and how is this affecting the grocery business?

Galen G. Weston: Canadian consumers are more discerning and informed than ever. They have a good idea what they want. There is growth in the ethnic/international and the natural/organic segments, and there is increasing interest in locally produced foods. In addition, the link between diet and health will be an increasingly important consideration for consumers. We need to strike a balance between serving the emerging food trends and keeping food prices at appropriate levels. We believe that Loblaw is very well positioned to help find solutions to these challenges.

InsideEdge: In 2009, Loblaw announced its Sustainable Seafood Commitment Initiative—a commitment that, by 2013, all of the fish sold in its stores will be sustainably harvested. Why did you launch this?

Galen G. Weston: While the demand for quality seafood is on the rise around the world, climate change, pollution, and overfishing are taking a toll on our seas and oceans. Seventy per cent of the world's fish stocks are at or beyond their capacity and on the verge of collapse. Imagine if that were true of our agricultural output. We would be taking radical action.

As Canada's largest buyer and seller of seafood, Loblaw has decided to take the necessary steps for positive change by launching our Sustainable Seafood Commitment.

We're committed to only selling sustainable seafood products. We aren't just talking about our own brands, but every brand we carry. Canned, frozen, fresh, wild, and farmed seafood products—as well as anything that contains seafood products, such as vitamins, pet food, and juices—will be 100 per cent sustainably sourced.

As we determine the status of certain species that are at risk, we stop selling those products and will only begin selling them again when we have found a sustainable third party-certified source for those species.

The first comprehensive sustainable seafood commitment of its kind in Canada and among the leading ones in the world, our Sustainable Seafood Commitment is aligned with one of our five corporate social responsibility principles: sourcing with integrity.

Retailers can lead change. We hope that others will follow.

InsideEdge: Obesity has been called an epidemic in Canada. What role can food companies and grocers play in helping people eat well?

Galen G. Weston: The four primary chronic illnesses in Canada, including obesity, are directly linked to diet, and we believe we can play a major role in helping Canadians make healthier and more informed choices. Today's Loblaw supermarkets offer a far wider selection of healthy foods, at much lower prices, than at any other point in our history. By offering healthier food options, by stocking our shelves with fresh and wholesome Canadian produce, by providing information and improving our customers' understanding of nutritional values, and by promoting active lifestyles, we can help to improve the health of Canadians.

Source: Excerpted reprinted with permission from The Conference Board of Canada. (2011, July 11). Leading change in the food sector. *Inside Edge*. Retrieved from www.conferenceboard.ca/insideedge/2011/july2011/jul11-5minutes-weston.aspx.

Compact fluorescent, High Intensity Discharge (HID) and Light Emitting Diode (LED) lighting is more energy-efficient compared to standard incandescent, fluorescent and halogen lighting. Energy efficient lighting also lasts much longer, requiring fewer replacements than standard lighting, thereby reducing materials, packaging and maintenance costs. Since all fluorescent and HID lights contain a small amount of mercury, it is important to choose the lowest mercury option available, and to recycle the bulbs at the end of their life. Some manufacturers offer very low mercury content lamps. LED lights are the best choice since they are the most energy efficient and contain no mercury.[66]

---

[66] Industry Canada. (n.d.). Corporate social responsibility: Top 10 sustainability shopping list. Retrieved from www.ic.gc.ca/eic/site/csr-rse.nsf/eng/rs00550.html.

As a food manufacturer, Kraft is one company that has reduced its use of water, energy and waste. In fact, some of its plants across North America have achieved *zero-waste-to-landfill* status, which means they are recycling and using 100% of their manufacturing waste, as well as turning manufacturing byproducts into other forms of energy. What have some of its plants achieved across North America? Let's consider Kraft's achievements in the following three states:

- *New York*: At its cheese plants in Lowville, New York, and Campbell, New York, Kraft is creating renewable energy by using its waste products. The plants generate biogas using anaerobic digesters that turn whey waste (a regular byproduct of cheese-making) into fuel. These two plants are creating enough renewable energy to heat about 2,600 typical homes in the northeast for one year.

- *Pennsylvania*: The Allentown, Pennsylvania, plant is a zero-waste facility. For example, a few years ago the plant was sending nearly 5 million pounds of mustard seed hulls (a byproduct of making Grey Poupon mustard) to landfills each year. Today, the seed materials are repurposed as animal feed.

- *Missouri*: The Columbia, Missouri, plant is repurposing its waste as compost. The plant sends used casings and wood ash from its hardwood smoking process (for Oscar Mayer hot dogs) to make compost for local residents' landscaping needs.[67]

Distribution

Distribution involves shipping a product to a potential buyer. **Sustainable distribution** involves any form of transportation of goods between the seller and the buyer that causes the least harm to the environment and the community. The transportation process can include packaging, shipping from storage, order processing, delivery to the buyer, and returning containers and packaging.

sustainable distribution Any form of transportation of goods between the seller and the buyer that causes the least harm to the environment and the community.

In the food industry, food manufacturers must distribute their products to grocery stores, restaurants, banquet halls, and other catering businesses. Let's revisit Kraft and consider its sustainable distribution achievements:

- *China*: Kraft Foods's Shanghai plant has replaced many inbound shipping containers with reusable cartons, reducing the amount of carton waste by 25%—this allows 90% of the containers to be reused.

- *Russia*: At Kraft Foods's Saint Petersburg coffee plant, incoming coffee bean shipping bags and pallets are reused.[68]

Retailing

Like manufacturers, retailers can also reduce, reuse, and recycle. While retailers can work with manufacturers or suppliers to reduce waste or limit environmental harm, retailers can also make purchase choices to buy green products that contain recycled components and reduced packaging.

---

[67] Atkinson, W. (2012, January 27). Kraft Foods continues a successful campaign against solid waste. Retrieved from http://www.sustainableplant.com/2012/01/kraft-foods-continues-a-successful-campaign-against-solid-waste.

[68] King, B. (2012, February 7). Kraft Foods cuts manufacturing waste by 50% since 2005. Sustainable Brands. Retrieved from www.sustainablebrands.com/news_and_views/feb2012/kraft-foods-cuts-manufacturing-waste-50-2005.

In 2011, Home Depot organized its first "Innovation for Sustainability" event, in partnership with the Ontario Ministry of Economic Development, Trade and Employment, where small manufacturers had an opportunity to pitch new product ideas to its merchandisers. From over 200 submissions, Home Depot selected 20 products to pilot test in selected stores. One product called Compostgenie encouraged individuals to compost and helped suppress odours from food waste. The product was made from organic ingredients such as sea salt, seaweed, molasses, bran, and probiotics and looked like small seeds. The event was a win-win for both Home Depot and small manufacturers. Home Depot had an opportunity to buy new green innovations while also helping support local entrepreneurs, manufacturers and communities.[69]

Whole Foods is a food retailer that has integrated reducing, reusing, and recycling into every part of its business. Whole Foods, for example has replaced plastic gift cards with cards made of paper. The paper cards are made with 50% postconsumer waste and are certified by the Forest Stewardship Council (FSC). The new cards are reusable, recyclable, compostable, and have a lower carbon footprint. The company also sells e-gift cards, which can be reloaded with a smartphone.[70]

Retailers can offer reusable shopping bags, too. While the debate between paper and plastic bags will surely continue, using a reusable shopping bag remains the best choice, as seen in Talking Business 11.6.

Marketing

What is sustainable marketing? According to the American Marketing Association, **sustainable marketing** or green marketing is

sustainable marketing Also referred to as green marketing, this is marketing of products that are environmentally safe; developing and marketing products that have minimal negative effects on society; and producing, promoting, packaging, and reclaiming products in an environmentally friendly way.

1. (retailing definition) The marketing of products that are presumed to be environmentally safe.
2. (social marketing definition) The development and marketing of products designed to minimize negative effects on the physical environment or to improve its quality.
3. (environment definition) The efforts by organizations to produce, promote, package, and reclaim products in a manner that is sensitive or responsive to ecological concerns.[71]

Retailers and others can appeal to their customers to do good by also marketing environmentally friendly products in a sustainable way.

In Canada, companies can market products that contain recycled materials or use less packaging, such as some goods sold in bulk. In the United States, companies can apply to use a new label called the How2Recycle Label to help market their products and their brand. The nonprofit organization GreenBlue and its Sustainable Packaging Coalition

[69] Galt, V. (2011, September 8). Home Depot stocks up on green inventions. *Globe and Mail*. Retrieved from www.theglobeandmail.com/report-on-business/small-business/home-depot-stocks-up-on-green-inventions/article593501.

[70] King, B. (2012, August 31). Whole Foods phases out plastic gift cards, powers kitchen facility with used cooking oil. Sustainable Brands. Retrieved from www.sustainablebrands.com/news_and_views/articles/whole-foods-phases-out-plastic-gift-cards-powers-kitchen-facility-used.

[71] American Marketing Association. (n.d.). Green marketing definition. Reprinted with permission. Retrieved from www.marketingpower.com/_layouts/Dictionary.aspx?dLetter=G.

Convenience Versus Sustainability: The Plastic and Paper Bag Debate

One Canadian newspaper columnist wrote that "banning plastic bags will do exactly nothing to save the planet." While this may be true, it is a start in the right direction toward reducing waste and the ultimate harm that they can cause. Certainly, as a society, we have become more accustomed to using plastic bags in our everyday lives, from carrying home groceries to lining trash bins and to collecting dog poop. But should we continue using them just for convenience when they ultimately harm the environment?[72]

According to the Greeener Footprints website, Canadians throw away between 9 and 15 billion plastic bags annually, enough to go around the earth 55 times! And since plastic bags can take up to 1,000 years to biodegrade, this adds up to a lot of waste.[73]

Because they are lightweight, plastic bags are easily blown around by wind and carried by water. They litter our streets and natural areas and accumulate in our oceans.

One research study by the University of British Columbia found that 93% of migratory seabirds (called northern fulmars) had stomachs full of plastic, a substantial increase since these birds were first tested in 1980. Stephanie Avery-Gomm, the head researcher, explained to the *Globe and Mail* that one bird had over 450 pieces of plastic in its belly. Researchers already know that plastic can kill birds as well as other marine species, including turtles and fish, since these species either eat the plastic or just get entangled in the stuff, limiting them from flying, eating, or getting to safety.[74]

Businesses, of course, use plastic too. Food is often packaged in plastic containers, delivered on crates wrapped in plastic, and so on. Many retailers prefer to use plastic bags because they are less expensive than paper. What makes plastic really essential when there is so much waste?

Plastic is a petroleum product, which means valuable fossil fuels are consumed in order to make it. In fact, nine plastic bags have enough of embodied petroleum to drive a car 1 kilometre.[75]

But are paper bags any better? Surely, at least paper comes from a renewable resource, and they can be composted and recycled, right? According to the Environmental Protection Agency in the United States, paper bags do not biodegrade all that much faster than plastic.[76]

The big problem with paper bags is not so much the paper bag itself, but the production process required to make them. Paper production emits air pollution—specifically, 70% more pollution than plastic bags. What kind of pollution? Greenhouse gases that are responsible for contributing to climate change across the planet. But paper bags are made from a renewable resource, you might argue. Though true, these same trees could be used in absorbing greenhouse gases emissions.

Paper bags also emit 50 times more pollutants than plastic bags. And water is consumed three times more in producing a paper bag than a plastic one.[77] While plastic

(continued)

[72] Suzuki, David. Are plastic bags really necessary? David Suzuki Foundation. August 2, 2012. http://www.davidsuzuki.org/blogs/science-matters/2012/08/are-plastic-bags-really-necessary/

[73] Suzuki, David. Are plastic bags really necessary? David Suzuki Foundation. August 2, 2012. http://www.davidsuzuki.org/blogs/science-matters/2012/08/are-plastic-bags-really-necessary/

[74] Suzuki, David. Are plastic bags really necessary? David Suzuki Foundation. August 2, 2012. http://www.davidsuzuki.org/blogs/science-matters/2012/08/are-plastic-bags-really-necessary/

[75] Suzuki, David. Are plastic bags really necessary? David Suzuki Foundation. August 2, 2012. http://www.davidsuzuki.org/blogs/science-matters/2012/08/are-plastic-bags-really-necessary/

[76] McGrath, Jane. Which is more environmentally friendly: paper or plastic? *How Stuff Works*. http://science.howstuffworks.com/environmental/green-science/paper-plastic.htm

[77] McGrath, Jane. Which is more environmentally friendly: paper or plastic? How Stuff Works. http://science.howstuffworks.com/environmental/green-science/paper-plastic.htm

bags use petroleum, paper bags require four times as much energy as plastic bags.[78]

Recycling is also an issue. While some jurisdictions recycle some plastic products, plastic bags are not typically one of them. Paper, on the other hand, is a better choice for recycling. However, it takes 91% more energy to recycle a pound of paper than a pound of plastic.[79] And paper has to be separated and put into a recycling bin or it ends up in a landfill, too.

So what did we do before the invention of plastic bags? Clearly, our grandparents were more accustomed to using paper bags before plastic ones became mainstream. But the other alternative is to use reusable bags, ones that aren't thrown away.

An outright ban on plastic bags may not be the best solution, but choosing more sustainable options makes sense for the environment and the future.

---

initiated this labelling system to conform to the Federal Commission's green marketing guides and to reduce consumer confusion about recycling.[80] General Mills, for example, is one food company that uses this labelling system.

Electronic media is another tool that can be used to educate customers and to sell products. A company's website or Facebook page can also promote "green" products.

Consumer Use/Consumption

Clearly, businesses need to do their part, but consumers also need to change their mindset to determine their needs versus their wants and purchase more sustainable products. After all, consumerism and sustainability are two conflicting behaviours. While *consumerism* embraces purchasing more consumer goods, *sustainability* discourages consumption and promotes reducing, reusing, and recycling. What is sustainable purchasing? Industry Canada defines **sustainable purchasing** as follows:

> **sustainable purchasing** The acquisition of goods and services in a way that gives preference to suppliers that generate positive social and environmental outcomes. It might even involve considering whether a purchase needs to be made at all.

[the] acquisition of goods and services ("products") in a way that gives preference to suppliers that generate positive social and environmental outcomes. It integrates sustainability considerations into product selection so that impacts on society and the environment are minimized throughout the full life cycle of the product. Sustainability purchasing entails looking at what products are made of, where they have come from, who has made them, how they will be ultimately disposed—even considering whether the purchase needs to be made at all. It encompasses environmental, social, and ethical dimensions and brings benefit to the environment and local and global communities and workers.[81]

[78] McGrath, Jane. Which is more environmentally friendly: paper or plastic? *How Stuff Works.* http://science.howstuffworks.com/environmental/green-science/paper-plastic.htm

[79] McGrath, Jane. Which is more environmentally friendly: paper or plastic? *How Stuff Works.* http://science.howstuffworks.com/environmental/green-science/paper-plastic.htm

[80] *Sustainable Food News.* (2012, November 29). On-package recycling label aims to appear on majority of consumer product packaging by 2016. Retrieved from www.sustainablefoodnews.com/printstory.php?news_id=17925.

[81] Industry Canada. (n.d.). Corporate social responsibility: Top 10 sustainability shopping list. Retrieved from www.ic.gc.ca/eic/site/csr-rse.nsf/eng/rs00550.html.

We already know that sustainable products involve not just renewable resources but also environmentally friendly processes that aim to do the least harm to the environment. Another consideration is the lifespan of the product. Is it a product that can potentially be reused and passed down to the next generation, like a watch, a piano, fine china, or handcrafted furniture?

Certainly, this will not be true in the food industry since food has a limited life and then will be thrown away. However, customers can make more sustainable choices by buying locally and reducing their food waste.

Buying locally produced food has been promoted as a better choice than buying food that is grown far away. Local food is usually fresher, tastes better, and helps preserve valuable farmland. Money, therefore, is spent on food that helps to support local communities and their economic development. Of course, there is also the main argument that local food significantly reduces greenhouse gas emissions from transportation. Local peppers, tomatoes, and other vegetables will have to travel less if grown in your own community rather than if they must be transported by truck, plane, or train from Mexico or across the ocean.

Certainly, North Americans do not have a food shortage. Our culture of fast food, super-sizing, and all-you-can-eat buffets encourages us to eat more, not less. However, the food that we don't eat—the kitchen scraps, the unwanted leftovers, and the spoiled food from our fridges—has turned into a $27 billion problem that ends up in landfills each year. According to a recent study by the Value Chain Management Centre, about 40% of our food in Canada is wasted every year.[82] This contributes to the growing problem of greenhouse gas emissions, including methane, which traps more heat than carbon dioxide in the atmosphere. "Already 38 percent of Canada's emissions come from landfills," according to Susan Antler, executive director of the Composting Council of Canada.[83]

How do we change our mindset to make better purchasing decisions? How do we separate our needs from our wants? As consumers, using only what we need, rather than what we want, may conflict with consumerism, but it would ultimately result in less waste and less harm to the environment.

End-of-Life/Disposal

When is the end of a product's life? The answer, of course, is that it depends. Typically, if a product can be reused, it can be donated to a charitable organization or sold for profit. The product's life therefore continues. However, when a product is broken or becomes obsolete because of technological change, there are usually two choices businesses and individuals have: Recycle a product's parts or dispose of them.

When old parts are recycled, materials can be reused and made into new products. Some items that can be diverted from a landfill into a recycling system include scrap metal, wood, cardboard, glass, paper, plastic, batteries, and other materials. On the other hand, disposing of a product usually means it will end up in a landfill, which has become a growing cost for taxpayers and has long-term environmental consequences.

In the food industry, food has a limited life and cannot easily be recycled. Food manufacturers and restaurants can participate in food-rescue programs like Second Harvest,

[82] Bain, J. (2011, January 14). Food waste: An unappetizing, $27B problem. *Toronto Star*. Retrieved from www.thestar.com/printarticle/920663.

[83] Chung, A. (2008, May 25). How we waste food. Toronto Star. Retrieved from www.thestar.com/printarticle/429617.

which picks up excess and donated food that may otherwise go to waste. A food-rescue program can provide fresh food to people in need. Food manufacturers may also be able to sell certain foods to farmers for livestock feed.

What about businesses in other industries? What can all businesses consider doing to become more sustainable in the long run? On a functional level, each company can consider how it can reduce, reuse, recycle, and improve its sustainable practices, as seen in Exhibit 11.14.

Exhibit 11.14 Implementing Sustainable Practices by Department

Department	Sustainable Action
Accounting and Finance	• Implement the triple bottom line approach to track, measure, and report sustainable practices to stakeholders
Human Resources	• Use an online database to accept résumés instead of mail-based applications to reduce paper
	• Implement telework and shared workspace options to reduce building space and heating/utility requirements
	• Promote benefits that include healthy food options and exercise facilities
	• Train employees on sustainable practices
	• Hire sustainability consultants to implement green initiatives
Marketing	• Use recyclable materials in packaging
	• Use electronic media for promotions
	• Provide discounts or other incentives for purchasing in bulk
Information Technology	• Develop policies to dispose of electronics safely
	• Convert to a paperless office by scanning documents, using online storage, etc.
	• Implement electronic management systems to reduce paper storage
	• Promote videoconferencing and teleconferencing technologies to reduce travel requirements
Research and Development	• Invest in products and services that promote sustainable practices
	• Use reusable or recycled products
	• Reduce materials, water, and energy in the manufacture of goods
Operations and Logistics	• Reduce packaging and waste
	• Reduce transportation
	• Reduce overall emissions
Public Relations and Communications	• Include sustainable practices as part of company's values and mission
	• Use electronic media sources to release announcements and other information to save paper
Facilities	• Build or rent green facilities that minimize energy and water usage
	• Implement a green waste management program
	• Ensure green cleaning and landscaping practices are used
Procurement	• Develop green purchasing policies
	• Ensure vendors share the company's sustainable values
Legal and Risk Management	• Evaluate risks of how products and services may negatively impact people and the environment

Source: Stringer, L. (2010). *The green workplace* (pp. 48–49). New York, NY: Palgrave MacMillan.

CHAPTER SUMMARY

Implementing sustainable business practices is a new challenge faced by many managers. Time, money, and lack of knowledge are a few obstacles in the way of obtaining this lofty goal. Yet sustainable businesses that achieve their economic, social, and environmental goals can expect to receive many benefits. Sustainable business practices have proven to help businesses in the long run by reducing costs, reducing risk, and improving customer relations. Clearly, environmental degradation cannot quickly be fixed, and businesses need to continue to consider their impact on the environment and society to be sustainable in the long term.

CHAPTER LEARNING TOOLS

Key Terms

biological diversity 420

carbon footprint 416

climate change 412

Ecological Footprint (EP) 422

ecosystem 421

fossil fuel 415

Genuine Progress Indicator (GPI) 425

greenhouse gas emissions 415

Index of Sustainable Economic Welfare (ISEW) 424

Living Planet Index (LPI) 420

nonrenewable resource 415

social equity 411

sustainable development 408

sustainable distribution 437

sustainable manufacturing 434

sustainable marketing 438

sustainable purchasing 440

sustainable resource 417

triple bottom line (TBL) 409

virtual water 413

Multiple-Choice Questions

Select the *best* answer for each of the following questions. Solutions are located in the back of your textbook.

1. Sustainable development as described by Brundtland includes
   a. meeting the needs of present and future generations
   b. meeting the needs of past generations
   c. development that does not compromise the needs of people
   d. both A and C

2. The triple bottom line approach can be a tool for reporting
   a. financial statement information
   b. a company's carbon footprint
   c. personal values on the environment
   d. both A and B

3. The triple bottom line approach reports information on
   a. economic, social, and environmental results
   b. people, profits, and the planet
   c. quantitative and qualitative information
   d. all of the above

4. The *economic* category of TBL reporting can include all of the following indicators *except*
   a. assets and liabilities
   b. the number of days employees volunteered their time to help social causes
   c. revenue by sector
   d. taxes paid

5. In TBL reporting, when Starbucks pays farmers a fair price for their coffee beans, this would be reported under the _____ category.
   a. social
   b. environmental
   c. both A and B
   d. none of the above

6. The most important environmental issues that exist today include all of the following *except*
   a. overconsumption of resources
   b. pollution from secondhand smoking
   c. greenhouse gas emissions
   d. depletion of natural resources

7. Virtual or embodied water is
   a. drinking water
   b. water used to produce, process, and transport goods
   c. both A and B
   d. none of the above

8. A fossil fuel is a
   a. renewable form of energy
   b. nonrenewable form of energy
   c. carbon dioxide
   d. none of the above

9. A benefit of the TBL approach is
   a. it is easy to measure with accuracy
   b. it allows results to be easily compared to other organizations
   c. it allows the organization to be flexible
   d. all of the above

10. A limitation of the TBL approach is that it
    a. is too subjective
    b. is too new and not flexible
    c. only satisfies shareowners
    d. is legally required

11. Businesses can be motivated to implement sustainable practices for all of the following reasons except
    a. to reduce risk
    b. to reduce costs
    c. to improve public relations
    d. to get free negative publicity

12. An obstacle for an organization to implement sustainable practices is
    a. time
    b. employee volunteer involvement
    c. tax credits
    d. both A and C

13. Improving business sustainable practices involves examining
    a. the product's life cycle
    b. department functions
    c. both A and B
    d. none of the above

14. The sustainability debate between plastic bags and paper bags generally considers
    a. product components
    b. process emissions
    c. landfill issues
    d. all of the above

15. A sustainable business must
    a. make a profit
    b. consider many stakeholders
    c. both A and B
    d. none of the above

Discussion Questions

1. Define sustainable development.
2. Discuss the three categories of the triple bottom line approach.
3. Explain the benefits and limitations of TBL reporting.
4. Identify three social indicators that could be used in TBL reporting.
5. What are greenhouse gas emissions and why should organizations try to reduce them?
6. Identify and compare four ways to measure sustainability.
7. Describe the business case for sustainability.
8. Explain three obstacles for organizations implementing sustainable initiatives.
9. Identify and describe the areas of a product's life cycle whereby sustainable practices should be assessed.
10. Identify three business departments and explain three examples of sustainable practices they could introduce.

CONCEPT APPLICATION   IS LOCAL FOOD SUSTAINABLE?

In recent years, there has been a cultural shift to eat local food—in other words, eating fresher food, closer to home, and supporting the local economy. Today, there are a growing number of farmers' markets, community gardens, and gourmet restaurants specializing in locally grown food. City councils have even debated the possibility of backyard chicken coops. And an increasing number of businesses are offering home-delivery services of fresh produce from local farms.

In conjunction with this trend, a growing number of consumers are demanding more information about their food, such as what's inside their food and where it comes from, putting pressure on the government and the food industry to provide greater transparency on food labelling. Certainly, buyers have concerns over chemicals and additives in processed foods and want to make more healthy choices. Savvy customers also want to protect the environment and purchase sustainable, environmentally friendly food.

There are many reasons to support locally grown food:

Steve Pepple/Shutterstock

Fresher tastes better

If you have picked a tomato from your own backyard, you know that fresher tastes better. Clearly, this is one advantage of locally grown food. It does not have to be flown in, shipped in, or trucked very far. The food has to go through fewer processes that may affect its quality and flavour. With food shipped from overseas, vegetables are often picked green and then ripened artificially upon arrival. Eating locally therefore means eating fresher and eating seasonally.

Less chemicals

As large agribusiness takes over more farmland, there are less farmers growing food and managing the land. In fact, less than 1% of the population provides food for the remaining 99%. To manage larger spaces, more fertilizer and pesticides are required. In the United States over 800 million tonnes of pesticides and 160 million tonnes of fertilizer go into the soil, depleting it of its natural fertility and contaminating the water supply.

More variety

Large businesses heavily focus on profit rather than sustainability, which often results in large quantities of uniform cash crops that are replanted year after year on the same land. Due to economies of scale, this strategy can force smaller farmers, who may offer a wider variety of fruits or vegetables, into bankruptcy. For example, local farmers can sell brandywines, early girls, and lemon boys instead of just "tomatoes." Mono-cropping also degrades soil and can result in less nutritious produce over time.

Less pollution

Since local food has less distance to travel, it uses less gasoline, packaging, storage, and refrigeration. This in turn means less fossil fuels are burned that contribute to harmful greenhouse gas emissions. According to OM Organics, the global food trade has quadrupled since 1961, with thousands of tonnes of food shipped annually. In fact, on average, corporate crops can travel between 1,500 to 2,500 miles before they arrive at your local neighbourhood grocery store.

Improved local economies

Purchasing local food means more than just supporting local farmers, it means supporting small business, entrepreneurship, and domestic job growth. Certainly, small towns benefit

Case Continued >

when local farmers do well, since farmers spend money on goods and services that contribute to the surrounding economy. Indeed, local farmers can keep more of the profits when there are few, if any, middlemen involved, unlike with corporate agribusiness.

While the trend toward "local food" appears to be growing, some question the validity of assertions that accuse large agribusinesses of unsustainable farming practices.

Is eating "local food" more sustainable than "nonlocal food"? While many observers would argue yes, others like University of Toronto geography professor Pierre Desrochers have questioned this assumption. Desrochers contends that much of the advances in food security and standards of living have been a result of corporate agribusiness and not due to small-scale subsistence farmers. One reason is that large multinationals are involved in international trade and have had the resources to specialize, create economies of scale, and make food safer and cheaper. This includes technological advancements such as genetically modified seeds, safer pesticides, more automated farming equipment, and safer food practices. However, this assertion has been disputed by other experts.[84]

Debbie Field, executive director of Foodshare, an Ontario community food program that provides local food to 141,000 children in a school nutrition program, explains that local farmers use new technology as well and local food does not always have to cost more. "I know a lot of young farmers in Ontario and they're some of the most technically sophisticated people in the world," she says.[85]

One of the main arguments that local food is more sustainable is that it contains less "food miles"—that is, local food does not have to travel as far from the farm to your plate. According to OM Organics,

> Typically, agribusinesses own large farmland plots and ship harvests across the country or internationally. In the U.S., food travels an average of 1500–2500 miles and 7–14 days to get to your plate. How fruits and vegetables last the journey is by chemical preservatives, additives, and/or genetic-engineering that retards spoilage. More than half our tomatoes are harvested and shipped green, and then artificially ripened at their final destination.[86]

In contrast, food from local farmers involves less transportation. Less transportation means less gasoline is burned, which means less greenhouse gases are released into the air causing climate change. Desrochers and his wife, Hiroko Shimizu, argue that food miles are deceiving. Why? Food miles are only one measure of how food contributes to global warming. However, some local food growers produce certain crops that use energy that is equally or more damaging to the environment. For example, a research report conducted in the United Kingdom compared local (UK) tomatoes with those imported from Spain. The results indicated that UK tomatoes, which had to be grown in heated greenhouses,

[84] McMahon, T. (2012, July 9). Is local food bad for the economy? *Maclean's*. Retrieved from http://www2.macleans.ca/2012/07/09/is-local-food-bad-for-the-economy.

[85] McMahon, 2012.

[86] Om Organics. (n.d.). Large agribusiness—Lower quality, less variety. Retrieved from www.omorganics.org/page.php?pageid=100.

"emitted nearly 2,400 kg of carbon dioxide per ton, compared to 640 kg for the Spanish tomatoes, which could grow in unheated greenhouses."[87]

This is another claim that not everyone agrees with. Other research has found that food miles only represent 4% of total food-related emissions. For instance, what about the energy used to produce food or the energy consumed to drive to the store to buy it? Air transportation only accounts for 1% of food miles. In addition, most food is transported by ship, which is the most fuel-efficient way to ship food.

Advocates of agribusiness, however, argue that such businesses can be equally cognizant of the health issues surrounding their products:

> Large corporations have brands to protect and budgets to devote to scrupulous food safety practices, compared to small farms, which usually aren't worth suing if they cause outbreaks of food-borne illnesses like *E.coli* or salmonella. . . . Large farms and food processing plants are also susceptible to outbreaks of food-borne illness—Maple Leaf Farms paid $25 million to settle claims from a 2008 listeria outbreak—but . . . they're easier to trace and correct than illnesses caused by small farms since they generate more media coverage and government oversight.[88]

According to many observers, there are numerous potential benefits to supporting local food, as described above. However, the debate about locally grown produce versus corporate agribusiness will surely continue.

Questions

1. Provide arguments *for* and *against* purchasing locally grown food. In your answer, refer to the social, economic, and environmental factors of sustainability.

2. Identify which type of farming (local or agribusiness) you believe to be more sustainable. Why?

3. What are "food miles"? What are the pros and cons of using food miles to determine the environmental impact of food?

---

[87] McMahon, 2012.

[88] McMahon, T. (2012, July 9). *Is local food bad for the economy?* Retrieved from http://www2.macleans. ca/2012/07/09/is-local-food-bad-for-the-economy/.

Chapter 12
Confronting Change
How Do Businesses Address the Challenge of Change?

© Gregory Holmgren/Alamy

Learning Objectives

After studying this chapter, you should be able to

1. Describe the forces encouraging change in organizations.
2. Define developmental change, transitional change, and transformational change.
3. Understand the value of Theory E and Theory O change.
4. Describe the process of transformational change.
5. Explain the relationship of learning with organizational change.
6. Explain the role of "the tipping point" and its impact on change.

To succeed in today's business environment requires the ability to quickly adapt to changing market conditions. Consequently, it is fitting that we devote specific attention to a discussion of the nature of change. What does change entail? What are the forces for change? In this chapter, we will examine the methods adopted to facilitate change. Within this discussion, the concept of the "learning organization" will be explored. In addition, we will consider how organizations may facilitate or impede change. The chapter ends with a discussion of the issue of the tipping point for organizational change.

THE BUSINESS WORLD

Indigo: Writing the Next Chapter in Canada's Book Industry

Have you bought a book in Canada lately? If you have, it was likely purchased at Canada's largest bookstore operator, Indigo, or through US online retailer Amazon. You might be lucky to find a smaller bookstore, but these are quickly dwindling in number. Besides fierce low-cost competitors such as Amazon, the cost of rent and high property taxes are reasons why many independent bookstores, such as The Book Mark, have closed their doors.

Indigo Books and Music Inc., which also operates Chapters and Coles stores, is a business in transition. While Indigo holds a quasi-monopoly on the Canadian in-store book market, fierce online competition has forced Indigo to rethink what it sells and how it competes.

In the past two years, Indigo has diversified into toys, gifts, and home décor merchandise to expand product offerings and to reduce losses in other areas. In 2011, revenue declined by 2.3% to $934 million, largely because of declining physical book sales. Currently, books sales make up 75% of Indigo's core business; however, Indigo forecasts that this will drop to 50% in a few years.[1]

CEO Heather Reisman calls it the right direction for the company. With the ease of buying books online, customers need other reasons to come into a bookstore. "I'm not interested in selling a bowl," Reisman said. "That's not the business I'm going to be in. I am interested in creating an experience around the table for the customer."[2]

According to Anthony Campbell, a brand strategist at consultancy firm Level5, "It is a big challenge—there are a lot of retailers in this [lifestyle, gift and home décor] space and it is where the world is going for a lot of other brands."[3] Indeed, it is a different industry with different rules. Traditionally, book companies have been able to return books to the publisher that they don't sell. But with general consumer goods, the risk is taken on by the retailer, not the supplier.

What else is Indigo doing differently? Indigo has introduced the Indigo Ideas Facebook page that allows customers to provide their suggestions, ideas, and feedback. The page is powered by an interactive app called SoapBox, created by 22-year-old Ryerson student and entrepreneur Brennan McEachran. The platform has been proven successful as it gives customers the option to be part of the process and change that lies ahead.[4]

SoapBox acts like a message board. Once key words are entered, the platform matches similar words already posted so that customers can lend their support for an idea. Customers, for example, suggested increasing the length of a popular blanket sold in Indigo stores. Once the idea was posted on the website, other comments soon appeared, and later 21 votes were made in favour of the idea. Indigo quickly responded and improved the blanket. Another suggested idea was a "customer wish list." Here, friends and family have access to preferred gift items for birthdays and other special occasions. Indigo responded quickly to this idea, too.

---

[1] Shaw, H. (2012, June 27). Indigo CEO Reisman grapples with future growth of e-books. *Financial Post.*

[2] Strauss, M. (2011, November 9). For Indigo CEO, it's time to think outside the box. *Globe and Mail.* Retrieved from www.theglobeandmail.com/globe-investor/for-indigo-ceo-its-time-to-think-outside-the-book/article4200507.

[3] Strauss, 2011 (November 9).

[4] O'Kane, J. (2013, February 28). Indigo gives its customers a Soapbox. *Globe and Mail.* Retrieved from www.theglobeandmail.com/technology/tech-news/indigo-gives-its-customers-a-soapbox/article9177365.

Since then, Indigo has seen over 400 suggestions and 700,000 interactions. The company has favourably implemented 56 ideas. Clearly, Indigo is learning from its customers. "We want to make sure as we go that we're getting as much real-time feedback as possible," says Lance Martel, senior vice-president of digital innovation at Indigo. "We thought, 'let's go where our most engaged consumers are and provide them a solution to submit their ideas and engage them on the transformation.' SoapBox did that very well."[5]

According to *Globe and Mail* writer Josh O'Kane, Indigo wants its customers to remain engaged and responsive. "The last thing Indigo Books and Music Inc. wants is for its customers to get cold feet. As e-readers transform the book world, Canada's largest book retailer is transforming too, shifting from a traditional book retailer to a book-lifestyle [and] cultural department store," says O'Kane.[6]

Indigo has also changed its rewards loyalty program to help boost sales by offering two different options to customers. The Plum Rewards program is free to join and allows customers to collect points on most products. On the other hand, its iRewards program costs $35 annually, but gives customers a 10% discount on books and a 5% discount on most nonbook products.[7]

The strategy is taken from Canada's largest drugstore retailer, Shoppers Drug Mart, whose rewards program has been very successful thus far. Shoppers Drug Mart's Optimum cardholders typically spend 60% more than noncardholders.[8] Indigo hopes its customers will do the same. Several years ago, Shoppers Drug Mart similarly needed to diversify its pharmacy business and now sells selected groceries, cameras, and much more.[9]

"It's a defining moment in physical book retailing, just as I think we're in some ways in a defining period for physical retailing," Reisman said. "If you don't do something, you're not going to be in business."[10]

In 2011, Indigo sold its e-reader, Kobo, to Rakuten, a Japanese firm, for US$315 million. While the digital book business initially looked promising, increasing losses were a drain on the company. E-readers had been slowly losing appeal. Although there is a loyal niche market of older adults who want to read a lot of books using one device, more consumers are opting to buy tablets, which can perform multiple tasks. Similarly, e-books, priced at about $10, deliver less than half of the profit from physical hardcover books, industry analysts' estimate.[11]

Amazon, the largest US online book retailer, has been the frontrunner in transforming the book industry in Canada, the United States, and around the world. Amazon, which sells books online, has also expanded into other consumer goods while selling them at rock-bottom prices. Indigo's largest competitor has been competing like no other retailer. Amazon has been accused of actively encouraging customers to check out goods in competitor physical stores and then to purchase them at a cheaper price online with Amazon.

---

[5] O'Kane, 2013.

[6] O'Kane, 2013.

[7] Strauss, M. (2011, April 5). Indigo launches rewards program. *Globe and Mail*. Retrieved from www.theglobeandmail.com/globe-investor/indigo-launches-rewards-program/article598396.

[8] Strauss, 2011 (April 5).

[9] Strauss, 2011 (April 5).

[10] Strauss, M. (2011, April 8). Indigo's Heather Reisman faces digital reckoning. *Globe and Mail*. Retrieved from www.theglobeandmail.com/globe-investor/indigos-heather-reisman-faces-digital-reckoning/article577337/?page=all.

[11] Strauss, 2011 (April 8).

The online company has benefited in other ways, too. The Internet giant has not only been able to keep costs low by avoiding physical stores that come with overhead costs such as labour, rent and utility expenses, Amazon has also been able to curtail tax laws in many foreign jurisdictions. Since Amazon does not maintain a "physical presence" in many countries (such as a retail store, warehouse, or sales office) governments cannot charge Amazon corporate income taxes nor enforce tax collection.

Many of Indigo's US peers continue to struggle. Borders filed for bankruptcy in 2011, and Barnes and Noble has been trying to expand its product offerings.

Certainly, Reisman is trying to position the company to succeed in the long term, but competing in this new industry is a learning process. "Book retailing, publishing as a whole, is going through a massive transformation," said Michael Serbinis, chief executive of Kobo. "That takes incredible will and mettle to go through."[12]

CHANGE AND THE ENVIRONMENT OF BUSINESS

Objective 1 Describe the forces encouraging change in organizations.

The Business World opening vignette underscores the significant challenges organizations face in confronting a changing environment. What are the sources of change directed at organizations? How do these changes affect the nature of organizations and work? In every chapter in this book, from management thought to business ethics, we have often recognized that just about every important area of business is undergoing some kind of change. How is the organizational environment changing? Consider a number of issues addressed in this book, including issues like globalization, free trade, deregulation, privatization, or the changing emphasis on corporate social responsibility. Much of what we have addressed involves issues that are undergoing dramatic change.

Regardless of the target for the change, it is critical to understand what factors in the organization's environment dictate the need for change.

Exhibit 12.1 Forces for Change

Forces for Change

As discussed in Chapter 1, organizations are open systems that are in continual interaction with their external environment. Success and survival require organizations to continually develop a "fit" with their dynamic and evolving environment. Consequently, the ability to change is central to the success of any organization. On the other hand, there is a paradox at play— while change is ultimately required to adapt to a changing environment, the success of any organization depends on the capability to maintain stable and reproducible organizational processes and outcomes. See Exhibit 12.1 for an illustration of the forces for change, which we discuss next.

[12] Strauss, 2011 (November 9).

Economic Changes   Is the economy healthy or weak? Clearly, organizations must adapt to changing economic conditions. Downsizings are more likely to occur in lean times than in rich. Organizational expansion cannot occur in an economic vacuum, as the following indicates:

> We have watched what the new workplace rules mean in periods of economic expansion. The decade long boom of the 1990s occurred just as downsizing became *de rigueur* at American companies. The greater efficiency with which companies allocated their human resources spurred enormous gains in economic growth and productivity. Companies hired contract consultants who could deliver specific expertise on a project, and they hired temporaries to handle the surge periods of the business day.[13]

This quote alludes to a few of the changes that resulted from changing economic circumstances. Certainly, such changes have also facilitated changes to the nature of the employer–employee relationship. Lifetime employment appears to be a thing of the past. Consider the 1950s or the 1970s: These were actually times where employment meant security. The dominant model was long-term employment—stability. However, a change to this implicit employment contract occurred sometime in the 1980s. And, as we identified in an earlier chapter, the age of downsizing began—with large, secure organizations beginning to lay off employees. Part-time and temporary work arrangements have become much more common than in the past:

> Organizations are typically responding to this challenging new organization world by becoming preoccupied with improving performance and bottom line results while losing sight of the importance of a people/performance balance in achieving lasting success. In these organizations, slashing costs, continuous restructuring, downsizing, trying endless quick fix programs and solutions, announcing new visions, values, and goals that everyone is expected to embrace, and lots of well intended talk about the importance of people and values is becoming common place. It is a push, cut, slash, slice, talk, quick fix management mentality and strategy that places a high emphasis on performance and a low emphasis on people and often creates an illusion of doing well while the organization is regressing and in some cases unraveling! It appear to employees to be a "built to sell or built to fail" strategy that assumes that you can manage or shrink your way to success.[14]

We have also witnessed a change with regard to the pattern of career movement within an organization. Traditionally, employees attempted to move up the corporate hierarchy throughout their career. However, the flattening of many organizational hierarchies has tended to substitute horizontal or lateral career movement for the former vertical movement, so that you might move around an organization into different areas rather than directly up the hierarchy. The following quote reflects the new era of the "free agent":

---

[13] Challenger, J.A. (2001). The transformed workplace: How you can survive. *The Futurist, 35*(6). Retrieved from www.questia.com/library/1G1-79382115/the-transformed-workplace-how-you-can-survive.

[14] Warrick, D.D. (2002). The illusion of doing well while the organization is regressing. *Organization Development Journal, 20*(1), 56–61.

Employees and workers must view their careers in terms of what skills they can offer. As individual identity has become uncoupled from a particular company, people have focused on functional career areas, such as law, human resources, financial, sales and marketing, and manufacturing. In the 1990s, professional associations and functional groupings have seen explosive membership gains. More and more people have sought community and networking opportunities in the company of like-minded career professionals.[15]

In recent years, some Canadian provinces have experienced an increase in structural unemployment caused by skill gaps, as seen in Talking Business 12.1.

TALKING BUSINESS 12.1

Making Skills Work in Ontario

There is growing concern about skills gaps in Ontario. Many employers can't find skilled people to fill positions, impeding their ability to grow and contribute economic value to the province. At the same time, many individuals lack the skills needed to find employment—over the past year, new job gains were concentrated among individuals with some form of post-secondary education. Across Canada, skills and labour shortages have been described by Diane Finley, Minister of Human Resources and Skills Development, as the "most significant socio-economic challenge to our success and competitiveness." But what do we really know about the causes and consequences of skills gaps in Ontario—and what questions remain?

The Skills and Labour Squeeze

Skills gaps are the result of fundamental changes to the province's industrial and demographic make-up. Ontario's economy has become more highly skilled and "creative," in the words of Richard Martin and Robert Florida. Many jobs require greater technical proficiency, as well as essential skills (e.g., critical thinking, teamwork, and communication) and innovation skills (e.g., creativity, risk-taking, and relationship-building). To be sure, Ontarians are highly educated—Ontario has the highest post-secondary education completion rate in Canada (57 per cent) and is well above the OECD average. But more is needed to meet the demands of tomorrow's economy. Some estimate that 77 per cent of individuals will require post-secondary credentials in the years to come.

Just as skills requirements for employment are rising, Ontario's workforce is aging, and many of those with the most experience are beginning to retire. Combined with lower population growth rates, Ontario will face labour shortages in addition to skills shortages. Previous Conference Board research has shown that the province could face a labour shortage of 364,000 workers by [next year], increasing to 564,000 by 2030.

The Risks of Inaction

Some have forecasted significant consequences of failing to address skills gaps. Miner, for example, projects that [in three years] there will be "almost 450,000 unskilled workers" who cannot find employment, combined with "500,000 skilled vacancies." Moreover, he suggests that the number of skilled vacancies may rise to a staggering one million by 2021, and almost two million by 2031, if no corrective action is taken.

The result would be far-ranging consequences for Ontario, its businesses and citizens. Many more individuals would be unable to find employment and the economic and social benefits it provides. Businesses would find themselves without the people they need to grow, innovate, and provide many of the services society requires. Ontario's Workforce Shortage Coalition notes that skills gaps could "jeopardize ongoing government priorities such as infrastructure renewal and environmental protection."

Source: Excerpted from Stuckey, J. (2013, June 19). *Making Skills Work in Ontario*. Reprinted with permissions from The Conference Board of Canada. Retrieved from www.conferenceboard.ca/topics/education/commentaries/13-06-19/making_skills_work_in_ontario.aspx?pf=true.

---

[15] Challenger, 2001.

Competitive Changes Chapter 7 underscored the importance of identifying how industries change or evolve over time. Competitive processes do evolve, and understanding what to expect and what drives evolution along the life cycle of an industry is critical for surviving turbulent times. As we identified in Chapter 7, there are major phases and milestones that mark an industry's evolutionary path from emergence and shakeout to maturity and decline. At each stage of the industry life cycle, the organizational skills and capabilities needed to survive and grow change in significant ways.

Organizations must adapt to change as competition evolves in markets from fragmented and fast growing to concentrated and declining. In addition, competition, both domestic and foreign, certainly has demanded an acceleration in innovation among firms in many industries. To compete effectively, organizations must continually create new and better methods of serving customers. For example, while globalization has opened up larger markets for businesses, it has also facilitated much higher levels of competition. Globalization, as discussed elsewhere in this book, opened the floodgates for competitors. Certainly, for some industries, change was not an option but a requirement for survival, as seen in Talking Business 12.2.

TALKING BUSINESS 12.2

Yes, There Is a Future for Manufacturing in Canada

Pengyou91/Shutterstock

One could be forgiven for believing that a perpetual fog of woe betides Canada's manufacturing industry. Despite the end of the recession nearly 3 years ago, headlines continue to trumpet plant closures and job losses. However, this is the common problem of confusing firm performance with sector performance. Manufacturing in Canada is not in decline—output today is up nearly 14 per cent from the nadir it reached during the recession. But manufacturing is most definitely in a state of change.

Many major segments of Canada's manufacturing sector are currently reporting rising production; some are even surging. For example, robust investment in the oil sands is driving very strong gains in production in the machinery and fabricated metal products industries, which are major suppliers. The ongoing recovery in North American vehicle sales is driving rising production in industries like transportation equipment, primary metals and plastics. A few industries have even attained production today that is above where it stood at the start of the recession; in short, they have fully recovered.

That said, the rising tide of manufacturing output is not lifting all boats. Canada's paper products and printing industries continue to suffer from the shift in information and entertainment away from print to electronic media. Building materials production, such as cement and aggregates, has failed to rebound due to the tepid performance of North American construction spending since the end of the recession. These underperforming segments may be giving the false impression of a more general manufacturing malaise.

Manufacturing employment is also perpetuating the impression of gloom. Although production has made healthy gains in the past couple of years, employment has not—it is little different today than it was in the summer of 2009. The combination of a recovery in output in many manufacturing segments but few job gains means that labour productivity is rising substantively. Unfortunately for frustrated workers in the manufacturing sector, this is an effective way for manufacturers to overcome the twin challenges of a strong dollar and rising global competition.

This ongoing improvement in labour productivity is part of the necessary and ongoing transformation that manufacturing must undertake in order to be successful beyond the post-recession rebound.

Ultimately, the manufacturing sector will have to change what it does here, and how it does it. Part of this transformation will involve further increasing engagement with emerging markets, both as customers and as links in the supply chain. For example, Canada's textiles and apparel industry has gone through a painful transformation over the past decade, shrinking by more than half as a result of competition from developing economies. However, the industry has achieved some success in recent years by focusing on high-value activities and products (such as high-end suits and safety attire), and by taking advantage of low-cost inputs from those same developing economies.

Increasing the amount of services that manufacturers provide with their products is another strategy. The Conference Board's recently-published study on small- and medium-sized manufacturers in Quebec reported that companies are increasingly providing services that complement their products. Linking products and services together helps to build competitive advantages, better client relationships and pricing power for manufacturers. As well, it diversifies firms' revenue mix away from the sale of physical products, which can be much more volatile.

Canada's manufacturing sector is and will still be here for many years to come, but not in its current form. The mix of what we produce will continue to change, and the performance among the manufacturing segments will vary. Growth in manufacturing employment growth may not be robust as firms concentrate on boosting productivity to stay globally competitive. It will not be manufacturing as we knew it a generation ago, but yes, there will be a manufacturing sector in Canada.

Source: Excerpted from Burt, M. (2012, April 10). Yes, There Is a Future for Manufacturing in Canada. Reprinted with permission from The Conference Board of Canada. Retrieved from www. conferenceboard.ca/economics/hot_eco_topics/default/12-04-10/ yes_there_is_a_future_for_manufacturing_in_canada.aspx.

Technological Changes   Technology is both a continuously changing variable and one that permits and demands organizational change. One scholar observed the following:

In recent years, there has been considerable discussion of whether the development and application of information and communications technology have changed the . . . economy in a fundamental way, promising a golden future of rapid growth, low unemployment and inflation, perpetual economic expansion, and a booming stock market. The change is sometimes called the "Information Revolution"; more commonly, it is called the "New Economy." . . . As the economy absorbs any new technology, what typically happens first is that existing economic activities are performed at lower cost. E-commerce is no exception . . . Only a few firms have gone through the deep organizational changes needed to become web-based organizations, but those that have done so have achieved remarkable results, like cutting administrative costs by 75 percent.[16]

Technology has been a double-edged sword for business—bringing both benefits and threats. It can create new industries and destroy old ones. For some workers, technology is a threat because it can replace jobs, but for other workers technology can create new opportunities in the knowledge economy, as seen in Talking Business 12.3. Benefits from technology have also included the ability to gain more flexibility in work arrangements, such as the practice of telework:

---

[16] Taylor, T. (2001). Thinking about a "new economy." *Public Interest, 143,* 3–19. Can be accessed at http:// timothytaylor.net/articles/public_interest_spr_2001.pdf

The idea of telecommuting isn't new, but companies still have a long way to go to fully exploit the benefits of a networked economy. Indianapolis pharmaceutical company Eli Lilly and Co. lets all its knowledge workers work from home occasionally, and a formal telework program lets a smaller number of employees keep their primary offices at home. Such telecommuting generally had been considered a concession to work-life balance, but these days, the company is also thinking about it as a means to drive productivity, say Candi Lange, director of workforce partnering. "We bring in such smart people who are responsible for so much important work in the company," she says. "Why not let them control their own schedules as well?"[17]

Digital Health: More than Just Health and Technology

With a population of 35 million spread across the second largest country in the world, it comes as no surprise that Canadians ranked as the world's most intensive Internet users. For the last decade, we have embraced new technologies with open arms. We can now manage with ease most of our daily activities online with a simple tap of the finger (e.g., searching information, managing our finances, booking a flight and connecting with others). Surprisingly, advancements of digital health in Canada have not caught up to today's technology standards, and that is not from a lack of trying. So what can we do to promote the advancement of health innovations in Canada? Digital health is more than the mere combination of health and technology; it is a collaborative effort between health specialists, technology experts and patients to create health solutions for everyone.

The explosive wave of technologies has allowed us to become experts in creating data. Most people do not even realize that we leave digital footprints everywhere we go (e.g., by sending messages from our mobile phone, checking in on our social media and browsing the web via Google searches). This wealth of information has given the public a strong voice that has a direct impact on business, philanthropy and politics. Similarly, crowd-sourced health information empowers people by connecting the world health community in real time. For those constantly fearing the next pandemic, Healthmap.org uses data from tens of thousands of different sources every hour to inform us of disease trends. The data collected from Canadian's Hacking Health does not necessarily involve tracking down diseases but instead, it uses the collaborative brain power of medicine and technology to find solutions to current health issues. Last fall, the 48-hour Toronto "Hackathon" hosted at the MaRS building attracted

more than 300 physicians and IT experts ready to push the envelope of digital health. The big game changer in digital health remains the long overdue standardization of electronic medical records. Collaborations between individuals and cutting-edge technology are vital in the development of digital health. These partnerships help deliver health information and services to patients in a more efficient way.

Provincial and federal governments recognize the benefits of e-health in improving communications and driving new efficiencies. With a grey tsunami approaching and 80 per cent of our health care money allocated to chronic illnesses, Canada hopes that investing in health information technology will reduce the cost of our $200 billion annual Medicare bill. The Internet has experienced great success stories in digital health by connecting people. Thanks to websites such as patientslikeme.com and lotsahelpinghands.com, communities of patients, caregivers and health professionals can find support and share their experiences remotely. The challenge of digital health is not simply a question of technological advancements but mostly one of humanism using technology. By providing cutting-edge patient-centric treatments, digital health will succeed into offering high caliber treatments that will transform patients' lives.

With the extensive amount of data created continuously, health specialists find strength in sharing their knowledge online. Naturally, with the accessibility of smart phones (and geolocation applications), the trend of connecting remotely will continue to expand with the goal of bringing patients and health communities closer together. Keeping up with the innovation of information technology plays an essential role in expanding e-health. But besides impressive new technologies that can reach a global audience, we need to remember

---

[17] Rezendes Khirallah, D. (2008, April 8). The tug of more. *InformationWeek*. Retrieved from www.informationweek.com/the-tug-of-more/6502154.

Source: Excerpted from Simon, P. (2013, February 14). Digital health: More than just health and technology. Reprinted with permission from The Conference Board of Canada. Retrieved from www.conferenceboard.ca/commentaries/healthinnovation/default/13-02-14/digital_health_more_than_just_health_and_technology.aspx.

that digital health's main goal is to deliver health services to improve the quality of life of patients. To advance digital health in Canada, provincial and federal governments need to reach and engage three types of people: individuals that create data, the panel of experts coming up with creative solutions and patients who represent the vital essence of medicine.

Part-time work has increased dramatically in recent years, and we also continue to see the increasing use of compressed workweeks and flextime—all in all, this means that the nine-to-five job is certainly no longer a fixed rule.

Global Changes   As we observed in Chapter 8, globalization has been among the most pervasive forces affecting not only business in Canada but in almost every corner of the world. We also noted the tremendous growth of "borderless" corporations. The increasing ability of multinational corporations to move freely across borders and set up business just about anywhere reflects the title "borderless corporation." The term *multinational* is a bit inaccurate, however, given that many of these companies do not claim any specific nationality but, in fact, gear their planning and decision making to global markets. For example, goods could be designed in one country, raw material obtained from a second country, the product could be manufactured in a third country, and shipped to consumers in another country.

Globalization has certainty allowed more people with specialized skills to obtain employment in other countries. The sports industry is no exception, as seen in Talking Business 12.4.

In a broader sense, globalization has also influenced profound changes in the relationship of business to its external stakeholders. As one observer noted, globalization has changed the nature of business and communities:

TALKING BUSINESS 12.4
Pro Sports and Globalization

Globalization has also become a factor of growing importance in pro sports that have international appeal. Forty years ago, more than 90 per cent of the players in the NHL were Canadian. Today, that share has fallen to about 50 per cent. The U.S. share of the NHL talent pool has grown to about 20 per cent, and Europeans now account for about 30 per cent (although this share is being challenged by the three-year-old Kontinental Hockey League in Russia). Baseball first looked to the Caribbean and Latin America to its expand its existing American player base, and has more recently spread its talent search to the Asia-Pacific region and Canada. The NBA has the most diversified talent pool. It draws players from around the globe. More than 30 countries are represented in the NBA, with foreign-born players accounting for about 20 per cent of NBA rosters. Expanding the pro sports talent pool has been key to maintaining a high standard of play at a time of steady expansion in all the North American leagues in recent decades. At the same time, international expansion of the talent pool has helped to grow the popularity of these sports in international markets.

Source: Excerpted from Hodgson, G., & Lefebvre, M. (2011, June). Pro league competitive conditions and how the NHL stacks up. Reprinted with permission from The Conference Board of Canada. Retrieved from www.conferenceboard.ca/reports/briefings/bigleagues/briefing-5.aspx.

Employees and communities were once critical factors in companies' long-term strategic decisions. Moving factories and jobs to another area of the country was unthinkable because of the damage it would do to the local community. In recent years, thousands of companies—including UPS, J.C. Penney, and Boeing—have moved their headquarters or operations from cities where they had deep roots. The old business structure—with a dominant CEO, a largely ceremonial board of directors, and employees willing to put the goals of the company first—is nearly extinct. . . . Several primary forces created systemic change in the American economy in the 1980s and 1990s, leaving the former system in shambles. One such factor was globalization, which forced the United States out of isolation. Companies began to look for new markets overseas. Coca-Cola and McDonald's spread throughout the world. NAFTA, GATT, and free trade brought down barriers that had prevented the flow of goods and services and human resources around the world. The law of unintended consequences worked its way into the American economy. Protected industries such as auto manufacturing faced serious competition from overseas for the first time, with devastating consequences.[18]

Legal/Political Changes Deregulation and privatization, discussed in an earlier chapter, are clear examples of the importance of considering governmental changes on business strategy. Are legal regulations facilitating or restricting certain strategies? The legal environment of business can dictate changes in how business competes, as well as what services it offers and how they can be offered:

The deregulation of protected industries in the 1980s and 1990s created competition for companies where none had previously existed. The telecom, banking, energy, and aerospace industries were ruled by the change. As the dominant companies in these sectors were forced to compete in an open market, they started letting sizable numbers of people go. The breakup of the Bell System into AT&T, Lucent, and the seven Baby Bells unleashed a surge of technology inventiveness. It was not surprising that telecom, financial services, and aerospace dominated the list of industries experiencing the heaviest downsizing in the early to mid-1990s.[19]

In the workplace, we have witnessed an increasing emphasis on organizational justice—that is, how employees are treated. This has translated into more laws governing fairness in the workplace. One such area that has been dramatically affected is compensation. Pay equity has been among numerous issues involved in redressing inconsistencies in pay treatment among men and women, for example. We have also witnessed an increasing emphasis on merit-based pay and pay for performance, which all attempt to more closely link actual effort to performance (versus seniority-based pay, which bases pay on the number of years you have been with the organization).

In recent years, we have also seen the reduction of tariffs on imported goods, such as in the apparel industry. A decrease in tariffs on some goods has allowed an increase in competition in Canada from foreign competitors. This has affected businesses in Canada and abroad, as seen in Talking Business 12.5.

Societal Changes Businesses must respond to society: Consumer tastes change, for example, and businesses must adapt to such changes. Similarly, the types of organizations that service societal demands can change. The aging population suggests greater emphasis needs to be placed on such industries as the health care sector:

---

[18] Challenger, 2001.

[19] Challenger, 2001.

How Canada Welcomed Bangladeshi Clothing Imports

age fotostock/SuperStock

The recent Bangladeshi garment factory collapse that has already killed over 500 workers was horrific—and avoidable. It is now considered the deadliest accident in the history of the garment industry. The building's owner has now been arrested, having reportedly ignored warnings about dangerous cracks in the building.

As is now well known, workers in the factory sewed clothes for consumers in rich countries, including some being made for Canada's Joe Fresh, owned by Loblaws. Loblaws has vowed to compensate the victims' families, to stay in Bangladesh, and to improve its facilities.

Less appreciated, however, is that the rise of Bangladeshi garment factories is something that Canada has encouraged. Canada made a significant policy change a decade ago, eliminating all tariffs and quotas on imports from the poorest countries. While the average tariff on all goods exported to Canada was less than 1 per cent, roughly 70 per cent of textile and clothing products subject to tariffs had tariffs greater than 15 per cent. The 49 poorest countries were not exempt.

The policy change was unveiled as part of a G8 Africa initiative. But, while most of the world's poorest countries are indeed in Africa, they export very little. By contrast, poor South Asian nations, such as Bangladesh and Cambodia, as well as the Caribbean nation of Haiti, had some capacity to take advantage of the duty-free access to Canada.

Canada's clothing imports from Bangladesh were $330 million in 2003 and soared to $1.1 billion by 2012. Similarly, Canada imported $83 million in clothing from Cambodia in 2003, and over half a billion by 2012.

As many have noted, conditions in garment factors are abysmal. The mostly women who labour in them endure long hours in poor conditions and earn low wages.

Yet, as history has shown, the textile sector serves as the first rung on the ladder to development and economic prosperity. And, according to some commentaries such as this one, it has fueled a social revolution in Bangladesh.

As they did in Europe and North America, garment factories offer workers a chance to enter the better-paying formal sector of the economy. Better wages raise living standards and lower poverty, particularly in cities and towns. Garment production represents a rare chance for many of the women employed in these industries to earn independent income. Their alternatives are usually subsistence farming in the villages they come from.

Textile and clothing exports also contribute to greater overall economic stability. This is because they come from an economic sector that is more stable and has a relatively higher value-added component than the agricultural sector, on which most of these countries depend for their exports. The textile and clothing sector also creates entrepreneurial opportunities and managerial jobs for members of the middle class who might otherwise emigrate.

In other words, Canada's decision to encourage more imports from these economies encourages exactly the type of activity that promotes development, sexual equality, and poverty reduction in the poorest countries. (Canada's recent decision to eliminate tariff preferences for more developed economies such as China will now make it even more attractive to import from Bangladesh. The benefits and costs of this more recent policy decision merit another discussion on their own.)

Many Canadian clothing imports now come from the poorest countries. In fact, 50 per cent of all Canada's imports come from outside of the US today (down from 35 per cent a decade ago). These imports come from both developed and developing markets.

In short, Canadian companies are now engaged with markets that are very different from Canada's. This means that our companies need to ensure that their entire supply chain meets reasonable working conditions and standards, at the least to protect their reputations that can be easily and quickly destroyed. After the horrific factory collapse in Bangladesh, consumers in Canada and other rich countries will now be able to apply much more pressure on companies to demand better working conditions in poor countries.

Source: Excerpted from Goldfarb, D. (2013, May 3). How Canada welcomed Bangladeshi clothing imports. Reprinted with permission from The Conference Board of Canada. Retrieved from www.conferenceboard.ca/economics/hot_eco_topics/default/13-05-03/how_canada_welcomed_bangladeshi_clothing_imports.aspx.

The growing number of people with advanced educational degrees is another force hurtling knowledge forward at a higher rate. As more people become educated, knowledge expansion increases geometrically simply because there are more people to move the cutting edge of knowledge ahead. Geniuses emerge who could not have appeared in past eras because they did not have access to the then-current state of knowledge necessary to push the thought boundaries. Unprecedented numbers of people today are working at the cutting edge of research in a variety of fields. And the glass ceiling is breaking apart because young women are achieving the advanced degrees necessary for economic and social advancement.[20]

The increasing education level of the workforce has also generated changes to the nature of work. As we discussed in an earlier chapter, for some time there has been a movement away from high job specialization, where jobs are broken down into simple, distinct packages. The trend has been to generate jobs that demand employees be multi-skilled to handle more challenging and enriched work. Consequently, employees are also tending to work more in teams and are responsible for a larger piece of the work, so to speak. Knowledge work demands a more highly educated workforce.

Clearly, changes in demographics will result in changes in consumer demand, and as the population ages there will be profound affects on business and the economy, as seen in Talking Business 12.6.

TALKING BUSINESS 12.6

Slow-Motion Demographic Tsunami about to Hit Canada's Economy

We often joke that there are only two inevitable things in life—death, and taxes. That may be true for us as individuals; but for societies and nations as a whole, the most inevitable and unstoppable force of all is demographics. The rate of population increase and the national age profile are critical drivers of economic growth—since demographics affect both the available workforce, and consumer demand. Canada is about to be hit by a demographic tsunami in slow motion, with profound and lasting impacts on our economy and our society.

Among its many economic outlook products, The Conference Board of Canada produces a long-term forecast for the country and each province, to 2035, and we are considering producing a long-term forecast for major cities. Rather than focusing on demand for goods and services, the long-term forecast is based on estimating Canada's capacity to supply goods and services. This is a

"pure" forecast—in that it is driven by the fundamentals of demographics, capital investment and productivity growth, and beyond the medium term, is unaffected by short-term risks or the economic cycle.

What does our long-term forecast for Canada say? It confirms that a slow-motion demographic tsunami is about to arrive. We expect that Canada's underlying growth potential will begin to fade over the next few years, just as the growth potential of other aging industrial nations like Japan and Italy has slowed sharply in recent years. We estimate that after 2015, sustainable growth in Quebec and in much of Atlantic Canada will have slowed to around 1.5 per cent in real terms (i.e., with the impact of inflation is removed). Ontario's sustainable growth rate will fall below 2 per cent after 2015, as we recently re-estimated in our study *Ontario's Fiscal Outlook: Challenges Ahead*. Western provinces will fare a bit better, but even

[20] Challenger, 2001.

they will see their collective growth potential fall to around 2.5 per cent as the effects of aging demographics kick in.

Governments, many businesses and the public have been slow to address Canada's aging demographics in a timely way, notwithstanding warnings from the Conference Board and others. We are now playing catch-up in terms of policy and practices.

What policy options are available for adapting the labour force to aging demographics? There are essentially three. Immigration policy can be re-energized, both by raising the annual level of immigration and re-focusing on the needs of the economy and of employers—as we proposed in our briefing "Canada's Future Labour Market: Immigrants to the Rescue?" in the July 2010 edition of *Policy Options*. Those changes have begun, but an immigration strategy that is even a more activist will be needed, ideally with the federal government, the provinces, employers and professional associations (which evaluate credentials) working together in an integrated way.

Next, we could enhance incentives to keep an aging population engaged longer in the workforce. The announced changes to Old Age Security are an opening salvo in improving incentives to work longer—not necessarily a popular move, but a necessary element. Equal consideration should be given to creating positive financial incentives to work longer, such as through changes to pension rules or to tax policy. Similarly, we should be opening doors to the labour force for under-represented groups, such as Aboriginal peoples and those with disabilities. And we need to make even greater investments in our educational system, to ensure that our human capital is as productive as possible.

Within organizations, employers will need to apply the same kind of creative thinking, by investing more in their workforce and fostering a positive workplace environment that helps to retain and engage all types of workers.

But the possible action steps shouldn't stop there if we are to offset the drag effect of aging demographics on the economy. Canada has suffered from chronically slow productivity growth for nearly three decades. There is no silver bullet or quick-fix solution on productivity, but a national debate and a defined productivity strategy would heighten our awareness of what needs to be done—things like enhanced infrastructure investment, a focus on advanced education, and eliminating barriers to commerce between provinces. And we need to embrace the globalization of Canadian business, through increased use of outward foreign investment to engage the huge available labour force outside our borders.

Alternatively, we could decide to sit back and do nothing exceptional. If that is the default option, Canada's growth potential will slowly fade away . . . making us eerily like Japan and Italy, which have not responded well to aging demographics and where real annual economic growth of around 1 per cent is now considered a normal year. If we choose to do nothing different, Canada would still be relatively wealthy—but with little dynamic energy, or revenue growth, for businesses and governments. That's not much of a future.

Source: Excerpted from Hodgson, G. (2012, July 10). Slow-motion demographic tsunami about to hit Canada's economy. Reprinted with permission from The Conference Board of Canada. Retrieved from www.conferenceboard.ca/economics/hot_eco_topics/default/12-07-10/slow-motion_demographic_tsunami_about_to_hit_canada_s_economy.aspx.

TYPES OF CHANGE

Objective 2 Define developmental change, transitional change, and transformational change.

According to Dean Anderson and Linda Ackerman Anderson, organizations may confront three fundamentally different types of change: developmental, transitional, and transformational.[21] Any organization must comprehend the nature of the change that it is attempting to undergo—this is a precursor to successfully managing any type of change (see Exhibit 12.2).

Developmental Change

Developmental change attempts to improve upon what the business is currently doing, rather than creating something completely new. This may include the improvement of

developmental change
Change that attempts to improve upon what the business is currently doing, rather than creating something completely new.

[21] Anderson, D., & Ackerman Anderson, L. (2005, April). What is transformation? Why is it so hard to manage? *Workforce Performance Solutions*. Retrieved from www.wpsmag.com/content/templates/wps_section.asp?articleid=124&zoneid=29.

Exhibit 12.2 Types of Change

Developmental change	Transitional change	Transformational change
• *Improves* existing skills, processes, methods, performance standards	• *Replaces* what already exists with something completely new • Requires the organization to depart from old methods	• *Transforms* the future state from the current state dramatically • Outcomes are unknown, unpredictable, and uncertain • Achieved through trial and error • Employees and their mindsets, behaviour, and culture must change to successfully implement this type of change

existing skills, processes, methods, performance standards, or conditions. For example, increasing sales or quality of goods, interpersonal communication training, simple work process improvements, team development, and problem-solving efforts may all be considered forms of developmental change.

Transitional Change

transitional change Change that replaces what already exists with something completely new. It requires the organization to depart from old methods of operation while the new state is being established.

Transitional change actually replaces what already exists with something completely new and requires the organization to depart from old methods of operating while the new state is being established. Examples of transitional change include reorganizations, simple mergers or acquisitions, creating new products or services that replace old ones, and information technology implementations that do not require a significant shift in culture or behaviour.

There are two factors that largely distinguish transitional from transformational change:

■ It is possible to determine the final destination or state in detail before the transitional change is implemented. This permits the change to be managed.

■ Transitional change largely impacts employees only at the levels of skills and actions, but not at the more personal levels of mindset, behaviour, and culture.

Transformational Change

transformational change A type of change where the future state of the business is dramatically different from the current operating state. This is the most challenging type of change to implement, because the future state is unknown, it requires employees to develop new mindsets and behaviours, and the entire organizational culture must change.

Transformational change is far more challenging to manage compared to the other types of change for at least two reasons. First, the future state or destination caused by the change is unknown when the transformation begins. Rather, the final state is determined through trial and error as new information is gathered. Consequently, transformational change cannot be managed with predetermined, time-bound, or "linear" plans. While an overarching change strategy can be created, the actual change process only really emerges, somewhat unpredictably, as the change is implemented. This means that managers and employees must operate in the "unknown"—where future outcomes are quite uncertain. Second, the future state is so dramatically different from the current operating state that employees and their culture must change to successfully implement this type of change. New mindsets and behaviours are required to adapt to this transformed state (see Talking Business 12.7).

Transformational Change: Starbucks Risks Core Business for New Unknown Ventures

Starbucks (SBUX) CEO Howard Schultz had a lot of positive news to highlight yesterday at the annual shareholder meeting. Since the company's low point in 2008, when the stock closed below $8, Starbucks has turned itself around, opening 1,400 stores worldwide, bringing the total to 17,200.

The company's stock has performed well as a result, with a 32% growth in profits for the end of its fiscal year in October 2, 2011, and the stock price has risen from $37 to $53 since that month. Now, the company hopes to maintain the momentum, with the aid of lower coffee prices, by pushing into new international markets and expanding its client base with new products.

Before Schultz retook control of the company in 2008, Starbucks had focused almost solely on its cafes in the US and inventing new coffee drinks. Spurred by the growing middle class in emerging economies and the shrinking middle class in Western nations, the company has changed course, with 600 of the 800 stores slated to open in 2012 opening in foreign countries, and China taking a quarter of that 600.

Starbucks also hopes to open its first store in India this year and to have 7,000 stores in South Korea by 2016. MorningStar analyst R.J. Hottvoy says the company has done a good job turning its business around by closing unprofitable stores, streamlining its supply chain, and offering higher-margin consumer products.

The new business ventures of the company will be equally important to profit growth, and investors and analysts will surely be keeping eye on these five new business concepts recently begun by the company. At yesterday's meeting, the company stated it aims to reach between 10% and 15% in annual revenue growth, and it forecasts earnings per share growth of 15% to 20%. UBS agrees with the company's predictions, as analyst David Palmer boosted the target price of the stock to $61, an increase of around 15%.

The success of these five new projects will determine if Starbucks can continue its robust profits growth.

1. Evolution Fresh

Starbucks' most recent addition to its business is its juice bar, called Evolution Fresh. The first store opened in Bellevue, Washington, this past Monday, and Starbucks looks to turn the brand name into another successful restaurant chain. Its success will depend on people's willingness to pay $8 for a 16-ounce cup of juice and $7 for a 16-ounce smoothie, which is more than the cost of a sandwich and nearly the same as a salad.

At first glance, the steep prices would suggest that the new store will struggle with its rival Jamba (JMBA) and its Jamba Juice stores, one store located only a short walk away from Evolution. Jamba Juice offers more selections for smoothies, and its 16-ounce smoothie costs half the price of Evolution's equivalent. However, Starbucks proved that people will pay high prices for coffee, and they seem willing to pay high prices for juice, too. According to local reports, people packed into the store to test the new drinks. The store offers delivery service and emphasizes a healthy lifestyle.

As it does its coffee products, Starbucks will also sell the store's juices at grocery stores, including Whole Foods (WFM).

2. Seattle's Best Coffee

Starbucks bought Seattle's Best Coffee last November after the chain had to close many of its locations in the former bookseller Borders. Starbucks is now expanding the stores around the country and describing Seattle's Best as a "billion dollar brand." A new store opened up in Northlake, Illinois, that features the chain's first drive-through (some Starbucks cafes already have drive-thrus) to appeal to the busy suburban middle class population.

This drive-through experiment will test never-before-seen coffee beverages and show its competitiveness against rivals such as the Dunkin' Brands Group (DNKN) and its Dunkin Donuts stores, many of which have drive-thrus.

Starbucks will also sell the Seattle's Best brand at Kmarts and at Chevron (CVX) gas station stores across the country.

3. Starbucks Bars

The Starbucks in Calabasas, California, is among the first Starbucks stores in California to file for a beer and wine license. The company wants to draw more traffic to its stores in the evening as the flow of customers tends to taper off later in the day. The company successfully experimented with selling alcohol at branches in its home base of Seattle in October 2010. Now, the company plans on having 25 more stores that sell alcohol by the end of the year, mostly concentrated in Atlanta, Chicago, and Southern California.

(continued)

4. Verismo Coffee Machine

Starbucks aims to get inside its customers' homes, too, with its Verismo single-cup coffee machine. When the machine lands on shelves later in the year, Starbucks fans will be able to make their own Starbucks espresso drinks and brewed coffee. Schultz wants to tap into this $8 billion market and to continue capitalizing on the consumer products group, which is the fastest growing branch of the company. He claims that it is "the fastest growing business within the global coffee industry."

Starbucks denies that it will hurt its partner Green Mountain Coffee Roasters (GMCR), which makes the Keurig Vue single-cup coffee makers. Green Mountain's stock dropped 20% minutes after the news two weeks ago, but the stock rose close to 10% after the two companies reached an agreement to expand their partnership by marketing Starbucks' Vue coffee packs for use in Green Mountain's Keurig machine, ideally increasing demand for the Keurig. Analysts remain skeptical, though, believing that Starbucks will cut out the middleman.

Whether Starbucks will destroy its partner remains to be seen, but analysts are confident that Starbucks will eat into Nestle's (NESN.VX) sale of its single-cup coffee machines, the Nespresso and the Nescafe Dolce Gusto. The fastest-growing market for Nestle is the US, but analyst Pablo Zuanic of Liberum Capital states the Verismo may steal 20% of Nestle's overall annual profit growth. Nestle's product sales jumped 20% to more than $3.8 billion last year with the

help of the Nespresso, and Starbucks wants a piece of these revenues. Analyst Johnny Forsyth of Mintel says single-cup coffee "machines are the future of coffee."

5. Refreshers

Starbucks will also begin carving out its own slice of the energy drink market at the end of next month. Yesterday, the company announced its new product Starbucks Refreshers, which will be the first energy drink to use flavorless green coffee extract. The new drink will compete with Red Bull and Rockstar energy drinks, and it will come in Raspberry Pomegranate, Strawberry Lemonade, and Orange Melon, all containing real fruit juice. This product line is another push by Starbucks to grab a larger foothold in grocery stores.

Starbucks' expansion in grocery stores makes some analysts a little hesitant. Peter Saleh from Telsey Advisory Group points out that 91% of revenues still come from Starbucks cafes and notes, "My concern would be that they get distracted from the real revenue and profit driver."

Investors, though, have so far responded favorably to Starbucks newest plans, with the stock up about 1% in morning trading.

Source: Excerpted from Witrak, C. (2012, March 22). Starbucks: 5 business moves that could change its brand Minyanville. *Yahoo Finance*. Retrieved from http://ca.finance.yahoo.com/news/starbucks-5-potential-brand-changing-200000507.html. Reprinted by permission.

Objective 3 Understand the value of Theory E and Theory O change.

METHODS OF CHANGE: THEORY E AND THEORY O CHANGE

Whether it is the presence of new competitors, new technologies, or changes to any of the other forces facing business, organizations often respond to the challenges of change with a variety of programs that might include the following:

Theory E change A theory of change that has as its purpose the creation of economic value, often expressed as shareholder value. Its focus is on formal structure and systems.

- structural change: mergers, acquisitions, and so on
- cost cutting: eliminating nonessential activities
- process change: reengineering
- cultural change: changes in its approach to doing business or changes in the relationship between management and employees

Theory O change A theory of change that has as its purpose the development of the organization's human capability to implement strategy and to learn from actions taken about the effectiveness of changes made.

In broader terms, Michael Beer and Nitin Nohria discuss two fundamentally different approaches to change. Each of these methods of change are based on different assumptions regarding what successful change tools must be employed to achieve a desirable final outcome for the organizations. These two different approaches are referred to as **Theory E change** and **Theory O change:**

Two dramatically different approaches to organizational change are being employed in the world today, according to our observations, research, and experience. We call these Theory E and Theory O of change. Like all managerial action, these approaches are guided by very different assumptions by corporate leaders about the purpose of and means for change. In effect these two approaches to organizational change represent theories in use by senior executives and the consultants and academics who advise them. By "theory in use" we mean an implicit theory that one can deduce from examining the strategies for change employed.[22]

Theory E has as its purpose the creation of economic value, often expressed as shareholder value. Its focus is on formal structure and systems.[23]

The central goal of this approach to change is based on the notion of maximizing shareholder value. The methods used to achieve this goal are changes to organizational structure and systems. The planning for this type of change tends to emanate from the highest levels of the organization, making it a "top-driven," programmatic approach to change. Among the specific mechanisms employed to achieve such change are performance bonuses, personnel reduction, asset sales, or strategic restructuring of business units.

An example of Theory E change can be seen in the changes implemented by Scott Paper, operating largely in the consumer package paper business. About a decade ago, Al Dunlap, CEO of Scott Paper, embarked on a series of changes. His main objective was to increase shareholder value by 200%. Among the changes were the following:

- Eleven thousand terminations were conducted throughout Scott Paper.
- Certain business units within Scott Paper were sold off.
- The location of the head office was moved.
- Financial incentives were given to executives that met new performance criteria.

The changes at Scott Paper were consistent with the spirit of Theory E change. While the short-term goal was achieved, the company did not achieve long-term viability and eventually was sold to Kimberly-Clark. There had been no lasting change achieved within the organization or its workforce.

Theory O has as its purpose the development of the organization's human capability to implement strategy and to learn from actions taken about the effectiveness of changes made.[24]

The central goal of Theory O change is to develop organizational capabilities. The focus is on developing an organizational culture that supports learning and a high-performance employee population. The planning for this type of change is essentially emergent and participative rather than programmatic and top-driven. The mechanisms employed to facilitate such change include the following: flatter structure (to increase involvement of employees), increased bonds between organization and employee, and employee commitment to the change.

[22] Beer, M., & Nohria, N. (2001, April 16). Breaking the code of change. Harvard Business School: Working Knowledge. Retrieved from http://hbswk.hbs.edu/item/2166.html.

[23] Beer & Nohria, 2001.

[24] Beer & Nohria, 2001.

An example of Theory O change involves the case of Champion International, operating in the same industry as Scott Paper. In response to poor performance, CEO Andrew Sigler of Champion International initiated an organizational change effort aimed at altering the culture and behaviour of management, unions, and workers. Sigler developed a vision of the new Champion, called the Champion Way, which reflected such values as involvement of all employees in improving the company, fair treatment of workers, support for the community around its plants, and openness in the company. In the years that followed, Champion's management implemented one of the most effective organization development efforts witnessed in several decades. Champion used a high involvement method called **sociotechnical redesign** to change its approach to organizing and managing people in all of its plants.

sociotechnical redesign An approach to work redesign that recognizes the complex interaction between people and technology in the workplace.

To support these changes, Champion improved its relations with its unions, and compensation systems were aligned with culture change objectives. A skills-based pay system was installed to encourage employees to learn multiple skills. A corporation-wide gains-sharing plan was introduced to help unify union workers and management with a common goal. Throughout this change effort, which occurred over a decade, there were no layoffs. Ironically, this Theory O change did not actually result in any improvement in shareholder value.

The advice from the experts is clear—Theory E and Theory O must be combined to achieve successful, long-term change. As Beer and Nohria assert,

> Where the objective is to enable an institution to adapt, survive, and prosper in the long run, Theory E change must be combined with Theory O. In effect we are arguing for the and/also, for the management of a paradox. It is the way to get rapid improvements in economic value while also building sustainable advantage inherent in building organizational capability.[25]

Theory E and Theory O are summarized in Exhibit 12.3.

Exhibit 12.3 A Comparison: Theory E and Theory O Change

	Theory E Change	Theory O Change
Timing	• Short term	• Short to long term
Goal	• Creates shareholder value	• Develops organizational capabilities
Focus	• Changes organizational structures and systems	• Develops an organizational culture that supports learning and high-performance employees
Planning	• Top-driven	• Participative
Mechanisms Used	• Performance bonuses	• Flatter structure
	• Personnel reductions	• Increases bonds between organization and employees
	• Asset sales	• Commits employees to change
	• Strategic restructuring of business units	

---

[25] Beer & Nohria, 2001.

THE PROCESS OF TRANSFORMATIONAL CHANGE: AN ILLUSTRATION

Objective 4 Describe the process of transformational change.

The story of transformational change at IBM is clearly told in the book *Who Says Elephants Can't Dance?* Specifically, it documents IBM's transformation from the period 1993 to 2002 under the leadership of Louis V. Gerstner, Jr. (also the author of the book). In the book's foreword, Gerstner writes that his reason for writing *Who Says Elephants Can't Dance?* is to "tell [the] story of the revival of IBM" to answer the questions posed by those who wanted to know how IBM was saved. Gerstner modestly acknowledges that he did not transform IBM alone,

© Andia/Alamy

and maintains that "without the heroes among [his] IBM colleagues" and the "thousands of IBMers who answered the call," IBM would not have been restored to its former glory.[26]

Understanding the Forces for Change

At a time when the external marketplace was changing rapidly, IBM had not realized that its customers, technology, and competitors had changed; nor had it adapted to meet those changes. Gerstner writes that "IBM's dominant position had created a self-contained, self-sustaining world for the company"; however, by the early 1990s, it woke up to find itself perilously close to bankruptcy.

Gerstner accepted the job at IBM after being told that the company needed and wanted a "broad-based leader and change agent" who was "skilled at generating and managing change." IBM's management team, led by Gerstner, had to quickly assess and react to the rapidly changing external environment.

As part of Gerstner's orientation into the company, he went out into the field to learn about IBM, the IT industry and the external business environment. He quickly learned that IBM had lost touch with the outside world and the external forces that were changing as IBM stood still, lost in time. One distinct advantage Gerstner held over IBM's previous leaders was that he was from the outside and had been one of IBM's former customers; therefore, he had first-hand knowledge of IBM's lack of customer focus.

According to Dick Beatty and Dave Ulrich, mature organizations "establish a relatively fixed mindset."[27] This creates a huge resistance to change. Gerstner, essentially, had to attempt to implement *transformational change* within IBM. Among the fundamental changes that Gerstner initiated are the elements highlighted below.

The Change Vision and Implementation

Gerstner had to develop and implement a program that would be accepted and adopted by the stakeholders (employees, customers, and shareholders). Gerstner writes that restructuring the organization, implementing a new compensation program, and consolidating its marketing plans was relatively easy compared to having to change the corporate culture and establishing strategies for the new business environment. Gerstner writes, "Fixing IBM was all about execution."

---

[26] Gerstner, L.V. (2002). *Who says elephants can't dance?* New York, NY: HarperCollins.

[27] Beatty, R.W., & Ulrich, D.O. (1991). Re-energizing the mature organization. *Organizational Dynamics, 20*(1), 16–30.

While management scholar Todd Jick warns that "change lists" and guidelines don't guarantee success, he nonetheless offers 10 "rules" that can be used as a tool to assist in the implementation process.[28] It appears that Gerstner did in fact follow most of these rules in one sense or another:

1. Analyze the organization and its need for change: Gerstner, as well as the business community, knew that IBM needed to change just to survive.

2. Create a shared vision and common direction: A common corporate focus was created—customer focus—which instilled a common direction.

3. Separate from the past: At his first meeting, Gerstner told IBM executives that "there was no time to focus on who created [IBM's] problems."

4. Create a sense of urgency: IBM's precarious cash flow problems made urgency a high priority.

5. Support a strong leader role: Based on his previous leadership record, Gerstner was selected by IBM's search committee as the one who could lead the organization.

6. Line up political sponsorship: Gerstner involved the IBM senior management team from the beginning, even including them in Operation Bear Hug.

7. Craft an implementation plan: "Win, Execute, and Team" became what Gerstner felt was what "all IBMers needed to apply in their goals."

8. Develop enabling structures: Gerstner restructured the organization and reset the compensation system to create a sense of ownership.

9. Communicate, involve people, and be honest: Just six days after his arrival, Gerstner wrote a note to his employees. From there he continued with a strong, open, honest employee communication strategy.

10. Reinforce and institutionalize change: Gerstner writes that "execution is all about translating strategies into action programs and measuring their results" and that "proper execution involves building measurable targets and holding people accountable for them."

The Need for Cultural Change   "Big Blue," an "institution" in its own right, had culture, behaviour, and beliefs uniquely its own. Traditions ran deep at IBM, and Gerstner candidly admits, "the company has been known as much for its culture as for what it made and sold."

Historically, IBM has been a paternalistic, family-oriented company, providing its employees with generous compensation and benefits packages, lifelong employment, and plenty of opportunities for advancement; as a matter of fact, IBM was not the standard—IBM set the standards. According to Denise Rousseau, there are two ways to change the psychological contract—that is, the set of implicit assumptions that underlie the expectations of employees with regard to their employment status:

1. accommodation, which means to modify or alter the terms "within the context of the existing contract so that people feel the old deal continues despite the changes."

2. transformation, which means a radical change that replaces the old mindset with new ones.[29]

---

[28] Jick, T.D. (2003). Implementing change. In T.D. Jick & M.A. Peiperl, *Managing change: Cases and concepts* (2nd ed.) (pp. 174–183). New York, NY: McGraw-Hill/Irwin.

[29] Rousseau, D.M. (1996). Changing the deal while keeping the people. *Academy of Management Executive*, 10, 50–59.

By all accounts, the psychological contract had been "transformed" by Gerstner's predecessor, who had made significant alterations to the company's commitment to lifelong employment by laying off tens of thousands of employees and capping future medical benefits. Gerstner further transformed the psychological contract by implementing a new compensation program, which was based on pay for performance rather than on corporate loyalty, long service, or entitlement.

By implementing a pay-for-performance compensation program, Gerstner followed the opinion of Bob Knowling, who says that "changing a culture from one of entitlement into a culture of accountability"[30] is a starting point for making a successful change.

According to Rousseau, "a core issue in the management of contract change involves how change is framed"; this means that the "reasons for the change" must be validated and communicated.[31] Gerstner knew and understood that it was "essential to open up a clear and continuous line of communications with IBM employees" and that the end result of a "successful corporate transformation" was to publicly acknowledge the "existence of a crisis." He felt that if the IBM employees didn't believe that there was a real threat, they wouldn't make or accept the need for the urgently needed changes.

Just in the manner in which Gerstner acknowledges the hard work and determination of the "thousands of IBMers who answered the call, put their shoulder to the wheel, and performed magnificently" and how he dedicates his book to acknowledge their efforts, it's evident that the IBMers responded to his plea for change. No stranger to change, Gerstner knew that "management doesn't change culture. Management invites the workforce itself to change the culture."

Leading Change Through Communication   Instrumental to the change was Gerstner's acceptance that he needed to assume the role of chief communicator, which he did willingly and in an outstanding fashion. Gerstner's outstanding communication and leadership skills were the most influential contributing factors in IBM's transformation. By becoming the change agent and the communicator Gerstner was able to express his passion about leading the company into a new era and visibly demonstrate that he was committed to the change and ready to face the challenges along with the rest of his leadership team. Rosabeth Moss Kanter writes in her article "The Enduring Skills of Change Leaders" that leaders should be "offering a dream, stretching their horizons, and encouraging people to do the same" rather than just "announce a plan, launch a task force, and then simply hope that people find the answers."[32]

Gerstner also championed many of the other skills recommended by Kanter, such as "transferring ownership to a working team." Gerstner's belief is that "Great institutions are not managed; they are led," meaning that managers should set goals and objectives and allow their teams to determine the most appropriate manner in which to attain these goals and objectives. Kanter also recommends perseverance; Gerstner admits that it takes time to implement large changes and that it took him "more than five years of daily attention" to transform IBM.

According to Mary Young and James E. Post, the most effective organizations are those that communicate openly, honestly, consistently, and continuously. They also developed a list of

[30] Tichy, N. (1997, April). Bob Knowling's change manual. *FastCompany Magazine*, 76–99. Retrieved from www.fastcompany.com/28813/bob-knowlings-change-manual.

[31] Rousseau, 1996.

[32] Kantner, R.M. (1999). The enduring skills of change leaders. *Leader to Leader, 13*(Summer), 15–22. Retrieved from www.hesselbeininstitute.org/knowledgecenter/journal.aspx?ArticleID=50.

factors that determine the effectiveness of employee communications.[33] It is evident that IBM's successful transformation was facilitated through Gerstner's adherence to these principles:

- The chief executive as the communications champion: Gerstner appointed himself to the position of chief communicator, realizing that this task could not be delegated to anyone else and that he had to personally set the example for others to follow.

- Matching words to actions: Gerstner led IBM by demonstrating his passion, his anger, his directness, which in his own words was "very un-IBM. Very un-CEO-like." Gerstner even went so far as to tell his team that he was "looking for people who make things happen, not who watch and debate things happening."

- Commitment to two-way communications: Gerstner went out into the field to listen to and solicit input from the field employees; he held customer focus sessions, used the internal messaging system to "talk to employees" as well as listen to their concerns, comments, and advice.

- Emphasis on face-to-face communications: Gerstner met regularly with executives and senior members of management; however, he omits to mention how often employees had opportunities to speak with him "live, face-to-face." Face-to-face communication is important; however, with 90,000 employees in 44 countries, *what* is communicated is certainly more important than the medium in which it is communicated.

- The bad news/good news ratio: Gerstner felt it was imperative that employees knew and understood that IBM was in crisis, otherwise they would continue to operate in the same manner; while he felt it was important to communicate the "crisis, its magnitude, its severity, and its impact," he also felt it was necessary to communicate "the new strategy, the new company model, the new culture."

- The employee communication strategy: Young and Post stress that communication is a process, not a product; communication should include the whys and hows, not only the whats; it should be timely, continuous, help employees understand their roles, and should allow employees to formulate their own feelings and opinions. Based on his actions, Gerstner followed this advice and developed an effective communication strategy that helped in IBM's transformation.

Reinforcing the Change   After assessing and reacting to the external environment, creating a new corporate strategy and vision, implementing the change program, convincing skeptical and resistant stakeholders of the need to change, Gerstner's last challenge was to instill a culture that may not necessarily embrace change, but at the very least would not shun and avoid change at any cost.

Gerstner believes that "great companies lay out strategies that are believable and executable" but also writes that "these plans are then reviewed regularly and become, in a sense, the driving force behind everything the company does." He also points out that "execution is all about translating strategies into action programs and measuring their results" and "holding people accountable for them."

Peggy Holman explains that "Change is a process, not an event" and that while "events can be helpful in focusing people's attention, they are only part of the change equation" and

---

[33] Young, M., & Post, J.E. (1993). Managing to communicate, communicating to manage. *Organizational Dynamics, 22*(1), 31–43.

explains that "organizations and communities also need to focus on actively supporting the plans and improvements achieved during the event," otherwise "without such ongoing support, conditions may return to what they were before the event occurred."[34]

Unfortunately, making people accountable and measuring results makes them feel as if they are being tested or evaluated; however, when it comes to objectively evaluating a change program there is no other objective manner in which to assess the program other than to use quantifiable measures. It is a vital part of the change process and can help determine what further changes are needed, because there is always room for continuous improvement.

Konstantin Chagin/Shutterstock

CREATING A LEARNING ORGANIZATION

Objective 5 Explain the relationship of learning with organizational change.

A view among many management scholars is that organizations that effectively change or adapt to changes in their environment are ones that have first "learned"—they have learned how to recognize the need for change, and they have learned what actions are necessary to adapt. This notion of the central role of change is reflected in one of the many definitions of a **learning organization**: "an organization that facilitates the learning of all its members and consciously transforms itself and its context."[35] Learning, in this sense, involves three aspects:

learning organization An organization that facilitates the learning of all its members and consciously transforms itself and its context.

- adapting to its environment
- learning from its people
- contributing to the learning of the wider community or context of which it is a part.

Organizations, like individuals, need to develop and grow—not necessarily in size, but in their capacity to function effectively. Clearly, this demands organizational change. **Organizational development** has been defined as the following:

organizational development A process of planned change that attempts to make organizations better able to meet their short- and long-term objectives.

> a process of planned system change that attempts to make organizations (viewed as social-technical systems) better able to attain their short- and long-term objectives. This is achieved by teaching the organization members to manage their organization processes, structures, and culture more effectively.[36]

Chris Argyris and Donald Schon made a tremendous contribution to the management literature and to the topic of organizational change through their examination of the issue of organizational learning.[37] How do organizations learn? Do organizations learn from their

---

[34] Holman, P. (1999). Unlocking the mystery of effective large-scale change. *At Work*, 8(3), 7–11.

[35] Pedler, J., Burgoyne, R., & Boydell, T. (1997). *The learning organization* (2nd ed.) (p. 3). Maidenhead, UK: McGraw-Hill.

[36] French, W.L., Bell, C.H., & Zawacki, R.A. (Eds.). (1994). *Organization development and transformation: Managing effective change* (4th ed.) (p. 7). Burr Ridge, IL: Irwin.

[37] Argyris, C., & Schon, D. (1978). *Organizational learning: A theory of action perspective*. Reading, MA: Addison-Wesley.

Exhibit 12.4
Organizational Learning

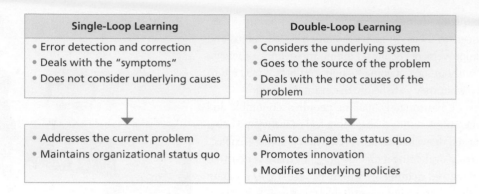

Single-Loop Learning	Double-Loop Learning
• Error detection and correction • Deals with the "symptoms" • Does not consider underlying causes	• Considers the underlying system • Goes to the source of the problem • Deals with the root causes of the problem
• Addresses the current problem • Maintains organizational status quo	• Aims to change the status quo • Promotes innovation • Modifies underlying policies

organizational learning
The detection and correction of error, or the collective experience of individuals within the organization that results in changes in organizational procedure. Three aspects of learning are adapting to the environment, learning from employees, and contributing to the learning of the wider community or context. Two types of learning are single-loop learning and double-loop learning.

single-loop learning The correction of errors that employees find in organizational methods of performance in order to keep the system working. Assumes that the organization has the right systems established but simply needs to fine tune them. Results in incremental improvements and improved efficiency. Addresses symptoms rather than root causes.

double-loop learning The assessment by individuals of whether an error or problem exists in an organization because the systems themselves need to be changed. Requires a deeper level of examination than single-loop learning and typically precedes significant organizational change. Uncovers root causes.

mistakes? This seems to be an abstract notion, and yet it is a very real topic. Argyris and Schon suggest that organizational learning represents the collective experience of individuals within the organization and comes about when organizational procedures change as a result of what has been learned. In this sense, **organizational learning** has been defined as the detection and correction of error.[38] Organizations can learn through individuals acting as agents in an effort to critically examine the methods and functioning of their organization. Argyris and Schon make a distinction between two types of learning: single-loop learning and double-loop learning. It is the latter that constitutes genuine organizational learning and that leads to significant organizational change (see Exhibit 12.4).

Single-loop learning involves the correction of errors that employees may find in organizational methods of performance in order to keep the system working. This approach assumes that the organization has the right systems established but simply needs to fine tune the present system. For example, an organization may find that downsizing permits it to be more flexible with lower costs. However, does reducing the workforce achieve flexibility? Individuals engaging in single-loop learning or adaptive behaviour are essentially functioning within the boundaries or constraints of the presented problem. Single-loop behaviour typically results in making *incremental* improvements and improving efficiency. Such behaviour involves, at best, the modification of strategies or assumptions underlying the strategies in ways that maintain the existing organizational approaches to problems. That is, single-loop learning results in the organization continuing its present policies or achieving its current objectives.

Double-loop learning requires that individuals assess whether an error or problem exists in an organization because the systems themselves need to be changed. Changing organizational systems or assumptions requires a deeper level of examination, and typically is a precursor to significant organizational change. For example, if an organization wants to achieve "flexibility," is this achieved simply through a reduction in the workforce? Perhaps the objective itself of "flexibility" needs to be reevaluated.

Double-loop learning leads to the organization modifying its underlying policies or goals. The double-loop learning process requires innovation and involves challenging the status quo within an organization. Individuals engaged in double-loop learning are not bound by the constraints of the presented problem. Rather, double-loop learning involves an examination of the assumptions and values underlying an organization's functioning. This critical examination culminates in fundamental changes to the present

---

[38] Argyris & Schon, 1978.

system and in recognition of new problems to be solved. These new problems and new solutions will ultimately transform current strategies and assumptions.

Single-loop learning results from addressing the *symptoms* of a problem, while double-loop learning results when individuals attempt to uncover the *root causes* of the problem—questioning why the problem arose in the first place.

What type of learning is dominant in most organizations? Many scholars have suggested that most organizations, at best, encourage single-loop but not double-loop learning. Moreover, it has been suggested that organizations typically create systems that in fact inhibit double-loop learning. For example, the bureaucratic nature of most organizations encourages employees to be methodical and disciplined and, consequently, less likely to question the basic assumptions of most organizational practices.

How do organizations change? According to Argyris and Schon, change is accomplished through double-loop learning. This demands that individuals increase their awareness of the nature of the status quo and of those elements that deserve and require change. What is the ultimate goal? As one scholar commented,

> [The] ultimate goal [is] to help individuals unfreeze and alter their theories of action so that they, acting as agents of the organization, will be able to unfreeze the organizational learning systems that also inhibit double-loop learning.[39]

Argyris and Schon assert that people tend to adopt a single-loop learning approach in organizations rather than developing double-loop learning skills.[40] Argyris states that "We strive to organize our individual and organizational lives by decomposing them into single-loop problems because they are easier to solve and to monitor."[41]

Is the job of management one that demands learning? This is an interesting question. Some critics suggest that management, with its emphasis on concrete results (typically measured in profits, dollars, costs, and so on), has traditionally deemphasized the importance of learning as a necessity of proper management (see Talking Business 12.8).

TALKING BUSINESS 12.8

The Learning Manager

Management scholar Steven Henderson noted the following:

> Why is it that managerial work is not generally as scientific, or learning-oriented, as it could be? In many ways, the process of scientific thinking would appear to be significantly different to that of management thinking, since managers rarely set knowledge as the prime target of their activity. Indeed, the so-called learning curve or learning effect is seen as a consequence of carrying out managerial activity (typically production) rather than prerequisite. Organizations structured along the lines of a "learning laboratory" remain isolated exceptions.

Source: Henderson, S. (1997). Black swans don't fly double loops: The limits of the learning organization? *The Learning Organization, 4*(3), 99.

---

[39] Argyris & Schon, 1978, 4.

[40] Argyris & Schon, 1978.

[41] Argyris, C. (1982). *Reasoning, learning, and action* (p. xii). San Francisco, CA: Jossey-Bass.

Double-Loop Learning and Shifting Paradigms

It would seem that radical organizational change can only come about when the members of an organization are encouraged to engage in double-loop learning. It is akin to making a dramatic departure from the present way of doing things. This has also been referred to in the notion of *shifting paradigms*. Joel Barker, a management consultant and author, in his popular book *Paradigms* (1993), talks about the failure of many organizations to adapt to change. Consider the case of the Swiss watchmakers. Way back in 1968, who dominated the watch industry? Yes—the Swiss, with about 65% of the unit sales in the world. And in fact, back then, if anyone was asked to predict who would remain the leader even 20 or 30 years later, they would probably say the Swiss. However, by 1980, who came to dominate the world watch market? You may have correctly guessed Seiko of Japan. By that year, the Swiss share had fallen to 10% of the market, while Japan (who had held about 1% of the market in 1968) was the dominant force, with Seiko owning about 33% of the world market. From 1979 to 1981 about 50,000 of the 62,000 Swiss watchmakers lost their jobs—a huge disaster for Switzerland. What happened? Well, Japan had focused on electronic technology—the electronic quartz was a natural outcome. Where did this technology come from that allowed Japan to demolish the Swiss's domination of the watch market? The technology came from a research institute in Switzerland.

This story has a particularly ironic twist, because it suggests that the Swiss could have easily maintained their market leadership. However, when the Swiss researchers presented their new idea to Swiss manufacturers back in 1967, the manufacturers rejected it! They considered it inferior—who would want to buy a watch that didn't have a mainspring, didn't need bearings nor almost any gears, and was electronic with battery power? So the manufacturers rejected it, but let their researchers display what they thought was useless technology at the world Watch Congress that year. Seiko, upon observing this invention, had a completely different view—and the result was a dramatic turnaround for Japan and a dramatic failure for the Swiss. What happened here, according to Joel Barker, was a failure to make a paradigm shift.

In Barker's view, change is all about adopting new paradigms. What is this strange concept called a paradigm, and how did it cause the downfall of the Swiss watch industry at that time?

The term **paradigm** can be considered as referring to our set of beliefs or mental framework for understanding how the world operates. We see the world through our paradigms. You might also think of a paradigm as our theories, our assumptions, our beliefs, and our customs. As Joel Barker writes: "A paradigm in a sense tells you that there is a game, what the game is and how to play the game according to the rules." Barker argues that overcoming resistance to change is all about being able to do two things:

paradigm Our mental framework for understanding how the world operates. Our theories, assumptions, sets of beliefs, and customs. Overcoming resistance to change means recognizing the current paradigms that govern our behaviour and shifting to a new paradigm.

1. Recognize the current paradigms that govern our behaviour.

2. Shift to a new paradigm.

So, how does this apply to our example of the Swiss watch industry?

You might consider the Swiss manufacturers as being prisoners of their old paradigm—they could not conceive of the watch industry as ever changing, so it was the old, traditional Swiss watches that would always dominate the market. However, the industry did, in fact, experience a paradigm shift brought about by Seiko, which did adapt its thinking to recognize new consumer tastes: The paradigm governing the rules of the watch industry game changed, but the Swiss still thought they could play the game by the old rules, based on the old paradigm. Consequently, they were victims of failing to adapt to changing conditions, failing to shift away from their old paradigm. The ability to critically examine our paradigms, how we see the world, is very much a part of our ability to accept change, both at the individual and at the organizational level.

Why don't organizations encourage double-loop learning and, consequently, innovation? Clearly, innovation is a desirable objective, yet organizations tend to manifest rules and regulations that facilitate consistency and stability—qualities needed to function effectively on a day-to-day basis. Ironically, it is innovation and the ability to change that are the skills necessary for long-term survival. Unfortunately, organizations do not tend to encourage double-loop learning. If organizations are guilty of inhibiting genuine learning (double-loop learning) and, consequently, failing to generate real change, what are the sources of this dysfunction? We will consider those sources next.

Do Organizations Encourage or Discourage Learning and Change?

Peter Senge, in many ways, popularized the concept of the learning organization as one that encourages all employees to engage in the learning process through dialogue, experimentation, and learning from each other.[42] It has been acknowledged that learning organizations cannot exist without "learning employees."[43] That is, organizational learning and development are facilitated through individual learning and development. The ability of organizations to adapt to and change with a changing environment is dependent on the ability of their members to change and adapt.

Individual change is really about learning—learning new skills, learning or developing new perspectives and new ways of dealing with everyday challenges. Do organizations facilitate individual learning and development? Can organizations provide a learning environment for their employees whereby employees can grow and develop throughout their careers? Given that the traditional bureaucratic organizational structures are rapidly being replaced with more organic structures, it would seem critical to similarly shift greater attention to a more adaptive, innovative type of employee who is better suited to the changing needs of the new organization and capable of changing and developing along with the organization.

Can Employees Learn? Workplace experiences comprise a significant portion of people's lives and, consequently, it is understandable that the manner in which individuals experience their workplaces will have a considerable impact on their growth and development.[44] Adults continue to learn throughout their lifetimes, and their past experience can help or hinder this learning.[45] A number of developmental theorists have emphasized the presence of challenge and stimulation in the environment as a means to encourage learning and development. Environments or experiences that challenge individuals will help bring about development.[46] The workplace is an important element in

---

[42] Senge, P. (1990). *The fifth discipline: The art and practice of the learning organization.* New York, NY: Doubleday.

[43] Dodgson, M. (1993). Organizational learning: A review of some literatures. *Organization Studies, 14,* 375–394.

[44] Glaser, J.S. (1992, June). Connecting the workplace and adult development theory: Self-directed work teams as a petri dish for adult development. Paper presented at the 7th Annual Meeting of the Society for Research in Adult Development. Toronto, Ontario.

[45] Brundage, D.H., & Mackeracher, D. (1980). *Adult learning principles and their application to program planning.* Toronto, ON: Ministry of Education.

[46] Mezirow, J. (1978). Perspective transformation. *Adult Education Quarterly, 28*(2), 100–110.

adult development, with the power to foster or impede development of its members. For example, organizations that encourage self-exploration and information seeking will facilitate individual growth and development.[47] The workplace's influence on individual development results from its ability to promote individual challenge and critical reflection through the introduction of new tasks and responsibilities.[48]

One firm that encourages new challenges as part of its culture is the social networking giant Facebook (see Talking Business 12.9).

TALKING BUSINESS 12.9

Facebook's Culture Promotes Learning and Change

A Bootcamp class, which can range from 3 to 40 new engineers, doesn't look much different during the program from any other group of Facebook engineers. There are lectures and talks from top executives like Vice President of Engineering Mike Schroepfer, and Bootcampers learn about the various product groups in preparation for deciding where they want to work. But for the most part, they work independently mastering Facebook's software code base, the long tables that support their large monitors cluttered with cans of Red Bull and Starbucks iced coffee.

One current Bootcamp attendee, Ali-Reza Adl-Tabatabai, was most recently the director of the programming systems lab and senior principal engineer at Intel Labs.

"You have people coming into the company—they are engineers, but within the week, you are allowing them to change a part of the product that then becomes visible to millions of users," said Adl-Tabatabai. "One thing that really surprised me was how open the culture is. It seems there are no secrets inside."

An early lesson in Bootcamp is that it's fine for any employee to walk up to Zuckerberg or Chief Operating Officer Sheryl Sandberg to talk about an engineering problem or a company issue.

"That is actually very hard to teach people," Seligstein said.

But it is a significant lesson.

"What makes (Facebook) flat is that Zuck is very hands-on with the product," [Joceyln] Goldfein said, [a Facebook director of engineering]. "When he wants to find out what's going on in his organization, he doesn't go talk to the VP, who talks

to the director, who talks to the manager, who talks to the engineer. Zuck goes and talks directly to the engineer."

The "Hacker Way":

CEO Mark Zuckerberg and others at Facebook believe the company's culture is an important element of its success. A look at some of Facebook's key internal values:

- Egalitarian: Facebook lacks hierarchical titles like "principal engineer" or "senior engineer."

- Flat: At no time should there be more than three layers of management between an engineer working on a product and CEO Mark Zuckerberg. Even for a major product like Facebook's new Timeline feature, engineering teams begin as a dozen people or fewer.

- Just Do It: Engineers are expected to tackle problems on their own accord, to build a prototype that fixes a problem, rather than debating how to do something, or spending too much time trying to get it perfect.

- "Hackathons" and "Hack-a-months": Every few months, Facebook engineers pull an all-nighter called Hackathon, trying out software ideas that sometimes turn into real products. Employees are encouraged to do temporary tours with other product teams, something called "Hack-a-month."

Source: Mike Swift, "A look inside Facebook's 'Bootcamp' for new employees, Published on April 18, 2012 via TheStar.com. San Jose Mercury News. Reprinted by permission from YGS Group.

---

[47] Kegan, R. (1982). *The evolving self: Problem and process in human development*. Cambridge, MA: Harvard University Press.

[48] Basseches, M. (1984). *Dialectical thinking and adult development*. Norwood, NJ: Ablex.

What Is Adult Learning Development? There is not one all-encompassing definition of adult learning or development. Among the streams of thought in adult learning and development theory is the notion that development grows out of the interaction of both internal/psychological events and external/social events.[49] Adult development is based on change rather than stability, and this change or growth occurs at a predictable rate and sequence.[50] Individuals can learn from their experience if they can effectively see what changes are involved and how they can be accomplished.[51]

Based on the views cited above, learning from experience essentially involves changing both what one does and how one sees things. As we identified earlier, according to Argyris and Schon, learning in organizations involves the process of detecting and correcting "error."[52] When individuals begin to question or confront the underlying organizational norms and goals that relate to this process of error detection and correction, this constitutes double-loop learning. The question of interest in this regard is, "Do organizations contain elements that encourage or impede challenge, confrontation, and inquiry as a means to facilitate double-loop learning or paradigm shifting in organizations among individuals?" A consideration of the "institutional" nature of organizations offers some insights in this regard.

Bureaucracies and Roles
To understand the ability of organizations to influence individuals in the manner described above, it is useful to consider a theory of organizational behaviour that considers the institutional nature of organizations: **institutionalization theory**.[53] To determine what institutionalization theory has to offer in terms of understanding the influence of organizations on adult learning and development, it is necessary to understand what this theory says about the nature of organizations and their influence on individual behaviour.

Institutionalization involves the processes by which shared beliefs take on a rule-like status. Institutionalization has been defined as a social process through which individuals create a shared definition of what is appropriate or meaningful behaviour.[54] John Meyer and Brian Rowan suggest that organizations that incorporate societally legitimated elements in their formal structures maximize their legitimacy and increase their resources and survival capabilities.[55] Essentially, this perspective acknowledges that organizations often generate "accepted practices" that tend to govern how things are done. These practices may continue even when they are no longer functional, simply because they have become an "ingrained" part of the organization.

Single-loop learning would seem to be a natural consequence of adherence to institutionalized structures. Single-loop learning is emphasized in organizations governed by institutionalized structures—following organizational policy without critically examining behaviour or the policy that dictates behaviour. This is reflected in the image of the "mindless bureaucrat" who follows rules and regulations without considering the necessity of such rules. On the other hand, when individuals are not forced to conform to myriad

institutionalization theory The theory that organizations are driven to incorporate practices and procedures defined by current concepts of work and those accepted or institutionalized by society. Taken-for-granted means of "getting things done" and, as such, not necessarily rational.

institutionalization The processes by which shared beliefs take on a rule-like status. A social process through which individuals create a shared definition of what is appropriate or meaningful behaviour. May generate "accepted practices" that continue even when they are no longer functional.

---

[49] Erikson, E. (1968). Identity and the life cycle. *Psychological Issues Monograph 1*(1).

[50] Erikson, 1968.

[51] Cell, E. (1945). *Learning to learn from experience*. Albany, NY: State university of New York Press.

[52] Argyris & Schon, 1978.

[53] Meyer, J., & Rowan, B. (1977). Institutional organizations: Formal structure as myth and ceremony. *American Journal of Sociology, 83*, 340–363; Zucker, L.G., (1977). Institutionalization as a mechanism of cultural persistence. *American Sociological Review, 42*(2), 726–742.

[54] Zucker, 1977; Meyer & Rowan, 1977.

[55] Meyer & Rowan, 1977.

rules and regulations, they are more likely to engage in thoughtful consideration of the utility of workplace policy to determine whether such policies are effective or ineffective. Consequently, organizations where institutionalized structures are deeply entrenched are less likely to provide an environment conducive to adult learning and development.

Cognitive Scripts   Organizational policy can discourage employees from thinking "outside the box," so to speak. This is also reflected in the notion of **cognitive scripts**. These are scripts we all carry with us in the performance of our jobs. Though they are not concrete or tangible, they are very real. That is, any organization possesses shared meaning regarding how its members should conduct themselves in the performance of their duties.[56] Cognitive scripts or schema have been described as mental pictures (most often unconscious) that serve to organize knowledge in some systematic fashion. Essentially, organizational members can function efficiently in organizations through the use of scripts or schema, to reduce the mass of information to be processed as a means to guide their performance. That is, cognitive scripts may guide thought and behaviour and are based on beliefs about people, situations, or behaviours. A *script* is a type of schema that serves to help understand and enact dynamic patterns of behaviour. A script provides knowledge about expected sequences of events, and guides behaviour for a given situation.

What are the implications of organizational scripts for learning and development in the workplace? **Cognitive learning** is one learning domain that assumes that people have characteristic ways of making sense of the world by organizing that world into abstract categories.[57] These categories change with age and, ideally, should move in the direction of growth. How do organizations impact cognitive learning? Individuals, within social settings, form and use categories in such processes as perception, decision making, and conceptualization. This categorization is intended to reduce the cognitive complexity of the environment. In other words, individuals within organizations often rely on preprogrammed methods of conduct (scripts) and cognitive pictures of their environment. In effect, scripts internalize a routinized approach to performance on the job. Similarly, the use of scripts to guide behaviour in the workplace can potentially discourage individuals from critically examining events and situations each time performance is required.

The reliance on cognitive scripts and schema in the workplace reduces the need to continually question and confront environmental cues. Rather, a preprogrammed approach to dealing with others in the workplace seems to develop. To the extent that reliance is placed on these scripts and schemas, confrontation and change will be discouraged and, consequently, learning and development will be impeded.

Employees can differ in the degree to which they rely on scripts or preprogrammed performance guidelines to govern their work conduct. Work behaviour that is largely scripted discourages employees from engaging in critical evaluation of how their work is conducted. Through their need to maintain reliability and consistency in employee performance, cognitive scripts that we use to function in our jobs can actually generate obstacles to individual-level change and learning. Organizations that encourage a critical evaluation of these scripts are more likely to motivate learning and development among members than are organizations that discourage the critique of established methods of work.

[56] Sims, J.P., Gioia, D.A., et al. (1986). *The thinking organization*. San Francisco, CA: Jossey-Bass.

[57] Piaget, J. (1954). *The construction of reality in the child*. New York, NY: Basic Books; Kohlberg, L. (1969). Stage and sequence: The cognitive developmental approach to socialization. In D.A. Goslin (Ed.), *Handbook of socialization theory and research* (pp. 347–480). Chicago, IL: Randy McNally.

cognitive scripts Mental pictures, usually unconscious, that serve to organize knowledge in some systematic fashion. In relation to business, these are scripts or schema used by organizational members to help them function efficiently by reducing the amount of information they need to process as a means to guide their performance. Can generate obstacles to learning and change.

cognitive learning A learning domain that assumes people have characteristic ways of making sense of the world by organizing that world into abstract categories.

IMPLEMENTING CHANGE THROUGH TIPPING POINT LEADERSHIP

What Is the Tipping Point?

Objective 6 Explain the role of "the tipping point" and its impact on change.

Malcolm Gladwell's 2002 book *The Tipping Point* offers a unique and thought-provoking framework for understanding change and serves to explain some of the reasons for change when it happens in rather unexpected ways. Through the use of terminology borrowed from epidemiology, Gladwell describes change as seeing a virus when it reaches critical mass, or, as he refers to it, "the boiling point." He develops this term to lend itself to an examination of what he refers to as "social epidemics." While the book speaks to many social phenomena dating back to the American Revolution, it also has great relevance to organizational change.

One of the ideas that he discusses is the phenomena of *word of mouth* and its ability to bring about change. As well, the book addresses the notion of change occurring as an epidemic within an organization, beginning at the periphery and moving to the core. Finally, contrary to the idea of slow and steady change, the premise of Gladwell's book is to understand change that happens quickly and successfully.

Three Rules of the Tipping Point

Gladwell has developed three rules of epidemics: (1) the law of the few—that is, there are exceptional people who possess social connections, personality, energy, and enthusiasm to be able to spread "the word" (idea or product) in epidemic proportions; (2) the stickiness factor—that is, there are specific ways to make a message memorable in terms of presenting and structuring information to influence the impact it will make; and (3) the power of context—discussed in two parts, essentially that "human beings are a lot more sensitive to their environment than they may think."[58]

The Law of the Few   The **law of the few** divides these "exceptional" people who essentially control the power of word-of-mouth epidemics into three categories. They are, as Gladwell has named them, Connectors, Mavens, and Salesmen.

Connectors, most simply put, know a lot of people. They are critical to the instigation of a word-of-mouth epidemic. Gladwell repeatedly uses the example of Paul Revere, who sparked the American Revolution by riding miles during the night to warn of Britain's impending attack. Gladwell contrasts the success of this word-of-mouth campaign with William Dawes, who, in collaboration with Revere, embarked on the same ride but with a lower success rate: Fewer people were called into action by Dawes than by Revere. This, Gladwell explains, attests to the fact that Revere was a Connector, someone who had a great social network. Connectors, Gladwell describes, are so well connected because "they manage to occupy many different worlds and subcultures and niches."[59] Hence, the ability to be able to diffuse an idea is greatly increased. Finally, he states, "that the closer an idea or product comes to a

law of the few One of the three rules of Malcolm Gladwell's tipping point theory that states there are exceptional people (Connectors, Mavens, and Salesmen) who possess social connections, personality, energy, and enthusiasm to be able to spread the word in epidemic proportions.

Connectors Individuals who know a lot of people, are well-connected socially, and therefore are critical to the instigation of a word-of-mouth epidemic.

---

[58] Gladwell, M. (2002). *The tipping point: How little things can make a big difference* (p. 29). New York, NY: Little Brown and Company.

[59] Gladwell, 2002, 48.

Connector, the more power and opportunity it has."[60] Therefore, based on this explanation, had Dawes been a Connector his success rate would have been greater.

The second category of people in the law of the few are **Mavens**, from the Yiddish word meaning "one who accumulates knowledge." This term, also employed as a marketing concept, is important to economists analyzing Mavens' effects on the marketplace. Mavens are people who have information "on a lot of different products or prices or places."[61] Gladwell introduces a Maven by the name of Mark Alpert, whom he describes as pathologically helpful, even so far as writing to *Consumer Reports* to offer corrections. Mavens, he describes, are important in starting word-of-mouth epidemics because "they know things the rest of us don't."[62] Mavens have the ability to start word-of-mouth epidemics not only because of their knowledge and social skills, but also because their motivation is pure, based on a desire to "help out"; therefore, they appear to be unbiased and people accept their message or information more willingly.

The final category, **Salesmen**, have the skills to persuade those who are not convinced by the data provided by the Mavens or the message spread by the Connectors. Salesmen possess natural exuberance and are finely tuned (albeit often subconsciously) to nonverbal communication. Moreover, it is the subtle, hidden, and unspoken communication that often determines the Salesmen's success. While Salesmen are known for their persuasiveness, it is not through overt tactics that they are able to persuade. It is a genuine interest that makes them mesmerizing and, in turn, persuasive.

The Stickiness Factor

The second rule of epidemics is called the **stickiness factor**— that is, the quality of a message to ensure that it "sticks"; it is the method of presenting information in a memorable way. The tangible descriptor Gladwell uses is the television program *Sesame Street* and how it was created to cause an epidemic of literacy in children. The creators of the television program endeavoured to create a program that would increase literacy in children through a medium that was not known to elicit such a reward. Gladwell describes a process of testing and reworking the program to arrive at a "sticky" version that accomplished its intended goal. The importance of "stickiness" is that the idea needs to resonate with people so that it becomes memorable. Gladwell poses a question as he considers the notion of stickiness in comparison to the importance of the messenger: "Is it so memorable, in fact, that it can create change, that it can spur someone to action?"[63]

Although the law of the few states that it is the exceptional people who start the epidemics and all that is required is you find them, stickiness has the same applicability— there is a simple way to present information to make it irresistible, and the only requirement is you find the right way. To sum, while the messenger is critical to spreading the message, the content of the message is equally important.

The Power of Context

The third rule of epidemics is called the **power of context**, which is described in two parts. The first part pertains to the environment: "epidemics are sensitive to the conditions and circumstances of the times and place in which they occur."[64] Gladwell illustrates this using the "broken windows" theory, borrowed from criminologists James Q. Wilson and George Kelling. The theory states that if a window is broken and left unrepaired, people will draw the conclusion that there is no place for

---

Mavens People who are knowledgeable and have a lot of information on products, prices, and places. They often start word-of-mouth epidemics because they have knowledge the rest of us don't, and many people rely on them to make informed decisions.

Salesmen Individuals who are unusually charismatic and have the skills to persuade even those who are unconvinced by Connectors or Mavens.

stickiness factor One of the three rules of Malcolm Gladwell's tipping point theory that states there are specific ways to make a message memorable in terms of presenting and structuring information to influence the impact it will have.

power of context One of the three rules of Malcolm Gladwell's tipping point theory that consists of two parts: (1) Word-of-mouth epidemics are sensitive to the environment in which they occur; and (2) groups play a significant role in spreading word-of-mouth epidemics.

---

[60] Gladwell, 2002, 55.

[61] Gladwell, 2002, 62.

[62] Gladwell, 2002, 67.

[63] Gladwell, 2002, 92.

[64] Gladwell, 2002, 139.

authority and order, and in turn more windows will be broken, inviting a graduation in the severity of crimes committed.[65] He posits that the broken window theory and power of context are one and the same in that the smallest changes in the environment can lead to an epidemic that can be tipped or reversed. He states that behaviour is a "function of social context" and that in this situation "what really matters is little things."[66]

The second part of the power of context is the critical role that groups play in social epidemics. Gladwell introduces the notion of groups and their importance in initiating and sustaining change by creating a community to practise and support the change. Borrowing from cognitive psychology and research by anthropologist Robin Dunbar, Gladwell describes the Rule of 150, which asserts that human beings are most capable of having genuine social interaction with a maximum of 150 individuals.[67] He describes an organization that uses this model and has had tremendous success. The strength behind this notion is that "in order to create one contagious movement, you often have to create many small movements first."[68]

Applying the Tipping Point to Organizational Change

As mentioned previously, human interaction is of great importance in how we receive information, specifically information pertaining to change. Therefore, the concept of the law of the few has strong relevance to the organizational context.

"Word-of-mouth" change may seem like an unorganized and unconventional approach to implementing change within an organization. For an organization to draw upon hidden resources such as the Connectors, Mavens, and Salesmen already within its ranks, there exists the potential to bring about a change epidemic.

Wanda Orlikowski and J. Debra Hofman discuss the need for change to be flexible and not based on a fixed beginning, middle, and end point. To accomplish this they suggest being more open to the opportunities that arise during change.[69] A word-of-mouth change "epidemic" in an organization requires at least some prior commitment by the "few" key organizational members.

A second approach to change based on Gladwell's framework is implementing change from the periphery (that is, small groups) in an organization and then moving to the corporate core, as is suggested by Michael Beer, Russell Eisenstat, and Bert Spector.[70] What the authors suggest is change that is mandated from the most senior levels within the organization and delivered in a "top-driven" fashion will not lead to success, as opposed to change that begins far from corporate headquarters and is initiated by line managers and employees. The underlying rationale is that at the "grassroots" level there is a greater understanding of the individual roles and responsibilities and the changes that are required to bring about change. Instead, senior management should create a culture for change and support initiatives at the grassroots level and allow it to move to the corporate core, as opposed to mandating change in the opposite direction.

---

[65] Gladwell, 2002, 141.

[66] Gladwell, 2002, 150.

[67] Gladwell, 2002, 179.

[68] Gladwell, 2002, 192.

[69] Orlikowski, W.J., & Hofman, J.D. (1997). An improvisational model for change management. *Sloan Management Review* (Winter), 11–21. [This article is directed at technological change; however, I am applying the model more broadly to change initiatives, as I think it has great relevance.]

[70] Beer, M., Eisenstat, R.A., & Spector, B. (1990). Why change programs don't produce change. In T.D. Jick & M.A. Peiperl (Eds.), *Managing change: Cases and concepts* (pp. 229–241). New York, NY: McGraw-Hill/Irwin.

Again, if we look at the law of the few and assume that an organization has a culture that encourages change, then it is possible that change can be initiated or "tipped" by either a Connector, Maven, or Salesmen. This outside/in-driven philosophy could remedy the failures that organizations encounter when attempting top-driven change. Of course, this philosophy does require participation and awareness from the senior levels, primarily in understanding and seeking out, perhaps from the human resources function, these Connectors, Mavens, and Salesmen and engaging them in an idea or further allowing them to engage the organization with their ideas.

The concept of identifying and allowing the role of a change agent to move from a senior leadership function to an employee-driven process for a change initiative to take hold and "tip" within an organization is a powerful notion. As suggested by Beer and colleagues, the potential for change could be significantly increased if initiated by employees and if the process of engagement is also employee driven. If employees see the value in the change and it is initiated by a respected peer (that is, a Salesman or Connector), employee support for the change would increase significantly as opposed to a mandated or programmatic change that does not have employee "buy-in" or support.

The power of context also has relevance here, as Gladwell states that groups also play a critical role in initiating and sustaining change. Further, as stated earlier, to have one contagious movement you often have to have many small movements first. Again, speaking to the power of change occurring at the *periphery* and moving inward, if there are many small movements started locally the power of these movements to grow into one large movement and eventually "tip" into large-scale change is a strong possibility and presents a compelling and lasting model for change.

If organizations are willing to accept some risk, to take some of the control away from senior management and place it in the hands of the Connectors, Mavens, and Salesmen and place more emphasis on the impact that employees can have on one another, the potential for any change to "tip" (that is, spread) within an organization is great. We must embrace the idea that change is possible, that people can change their behaviour, and that it can happen quickly. All we need to do is consider the right "triggers" to make it all happen. As Gladwell suggests,

> What must underlie successful epidemics, in the end, is a bedrock belief that change is possible, that people can radically transform their behaviour or beliefs in the face of the right kind of impetus.[71]

CHAPTER SUMMARY

Every organization must contend with a changing environment. These changes may stem from economic, labour, global, competitive, legal/political, technological, or societal sources. This chapter emphasized the importance of understanding how organizations facilitate or resist change. We considered the notion of double-loop and single-loop learning, and how organizations might effect these types of learning among their employees. We discussed the tipping point for change as a theory of how to spread change in an organization. Sources of resistance to change were specifically identified, as well as organizational responses to resistance.

---

[71] Gladwell, 2002, 258.

CHAPTER LEARNING TOOLS

Key Terms

cognitive learning 478

cognitive scripts 478

Connectors 479

developmental
  change 461

double-loop learning 472

institutionalization 477

institutionalization
  theory 477

law of the few 479

learning organization 471

Mavens 480

organizational
  development 471

organizational
  learning 472

paradigm 474

power of context 480

Salesmen 480

single-loop learning 472

sociotechnical redesign 466

stickiness factor 480

Theory E change 464

Theory O change 464

transformational
  change 462

transitional change 462

Multiple-Choice Questions

Select the *best* answer for each of the following questions. Solutions are located in the back of your textbook.

1. When a business makes a small improvement in something it is currently doing, this type of change is called a
   a. technological change
   b. transitional change
   c. competitive change
   d. developmental change

2. When a business replaces an old product for a new one, this type of change is called a
   a. competitive change
   b. transitional change
   c. developmental change
   d. transformational change

3. Trying something completely new where the result is unknown and uncertain is called a
   a. transformational change
   b. developmental change
   c. competitive change
   d. developmental change

4. Theory E change can involve
   a. maximizing shareholder value
   b. changes to organizational structure and systems
   c. the participation of employees
   d. both A and B

5. Theory O change can involve
   a. developing organizational capabilities
   b. developing a culture that supports learning
   c. the participation of all employees
   d. all of the above

6. Which type of learning involves finding and correcting an error?
   a. Single-loop   b. Double-loop
   c. Theory E   d. Theory O

7. Which type of learning involves changing the company's status quo and modifying underlying policies?
   a. Theory E
   b. Theory O
   c. Double-loop
   d. Single-loop

8. The meaning of *paradigm* can refer to
   a. our ability to learn new skills
   b. our set of beliefs or our mental framework for understanding the world
   c. a model of learning
   d. a learning organization

9. The meaning of *institutionalization* can be referred to as
   a. a special process in which individuals share an idea of what is appropriate behaviour
   b. a form of management structure
   c. how organizations generate a set of accepted practices
   d. both A and C

10. The word-of-mouth approach is associated with the
    a. societal force   b. tipping point
    c. cognitive scripts   d. none of the above

11. Exceptional people who possess energy and enthusiasm to spread the word is a rule of
    a. societal force   b. cognitive scripts
    c. the law of the few   d. learning organizations

12. Connectors typically
    a. know a lot of people
    b. are important to the word-of-mouth epidemic
    c. ensure the quality of the message so it sticks
    d. both A and B

13. The stickiness factor involves making information
    a. memorable
    b. sticky
    c. irresistible
    d. all of the above

14. Mavens are people who
    a. have information
    b. appear unbiased
    c. know things the rest of us don't
    d. all of the above

15. In the power of context, two important factors are
    a. Salesmen and Mavens
    b. Connectors and word of mouth
    c. the environment and groups
    d. none of the above

Discussion Questions

1. Identify and discuss the forces of change.

2. Compare and contrast developmental, transitional, and transformational change.

3. Explain the difference between Theory E and Theory O change.

4. Discuss what type of change is required for long-term change.

5. What are the differences between single-loop and double-loop learning?

6. What is the meaning of a paradigm shift?

7. Explain the three rules of the tipping point theory.

8. Discuss the law of the few and the three categories of people who control the power of the word of mouth.

9. What is adult learning development?

10. What is the meaning of institutionalization?

CONCEPT APPLICATION   WHEN GOOD COMPANIES GO BAD: THE CASE OF KODAK

The Eastman Kodak company was established by George Eastman in 1880. Eastman Kodak sold the world's first flexible roll film in 1888 and continued to transform photography into a major sensation with a $1 Brownie camera in 1900. Among its greatest innovations was Kodachrome, a slide and motion-picture film embraced for 74 years. While colour photography had existed since the 1860s, Eastman Kodak Company's introduction of its Kodachrome film in 1935 made the old system of dealing with heavy glass plates, tripods, an exacting development procedure, and inferior quality pictures all obsolete.[72]

The Kodachrome process was invented by Leopold Godowsky Jr. and Leopold Mannes, two scientists who worked at Kodak's research facility in Rochester, New York. The film's high quality and relative ease of use made it the dominant film for both professionals and amateurs for much of the 20th century. Kodak and its Kodachrome process were responsible for providing images that became historical icons of the 20th century, including capturing a colour version of the Hindenburg's fireball explosion in 1936, and President Kennedy's

---

[72] Suddath, C. (2009, June 23). A brief history of Kodachrome. *Time Magazine*. Retrieved from http://content.time.com/time/arts/article/0,8599,1906503,00.html.

assassination in 1963.[73] During the 1960s, Kodak's easy-load Instamatic 126 became one of the most popular cameras in history, replacing the old box cameras.

It's not surprising, then, that by 1976 Kodak was responsible for 90% of film sales and 85% of camera sales in the United States. It was consistently ranked as one of the world's five most valuable brands.[74] So it seemed impossible to anyone that a company this large and successful company could ever disappear.

Fast forward to September 2011, when Kodak's stock, which had reached $94 in 1997, slid below $1 a share for the first time and, by January 6, 2012, hit an all-time closing low of 37 cents.[75] It filed for bankruptcy protection that same year. Essentially, Kodak had dominated the market until the 1990s, but by then things started to fall apart. What happened? How could this once great company go bad?

On the face of it, the answer is relatively straightforward. Undoubtedly, the digital revolution buried the film business that was once Kodak's mainstay. Essentially Kodak neglected to fully acknowledge the threat that digital technology posed to its business until it was too late.

However, there is a major ironic twist in this story: Kodak invented the digital camera in 1975. By 1975, employing a new type of electronic sensor, engineer Steven Sasson created the first prototype digital camera, capturing black-and-white images at a resolution of 0.1 megapixels. In 1979, a Kodak executive even generated a report that estimated how different segments of the market would switch from film to digital by 2010. The report was eerily accurate, albeit the date of this switch could likely be pinpointed to even earlier than 2010.[76]

From about the mid- to late 1990s, digital camera sales start to significantly increase. While competitors pursued methods of enhancing the digital future of the camera, Kodak largely remained inactive. Film was slowly becoming outdated. By the early 2000s, with deteriorating film sales, Kodak attempted to profit from other markets like drugs and chemicals, but with largely mixed results. In 2003, Kodak launched its Easyshare printer dock 6000, focusing on printing quality photos.

Once Kodak did begin to seriously enter the market it neglected to focus its efforts on the youth-driven consumer. At this point, digital cameras had become a huge item, so Kodak faced many competitors. Kodak could have used its leading-edge technologies to develop other items, such as cellphones, but instead it kept its focus on printers. In 2004, Kodak was forced to cut thousands of jobs and close factories. This sense of urgency had only now become real for the company. During the mid-2000s, Kodak attempted to rebrand itself but at that point it could no longer effectively compete nor attract enough interest within the digital camera market. As of 2013, Kodak still struggled to emerge from bankruptcy and failed to regain its past glory. At that point, its aim was simply to entirely leave the consumer business and focus instead on providing products and services to the commercial imaging market.

So, looking at the facts, Kodak was certainly not taken by surprise by the new digital technology. It not only had ample warning but ironically it was the prophet of

[73] Suddath, 2009.

[74] Naughton, J. (2012, January 22). Could Kodak's demise have been averted? *The Guardian*. Retrieved from www.theguardian.com/technology/2012/jan/22/john-naughton-kodak-lessons.

[75] Rubin, J. (2012, January 19). Kodak's snapshot of an era. *Toronto Star*. Retrieved from www.thestar.com/business/2012/01/19/kodaks_snapshot_of_an_era.html.

[76] Bertucci, K. (2012, January 30). Kodak moments now a thing of the past: The rise and fall of the great American company. *Gadget Review*. Retrieved from www.gadgetreview.com/2012/01/kodak-moments-now-a-thing-of-the-past-the-rise-and-fall-of-a-great-american-company.html.

Case Continued >

its own demise. It developed the technology that essentially revolutionized its industry. Unfortunately, it neglected to exploit that lead. Why?

Clayton Christensen's *The Innovator's Dilemma* explains why and how successful firms can be destroyed by disruptive innovations. That is, even companies that seem to be doing everything correctly from listening to customers to investing in research and

© Stuwdamdorp/Alamy

development can be undermined by innovation. Christensen argues that large companies are adept at nurturing "sustaining" innovations (innovation that enhances their position in established markets). However, those same companies are incapable at dealing with innovations that entirely disrupt those markets.[77]

Imagine how difficult it would be for a company that had close to a monopoly on the market to give that up and take a chance on this new technology. And ironically, if that technology proved successful, it would reduce the company's profit margins! So, imagine Kodak discovering this technology and then considering its options. If it introduced this technology it risked cannibalizing its existing products. And if it invested all this money into this new technology and it failed, it could have lost a tonne of money. Why take the risk?

According to some observers, the biggest lesson to be learned from Kodak's failure is that even successful companies need to continually innovate. A case in point has been Apple. Apple has always struggled to transform its most popular products into better versions of themselves. This company consistently attempts to transform the industry it operates within by launching "game changing" products. The fact is, Kodak had a lot in common with Apple. It did innovate and was the first to release the digital camera—definitely a game-changing product. However, it failed to follow through with its technology and consequently they were left behind. Similarly, Apple can only lead the market for as long as it can innovate.[78]

Change management expert and Harvard Business School professor John Kotter sums it up nicely:

> How can CEOs learn from Kodak's failure? . . . One key to avoiding complacency is to ensure these innovators have a voice with enough volume to be heard (and listened to) at the top. . . . If they are given the power to lead, they will continue to innovate, help keep a culture of urgency and affect change.[79]

Questions

1. What were the forces of change acting on this industry?
2. Why was it so difficult for Kodak to adapt to change?
3. Discuss the notion of a paradigm and double- and single-loop learning and their role in the case of Kodak.

---

[77] Naughton, 2012.

[78] Bertucci, 2012.

[79] Kotter, J. (2012, May 2). Barriers to change: The real reason behind the Kodak downfall. *Forbes*. Retrieved from http://www.forbes.com/sites/johnkotter/2012/05/02/barriers-to-change-the-real-reason-behind-the-kodak-downfall.

Appendix: Answers to Multiple-Choice Questions

Chapter 1

1. B 2. D 3. B 4. C 5. D 6. D 7. D 8. D 9. D
10. B 11. A 12. D 13. B 14. C 15. B

Chapter 2

1. D 2. B 3. A 4. B 5. C 6. D 7. D 8. D 9. B
10. D 11. D 12. C 13. A 14. C 15. D

Chapter 3

1. B 2. D 3. A 4. C 5. D 6. A 7. D 8. B 9. D
10. B 11. C 12. C 13. D 14. D 15. C

Chapter 4

1. D 2. A 3. C 4. A 5. B 6. A 7. A 8. D 9. C
10. A 11. D 12. B 13. A 14. A 15. D

Chapter 5

1. D 2. B 3. A 4. D 5. D 6. A 7. D 8. D 9. D
10. B 11. C 12. C 13. C 14. D 15. D

Chapter 6

1. B 2. C 3. D 4. C 5. D 6. D 7. A 8. C 9. D
10. B 11. A 12. D 13. C 14. A 15. B

Chapter 7

1. B 2. D 3. A 4. D 5. B 6. A 7. D 8. B 9. B
10. B 11. C 12. C 13. D 14. D 15. B

Chapter 8

1. D 2. D 3. A 4. A 5. D 6. D 7. D 8. A 9. D
10. B 11. C 12. C 13. C 14. D 15. A

Chapter 9

1. A 2. D 3. D 4. A 5. D 6. C 7. A 8. D 9. A
10. A 11. B 12. D 13. C 14. D 15. C

Chapter 10

1. D 2. D 3. B 4. A 5. D 6. A 7. C 8. D 9. D
10. B 11. D 12. D 13. D 14. D 15. D

Chapter 11

1. D 2. D 3. D 4. B 5. A 6. B 7. B 8. B 9. C
10. A 11. D 12. A 13. C 14. D 15. C

Chapter 12

1. D 2. B 3. A 4. D 5. D 6. A 7. C 8. B 9. D
10. B 11. C 12. D 13. D 14. D 15. C

Glossary

acquisition A way to achieve diversification, when a firm acquires the majority of shares in another firm. 185, 286

activist government A government that intervenes in the employment relationship by passing laws that restrict freedom of contract, such as employment standards, human rights, health and safety, and employment equity laws. 51

administrative management Henri Fayol's philosophy of management, one of the three major classical approaches (the others being scientific and bureaucratic management). It focuses on the principles of division of work, unity of command, subordination of employees' individual interests to the common good, and *esprit de corps*. *See* bureaucratic management and scientific management. 92

Asia-Pacific Economic Cooperation (APEC) A trading bloc formed in 1989. Among the members are the People's Republic of China, Hong Kong, Japan, Indonesia, Malaysia, South Korea, Canada, and the United States, to name a few of the 21 members. 297

Association of Southeast Asian Nations (ASEAN) The first major free trade bloc in Asia. It aimed to promote greater cooperation in areas such as industry and trade among its members. 297

"at will" employment A concept used in US labour law that allows employers to terminate employees without any notice for any reason. At-will employment does not exist in Canada. 57

attribute A business advantage of some kind, which might include having a highly skilled staff, a patented technology, a unique marketing strategy, a well-known brand, or something else that makes the company a leader in its field. *See* competitive advantage. 16

authoritative culture A culture where rules are dictated and individual discretion is limited; has the effect of suppressing the development of ethical decision making. 370

backward integration A type of diversification that refers to an extension or expansion of firm value chain activities by integrating productive processes (backward) toward the source of raw materials. 184

bailout A type of government support to business to prevent an organization or industry from financial collapse, often in the form of a loan or loan guarantee. 329

balance of trade The value of all goods and services a country exports minus the value of goods and services it imports. 215

Bank of Canada Canada's central bank, which is a Crown corporation of the federal government. It regulates the banking and financial industry to ensure low inflation, high employment levels, and positive long-term economic growth for Canada. 225

bank rate The rate at which the Bank of Canada loans money to financial institutions. 225

bargaining power The amount of power workers have to determine their conditions of employment with their employer, such as wages, hours, training, vacation time, health and safety measures, and other factors. 51

bargaining power of buyers The power held by individuals or organizations that purchase incumbents' products or services. Buyers can exert power by demanding lower prices, better quality or services, or playing incumbents against one another. 167

bargaining power of suppliers The power held by firms, organizations, and individuals that provide raw materials, technologies, or skills to incumbents in an industry. Suppliers can exert power by demanding better prices or threatening to reduce the quality of purchase goods or services. 166

barriers to entry Obstacles that may prevent another company from entering a given market. Could include high capital costs, government regulations, customer brand loyalties, intellectual property, and high switching costs. 204

behavioural approaches to management Managerial perspectives that consider the social or human side of organizations and address the challenges of managing people. Assume that achieving maximum productivity requires understanding the human factor of organizations and creating an environment that permits employees to fulfill social, not only economic, needs. *See* classical approaches to management. 98

Big Six Canada's six largest banks, including CIBC, Scotiabank, TD Canada Trust, BMO, RBC, and National Bank. 15

biological diversity The different forms of life and number of species on earth. It includes people, plants, animals, bacteria, and other living organisms. 420

borderless corporation or transnational corporation (TNC) A multinational corporation that is not linked with one specific home country. Such an enterprise thus has no clear nationality. 288

bounded rationality The idea that humans often do not make decisions that would maximize their personal utility because they either lack the necessary information to assess the various options or lack the capacity to assess the information they have. 51

branch plants Subsidiaries (of companies in another country) that do not perform the complete range of functions necessary to offer a product in the marketplace. Typically, subsidiaries defer responsibility of higher-level strategic functions to the parent company. 24

budget deficit The negative difference between incoming tax revenues and outgoing government expenditures. Like a bank overdraft, a deficit means the cash outflows are greater than the cash inflows in a given period. 219

bureaucratic management One of the classical approaches to management (the others being scientific and administrative management) that focuses more broadly on the organization as a whole and incorporates the ideas of rules and procedures, hierarchy of authority, division of labour, impersonality, and selection and promotion. Associated with Max Weber. *See* scientific management and administrative management. 92

business cycle The rise and fall of economic activity over time. There are five stages: expansionary, peak, contraction, trough, and recovery. 210

business enterprise system The system all developed countries possess that determines what goods and services are distributed to society and how those goods and services are produced and distributed. The decisions may be made by government or by business or both. 312

business ethics The rules, standards, principles, or codes giving guidelines for morally right behaviour in certain contexts. 358

business-level strategy A strategy a firm uses to compete in a given market. Three business-level strategies are cost leadership, product differentiation, and focus. 173

Cabinet Members of Parliament who are appointed by the prime minister to oversee an assigned government ministry or department. 317

capital One of the five factors of production. Includes buildings, machines, tools, and other physical components used in producing goods and services. 198

capitalism An economic system based on the rights of the individual, the rights of private property, and competition and minimal government interference. 312

carbon footprint A measurement of the total amount of greenhouse gas emissions from a person, product, event, or organization. 416

categorical imperative The assertion by the philosopher Immanuel Kant that moral actions are, by definition, actions that respect others. 358

centralization The degree to which decision-making authority in an organization is concentrated at the top level. 128

change A shift in how an organization operates. 5

Charter of Rights and Freedoms A part of the Canadian Constitution that governs the relationship between governments and citizens by protecting fundamental rights and freedoms of Canadians against state interference. 59

Chester Barnard An organizational practitioner who served as president of the New Jersey Bell Telephone company; he was interested in organizational structure, but he considered organizations to be social systems. He focused on communication and authority in management practices. 100

classical approaches to management The oldest of the formalized perspectives of management, which arose in the late 19th and early 20th centuries during a period of rapid industrialization in the US and European business sectors. Includes scientific, administrative, and bureaucratic management. *See* scientific, administrative, and bureaucratic management. 88

climate change Changes in climate caused by a significant change in weather patterns, either from natural causes like oceanic processes, or unnatural causes like human interference. 412

cloning forces Pressure on organizations to imitate the behaviour of industry leaders. "Jumping on the bandwagon," or "keeping up with the corporate Joneses." 154

closed systems Entities viewed as being fully self-sufficient and thus requiring no interaction with the environment, which is difficult to find in practice. 126

codes of conduct Rules created by business to reflect the general values of society in business practices; one means of "institutionalizing" ethics in corporations. This involves incorporating ethics formally and explicitly into daily business life. 370

cognitive learning A learning domain that assumes people have characteristic ways of making sense of the world by organizing that world into abstract categories. 478

cognitive legitimacy The level of public knowledge about a new industry and its conformity to established norms and methods reflected in the extent to which it is taken for granted as a desirable and appropriate activity. 241

cognitive scripts Mental pictures, usually unconscious, that serve to organize knowledge in some systematic fashion. In relation to business, these are scripts or schema used by organizational members to help them function efficiently by reducing the amount of information they need to process as a means to guide their performance. Can generate obstacles to learning and change. 478

collaboration In behavioural approaches to management, the consequence of managers and workers viewing themselves as collaborators or partners. 101

collective bargaining A process of negotiation measures between a group of employees (through a union) and an employer (or group of employers) leading to a collective agreement that applies to the entire group of employees. 51

commoditization The process by which a differentiated good becomes undifferentiated in the market. Consumers, thus, become more focused on price, which in turn forces firms to continuously squeeze out more cost savings from their production processes. 250

common law of the employment contract All of the rules of interpretation of employment contracts applied by judges over the years, as recorded in legal decisions. 56

common market Economic integration that goes beyond free trade areas and customs unions and includes, for example, freer flow of labour and capital across members' borders and a common trade policy regarding nonmembers. *See* free trade area, customs union, and economic union. 295

communism An economic system where the government owns or controls essentially all of a country's economic resources. 202

compartmentalizing In scientific management, the result of Frederick Taylor's pursuit of the one best method of performing a job, which involves breaking the job down into its most fundamental steps or components. Also called specializing. 90

competition When two or more sellers offer the same or similar products or services to consumers. 204

competitive advantage Achieved when an organization excels in one or more attributes that allow it to outperform its competitors. *See* attribute. 16

competitive forces The domestic and foreign competitor influences on organizational decisions. Competitors are organizations operating in the same industry and selling similar products and services. However, competitors may compete in different ways. 8

competitive markets Markets in which there are a sufficient number of participants competing for the same goods, services, and customers. Market forces tend to fix prices at a point where the supply of a good or service equals the demand for that good or service. 49

connectors Individuals who know a lot of people, are well-connected socially, and therefore are critical to the instigation of a word-of-mouth epidemic. 479

consolidation strategy An alternative for firms that are in the decline phase of their industry life cycle whereby a firm acquires the best of the remaining firms in the market to enhance its market power, to generate economies of scale, and to allow for synergies. 253

constraining forces Practices that come to define what are perceived as legitimate management structures and activities and that, consequently, place pressure on organizations to conform to these institutional roles. 153

consumer price index (CPI) A price index that measures commodities commonly purchased by households, such as food, clothing, transportation, education, shelter, and recreation. 224

contingency approach to management The acknowledgement that there is no one best way to manage and that different conditions and situations require the application of different approaches or techniques. Includes consideration of organization size, environmental uncertainty, routineness of task technology, and individual differences. 102

contingency theory A natural outgrowth of systems theory, which recognizes that all organizations are open systems that can only survive through continuous and successful interaction with their environment. A central philosophy underlying contingency theory is that there is no one ideal way to organize. 133

contraction phase A phase in the business life cycle that is characterized by declining economic activity and falling profits. 211

control Typically achieved when a company or individual owns greater than 50% of the shares of another company. However, it can sometimes be achieved by other factors, such as management influence. 281

coordination In behavioural approaches to management, the harmonizing of workers and activities to maximize productivity. Mary Parker Follett argued that management needed to be closely involved with subordinates in the daily conduct of their work, rather than simply being people who made and enforced rules. 101

corporate-level strategy A strategy a firm uses to determine what businesses or markets it should compete in, and how these businesses or markets can be managed to create synergy. 179

corporate memory The knowledge of individuals who are a central part of an organization's knowledge base. If they are eliminated by downsizing there is a significant loss of informal bridges, business relationships, customer ties, friendship ties, and so on that bond people together in the workplace. 151

corporate social responsibility (CSR) Obligations or responsibilities of an organization to go beyond the production of goods or services at a profit, and beyond the requirements of competition, legal regulation, or custom, thus acting in a way desirable in terms of the values and objectives of society. This includes a business's economic, legal, ethical, and philanthropic responsibilities. 383

corporate welfare A term used to refer to government assistance given to businesses. 337

cost leadership strategy A business-level strategy that aims to reduce economic costs below that of all competitors to gain a competitive advantage. The strategy often requires aggressive construction of efficient-scale facilities, vigorous pursuit of cost reductions from experience, tight cost and overhead control, avoidance of marginal customer accounts, and cost minimization in areas like R&D, service, sales, marketing and advertising, and general administration. 173

cost-push inflation A type of inflation that occurs when increases in production costs for businesses "push" up the final price that consumers have to pay. 224

creative destruction A term that explains how innovations sweep away old technologies, skills, products, ideas, and industries and replace them with new ones. 258

critical perspective A perspective that believes the interests of labour (workers) and capital (the owners and managers of economic organizations) are irreconcilably in conflict. The objective of capital is to extract from labour maximum effort and control at minimal cost. Since workers depend on capital for their basic needs in a capitalist system, and there are almost always more workers than jobs, labour is inherently disadvantaged and subject to exploitation at the hands of the more powerful capitalists. 52

cross-functional teams Work groups that bring together members from various parts of the organization. 121

Crown corporation A federal or provincial-run government agency, also called a public enterprise, that is accountable to Parliament for its operations through a minister. Examples include Canada Post (federal) and the Liquor Control Board of Ontario (provincial). 320

currency risk The potential risk of financial loss due to transactions in multiple currencies. 218

customs union Economic integration with the removal of trade barriers in goods and services among the member countries. A greater degree of integration than free trade areas, but with less member autonomy in how nonmember countries are dealt with. *See* free trade area, common market, and economic union. 295

cyclical unemployment Unemployment caused by changes in the business cycle or pace of the economy. When the economy slows down or is in a recession, cyclical unemployment is high. Alternatively, when the economy is growing and expanding, cyclical unemployment is low. 227

de facto **standard** A standard that arises by virtue of common usage and is not officially sanctioned by any authority. It is a standard "in fact" or "in practice," rather than in law. 245

de jure **standard** A standard that is legally mandated and enforced by a government or standards organization. 245

decentralization The degree to which decision-making authority in an organization is spread to the lower levels. 128

decisional roles One of Mintzberg's three broad categories of roles that managers play, where information is processed and decisions made. Includes entrepreneur, disturbance handler, resource allocator, and negotiator. *See* informational roles, interpersonal roles, entrepreneur, disturbance handler, resource allocator, and negotiator. 83

decline phase The last phase in the industry life-cycle model, where aggregate sales drop and rivalry further heats up. 251

deflation When the price level of goods is falling; the opposite of inflation. 225

delayering Flattening organizational hierarchies so that they have a wider span of control; the elimination of hierarchical layers, often involving downsizing. *See* span of control. 120

demand-pull inflation A type of inflation that occurs when the demand for goods and services exceeds the supply, which tends to "pull" prices up. 224

democratic culture A culture where individuals are encouraged to take responsibility for their actions. 370

depression A phase in the business life cycle that is characterized by longer economic periods of declining economic activity, high unemployment, and high levels of personal and commercial bankruptcies. A depression is a severe recession. 211

deregulation A reduction in the number of laws or regulations affecting business activity. 339

designated groups The four designated groups under Canada's Employment Equity Act: women, Aboriginal peoples, persons with disabilities, and members of visible minorities. 62

developmental change Change that attempts to improve upon what the business is currently doing, rather than creating something completely new. 461

disseminator One of the three informational roles that managers play (the others being monitor and spokesperson), where the information obtained through monitoring is shared and distributed. *See* monitor and spokesperson. 83

disturbance handler One of the four decisional roles that managers play (the others being entrepreneur, resource allocator, and negotiator), where the manager deals with and attempts to resolve conflicts, such as dealing with a difficult or uncooperative supplier. *See* informational roles, interpersonal roles, entrepreneur, resource allocator, and negotiator. 83

diversification A corporate-level strategy where a firm operates in more than one market simultaneously. 179

domestic trade Trade that involves the purchase, sale, or exchange of goods between provinces, cities, or regions within the same country. 290

dominant design The dominant approach or design established in a product class. 245

double-loop learning The assessment by individuals of whether an error or problem exists in an organization because the systems themselves need to be changed. Requires a deeper level of examination than single-loop learning and typically precedes significant organizational change. Uncovers root causes. *See* organizational learning and single-loop learning. 172

downsizing The planned reduction in breadth of an organization's operations, typically involving terminating relatively large numbers of employees or decreasing the number of products or services the organization provides. 145

dumping An accusation against an exporting country of pricing its product below cost or below the cost of the target country's product. 334

duty to accommodate A legal obligation required by human rights statutes requiring employers to accommodate employees who otherwise would not be able to perform the requirements of a job because of a reason related to a prohibited ground, such as religion or disability. 62

dynamic environment One of the two broad classifications of environments of organizations (the other being static). The dynamic environment contains much uncertainty and change. *See* static environment. 133

Ecological Footprint (EP) The amount of biologically productive land and sea area that is required to meet the demands of human consumption for a particular population or country. 422

economic environment The economic conditions in which an organization operates. Key groups that make up an economic environment are individuals, businesses, and the government. 197

economic forces The economic influences on organizations, such as the state of the economy, unemployment, inflation, interest rates, and gross domestic product. For example, high unemployment numbers may indicate lower overall consumer spending, and business sales could be negatively affected. If sales go down significantly, businesses may need to reduce production, cut costs, or lay off workers. 8

economic responsibilities The responsibilities of a company to make profits and minimize costs. 384

economic stability An economic state that occurs when the amount of money available and the goods and services produced grow at approximately the same rate. 223

economic system The way that the five factors of production are managed. Can be classified as either public (where the government makes decisions about production and allocation of resources) or private (where individuals can own their own property and make their own decisions). There are four types of economic systems: a market economy, communism, socialism, and a mixed system. 202

economic union A higher level of economic integration than a common market, with harmonization of fiscal, monetary, and tax policies and often a common currency. There is comparably very little member autonomy. *See* free trade area, customs union, and common market. 296

economies of scale Spreading the costs of production over the number of units produced, which can provide incumbent firms with cost advantages that create a barrier to entry for new entrants. 164

economies of scope The situation where the total costs for serving two markets or producing products for two markets are less than the costs for serving them or producing them alone. 181

ecosystem A set of complex relationships among all living organisms and their environment. 421

effectiveness The pursuit and achievement of goals that are appropriate for an organization. 81

efficiency Using the fewest inputs to produce a given level of output. 81

employee A person hired by an employer to perform work according to the terms of an employment contract. 44

employment A relationship between an employer and an employee involving an exchange of labour power (work) for something of value, such as wages or benefits. 44

employment contract A contract that defines the terms and conditions of a contractual relationship between an employer and an employee. The contract may include reference to services to be performed, working hours, compensation, and other work-related obligations of the employer and the employee. 44

employment equity A term that was developed by Justice Rosalie Abella, commissioner of the Royal Commission on Equality in Employment (1984), to describe a model designed to remove systemic barriers that have historically led to underrepresentation in Canada's labour market of people from the four designated groups. 68

end-point ethics Assessing the rightness or wrongness of an action by its outcomes. Its modern counterparts are cost-benefit and risk-benefit analysis. *See* rule ethics. 361

entrepreneur (1) One of the four decisional roles that managers play (the others being disturbance handler, resource allocator, and negotiator), where the manager develops and initiates new projects. *See* informational roles, interpersonal roles, disturbance handler, resource allocator, and negotiator. (2) One of the five factors of production. Individuals who establish a business in the pursuit of profit and to serve a need in society. They are the owners, decision makers, and risk takers of the business. 83, 199

environmental uncertainty The rate at which market conditions and production technologies change, producing

dynamic or static environments. *See* dynamic environment and static environment. 133

equity alliance A form of strategic alliance that involves an arrangement between two or more firms where one firm has partial ownership in the other firm and the two firms work together to pursue common goals. 187

esprit de corps In administrative management, generating organizational cohesiveness and unity by encouraging team spirit and harmony among workers. 92

ethical responsibilities The responsibilities of businesses to engage in business practices that are in line with what society considers acceptable, fair, and just. 384

ethics The study of morality or moral judgments, standards, and rules of conduct. 358

European Union (EU) A common market with a single currency and a free flow of money, people, products, and services within its member countries. 296

exchange rate (currency rate) The value of a foreign currency compared to a home currency. 218

exit barriers The economic, strategic, and emotional factors that keep firms competing even though they may be earning low or negative returns on their investments. 168

exit early strategy An alternative for firms that are in the decline phase of their industry life cycle whereby the firm recovers some of its prior investments by selling off assets to others and exiting the market. 253

expansionary phase A phase in the business life cycle, where economic activity is rising. 210

external stakeholders Individuals or groups who bear some kind of risk, whether financial, physical, or other, as a result of a corporation's actions. They include such parties as suppliers, the government, and society in general. There are ethical as well as practical reasons to attend to all of their interests, even when they conflict. *See* general environment. 7

family income A historical term used to describe the amount of money working men were able to bring home to support their spouses and children. Today, *household income* is used to describe the total amount of income brought in by all members of a household or place of residence. 54

federal level of government The highest level of government that governs all Canadian citizens, residents, and others across Canada. 314

figurehead One of the interpersonal roles that managers play (the others being leader and liaison). Typically ceremonial or symbolic in nature, such as handing out "employee of the month" awards. 82

financial resources Resources used by a firm that include debt, equity, retained earnings, and so on. 170

first-mover advantage The benefits of being among the first to establish strong positions in important world markets. 272

five factors of production The five key inputs in an organization, which include natural resources, labour, capital, knowledge, and entrepreneurs. 197

five-forces model A prescriptive model developed by Michael Porter (1980) that allow for the systematic assessment of the industry environment. The five forces include the threat of new entrants, the bargaining power of suppliers, the bargaining power of buyers, the threats of substitutes, and rivalry among existing firms. 164

fixed rate A permanent interest rate that cannot be changed for the term of a loan. Usually higher than a variable rate. 225

focus strategy A business-level strategy that targets a particular buyer group, a segment of the product line, or a geographic market. Specifically, the focus strategy rests on the premise that a firm is able to compete efficiently or effectively by targeting a particular narrow market. The firm can thus achieve either differentiation by better meeting the needs of a particular buyer group or lower costs in serving this group or both. Accordingly, the firm may potentially earn above-normal returns by adopting either a focused low-cost strategy or a focused differentiation strategy. 177

foreign direct investment (FDI) The purchase of physical assets or an amount of share ownership in a company from another country to gain a measure of management control. 281, 334

formalization The degree to which rules, regulations, procedures, and so on govern how work is performed; the degree of the standardization of jobs in the organization. The greater the degree of formalization, the lower the reliance on individual discretion and the greater the assurance of consistent and reliable performance. 130

forward integration A type of diversification that refers to an extension or expansion of firm value chain activities by integrating processes (forward) toward the ultimate customers. 184

fossil fuel A nonrenewable resource that takes millions of years to form. Burning fossil fuels causes carbon dioxide to be released into the atmosphere and causes the earth's surface temperature to rise. 415

franchisee The dealer in a franchising arrangement who is permitted to sell the goods/services of the franchisor in exchange for some payment. 281

franchising A method of distribution or marketing where a parent company (the franchisor) grants to another individual or company (the franchisee) the legal right to sell its products or services, with exclusive rights to a particular area or location. 281

franchisor The supplier in a franchising arrangement, who permits a franchisee to sell its goods/services in exchange for some payment. 281

free enterprise system Another term for *laissez faire*, or the capitalist notion that the government should not interfere too much in business affairs. 313

free trade The trade of goods and services in open markets where a level playing field is created for businesses in one country to compete fairly against businesses in other countries. Government intervention is therefore kept at a minimum. 290

Free Trade Agreement (FTA) An agreement established in 1989 between Canada and the United States to remove trade barriers and to produce a common market between the countries. 298

free trade area The lowest degree of regional economic integration, where tariffs and nontariff trade barriers on international trade in goods and services among the member countries are removed. *See* customs union, common market, and economic union. 295

frictional unemployment Unemployment that is caused by normal labour market turnover, not a downturn in the economy. 226

full employment A situation that occurs when only frictional unemployment exists. 228

functional specialization The dividing up of jobs into their smallest components so that workers perform simple, specific, and repetitive tasks. 128

G7 A group of seven developed, industrialized nations with large economies. Includes France, Germany, the United States, the United Kingdom, Italy, Japan, and Canada. 219

GDP per capita The gross domestic product per person in a country. Calculated by dividing the total GDP by the total population of a country. 214

General Agreement on Tariffs and Trade (GATT) An agreement among approximately 100 countries to reduce the level of tariffs on a worldwide basis. 294

general environment The environment shared by all organizations in a society, such as the economic and political environments, and technological, societal, and global forces. *See* specific or task environment, technological forces, societal forces, and global forces. 7

Genuine Progress Indicator (GPI) A tool used to measure a country or region's economic growth and social well-being. It includes all variables calculated under the GDP, but subtracts the negative effects of economic growth that cause social harm to a community. 425

global business A business that engages directly in some form of international business activity, including such activities as exporting, importing, or international production. 286

global forces The global influences on organizations that could be considered as part of the general economic, political, technological, or societal forces, but are international in nature. *See* technological forces and societal forces. 9

globalization Although there is no universally agreed-upon definition, it may be considered as a process involving the integration of national economies and the worldwide convergence of consumer preferences; the process of generating a single world economic system. 9, 271

government economic regulation The imposition of constraints, backed by the authority of the government, to significantly modify economic behaviour in the private sector. The motive may include protection of the consumer or of the environment, or protection of fair competition among businesses. 325

Governor General The holder of executive authority in Canada's government. This person typically plays a passive administrative role and usually follows the advice of the prime minister, but he or she must sign bills before they become law. 316

greenhouse gas emissions Gas emissions that result from burning fossil fuels to carry out many of our daily functions in industrialized society, such as to make electricity, to heat homes and buildings, to process industrial and commercial activities, to power transportation, and to allow agricultural and other miscellaneous processes. 415

gross domestic product (GDP) The total value of a country's output of goods and services in a given year. 13, 211

gross national product (GNP) The value of all final goods and services produced by a national economy inside and outside of the country's borders. (In Canada, this is the the income received in Canada, whether earned in Canada or abroad.) 211

growth phase The second phase in the industry life-cycle model that occurs after the industry coalesces around a particular approach and a dominant model. This leads to a shakeout, where many firms exit the industry. 245

habitual routines Commonly accepted methods for performing a task with, potentially, both functional and dysfunctional consequences. For example, once a behaviour is accepted as a legitimate means of accomplishing the work, its actual effects (efficiency or otherwise) are not readily questioned. 373

harvesting profits strategy An alternative for firms that are in the decline phase of their industry life cycle, whereby the firm tries to squeeze as much remaining profit as possible from the industry by drastically reducing costs. 253

Hawthorne effect The discovery that productivity can be enhanced by giving employees special attention rather than by simply improving their physical working conditions. 100

horizontal differentiation The degree of differentiation between horizontal (as opposed to vertical) units of the organization, based on things such as the orientation of the members, the nature of their jobs, and their education or training. Includes job specialization, which is divided into functional and social specialization. *See* vertical differentiation, functional specialization, and social specialization. 127

House of Commons The lower house of Parliament, where Members of Parliament (MPs) sit to discuss, debate, and amend bills to pass legislation. 317

human relations movement One of the schools of behavioural management developed by Elton Mayo, who emphasized that social factors had a greater impact on productivity than actual working conditions. Focuses on organizations as social systems. *See* Hawthorne effect. 100

human resources The experience, knowledge, judgment, risk-taking propensity, and wisdom of the individuals associated with a firm. 170

imperfect competition A fundamental shortcoming in the market system that necessitates government involvement. It occurs when fewer than the optimal number of competitors exist to ensure fair pricing and distribution of goods and services at the highest possible level of quality. 327

import quota A limitation on the amount of a product that can be imported to ensure that domestic producers retain an adequate share of consumer demand for their product. 293

income inequality The unequal distribution of wealth to individuals or households in an economy. 48

incremental innovations Making relatively minor improvements or modifications to an existing product or practice in the hopes of differentiating it from the competition. It is also a way to extend the life cycle of the product, delaying the inevitable onset of the decline stage. 255

independent contractor Independent contractors or the self-employed provide labour services in exchange for compensation. They run their own businesses rather than serving as an employee for another organization or person. 44

Index of Sustainable Economic Welfare (ISEW) An index that attempts to measure both positive and negative activities that affect a society's well-being. 424

industrial pluralist perspective A perspective that emphasizes the imbalance of power between workers and employers and the value to society and economies of striking a reasonable balance between the *efficiency* concerns of employers and the *equity* concerns of workers. Pluralists believe that unions and collective bargaining are beneficial to society and the economy because they give workers "voice" and ensure a fairer distribution of wealth throughout society than a system in which workers bargain employment contracts with employers on their own. 50

Industrial Revolution A period of time when manufacturing practices developed, between 1760 to 1840, changing the nature of work from manual hand production methods to machine use and mass production. 89

industry A group of organizations that share similar resource requirements, including raw materials, labour, technology, and customers. 163

industry life-cycle model An inverted U-shaped growth pattern that is seen in almost all industries given a long enough period of observation. The number of organizations rises initially up to a peak, then declines as the industry ages. 237

inflation The rise in the price level of goods and services. 223

informational roles One of Mintzberg's three broad categories of roles that managers play, where managers are communication sources for the organization, whether between parties in the organization or to parties outside it. Includes monitor, disseminator, and spokesperson roles. *See* decisional roles, interpersonal roles, monitor, disseminator, and spokesperson. 82

information sharing Workers sharing knowledge with other workers in the organization to help better meet the organization's goals and needs. Information sharing is an important component of the team-based approach. 121

input Something a company contributes to creating its products or services, such as materials, labour, or overhead. 215

institutionalization The processes by which shared beliefs take on a rule-like status. A social process through which individuals create a shared definition of what is appropriate or meaningful behaviour. May generate "accepted practices" that continue even when they are no longer functional. 477

institutionalization theory The theory that organizations are driven to incorporate practices and procedures defined by current concepts of work and those accepted or institutionalized by society. Taken-for-granted means of "getting things done" and, as such, not necessarily rational. 152, 477

interest rate A fee charged, usually a percentage, by a lender to a borrower for the use of funds. 225

interfirm dynamics A motive for diversification that includes market power enhancement, a response to competition, and imitation. 181

International Monetary Fund (IMF) An international organization established after World War II to provide short-term assistance in the form of low-interest loans to countries conducting international trade and in need of financial help. 294

international trade Trade that involves the purchase, sale, or exchange of goods or services across countries. 290

intern A worker who receives on-the-job training at a workplace. The internship may or may not be a formal requirement of an educational program and can be paid or unpaid. Whether an intern is considered an "employee" and is therefore entitled to legal entitlements available to employees in Canada, such as a minimum wage, depends on how a province's employment standards laws define an employee. Some unpaid internships are unlawful, while others are not. 44

interpersonal roles One of Mintzberg's three broad categories of roles that managers play. Those tasks that arise from the manager's formal authority base and involve relationships with either other organizational members or external parties. Includes figurehead, leader and liaison roles. *See* decisional roles, informational roles, figurehead, leader, and liaison. 82

intrafirm dynamics A motive for diversification that can include growth and managerial self-interests. 179

introductory phase The first phase in the industry life-cycle model, where many entrepreneurial firms enter the industry, hoping to emerge as a market leader. New industries tend to be highly fragmented (that is, with many small competitors) and characterized by experimentation with novel technologies and business models. 238

invisible hand of the market Adam Smith used the "invisible hand" metaphor in his book *The Wealth of Nations*, published in 1776. Smith argued that, by pursuing their own self-interest, individuals "are led by an invisible hand" to promote the greater public interest, even if that is not their intention. 49, 313

joint venture A form of strategic alliance that involves an arrangement between two or more companies joining to produce a product or service together, or to collaborate in the research, development, or marketing of that product or service. 187, 284

keiretsu The Japanese term for networking of major enterprises—creating loosely affiliated collections of companies These are quite common in Japanese industry and banking. 123

knowledge One of the five factors of production. It is captured in the individuals who work for an organization and the specialized education, skills, training, and experience they bring to their role. In today's business environment, it has become the most important factor of production. 198

knowledge-based economies Economies that involve the production, distribution, and consumption of knowledge and information. 198

knowledge workers People employed in knowledge-intensive industries, such as the high-tech industries, where specialized and frequently changing knowledge is required. Knowledge work is thus harder to routinize than, for instance, service work. 21

labour One of the five factors of production. Includes all workers in an organization who contribute their talents and strengths to create goods and services. 5, 197

labour relations statutes Laws that govern labour issues in a particular province. In Canada, each province has the power to enact its own labour laws. 53

laissez faire A term meaning that businesses or manufacturers should be free to make and sell what they please and, consequently, reflects the notion that government should not interfere with the economic affairs of business. 89, 313

law of the few One of the three rules of Malcolm Gladwell's tipping point theory that states there are exceptional people (*See* connectors, mavens, and salesmen) who possess social connections, personality, energy, and enthusiasm to be able to spread the word in epidemic proportions. 479

leader One of the three interpersonal roles that managers play (the others being figurehead and liaison), wherein the manager may serve as a motivator, communicator, and coordinator of subordinates' activities, such as by conducting performance appraisals. *See* informational roles, interpersonal roles, figurehead, and liaison. 82

leadership How people are managed within an organization. 4

leadership strategy An alternative for firms that are in the decline phase of their industry life cycle whereby the firm continues to invest in marketing, support, and product development, hoping that competitors will eventually exit the market. 253

learning forces Lessons that result from institutionalized management practices and that are taught to future managers and business leaders in the course of their formal education. 154

learning organization An organization that facilitates the learning of all its members and consciously transforms itself and its context. 471

legal responsibilities The responsibilities of businesses to honour all relevant laws and regulations governing business activities. 384

liaison One of the three interpersonal roles that managers play (the others being figurehead and leader), including developing relationships with members of the organization outside the manager's area of authority, such as with other departments. *See* interpersonal roles, figurehead, and leader. 82

licensing agreement An arrangement whereby the owner of a product or process is paid a fee or royalty from another company in return for granting it permission to produce or distribute the product or process. 280

limited monopoly A type of monopoly that occurs when a company has a patent that protects its product or idea for a limited time period. 206

Living Planet Index (LPI) Created by the World Wildlife Fund, this index aims to measure changes to the world's biological diversity. 420

machine metaphor (of an organization) A metaphor used to describe organizations that function like a machine—that is, in an orderly, prescribed, rational, and controlled manner. The classical school of management viewed organizations as entities devised to perform work that led toward specific goals, structure, and technology. 125

macroeconomics The study of larger economic issues involving the economy as a whole; examples include unemployment, consumption, inflation, gross domestic product, and price levels. 200

management The process of administering and coordinating resources effectively and efficiently in an effort to achieve the organization's goals. 81

managerial perspective A perspective associated with the human resource management school. Managerialists believe that employees and employers share a common goal of maximizing productivity and profits, so there need not be conflict between them. As long as employers treat employees decently, the employees will work hard in the employer's interests. 50

mandatory minimum statutory notice The minimum job termination notice employers must give their employees. It is found in employment standards statutes and varies from province to province. 57

market economy A free market system in which businesses compete with others in a marketplace where supply and demand determine which goods and services will be produced and consumed. Individuals can decide to be either workers for an employer or owners of a business. 202

Mary Parker Follett A social philosopher who made a number of significant contributions to the field of management in the first decades of the 20th century. She focused on coordination, self-management, and collaboration. 100

mature phase The third phase in the industry life-cycle model, where the market stabilizes and sales grow more slowly. Firms must become more efficient during this stage. 248

mavens People who are knowledgeable and have a lot of information on products, prices, and places. They often start word-of-mouth epidemics because they have knowledge the rest of us don't, and many people rely on them to make informed decisions. *See* law of the few. 480

mechanistic organizations The extreme opposite from organic organizations in organizational design. These organizations are exemplified by the machine bureaucracy. Machine bureaucracies, or mechanistic organizations, maintain jobs that are narrow in scope, decision making is centralized at the top of the organizational hierarchy, there is a narrow span of control, and work is conducted within highly formalized rules and procedures. 131

mercantilism The trade theory that dominated economic thinking for the 15th, 16th, and 17th centuries, where a country's wealth was believed to be a matter of its holdings of treasure, especially gold; the economic policy of accumulating wealth through trade surpluses. In the modern era, Japan has often been called a mercantilist country because of its high trade surpluses. *See* trade surplus. 290

merger A way to achieve diversification, when two firms come together to create a new firm with a new identity. 185, 284

microeconomics The study of smaller components of the economy, such as individuals and businesses. 200

minimum wage An employment standards law that mandates the minimum hourly wage that must be paid to an employee. Each province sets its own minimum wage. 49

ministries (federal) The various departments of the federal government that specialize in various functions (for example, health, fisheries, justice, national defence). Each ministry is headed by a Cabinet minister. 317

mixed economy An economic system where the government (public) and businesses (private) influence the economy. 203

mixed system An economic system that involves a capitalist economy with an important government role. Most economies today are considered mixed systems. 25, 312

modern behavioural science The school of thought that consists of sociological, psychological, and anthropological perspectives based on the premise that motivating workers is preferable to controlling them. It has produced an enormous number of theories, including need-based and cognitive-based theories of motivation. 102

monitor One of the three informational roles that managers play (the others being disseminator and spokesperson), where the internal and external environments of the organization are constantly monitored for information useful in decision making. *See* disseminator, spokesperson, internal environment, and external environment. 83

monopolistic competition A form of competition where a large number of small and large firms have a similar product or service that is perceived as slightly different from the others due to branding, style or design, and advertising. 208

monopoly A form of competition that occurs when only one company produces a particular product or service in a given market and, as a result, there are no competitors. 206

multinational corporations (MNCs) Business enterprises that control assets, factories, and so on that are operated either as branch offices or affiliates in two or more foreign countries. It generates products or services through its affiliates in several countries and maintains control over their operation, managing from a global perspective. 286

municipal level of government   The lowest level of government in Canada that governs a city or smaller community, such as a town, village, or parish. 315

national debt   Debt that is accumulated by the federal government. It can impact businesses because it has an effect on the entire country's economy. 219

natural monopoly   A type of monopoly that occurs when economic and technical conditions only allow for one efficient producer. An example is water supplied by a municipality. 206

natural rate of unemployment   The total amount of frictional and structural unemployment combined. 228

natural resources   One of the five factors of production. Includes land and raw materials that are found either below or above the ground, such as soil, rocks, minerals, vegetables, and so on. Can also include living organisms like fish and agricultural products. 197

negotiator   One of the four decisional roles that managers play (the others being entrepreneur, disturbance handler, and resource allocator) involving negotiation in all its forms, whether with customers, employees, or other departments. *See* informational roles, interpersonal roles, entrepreneur, disturbance handler, and resource allocator. 83

neoclassical perspective   One view of how the economy should function. It contends that competitive markets are the best means of organizing complex economies and societies. The forces of supply and demand, if left to operate freely with limited government interference, will ensure optimal assignment of skills and expertise throughout the economy as well as the fairest distribution of wealth. 49

networking   Organizations engaging in cooperative relationships with suppliers, distributors, or competitors with the aim of improving efficiency and flexibility in meeting consumer needs. The Japanese version is called *keiretsu*. *See keiretsu*. 143

niche strategy   A strategy whereby the firm focuses on a specific segment of the industry where it can expect to possess some form of competitive advantage. 253

nominal GDP   Gross domestic product that is not adjusted for inflation and is measured in current dollars. 211

nonequity alliance   A form of strategic alliance that involves an arrangement between two or more companies that work together based on contractual agreements. 187

nonrenewable resource   A form of energy that takes millions of years to form. 415

nonroutine technology   Nonstandardized technology. Might include anything from conducting genetic research to making custom furniture. 132

nonstandard employment (NSE)   A less stable form of employment than the SER that is characterized by part-time, temporary, or variable working hours; lower pay; fewer employer-provided benefits; shorter job tenure; and is usually non-unionized. 47

North American Free Trade Agreement (NAFTA)   An agreement established in 1994 between Canada, the United States, and Mexico to remove trade barriers and to produce a common market between the countries. The agreement replaced the FTA from 1989. 298

oligopoly   A form of competition when only a few large producers sell a certain product or service in a given market. 206

open systems   Entities that are embedded in and dependent on exchanges with the environment within which they operate. The interdependence of elements means that the entity (the organization) is more than the sum of its parts; it interacts with its environment. 126

opportunity cost   The cost of the best foregone alternative. 197

organic organizations   The extreme opposite from mechanistic organizations in organizational design. Organic organizations tend to have jobs that are enriched with more variety and task responsibilities (wide work specialization); typically, there is a team-based approach rather than a "top-down" approach to authority, and decision making is decentralized throughout the organization. There is a wide span of control. The worker is also less restricted with fewer rules and regulations. These organizations tend to be innovative and flexible. 131

organism metaphor (of an organization)   A metaphor used to describe organizations as systems of mutually connected and dependent parts that share a common life. This metaphor suggests that we can conceive of organizations as living organisms that contain a combination of elements that are differentiated yet integrated, attempting to survive within the context of a wider environment. 125

organizational culture   A set of shared beliefs regarding how members of the organization should behave and what goals they should seek. 368

organizational development   A process of planned change that attempts to make organizations better able to meet their short- and long-term objectives. 471

organizational learning   The detection and correction of error, or the collective experience of individuals within the organization that results in changes in organizational procedure. Three aspects of learning are adapting to the environment, learning from employees, and contributing to the learning of the wider community or context. Two types of learning are single-loop learning and double-loop learning. 12, 472

organizational resources   The history, relationships, trust, and organizational culture that permeates a firm, along with the firm's formal reporting structure, management control systems, and compensation policies. 170

organizational role theory   The theory that organizational roles have a psychological reality to the individuals occupying them, whereby they fulfill role requirements based on internalized expectations concerning responsibilities of the role. 377

organizational structure A deliberately planned network or pattern of relationships that exists among individuals in various roles or positions. 127

output A finished unit of product (or service) ready to be sold. 215

outsourcing Hiring external organizations to conduct work in certain functions of the company. *See* downsizing. 140, 280

paradigm Our mental framework for understanding how the world operates. Our theories, assumptions, sets of beliefs, and customs. Overcoming resistance to change means recognizing the current paradigms that govern our behaviour and shifting to a new paradigm. 474

partners Individuals who share part ownership in a business. There can be two or more partners in a partnership. 44

patent A form of intellectual property rights whereby a country grants exclusive rights to an inventor to protect his or her product or idea for a limited period of time. 206

peak The point in the business life cycle when the economy has reached its highest point, thus marking the end of the expansionary phase and the beginning of the contraction phase. 210

perfect or pure competition A form of competition where many small and medium firms produce the same product or service and no single seller has the power to influence the price of that product or service. 204

philanthropic responsibilities The responsibilities of businesses to engage in activities that help to improve society. 384

physical resources The machines, production facilities, and buildings that firms used in their operations. 170

piece-rate system In scientific management, motivating workers by tying compensation to performance according to output, so that a standard level of output produces a standard level of pay, and above-average output produces above-average pay. 91

political forces Governmental influences on an organization's decisions through laws, taxes, trade relationships, and other related political factors. 10

power of context One of the three rules of Malcolm Gladwell's tipping point theory that consists of two parts: (1) Word-of-mouth epidemics are sensitive to the environment in which they occur; and (2) groups play a significant role in spreading word-of-mouth epidemics. 480

price index A measure of the average change in a group of prices over time. 224

price level The average level of prices. 224

prime minister The head of the Canadian government; elected by Canadian voters. 316

Prime Minister's Office (PMO) The office that assists the prime minister with daily activities. 316

privatization Divesting of government involvement in the operation, management, or ownership of business activities, involving transfer of activities or functions from the government to the private sector. 344

Privy Council Office (PCO) An important policy-advising agency that serves the prime minister. 317

producer price index (PPI) A price index that measures the prices of inputs to producers and wholesalers, including finished products for resale, partially finished goods, and raw materials. 224

product differentiation strategy A business-level strategy whereby a firm attempts to gain a competitive advantage by increasing the perceived value of its products or services relative to that of other firms' products or services. 174

productivity A measure of the level of output versus the level of input in an organization. 215

prohibited grounds Those grounds listed in human rights statutes. Discrimination is prohibited in employment on the prohibited grounds only. Prohibited grounds vary from province to province, but all include common grounds such as race, colour, ethnicity, religion, age, disability, sex, and sexual orientation. 60

provincial level of government A regional level of government in Canada that only affects those citizens and residents who reside in a particular province. 315

pull factors Positive outcomes a business would gain from entering the global market; include the potential for sales growth and the opportunity of obtaining needed resources. *See* push factors. 271

punctuated equilibrium A pattern that shows, over long periods, that technological discontinuities tend to appear at rare and irregular intervals in industries. 260

purchasing power of money The value of what money can buy. If prices increase, then individuals and businesses have less money to spend on other items. 223

push factors Forces that act on all businesses to create an environment where competing successfully means competing globally; include the forces of competition, the shift toward democracy, the reduction in trade barriers, and improvements in technology. *See* pull factors. 271

radical innovations When a new technical process or advancement marks a significant departure from existing practices; they often create a whole new industry (such as automobiles or wireless phones have done). These innovations are often referred to as *discontinuous* because they do not continue to build on the previous technological regime, but instead mark a shift to a completely new technology. An example would be the shift to jet engines in aircrafts, which did not build on the previous propeller-based technology. 254

real GDP Gross domestic product adjusted to reflect the effects of inflation. 211

reasonable notice The amount of time in advance that employers must inform employees that their services are no longer necessary and their employment contract is ending. How much notice is "reasonable" is decided by judges and depends on a number of factors, including the length of the employee's service, the employee's age, and the type of work the employee performed. 56

recession A phase in the business life cycle where there are two or more consecutive quarter periods of negative or falling economic activity. 211

recovery phase The phase in the business life cycle that occurs after a trough, where economic activity slowly begins to rise again and the demand for goods and services increases. 211

reengineering The fundamental rethinking and radical redesign of business processes to achieve dramatic improvements in measures of performance. It often advocates the collection of individual tasks into a greater number of whole jobs. 136

regional economic integration Bringing different countries closer together by reducing or eliminating obstacles to the international movement of capital, labour, and products or services. 295

regional trading bloc A collection of countries within an integrated economic region. 295

related diversification A type of diversification that refers to situations where a firm expands its core businesses or markets into related businesses or markets. Such an expansion usually involves horizontal integration across different business or market domains. It enables a firm to benefit from economies of scope and enjoy greater revenues if the businesses attain higher levels of sales growth combined than either firm could attain independently. 181

resource allocator One of the four decisional roles that managers play (the others being entrepreneur, disturbance handler, and negotiator), where it is decided how resources such as money, equipment, personnel, and time will be allocated. *See* informational roles, interpersonal roles, entrepreneur, disturbance handler, and negotiator. 83

resources and capabilities All of the financial, physical, human, and organizational assets used by the firm to develop, manufacture, and deliver products or services to its customers. 170

restrictive or regulatory taxes One of two broad forms of taxes, the other being revenue taxes. This form of taxation consists of two types: excise taxes and customs duties or tariffs. Excise taxes are applied to goods and services that the government wants to restrict the purchase of. *See* revenue taxes and tariffs. 318

revenue taxes One of two broad forms of taxes, the other being restrictive or regulatory taxes. This money is collected to help fund government services and programs and includes individual income taxes, corporate income tax, property tax, and sales tax. *See* restrictive or regulatory taxes. 318

routine technology Automated and standardized technology and operations typical of mass production operations. 132

rule ethics Judging actions to be right or wrong according to absolute rules regardless of the consequences. Such rules may be based on religious beliefs, family values, education, experience, and so on. *See* end-point ethics. 363

salesmen Individuals who are unusually charismatic and have the skills to persuade even those who are unconvinced by connectors or mavens. *See* law of the few. 480

scientific management Frederick Taylor's philosophy that the fundamental objective of management is "securing the maximum prosperity for the employer coupled with the maximum prosperity for each employee" by standardizing and compartmentalizing work practices. This is one of the three central classical approaches to management, the others being the administrative and the bureaucratic. *See* administrative and bureaucratic management. 89

seasonal unemployment Unemployment that is caused by the seasonal nature of the job. 228

self-management In behavioural approaches to management, Mary Parker Follett's emphasis on the fact that the person doing a job is often the best one to decide how best to do it, rather than managers who are not familiar with the task. 101

self-managing work teams Teams that are given the power to manage themselves and make decisions without the approval of formal management. 121

Senate The upper house of Parliament, where a bill is passed after it has been approved by the House of Commons. If approved by the Senate, the bill is passed to the Governor General to sign and enact into law. 317

shakeout A large number of exits from the market at the same time as the aggregate output of the industry increases; a natural and healthy, though painful, process for an industry to purge and weed out the weaker competitors. 245

single-loop learning The correction of errors that employees find in organizational methods of performance in order to keep the system working. Assumes that the organization has the right systems established but simply needs to fine tune them. Results in incremental improvements and improved efficiency. Addresses symptoms rather than root causes. *See* organizational learning and double-loop learning. 472

social contract ethics This model of ethics posits that the rules by which people live are those that they would agree to live by if given the opportunity to make a choice based on reason or knowledge. 378

social equity In general terms, fair and equitable business practices toward employees and the community. It involves such things as fair salaries, a safe workplace, reasonable working hours, adherence to employment laws, and respect for diversity and human rights. 411

social identity theory The theory that individuals classify themselves and others into social categories (organizational membership, age, gender, and so on) defined by typical characteristics of the members. 376

socialism An economic system where the government has large ownership in or control over major industries essential to the country's economy. 203

socialization of ethics The process of conveying the organization's goals and norms to employees so that they internalize organizational ethical standards. 369

social media Web-based or mobile technologies that allow people to communicate in an interactive way. 395

social specialization The specialization of individuals rather than jobs, which is accomplished through employment of professionals whose skills cannot be easily routinized. *See* functional specialization. 128

societal forces A wide range of influences in society in general, including, for example, changes in public opinion on ethical issues like organizational justice (how employees are treated), that affect all organizations and to which businesses must respond. 10

sociopolitical legitimacy The endorsement of an industry, activity, or organizational form by key stakeholders and institutions such as the state and government officials, opinion leaders, or the general public. 241

sociotechnical redesign An approach to work redesign that recognizes the complex interaction between people and technology in the workplace. 466

span of control The number of employees reporting to a supervisor. *See* horizontal and vertical differentiation. 129

specialization Also called *division of labour*, refers to the degree to which organizational tasks are subdivided into separate jobs. There are fundamentally two different kinds of specialization: functional and social specialization. *See* horizontal differentiation, functional specialization, and social specialization. 128

specific or task environment The environment within which a particular organization operates, which is ultimately shaped by the general environment and includes stakeholders, customers, competitors, suppliers, and so on. *See* general environment and stakeholders. 7

spokesperson One of the three informational roles that managers play (the others being monitor and disseminator), where information is transmitted to individuals outside the manager's area of authority. *See* decisional roles, interpersonal roles, monitor, and disseminator. 83

stakeholder An individual or group with whom a business interacts and who has a "stake," or vested interest, in the business. 382

standard employment relationship (SER) A form of employment relationship characterized by regular, full-time hours at a single employer, often spanning an entire working career. Employees working under an SER usually receive periodic pay raises, and their employers usually provide health benefits and pension plans. 47

standardizing In scientific management, the establishment of clear rules regarding how to perform a job, leaving little or no room for individual discretion, thus assuring consistent performance. 90

static environment One of the two broad classifications of environments of organizations (the other being dynamic). The static environment exhibits little if any change. *See* dynamic environment. 132

stickiness factor One of the three rules of Malcolm Gladwell's tipping point theory that states there are specific ways to make a message memorable in terms of presenting and structuring information to influence the impact it will have. 480

strategic alliance A way to achieve diversification by two or more organizations working together to achieve certain common goals. Strategic alliances can take various forms and serve various purposes. 187, 284

strategic management An ongoing process that requires managers of a firm to constantly analyze their external and internal environments, make decisions about what kinds of strategies they should pursue, implement the strategies, and evaluate the outcomes to make any changes, if necessary, in order to create and sustain its competitive advantages. 162

strategy The decisions made by business managers about how the company will address political, economic, global, societal, competitive, and technological forces. 4

structure A deliberately planned network or pattern of relationships that exists among individuals within an organization. It determines such things as division of labour, span of control, level of formalization, and how centralized decision making is. 6

structural unemployment Unemployment that occurs either because the available jobs do not correspond to the skills of the labour force or unemployed individuals do not live in a region where jobs are available. 227

subsidiaries A legally separate company owned and controlled by a parent company and through which the enterprises can produce or market goods and services. 286

subsidies Government assistance to businesses that are either in the form of cash payments, low-interest loans, or reduced taxes. In a global context, subsidies are mean to assist domestic industry to compete against foreign businesses. 331

sustainable development Development that meets the needs of the present without compromising the ability of future generations to meet their own needs. 408

sustainable distribution Any form of transportation of goods between the seller and the buyer that causes the least harm to the environment and the community. 437

sustainable manufacturing Creating manufactured products using processes that are nonpolluting, that conserve energy and natural resources, and that are economically sound and safe for employees, communities, and consumers. 434

sustainable marketing Also referred to as green marketing, this is marketing of products that are environmentally safe; developing and marketing products that have minimal negative effects on society; and producing, promoting, packaging, and reclaiming products in an environmentally friendly way. 438

sustainable purchasing The acquisitions of goods and services in a way that gives preference to suppliers that generate positive social and environmental outcomes. It might even involve considering whether a purchase needs to be made at all. 440

sustainable resource A resource that can be replenished at the same rate as it is used. It typically derives from renewable resources or recycled materials. 417

sustainability In business, the relationship between the three Ps: people, profits, and the planet. 11

switching costs The costs, both monetary and psychological, associated with changing from one supplier to another from a buyer's perspective. 164

SWOT analysis An analysis of the strengths and weaknesses of an organization and of external opportunities and threats it is exposed to. The strategic planning team can use this information to reexamine the organization's mission statement to capitalize on opportunities and reduce threats. 172

systemic discrimination Internal policies, practices, patterns, or biases that tend to disadvantage some groups and favour others. It might not be deliberate, but it has the effect of excluding certain classes of people. 68

systems theory A theory that recognizes that all organizations are open systems that can only survive through continuous and successful interaction with their environment. 133

tariff A tax on imported goods traditionally employed with the intent to ensure that they are not less expensive than domestically produced goods. 291

technological forces The technological environment that exerts influence across industries, playing a central role in how an organization functions, obtains resources, and competes. Changes in technology both permit and demand organizational change. *See* general environment. 9

temporary placement organizations A business that helps match workers looking for jobs with businesses that require temporary help. Also called an employment agency. 44

Theory E change A theory of change that has as its purpose the creation of economic value, often expressed as shareholder value. Its focus is on formal structure and systems. 464

Theory O change A theory of change that has as its purpose the development of the organization's human capability to implement strategy and to learn from actions taken about the effectiveness of changes made. 464

time and motion studies In scientific management, the scientific analysis of work, often using a movie camera and a stopwatch to closely scrutinize the elements of performing a task. *See* scientific management. 90

trade barriers A government barrier that prevents the free trade of imported goods and services into a country via tariffs, quotas, subsidies, and so on. 273

trade deficit When a country imports more than it exports to the degree that the value of its imports exceeds the value of its exports. Also referred to as a negative balance of trade. 218, 291

trade protectionism Protecting a country's domestic economy and businesses by restricting imports to prevent domestic producers from losing business to producers of low-priced foreign goods, and to prevent a trade deficit, where more

money leaves the country than enters it because imports exceed exports. *See* trade deficit. 291

trade surplus When a country's exports exceed its imports, so that more money enters the country than leaves it. Also referred to as a positive balance of trade. 218, 291

transformational change A type of change where the future state of the business is dramatically different from the current operating state. This is the most challenging type of change to implement, because the future state is unknown, it requires employees to develop new mindsets and behaviours, and the entire organizational culture must change. 462

transitional change Change that replaces what already exists with something completely new. It requires the organization to depart from old methods or operation while the new state is being established. 462

triple bottom line An accounting framework that can be voluntarily used by organizations to report performance on social, economic, and environmental results for a project or reporting period. 11, 409

trough The point in the business life cycle when the economy has reached its lowest point, thus marking the start of the recovery phase. 211

trust One's perception of the integrity and openness of others, one's comfort with the expected actions of others, one's faith in how others will react, and one's willingness to become vulnerable to the actions of others. 107

undue hardship The meaning of undue hardship can vary across provinces, but is generally considered to occur when the accommodation necessary to enable a worker to perform a job requirement is too onerous for an employer to implement. It is a very high standard for employers to meet. 62

unemployment A situation that occurs when qualified individuals who are actively looking for work are unable to secure employment. 226

unemployment insurance program A federal government program that requires employers and employees to make contributions into an unemployment insurance fund. To access benefits, unemployed individuals must satisfy a series of conditions, including having paid into the fund for a specified period of time and actively searching for employment. The amount of benefits payable are based on a percentage of the employee's prior earnings up to a maximum amount, and benefits last for only a fixed period of time (usually several weeks) and vary according to the level of unemployment in the region where the worker lives. 58

unemployment rate The percentage of people who are unemployed out of the total labour force and who are actively seeking work. 55

unethical behaviour Behaviour that in some way has a harmful effect on others and is either illegal or morally unacceptable to the larger community. 358

union density A measure of the percentage of employees who are members of a union out of the total employees in the labour market. 54

union wage premium   The additional amount of wages paid to unionized over non-unionized workers. 54

unity of command   In administrative management, avoiding confusion and conflicting instructions by having each employee report to only one boss, preferably in the upper levels of the organization. *See* administrative management. 92

unrelated diversification   A type of diversification where a firm diversifies into a new market that is not similar to its current market(s). This kind of diversification tends to provide little synergies for a firm, given that there are few opportunities for sharing activities or leveraging resources and capabilities. Firms pursuing this strategy tend to have the synergies created (or believe that the synergies will be created) through corporate office's management skills. 182

utilitarianism   First articulated by John Stuart Mills in response to the Industrial Revolution, a way to determine if an action is right or wrong by assessing the likely consequences of the action, including tangible economic outcomes or intangible outcomes. *See* end-point ethics. 361

variable rate   An interest rate that fluctuates over the term of the loan. Since there is more risk for the borrower, variable rates are usually lower than fixed rates. 225

vertical differentiation   The number of managers and levels in the organizational hierarchy. *See* horizontal differentiation. 129

vertical integration   A type of diversification that refers to an extension or expansion of firm value chain activities by integrating preceding or successive productive processes. 182

virtual organization   An organization that attempts to maximize its fluidity, flatness, and integratedness with the environment. Outsourcing, networking, and shedding noncore functions are three ways organizations can become more virtual. 140

virtual water   Water necessary to produce, process, and transport products for consumption. Also called embodied water. 413

volunteers   An unpaid individual who performs services for an organization voluntarily. A volunteer is not an employee under the law. 44

VRIO model   A model that examines an individual firm's value, rareness, imitability, and organization to determine its relative strengths in comparison to its competitors in the industry. 169

vulnerable or precarious workers   Individuals who perform work in a nonstandard employment relationship. They are always at risk of unemployment since their jobs are insecure, and because their pay is low they live on the cusp of poverty. 48

worker empowerment   A move toward shifting greater levels of responsibility back to employees, so that in a sense they are at least partly their own bosses. One popular example of the trend toward less emphasis on one boss is the use of self-managing work teams. 128

workforce reduction   A short-term strategy that is aimed at reducing the number of employees through attrition, early retirement, voluntary severance package, layoffs, or terminations. 145

World Bank   An international organization that provides long-term loans to countries for economic development projects. Typically, the World Bank will borrow funds from more developed countries and offer low-interest loans to under-developed nations. 294

World Trade Organization (WTO)   An international organization created to develop and administer agreed-upon rules for world trade and discourage protectionist laws that restrict international trade. 294

zero-sum gain   The assumption of mercantilism that the world's wealth is a fixed amount, so that a nation can only increase its share by forcing other nations to reduce their share. *See* mercantilism. 293

Index